# VITAL RECORDS

OF

# ROXBURY

MASSACHUSETTS

TO THE END OF THE YEAR 1849

VOLUME II.—MARRIAGES AND DEATHS.

PUBLISHED BY
THE ESSEX INSTITUTE
SALEM, MASS.
1926

NEWCOMB & GAUSS
Printers
SALEM, MASS.

# EXPLANATIONS

The following records of births, marriages and deaths include all entries to be found in the books of record kept by the town clerks; in the church records; in the cemetery inscriptions; and in private records. These records are printed in a condensed form in which every essential particular has been preserved. All duplication of the town clerks' record has been eliminated, but differences in entry and other explanatory matter appear in brackets. Parentheses are used when they occur in the original record; also to indicate the maiden name of a wife.

When places other than Roxbury and Massachusetts are named in the original records, they are given in the printed copy. Marriages and intentions of marriage are printed under the names of both parties. In all records the original spelling of names is followed and in the alphabetical arrangement the various forms should be examined, as items about the same family may be found under different spellings.

# ROXBURY

The Town of Roxbury was first mentioned in the list of plantations on Sept. 28, 1630. Mar. 4, 1633, bounds between Roxbury and Boston established. Apr. 7, 1635, bounds between Roxbury and Newe Towne established. May 25, 1636, and May 2, 1638, certain lands granted to Roxbury. May 16, 1638, bounds between Roxbury and Dedham established. Oct. 7, 1641, the bounds between Boston and Roxbury at Muddy River were established. Mar. 16, 1660, certain lands granted to Roxbury. May 12, 1675, bounds between Roxbury and Dedham established. Mar. 16, 1836, bounds between Boston and Roxbury were established. Apr. 19, 1837, bounds between Boston and Roxbury were established. Apr. 23, 1838, part of Newton was annexed to Roxbury. Feb. 24, 1844, part of Roxbury annexed to Brookline. Town of Roxbury incorporated as a city, Mar. 12, 1846. May 3, 1850, bounds between Roxbury and Boston established. May 24, 1851, part of Roxbury established as West Roxbury. Apr. 3, 1860, part of Roxbury annexed to Boston, which Act was accepted by Roxbury Apr. 16, 1860, and by Boston May 8, 1860. June 1, 1867, the City of Roxbury was annexed to Boston. Sept. 9, 1867, the Act was accepted by Boston and Roxbury. Jan. 5, 1868, the Act of June 1, 1867, took effect.

The population of Roxbury at different periods has been as follows:

| | | |
|---|---|---|
| 1765.....1,487 | 1810.....3,669 | 1840......9,089 |
| 1790.....2,226 | 1820.....4,135 | 1850.....18,373 |
| 1800.....2,765 | 1830.....5,247 | 1860.....25,137 |
| | | 1870.....34,772 |

# ABBREVIATIONS

*a.*—age.
*abt.*—about.
*b.*—born.
*bef.*—before.
*bet.*—between.
*bp.*—baptized.
*bur.*—buried.
C. R. 1.—church record, First Religious Society (Unitarian).
C. R. 2.—church record, First Congregational Parish of West Roxbury (Unitarian).
C. R. 3.—church record, First Congregational Society of Jamaica Plain (Unitarian).
C. R. 4.—church record, Dudley St. Baptist Church.
C. R. 5.—church record, St. James Episcopal Church.
C. R. 6.—church record, Eliot Congregational Church.
C. R. 7.—church record, South Congregational Church, West Roxbury.
*certif.*—certificate.
*ch.*—child.
*chn.*—children.
*Co.*—county.
CT. R.—court records, Suffolk Co. Quarterly Court.
*d.*—daughter; day; died.
*Dea.*—deacon.
*dec.*—deceased.
*dup.*—duplicate entry.
G. R. 1.—gravestone record, Eliot Cemetery.
G. R. 2.—gravestone record, Westerly Cemetery.
G. R. 3.—gravestone record, Walter St. (West Roxbury) Cemetery.
G. R. 4.—gravestone record, Jamaica Plain Cemetery.
G. R. 5.—gravestone record, Warren Cemetery.
*h.*—husband; hour.
*inf.*—infant.
*int.*—intention of marriage.
*jr.*—junior.
*m.*—male; married: month.

5

N. R. 1.—newspaper record of deaths, Boston News Letter.

N. R. 2.—newspaper record of deaths, Boston Gazette.

N. R. 3.—newspaper record of deaths, Massachusetts Centinel.

N. R. 4.—newspaper record of deaths, Columbian Centinel.

N. R. 5.—newspaper record of deaths, Boston Post.

P. R. 1.—Bible record now in possession of Walter E. Thwing.

P. R. 2.—Bible record now in possession of Mrs. George M. Read.

P. R. 3.—Bible record now in possession of Miss Griggs.

P. R. 4.—Bible record now in possession of Wm. S. Leland.

P. R. 5.—Bible record now in possession of the Misses Rumrill.

P. R. 6.—Bible record now in possession of William Rumrill.

P. R. 7.—Samplers in the possession of the Misses Rumrill.

*rec.*—recorded.

*rem.*—removed.

*ret.*—return.

*s.*—son.

*sr.*—senior.

*T. C.*—Town copy.

*unm.*—unmarried.

*w.*—wife; week.

*wid.*—widow.

*widr.*—widower.

*y.*—year.

# ROXBURY MARRIAGES

**ABBE,** Elizabeth F., and Abner J. Phipps of Andover, int. Nov. 20, 1842.

**ABBOT** (see also Abbott), George, and Mary Chandler, Dec. 12, 1646.

Isaac C., of Groton, and Mary Jane Jenkins of Dorchester, Oct. 23, 1834.

Lydia, of Billerica, and Nathaniel Stevenson, int. Mar. 7, 1819.

Rebecca, jr., Mrs., and Rev. Natha[nae]ll Walter, Apr. 24, 1735.

Sarah, of Sudbury, and Lemuel Veazy, at Sudbury, Dec. 26, 1771.

Thomas, Rev., and Hannah Hesilrige, July 18, 1776.

William, s. George, and Elisabeth Gary, June 19, 1682.

William, and Rebecca Boylstone, May 25, 1708.

**ABBOTT** (see also Abbot), Betsey, and Samuel R. Farmer, both of Ossipee, N. H., Jan. 17, 1849.*

David, of Charlestown, and Emily G. Richards, int. Dec. 11, 1847.

Samuel P., Rev., of Houlton, Me., and Hannah Barker, int. May 2, 1841.

Sarah F., a. 22 y., d. Asa and Esther, and James O. Brooks of Lawrence, a. 25 y., carpenter, s. Barker and Margarett, Sept. 8, 1847.*

Sophia R., and Joel Davis, int. Mar. 15, 1818.

**ABRAMS,** Mary, of Milton, and Winter Boson, at Milton, ——, 1761.

Sarah, of Brookline, and John Randall, int. Apr. 9, 1812.

**ACHINSON,** see Ackin.

**ACKERS,** Elizabeth, and Samuel Bacon of Dedham, July 3, 1705.

* Intention also recorded.

7

ACKERS, John, and Hannah Ruggles, May 26, 1715.
Nancy, of Brookline, and Capt. Belcher Hancock, int. Sept. 30, 1787.

**ACKIN,** Michael [Achinson. int.], and Sarah McKenna, both b. Ireland, Nov. 6, 1849.*

**ADAMS** (see also Addams), Amos, Rev., and [Mrs. dup.] Abigail Mears, Feb. 15, 1770.
Betsey, and Sherman Leland, Oct. 13, 1811. P. R. 4.
Catherine S., of West Townsend, and Joseph H. Chadwick, int. Sept. 6, 1849.
Eliza, and Simon Willard, jr., Dec. 6, 1821.*
Elizabeth [Betsey of Lynnfield. int.], and Rev. John [Joseph. int.] Bullard [resident. int.], Nov. 9, 1779.*
Elizabeth, and Rev. William H. Dalrymple of Arlington, July 9, 1835.
Ephraim, and Catherine Callaghan, int. Sept. 18, 1842.
Fanny, and Milton Willis, Mar. 3, 1822.*
George, and Mary Ann Leach, int. Aug. 28, 1836.
Hannah, of Watertown, and Barachias Lewis, at Watertown, Dec. 4, 1734.
Henry C., and Eliza Johnson of Holliston, int. Mar. 11, 1832.
James, and Mary Williams, Feb. 9, 1812.*
James, and Mary Long, int. Aug. 7, 1847.
James E., and Maria F. I. Adams of Dorchester, int. Sept. 13, 1840.
Jane E., of Dorchester, and John Erskine, int. June 11, 1847.
John, of Framingham, and Elizabeth Goddard, at Framingham, June 27, 1706.
John [of Wrentham. C. R. 2.], and Rachel Heley, Nov. 15, 1739.
John, and Abby May of Beverly, int. Aug. 24, 1828.
Joseph, and Ruth Whitney, Apr. 22, 1701.
Julia A., and James G. Young, Apr. 26, 1846.*
Maria F. I., of Dorchester, and James E. Adams, int. Sept. 13, 1840.
Mary, and James Shed of Brookline, at Brookline, June 12, 1712.
Mary, and William Evans, May 30, 1844.*
Mary P., and John A. Dodd, June 16, 1842.*
Nancy Jackson, of Pepperell, and Charles Fitch, int. Sept. 15, 1833.

* Intention also recorded.

ADAMS, Pharez, and Susannah Wilson, Feb. 20, 1814.*

Philip, and Mary Goodwin, Sept. 30, 1827.

Rebecca, and Joseph Harris of Brookline, at Boston, June 10, 1731.

Sarah, and Henry Smith, May 26, 1713.

Susannah, and John Vinal, Apr. 18, 1793.

Theoda H., a. 24 y., d. James and Mary, and John A. Dodd, widr., a. 36 y., merchant, s. John and Harriet, Sept. 9, 1847.*

Zabdiel, and Mrs. Nabby [Heath int.] Richardson, May 23, 1813.*

Zebdiel, and Rachel Lyon, int. May 6, 1792.

**ADDAMS** (see also Adams), Thomas, of Canterbury, and Abigail Davenport of Dorchester, Feb. 23, 1714-15.

**ADIS,** Ruth, and Joseph Metcalf of Dedham, at Dedham, Feb. 21, 1764.

**ADKINSON,** Jane [Atkinson. CT. R.], and Thomas Cheaney, Jan. 11, 1655. [11 : 12 m : 1655. CT. R.]

**ADLER,** George M., and Martha A. Dean, int. Oct. 8, 1843.

John, of Dorchester, and Elizabeth Leonard, int. Oct. 6, 1844.

**AGIN** (see also Aigin), Daniel, and Mary Tarrall of Cambridge, int. May 25, 1846.

**AIGIN** (see also Agin), Margarett, b. Ireland, and Luke Kelly, b. Ireland, Sept. 30, 1849.*

Thomas, and Julia Burk, int. Dec. 20, 1849.

**AINSWORTH,** Amelia A[nn. int.], and Charles S[aunders. int.] Nichols of Salem, Apr. 21, 1845.*

Edward, and Joanna Hemingway, Jan. 11, 1687-8.

**ALBEE** (see also Allbee), Pardon, of Sutton, and Lampetia Fechem, Jan. 4, 1825.*

**ALCOCK,** Elizabeth, and Henry Dingam, Apr. —, 1641.

**ALDEFT,** John, and Mehittabel Haus of Dedham, at Dedham, May 15, 1733.

**ALDEN** (see also Aldin, Alding), Julia A., of West Randolph, and Henry W. Smith, int. Mar. 17, 1847.

* Intention also recorded.

ALDEN, Susan [Sukey. c. r. 2.], and Leonard Whiting, June 11, 1809. c. r. 2.*

ALDERCHURCH, Elisabeth, Mrs., and William Fuller, Aug. 2, 1759.

ALDIN (see also Alden), Polly, and Jacob Chamberlain, Nov. 9, 1788.*

ALDING (see also Alden), Sally, and Cyrus Wood, int. May 8, 1803.

ALDIS, Abigail, and Gideon Draper, Apr. 22, 1713.
Nathan, and Eunice Draper, June 24, 1708.
Rachel, and James Draper, May 2, 1716.
Sarah, and Thomas Perry, May 30, 1710.

ALDRIDGE (see also Eldridge), Mary, and Joseph Lyon of Braintree, Dec. 5, 1701.

ALEXANDER, Catharine S., and Charles Cary, int. Oct. 16, 1825.
Giles, and Susannah Fowle [Sukey Fowl. int.], at Boston, Apr. 2, 1797. [Mar. 18, 1798. int.]*
Gyles, and Sarah Williams, May 4, 1773.

ALGER, Hepzibah, of North Bridgwater, and Joseph E. Davis, int. Dec. 23, 1827.

ALKER, Samuel B., of Cambridge, and Mary Godell, int. Mar. 28, 1830.
Thomas, of Princeton, and Deborah G. Shattuck, Dec. 13, 1827.*

ALLARD, Elizabeth, and Robart Sever, Dec. 10, 1634.

ALLBEE (see also Albee), John, Capt., of Mendon, and Mrs. Sarah Bugbee, Aug. 24, 1790.*

ALLEN (see also Allin), Abel, and Lucinda McIntosh, int. Mar. 6, 1842.
Andrew, and Margaret Riley, Mar. 12, 1806.*
Ann, of Newton, and Ebenezer Stetson, at Newton, Sept. 11, 1755.
Ann, of Brookline, and Stephen Davis, at Brookline, Nov. 12, 1761.
Ann, and James Ward, May 12, 1811.*

* Intention also recorded.

ALLEN, Augustus, and Adeline Smith, Dec. 11, 1842.*

Byran, of Bridgewater, and Elizabeth Child, resident, int. Jan. 15, 1786.

Calvin, and Mrs. Abagail Richards, Apr. 16, 1801. c. r. 2.*

Calvin, and Ann Priscilla Watson, Apr. 8, 1839.*

Caroline, and Joseph H. Clapp, Sept. 8, 1835.*

Caroline and George Dean, Apr. 27, 1845.*

Catharine Hinsdale, of Dedham, and William Hervey Spear, int. May 1, 1831.

Charles E., and Anna C. Weatherwas, int. Apr. 26, 1835.

Christian H., and William Briar, int. Apr. 13, 1823.

Elisha, and Jane Cottle of Watertown, int. Nov. 27, 1828.

Eliza, and Samuel Slocomb of Cambridge, int. Jan. 8, 1826.

Eliza Ann, a. 28 y., d. Gersham and Margarett, and Andrew G. Chambers, a. 25 y., laborer, s. John and Mary, Oct. 8, 1846.*

Elizabeth, and Benjamin Lyon, Oct. 16, 1796.*

Ethan, and [Mrs. int.] Nancy Batchelder, Nov. 3, 1825.*

Frances E., and James M. Coye, Apr. 20, 1845.*

Hannah A., Mrs., and Aaron Cass, int. June 16, 1833.

Harry, 2d m., a. 55 y., pianoforte maker, b. Leominster, s. Silas, and Hannah C. Dodge, 2d m., a. 37 y., b. N. H., d. George Blanchard, Oct. 6, 1849.

Hervey D., and Ann Maria Rider, Dec. 22, 1844.

James, and Hannah Billings, int. May 9, 1819. [June 8. c. r. 2.]

John, a. 34 y., reformer, s. Solomon and Abigail, and Ellen Lazarus of Wilmington, N. C., a. 23 y., d. Aaron and Rachel, Oct. 4, 1848.*

John W., and Pametia Knights, Sept. 4, 1821.*

Joseph, and Susannah Wood, Oct. 3, 1745.

Joseph Henry [Rev. int.], a. 25 y., clerk, s. Joseph and Lucy C., and Anna Minot Weld, a. 25 y., d. William G., May 22, 1845.*

Levi H., and Eliza Weatherspoon, int. Oct. 8, 1820.

Louisa, and James Copps, Jan. 23, 1821.*

Lucy, and Capt. William Lingham, Apr. 3, 1825.*

Lucy Jane, and William H[enry. int.] Ivers, Apr. 22, 1845.*

Mary, and Addington Gardner of Brookline, at Brookline, ——, 1718.

Mary, of Sturbridge, and Eben[eze]r Sessions, int. Nov. 27, 1808.

Mary, and James Blackman, July 11, 1813.*

* Intention also recorded.

ALLEN, Mary Ann, and Josiah D. Jenness, Apr. 29, 1841.*
Mehetabel, of Bridgewater, and John Clap, jr., int. Apr. 1,
    1804.
Richard, and Mrs. Hannah Thayer, int. May 29, 1791.
Rufus S., and Direxa P. Odiorne, int. Apr. 19, 1840.
William H., a. 22 y., carpenter, s. Oliver N. and Frances O.,
    and Harriet S. Trask, a. 18 y., d. Lyman P. and Caroline,
    May 21, 1849.*

ALLENDOFF (see also Allendorf), Adam, and Bridget Ken-
    ney, int. May 13, 1838.

ALLENDORF (see also Allendoff), Adam, and Margarett
        Clenan, int. Nov. 8, 1848. (null and void.)
Adam, and Winneford McGennis, int. Dec. 14, 1848.

ALLESSON, Martha, and Stephen Mills, Aug. 4, 1768.

ALLIN (see also Allen), Daniel, and Hannah Davis of Muddy
    River, Oct. 26, 1705.
Ephraim, and Susanna Beacon, Nov. 28, 1716.

ALWARD, Judith, [maid servant. c. R. 1.], and John Graves,
    Dec. —, 1635. [bef. 1636. c. R. 1.]

AMAZEEN, Robert W., and M. Anna Hickey, int. June 12,
    1847.

AMBROOK, Catherine, and Patrick McCormic, int. Oct. 12,
    1846.

AMBUSH, Alexander, of Quincy, and Mary Ann Golden, int.
    Sept. 15, 1849.

AMES, Almira, and William L. Stodder, Aug. 10, 1820.*
Asa, and Mary C. Warner of Townsend, int. Oct. 28, 1838.
Harriot, and Samuel M. Hersey, int. Nov. 23, 1828.
Henry, and Margarett Dyer, int. July 20, 1848.
Mary, and Moses Winchester, Oct. 25, 1757.
Mary Ann, and William C. Moore, May 22, 1823.*
Mercy Maria, of Belfast, Me., and John Richardson, int. Nov.
    5, 1846.
Robert W., and Louisa Danforth, July 2, 1835.*
Robert W. [a. 34 y. in pencil. int.], and Frances Tilden, Mar.
    4, 1844.*

* Intention also recorded.

**AMORY,** Catharine Greene, and Joseph Lewis Cunningham, int. May 11, 1828.

Harriet Bowen, and Robert Ives of Providence, R. I., int. Sept. 16, 1827.

Helen M., and [Willia]m Raymond Lee, July 7, 1842.*

Julia Bowen, and Rev. Mark Anthony DeWolf Howe, Oct. 16, 1833. c. r. 5.*

Letitia Sullivan, a. 17 y., d. Jon[atha]n and Letitia, and Lucius Manlius Sargent, jr., a. 20 y., artist, s. L. M. and Sarah C., Sept. 22, 1847.*

Rebecca, and John Lowell, jr., int. May 26, 1793.

**AMOS,** Sarah, and John Fairbanks [of Dedham. c. r. 2.]. ——, 1749. [Jan. 3, 1749-50. c. r. 2.]

William, and Sarah Youngman, Apr. 30, 1733.

**ANAN,** John, and Isabella Smith, int. Nov. 22, 1816.

**ANDERSON,** Archibald C., and Caroline F. Burrill, Feb. 17, 1828.*

Arthur F., and Susan Drown, int. Dec. 13, 1829.

James, and Martha E[lizabeth. int.] Sumner, ——, 1832. [Oct. 23, 1831. int.]*

Joseph, and Ann Kelley, int. Aug. 4, 1848.

Rebecca F., and Henry A. Robinson, Oct. 26, 1845.*

**ANDRESS** (see also Andrews), Mary [Andross. c. r. 2.], and Samuel Harris, Nov. 11, 1753.

**ANDREWS** (see also Andress, Androws), Dennis, and Tamar Stiles of Boylston, int. Aug. 22, 1813.

Dudley, and Hepza Dana Sampson, May 5, 1816.*

Henry [of Boston. c. r. 3.], and Mary Prince Apthorp, Nov. 7, 1811.*

John, jr., and Elizabeth Wales of Dorchester, at Dorchester, Sept. 21, 1738.

Joseph, and Elizabeth Bill of Dorchester, May 10, 1705.

Joseph, widr., a. 40 y., engraver, s. Ephraim and Lucy of Hingham, and Frances Hallet, d. George and Eliza, May 19, 1847.*

Joseph E., and Frances S. Norton, int. May 20, 1837.

Lyman, and Susan P. Webster of Manchester, int. Dec. 13, 1835.

Pierre [Peter. c. r. 5.] S. M., of Lynnfield, and Mary F[rances. c. r. 5.] Oliver, June 17, 1841.*

* Intention also recorded.

ANDREWS, Thomas [M. C. R. 3.], of Hallowell, Me., and Margaret Curtis, Apr. 14, 1831.
William C., of Dedham, and Eleanor Forest, May 10, 1845.

ANDROWS (see also Andrews), John, and Mary Dowse, Oct. 2, 1781.

ANGIER, Margaret, and Benjamin Searl, at Dorchester, Aug. 29, 1738.

ANJEMA, Charles J., and Sarah Jane Strong, int. May 19, 1844.

APPLETON, Almira Jane, wid., a. 37 y., d. Aaron and Phebe Melcher, and Thomas H. Child, a. 38 y., gauger and measurer, s. Thomas and Charlotte, Nov. 24, 1846.*
William C., and Mary Ann L. Smith, int. Mar. 23, 1845.

APTHORP, Mary Prince, and Henry Andrews [of Boston. C. R. 3.], Nov. 7, 1811.*

ARCHER, Henry, and Elize[be]th Stow, Dec. 4, 1639.

ARKERSON, George W., of Cambridge, a. 29 y., carpenter, s. W[illia]m and Sarah, and Hannah R. Homan, a. 18 y., d. Milton and Ann, Dec. 25, 1846.*
James, and Elizabeth Symmes, Sept. 17, 1837.*

ARMSBY, Eliza K., of Sutton, and Nath[anie]l Colburn, int. Mar. 10, 1822.
Rena, of Sutton, and Capt. Thomas Davis, int. Oct. 6, 1816.

ARMSTRONG, Benjamin, and Caroline R. Williams, Aug. 7, 1842.
John, and Mary [Mercy. int.] Gibson, Jan. 6, 1834.*
Margaret, and William Breaden of [Kingston, int.], Upper Canada, May 17, 1838.*

ARNOLD, Adeline, and William Macintosh, int. Mar. 14, 1841.
Elizabeth, and Martin Perry of Ludlow, Vt., June 1, 1831.*
Eunice L., and Jonathan Avery, Apr. 8, 1834.*
Jane, and John L. Meder, Mar. 17, 1831.*
Joseph A., and Martha Arnold, Nov. 18, 1830.*
Joseph, jr., and Mary Ann Hastings of Brighton, int. Mar. 3, 1833.

* Intention also recorded.

ARNOLD, Maria F., and Nathaniel R. Meder [of Boston. C. R. 2.], Nov. 18, 1830.*

Martha, and Joseph W. [A. C. R. 2.] Arnold, Nov. 18, 1830.*

Mary, and Benjamin Lyon, int. Feb. 23, 1823.

Mottrom V., of Quincy, and Sarah M. Dudley, Jan. 15, 1835.*

**AROTRIGE,** Anne, and Thomas Barry, int. June 20, 1847.

**ASHLEY,** Mary, and John Webb of Braintree, Mar. 23, 1701-2.

**ASPINWALL,** Caleb, resident, and Mrs. Betsey Freeman, int. Mar. 13, 1785.

Catharine Sparhawk, of Brookline, and Edward Brewer, int. Oct. 1, 1786.

Elizabeth, Mrs., and Capt. Benjamin White, both of Brooklyn, Feb. 19, 1756.

Joanna, of Brookline, and John Brewer, at Brookline, Nov. 24, 1761.

Mehitable, of Brookline, and Samuel Craft, at Brookline, ——, 1725.

Samuel, and Mary Holbrook, Feb. 26, 1761.

**ATHERTON,** Daniel, and Sophronia Emerson of Candia, N. H., int. Nov. 15, 1835.

Elizabeth, and Peter Briggs, ——, 1701.

Henry, and Naomi Porter, Jan. 30, 1804.*

Roxanna, and Judson Chapin, int. Oct. 1, 1826.

Sophia, and James Dugan, int. Mar. 29, 1818.

**ATKINS,** Mary S., a. 32 y., seamstress, d. Charles and Rebecca, and Rufus F. Fletcher, a. 32 y. farmer, s. Alpheus and Ruth, Oct. 27, 1845.*

Zacheus, of New Sharon, Me., and Marcia Grozer, June 23, 1840.*

**ATWOOD,** Clarissa, and Amasa C. Wiswall, Jan. 7, 1830.*

Daniel, Capt., and Nancy Hallowell of Framingham, int. May 13, 1821.

Hannah, and Elijah Trescott [of Boston. C. R. 3.], Dec. 3, 1835.*

James T., and Abby W. Mason of Attleboro, May 16, 1843. C. R. 7.

Jane R., of Frankfort, Me., and Samuel D. Rumrill, int. July 25, 1846.

* Intention also recorded.

ATWOOD, Mary L., of Middleboro, and Capen R. Spurzheim, int. Oct. 18, 1849.

**AUSTIN,** Abner, and Sally Edes, Dec. 1, 1825.*
Arthur W., of Charlestown, and Sarah C[hild. c. R. 3.] Williams, May 29, 1834.*
Cordelia C., and Sylvanus Jordan, Aug. 23, 1831.*
John, and Mary Ann Craig, Jan. 26, 1844.
Margarett, and William P. Dexter of Brookline, int. Mar. 26, 1847.
Moody, of Bellingham, and Ann Carter, Dec. 28, 1820.*
Sarah F., and George Nixon, Feb. 18, 1836.*
Susanna, and Wyatt Herring, Oct. 5, 1794.*
William, of Charleston, and Charlotte Williams, June 19, 1806. [June 17. c. R. 3.]*

**AVERBECK,** Lydia, and Josiah Crosby, int. Apr. 27, 1834.

**AVERILL,** Charlotte H., and William H. Holmes, Oct. 20, 1835.*
Emily A., and William C. Mellus, Jan. 1, 1845.*
James W., and Philander [Phylindia. int.] Richardson, Dec. 3, 1843.*
Mary Ann, a. 21 y., d. James and Elizabeth, and Levi Philbrook, a. 27 y., sash and blind maker, s. Henry and Betsey, Jan. 23, 1848.*
Susan Jane, a. 18 y., d. Nathaniel and Ann, and George Robinson, a. 24 y., carpenter, s. Stephen and G., Aug. 9, 1846.*
Susannah R., and Job H. Perkins, Jan. 1, 1846.*

**AVERY,** Jonathan, and Eunice L. Arnold, Apr. 8, 1834.*
Nancy, of Holden, and W[illia]m White, int. Dec. 7, 1806.

**AVIS,** Tho[ma]s, [of Boston. c. R. 3.], and Katherine May, [Mar. 10. int.; Oct. 17. c. R. 3.], 1799.*

**AYER** (see also Ayers), Diana, and W[illia]m E. Smith, Jan. 1, 1840.*

**AYERS** (see also Ayer, Ayres, Eayres), Adin, and Mrs. Eliza Davis, June 30, 1802.*
Benj[amin] F., and Almira Hodgdon, Oct. 1, 1837.*
B[enj[ami]n. int.] F., and Zilpha Hodgdon, Sept. 4, 1842.*
Ebenezer, and Eleanor Richards, Jan. 3, 1803. c. R. 2.*
Emely, and Abram Hodgdon, Dec. 25, 1825.*

* Intention also recorded.

AYERS, Emiley, of Ossipee, N. H., and James S. Marble, int. Aug. 9, 1829.

John, of Needham, and Mrs. Hannah Dana of Dedham, July 5, 1757.

John, and Susan Stowers, int. May 4, 1845.

Otis, and Eliza Hazelwood, Dec. 24, 1835.*

Robert, and Dolly Turner, Nov. 28, 1801.*

Solomon, and Mrs. Elizabeth Gridley, Mar. 18, 1752.

AYLING, Maria R., and Elizah B. Phillips, int. Dec. 29, 1844.

AYRES (see also Ayers), Benjamin F., and Jane F. Cheney, Oct. 16, 1834.*

Rebecca G., and Jonathan Shapleigh, Oct. 20, 1833.*

BABBIT, Benjamin, and Polly Tower, May 13, 1805.*

BABCOCK, Joseph, Esq., of Dorchester, and Mrs. Grace Draper, int. Oct. 26, 1800.

Robert G., and Sally Otis, Aug. 3, 1818.*

Robert G., and Lucy Blackman of Dorchester, int. Apr. 4, 1822.

Rufus, and Mary Child, May 3, 1807.*

Sally, of Milton, and William J. Newman, int. Feb. 24, 1810.

BACHELDER (see also Batchelder), Charles G., and Susan W. Curtis, both of Hallowell, Me., Dec. 9, 1841. C. R. 3.

BACHELER (see also Batchelder), Olis R., and Catherine E. Palmer, int. Apr. 26, 1840.

BACHI, Peter, and Abigail Fisher, Feb. 14, 1826.*

BACON (see also Beacon, Becon), Abigail [of Dorchester. C. R. 3.], and John Carpenter of Foxborough, Oct. 13, 1825.

Asenath, Mrs., and Otis Gould, Dec. 1, 1814.*

Ebenezer, and Jane Everton, Nov. 13, 1729.

Ede Goulding [Goulder. int.], of Natick, and Clarke Travis, Apr. 15, 1824.*

Eliza A. H., and Charles E. Grant, June 26, 1839.*

Elizabeth, and John Jones, Feb. 4, 1713.

Ephram, and Elizabeth Griggs, at Dedham, Aug. 28, 1700.

George, and Mary Davis, May 4, 1699.

George [Baken. int], and Mrs. Hepzibah Crease [Creese. int.], both residents, June 15, 1784.*

* Intention also recorded.

BACON, Henry, and Sophia Smith, May 11, 1813.*
Horace, and Miranda Woods, int. Jan. 7, 1838.
Isaac, and Abigail Brodhurst, Jan. 1, 1710-11.
Jacob, and Dorothy Bradhurst, Dec. 24, 1700.
John, and Mary Baker, Mar. 17, 1707-8.
Joseph, and Margaret Bowen, Nov. 6, 1688.
Joseph, resident, and Elizabeth King, int. Apr. 14, 1793.
Margaret, and Timothy Whitney, June 12, 1706.
Mary, and Thomas Hammond, Aug. 8, 1705.
Mary [Boson. c. r. 2.], and Nathanael Carpenter [of Attle-
    borough. c. r. 2.], Nov. 13, 1716.
Phillip, and Patience Craft, Nov. 17, 1726.
Samuel, of Dedham, and Elizabeth Ackers, July 3, 1705.
Sarah K., of Dedham, and Charles Winship, int. Mar. 15,
    1829.
Timothy, and Martha Morse, Dec. 16, 1714.
William, and Elizabeth Wyman, Jan. 15, 1815.*
William, jr., a. 34 y., trader, s. William and Elizabeth, and
    Mary C. Hunneman, a. 33 y., d. William C. and Hannah,
    June 10, 1849.*

BADEN, Jane, and Jonathan Clap, Sept. 8, 1793.*

BADES, Edward, and Bridget Condry, int. May 1, 1836.

BADGER, Abigail F., and Job T. Grush, int. Oct. 6, 1822.
Mary B., a. 49 y., d. John and Sarah, and Job T. Grush, widr.,
    a. 47 y., currier, s. Thomas and Esther, Feb. 23, 1848.*

BADLAM, Clarissa, of Dorchester, and Ebeneser Dorr, int.
    Oct. 1, 1815.

BAHERN, Bridget, and Hugh Cooney, int. Sept. 15, 1844.

BAILEY (see also Baley, Bayley, Baylie, Baylies), Ellen M.,
    a. 22 y., d. John, and Alexander C. Washburn, a. 29 y.,
    attorney at law, s. Calvin and Lydia, May 7, 1849.*
Joseph, jr., a. 24 y., carpenter, s. Joseph and Sarah, and Mary
    L. Sanborn, a. 17 y., d. Shubael and Mary, Nov. 26,
    1846.*
Luther C., a. 24 y., s. Phineas and Dorcas, and Mary W. Whit-
    ney, a. 42 y., Dec. 31, 1848.*
Timothy, and Eunice Sweetser of South Reading, int. Nov.
    24, 1816.

* Intention also recorded.

**BAKER,** Abigail, and Samuel Gridley, Apr. 23, 1747.

Abigail, and Jonathan Parker, Feb. 11, 1752.

Ann, and Nathaniell Mills, Oct. 29, 1718.

Ann H., and Col. Edmund Foster of Dorchester, Oct. 20, 1825.*

Benjamin, and Anne Parker of Needham, at Needham, July 23, 1766.

Benj[ami]n D., of Salem, and Mrs. Mary Ward, int. Oct. 16, 1836. [Nov. 5, 1837. dup.]

Calvin, and Roxana Mayo, Sept. 21, 1815.*

Charlotte W., and Cyrus Grant, int. Nov. 8, 1840.

Dana, and Sarah Leeds, Feb. 3, 1822.*

David, and Hannah Googins, July 23, 1778.

David, and Polly How of Dorchester, int. Nov. 29, 1801.

David, and Amy Williams, Mar. 22, 1809.*

Dorothy, and Jacob Davis, Oct. 30, 1764.

Eliphalet, and Lucretia O. Harrington, Jan. 1, 1834.*

Eliza J., a. 20 y., d. Theodore and Ann, and John D. Fowle [Fowel. int.], a. 25 y., upholsterer, s. John and Prudence, July 19, 1849.*

Elizabeth, and William Richards, May 30, 1733.

Ellis, and Mrs. Mary Wardel, Mar. 14, 1782. c. r. 2.

Hannah, and Samuel Peck, June 11, 1809. c. r. 2.*

Henry P., of New Bedford, and Emily Eastham, Apr. 14, 1839.

Henry T. [Henry F. of Boston. c. r. 3.], and Caroline Boit, Nov. 25, 1822.*

John, and Sarah Ellis, Apr. 6, 1748.

John, Ens., and Abigail Draper, Feb. 23, 1762.

John, Ens., and Lucy Haws, Jan. 8, 1775.

John, and Lydia Teel, int. May 4, 1806.

John, and Elizabeth Brooks, June 25, 1844.*

John, jr., and Abigail Colbourn, Sept. 6, 1732.

John, jr., and Mrs. Mary Breck of Dorchester, at Dorchester, Nov. 20, 1771.

John, jr., and Charlotte White, at Sharon, Feb. 4, 1798.*

Joseph, and Hannah Lovewell, May 31, 1739.

Joseph, and Mary Haycle, July 14, 1822.*

Judith, Mrs., of Dorchester, and Aaron Wilson, at Dorchester, Nov. 19, 1778.

Lemuel, and Abigail Griggs, Nov. 17, 1785.*

Louis, and Joseph Weld, int. June 1, 1783.

Mary, and John Bacon, Mar. 17, 1707-8.

* Intention also recorded.

BAKER, Mary, Mrs., and Rev. Enoch Pond of Ashford, Conn., Nov. 12, 1801.*

Mary N., and Moses C. Grant, Feb. 4, 1839.*

Mary, of Shapleigh, Me., and George H. Pike, int. Aug. 4, 1848.

Mercy, of Lincoln, and Benjamin Warden Child, int. Dec. 28, 1806.

Nabby, and Solomon Jones, Apr. 11, 1799.*

Rhoda, and George L. Farrington, Oct. 10, 1805.*

Sally, and Nathaniel Everett, int. Feb. 1, 1801. [Apr. 12, 1801. C. R. 2.]

Sarah, and Jonathan Daviss, Feb. 14, 1721-2.

Sarah, and Lemuel Tucker, Feb. 11, 1768.

Sarah, of Dorchester, and Joseph Muncreif, Aug. 8, 1793.

Susanna, and George Griggs [of Brookline. C. R. 2.], Sept. 3, 1747.

Tamerin [Tamesine. C. R. 2.], and Edw[ar]d Jackson Felton, Sept. 19, 1782. C. R. 2.*

Thomas, and Marie Gambling, May 27, 1663.

Thomas, and Sarah Pike, May 28, 1702.

Thomas, and Hannah Park of Newton, at Watertown, Aug. 2, 1722.

Thomas, jr., and Hannah Child, Apr. 18, 1734.

Thomas, and Betsey Rhoads [Rhoades. int.], Dec. 25, 1814. C. R. 2.*

BALCH, Caroline W., and Dr. Isaac G. Bramin of Georgetown, int. Oct. 18, 1840.

Edward L. [of Boston. C. R. 3.], and Martha W. Lincoln, Dec. 1, 1844.*

Jonathan, and Abigail Williams, Dec. 5, 1771.

Joseph W., a. 26 y., merchant, s. Jos[eph] and Caroline A. B., and Maria Hallet, a. 25 y., d. George and Eliza, June 8, 1846.*

Mary R., and George W. Pettes, Dec. 8, 1846.

Sarah B., and Stephen M. Weld, June 6, 1838.*

Thomas, Rev., of Dedham, and Mrs. Mary Sumner, Oct. 11, 1737.

BALDNER (see also Baldnor), Elisabeth, and Jacob Weing of Boston, int. Sept. 4, 1846.

V[irginia. int] Catharine, and Charles Schwaz, Aug. 8, 1839.*

* Intention also recorded.

**BALDNOR** (see also Baldner), Mary, and George Souner, int. Mar. 5, 1843.

**BALDWIN,** Anna, of Newton, and Ebenezer Smith, at Newton, Dec. 22, 1767.
Edward, and Ellen W[atson. int.] White, Aug. 8, 1838.*
Elizabeth W., of Grafton, and Amos Stevens, int. Sept. 19, 1849.
Lucy Ann, and John Collins, Aug. 29, 1837.*
Mary, of Shrewsbury, and Moses Gill, A. M., int. Sept. 16, 1810.
Reuben, and Mrs. Mary Stone, int. Mar. 10, 1844.
Thomas Williams, and Margaret Josephine Bawn, int. Oct. 12, 1834.

**BALEY** (see also Bailey), James, and Elisabeth Child, May 3, 1768.

**BALL,** Anne, and Bernard Foley, int. Oct. 10, 1846.
Elizabeth, Mrs., of Dorchester, and Ebenezer Spear, at Dorchester, Mar. 19, 1772.
James, and Lydia Johnson, int. Oct. 13, 1844.
Jane, and Joshua Pond of Dedham, June 21, 1744. c. r. 2.
Mary, and Peter Dusey, Sept. 3, 1718.
Mary Ann P., and George R. Mead, int. Nov. 12, 1837.
Mary Vila, and Charles Davis, int. Aug. 24, 1845.
Rufus, and Sarah Fruean, int. Apr. 5, 1835.
Sarah, of Dedham, and Janett Perry, at Dedham, Apr. 4, 1732.
Thankfull, and John Perry, jr., Apr. 24, 1740.

**BALLARD,** Mary, and Daniel Chamberlain, June 22, 1825. c. r. 2.*

**BALLCOM,** Nathan, and Sarah Jewell, Jan. 12, 1768.

**BALNEY,** Mary, and Samuel Bowen, Feb. 14, 1771.

**BAMBOER,** Daniel, and Elizabeth Ortman, int. Nov. 23, 1848.

**BANCROFT,** Abigail, and Jonathan Hamlet, int. Nov. 24, 1822.
John, and Hannah Harrison, int. Nov. 27, 1836.
Joseph, and Hannah Pierpont Fellowes, May 12, 1811.*
Robert, and Sally Robbins, July 20, 1818.*

* Intention also recorded.

**BANDLEN,** Frederick, and Mary Spendler, int. Dec. 22, 1847.

**BANKS,** Thomas S., and Amelia R. Barker, Sept. 1, 1836.*

**BANNON,** Patrick, and Mary Kelly, int. Apr. 27, 1848.

**BANTON,** Tabitha Eliza, and William Stevenson, Oct. 23, 1814.*

**BARANE,** Thomas, and Ann King, int. Sept. 20, 1845.

**BARBER** (see also Barbour), Achsah, of Medway, and John H. Hawes, int. Nov. 16, 1806.
Elizabeth, and John Woods, jr., Oct. 31, 1742.

**BARBOUR** (see also Barber), Henry M., of Worcester, a. 25 y., geologist, s. Isaac R. and C. P., and Ellen M. Thayer, a. 25 y., d. Robert H. and Abigail, May 30, 1848.*
Louisa P., and John W. Blanchard, Nov. 14, 1844.*

**BARDEN,** Joseph H., and Catherine Harvey, Dec. 25, 1848.*

**BARKER,** Amelia R., and Thomas S. Banks, Sept. 1, 1836.*
Daphne C., of Cambridge, and John W. Morey of Boston, Oct. 11, 1840. c. r. 3.
Hannah, and Rev. Samuel P. Abbott of Houlton, Me., int. May 2, 1841.
Maria B., and James W. Russell, int. Aug. 14, 1831.
Mary, a. 22 y., d. George and Susan, and John D. Wilson, a. 21 y., merchant, s. Joseph and Jane J., June 23, 1849.*
Messer, of [Plymouth. int.], Ohio, and Lydia F. Simmons, Oct. 9, 1843.*
Susan, and Dr. Charles May Windship, int. Feb. 27, 1831.
William B., and Sarah Ann Noyes, Apr. 24, 1836.*

**BARKMAN,** Sarah C., and William H. Stodder, int. May 4, 1848.

**BARLOW,** Ellen H., and Edwin Garfield, July 2, 1837.*
Joseph K., and Sarah P. Bills, Oct. 31 1844.*
Lucy B., and James P. [B. int.] Barrows, Oct. 24, 1848.*
Royal J., and Sarah E. Hayden, Aug. 12, 1838.*
Royal M., and Lucy P. Pope of South Reading, int. Apr. 30, 1837.

* Intention also recorded.

**BARNARD,** Abigail, and Isaac Withington, jr., Oct. 14, 1841.*

Ebenezer, and Elizabeth Foster, at Dorchester, Sept. 29, 1715.

Emily, and William Jones, int. Feb. 26, 1849.

James H., of Waterbury, Conn., and Mary N. Goss of Newton, Dec. 5, 1844.

Joseph, Rev., of Salem [of New York. int.], and Martha R[uggles. int.] Prentiss, Sept. 2, 1835.*

Mary [of Watertown. c. r. 2.], and Jonathan Smith, June 6, 1738.

Samuell, and Sarah Williams, May 22, 1718.

Sarah, and John Woods, at Boston, Aug. 20, 1747.

William, and Hester Hyde of Needham, int. July 16, 1826.

**BARNES** (see also Barns), Maria Catharine, and Charles Blake, Feb. 21, 1843.*

Seth H[illman. int.], and Maria L. Brinley, Nov. 21, 1837.*

William [Barns. int.], and Jane Thompson, Nov. 29, 1793.*

William, and Sarah H. Hall, Apr. 21, 1840.*

**BARNETT,** Lydia H. Mrs., of Dorchester, and Capt. Joshua Lewis, Apr. 19, 1827.*

**BARNEY,** Susan, of Newton, and Edwin F. Farwell, int. Apr. 4, 1844.

**BARNS** (see also Barnes), Mary A., and John S. White, Aug. 17, 1844.

**BARREL,** James E., and Rebecca E. Cheney, Oct. 17, 1841.*

**BARRET** (see also Barrett), Roswell, and Olive Rice, Dec. 12, 1810.*

Samuel [Barrett. c. r. 3.], of Windsor, Vt., and Elizabeth Field, Nov. 15, 1814.*

**BARRETT** (see also Barret, Barrit), Charlotte, and John Adams Lyon of Brookline, int. Dec. 15, 1800.

Margarett, and Jeremiah Cronin, int. Jan. 5, 1847.

Mary, and Nicholas Parker, int. Oct. 11, 1849.

**BARRIT** (see also Barrett), Mary, and James Fay, int. June 4, 1847.

**BARRON,** Lemuel, Dr., and Martha Osgood Kittredge of Andover, int. Sept. 17, 1809.

**BARROWS,** Calvin, of Lexington, a. 29 y., s. Samuel S. and Belinda, and Caira R. Whitney, a. 23 y., d. Eli and Sally, Oct. 14, 1849.

* Intention also recorded.

BARROWS, James P. [B. int.], and Lucy B. [P. int.] Barlow, Oct. 24, 1848.*

**BARRY,** Catharine, and Dan McCarthy, int. Aug. 17, 1845.
Charles, and Mrs. Mary W. Wharf, int. Sept. 6, 1829.
Eliza, and Patrick McCarty, int. Dec. 1, 1848.
Hannah, and John Coy, May 24, 1848.*
James, jr., and Sophia Patterson, int. Sept. 30, 1821.
Samuel, and Nancy Swift of Milton, int. May 21, 1786.
Samuel, and Rebecca Marshall of Brookline, Oct. 17, 1802.
Thomas, and Anne Arotrige, int. June 20, 1847.

**BARTHOLMEW,** Willyam, and Mary Johnson, Dec. 17, 1663.

**BARTLETT,** Aaron, and Melinda Bean, Apr. 6, 1818.*
Ann Matilda, and Edward Brinley, Nov. 18, 1835.*
Charles, of Concord, and Elizabeth Walker, int. Sept. 11, 1842.
Clement, of Dedham, and Fanny T. Whittemore, Sept. 26, 1824.*
George, Dr., and Catharine Amelia Greenwood, int. Oct. 23, 1834.
George F., and Martha M. Rogers, Sept. 2, 1824.*
Henry, M. D., and Hannah Everett of Dorchester, int. Mar. 23, 1828.
Isaac, and Ann Lyon, int. Oct. 3, 1824.
John, Dr., and Abigail Williams, Feb. 17, 1789.*
Julia, and Thomas Hill, Sept. 27, 1825.*
Martha, and Jonathan Brett, int. Aug. 26, 1827.
Martha, of Norway, Me., and William D. Fisher, July 8, 1848.
Nathan, and Polly Dennis of Marblehead, int. May 18, 1817.
Sarah, of Newton, and Moses Davis, at Newton, Apr. 28, 1768.
Sarah Bass, a. 40 y., d. Enoch and Sarah, and Allen Putman, widr., a. 43 y., merchant, s. Daniel and Susannah, of Danvers, June 10, 1846.*
Sarah K., and Thomas M. Hayes of Haverhill, Jan. 16, 1844.*
Theoda Williams, and John S. Foster, June 23, 1811.*
William, and Mary O. Phillips of Easton, int. June 11, 1837.

**BARTON,** William, and Harriet A. Everett [Everell. int.], May 17, 1844.*

**BASFORD,** Caroline, and Jeremiah Sanborn, Jan. 11, 1831.*
Henry, and Mary Jane Waterman, May 23, 1839.*

* Intention also recorded.

BASFORD, John K., and Margaret A. Burns of Boston, int.
Aug 18, 1849.

**BASS,** Benjamin, and Mary Gore, Dec. 7, 1757.
John W., of Eastport, Me., and Adelaide C. Norcross, Nov.
26, 1844. c. r. 3.*
Mary, of Dorchester, and Joseph Williams, at Dorchester,
Jan. 1, 1750.

**BASSETT,** Elizabeth H., of Bridgewater, and William H.
Davis, int. July 15, 1838.

**BASTO,** Mason, and Hannah Wheelwright, int. Apr. 29, 1827.

**BATCHELDER** (see also Bachelder, Bacheler), Albert, a. 26
y., box manufacturer, s. Jeremiah and Sally, and Hannah
L. Chase, a. 25 y., d. Anthony and Jane, May 23, 1848.*
Charles Greenleaf, of Hallowell, Me., and Susan W. Curtis,
Dec. 9, 1841.
Joseph, and Betsey K. Tucker of South Bridgewater, int. May
8, 1847.
Joshua, and Harriet Hearsey, int. Dec. 12, 1824.
Joshua, and Martha Ann Jones, int. Sept. 9, 1827.
Nancy [Mrs. int.], and Ethan Allen, Nov. 3, 1825.*

**BATES,** Caleb, of Concord, and Lydia Mason, Nov. 13, 1823.*
Daniel C., and Mary W. Bugbee, Jan. 25, 1841.*
Emeline D., of Providence, R. I., a. 21 y., and Daniel M.
Black, a. 29 y., carpenter, s. Edmund and Comfort, of
Palermo, Me., Dec. 17, 1846.*
Hannah, and Samuel Winchester, Dec. 10, 1801.*
Jane, Mrs., and Moses Pain, June 18, 1679.
Joseph C., and Abby L. Carleton, int. May 5, 1839.
Mary A., and David F. White of Watertown, June 29, 1841.*
Sally A., of Weymouth, and Joseph Harlow, int. Feb. 6, 1847.

**BATIE,** John C., and Ellen McCairn, int. Sept. 22, 1847.

**BATTS,** Timothy, and Sally Newell, Oct. 19, 1800.*

**BAUER,** Elizabeth, and Henry Lehman, Oct. 12, 1834.*

**BAWN,** Margaret Josephine, and Thomas Williams Baldwin,
int. Oct. 12, 1834.

**BAXTER,** Lewis, jr., of Quincy, and Susan E. Kennan, int.
Dec. 25, 1842.

* Intention also recorded.

BAXTER, Maria, and John Creed, May 1, 1836.*
Oliver [Charles, of Braintree. c. R. 2.], and Mary Stone, Feb. 18, 1762.

BAYLEY (see also Bailey), Anna, and John Prentice of Lancaster, Oct. 11, 1728.
Samuell, and Mrs. Anna Richardson, Dec. 17, 1730.

BAYLIE (see also Bailey), James, and Sarah Goddard, at Boston, Apr. 13, 1720.

BAYLIES (see also Bailey), Henry, of Ashland, a. 28 y., tailor, s. Daniel and Lucy, and Catherine R. Newell, of Ashland, a. 25 y., d. Willard and Sarah, Apr. 4, 1849.

BEACH, Martha E., and Isaac M. Staniels, Dec. 10, 1829.

BEACHMAN, Eliza, a. 19 y., d. Anthony and Catherine, and John Murphy, a. 21 y., shoemaker, s. Edward and Lucy, Feb. 15, 1849.*

BEACON (see also Bacon), Abiel, and Jonathan Puffer [of Dorchester. c. R. 2.], July 18, 1717.
Elizabeth, and Ebenezer Edmunds, Sept. 12, 1717.
John, and Abiel Curtiss, Nov. 21, 1693.
Susanna, and Ephraim Allin, Nov. 28, 1716.

BEAGLEY, Joseph, and Eliza Ann Payne, int. July 7, 1846.

BEAL (see also Beals), Grace, and Oliver Shed, July 17, 1787.*
Mary, of Brookline, and Asa Brown, Nov. 4, 1824.*
Sarah, and William Bird, Dec. 1, 1837.
Thomas, and Ruth O. Spencer, July 31, 1842.*

BEALS (see also Beal), Ann, Mrs., and Otis Kenney, both of Canton, June 12, 1826.
Betsy, and Nehemiah Blanchard, Apr. 28, 1807.*
Caroline P., and Henry M. Stearns of Charlestown, int. Dec. 28, 1834.
Lydia [Mrs. int.], and John Pierce, Mar. 20, 1818.*
Lydia B., and William A. Stearns, int. May 31, 1835.
Sarah P., and George Penny of Hingham, ——, 1832. [Dec. 11, 1831. int.]*
Thomas, and Lydia Dammon, int. Apr. 30, 1809.

* Intention also recorded.

**BEAN,** James H., and Abigail Roberts, int. Aug. 26, 1832.
Melinda, and Aaron Bartlett, Apr. 6, 1818.*

**BEARD** (see also Beaver), Sarah, and Aaron Robbins, Feb. 9, 1817.*

**BEATH,** Mary, and Rev. Matthias H. Smith of Guilford, Vt., int. Mar. 20, 1831.

**BEATTY,** John [Beaty. c. r. 5.], and Mary F. Snowdon, July 7, 1844.*

**BEAUMONT,** Charles, and Lawrans [Laurana. c. r. 5.] R. Brewer, Mar. 7, 1833.

**BEAVER** (see also Beard), Lucy [Beard. int.], and Ben[ja-mi]n Burrill, Oct. 29, 1805.*

**BECK** (see also Peck), David, and Mary Ann Stowell, int. Dec. 27, 1849.
Elizabeth, and Andrew Corporal, Oct. 27, 1839.*
John, and Sarah Woods, June 22, 1807.*

**BECKWITH,** George W., of Boston, and Sarah Whittemore, Nov. 26, 1848.
John P., and Rebecca Whittemore of Boston, Nov. 19, 1843. c. r. 7.

**BECON** (see also Bacon), Elizabeth [Beacon. c. r. 2.], and Ebenezer Child of Woodstock, Nov. 30, 1720.

**BEECHER,** John, and Nancy Wallace, int. Oct. 5, 1846.

**BEETHAM,** Betsey, and Christan Castin, Mar. 8, 1812.*
Marcy, and John Smailes, May 12, 1811.*

**BEETON,** Thomas, of Westborough, and Olive Lyon, int. Dec. 1, 1816.
**BEHAN,** John, and Eliza O'Bryan, int. Nov. 17, 1844.

**BELCHER,** Rebecca, Mrs., of Dedham, and Thomas Walter, at Dedham, Dec. 25, 1718.
Sally, of Randolph, and Caleb Pond, int. Nov. 30, 1806.

**BELDING,** Samuel [jr. int.], and Philana Miner, June 5, 1828.*

**BELKNAP,** Charles, and Mercy Webb, Feb. 15, 1773.

* Intention also recorded.

BELKNAP, Charles, jr., and Rebeca Dickerman, Oct. 1, 1803.*
Isaac, and Rebecca Elvill, at Boston, July 17, 1781.

BELL, Amory, and Anna Curtis, Apr. 13, 1823.*
Anna C., d. Amory and Ann, and Frederick E. Wright of Cambridge, Nov. 28, 1847.*
Catherine W., a. 23 y., d. James and Sarah, and Rufus Chapman, a. 27 y., patent leather manufacturer, s. Francis and Elizabeth, Oct. 11, 1846.*
Elizabeth, Mrs., and Lt. Henry Howell Williams, Jan. 28, 1762.
Harriet [B. int.], and Eben H. Folsom, Mar. 26, 1843.*
Harriot, and Nathaniel Brewer, Dec. 29, 1816.*
Margaret, and Isaac Curtis, Aug. 31, 1809.*
Mary, and David Morse of Cambridge, int. Nov. 17, 1822.
Mary E., and Benjamin S. Goodhue, Mar. 12, 1835.
Nancy, a. 23 y., d. Ben[jamin] and Sarah, and Lerenzo [Lorinzo. int.] White, a. 24 y., cabinet maker, s. Joseph and Ruth, of Portsmouth, N. H., Sept. 2, 1846.*
Sarah R., of Brookline, and James Tinkham, June 18, 1835. c. r. 7.
William, and Letitia Porter, int. Aug. 6, 1849.

BELLOWES (see also Bellows), Nancy, [of Boston. c. r. 3.], and James S. Hanscomb, Dec. 25, 1833.*

BELLOWS (see also Bellowes), Abigail, and Luke Smith, Dec. 1, 1765.
Sally, and Jeremiah Evans, Feb. 18, 1827.*

BELSON, Tamor, and John Harding of Newton, int. Mar. 30, 1806.

BELTMAN, John, and Kazienna Kempis, int. Aug. 11, 1849.

BEMAN, David, and Elizabeth Withington, Nov. 2, 1806.*

BENDER, John, and Martha Swan, int. Mar. 3, 1839.

BENIT (see also Bennett), Marie, and Richard Meads, Nov. 6, 1678.

BENJAMIN, Acenith B., a. 23 y., d. John and Esther, and Thomas Cobb, a. 31 y., oyster dealer, s. Thomas and Lucy, Apr. 30, 1848.*
Daniel, and Mary Phillips, Apr. 13, 1746. [1756?]

* Intention also recorded.

BENJAMIN, Esther J., of Athens, Me., a. 19 y., d. John and Esther, and John A. Dyer, a. 22 y., carpenter, s. William and Sally, Sept. 13, 1846.*

Susannah, and Ebenezer Weld, jr., int. ——, 1802.

BENNET (see also Bennett), Jonathan, and Jane Frances, Nov. 9, 1763.

Timothy [W. int.], and Mary Wiswall, Nov. 5, 1826.*

BENNETT (see also Benit, Bennet, Bennit), Anne [Ann. int.], and Ebenezer Dodge, jr., Aug. 3, 1845.*

Mary, and Phillip Doyle, Apr. 9, 1767.

Sarah, and Joseph Newcomb, int. Feb. 16, 1848.

Timothy W., of Brighton, and Phebe Titcomb, Dec. 27, 1829.*

BENNIT (see also Bennett), Susannah [Bennet. dup.], Mrs., d. John, and James Winter, Oct. 9, 1762.

BENT, Deborah, Mrs., and Ebenezer Trescott of Dorchester, at Dorchester, June 19, 1776.

George, of East Sudbury, and Esther Marshall, Jan. 17, 1821.*

BENTLEY, Thomas, and Mrs. Hannah Gould, int. Dec. 25, 1825.

Thomas, and Susannah Frisell, int. Feb. 25, 1827.

BERCE, Artemas, and Mary A. Snell of Dedham, Mar. 18, 1847. C. R. 7.

BERGIN, John, and Margaret Carthy, int. Dec. 31, 1843.

BERR (see also Kerr), William [Kerr. int.], and Elizabeth Coney, Mar. 27, 1796.*

BERRAN (see also Berrien), Bridget, and John Berran, int. July 13, 1847.

John, and Bridget Berran, int. July 13, 1847.

BERRIEN (see also Berran), Benedict, and Susanna A. Williams, int. Aug. 28, 1848.

BERRY, John, and Sarah Burgeen, Feb. 12, 1768.

John [Berg. int.], and Catharine M. Smith, Nov. 27, 1843.*

Moses N., of Lowell, a. 25 y., powder maker, s. David and Nancy, and Emeline Braley of Lowell, a. 19 y., operative, d. Joseph and Julina, Nov. 27, 1845.

**BESSE,** Roxanna, and George Dwight [Wright. int.], Feb. 22, 1846.*

**BESTO,** Susanna, and Roger Stayner, June 22, 1705.

**BETTUES,** Arno, and Pamelia Melcher of Kensington, N. H., int. Jan. 25, 1818.

**BEVERSTOCK,** Francis P., a. 21 y., morocco dresser, s. Edward and Hannah, and Laura Ann Wheeler, a. 22 y., d. Silas and Laura Ann, Mar. 19, 1848.*

**BICKFORD,** Frederick L., and Sarah E. Green of Dedham, Nov. 29, 1832.

**BICKNELL,** Charles, and Catharine P. Haskell, int. May 22, 1825.
Charles, and Mary Tarr, Sept. 13, 1827.*
Humphry, and Jemima Jackson, July 19, 1789.*
James T. [Bicknall. int.], and Caroline Newell, May 23, 1841.*
Mary Ann J., and Francis Holden, ——, 1832. [May 9, 1831. int.]*

**BIGELOW,** Rufus, [of Boston. c. R. 3.], and Pamelia Hill, Sept. 3, 1820.*
Thomas, and Elizabeth Wales, Nov. 24, 1774.

**BILL** (see also Bills), Elizabeth, of Dorchester, and Joseph Andrews, May 10, 1705.
Joseph, and Rebecca Pepper, at Boston, Nov. 5, 1736.
Rebecca, and Abraham Dorr, Sept. 10, 1786.*

**BILLEG,** Godfrey, a. 25 y., carpet weaver, s. Matthias and Mary, and Mary Hoy, a. 20 y., carpet weaver, Jan. 19, 1848.*

**BILLINGS,** Benjamin, and Susana Weld, Apr. 18, 1790.*
Charles H., and Sarah Mason, Apr. 1, 1841.*
Eliza, and Isaac Child, Nov. 22, 1821. c. R. 2.*
George, and Lucy E. Parker, Dec. 26, 1843.*
Hannah, of Sharon, and Warren Hartshorn, int. Nov. 17, 1805.
Hannah, and James Allen, June 8, 1819. c. R. 2.*
Joseph, of Stoughton, and Mary Gookin, int. Jan. 3, 1790.
Joseph H., and Sarah Keith, Oct. 22, 1835.*

* Intention also recorded.

BILLINGS, Lemuel, and Han[na]h Whiting, May 24, 1781.
C. R. 2.

Sarah W., and George Dana, Nov. 30. 1820. C. R. 2.*

Susanna, and Jeremiah Gore, jr. of Portland, Oct. 16, 1819.
C. R. 2.*

BILLS (see also Bill, Bils), Clara M., a. 23 y., d. Shubael and
Harriet, and William H. Burroughs, a. 25 y., nail maker,
s. John and Mary, June 4, 1846.*

Gustavus, and Ann Augusta Kennon of Quincy, int. May 7,
1843.

Harriet Jane [a. 27 y. in pencil. int.], and Henry Onion [a.
25 y. in pencil. int.], Apr. 11, 1844.*

Jesse, and Sarah Ann C. Bliss of Rehoboth, int. Oct. 12, 1828.

Jesse, and Elizabeth K. Whitney, int. Dec. 15, 1833.

Mark, and Maria D. Granger, both of Cambridge, Aug. 18,
1835.

Samantha, and Andrew Horn, Apr. 11, 1826.*

Sarah P., and Joseph K. Barlow, Oct. 31, 1844.*

BILS (see also Bills), Mather [Byles. C. R. 2.], Rev., of New
London, and Mrs. Rebeckah Walter, May 12, 1761.

BINGHAM, Benjamin, and Mary Shepard, Sept. 7, 1823.*

Boyden [Boydin. C. R. 2.], and Rebecca Crane, int. Feb. 5,
1809.

BINNEY, Matthew, and Sarah R. Ellis, Sept. 13, 1827.*

BIRD (see also Burd), Abiel, of Dorchester, and Mindwell
Weeks, Jan. 29, 1704-5.

Ann, of Dorchester, and John Williams, jr., at Dorchester,
May 25, 1749.

Calvin, and Nancy S. Briggs of Dartmouth, int. Nov. 5, 1843.

Calvin, and Mary H. Gulliver, both of Dorchester, June 13,
1848.

Catherine, and John Hewes, Sept. 8, 1848.

Edward, of Dorchester, and Sarah B. Willard, int. May 10,
1829.

Eliza L., and John Green, jr., May 23, 1813.*

Elizabeth, and Richard Fox, Nov. 6, 1760.

Elizabeth, and Daniel Lyon, May 9, 1771.

Elizabeth D., and John H. Houghton, int. Mar. 27, 1831.

Hannah, and Francis F. Morey, int. Nov. 6, 1848.

Jinner, and Elizabeth Cook, Nov. 2, 1817.*

* Intention also recorded.

BIRD, Joanna, of Dorchester, and Samuel Ward, at Dorchester, Nov. 20, 1799.*

John, of Needham, and Mary Lyon, at Needham, May 21, 1785.

Katharine, and Israel Dean, Mar. 27, 1704-5.

Lydia J., of Dorchester, and James W. Felker of Nottingham, N. H., Oct. 9, 1846.

William, and Sarah Beal, Dec. 1, 1837.

**BIRMINGHAM,** Catharine, and Patrick Galher, int. Jan. 9, 1847.

**BISBE** (see also Bisbee), Jonathan [Bisbey, of Boston. c. r. 3.], and Sarah Payson, int. Mar. 12, 1797.

**BISBEE** (see also Bisbe, Bisby), Caroline R., and John Blackburn, int. Mar. 22, 1829.

Harriet N., of Waterville, and Charles F. Tower, int. June 12, 1847.

**BISBY** (see also Bisbee), John, and Sarah Payson, Apr. 11, 1797.

Theop[hilus] F., and Anna Fisk of Groton, int. Feb. 10, 1805.

**BISCON,** Margarett, and William Philleps, Sept. 16, 1713.

**BISHOP,** Elizabeth, and John Druce, May 23, 1700.

Margarett, and Zechariah Chandler, Jan. 18, 1715-16.

Thomas, and Anne Gary, June 7, 1683.

**BLACK,** Daniel M., a. 29 y., carpenter, s. Edmund and Comfort of Palermo, Me., and Emeline D. Bates of Providence, R. I., a. 21 y., Dec. 17, 1846.*

Mary, and John McDaniel, int. Oct. 19, 1848.

Robert, and Elizabeth Fulton, Feb. 15, 1844.*

**BLACKBURN,** John, and Caroline R. Bisbee, int. Mar. 22, 1829.

**BLACKMAN,** Abigail, of Dorchester, and Charles Bridgham, both of Dorchester, May 10, 1827.

Eliakim, of Dorchester, and wid. Sarah Parker, Oct. 18, 1789.*

Henry, and Caroline Enslin, July 9, 1822.*

James, and Betsy Mellish, both of Dorchester, Sept. 28, 1797. c. r. 3.

James, and Mary Allen, July 11, 1813.*

* Intention also recorded.

BLACKMAN, Jerusha, of Dorchester, and Joseph Bugbee, int. May 27, 1821.

John, jr., of Dorchester, and Abigail How, at Dorchester, Jan. 1, 1746.

Lucy, of Dorchester, and Robert G. Babcock, int. Apr. 4, 1822.

Samuel, jr., of Dorchester, and Mrs. Elizabeth Oldman, at Dorchester, Feb. 28, 1780.

Tryphene, and William Sprague, Feb. 19, 1764. [Feb. 9. c. r. 2.]

William M., and Eunice Holden, both of Dorchester, Oct. 15, 1823.

**BLAGGE,** Benjamin, and Elisabeth Ann Hatch, int. Aug. 6, 1815.

**BLAIR,** Mary Ann, and George S. Peters, int. May 18, 1828.

**BLAISDELL** (see also Blasdel), George J., and Jane N. Harris, Apr. 27, 1841.*

Maria A., and W[illia]m B. Jones, Oct. 13, 1844.*

**BLAKE,** Ann, b. Ireland, and Peter Tay, b. Ireland, Oct. 30, 1849.*

Charles, and Maria Catharine Barnes, Feb. 21, 1843.*

Dearborn, and Mrs. Polly S. Heath, July 21, 1824.*

Ellen, and Thomas Gannon, int. Apr. 4, 1841.

Eunice, and Simeon Noyes, jr., Sept. 21, 1841.*

George W., a. 23 y., box maker, b. Keene, N. H., s. Joseph and Sarah, and Mary A. Boynton, a. 22 y., b. Alna, Me., d. John and Mary, Oct. 28, 1849.*

Jeremiah, a. 23 y., engraver, s. Jeremiah and Lucy, and Eliza A. W. Evans, a. 18 y., d. Cha[rle]s and Emeline, Nov. 9, 1847.*

Jesse, and Nancy Henery [Hennery. int.], June 2, 1844.*

Joseph, and Elisa McClure, May 29, 1814.*

Mehetable, of Holden, and Aaron Goodale, int. Dec. 23, 1804.

Oliver, and Harriet Hayden, int. Apr. 5, 1835.

Peter, of Dorchester, and Fanny Colburn, Apr. 13, 1820.*

Rachel, and John Pierce, both of Dorchester, June 13, 1793.

Samuel, and Hannah Curtiss, May 15, 1712.

Samuel, and Caroline Temple of Dorchester, int. Nov. 30, 1828.

Thomas, and Elizabeth J. Smith, Oct. 2, 1839.*

* Intention also recorded.

BLAKE, Ursula A., of Wrentham, and Asa B. Lowell, int. Mar. 4, 1838.

William, a. 27 y., patent leather dresser, s. William and Abigail, and Francis P. D. Kelly, a. 26 y., visor maker, d. Joseph and Betsey, Feb. 4, 1846.*

**BLANCHARD** (see also Blancher), Charles H., a. 24 y., merchant, s. Jedidiah and Sarah, and Mary E. Stephenson, a. 19 y., d. Benj[ami]n and Mary, Oct. 20, 1846.*

Eliza, and Thomas Sealy, Dec. 5, 1824.*

Elizabeth, and William Snell, June 28, 1827.*

Frances, and Seth Snell, Apr. 24, 1834.*

Francis, resident, and Thankfull Stevens of Braintree, int. July 25, 1784.

Harriot, and Theodore Otis, Dec. 1, 1841.

John W., and Louisa P. Barbour, Nov. 14, 1844.*

Joshua, and Ruhamey Lovering of Exeter, N. H., int. Oct. 28, 1792.

Mary Ann, and Jerome Prescott, May 30, 1835.

Nath[anie]l, and Elizabeth Perry, May 24, 1759.

Nehemiah, and Betsy Beals, Apr. 28, 1807.*

Sarah, and Emmons Slocomb, jr. of Cambridge, Mar. 21, 1824.*

William, Capt., of Dorchester, and Harriet Lambert, int. Sept. 8, 1816.

**BLANCHER** (see also Blanchard), Ephraim, and Mary Everett, May 5, 1752.

John, and Mary Perry, Nov. 14, 1737.

**BLANEY,** Aaron, and Eunice Seager, Dec. 6, 1770.

Abigail, and Asa Huntting, Oct. 18, 1789.*

Ambrose, [of Boston. c. r. 3.], and Ann Mears Blaney, May 19, 1819.*

Ann Mears, and Ambrose Blaney [of Boston. c. r. 3.], May 19, 1819.*

Elizabeth, and Thomas Nolan, Feb. 20, 1762.

Hannah A., and Gilman Page of Cambridge, May 20, 1835.*

Lidia, and William Gridley, Dec. 4, 1755.

Mary, Mrs., and George Zeigler [Zegler. int.], Sept. 9, 1784.*

Samuel, and Anna Curtis, June 12, 1791.*

William, and Mary Gridley, Feb. 17, 1755.

William, and Mrs. Catharine Mears, May 8, 1783.*

* Intention also recorded.

**BLANK,** Joseph, and Pauline E. Waldmire, int. Dec. 29, 1844.

**BLASDEL** (see also Blaisdell), Ruth, and Solomon Goldsmith, int. Aug. 23, 1829.

**BLEESZ,** Charles, and Catherine Ilig, int. Dec. 23, 1846.

**BLEMUS,** Willet C., of Dedham, a. 24 y., cabinet maker, s. Thomas and Pheby, and Eliza A. Homer of Dorchester, a. 22 y., d. Joseph and Mary, July 8, 1849.

**BLENDELL,** George H., and Sophia M. Farrington, Aug. 9, 1827.*

**BLISS,** Elijah, of Lebanon, and Rebecca Bradley [Feb. or Mar. ?], 1782.
Elizabeth, and Caspar Esser, int. Nov. 7, 1848.
Sarah Ann C., of Rehoboth, and Jesse Bills, int. Oct. 12, 1828.

**BLODGET** (see also Blodgett), John, and Rebecca Mitchell of Boxford, int. Aug. 4, 1833.

**BLODGETT** (see also Blodget), Susan S., of Lexington, and Amos H. Richardson, int. Aug. 18, 1844.

**BLOOD,** Eliza, and William M. Crehore, int. July 1, 1832.
Sylvanus, and Lydia Brown of Brookline, int. Dec. 22, 1793.
Unice, and William Shattuck, residents, July 16, 1788.*

**BLOSSOM,** Delia C., of West Barnstable, and Henry H. Prouty, int. Mar. 22, 1835.

**BOARDMAN** (see also Bordman), Mary, of Cambridge, and Ebenez[e]r Dorr, at Cambridge, Feb. 16, 1709-10.

**BODGE,** Angeline, and Timothy Hunt, Jan. 17, 1840.*
Charles, and Louisa Trefrey, int. July 12, 1829.
John, and Abagail Sweat, int. Nov. 23, 1800.
John, and Polly Page, Sept. 3, 1821.*
Lucius B., a. 23 y., gentleman, s. John and Mary, and Sarah E. Sumner, a. 16 y., d Arthur and Mary, Nov. 26, 1847.*
Lydia, Mrs., and Nathan Henderson, Feb. 21, 1802.*
Samuel W., and Angeline Drew, int. Oct. 16, 1836.

**BODOWIN** (see also Bowden), Experience, and Thomas Cobbet, May 20, 1709.

* Intention also recorded.

**BOFFEE,** Elizabeth, and Robart Harris, Jan. 24, 1642.

**BOGLE,** Sara, of Brighton, and Joel G. Davis, int. Nov. 8, 1840.

**BOID,** see Bond.

**BOILSTON** (see also Boylston), Hannah, and Beza Cushing, Feb. 15, 1753.
Mary, and Daniel Bugbe, jr., May 20, 1762.
Robert, and —— ——, Mar. 29, 1750.

**BOILSTONE** (see also Boylston), Luce, and Benjamin Phillips of Charlestown, Mar. 10, 1702-3.

**BOIT** (see also Boyde), Caroline, and Henry T. [F. c. r. 3.] Baker [of Boston. c. r. 3.], Nov. 25, 1822.*

**BOLIN,** John, and Abby A. Tufts of Wilton, N. H., int. Sept. 1, 1844.

**BOLLES** (see also Bowles), John A., Esq., and Catharine H. [Dix. int.], Nov. 11, 1834.*

**BOLTER,** Benjamin, and Polly Nolen, Dec. 21, 1794.*

**BOLTON,** Caroline A., a. 18 y., d. Leonard and Mary Ann, and William O. Frost, a. 21 y., laborer, s. Benj[amin] and Eliza, Jan. 14, 1847.*

**BOMAN** (see also Bowman), John, and Martha Goding, Mar. 4, 1821.*

**BONAR,** John, and Margarett Donally, int. Dec. 27, 1849.

**BOND** (see also Boyde), Caroline [Boid. c. r. 5.], and J. Phillips George, Oct. 13, 1844.*
Elizabeth, and Bagley Carter of Dorchester, July 8, 1824.*

**BONEMORT** (see also Bonnmort), Nicholas, and Mary Gill of Dorchester, int. Mar. 18, 1832.

**BONNEY,** William C., and Dolly Currier of Amesbury, int. Jan. 5, 1848.

**BONNMORT** (see also Bonemort), Clementina, and Charles Mason, Dec. 25, 1817. c. r. 2.*

**BOOS,** Valentine, and Sophia Minot, Aug. 21, 1834.

* Intention also recorded.

**BOOTH,** Phidelia A., and William P. Pierce, int. Feb. 10, 1849.

Susan, and Ephraim Walcutt, int. June 21, 1829.

**BOOTHBY,** Roxanna, and Daniel Torrey [Torsey. int.] of Lowell, Dec. 22, 1844.*

**BORDEN,** Louisa, and Freeborn Payne, Apr. 3, 1836.*

**BORDMAN** (see also Boardman), Andrew, and Sarah Goddard, Oct. 20, 1715.

Sarah, and Benjamin Eaton, Apr. 17, 1735.

**BOSON** (see also Bosson), Dorothy, and Elias Monk, Aug. 5, 1714.

Winter, and Mary Abrams of Milton, at Milton, ——, 1761.

**BOSS,** John W., of Eastport, Me., and Adelaide C. Norcross, Nov. 26, 1844.

**BOSSON** (see also Boson), Deborah, and William White; Dec. 22, 1767.

John, and Eleanour Nissbit, Sept. 3, 1747.

Mary, and John Brown, Aug. 4, 1777.

Nancy B., and Isaac Shaw, Nov. 30, 1794.*

Sarah, and William Patrick, May 3, 1758.

Sukey, and Jonathan Hills, Dec. 19, 1803.*

William, and Mrs. Ruth Curtis of Dorchester, at Dorchester, July 9, 1767.

William, and Sarah Hawes, Jan. 24, 1771.

William, jr., and Abigail Partridge, Aug. 15, 1745.

William, jr., and Prudence Mayo, Sept. 18, 1777.

William, jr., and Susanna Mayo, int. Oct. 31, 1784.

**BOSSUET,** Louisa, and Daniel Kyburz, int. May 6, 1832.

**BOUGE,** Edward, and Mrs. —— Burchett, int. July 6, 1849.

Hannah, b. Ireland, and Patrick Donnogan [Downey. int.], b. Ireland, Sept. 11, 1849.*

**BOURN** (see also Bourne, Bourns), Sarah, and Lt. Richard Humphry Greaton, Feb. 6, 1787.*

Sheerjashub, Rev., of Scituate, and Mrs. Susannah [Jehannah. c. r. 2.] Stevens, Nov. 10, 1757.

**BOURNE** (see also Bourn), Ann M., and James D. Kent, Mar. 24, 1841.

* Intention also recorded.

BOURNE, Mary, and Alvah Cook, int. Jan. 8, 1843.

**BOURNS** (see also Bourn), Ezra [Bourns. int.] of Falmouth, and Nancy Swift, Nov. 28, 1799.*

**BOUTELLE,** Rosetta A., of Antrim, N. H., a. 20 y., d. Charles and Betsey, and George H. Newell, a. 21 y., cabinet manufacturer, s. Willard and Sarah, July 12, 1849.*

**BOUVE,** Frances L., and T. B. Moses, int. June 9, 1844.

**BOWDEN** (see also Bodowin), Mary, and Thomas Larabee, Nov. 30, 1828.*

**BOWDITCH,** Galen, and Martha W. Child, June 12, 1833.*
Galen, and Susan Child, Feb. 10, 1836.*

**BOWELS** (see also Bowles), Mary E., and William Crosby, Sept. 9, 1845.

**BOWEN** (see also Bowin), Abby F., and Sylvanus Page, int. Feb. 5, 1843.
Elisabeth, and Edward Morriss, May 24, 1683.
Elizabeth, Mrs., and Simon Rogers, July 10, 1728.
Henry, and Elizabeth Johnson, Dec. 20, 1658.
Henry, and Susanna Heath, Apr. 14, 1685.
John, and Mehetabell May, June 6, 1734.
John, and Ann Roby of East Sudbury, at East Sudbury, Apr. 15, 1798.*
Joshua, and Abigail Smith of Bridgewater, at Bridgewater, May 26, 1782.
Margaret, and Joseph Bacon, Nov. 6, 1688.
Margret, and John Weld, Dec. 24, 1647.
Samuel, and Mary Blaney, Feb. 14, 1771.
William, and Jane F. Dunkin, int. Aug. 7, 1848.

**BOWERS,** Amanda P., and Benjamin H. Ropes, int. June 3, 1838.
George P., and Waitstill A. Savery, of Carver, int. Sept. 29, 1844.
Mary, and William Nanahan of Deering, N. H., May 16, 1830.*
Sarah A., and Albert Clark of Brookline, Feb. 15, 1842.*

**BOWIN** (see also Bowen), Abigail, and Caleb Kindrick of Newton, Sept. 14, 1721.

* Intention also recorded.

Bowin, Hannah, and John Chamberlain, Dec. 30, 1725.
Isaack, and Elizabeth Tucker, Apr. 15, 1720.

BOWKER, Lois [Louis Bouker. int.], of Sudbury, and
Stephen Chamberlain [jr. int.], at Sudbury, Apr. 13,
1793.*

BOWLES (see also Bolles, Bowels, Bowls), Catherine, a. 22
y., d. John and Mary, and William J. Burges, a. 22 y.,
blacksmith, s. John and Ann, Jan. 30, 1848.*
Elizabeth Wallace, a. 19 y., d. Stephen J. and Elizabeth T.,
and J. Wingate Thornton [of Boston. int.], a. 29 y., an
attorney at law, s. James B. of Saco, Me. and Eliza
Gookin of Northampton, N. H., May 31, 1848.*
Francis E. B., and Cushing Stetson of Baltimore, Md. [of
Charlestown. int.], Oct. 23, 1838.*
John, and Elizabeth Heath, Apr. 2, 1649.
Jôhn, and Sarah Eliot, Nov. 16, 1681.
Mary, Mrs., and Walter Goodridge, Feb. 8, 1727-8.
Mary E., and William Crosby, int. July 20, 1845.
William [of Boston. c. r. 3.], and Frances Elizabeth Bur-
rows, Oct. 4, 1826.*

BOWLS (see also Bowles), Mary, and Thomas Gardner, Nov.
17, 1673.

BOWMAN (see also Boman), Brooks, and Achsah Tufts, Aug.
6, 1826.*
Charles C., and Sarah H. Smith of Waltham, June 3, 1847.
Emeline A., a. 19 y., d. Brooks and A., and John Robinson,
a 23 y., blacksmith, s. John and Lucy, July 21, 1847.*
Joanna B., of Boston, and James W. L. Gridley, int. July 9,
1847.
Nancy, and Miles Sweeney, int. Feb. 17, 1849.
Rebecca, Mrs., of Cambridge, and Stephen Choat, Feb. 4, 1730-
31.
Sarah, and Benja[min] Thompson, at Boston, Sept. 22, 1724.
William, and Lucy Sumner, June 5, 1777.

BOWMASTER, Francis, and Victoria Miller, int. Aug. 25,
1847.

BOWNISTER, Joseph, and Christeanna Woolrush, int. Jan. 4,
1846.

* Intention also recorded.

**BOYD** (see also Boyde), Thomas, of Dorchester, a. 25 y., s.
Sam[ue]l and Sarah, and Nancy Rice of Dorchester, a.
17 y., d. Adam and Margaret, Apr. 8, 1847.

**BOYDE** (see also Boid, Boit, Boyd), John C. [Boyd.int.],
and Catharine G. Smith, Oct. 7, 1845.*
Margarett C. [Boyd. int.], a. 19 y. d. James and Margarett,
and Edward Wyman, a. 27 y., merchant, s. Rufus and
Ann, Sept. 23, 1845.*
Patrick, b. Ireland, and Margarett Dugan, b. Ireland, Dec.
18, 1849.*

**BOYDEN** (see also Boydon), Eliza, and William Marden of
Franklin, boat builder, Oct. 24, 1847.*
Obed A., and Charlotte Shertliff, int. June 1, 1828.
Thomas, and Mrs. Abigail Welch, Sept. 28, 1780.

**BOYDON** (see also Boyden), Lemuell, and Mary Seaver, Dec.
22, 1757.

**BOYLAN,** James, and Mary O'Brien, int. May 9, 1848.

**BOYLE,** John, and Ann Sweeney of Boston, int. Mar. 20,
1849.
Patrick, and Mary Donovan, int. Oct. 11, 1849.
Richard, and Jane Hunt, int. Jan. 30, 1847.

**BOYLSTON** (see also Boilston, Boilstone, Boylstone), Ben-
jamin, of Brookline, and Mrs. Eliz[abe]th Sumner, Nov.
30, 1727.
Elisabeth, and Benjamin Williams, Mar. 9, 1756.
John Lane, and Sally Brooks of Princeton, int. May 9, 1813.
Susanna, and Samuel Sumner, Aug. 18, 1757.

**BOYLSTONE** (see also Boylston), Ann, and Robert Williams,
Mar. 29, 1750. c. r. 2.
Rebecca, and William Abbot, May 25, 1708.

**BOYNTON,** Mary A., a. 22 y., b. Alna, Me., d. John and
Mary, and George W. Blake, a. 23 y., box maker, b.
Keene, N. H., s. Joseph and Sarah, Oct. 28, 1849.*

**BRACKEN** (see also Brackin), William, and Esther Doyle, int.
Oct. 7, 1848.

**BRACKET** (see also Brackett), John, and Rebecca Ruggles,
Apr. 10, 1705.

* Intention also recorded.

BRACKET, Kezia, and John Pattison, June 11, 1706.

**BRACKETT** (see also Bracket), Charles, of Quincy, and Betsey Bugbee, Nov. 15, 1801.*
Isaac, and Mary Clay, Oct. 7, 1819.*
James S., of Portland, and Ann M. Jones, int. Dec. 16, 1838.
Samuel, and Elizabeth Corey, Nov. 17, 1748.
William, of Newton, and Ann Hancock, Feb. 21, 1813.*

**BRACKIN** (see also Bracken), James W., and Rebecca T. Reed, int. Apr. 28, 1848.

**BRADBURST** (see also Bradhurst), Ralph, and Hannah Galeucia, Mar. 28, 1716.

**BRADBURY**, Edward, and Abagail Hill of Cambridge, int. Sept. 16, 1804.
Phebe, and William C. Twombly, Aug. 26, 1844.*

**BRADEENE** (see also Breaden), Nancy H., of Dedham, and Addison P. Tuck, int. May 8, 1836.

**BRADFORD**, Charles F., and Eliza E. Hickling, Nov. 15, 1843.*
Elizabeth, Mrs., and Edmund F. Pope, June 6, 1836.*
Louisa E., and Cha[rle]s H. Thomas of Hingham, Dec. 12, 1833.*
Sarah P., and Julius B. Champney, int. Aug. 25, 1833.

**BRADHERS** (see also Bradhurst), Ralph, and Hannah Gore, June 13, 1677.

**BRADHURST** (see also Bradburst Bradhers, Brodders, Brodhurst), Dorothy, and Jacob Bacon, Dec. 24, 1700.
Rhoda, and John Colburn, Mar. 13, 1703-4.

**BRADLEE** (see also Bradley), Adeline, and Ebenezer B. Scott [jr. int.], Oct. 9, 1825.*
Amerinta, and Thomas Faxon, int. Dec. 13, 1829.
Elizabeth, and James E. Hewes, Mar. 30, 1828.*
George W., and Elizabeth S. Jewett of Pepperell, int. Oct. 11, 1840.
Lemuel, and Sarah Derby of Brookline, int. Apr. 30, 1820.
Lemuel, and Susan Leonard, July 4, 1824.*
Mary, and Thomas T. Wadsworth of Milton, June 3, 1829.*
Stephen H., and Lydia R. Snowdon, Dec. 15, 1844.*
Thomas, and Catharine Pendergast, int. Oct. 10, 1830.

* Intention also recorded.

**BRADLEY** (see also Bradlee), Dominick, and Ann Gibbons, int. Apr. 25, 1849.

Edward W., and Elizabeth W. Williams, May 25, 1825.*

Edward W., and Sarah Davis, Apr. 4, 1826.*

Isaac, and Joanna Hawes, both residents, June 11, 1789.*

James, and Catherine Roach, int. Apr. 18, 1848.

John, and Margarett Gillespie, int. Nov. 5, 1849.

Josuha, and Mrs. Sarah Clap of Dorchester, at Dorchester, Jan. 9, 1770.

Lemuel, and Mrs. Patience Howe, Jan. 23, 1783.*

Lemuel, and Mary Burrill of Brookline, July 21, 1796.*

Rebecca, and Elijah Bliss of Lebanon [Feb. or Mar. ?], 1782.

Robert, and Catharine Killan, int. Apr. 12, 1846.

Sarah A., a. 25 y., d. Charles and Sarah, and Nathaniel S. Howe of Jonesville, Mich., a. 29 y., lawyer, s. Isaac R. and Sarah S., May 26, 1846.*

Sarah D., a. 23 y., d. Lemuel and Sarah, and John E. Sheafe, widr., a. 28 y., woodturner, s. John and Joanna, May 31, 1846.*

**BRADSHAW,** Elizabeth, of Medford, and Andrew Floyd, at Medford, Oct. 31, 1765.

**BRADSTREET,** Samuel H., of Charlestown, and Elizabeth [Betsey, C. R. 3] Weld, July 30, 1811.

**BRADY** (see also Briady), Ann, and Phillip O. Reilly, int. Sept. 24, 1846.

Ann, and John Roan, int. Feb. 7, 1848.

Ann, and John Brady of Randolph, int. Feb. 17, 1848.

Ann, and John McKenna, int. Oct. 28, 1848.

Ellen, and Charles Kearin, int. July 21, 1849.

John, and Elizabeth Donnelly, int. Jan. 13, 1846.

John, of Randolph, and Ann Brady, int. Feb. 17, 1848.

John, b. Ireland, and Margarett Gillispie, b. Ireland, Nov. 19, 1849.

Mary, and Peter Gafney, int. May 18, 1847.

**BRAGG,** Abigail, and Joseph Harper, int. Sept. 8, 1833.

Horatio N., and Mary Hatton, int. July 29, 1832.

**BRAID,** John B., and Meriam P. Channel, Nov. 30, 1797.*

* Intention also recorded.

**BRALEY** (see also Brawley, Brayley), Emeline, of Lowell, a. 19 y., operative, d. Joseph and Julina, and Moses N. Berry of Lowell, a. 25 y., powder maker, s. David and Nancy, Nov. 27, 1845.

**BRAMAN** (see also Bramin), Jenette E., of Providence, R. I., and Luther Tinkham, int. May 4, 1845.

**BRAMIN** (see also Braman), Isaac G., Dr., of Georgetown, and Caroline W. Balch, int. Oct. 18, 1840.

**BRAN**, William F., a. 23 y., carpenter, s. William, and Mary S. Mellus, a. 19 y., d. John and Mary, May 31, 1848.*

**BRANAN** (see also Brennon), Bridget, and John Dolan, int. July 3, 1846.

**BRAND,** George, and Mathew [sic.] Heath, July 24, 1643.

**BRANHAM,** Emily, and Francis Tracy, int. Jan. 15, 1848.

**BRAWLEY** (see also Braley), Henry, and Margarett Murphy, int. Oct. 23, 1847.

**BRAY,** Eunice S., and Hiram W. C. Burnham, int. Oct. 6, 1833.
Mary, and Peter Linen, int. Oct. 2, 1836.

**BRAYLEY** (see also Braley), Nancy, of Grafton, and Thomas Sweet, Dec. 27, 1840.*

**BRAZIER,** James, and Elizabeth H. Hunt, int. Mar. 15, 1818.
Margaret E., and Abiel E. Thompson of Concord, N. H., May 22, 1822.*

**BREADEN** (see also Bradeene, Bruden), William, of [Kingston. int.], Upper Canada, and Margaret Armstrong, May 17, 1838.*

**BRECK,** Mary, Mrs., of Dorchester, and John Baker, jr., at Dorchester, Nov. 20, 1771.

Reuben, and Emeline Littlefield of Medway, int. Oct. 30, 1825.

**BREDEGER,** Eliza, and John Veatt, int. Nov. 9, 1849.

**BREED,** Mary, and John H. Webber, int. Sept. 16, 1838.

**BREHIN,** Francis J., and Catherine Ellen, int. Oct. 7, 1848.

* Intention also recorded.

**BRENNON** (see also Branan, Brinnen), Hannah, and Michael Keagan, May 15, 1848.*

**BRETT,** Jonathan, and Martha Bartlett, int. Aug. 26, 1827.

**BREWER** (see also Bruer), Adeline, and William Shepherd, Nov. 20, 1822.*
Anna C. B., and Moses Johnson, Aug. 8, 1824.*
Dolly, and George Woods, Oct. 15, 1766.
Dorothy, and John Williams, Mar. 15, 1715-16.
Dorothy, and Henry Winchester, jr. [of Brookline. c. r. 2.], Mar. 3, 1748. [1747-8. c. r. 2].
Ebenezer, and Mary Foster, Dec. 24, 1794.*
Ebenezer, and Elizabeth White, Apr. 8, 1807.*
Edward, and Catharine Sparhawk Aspinwall of Brookline, int. Oct. 1, 1786.
Elizabeth, and John Ward, May 24, 1807.*
Elizabeth, and Samuel Weld, Jan. 19, 1741-2.
Gardner, and Mary Weld, Apr. 1, 1831.*
Joanna, and Samuel Goddard, May 28, 1782.
Johanna, and Daniel Harriss, s. Robert, Nov. 14, 1682.
John, and Margaret Rogers, at Boston, June 30, 1737.
John, and Joanna Aspinwall of Brookline, at Brookline, Nov. 24, 1761.
Joseph, and Rebeckah Weld, Oct. 20, 1748.
Joseph, and Abigail May, Apr. 15, 1798.*
Lawrans [Laurana. c. r. 5.] R., and Charles Beaumont, Mar. 7, 1833.
Margarett, and Joseph Winchester [of Brookline. c. r. 2.], Nov. 27, 1740.
Mary, and Reuben Whitney, Dec. 12, 1763. c. r. 2.
Mary, and Joseph Smith, Sept. 17, 1766.
Mary, and William Brewer, May 19, 1803.*
Mary F., and Thomas A. Brewer of Brookline, Oct. 3, 1820.*
Moses, and Abigail May, Dec. 23, 1798. *
Nathanael, and Elizabeth Sunderland, Dec. 26, 1705.
Nathanael, and Elizabeth Mayo, Apr. 10, 1717.
Nathaniel, and Elizabeth Rand, Dec. 6, 1661.
Nathaniel, and Margaret Weld, Mar. 17, 1692.
Nathaniel, and Margaret Wheeler, at Boston, Dec. 6, 1763.
Nathaniel, and Elizabeth Curtis, Nov. 6, 1788.*
Nathaniel, and Harriot Bell, Dec. 29, 1816.*
Rebecca, and Robert Champney, Oct. —, 1767.
Rebecca, and Samuel Craft of Brookline, Dec. 1, 1811.*

* Intention also recorded.

BREWER, Rebeckah [Rebekah. int.], and William Brewer, Aug. 12, 1784.*

Sarah, and John Goddard [of Brookline. C. R. 2.], June 30, 1753.

Sarah, and Perly Morse, May 1, 1817.*

Susan C., and Thomas W. Scott, Sept. 28, 1818.*

Susan Davenport, and Samuel Dudley, Nov. 18, 1810.*

Susana, Mrs., and Joseph Devenport, Apr. 3, 1783.

Thomas A., of Brookline, and Mary F. Brewer, Oct. 3, 1820.*

William, and Rebeckah [Rebekah. int.] Brewer, Aug. 12, 1784.*

William, and Mary Brewer, May 19, 1803.*

**BREWSTER,** Elisha, and Mrs. Jane Williams, Feb. 1, 1779.

Ruth A., of Medford, a. 20 y., d. John and Elizabeth, and Daniel P. Quckenbush of Lansing, Mich., a. 24 y., artist, Oct. 15, 1848.*

**BRIADY** (see also Brady), Mary, and Thomas O'Reilly, int. Sept. 1, 1844.

**BRIAN** (see also Brine), Catharine, and James Gurrey, int. Oct. 21, 1845.

**BRIAR,** William, and Christian H. Allen, int. Apr. 13, 1823.

**BRICK,** Edward, of Dorchester, and Mrs. Sarah Williams, May 22, 1735.

**BRICKETT,** Nath[anie]l, jr., and Catharine G. Stoddard, int. Aug. 9, 1840.

**BRIDE,** Mary, and William McCloud, int. Apr. 18, 1830.

**BRIDGE,** Abigail, and Joseph Child of Woodstock, Nov. 29, 1722.

Abigail, Mrs., and Benjamin Curtis, Oct. 17, 1751.

Christian, and Joseph Heath, at Boston, June 18, 1732.

Edward, and Mary Brooks, May 27, 1690.

Edw[ar]d, and Rebeckah Gridley of Brookline, Sept. 16, 1759.

Edward, jr., and Mrs. Anna Child of Brooklyn [Brookline. C. R. 2.], Nov. 7, 1728.

Elizabeth, and Daniel Harris of Dudley, June 20, 1745.

Elizabeth, and Thomas Serjeant, May 11, 1765.

Hannah, and John Cheever, Nov. 9, 1732.

Hannah, and Samuel White, jr., May 21, 1763.

* Intention also recorded.

BRIDGE, John, and Elizabeth Mayo, Apr. 6, 1727.
Mary, d. John, and Joseph Lyon, s. William, Mar. 23, 1680-81.
Mary, and Benjamin Savell, Jan. 10, 1716-17.
Mary, and Capt. Ebenezer Dorr, at Boston, Sept. 25, 1749.
Mary, and Obadiah Druce [of Brookline. c. r. 2.], Feb. 1,
    1750. [1749-50. c. r. 2.]
Prudence, and John May, June 2, 1684.
Prudence, and William Heath, Apr. 24, 1716.
Prudence, and Isaiah Whiting, June —, 1754. c. r. 2.

**BRIDGHAM** (see also Brigham), Charles, and Abigail
    Blackman, both of Dorchester, May 10, 1827.

**BRIGDEN,** Thomas G., of Middleborough, and Eliza S.
    Smith, int. Mar. 28, 1841.

**BRIGGS,** E. Foster, and Harriet Guild, Nov. 13, 1845.*
Joshua, a. 24 y., cabinet maker, s. Cornelius and Mary, and
    Deborah J. Cushing, a. 21 y., d. John and Sarah, May 8,
    1849.*
Nancy S., of Dartmouth, and Calvin Bird, int. Nov. 5, 1843.
Otis, and Dorothy A. Colburn, int. Jan. 5, 1806.
Peter, and Elizabeth Atherton, —, 1701.
Sarah H., a. 21 y., d. Cornelius and Mary, and James W.
    Cushing, a. 23 y., clerk, s. John and Sarah, Jan. 3, 1849.*
William, and Mary Ann Farrer, Mar. 19, 1838.*

**BRIGHAM** (see also Bridgham), Catharine, and William
    Henry Jones, int. Apr. 7, 1833.
Elizabeth T., and Samuel Spurr, jr., int. May 30, 1841.
Lydia Ann, and Isaac Stevens, Mar. 25, 1838.*
Mary R., and Oliver A. Richardson of Lowell, Jan. 23, 1834.
Nathaniel, and Nancy Brown, Mar. 20, 1808.*
Peter, and Susan C. Clark, int. Aug. 29, 1841.
Simon, and Mrs. Hannah Roe, int. —, 1804.
Stephen, and Lucy White, Feb. 22, 1804.*

**BRIGHT,** Anna, and Samuell Ruggles, May 26, 1670.

**BRIGNEY,** William, and Hannah Welch, int. Jan. 6, 1848.

**BRIMMER,** Susan, and Henderson Inches of Boston, Sept. 15,
    1802.*

**BRINE** (see also Brian), Catherine [Bridget Bryan. dup.],
    and Michael Doland [Dolan. dup.], int. Jan. 17 [18.
    dup.], 1848.

* Intention also recorded.

**BRINLEY,** Edward, and Ann Matilda Bartlett, Nov. 18, 1835.*

Maria L., and Seth H[illman. int.] Barnes, Nov. 21, 1837.*

**BRINNEN** (see also Brennon), Bridget, and Edward Rooney, int. Dec. 29, 1846.

**BRINTNALL,** Jonathan, and Mary Williams, July 12, 1781.

**BRISTOR,** Dolly, and Nahum Rand, Feb. 11, 1842.*

Jerusha, of Rumford, Me., a. 33 y., and Obed Taylor, laborer, Sept. 7, 1846.*

**BROAD,** Betsey, of Natick, and Charles S. White, int. Jan. 1, 1826.

Calvin, and Priscilla McIntosh of Needham, int. Mar. 6, 1814.

Charlotte, and Ephraim Willis, int. May 4, 1828.

Dorothy C., and Sherman Derby of Dublin, N. H., Nov. 14, 1837.*

John, and Mary Richards, Sept. 30, 1801. c. r. 2.*

Wilder, and Elvira W. Shepard of Canton, int. Sept. 22, 1833.

**BROADRICK** (see also Broderick), Susan S., and John Glyn, int. Aug. 18, 1839.

**BROBSTON,** Nancy, and John Palmer, May 21, 1825.

**BROCK,** William, a. 27 y., blacksmith, s. Luke and Jane, and Charlotte Stevens, a. 21 y., d. John and Lucy, Oct. 29, 1848.*

**BODDERS** (see also Bradhurst), Michael [Broaders. int.], b. Ireland, and Margarett Hennessy, b. Ireland, Aug. 3, 1849.*

**BRODERICK** (see also Broadrick, Brodrick), Bridget, and Thomas Farrell, int. Sept. 25, 1842.

Bridget, and John Dolan, int. Jan. 1, 1843.

Margarett, and John Melody, int. Feb. 8, 1849.

**BRODHURST** (see also Bradhurst), Abigail, and Isaac Bacon, Jan. 1, 1710-11.

Hannah, and Timothy Peirce, Oct. 12, 1709.

**BRODRICK** (see also Broderick), David, and Winefred Dollon, int. Sept. 20, 1845.

* Intention also recorded.

**BRONLY,** Michael, and Hannah Greely, int. July 31, 1848.

**BRONSDEL,** Benjamin [Bronsdon, int.], of Milton, and Salley Kneeland, Jan. 15, 1786.*

**BROOK** (see also Brooks), Enos, and Polly McGlaffling, Dec. 25, 1800. c. r. 2.*

**BROOKER,** Benja[min] [Broker, int.], and Harriet Grandison of Scituate, at Scituate, Jan. 27, 1791.*

**BROOKES** (see also Brooks), Tabitha, and Benjamin Dows, May 11, 1708.

**BROOKS** (see also Brook, Brookes), Elizabeth, and John Baker, June 25, 1844.*

Elizabeth H., of Boston, and Benjamin B. Converse, int. Oct. 26, 1847.

Emily C., a. 20 y., d. Benjamin and Louisa, and Richard B. Howard of Cayuga Falls, O., a. 21 y., baker, s. John B. and Deborah, Aug. 26, 1849.*

Harriet L., a. 18 y., dressmaker, d. Benj[amin] and Louisa, and William Mason, widr., a. 30 y., cabinet maker, s. Thomas and Mary, Aug. 3, 1845.*

Helen E., of Boston, and Joseph Morrill, jr., int. Dec. 13, 1849.

James O., of Lawrence, a. 28 y., carpenter, s. Barker and Margarett, and Sarah F. Abbott, a. 22 y., d. Asa and Esther, Sept. 8, 1847.*

Jarusha, and William Foss, int. Jan. 17, 1819.

John, and Avis Hazlett, Oct. 5, 1823.*

John, and Sarah M. Burlingame of Brighton, int. Mar. 22, 1835.

Jonathan, and Nancy Pierce of Dorchester, int. Jan. 19, 1840

Kendall, and Mary Patee of Dedham, int. Nov. 8, 1818.

Kendall, 2d, and Lucy Ann Munroe, int. Apr. 23, 1843.

Mary, and Edward Bridge, May 27, 1690.

Nathan W., and Olive B. Pratt, int. May 26, 1822.

Patrick, and Mary Ann Mahon, int. Apr. 16, 1843.

Sally, of Princeton, and John Lane Boylston, int. May 9, 1813.

Sarah, and Francis Mahon, int. Dec. 29, 1844.

William, and Caroline Curley, int. Apr. 21, 1844.

Wyman, a. 36 y., carpenter, b. Robbinston, Me., s. Abel and Mary, and Mary M. Ladd, a. 22 y., b. Holderness, N. H., d. Asa and Betsey, Nov. 4, 1849.*

* Intention also recorded.

**BROUGH,** John, and Mary Kite, Sept. 24, 1847.

**BROWN** (see also Browne), Abby, and Joseph Cheney, Oct. 5, 1843.*

Abigail, and Henry Payson, June 15, 1789.*

Agnes, a. 22 y., and William Drinkwater of Merrimac, N. H., a. 24 y., s. William and Sarah, Oct. 21, 1847.*

Amanda, of Brighton, and Nathan Merrill, of Watertown, Oct. 31, 1847.

Arackzien S., of Pittston, Me., and William Demeritt Hall, int. Mar. 17, 1844.

Asa, and Mary Beal of Brookline, Nov. 4, 1824.*

Calvin, and Susan W. Seger, int. May 6, 1838.

Charles, and Mary Pearson, Dec. 2, 1821.*

Charles, and Eliza Jane Sargent, int. Oct. 5, 1845.

Charles W., and Cornelia M. Murdock, of Lowell, int. Nov. 6, 1836.

Charlotte, and Joseph Howe, Apr. 6, 1814. c. r. 2.*

Charlotte, Mrs., and Benjamin Mirick, Nov. 2, 1826.*

Clarissa, and Moses Weare, Apr. 6, 1818.*

Daniel, and Patty Gould, Nov. 24, 1802.*

Daniel M., and Alice J[ane. int.] C. Dunning, Apr. 22, 1846.*

Ebenezer, Maj., of Lenox, and Catharine Parker, int. June 8, 1788.

Edward, and Margaret Mecuen, Nov. 17, 1839.*

Eliphalet, of Dorchester, and Martha Pratt, Oct. 18, 1821.*

Eliza, and Nathan F. Perry, Oct. 3, 1821.*

Elizabeth, and Beriah Sherman, June 13, 1776.

Ellen, and John G. Wilkinson, Oct. 6, 1844.*

Eunice, and Daniel Gould, int. May 6, 1792.

Ezekiel [Hezek[ia]h. int.], and Polly Doyle, Dec. 12, 1799.*

George, of Dedham, and Lucy A. Weld, Nov. 15, 1838. c. r. 3.*

George, and Frances Walker, May 28, 1848.*

Gershom, and Edith Wyman, Mar. 3, 1802.*

Hannah, and Edward Glover of Brookline, Jan. 1, 1805. c. r. 2.*

Hannah, and James Kelley, int. Oct. 1, 1843.

Henry, and Adeline S. Thomas, int. May 18, 1845.

James, and Sarah Bullard of Walpole, int. Nov. 13, 1831.

James S., and Louisa S. Gay, May 29, 1825.*

Jesse, and Abigail Pearson, Dec. 4, 1816.*

Joan, and George Mirick, int. June 16, 1833.

* Intention also recorded.

BROWN, John, of Rutland, and Jane Paterson, July 27, 1720.
John, and Mary Bosson, Aug. 4, 1777.
John, of Charleston [Charlestown, c. R. 2.], and Abigail H.
    Dudley, Oct. 13, 1835.*
John A., and Maria J. Wilson, int. Feb. 16, 1834.
John I., and Emily W. Fiske, int. Nov. 30, 1837.
Jonathan, of Cambridge, and Mrs. Hannah Gore, Nov. 4, 1731.
Joseph, and Sally H. Burrill, int. Mar. 2, 1823.
Joseph D., and Louisa C. Burrell, Mar. 26, 1844.*
Joshua, and Hannah Clark, Apr. 3, 1777.
Lewis, and Caroline M. Wood of Plymouth, int. Aug. 14,
    1836.
Lewis, and Bridget Maguire, Mar. 3 [24. c. R. 3.], 1844.*
Lucy, and Daniel Fuller of Marlborough, Apr. 17, 1814.*
Lydia, of Brookline, and Sylvanus Blood, int. Dec. 22, 1793.
Lydia, and John McEwin, Apr. 19, 1811.*
Lydia, of Brimfield, and Nathaniel Parker, int. Oct. 4, 1818.
Lydia, and Tho[ma]s S. Seaver, Nov. 25, 1841.*
Margaret, and Ichabod Hemingway, Dec. 10, 1702.
Margarett, and James Thomas, Sept. 16, 1845.
Maria E., and Joseph Stetson, int. Jan. 19, 1845.
Mary, and Thomas Cummings, both residents in Brookline,
    Nov. 26, 1759.
Mary, of Needham, and Ebenezer Fuller, resident, int. Apr.
    11, 1784.
Mary A., of Brunswick, Me., and Joseph G. Richards, Aug.
    10, 1844.*
Mary H., of Wenham, and Samuel Wyat, int. Jan. 5, 1823.
Mary W., and George Clapp of Dorchester, int. Aug. 31,
    1823.
Mehetabell, and Michal Pike of Framingham, at Framingham,
    May 28, 1706.
Nancy, and Nathaniel Brigham, Mar. 20, 1808.*
Nancy L., of Mason, N. H., and Isaac Williams, int. Feb. 9,
    1848.
Salley, and John Walker of New Ipswich, N. H., int. Mar.
    18, 1787.
Sally, and Charles Whitehouse, Feb. 2 [9. c. R. 3.], 1817.*
Sally, and Cyrus Marshall, Nov. 26, 1826.*
Samuel R., a. 23 y., carpenter, s. Edward, and Eliza P. Wat-
    son, a. 22 y., d. James and Mary Patricks, July 4, 1847.*
Sarah J., and William S. Towne, int. July 2, 1846.

* Intention also recorded.

BROWN, Sarah Jane, and Levi P. Dudley of Dedham, int. Nov. 9, 1845.

Sarah M., and William Webb, int. Apr. 7, 1839.

Silas R., and Abigail Wiggins, int. Nov. 27, 1836.

Susan A., and Ephraim H. Chenery, int. Mar. 3, 1833.

Timothy D., and Maria Sumner, Apr. 25, 1813.*

William, and Eliza White of Deering, N. H., int. Sept. 27, 1835.

William H., and Jane Laughton of Brookline, int. Aug. 27, 1820.

William H., and Jane Whitney of Marlborough, int. Nov. 16, 1828.

**BROWNE** (see also Brown), D. N. St. Johns, and Phebe C. Howes of Lynn, int. Sept. 16, 1847.

**BRUCE,** Benjamin, and Sally Wheat, int. Apr. 2, 1818.

Nancy, Mrs., and Stephen Harrington, Apr. 18, 1804.*

Sally, and Samuel Withington, Nov. 13, 1804.*

Thaddeus, and Anna [Nancy. dup.] Dana, June 1, 1786.

**BRUCHER,** John, and Augusta Mott, int. Nov. 27, 1847.

**BRUDEN** (see also Breaden), Hannah [F. Breeden of Malden. int.], and Otis Burbank, July 23, 1843.*

**BRUER** (see also Brewer), Daniel, and Hanna Morrell, Nov. 5, 1652.

Sarah, and John Mayes, Nov. 19, 1656.

**BRUNIAN,** Bridget, and Patrick Clansey, int. June 26, 1846.

**BRYANT,** Baker, and Mary Pierce, Jan. 1, 1827.*

Caroline L., of Medford, a. 22 y., d. Nathan and Mary, and William Emerson, a. 24 y., provision dealer, s. Oliver and Elizabeth, Nov. 26, 1847.*

Caroline W., of Lynnfield, and Robert Sweetser, int. June 8, 1834.

Charles B., a. 24 y., currier, s. Edward and Mary, and Elizabeth S. Williams, a. 18 y., d. Thomas and Mary, May 14, 1846.*

James, and Mary A. Tucker, int. Nov. 27, 1831.

James, and Lucy Cushing of Dorchester, int. Apr. 16, 1837.

Jane C., and Gilbert W. Holman [Homan. int.], Jan. 2, 1844.*

* Intention also recorded.

BRYANT, Rosannah, a. 20 y., d. Ichabod and Betsey, and Samuel T. Reckard, a. 19 y., laborer, s. Perez T. and Zenith E., Nov. 8, 1846.*

Thomas, and Frances M. Leroy of Sterling, int. Aug. 8, 1846.

**BUCKLEY** (see also Buckly), Dennis, and Mary J. Smith, int. July 12, 1849.

Johannah, and Michael Donovan, int. Dec. 29, 1848.

John, and Hanora Conlay, int. Nov. 19, 1843.

▸ **BUCKLY** (see also Buckley), Bridget, and Patrick Burk, int. Feb. 8, 1849.

**BUCKMAN,** Sally [Putman. int.], and Luther Parker, Jan. 7, 1807.*

**BUCKMINISTER** (see also Buckminster), Lydia, and John Clarke, Nov. 18, 1680.

**BUCKMINSTER** (see also Buckminister), Joseph, and Martha Sharp, May 12, 1686.

**BUCKNAN,** James, of Malden, and Mary Goddard, Sept. 17, 1747.

**BUFFINGTON,** Jonathan, and Mary Ann Churchill, May 2, 1837.*

**BUGBE** (see also Bugbee), Thomas, and Elizabeth Daviss, Nov. 1, 1722.

Daniel, jr., and Mary Boilston, May 20, 1762.

**BUGBEE** (see also Bugbe), Abigail, and Joseph Trescot, Feb. 19, 1718.

Abigail, and John Capen of Dorchester, at Dorchester, Jan. 3, 1757.

Asa, and Jane K. Robinson of Brookline, int. Apr. 23, 1820.

Betsey, and Charles Brackett of Quincy, Nov. 15, 1801.*

Charles, and Sarah Ann Gunnison of Dorchester, int. Nov. 25, 1827.

Daniel, and Abigail Rice, June 21, 1733.

Daniel, and Sarah Gore, Oct. 29, 1765.

Ebenezer, and Mary White, July 31, 1777.

Elizabeth, and Robert Williams, Apr. 28, 1774.

Joanna, and Philip Rich, Oct. 4, 1710.

John, and Ruth Paul of Dorchester, at Dorchester, Nov. 15, 1721.

* Intention also recorded.

BUGBEE, John, jr., and Hannah Munk, Oct. 29, 1741.

Joseph, and Jerusha Blackman of Dorchester, int. May 27, 1821.

Mary, and Joseph Goddard, May 29, 1716.

Mary, and John Maxfield, May 12, 1767.

Mary Ellery, and John Morgridge of Calais, Me., Apr. 8, 1830.*

Mary W., and Daniel C. Bates, Jan. 25, 1841.*

Nancy, and Aaron D. Williams, Dec. 8, 1814.*

Ruth, and Nehemiah Norcross, June 26, 1764.

Sarah, and Edward Child, jr., July 3, 1744. c. R. 2.

Sarah, and Jacob Cummings, May 12, 1767.

Sarah, Mrs., and Capt. John Allbee of Mendon, Aug. 24, 1790.*

Sarah E., and George Lindsey [of St. Stevens, New Brunswick. int.], Aug. 26, 1844.*

Thomas, and Sarah Peake, June 4, 1701.

William, and Hannah Maxfield, Nov. —, 1766.

**BULGER,** James, of Beverly, and Mary O'Flaherty, int. June 4, 1843.

**BULLARD,** Anna, of Dedham, and Jonathan Whiting, at Dedham, Jan. 27, 1725-6.

Baalis, of Dorchester, and Joanna Pierce, May 27, 1804.*

Charles, and Elizabeth Paul of Dedham, int. Nov. 10, 1822.

Delina, of Walpole, and Asa Clap, int. Apr. 23, 1826.

Frances M., and Oliver H. Whittemore of Sharon, Nov. 9, 1842.*

Joanna, and Reuben Nichols, Jan. 20, 1830. c. R. 2.*

John, Rev., and Elizabeth Adams, Nov. 9, 1779.

Joseph, resident, and Betsey Adams of Lynnfield, int. Oct. 17, 1784.

Mary, of Framingham, and Richard Sever, at Framingham, Nov. 13, 1745.

Rachel, and Benjamin Moss of Medfield, Sept. 28, 1702.

Sarah, of Walpole, and James Brown, int. Nov. 13, 1831.

Willard, and Mrs. Susan Day of Walpole, int. Oct. 11, 1835.

Willard, jr., and Mary Ann Tappan of Boston, int. May 21, 1847.

**BULLEN,** Thaddeus [Bullin. int.], and Emily H. Page, May 5, 1844.*

* Intention also recorded.

**BULLOCK,** Almira, of Lowell, and Isaac G. Davis, int. July 24, 1843.

James D., and [Mrs. int.] Olive Gale, June 8, 1845.*

W[illia]m H., and Maria D. Caswell of Windsor, Vt., int. Dec. 23, 1848.

**BUNKER,** Dorathy, of Cambridge, and Martin Twombley, int. July 11, 1830.

Olive N., and John R. Peary, Sept. 10, 1844.

Valentine, and Mrs. Clarissa Rumrill, Jan. 29, 1826.*

**BURBANK,** Ebenezer G., and Sarah Patterson, int. Dec. 7, 1828.

Lois, Mrs., and Ambrose Farrell, Aug. 17, 1828.*

Naomi P., and Charles P. Gould, Dec. 19, 1830.*

Otis, and Hannah Bruden [Hannah F. Breeden of Malden. int.], July 23, 1843.*

**BURBECK,** Samuel N., and Eliza P. Irving, int. Mar. 20, 1831.

**BURCHETT,** ——, Mrs., and Edward Bouge, int. July 6, 1849.

**BURD** (see also Bird), Samuel, and Margaret Craft of Newton, int. Dec. 1, 1799.

**BURDEKIN,** James, and Patty Jackson, at Boston, June 6, 1791.*

**BURDEN** (see also Burdin), Sarah, and John Mayo, July 8, 1685.

**BURDIN** (see also Burden), Sarah, and Eliphilet Flint of Weathersfield, Mar. 21, 1776.

**BURDITT,** Harriet, and Israel E. Glover, int. July 31, 1820.

Nathan, and Elizabeth Newhall, Oct. 4, 1791.*

**BURGEEN,** Sarah, and John Berry, Feb. 12, 1768.

**BURGES** (see also Burgess), William J., a. 22 y., blacksmith, s. John and Ann, and Catherine Bowles, a. 22 y., d. John and Mary, Jan. 30, 1848.*

**BURGESS** (see also Burges), Susan D., of Boston, and Moses H. Webber, int. May 20, 1846.

* Intention also recorded.

**BURGWYN,** Henry [K. int.; Henry King Burgynen. c. r. 3.], of Newbern, N. C., and Anna Greenough, Nov. 28, 1838.*

**BURIKES,** Barbara, and George P. Hinds, int. Mar. 22, 1835.

**BURK** (see also Burke), Bridget, and Michael Hastings, int. Feb. 10, 1849.

Daniel, of Providence, R. I., and Rebecca McGuire, int. Oct. 15, 1849.

Julia, and Thomas Aigin, int. Dec. 20, 1849.

Patrick, and Bridget Buckly, int. Feb. 8, 1849.

**BURKE** (see also Burk), Joseph H., and Betsey Yoaton, int. Dec. 11, 1842.

Mary A., of Eaton, N. H., and Charles R. Draper, int. Apr. 20, 1845.

Nancy, and J. P. Saxton, int. July 31, 1847.

Thomas, and Catherine Corcoran, int. Oct. 7, 1848.

**BURLEY,** Mary H., and Andrew J. Hammond, Oct. 20, 1844.

Reuamah, and Sylvester G. Louger, Dec. 31, 1844.*

**BURLINGAME,** Albert S., of Brighton, and Elizabeth Hazlett, int. Sept. 26, 1830.

Sarah M., of Brighton, and John Brooks, int. Mar. 22, 1835.

**BURNAP,** Sarah A., of Lowell, and Thomas L. Tuxbury, June 2, 1842. c. r. 7.

**BURNETT,** Benjamin, and Anna Simpson, int. Oct. 18, 1789.

Sarah, and James Duff, May 28, 1753.

**BURNHAM,** Ann M., and Thomas M. Wentworth, Oct. 31, 1839.*

Emily A., a. 27 y., upholsteress, d. Enoch and Judith, and Page Moore, a. 34 y., operative, s. James and Nancy, Feb. 6, 1845.

George P., and Achsah B. Nye of Falmouth, int. May 6, 1838.

Hiram W. C., and Eunice S. Bray, int. Oct. 6, 1833.

Ira, and Hannah M. Joslyn, int. Sept. 13, 1835.

Lemuel, and Mary Doland, int. July 24, 1836.

Thomas Mickell, and Elizabeth Herrick Willur, int. Oct. 6, 1844.

**BURNS** (see also Byrne, Byrnes, Byrns), Ann, and Patrick Waters, int. Apr. 13, 1849.

* Intention also recorded.

BURNS, Bridget, and Patrick Moore, int. May 12, 1848.
Eliza, and Michael Flood, int. Jan. 13, 1849.
Ellen, and Jeremiah Tuley [Furey. int.], Aug. 10, 1848.*
Hannah, and Francis Dwyre, int. July 14, 1844.
John, and Julia Feely, int. Dec. 10, 1837.
John, and Bridget Gallagher, int. Nov. 3, 1844.
Margaret A., of Boston, and John K. Basford, int. Aug. 18, 1849.
Mary, and Roger Clooman, int. July 11, 1848.
William, a. 25 y., shoemaker, s. George and Martha, of Ireland, and Jane Miller, a. 21 y., d. John, Nov. 5, 1846.*

BURRAGE, William [of Boston. c. r. 3.], and Mary Ann Jackson, May 14, 1835.*

BURREL (see also Burrill), Frances, and Eli Thurston of Cambridge, Apr. 27, 1806.*
Jerusha, and Theodore Kingsbury, May 25, 1806.*
Lucy, and Stephen Stephens, Jan. 1, 1809.*

BURRELL (see also Burrill), Abigail, and Aaron Pomroy, Oct. 25, 1801.*
Benj[ami]n, and Lucy Beaver [Beard. int.], Oct. 29, 1805.*
Clarissa, and John Howe, int. Dec. 25, 1808.
Isaac S. [Buriell. int.], a. 27 y., wheelwright, s. Benj[amin] and Lucy, and Maria A. Newell, d. Luther and Sarah, Jan. 23, 1848.*
Louisa C., and Joseph D. Brown, Mar. 26, 1844.*
Nancy, and Elisha Forbes, Dec. 29, 1799.*
Sussanah, and Jeremiah P. Smith, Nov. 27, 1808.*

BURRIL (see also Burrill), James, and Elizabeth Johnson, Dec. 7, 1775.
Mary, and Thomas Dudley, Feb. 8, 1807.*
Mercy, and Samuel Griggs, both residents, Aug. 5, 1788.*
Silvanus, and Mrs. Mary Williams, Jan. 16, 1783.*

BURRILL (see also Burrel, Burrell, Burril), Abigail, of Dedham, and Titus Smith, Mar. 22, 1832.*
Benj[ami]n H., and Harriet E. Morse, int. Sept. 4, 1836.
Caroline F., and Archibald C. Anderson, Feb. 17, 1828.*
Hannah, of Dedham, and Benj[ami]n J. G., int. Apr. 10, 1825.
James, and Mrs. Rachel Livermore, Nov. 26, 1812.*

* Intention also recorded.

BURRILL, Lucy H., and Reuben Howard, int. Mar. 9, 1834.
Mary, of Brookline, and Lemuel Bradley, July 21, 1796.*
Mary Ann, and Samuel Cummins, Jan. 8, 1809.*
Sally H., and Joseph Brown, int. Mar. 2, 1823.
Sarah, and William Robbins, May 14, 1797. C. R. 3.*
Sarah B., and John P. Chandler, int. Oct. 25, 1840.

BURROUGHS (see also Burrows), John, and Elisabeth Stodder of Hingham, int. Mar. 24, 1816.
William H., a. 25 y., nail maker, s. John and Mary, and Clara M. Bills, a. 23 y., d. Shubael and Harriet, June 4, 1846.*

BURROWS (see also Burroughs), Calvin, of Lexington, and Caira R. Whitney of Boston, Oct. 14, 1849. C. R. 3.
Frances Elizabeth, and William Bowles [of Boston. C. R. 3.], Oct. 4, 1826.*
Sylvia, and Charles Harriman, int. Aug. 17, 1834.

BURT, Calvin, of Longmeadow, and Mrs. Elizabeth Edes, Oct. 16, 1835.*
David, and Sally Hawes, Feb. 23, 1812.*

BURTON, George H., a. 24 y., carpenter, s. Thomas and Mary, and Hannah D. Pierce, a. 19 y., d. Levi and Hannah, Oct. 15, 1848.*
John, and Louisa P. Rumrill, Nov. 10, 1812.*
Sarah J., and Silas Estabrook, Dec. 5, 1846.

BUSH, Solon W., Rev., of Burlington, Vt., a. 31 y., clergyman, s. Thomas and Mary B., and Theoda D. Foster, a. 37 y., d. John S. and Theoda W., June 28, 1849.*

BUTCHER, Sarah, and Robert Man, Oct. 18, 1705.

BUTLER, Bernard, and Maria Conway, int. Oct. 6, 1844.
Edward, and Elizabeth Eagen, Nov. 6, 1743.
John H., of Moultonborough, N. H., and Elizabeth B. Poole, Sept. 1, 1844.*
Margaret, and Michael Dwir, int. Oct. 15, 1845.
Mary, of Malden, and Moses G. Kingsbury, int. Jan. 6, 1839.
Sarah C., of Pelham, N. H., and William H. Rook, int. Sept. 16, 1848.
Simeon, and Hannah Cheny, Sept. 11, 1712.
Simeon, of Chelsea, and Sarah Russell [Russel. dup.; of Boston. C. R. 5.], July 29, 1848.

* Intention also recorded.

BUTLER, Simeon D., and Joanna F. Russell of Dedham, Aug. 31, 1843. C. R. 7.

BUTT, Joseph, and Abigail Cheney, Oct. 13, 1743.

BUTTERFIELD, John B., and Mary Miller of Charlestown, int. Sept. 1, 1811.
Leonard, and Susan Lamson, int. Sept. 2, 1832.

BUTTERS, George W., and Sarah F. Putnam of Waltham, int. Apr. 17, 1842.

BUZZARD, Clarissa, and Abraham S. Sanborn, int. Oct. 5, 1817.
Elizabeth, and William Conn, Dec. 3, 1834.*

BYLES, see Bils.

BYRNE (see also Burns), Ignatus [Igntious Burns. int], b. Ireland, and Jane Driscoll [Jean Drischal. int.], b. Ireland, Nov. 14, 1849.*
John [Byron. int.], b. Ireland, and Bridget Kenney, b. Ireland, Nov. 29, 1849.*

BYRNES (see also Burns), Bryan, and Mary Mylay, int. Dec. 21, 1847.

BYRNS (see also Burns), Catharine, and Patrick Manning, int. Jan. 19, 1845.

BYROM, Thomas, and Sophia Dodgeman, Sept. 25, 1832.

CABALL, John H. [Cahall. int.], b. Ireland, and Mary Shea, b. Ireland, Nov. 10, 1849.

CABOT, Mary Ann, and Stephen Griggs, int. Aug. 11, 1822.

CACHMAN (see also Cashman), Cornelius, and Mary Collins, int. Aug. 11, 1844.

CADY, Catharine, and John Murphy, int. May 13, 1845.
Mary, and James Hannagan, int. May 30, 1841.
Sarah, and Michael Linnen, int. July 9, 1843.

CAFFIN (see also Coffin), Francis G., and Elizabeth B. Lauriatt, Oct. 8, 1826.

CAIN (see also Caine, Kaime, Kane), Bridget, and Peter Gannon, int. Oct. 1, 1843.

* Intention also recorded.

CAIN, Hannah, and Eben [Edmund. int.] Wheeler, Jan. 1, 1804. C. R. 2.*

James, and Rose Cain, int. Dec. 13, 1847.

John, and Bridget Dolan, int. Jan. 22, 1847.

John, and Catharine McCarty, int. May 28, 1847.

Mary, and Joseph Kirk, int. July 16, 1849.

Rose, and James Cain, int. Dec. 13, 1847.

Sally, and William Harvey, Oct. 6, 1811. C. R. 2.*

CAINE (see also Cain), Judith, and Samuel Whittemore, Mar. 31, 1811. C. R. 2.*

Thomas, and Margaret Mahan, int. Dec. 29, 1844.

CALAHAN (see also Callehan), Barnard, and Catharine Sheridan, int. July 15, 1838.

CALBURY, John, and Margaret Callduff, int. Sept. 23, 1838.

CALDER, Abby L., and Levi F. Snow of Dorchester, Nov. 25, 1844.

Catherine, and Willard Martin, int. Dec. 1, 1816.

Jane G., and Joseph D. Snell, Sept. 15, 1811.*

Lydia, Mrs., of Dorchester, and Samuel Stowell, int. Nov. 3, 1805.

CALDWELL, Jonathan J., and Margarett Little of Goffstown, N. H., int. Dec. 29, 1847.

Margarett, and Dependence Shapleigh, Jan. 1, 1823.*

Pamelia, and John Hammond, Nov. 23, 1823.

CALFE, Joseph, and Clarissa Worthen, int. Apr. 26, 1835.

Mary, and Samuel Stevens, Oct. 9, 1712.

CALLAGHAN (see also Callehan), Catherine, and Ephraim Adams, int. Sept. 18, 1842.

CALLAHAN (see also Callehan), John, and Sarah Cavanagh, int. Mar. 27, 1849.

CALLDUFF, Margaret, and John Calbury, int. Sept. 23, 1838.

CALLEHAN (see also Calahan, Callaghan, Callahan, Culligin), Joanna, and Cornelius Dunavin, int. Jan. 29, 1843.

CALLEN (see also Cullin), James, and Catherine Cochran, int. July 25, 1846.

* Intention also recorded.

**CALLENDER,** Benjamin, and Sarah Elizabeth Hersey, int. May 24, 1835.

Harriet L., a. 20 y., d. Joseph and Mary, and James Harris, a. 21 y., carpenter, s. John and Elizabeth, Dec. 27, 1846.*

Mary B., a. 20 y., d. Joseph and Mary, and Greenleaf C. George, a. 21 y., clerk, s. Joseph and Abigail, Dec. 17, 1846.*

**CALVIN,** James, and Margaret Gurigh, int. Oct. 21, 1838.

**CAMBERLIN** (see also Chamberlain), Sarah, and Joseph Davis, Oct. 28, 1670.

**CAMELL** (see also Campbill), Elizabeth, and John Milan, int. Apr. 10, 1848.

**CAMPBELL** (see also Camell, Campbill), Anne, and Michael Fahy, int. Feb. 2, 1845.

Benjamin F., and Eliza M. Everett, int. Apr. 26, 1829.

Bulah, and Boylston Fullum, int. May 29, 1825.

Hannah, and Thomas M. Lewis, int. Jan. 2, 1842.

James, and Ann McGaugen, int. Aug. 3, 1848.

John, and Deborah Lovett, int. Jan. 11, 1829.

Margarett, b. Ireland, and John Fitzgerald, b. Ireland, Dec. 28, 1849.

Mary, and James McClaren, int. June 8, 1817.

Mary, and John Fitzgerald, int. Dec. 14, 1849.

Mary J., and Barnard McLaughlin, int. Jan. 14, 1838.

Micah, and Mary E. Thompson, int. Aug. 7, 1842.

Robert C., and Rebecca R. Cheney, July 10, 1837.*

William, and Lucretia Williams, Jan. 28, 1779.

**CAMPBILL** (see also Campbell), Robert, and Sarah Winchester, Jan. 20, 1763.

**CANCK,** Cecilia, and Francis A. Herr, int. Jan. 27, 1849.

**CANN,** William B., and Josephine Gurney, int. Dec. 28, 1845.

**CANNAWAY,** James, and Rosanna Reddahan, int. Dec. 11, 1849.

**CANNIFF,** Thomas, and Mary Kenedy, int. Jan. 15, 1848.

**CANNON,** Thomas, and Mary Joice, int. July 24, 1845.

**CANREY,** Catharine, and Patrick Linard, int. Jan. 19, 1845.

* Intention also recorded.

**CANTERBURY,** Ira, of Medfield, and Sarah Daniels, Apr. 6, 1820.*

**CAPELL,** Elizabeth, of Newton, and William Saller, jr., at Newton, Apr. 20, 1773.

**CAPEN** (see also Capin, Capron), Benjamin, and Rebeckah Sanger of Sherburne, Oct. 27, 1822.

Benjamin, and Thankful H. Hatch of Dorchester, Apr. 24, 1827.

Catharine E., and James Day, June 9, 1833.*

Elizabeth, of Dorchester, and Samuel Lion, at Dorchester, Dec. 1, 1703.

Ephraim, of Dorchester, and Mary T. Lucas, resident, May 4, 1842.

John, of Dorchester, and Abigail Bugbee, at Dorchester, Jan. 3, 1757.

John, jr., and Patience Davis, Dec. 17, 1772.

Lemuel [Rev. int.], of Sterling, and Mary Ann Hunting, Oct. 11, 1815.*

Mary, of Dorchester, and Steven Williams, at Dorchester, June 18, 1700.

Mary, Mrs., and Samuel Williams, at Dorchester, Feb. 3, 1713-14.

Phebe, and Newman Greenough, int. Apr. 14, 1822.

**CAPIN** (see also Capen), Samuel, of Dorchester, and Miriam Child, Nov. 20, 1793.

**CAPRON** (see also Capen), Charles, and Sarah Whitmore, both of Brookline, Aug. 20, 1792.

**CARBERRY,** Anne, and Michael Donnelly, int. May 2, 1845.

Bridget, and Dennis Jolly, int. May 2, 1846.

**CARD,** James, and Lucy G. Morse, int. June 14, 1835.

**CARE** (see also Carr), Mary, and John McFall, May 9, 1844.*

**CAREY** (see also Cary), Bridget, and Peter McKenney, int. July 10, 1847.

Mary, of North Bridgewater, and Samuel W. Clapp, int. Apr. 3, 1845.

Nathan C., and Fanny T. Wilson, May 30, 1845.

**CARIN,** Ellen, and Daniel Spleen, int. May 29, 1849.

* Intention also recorded.

**CARL,** William, and Ellen Lally, int. Oct. 11, 1848.

**CARLETON** (see also Carlton), Abby L., and Joseph C. Bates, int. May 5, 1839.
Guy, and Charlotte Howe, Dec. 23, 1841.*

**CARLON** (see also Carlton), Mary, and Martin Coon, int. Mar. 23, 1845.

**CARLTON** (see also Carleton, Carlon), Betsey, and James Reed, Feb. 2, 1812.*
Guy, and Abigail Hovey of Bradford, int. Oct. 27, 1811.
Lewis, of Brooksville, Me., and Harriet Estabrook, int. Aug. 1, 1847.
Polly, and Thomas James, jr., int. Oct. 30, 1808.

**CARLYLE,** William, and Mary B. Forbes, Mar. 8, 1845.*

**CARNEY,** Catherine, and Patrick Gorman, int. Apr. 26, 1848.
Ellen, and Martin Scandlin, int. Nov. 9, 1848.
James, and Mary Ann Finn, June 8, 1848.
Martin, of Boston, and Bridget Mannion, int. May 8, 1847.
Mary, and Thomas Earlay, int. Aug. 9, 1849.
Michael, and Margarett Twigg, int. Sept. 8, 1849.
Peter, of Brookline, and Catherine Kelly, int. July 25, 1846.

**CARPENTER,** Catherine, and James Cassady, int. Jan. 25, 1848.
Eliphalett, and Rebecca Gardner, June 31, 1702.
Hannah, of Rehoboth, and Edward Preston, resident, at Rehoboth, May 15, 1746.
Jedediah, and Hannah Stratton of Foxborough, int. Feb. 12, 1809.
John, of Foxborough, and Abigail Bacon, Oct. 13, 1825.
Nathanael [of Attleborough. c. r. 2.], and Mary Bacon [Boson. c. r. 2.], Nov. 13, 1716.
Preston, and Nancy Skidmore, June 26, 1823.*
Sullivan, and Lucinda W. Goddard, Oct. 27, 1833.

**CARR** (see also Care), Ann, and Hugh Gray, int. Dec. 24, 1847.
Harriet, and John M[arden. int.] Plummer, Sept. 26, 1833.*
Henry W., and Martha C. Curtis, int. Nov. 6, 1836.
Margarett, and Patrick Curley, int. Nov. 23, 1847.
Sarah J[arvis. int.], and [Dr. int.] W[illia]m Le Baron of Andover, June 7, 1841.*

* Intention also recorded.

**CARRALL** (see also Carroll), Elizabeth, and Luke MaGeverey. int. Dec. 12, 1846.

**CARREL** (see also Carroll), Jonathan [Carriel, of Groton, int.], Capt., of Groton. int. and [Mrs. int.] Sarah Hancock, May 22, 1783.*

**CARRIGAN,** Catherine D., b. Ireland, and John Slenton, b. Ireland, Nov. 18, 1849.

**CARROL** (see also Carroll), Bridget, and John Killian, int. May 16, 1849.

**CARROLL** (see also Carrall, Carrel, Carrol), Jane, and Bernard Conoboy, int. Nov. 8, 1840.

Martin, and Ellen Fay, int. Jan. 15, 1837.

Patrick, b. Ireland, and Catherine Cronin, b. Ireland, Aug. 6, 1849.*

Rosanna, and Patrick Cunningham [of Pawtucket, R. I. int.], Sept. 19, 1848.*

Samuel [Caroll. int.], and Elizabeth Riley, Sept. 18, 1806. C. R. 2.*

**CARSON** (see also Corson, Curson), George, a. 24 y., carpenter, s. George and Margarett, and Amanda Morton, a. 21 y., d. William, Oct. 4, 1846.*

**CARTER,** Ann, and Moody Austin of Bellingham, Dec. 28, 1820.*

Bagley, of Dorchester, and Elizabeth Bond, July 8, 1824.*

Caroline, of Natick, and Calvin Warren, int. Dec. 11, 1814.

Charlotte A., and Alvin Hayes, int. Mar. 22, 1849.

Clariss H., and John Howard, int. Apr. 30, 1820.

Elizabeth [Newton. int.], and Antipas Newton, Apr. 4, 1808.*

Esther, and Thomas Howe, Mar. 7, 1819.*

George, and Bridget Quinn, int. Feb. 14, 1848.

Judith, and James Harper of Brighton, int. Aug. 24, 1828.

Merriam, and James Houghton of Dorchester, Dec. 11, 1834.*

William, and Mary Davis, Oct. 26, 1726.

**CARTHY** (see also McCarty), Margaret, and John Bergin, int. Dec. 31, 1843.

**CARTNALL,** James, and Margarett Otis, int. Oct. 23, 1847.

**CARTRET,** Lydia, and William Gale, Dec. 16, 1821.*

* Intention also recorded.

**CARTY** (see also McCarty), Catharine, and Timothy Clary, int. May 7, 1837.

John, and Ann Gately, int. June 22, 1849.

**CARVER,** Ezekiel [Cheever. c. r. 2.], and Mary Polley, Jan. 26, 1738.

William, and Rachel Noble, Aug. 2, 1804.*

**CARY** (see also Carey), Catherine, and Thomas McDaniel, Sept. 30, 1848.*

Catherine, and Michael Donlin, int. Dec. 8, 1849.

Charles, and Catherine S. Alexander, int. Oct. 16, 1825.

Ellen, and George Plunket, int. Apr. 11, 1841.

Hannah, and Benjamin West, Dec. 13, 1781. c. r. 2.

Isaac, and Julia Willard, int. Dec. 26, 1830.

Isaac H., and Phebe P. Pratt, ——, 1832. [Sept. 4, 1831. int.]*

James, and Catherine Flynn, int. Dec. 1, 1848.

John, and Mary Doyle, int. July 31, 1848.

Rosanna, and Patrick Quoe, int. Sept. 14, 1845.

Susanna, and Joshua Lamb, Oct. 1, 1702.

**CASBURY,** Eliza, and John Follen, int. Apr. 2, 1846.

**CASE** (see also Cass), Anne, and Thomas Lyon, jr., Nov. 1, 1692.

Ebenezer, and Patience Draper, Mar. 13, 1689-90.

**CASEY,** Ellena, and Solon W. Chaplin, Jan. 30, 1849.

**CASHMAN** (see also Cachman), Benjamin P., and Matilda B. Smith, int. June 21, 1849.

**CASNAR,** Michael, and Aristena Trepend, int. July 10, 1846.

**CASS** (see also Case, Casse), Aaron, and Priscilla Whiting, Apr. 24, 1825. c. r. 2.*

Aaron, and Mrs. Hannah A. Allen, int. June 16, 1833.

Abigael, and John Torbot, at Dedham, Nov. 17, 1698.

Eliza P., a. 20 y., d. Benj[amin] and Roxana, and Daniel Jones, a. 29 y., July 31, 1848.*

Lucy W., a. 24 y., d. Moses and Tanny, and William W. Stickney [of Boston. int.], a. 25 y., victualler, s. Charles and Lucy, of Grafton, N. H., Nov. 26, 1846.*

**CASSADY,** James, and Catherine Carpenter, int. Jan. 25, 1848.

* Intention also recorded.

**CASSE** (see also Cass), Elisabeth, and John Griggs, jr., [June ?], 1682.

**CASSELL,** Sarah L., of Dorchester, and John L. Duncan, int. Jan. 4, 1848.

**CASTIN,** Christan, and Betsey Beetham, Mar. 8, 1812.*

**CASTOLAND,** Ellen, and Michael Leonard, int. Nov. 10, 1844.

**CASWELL,** Ann, of Berkley, and John Savage, int. Feb. 23, 1812.
Lydia A., and Jeremiah M. Sweat, int. Jan. 18, 1846.
Maria D., of Windsor, Vt., and W[illia]m H. Bullock, int. Dec. 23, 1848.
Mason P., and Harriet G. Rumrill, int. Nov. 12, 1837.
Phebe, of Berkley, and Caleb Long, int. Feb. 26, 1809.
William, and Mary S. Lewis, Nov. 27, 1806.*

**CATE,** Thomas J., and Sarah Wiggin, int. Oct. 21, 1838.

**CATEN,** James, and Mary Ann Claffee, int. Oct. 16, 1842.

**CAUGHLAY,** Thomas, and Jane Kelley, int. May 3, 1849.

**CAUSENS,** Deborah D., and Joseph P. Jordan, both of Dorchester, Sept. 29, 1822.

**CAUSGRIVE,** Ellen, and John O'Horo, int. Aug. 8, 1848.

**CAVANAGH** (see also Cavanah, Cavanough, Kavanah), Ellen, and John M. Coen [McCoen. int.], July 25, 1848.*
Sarah, and John Callahan, int. Mar. 27, 1849.

**CAVANAH** (see also Cavanagh), James [Cavno. int.], b. Ireland, and Honora Mulray [Mulrey. int.], b. Ireland, Nov. 27, 1849.*

**CAVANOUGH** (see also Cavanagh), Mary, and Patrick Lyons, int. July 24, 1836.

**CAWLEY,** Ann, and Michael G. Minon of Boston, int. May 13, 1848.
Patrick, and Bridget Curley, int. July 19, 1849.

**CAYLE,** Patrick, and Hannah Fennelton, int. Dec. 2, 1848.

**CAYRS,** Ebenezer, and Clement Weld, int. Nov. 14, 1784.

* Intention also recorded.

**CELLEY,** Benjamin, and Jane M. Sawyer, int. Feb. 19, 1837.

**CHADDOCK,** Daniel [of Attleborough. c. R. 2.], and Hannah Smith, May 25, 1738.

Ephraim, and Hannah Ware, both of Dorchester, June 23, 1845.

**CHADWICK,** Joseph H., and Catherine S. Adams of West Townsend, int. Sept. 6, 1849.

Rhoda E., and Francis Freeman, Aug. 25, 1844.*

William T., a. 24 y., provision dealer, s. W[illia]m and Betsey, and Mehitable Sloman, a. 26 y., d. John and Betsey, May 14, 1848.*

**CHAFFEE,** Daniel D., and Sarah F. Morris of Wilbraham, int. Apr. 21, 1833.

**CHAFFIN,** Tilla [jr. int.], of Holden, and Mrs. Sarah Foster, May 20, 1829.*

**CHAMBERLAIN** (see also Camberlin, Chamberlaine, Chamberlin), Abel, and Mrs. Susanna Leeds of Dorchester, at Dorchester, Apr. 11, 1775.

Abigail, and Sylvanus Lindall, Apr. 5, 1819. c. R. 2.*

Daniel, and Mary Ballard, June 22, 1825. c. R. 2.*

Elizabeth, and David Howe, May 16, 1780.

George W., and Emma R. Sanborn of Boston, int. Dec. 8, 1847.

Hackabath [Hackaliah. int.], and Charlotte Harris, Dec. 24, 1801.*

Hannah, and Nath[anie]ll Parker, Jan. 1, 1756. c. R. 2.

Isaac, and Sarah White of Dedham, at Dedham, [bet. 1796 and 1800?]. [Nov. 6, 1796. int.]*

Jacob, and Mary Childe, Jan. 24, 1693-4.

Jacob, and Sarah Weld, Apr. 29, 1719.

Jacob, and Polly Aldin, Nov. 9, 1788.*

John, and Hannah Bowin, Dec. 30, 1725.

John [jr. c. R. 2.], and Sarah Trott, Mar. 24, 1768.

John, and Mary E. Fuller, int. June 16, 1844.

Lucy, and Moses Chamberlain, Dec. 20, 1807. c. R. 2.*

Margaret, of Newton, and James Ryan, at Newton, June 6, 1771.

Moses, and Lucy Chamberlain, Dec. 20, 1807. c. R. 2.*

Moses, and Ann Hayes, Jan. 7, 1845.*

Nehemiah, and Sarah Steadman, Feb. 25, 1783. c. R. 2.*

* Intention also recorded.

CHAMBERLAIN, Samuel, and Lucy Stevens, Nov. 18, 1742.

Sarah, Mrs., and Samuell Scot, Nov. 4, 1730.

Sarah, and Richard Daniels, May 20, 1829. C. R. 2.*

Sarah E., and Henry W. Farley, int. Dec. 22, 1849.

Stephen, and Sarah Weld, Aug. 7, 1755. C. R. 2.

Stephen [jr. int.], and Lois Bowker [Louis Bouker. int.] of Sudbury, at Sudbury, Apr. 13, 1793.*

Stephen, jr., and Mary Ann Morse of Dorchester, int. May 4. 1823.

Susan, and Joseph Nealey, Feb. 7, 1828. C. R. 2.*

**CHAMBERLAINE** (see also Chamberlain), Elizabeth, and Joseph Weld, May 22, 1711.

Mary, and Samuel Davis, June 23, 1709.

Mary, and John Trott of Dorchester, Jan. 23, 1733-4.

**CHAMBERLIN** (see also Chamberlain), Abraham, and Mary Whitney of Watertown, at Watertown, Oct. 26, 1716.

Edward, and Mary Turnor, Jan. 4, 1646.

**CHAMBERS**, Andrew G., a. 25 y., laborer, s. John and Mary. and Eliza Ann Allen, a. 28 y., d. Gersham and Margarett, Oct. 8, 1846.*

Joseph G., and Mary Ann Pratt, Jan. 5, 1840.*

**CHAMPION**, Ruth, and Jacob Wentworth, Apr. 23, 1843.*

Samuel, and Mary Kelly, int. Sept. 19, 1846.

Samuel S., of Watertown, and Nancy Wentworth of Brookline, Nov. 26, 1829.

**CHAMPNEY**, Elizabeth, Mrs., of Dorchester, and Jacob Whittemore, at Dorchester, Oct. 7, 1777.

Elizabeth, and Daniel Whitney, Nov. 14, 1802.*

Elizabeth, and Samuel Hewes Hunneman, June 30, 1825.*

Erastus, of Brookline, and Abigail Prentiss, int. Apr. 13, 1823.

John, and Lydia Howe, Mar. 11, 1804.*

John, and Maria S. Wells, Aug. 28, 1837.

John, jr., and Harriet Morse, at Brookline, May 28, 1843.*

Jonathan, and Mrs. Elizabeth Pierce, jr. of Dorchester, at Dorchester, Mar. 2, 1773.

Joseph [resident. int.], and Elizabeth Weld, Apr. 4, 1786.*

Julius B., and Sarah P. Bradford, int. Aug. 25, 1833.

Mary, Mrs., of Dorchester, and John Williams, at Dorchester, May 15, 1770.

* Intention also recorded.

CHAMPNEY, Mary, S., and Henry Wilson, int. May 24, 1835.

Robert, and Rebecca Brewer, Oct. —, 1767.

Sarah, Mrs., of Dorchester, and Jacob Green, at Dorchester, Mar. 14, 1771.

Susannah R., and Joseph C. Spear of New York City, Aug. 3, 1837.*

**CHANDLER,** Ann, and John Dane, July 2, 1643.

Delia F., of Boston, and Ansel W. Putnam, int. Sept. 7, 1846.

Elisabeth, and Robert Mason, Nov. 18, 1680.

Elizabeth, of Andover, and John Lowder, jr., at Andover, May 4, 1769.

Gardiner D., and Elizabeth H. Cleveland, of Salem, int. Apr 20, 1845.

Hannah, and Moses Draper, July 7, 1685.

Hannah, Mrs., and Samuel Williams, May 17, 1750.

Harvey, and Sarah Hall, Dec. 26, 1821.

John, and Elizabeth Dugglas. Feb. 16, 1658.

John P., and Sarah B. Burrill, int. Oct. 25, 1840.

Margaret, and Thomas Hake of Boston, at Boston, Nov. 6, 1754.

Mary, and George Abbot, Dec. 12, 1646.

Mary, and John Lowder, Mar. 12, 1744-5.

Sarah, and William Cleaves, Nov. 4, 1659.

Zechariah, and Margarett Bishop, Jan. 18, 1715-16.

**CHANNEL,** Meriam P., and John B. Braid, Nov. 30, 1797.*

**CHANNING,** Walter, and Eliza Wainwright, ——, 1832.

**CHAPIN,** George A., a. 22 y., clerk, s. Aaron and Lucy W., and Sarah H. Davis, a. 20 y., d. Gilman and Sarah H., June 2, 1846.*

Judson, and Roxanna Atherton, int. Oct. 1, 1826.

Judson, and Emeline Fletcher of Northbridge, int. May 5, 1839.

**CHAPLIN,** Ann, and Joseph Gorde [Gord. dup.], Mar. 23, 1680-81.

Lucy, and Reuben Whittier, Feb. 25, 1808.*

Solon W., and Ellena Casey, Jan. 30, 1849.

**CHAPMAN** (see also Chepman, Chipman), Prince, and Eliza Ann Reed of Framingham, int. Sept. 15, 1846.

Rufus, a. 27 y., patent leather manufacturer, s. Francis and Elizabeth, and Catherine W. Bell, a. 23 y., d. James and Sarah, Oct. 11, 1846.*

* Intention also recorded.

**CHARLTON,** John, and Mary Galvin, int. Jan. 6, 1833.

**CHASE,** Andrew, jr., and Mary Jane Curtis, int. Oct. 6, 1833.

Hannah L., a. 25 y., d. Anthony and Jane, and Albert Batchelder, a. 26 y., box manufacturer, s. Jeremiah and Sally, May 23, 1848.*

John, and Sarah Morto, int. Feb. 21, 1819.

Mary E., and Horase Littlefield of Lebanon, Me., int. Oct. 21, 1832.

Osgood, and Ann Tuttle, Feb. 24, 1828.

Samuel S., and Elizabeth Curtis, June 4, 1840.*

Sarah Ann, and Abner Littlefield, int. Apr. 5, 1829.

Susan B., of Stratham, N. H., a. 20 y., d. Andrew and Sarah, and George S. Head, a. 24 y., mason, s. Richard and Abigail, Apr. 23, 1848.*

**CHEANEY** (see also Cheney), Ellen, and Umphry Johnson, Mar. 20, 1642.

Judith, of Newton, and Henry Tucker, at Newton, Jan. 16, 1731-2.

Thomas, and Jane Adkinson [Atkinson. CT. R.], Jan. 11, 1655.

**CHEANY** (see also Cheney), Polly, and Samuel Swift, Nov. 2, 1806.*

**CHEESMAN** Benjamin, and Sarah Howe, [Dec. ?], 1778.

**CHEEVER** (see also Chever), John, and Hannah Bridge, Nov. 9, 1732.

John, and Margaret Man [both resident. C. R. 2.], July 1, 1736.

W[illia]m, and Caroline P. Whitington, Dec. 5, 1839.*

**CHEINY** (see also Cheney), Mary, and John Holbrooke, Sept. 24, 1684.

Thomas, and Hannah Wooddis, Sept. 24, 1684.

**CHENERY** (see also Cheney), Emily W., and Joseph B. Nichols, Nov. 20, 1823.*

Ephraim, and Rebecca Whittemore, Apr. 27, 1800. C. R. 2.*

Ephraim H., and Susan A. Brown, int. Mar. 3, 1833.

John L., and Augusta A. Whittemore, int. Mar. 5, 1843.

Solomon, and Rebeccah Pond, Mar. 29, 1798. C. R. 2.*

**CHENEY** (see also Cheaney, Cheany, Cheiny, Chenery, Cheny), Abigail, and Joseph Butt, Oct. 13, 1743.

Abigail, Mrs., and William Cunningham, Feb. 7, 1782.

* Intention also recorded.

CHENEY, Amos, of Cambridge, and Mary Holmes Morse, May 8, 1823.*

Catharine C., and Willard Onions, June 14, 1823.*

Ebenez[e]r, and Mrs. Elis[abe]th Palmer of Middlebury, Dec. 25, 1729.

Ebenezer, Lt., and Mrs. Abigail Stone, May 14, 1772.

George S., a. 22 y., tinplate worker, s. W[illia]m and Rebecca, and Lucy A. Sprague, a. 19 y., d. Hiram and Mary, Apr. 23, 1848.*

Henry, and Mary Cheney, at Boston, June 22, 1726.

Jane F., and Benjamin F. Ayres, Oct. 16, 1834.*

Joseph, and Abby Brown, Oct. 5, 1843.*

Margaret D., and David P. Hall, Dec. 15, 1836.*

Mary, and Henry Cheney, at Boston, June 22, 1726.

Mary, and Benjamin Cotterell, Nov. 26, 1765.

Mary, and John Mory, Sept. 9, 1768.

Mary, and Freeman —— of Connecticut, Jan. 5, 1776.

Rebecca E., and James E. Barrel, Oct. 17, 1841.*

Rebecca R., and Robert C. Campbell, July 10, 1837.*

Rebeckah, and Joseph Heath, Dec. 2, 1747.

Sarah, and Nathan[ie]l Parker, Apr. 12, 1753.

Thomas, and [Mrs. c. r. 2.] Deborah Parker, Mar. 25, 1747.

Thomas, and Jane Foster, Apr. 6, 1780.

Thomas, and Sarah Rice, Feb. 18, 1810.*

Thomas, and Ruth Sawyer, Feb. 5, 1829.*

William, and Rebecca Richards, July 14, 1811, c. r. 2.*

CHENY (see also Cheney), Clarissa, of Hopkinton, and Nathan Kennie, int. July 28, 1805.

Hannah, and Simeon Butler, Sept. 11, 1712.

Margarett, and Ebenezer Tucker, Jan. 10, 1711.

Rebecca, and Josiah Sabin, June 18, 1701.

William, and Rebecca Newel, May 24, 1686.

William, and Abigail Davis, Apr. 7, 1715.

CHEPMAN (see also Chapman), Edmund [Chipman. int.; Chessman, of Boston. c. r. 3.], and Elizabeth Gould, Jan. 30, 1820.*

CHEVER (see also Cheever), Hannah, and Caleb Wooodward [of Brookline. c. r. 2.], Nov. 21, 1751.

CHICK, Joseph P., and Aurelia T. Grosvenor, Dec. 22, 1845.*

* Intention also recorded.

CHIDESTER, Aletta, of Charlestown, and Abraham Crawley, int. Dec. 26, 1814.

CHILD (see also Childe, Childs), Aaron, and Susanna Gridley, Nov. 9, 1769.

Abag[ai]l, of Sudbury, and Richard Sheldon, int. Nov. 27, 1808.

Abigail [of Brookline. c. r. 2.], and James Draper, Nov. 12, 1719.

Abner, and Eliz[abet]h Richards of Dedham, int. Feb. 9, 1800.

Ann Parker, and Benjamin May Parker [of Baltimore. int.], Oct. 1, 1823.*

Anna, Mrs., of Brooklyn [Brookline. c. r. 2.], and Edward Bridge, jr., Nov. 7, 1728.

Benjamin Warden, and Mercy Baker of Lincoln, int. Dec. 28, 1806.

Betsy, and Oliver Fisher, May 5, 1803. c. r. 2.

Betsy, and Aaron Rhoades [Rhodes. c. r. 3.], Nov. 8, 1812.*

Caleb [of New Medfield. c. r. 2.], and Rebeckah Dana, Oct. 19, 1838.

Daniel F., and Mary D. Guild, Nov. 14, 1839.*

Dorothy, of Brookline, and Ebenezer Draper, May 2, 1723.

Ebenezer, of Woodstock, and Elizabeth Becon [Beacon. c. r. 2.], Nov. 30, 1720.

Edward, and Margarett Weld, June 2, 1712.

Edward, jr., and Sarah Bugbee, July 3, 1744. c. r. 2.

Elijah, and Hannah Harris of Brookline, int. Feb. 2, 1783.

Elisabeth, and James Baley, May 3, 1768.

Elisabeth [of Brookline. c. r. 2.], and John Payson, June 16, 1738. [June 15. c. r. 2.]

Elizabeth, resident, and Byran Allen of Bridgewater, int. Jan. 15, 1786.

Elizabeth, and Gorshom Tufts, Jan. 26, 1790.*

Esther, and John Child, Jan. 26, 1742-3.

Esther, and Dea. Nathaniel Weld, Sept. 10, 1793.*

Fanny, and Gabriel Titterton, both residents, Sept. 11, 1787.*

Hannah, and Thomas Baker, jr., Apr. 18, 1734.

Hannah, Mrs., and Abner Craft, Mar. 17, 1774.

Harriet, and Augustus Perrin [of Boston. c. r. 3.], Mar. 10, 1817.*

Isaac [of Brookline. c. r. 2.], and Sarah Newel, Nov. 4, 1713.

Isaac, and Elizabeth Weld, Apr. 18, 1716.

* Intention also recorded.

CHILD, Isaac, jr. [of Brookline. c. r. 2.], and Elisabeth Weld, Dec. 12, 1745.

Isaac, and Eliza Billings, Nov. 29, 1821. c. r. 2.*

James, and Julia Pearson, int. Dec. 25, 1836.

Jerusha, and Alvan Newton, int. Mar. 9, 1817.

John, and Esther Child, Jan. 26, 1742-3.

John R., and Hannah Richards, June 4, 1820. c. r. 2.*

John W., and Sally Richards of Dedham, int. Mar. 9, 1817.

Joseph, of Woodstock, and Abigail Bridge, Nov. 29, 1722.

Joshua, and Deborah Weld, Sept. 6, 1715.

Joshua, of Brooklyn [of Brookline. c. r. 2.], and Bethia Davis, Jan. 31, 1732-3.

Joshua, and Lucretia Dorr, Aug. 5, 1816.*

Lemuel, and Mary Hall, Sept. 20, 1768.

Louisa, and Leonard Newton, Apr. 28, 1831.*

Lucy, of Newton, and Jonas Lewis, at Newton, Apr. 9, 1766.

Margaret, and [Capt. int.] Benjamin Payson Williams, Feb. 3, 1814.*

Martha, Mrs., and Joseph Weld, June 4, 1729.

Martha W., and Galen Bowditch, June 12, 1833.*

Mary, and Peter Walker [Walter of Rehoboth. c. r. 2.], June 9, 1715.

Mary, and John Newland, Sept. 5, 1770.

Mary, and Rufus Babcock, May 3, 1807.*

Mary Leeds, and Shubael Sanborn, Mar. 23, 1828. c. r. 2.*

Mary M., and David Hall, Jan. 28, 1829.*

Mehitabel, and John Weld, Dec. 3, 1712.

Miriam, and Samuel Capin of Dorchester, Nov. 20, 1793.

Phinehas, and Susanna White [Whiting. int.], Sept. 20, 1801.*

Rachel, and Payson Williams, June 13, 1776.

Rebecca D., and Hiram Hall, Dec. 18, 1836.*

Rebecca W., and Reuben M. Stackpole, ——, 1833. [May 27, 1832. int.]*

Sally, and Enoch Hutchins, Mar. 25, 1819.*

Sarah, of Brooklyn [Brookline. c. r. 2.], and Ezra Davis, Dec. 1, 1737.

Sarah, and James Wheaton, Jan. 20, 1771.

Sophia B., and James Guild, int. Aug. 28, 1842.

Stephen, and Sarah Weld, May 25, 1786.*

Stephen, and Rebecca Williams, Dec. 22, 1803.*

Stephen, 3d, and Hepzibah C. Richards of Dedham, int. Sept. 5, 1813.

* Intention also recorded.

CHILD, Susan, and Galen Bowditch, Feb. 10, 1836.*

Thomas, and Harriet Williams, int. Nov. 8, 1835.

Thomas H., a. 38 y., gauger and measurer, s. Thomas and
     Charlotte, and Almira Jane Appleton, wid., a. 37 y., d.
     Aaron and Phebe Melcher, Nov. 24, 1846.*

William, and Deborah Goddard of Brookline, at Brookline,
     Jan. 16, 1723.

**CHILDE** (see also Child), Benjamin, and Grace Morriss, Mar.
     7, 1682-3.

Joshua, and Elisabeth Morriss, Mar. 9, 1685.

Mary, and Jacob Chamberlain, Jan. 24, 1693-4.

**CHILDS** (see also Child), Betsy, of Natick, and Curtis Travis,
     int. Apr. 5, 1818.

Emely, and Geo[rge] C. Hodges, May 2, 1833.*

Louisa, and Leonard Newton, Apr. 28, 1831. c. r. 3.

Nathaniel R., and Eliza E. Stone, Apr. 30, 1846.*

Sarah W., a. 29 y., d. Stephen and Rebecca, and William J.
     Hyde of Brookline, a. 31 y., yeoman, s. Leonard and
     Jerusha, June 1, 1848.*

**CHIPMAN** (see also Chapman), John, Rev., and Mrs. Hannah
     Warren, Nov. 20, 1751.

**CHITTENDEN,** Ann, Mrs., and Sears Hersey, Apr. 15, 1827.*

Eliza [Eliza Ann. int.], and Sam[ue]l M. Cummings, Oct.
     13, 1842.*

**CHOAT** (see also Choate), Stephen, and Mrs. Rebecca Bow-
     man of Cambridge, Feb. 4, 1730-31.

**CHOATE** (see also Choat, Chote), John, and Sarah G. Fair
     field, Nov. 9, 1819.*

**CHOTE** (see also Choate), Samuel, and Mary Williams, at
     Ipswich, 23: 9br: 1688.

**CHRISTEEN,** Sarah, and Frederick Peterson, int. June 14,
     1837.

**CHUCBUCK,** Eliz[abeth] F., and Geo[rge] M. Thompson of
     Southborough, Apr. 9, 1840.*

**CHURCHILL,** Mary Ann, and Jonathan Buffington, May 2,
     1837.*

Phebe Ann, and Hezekiah B. Harris, Aug. 25, 1834.

* Intention also recorded.

CHURCHILL, Samuel, and Sarah Sumner, Mar. 21, 1803.*
Susan, of Plympton, and Jabash Wright, int. May 6, 1821.

CIAGINLN, Christian, and Anthony Frink, int. Apr. 2, 1843.

CILLEY, see Celley.

CLAFFE (see also Claffy), Ellen, and Anthony McNeal, int. Jan. 9, 1842.

CLAFFEE (see also Claffy), James, and Maria Horn, int. Sept. 18, 1842.

Mary Ann, and James Caten, int. Oct. 16, 1842.

CLAFFIN (see also Claflin), William [jr. int.], and Susan F. Fairbanks, Feb. 9, 1823.*

CLAFFY (see also Claffe, Claffee), Bridget, and Thomas Harney, int. May 16, 1841.

James, and Ellen Gaffy, int. Jan. 23, 1842.

Mary E., and Michael Shine, int. July 16, 1843.

CLAFLIN (see also Claffin), John, and Clarinda Mellish, Jan. 13, 1805.

Warner [Warren. int.], and Nancy Pond, Nov. 8, 1801. C. R. 2.*

CLANCEY (see also Clansey), Morris, and Margaret Hefran, int. May 12, 1849.

CLANSEY (see also Clancey), Patrick, and Bridget Brunian, int. June 26, 1846.

CLAP (see also Clapp), Abner, of Dorchester, and Hannah Hoits, at Dorchester, Nov. 2, 1757.

Asa, and Delina Bullard of Walpole, int. Apr. 23, 1826.

Barbary, and Joseph Weld, Apr. 20, 1639.

Charles, of Dorchester, and Mary P. Richards, int. Sept. 19, 1846.

Charlotte Cushing, and Jabesh Wright, Jan. 1, 1811.*

Eliphaz [Eliphas. C. R. 3.], and Hannah Jones, Apr. 27, 1817.*

Elizabeth, and Edward Sumner, Sept. 25, 1701.

Elizabeth, and Aaron Rumry, Apr. 1, 1762.

Elizabeth, of Dorchester, and James Howe, June 30, 1803.

Elizabeth, and William Whittemore, Apr. 9, 1812.*

Eunice, and Caleb Williams, both of Dorchester, May 2, 1793.

George, and Magarett Goding, Oct. 18, 1821.*

* Intention also recorded.

CLAP, Hannah, of Scituate, and Charles James, Ens., int. Sept. 22, 1799.

Hannah, and Abiel Smith, Feb. 23, 1817.*

James, jr., and Peggy Lawrence of Dedham, int. Mar. 10, 1805.

Jane, and Moses Withington, Oct. 8, 1839.*

John, and Susanna [Sukey. int.] Robinson of Dorchester, at Dorchester, Nov. 20, 1794.*

John, and Priscilla Holden, Nov. 6, 1803.*

John, and Mrs. Ann Hawes, May 22, 1823.*

John, jr., and Mehetable Allen of Bridgewater, int. Apr. 1, 1804.

Jonathan, and Jane Baden, Sept. 8, 1793.*

Lydia, of Dorchester, and James Pierce, at Dorchester, June 20, 1796.*

Mary, and Antepas Jackson, jr., Dec. 10, 1823.*

Sarah, Mrs., of Dorchester, and Joshua Bradley, at Dorchester, Jan. 9, 1770.

Sarah, of Dorchester, and John Holdin, Dec. 3, 1793.*

Sarah Ann, and Otis Withington of Brookline, Nov. 27, 1828.*

Seth, and Sarah Haws, both of Dorchester, Sept. 10, 1793.

Susannah Robinson, and Benjamin Baker Davis of Brookline, July 8, 1818.*

**CLAPP** (see also Clap), A. W. H. [Col. int.], of Portland, Me., and Julia M. Dearborn, June 24, 1834.*

Abba S. H., and Sam[ue]l Fisk, June 20, 1833.*

Daniel, and Fanny Snell, Aug. 14, 1845.*

George, of Dorchester, and Mary W. Brown, int. Aug. 31, 1823.

Jacob, and Elizabeth A. Downer, Oct. 17, 1819.*

Joseph, and Milley G. Everett of Dedham, int. Oct. 16, 1825.

Joseph H., and Caroline Allen, Sept. 8, 1835.*

Lydia, of Walpole, and Isaac Davis, int. Sept. 28, 1806.

Perez C., of Dedham, and Sarah J. Collins, int. Dec. 8, 1848.

Samuel W., and Mary Carey of North Bridgewater, int. Apr. 3, 1845.

**CLARA**, Ann, and Thomas McNamarra, int. Sept. 11, 1848.

**CLARK** (see also Clarke), Abigail, and Thomas Lyon, at Dedham, July 8, 1698.

Albert, of Brookline, and Sarah A. Bowers, Feb. 15, 1842.*

Ann Maria, and James McGlinn, int. July 11, 1830.

* Intention also recorded.

CLARK, Asa, and Susan Patee, int. Sept. 13, 1818.

Caroline, of Amherst, N. H., and Daniel Dodge, int. Nov. 27, 1834.

Catharine S., of Gilmanton, N. H., and Capt Stephen Lemist, int. Jan. 20, 1839.

Charles, and Ruby A. Richardson, Aug. 9, 1840.*

Charles M., a. 21 y., laborer, s. Ezra and Amanda, of Amherst, N. H., and Sarah A. Head, a. 19 y., Jan. 7, 1847.*

Chenery [Clarke. int.], and Lucy Davis, Oct. 3, 1805. C. R. 2.*

Daniel T., of Medford, and Deborah Waugh, int. Oct. 5, 1845.

Eliza [beth], and Eben[eze]r Tucker, Nov. 22, 1743. C. R. 2.

Elizabeth, and John Kalbfus, int. Dec. 5, 1841.

Elizabeth R. C. [C. R. int.], a. 23 y., and Henry A. Folsom, a. 24 y., carpenter, Dec. 14, 1847.*

Franklin, and Ann Davis, at Danvers, Mar. 7, 184-. [1847. int.]*

Hannah, and Samuel Wyman, Now. 23, 1756.

Hannah, and Joshua Brown, Apr. 3, 1777.

Jane, Mrs., and Benjamin Thair, both of Brookline, Mar. 9, 1769.

John, and Sarah Lethbridge, both residents, July 21, 1735.

John, jr., and Sarah M. Haynes, both of Framingham, Nov. 19, 1848.

Joseph [Clarke. int.], and Lydia Sparhawk, at Boston, Aug. 12, 1788.*

Katharine, and Robert Robison, at Boston, May 17, 1764.

Mary, and William Thomson, Dec. 3, 1760.

Mary, and John Mooney, int. Jan. 1, 1849.

Meshech, and Lydia Clarkson, int. Sept. 14, 1823.

Mianda, and W[illia]m G. Pike of Newton, Mar. 23, 1841.*

Mona, of Medfield, and W[illia]m Langley, int. Sept. 18, 1808.

Patrick, and Ann Spellman, int. Dec. 31, 1847.

Roland, and Mary Weld, May 25, 1778.

Samuel, and Mary Oatiss, Mar. 28, 1743.

Sam[ue]l N., of Illinois, and Polly H. Patten, July 26, 1844.*

Sarah A., and Samuel R. Homer, int. Oct. 26, 1845.

Sarah Weld, and William Crehore, Mar. 28, 1810. C. R. 2.*

Susan C., and Peter Brigham, int. Aug. 29, 1841.

Thomas, and Sarah Lewis of Dedham, at Dedham, Dec. 21, 1775.

* Intention also recorded.

CLARK, Thomas, and Lois Williams, July 24, 1777.

Thomas A., and Sally Perkins of Rochester, N. H., int. July 25, 1824.

William, and Hannah Searl, Oct. 1, 1723.

William D., and Eliza S. Mead. int. Apr. 16, 1837.

**CLARKE** (see also Clark), Elizabeth, and William Marean, Jan. 7, 1701-2.

George, of Dorchester, and Sally Starr of Dedham, Feb. 28, 1796.

James, and Hanah Heath, Apr. 27, 1681.

Jane F., and Solomon Dodge, May 20, 1840.*

John, and Lidia Buckminister, Nov. 18, 1680.

John, and Mary Tucker, Jan. 29, 1712.

John Jones, Esq., and Rebecca Cordis Haswell, May 25, 1830.*

Lucy, and Isaac M. Mellen, June 5, 1825.*

Manlius S., and Frances C. Lemist, Dec. 1, 1841.

Mary A., and Nath[anie]l Dowse of Sherburne, Apr. 12, 1838.*

Mary C., of Exeter, N. H., and John Sawyer, int. Feb. 16, 1845.

Timothy, of Medfield, and Sarah Medcalfe, Nov. 22, 1705.

William, and Sophronia Drew of Plymouth, int. Aug. 14, 1842.

**CLARKSON,** Lydia, and Meshech Clark, int. Sept. 14, 1823.

**CLARY** (see also Cleary), Timothy, and Catharine Carty, int. May 7, 1837.

**CLAY,** Mary, and Isaac Brackett, Oct. 7, 1819.*

**CLEARY** (see also Clary), Joanna, b. Ireland, and John Grace, b. Ireland, Oct. 22, 1849.

**CLEAVELAND** (see also Cleveland), Sophronia Ann, and W[illiia]m H. Kelley, Jan. 18, 1842.

**CLEAVES,** William, and Sarah Chandler, Nov. 4, 1659.

**CLEMENT** (see also Clements), Jeremiah [of Boston, int.], a. 30 y., grocer, s. Ebenezer and Sarah, and Sarah A. Seaver, a. 24 y., d. John and Betsey, Sept. 16, 1847.*

**CLEMENTS** (see also Clement), Hannah of Hopkinton, and Reuben Perkins, at Hopkinton, Feb. 26, 1795.

* Intention also recorded.

CLEMENTS, William B., and Mary M. Hill, Oct. 18, 1840. [Oct. 1, 1840. c. r. 5.]*

CLENAN,Margarett. and Adam Allendorf, int. Nov. 8, 1848. (null and void.)

CLENTON (see also Clinton), Catherine, b. Ireland, and Patrick McGovern [McGown. int.], b. Ireland, Dec. 30, 1849.*

CLEVELAND (see also Cleaveland), Elizabeth H., of Salem, and Gardiner L. Chandler, int. Apr. 20, 1845.
John, and Susanna Hardin Torrance of Dedham, int. July 5, 1812.

CLEWLEY (see also Clewly), Bathsheba, and Thomas Wetherbee, Nov. 4, 1751.
Sarah, and William Reynolds [Renalds. c. r. 2.], Mar. 31, 1748.

CLEWLY (see also Clewley), Elizabeth, and Dr. John Wellman, at Newton, Aug. 29, 1776.

CLIFFORD, Patrick, and Margarett Sullivan, int. Apr. 9, 1849.
Sarah C., and William C. Decker of Boston, int. Oct. 28, 1848.

CLINTON (see also Clenton), Patrick, and Jane Duffy, int. Feb. 22, 1848.
Patrick, and Elizabeth Finn, int. May 5, 1849.

CLOGHER (see also Clougher), Bridget, and Michael Ward, int. Jan. 3, 1841.

CLOGSTON, Matthew L., and Hannah Nute, Aug. 12, 1832.*

CLOOMAN, Roger, and Mary Burns, int. July 11, 1848.

CLOUGH (see also Cloughe), Elizabeth, and Daniel B. Eddy, int. Oct. 13, 1844.
Elizabeth W., and Martin Eddy, Oct. 28, 1845.*
Gilman, and Elizabeth Leonard, Aug. 19, 1827.*

CLOUGHE (see also Clough), Margarett, and Thomas Foren, int. June 13, 1846.

* Intention also recorded.

**CLOUGHER** (see also Clogher), Hannah, and Patrick Gafney, int. Oct. 28, 1845.
John, and Hanna Follen, int. Mar. 31, 1844.

**CLOUNEY,** Julia, and Cornelius Dricoll, int. Sept. 11, 1844.

**COAN,** Thomas, and Hannah Kelly, int. Apr. 29, 1846.

**COBAIN,** Thomas, a. 22 y., engineer, b. Ireland, s. William
and Betsey, and Eliza Hamilton, a. 20 y., b. Ireland, Dec.
27, 1849.*

**COBB,** Abigail, and Henry Glynn, May 28, 1839.*
Andrew Jackson, a. 27 y., s. W[illia]m and Sarah, and Eliza
Ann Mackintosh, a. 19 y., d. John and Maria, Nov. 5,
1846.*
Elizabeth, and Holman Page, int. Sept. 8, 1833.
George W., and Mary L. Stanton, May 9, 1845.*
Jonathan Holmes, Esq., of Dedham, and Sophia Doggett, Sept.
26, 1822.*
Joseph L., and Elizabeth M. S. Watson, June 7, 1826.*
Joseph Warren, a. 23 y., morocco dresser, s William and Sarah,
and Mary Ann Withers [Whethers. int.], a. 19 y., d.
James and Margarett, Apr. 18, 1847.*
Rebeccah, and Daniel B. Green, Mar. 10, 1825.*
Sally [Sarah. int.], of Taunton, and Ransom Green, Aug. 30,
1827.*
Sarah, and Charles Pratt, int. Apr. 8, 1841.
Thomas, widr., a. 31 y., oyster dealer, s. Thomas and Lucy,
and Ascenith B. Benjamin, a. 23 y., d. John and Esther,
Apr. 30, 1848.*
William, and Sally Randall, Jan. 6, 1811.*
William, and Jane F. [Tatman. int.] Hobart, Oct. 12, 1837.*

**COBBET** (see also Cobbit), Thomas, and Experience Bodowin,
May 20, 1709.

**COBBIT** (see also Cobbet), Thomas, and Martha Collins of
Dedham, at Dedham, Feb. 24, 1747-8.

**COBLY,** Lucy, and William Marean, both of Brookline, Aug.
3, 1823. c. r. 3.

**COBURN** (see also Colburn), Caty, and Abijah Meriam, Nov.
21, 1805.*

* Intention also recorded.

COBURN, Cynthia [Colburn. int.], d. Phineas and Cynthia, and George W. Ricker, farmer, s. Henry and Margarett, Dec. 11, 1848.*

Nelson, of Charlestown, and Rosanna Esters of Rome, Me., Dec. 11, 1848.

Rebecca [Colburn. Mrs. c. r. 3.], and Cascamer Peck [Pike. int.; Cascamier Beck. c. r. 3.], of Dorchester, Aug. 17, [15. c. r. 3.], 1802.*

**COCHRAN** (see also Cockran), Catharine [Coughran. int.], and W[illia]m Fagender [Faulkner. c. r. 5.], Dec. 26, 1844.*

Catherine, and James Callen, int. July 25, 1846.

Edward C., and Joanna G. Nichols of New Hampton, N. H., int. Sept. 13, 1835.

Mary, and Edward Nielan, int. June 26, 1849.

Mary, and Felix Rafferty of Lowell, int. Dec. 29, 1849.

Michael, of Boston, and Margarett Hackey, int. Apr. 7, 1849.

Michael, of Boston, and Mary Kitch, int. Sept. 27, 1849.

Nathaniel R., and Jane A. Lees of Lowell, May 4, 1841.*

Thomas, and Catherine Lawson, int. Sept. 11, 1846.

William K., and Lydia Swasey, ——, 1832. [Oct. 9, 1831. int.]*

**COCKRAN** (see also Cochran), John B., and Elizabeth Fletcher, both of Lowell, at Lowell, Sept. 1, 1839.

**CODY,** William, and Catharine Connors, int. May 4, 1845.

**COE** (see also Coes), Isaac, and Martha Ramsey, Sept. 11, 1706.

**COEN,** John M., and Ellen Cavanagh, July 25, 1848.

**COES** (see also Coe), William, and Mary Welch [both residents. int.], Dec. 3, 1786.*

**COFFEE** (see also Coffey, Coffy), John, and Eliza Wallace, int. Dec. 28, 1846.

**COFFEY** (see also Coffee), John, and Maria Norton, int. June 8, 1849.

**COFFIN** (see also Caffin), Isaac F., and Martha Anne Prince, int. Apr. 6, 1845.

Patrick, and Maria Watts, int. July 17, 1848.

* Intention also recorded.

**COFFY** (see also Coffee), Patrick, and Maria Woods, int. Sept. 10, 1849.

**COGGESHALL, J. H.,** and Eliza M. Jones, Oct. 13, 1842.*

**COGHNANTON,** Bridget, and Michael Killion, int. Jan. 12, 1845.

**COGSWELL,** Margarett [Cogswell. int.], a. 24 y., and William McDonald, a. 29 y., s. W[illia]m and Sarah, Apr. 5, 1848.*
Mary Ann, a. 24 y., b. Nova Scotia, and James Morris of Nova Scotia, 2d m., a. 28 y., master mariner, b. Nova Scotia, s. Henry and Jane, Dec. 4, 1849.*

**COKELY,** Ellen, and William Crawley, int. July 25, 1849.

**COLAMER,** Peter, and Abigail Davis, at Scituate, Nov. 8, 1694.

**COLBETH,** Charles G. [Colbath. c. r. 3.], and Elizabeth Moulton, May 6, 1840.*

**COLBOURN** (see also Colburn), Abigail, and John Baker, jr., Sept. 6, 1732.
Rhoda, and Ebenezer Whiting, July 11, 1728.

**COLBURN** (see also Coburn, Colbourn), Dorothy A., and Otis Briggs, int. Jan. 5, 1806.
Elizabeth, and William H. Randall, Oct. 19, 1828.*
Emeline K., a. 23 y., d. Jonathon and Betsey, and John M. Parkhurst of Milford, a. 27 y., merchant, s. Alexander and Mary, May 28, 1846.*
Fanny, and Peter Blake, of Dorchester, Apr. 13, 1820.*
John, and Rhoda Bradhurst, Mar. 13, 1703-4.
Levi, of Needham, and Rebeckah Strobridge [Rebekah Trowbridge. int.], at Needham, Sept. 18, 1783.*
Mary, and Natha[nae]ll Richards, Aug. 12, 1736.
Nath[anie]l, and Eliza K. Armsby of Sutton, int. Mar. 10, 1822.
Nathaniel [Capt. int.], and Anna Fowle, Dec. 2, 1830.*

**COLBY,** Caroline, and Andrew H. Smith, Apr. 13, 1845.*

**COLE,** Abigail, and Hezekiah Turner, jr., Oct. 10, 1737.
Anna S., of Lynn, and Theodore S. Richardson, int. Mar. 25, 1848.

* Intention also recorded.

COLE, Caroline, of Watertown, and Andrew W. Newman, int. Nov. 15, 1835.

Charles, and Abigail G. Harvey, May 15, 1831.*

Edmund, and Abigail Sever, Mar. 29, 1705.

Judith, and John Hayden, Nov. 2, 1797.*

Louisa, of Watertown, and Charles Morse, int. Dec. 2, 1832.

Mary A., of Providence, R. I., and Rev. William Leverett, int. Mar. 13, 1825.

Rainsford A., of Utica, N. Y., and Williamina Ross, int. Dec. 31, 1849.

Sarah, and Ebenezer Warren, Aug. 22, 1746.

Thomas, and Sarah Ruggles, Apr. 3, 1732.

**COLEGATE,** W[illia]m A., and Louisa Stevens, Apr. 6, 1842.*

**COLLER,** Geartant, and Joseph Fex, int. Apr. 11, 1848.

**COLLINS,** Betsey, and Joseph Moore of Malden, int. Oct. 27, 1805.

James, and Eunice French of Braintree, Jan. 5, 1804.*

James, and Mary Kelly, int. Apr. 26, 1845. [Apr. 26, 1846. dup.]

John, and Lucy Ann Baldwin, Aug. 29, 1837.*

John, and Elizabeth Fintin, int. Jan. 8, 1843.

John, and Mary Donovan, int. Sept. 17, 1843.

John, and Hannah Murphy, int. Apr. 4, 1844.

Martha, of Dedham, and Thomas Cobbit, at Dedham, Feb. 24, 1747-8.

Mary, and Cornelius Cachman, int. Aug. 11, 1844.

Mary, and Patrick Young, int. Mar. 18, 1847.

Mary, and Thomas Hewes, int. Jan. 5, 1848.

Michael, and Margaret Hackney, int. July 9, 1837.

Moses, and Lydia Whittemore of Malden, at Malden, May 20, 1746.

Patrick, b. Ireland, and Ann Mulray [Mulry. int.], b. Ireland, Oct. 20, 1849.*

Richard, b. Ireland, and Mary Maloy [Malay. int.], b. Ireland, Sept. 6, 1849.*

Sarah J., and Perez C. Clapp of Dedham, int. Dec. 8, 1848.

Syranus, of Connecticut, and Hannah Williams, May 22, 1777.

**COLMAN** (see also Coltman), Joseph, and Ruth Spur, Oct. 10, 1793.

* Intention also recorded.

COLMAN, Mary, and Edward [William. c. r. 2.] King, Apr. 19, 1750.

Sarah Devereux, Mrs., and Samuel Shepard Gilbert, int. Sept. 25, 1836.

Sarah, and John Manahan, int. May 4, 1845.

William W., and Elizabeth Marden, int. Apr. 2, 1837.

COLSON, Joseph, and Mirian Withington of Stoughton, at Stoughton, Sept. 19, 1771.

Vashti, and Ebenezer Goddard, May 18, 1800.*

COLTMAN (see also Colman), Henry W., and Mary Ann Orton, int. Feb. 4, 1847.

COLTON, Elizabeth H., a. 33 y., and Cornelius Horgan, a. 39 y., laborer, Sept. 6, 1847.

Sarah, b. Ireland, and Patrick Kavanah, b. Ireland, July 24, 1849.

COMBS, Mary Ann G. [Coombs. int.], b. Ireland, and Joel W. Pelton, b. Ireland, Dec. 16, 1849.*

COMER, Mary, and John Killian, int. July 21, 1849.

COMMENGES, Jacob, and Martha Paine, July 15, 1740.

COMMERFORD, Elizabeth, and Patrick Kelly, int. Aug. 28, 1847.

CONANT, Elizabeth C., a. 21 y., d. Mrs. Elizabeth Thayer and Noble H. Hill [of Boston. c. r. 5.], a. 27 y., merchant, s. David and Lucinda, July 5, 1849.*

Ezra, a. 36 y., manufacturer, s. Ezra and Anna, and Marcella A. Conant, of Felchville [Fletcherville. Vt. int.], a. 24 y., d. Lott and Hannah, Sept. 28, 1848.*

Henry, Capt., and Cynthia A. Scott, int. Dec. 21, 1823.

Marcella A., of Felchville [Fletcherville, Vt. int.], a. 24 y., d. Lott and Hannah, and Ezra Conant, a. 36 y., manufacturer, s. Ezra and Anna, Sept. 28, 1848.*

Mary Ann, of Shapleigh, Me., and Sylvester L. Ward, int. Apr. 30, 1849.

Nathan D., a. 25 y., s. Nathaniel and Rachel, and Elizabeth C. Simpson, a. 25 y., d. Lewis and Mary, Oct. 17, 1849.*

[Sylvanus. c. r. 2.], Rev. [of Middleborough. c. r. 2.], and Mrs. Sarah Williams, May 16, 1751.

CONATY, Ann, and Michael Gilligan, int. Sept. 6, 1847.

* Intention also recorded.

**CONBOY** (see also Conoboy), Ellen G., and William Lennon, int. Nov. 5, 1843.

**CONBRAY,** Michael, and Ann Cratton, int. Feb. 5, 1849.

**CONCKLING,** Helen Frances, and William [F. int.] Remick of Dorchester, Jan. 1, 1843.*

**CONDRA** (see also Condry), Bridget, and James Kelley, int. Oct. 31, 1837.

**CONDREN** (see also Condry), Bridget [Condrin. c. r. 5.], and John [Stephen. int.] Downes, May 15, 1842.*

**CONDRY** (see also Condra, Condren), Bridget, and Edward Bades, int. May 1, 1836.

**CONE,** Bridget, b. Ireland, and Thomas McLaughlin, b. Ireland, Nov. 24, 1849.*
James, b. Ireland, and Bridget Curley [of Boston. int.], b. Ireland, Oct. 12, 1849.*

**CONEY,** Elizabeth, and William Berr [Kerr. int; Berr. dup.], Mar. 27, 1796.*
Hannah Ellis, and George Henry Williams, Sept. 27, 1838. c. r. 3.
Irene, and John Evans Williams, Mar. 21, 1833.*
Joseph, of Stoughton, and Sarah Savels, at Stoughton, Sept. 1, 1748.
Mary, and Charles Lincoln, Feb. —, 1805. c. r. 3.
Nathaniel, and Esther Thayer, int. Mar. 22, 1801.
Salley, and Luther Gay, both residents, int. Mar. 12, 1786.
Sally [G. c. r. 3.], and Charles S. Hersey [Hearsey. c. r. 3.], Jan. 24, 1828.*

**CONITEE,** Mary, and Timothy Kenney, int. Mar. 27, 1842.

**CONLAN,** Patrick, and Hannah Golden, int. Jan. 18, 1848.

**CONLAY,** Hanora, and John Buckley, int. Nov. 19, 1843.

**CONN,** William, and Elizabeth Buzzard, Dec. 3, 1834.*

**CONNALLY** (see also Connelly), Ellen, of Brookline, and Patrick Graham, int. May 25, 1846.

**CONNAWAY,** Mary, and Michael McDaniel, int. June 12, 1846.

* Intention also recorded.

CONNEFF (see also Conniff), John, and Mary F. Goodman, int. July 13, 1845.

CONNELL (see also Connill), Bernard [Barnard. int.], b. Ireland, and Ellen Shiny [Sheing. int.], b. Ireland, July 10, 1849.*

Margaret, and William Edmunds, Mar. 27, 1835. [Apr. 5. int.]*

CONNELLY (see also Connally, Connilly, Conoly), Ann, and James C. Manning, June 14, 1848.*

Michael, and Margaret Flynn, int. Nov. 3, 1844.

Peggy, and Moses Griggs, Apr. 30, 1797. C. R. 2.*

Peter, and Rosannah McClure, int. Sept. 22, 1849.

CONNER (see also Connors), Bridget, and Thomas Malone, int. May 25, 1845.

Margaret, and Daniel Findley Flinn, int. Apr. 27, 1791.

CONNERS (see also Connors), Catherine, and Roger Lyons, int. Sept. 25, 1847.

CONNERTY, Bridget, b. Ireland, and James Edward [Edwards. int.], b. Ireland, Aug. 12, 1849.*

James, and Margarett Glinnen, int. Nov. 21, 1848.

CONNIFF (see also Conneff), Bridget, and John McSorsey, int. Apr. 27, 1849.

CONNILL (see also Connell), Catherine, and Owen Gibbons, int. May 13, 1848.

CONNILLY (see also Connelly), Martin, and Mary Curley, int. Sept. 15, 1847.

CONNIN, Patrick, and Margaret Lary, int. July 29, 1838.

CONNOR (see also Connors), John [Conner. int.], b. Ireland, and Ann McCoen [McCuen. int.], b. Ireland, Feb. 24, 1849.*

Mary, b. Ireland, and John Killian, b. Ireland, Aug. 4, 1849.

CONNORS (see also Conner, Conners, Connor, O'Conner, O'Connors), Catharine, and William Cody, int. May 4, 1845.

Martin, and Margarett Gaffigan, int. Jan. 19, 1849.

Thomas, and Winefred Norton, int. Dec. 20, 1845.

* Intention also recorded.

**CONOBOY** (see also Conboy), Bernard, and Jane Carroll, int. Nov. 8, 1840.

**CONOLY** (see also Connelly), Mary, and Michael O'Keefee, int. Feb. 5, 1843.

**CONREY** (see also Conry), Patrick, and Ann Dunlary, int. Sept. 29, 1845.

**CONRY** (see also Conrey), Sarah, and John Maley, int. Jan. 19, 1849.

**CONVERSE**, Benjamin B., and Elizabeth H. Brooks of Boston, int. Oct. 26, 1847.
Joseph H., and Sophia G. Prentiss, int. May 30, 1849.
Rufus, and Betsy Post Hill, May 17, 1809.*

**CONWAY**, Maria, and Barnard Butler, int. Oct. 6, 1844.

**COOK** (see also Cooke), Abigail B., of Brighton, and James B. Leeds, Feb. 7, 1822.*
Alice, of New York, and John W. A. Scott, May 12, 1842.*
Alvah, and Mary Bourne, int. Jan. 8, 1843.
Caroline B., and John Timson, jr., Feb. 25, 1830.
David, Capt., and Jane Tyler, Nov. 20, 1779.
Elias, and Mary Mayo, Jan. 27, 1793.*
Elizabeth, and Jinner Bird, Nov. 2, 1817.*
Elizabeth M., of Lexington, and Hezekiah Park, int. Mar. 11, 1832.
Isaac, jr., of Brookline, and Harriet W. Wilson, int. May 13, 1827.
James, a. 23 y., carpenter, s. Thomas and Nancy, and Rosannah L. Harmon, a. 20 y., tailoress, d. Daniel and Loratisha, Apr. 20, 1845.*
Jonathan F., and Mary Little, Sept. 21, 1806.*
Margarett, and James McGoverin, int. Aug. 6, 1849.
Mary Z., and John G. Lewis, int. Apr. 7, 1833.
Matilda, and Patrick Curley, int. Dec. 17, 1849.
Nancy, and Increase Sumner Davis, May 14, 1818. c. r. 2.*
Nancy, of Wakefield, N. H., and Jacob C. Stanton, int. Nov. 4, 1832.
Spencer, and Almira L. Smith, Jan. 12, 1842.*
William B., and Sarah Jane Moore, int. July 25, 1814.

**COOKE** (see also Cook), Mercy, and Joshua Sever, Feb. 27, 1706-7.

* Intention also recorded.

**COOLEDGE** (see also Coolidge), Harvey S., and Abby D. Pierce, int. Sept. 20, 1849.

Matilda C. [Coolidge. c. r. 3.], and [Capt. int.] George J. Curtis, Nov. 4, 1834. [Nov. 11, 1835. c. r. 3.]

**COOLIDGE** (see also Cooledge, Coolige), Daniel, and Anne Sheppard, May 26, 1773.

Obadiah, and Mrs. Sarah Davis, July 30, 1750.

**COOLIGE** (see also Coolidge), Isaiah, and Hannah Herrington, Mar. 27, 1759.

**COOMBS,** see Combs.

**COON,** Martin, and Mary Carlon, int. Mar. 23, 1845.

William, and Ruth Drury, int. Aug. 24, 1828.

**COONAY,** Hugh, and Bridget Bahern, int. Sept. 15, 1844.

**COOPER,** John D., Jr., and Margarett E. Sunderland, of Charlestown, June 27, 1849.

Sarah Hall, and Jacob Porter, Dec. 6, 1789.

**COPELAND,** Benjamin F., and Julia F. Ruggles, Nov. —, 1823.*

Franklin, and Elizabeth Marion Ellis, int. Dec. 27, 1849.

**COPLIN,** Tiley, of Stoughton, and Jonathan Draper, at Stoughton, May 11, 1775.

**COPPS,** James, and Louisa Allen, Jan 23, 1821.*

**CORBETT** (see also Corbut), Ann, and John Kelly, int. Dec. 18, 1846.

Elizabeth [Corbell. int.], a. 23 y., tailoress, d. Robert and Catharine, and William E. McRobert, a. 23 y., carpenter, s. Edward and Abigail, Sept. 16, 1845.*

George W., and Marion M. Cutter of Lowell, int. Jan. 5, 1847.

Margarett Jane, a. 19 y., d. David and Margarett, and George Pratt, 2d m., a. 34 y., cabinet maker, s. Thomas and Mary, Sept. 19, 1849.*

Robert L., and Frances Pamelia Parrott of Marblehead, Nov. 10, 1847.

**CORBIN,** Sam[ue]ll [Corban. c. r. 2.], of Dudley, and Jane Davis, Jan. 6, 1735. [1736. c. r. 2.]

* Intention also recorded.

**CORBUT** (see also Corbett), Lawrence, and Bridget Heavy, int. Apr. 24, 1842.

**CORCORAN,** Catherine, and Thomas Burke, int. Oct. 7, 1848.

**CORDWELL,** George B., and Susan H. Jones, int. Dec. 20, 1835.

**COREY** (see also Cory), Anna, Mrs., and Col. Moses Mann, [of Dedham. int.], Jan. 1, 1804. c. r. 2.*
Benjamin, and Elizabeth Weld, Jan. 18, 1789.*
David, and Sarah Murdock, May 22, 1791.*
Ebenezer, and Hannah Smith, Dec. 1, 1747.
Eben[eze]r, and Anna Richards, int. Sept. 21, 1783.
Elizabeth, and Samuel Brackett, Nov. 17, 1748.
John, and Hannah Smith, Mar. 11, 1740-41.
Jonathan [resident in Cambridge. c. r. 2.], and Ruth Winchester, ——, 1753. [May 10. c. r. 2.]
Joseph, and Hannah Sables, Sept. 10, 1752.
Joseph, and Elizabeth Mills of Needham, at Needham, May 25, 1758.
Mary, and James Fenno, resident, int. Jan. 11, 1784.
Mary, and Dr. John Dwight, May 18, 1812. c. r. 2.*
Nathaniel, and Esther Thayer, Apr. 9, 1801. c. r. 2.
Sarah, and John Henshaw, Aug. 12, 1790.*

**CORLEY** (see also Curley), Ellen, and Thomas Kelly, int. Apr. 24, 1847.

**CORNELIUS,** Catharine, and Larkin Dolan, int. Jan. 7, 1845.

**CORNELL,** David, and Octavia S. Mitchell, int. June 5, 1836.

**CORNISH,** James, and Sarah West, Apr. 20, 1765.

**CORNSON,** Moses, and Frances H. Prouty, both of Newton, Sept. 2, 1847.

**CORPORAL,** Andrew, and Elizabeth Beck, Oct. 27, 1839.*
George, and Martha Jenkins, July 8, 1838.*
Louisa A., and John Egan, June 9, 1838.*
Lucy S., a. 18 y., and Hawley Folsom of Acton, Me., a. 23 y., blacksmith, s. Benjamin and Sarah, Nov. 24, 1847.*
Mary, and Ephraim Holmes, int. May 11, 1845.

* Intention also recorded.

**CORRIGAN,** Catherine D., and John Slenten, int. Nov. 3, 1849.

James, and Ellen Sheridan, int. July 30, 1837.

**CORSON** (see also Carson), Mehitabel P., and William Curtis, int. Feb. 17, 1849.

Peter R., and Mary Ann Henderson of Dover, N. H., May 29, 1838.*

**CORTLIN,** Mary, and John Haley, int. Aug. 19, 1838.

**CORY** (see also Corey), Caroline, of Braintree, and John Heath, int: Jan. 14, 1827.

John, and Mary Griggs, May 13, 1713.

**COSGRAVE** (see also Cosgrove), Celia, and Timothy Kelley, int. Oct. 11, 1848.

Maria, and Michael Cosgrave, int. Dec. 9, 1848.

Michael, and Maria Cosgrave, int. Dec. 9, 1848.

**COSGROVE** (see also Cosgrave), Patrick, b. Ireland, and Mary Griffin, b. Ireland, Dec. 11, 1849.*

**COSTELLO** (see Costolo), Ellen C., a. 19 y., and William C. Johnston [both of Boston. c. r. 5.], a. 19 y., glass blower, s. William, July 30, 1849.

**COSTERLY,** Ann, and John Killian, int. May 4, 1847.

**COSTOLO** (see also Costello), Mary [Costly. int.], and Thomas Dolan, both b. Ireland, Feb. 16, 1849.*

**COTRELL** (see also Cotterell), Elizabeth, and Elijah Weld, Oct. 17, 1782.

**COTRILL** (see also Cotterell), Eliz[abet]h, and Elijah Weld of Cambridge, int. June 2, 1782.

**COTTER,** Elizabeth S., and Chester M. Huggins, int. Oct. 1, 1837.

Joanna, and William Harris, int. Aug. 2, 1848.

**COTTERELL** (see also Cotrell, Cotrill, Cotterill), Benjamin, and Mary Cheney, Nov. 26, 1765.

Sarah, and Thomas Maccarty, Dec. 16, 1772.

**COTTERILL** (see also Cotterell), Mary, and John Montgomery, resident, Mar. 27, 1788.*

* Intention also recorded.

COTTING, Amos, widr., of Brookline, a. 49 y., clerk, s. Amos and Dinah, and Helen Augusta Dorr, a. 3|1 y., d. A. C. and Charlotte, Nov. 12, 1846.*

COTTLE, Jane, of Watertown, and Elisha Allen, int. Nov. 27, 1828.

COTTON, Martha, and Caleb Hayward, Dec. 9, 1773.
Thomas, of Brookline, and Martha Williams, Apr. 14, 1725.

COUGHLIN, Julia, and Cornelius Leary, int. July 31, 1846.

COURSEY, Anna, and David Wallis, int. Mar. 3, 1844.

COVERLY, Lucy, and Isaac Morse, int. July 17, 1831.

COWDIN, Joseph, of Fitchburg, and Charlotte May Winship, Dec. 1, 1813.*

COWEN (see also · Cowing), Jane, and Samuel Twomley, Mar. 25, 1828.

COWING (see also Cowen), Cornelius, and Sarah Stranger of Boston, int. Dec. 3, 1849.

COWLES, George, of Montgomery, Alabama, a. 34 y., merchant, s. Roswell and Laura, and Ellen W. Tyler, a. 19 y., d. Abraham and Susan G., Sept. 7, 1848.*

COWLEY, Catharine [Calder. int; of Boston. c. R. 3.], and Willard Martin, Jan. 5, 1817.*

COX, Elizabeth, and Robert J. Douglass, Jan. 1, 1843.
Lemuel, and Mary Trask, int. Jan. 3, 1819.
Maria, and Thomas Whealen, int. Aug. 3, 1845.

COY (see also Coye), John, and Hannah Barry, May 24, 1848.*

COYE (see also Coy), James M., and Frances E. Allen, Apr. 20, 1845.*

COYEN (see also Coyne), Mary, and Patrick Dolan, int. June 5, 1848.

COYLE, Dennis, b. Ireland, and Hannah Nolen [Neilen. int.], b. Ireland, Dec. 14, 1849.*
Ellen, and George W. Nelson, int. Sept. 27, 1847.

* Intention also recorded.

COYLE, George, and Margarett E. Glynn of Boston, int. Oct. 9, 1847.

James, and Mary Higney, int. May 9, 1849.

Mary, and Teophile Joyal, int. Dec. 21, 1845.

Michael, and Catherine Griffen, int. Feb. 16, 1848.

COYNE (see also Coyen), James, and Ann Mulligan, int. June 18, 1849.

CRACKLIN, Joseph, a. 31 y., painter, s. W[illia]m and Frances, and Julia A. McDuffie of Manchester, N. H., a. 20 y., d. John and Elizabeth, Apr. 27, 1848.*

Mary Ann, and John F. Davis, Nov. 6, 1842.*

CRAFFY (see also Cruffy), Ann, and Michael McNeil, int. Jan. 10, 1848.

Mark, and Mary Davis, June 22, 1848.*

CRAFT (see also Craftes, Crafts, Kraft), Abigail, and Daniel Holbrooke, May 29, 1698.

Abner, and Mrs. Hannah Child, Mar. 17, 1774.

Allis, and Robert Loverain, Jan. 3, 1704-5.

Anna [of Newton. int.], and John Curtis [Curtiss. int.], Sept. 9, 1804. C. R. 2.*

Benjamin, and Abigail Harriss, Jan. 10, 1704-5.

Betsey, and Amos Holbrook, Nov. 16, 1806.*

Ebenezer, and Elizabeth Weld, Nov. 14, 1700.

Eleanor, and George Soler, July 28, 1835.*

Elizabeth, and James Shed, May 8, 1718.

Ephraim, and Hannah Reed [Read. dup.] of Chelmsford, at Chelmsford, May 15, 1699.

Griffin, and wid. —— Robison, at Dorchester, 15 : 5 m : 1673.

Hannah, and Edward Ruggles, Jan. 24, 1715-16.

Hannah Mrs., and Jeremiah Mosher, Nov. 29, 1750.

John, and Elizabeth Youngman, Feb. 5, 1722-3.

Jonathan, and Susanna Gore, Apr. 22, 1836.

Joseph, and Betsey Mellish, Jan. 1, 1801.*

Margaret, of Newton, and Samuel Burd, int. Dec. 1, 1799.

Mary, and Ebenezer Weld, Nov. 18, 1725.

Mehitabel, and Isaac Curtis, Apr. 13, 1727.

Nathaniel, and Patience Topliff of Dorchester, at Dorchester, Nov. 26, 1701.

Nathaniell, and Hanah Daviss, May 24, 1722.

Patience, and Phillip Bacon, Nov. 17, 1726.

* Intention also recorded.

CRAFT, Prissilla, and Benjamin Hurd, Sept. 15, 1774.
Rebecca, and Samuel Wright, May 11, 1686.
Samuel, and Elisebeth Sever, Oct. 16, 1661.
Samuel, and Elizabeth Sharp, Dec. 25, 1693.
Samuel, and Mehitable Aspinwall of Brookline, at Brookline,
——, 1725.
Samuel, of Brookline, and Rebecca Brewer, Dec. 1, 1811.*
Sarah, Mrs., and Joseph White of Brooklyn, May 26, 1730.
Sarah, and Jonathan Winchester [both of Brookline. c. R. 2.],
May 5, 1748.
Sarah, Mrs., and Edward Payson Williams, May 21, 1772.
Susanna, and Luther Richardson, Aug. 3, 1803.*
Susannah, and John Heath, Jan. 12, 1758.
Susannah, and Aaron Davis, Nov. 20, 1760.
Thaddeus C., of Baltimore, Md., a. 30 y., merchant, s. George
and Eleanor, and Sarah J. Newman, a. 29 y., d. W[illia]m
J. and Sarah, June 27, 1847.*
Thankful, and Ephraim Hall, Sept. 23, 1731.

**CRAFTES** (see also Craft), John [Crafts. CT. R.], and
Rebecca Wheelock [Whelock. CT. R.], June 7, 1654.

**CRAFTS** (see also Craft), Abigail, and John Hayden of Cam-
bridge, July 10, 1811.*
Abigaile, and John Ruggles, Jan. 24, 1650.
Hanna, and Nathanael Wilson, Apr. 2, 1645.
John, and Mary Hudsonn of Lynn, Mar. 30, 1669.
Moses, and Rebecah Gardner, June 24, 1667.
Nancy, and Zerubbabel Hearsey, Sept. 21, 1820.*
Percia, and John Doane, int. Mar. 16, 1794.
Susan H., and J. Henry E. [John H. E. int.] Gallup, Jan.
11, 1844.*

**CRAGG**, Mary, and Thomas Stone, Dec. 4, 1639.

**CRAIG** (see also Craige), Mary Ann, and John Austin, Jan.
26, 1844.

**CRAIGE** (see also Craig, Craigge), Daniel, and Mary White,
int. May 10, 1827.
Thomas [Craig. c. R. 5.], and Mary Leach [Leech. c. R. 5.],
Dec. 4, 1845.

**CRAIGGE** (see also Craig), Samuel [Craige. c. R. 3.], and
Clarissa H. [K. int.] Perkins [of Boston. c. R. 3.], Sept.
14, 1826.*

* Intention also recorded.

**CRAIN** (see also Crane), Lydia, and Joseph Lewis, Sept. 7, 1806. C. R. 2.

**CRANE** (see also Crain), Charles, and Harriet H. Miles of Stowe, int. Nov. 3, 1833.

Deborah, and Thomas Wilson, June 25, 1811.*

Elizabeth, [of Dorchester. int.], and Alvan Howe, Apr. 29, 1827. C. R. 2.*

Ellen, a. 29 y., housewife, d. John T. G. and Abigail, and George W. B. McDonald, a. 25 y., stairbuilder, s. Elisabeth, Apr. 30, 1846.*

Harriet H., and William Williams, int. Nov. 9, 1845.

Lemuel, of Dorchester, and Elizabeth Davis, Oct. 2 [20. C. R. 2.], 1793.*

Lydia G., of Canton, and Greenleaf Turner, int. Mar. 10, 1833.

Rebecca, and Boydin [Boyden. int.] Bingham, Feb. 26, 1809. C. R. 2.*

**CRATTON,** Ann, and Michael Conbray, int. Feb. 5, 1849.

**CRAWFORD,** Esther, and Samuel Freeman, in Brewster, Sept. 6, 1841.*

Isabella M., a. 30 y., and Leonard Plumer, a. 26 y., stairbuilder, Aug. —, 1846.*

**CRAWLEY** (see also Crowley), Abraham, and Aletta Chidester of Charlestown, int. Dec. 26, 1814.

John, and Susannah Peet, at Boston, Nov. 25, 1756.

Sarah [Crowley. int.], and Nathaniel Withington, Nov. 26, 1807. C. R. 2.*

William, and Ellen Cokely, int. July 25, 1849.

**CRAWLY** (see also Crowley), Polly [Crawley. int.], and Allen Willis, June 26, 1800. C. R. 2.*

**CREASE,** Elizabeth, and Charles Howland, July 8, 1793.*

Hephzibah [Creese. int.], Mrs., and George Bacon [Baken. int.] both residents, June 15, 1784.

Mary, and Samuel Eastabrooks of Brookline, Aug. 22, 1791.*

Samuel, and Catherine Goddard, Oct. 18, 1807.*

**CREED,** John, and Maria Baxter, May 1, 1836.*

**CREELAN,** Mary [Crehan. int.], b. Ireland, and Patrick Norton, b. Ireland, Oct. 18, 1849.*

* Intention also recorded.

**CREHORE,** Mary [Mrs. int.], and Abraham F. Howe [Esq. int.], Oct. 2, 1842.*

William [of Milton. int.], and Sarah Weld Clark, Mar. 28, 1810. C. R. 2.*

William M., and Eliza Blood, int. July 1, 1832.

**CREOHEN,** Julia, and Marks Loan, int. Nov. 15, 1847.

**CRIGUE,** Thomas, and Mary Leach, int. Nov. 10, 1845.

**CRIMBEL,** Elizabeth, and Andrew McCubry, Sept. 7, 1835.

**CROAK,** Ann, and George W. Richardson, int. Nov. 9, 1828.

**CROCKER,** Abigail, and James Watson of Boston, Dec. 1, 1811. C. R. 3.*

Elisha, of Charleston, S. C., and Helen Matilda Howe, int. Aug. 5, 1827.

Gersham, and Lydia Herring, Nov. 14, 1802. C. R. 2.*

Henry S., of Brooklyn, N. Y., a. 26 y., ropemaker, b. Brooklyn, s. Warren and Olive P., and Charlotte W. Smith, a. 19 y., d. Henry and Elizabeth, Nov. 29, 1849.*

Mary Ann, and Thomas Sloan, May 10, 1838.*

**CROCKET,** Sarah, and Stephen Pepper, at Boston, Feb. 12, 1728.

**CROMBIE,** William, and Elizabeth Perry, int. Oct. 20, 1847.

**CROMEL,** Jacob, and Anna Patterson of Cambridge, at Sudbury, May 30, 1769.

**CRONIN,** Catherine, b. Ireland and Patrick Carroll, b. Ireland, Aug. 6, 1849.*

Jeremiah, and Margarett Barrett, int. Jan. 5, 1847.

**CROOKE** (see also Crooks), Rebecca, and Peter Gardner, May 9, 1646.

**CROOKS** (see also Crooke), Sam[ue]l, and Esther Mc-Ccombs, June 8, 1845.

**CROOME,** William, of Lancaster, and Sarah H. Curtis, Dec. 26, 1833.*

* Intention also recorded.

**CROSBEE** (see also Crosby), Abigail, and Ephraim Lyon, June 13, 1709.

**CROSBY** (see also Crosbee), Abiel, and Eliza A. Treworgy, Nov. 26, 1848.

Deborah, and Joel Seaverns of Weston, Oct. 15, 1797.*

Frances C., of Lowell, and Henry A. Martin, int. July 24, 1848.

Harriet, of Billerica, and Lyman Ward, int. July 17, 1836.

Jesseniah, and Sarah Phipps, Dec. 29, 1774.

Josiah, and Lydia Averbeck, int. Apr. 27, 1834.

Josiah, and Alice Ross, int. Dec. 11, 1842.

Mary E., of Nashua, N. H., and John A. Kendrick, int. Aug. 13, 1843.

Nancy, and Stephen Mansfield, Oct. 10, 1786.*

Sarah, Mrs., of Dorchester, and William Williams [jr. int.], at Dorchester, Dec. 25, 1782.*

Tamzin G., and Reuben Gale, Sept. 12, 1839.*

William, and Mary E. Bowles, Sept. 9, 1845.*

**CROSFIELD,** Timothy [A. int.], of New York, and Lucy Dinsdell, Aug. —, 1796.*

**CROSS,** David I., and Abby R. Curtis of Stoughton, int. Feb. 9, 1847.

Silas, and Rachel Thayer, int. Sept. 30, 1798.

**CROSSLEY,** Thomas, and Ardelia L. Whitney, Oct. 29, 1848.*

**CROSSMAN,** George, and Amelia Keith of Taunton, June 11, 1797.*

Nathaniel W., and Asenath Mitchell, Dec. 25, 1836.*

**CROWLEY** (see also Crawley, Crawly), Catherine, and John Swetnam, int. Aug. 30, 1847.

David, a. 34 y., laborer, b. Ireland, s. Charles and Julia, and Elizabeth Ferry, a. 21 y., b. Ireland, d. John and Elizabeth, Dec. 8, 1849.*

Jeremiah, and Julia Ford, int. Sept. 2, 1846.

**CROWN,** Bridget, and Daniel Read, both of Dorchester, May 16, 1803.

* Intention also recorded.

CROXFORD, Mary, and Stephen Jennings, Apr. 23, 1772.
Nancy, and Elijah Hayden of Quincy, int. Mar. 16, 1806.
Samuel, and Lydia Thayer of Braintree, at Braintree, Dec. 4, 1774.

CRUFFY (see also Craffy), Ann [Cruffey. int.], b. Ireland, and Michael Curley, b. Ireland, July 25, 1849.*

CUDDY, Ann, and John Mahoney, int. Feb. 14, 1848.
Margarett, and Francis McDonough, int. Feb. 1, 1847.

CUDLIS, Mehet[ab]le, and George Laughton, at Boston, July 29, 1725.

CUDWORTH, see Gudworth.

CULLIGIN (see also Callehan), Thomas, and Mary Ann Paine, int. Sept. 3, 1843.

CULLIN (see also Callen), Catherine, and Thomas McGowan, int. Sept. 10, 1847.

CULLINAN, William, and Margret Hollen, int. Apr. 15, 1838.

CUMINGS (see also Cummings), Martha, and David Williams, Dec. 17, 1797.*

CUMMINGS (see also Cumings, Cummins), Betsey, and Truman [Freeman. int.] Woodman, Sept. 7, 1834.*
Jacob, and Sarah Bugbee, May 12, 1767.
Margaret, and John Murphy, int. Apr. 25, 1841.
Martha, and Thomas M. Frost, int. Nov. 12, 1843.
Sam[ue]l M., and Eliza [Eliza Ann. int.] Chittenden, Oct. 13, 1842.*
Thomas, and Mary Brown, both residents in Brookline, Nov. 26, 1759.
Thomas, and Mehitable T. Parker, Jan. 19, 1830.*
William, and Mrs. Polly Mayo, Mar. 10, 1793.
W[illia]m, and Susan S. Langley, May 27, 1830.

CUMMINS (see also Cummings), Flora, and Peter Fraizer, int. Sept. 24, 1809.
Patrick, and Elizabeth Mooney, int. Aug. 2, 1840.
Samuel, and Mary Ann Burrill, Jan. 8, 1809.*

CUMSKY, Ann, and Abram Hampson, int. Feb. 17, 1849.

* Intention also recorded.

**CUNIFF** (see also Cunniff), Bridgett, and Thomas Kelly, int. Nov. 4, 1848.

**CUNNIFF** (see also Cuniff), Winnefred, of Dorchester, and John Kelley, int. Dec. 31, 1843.

**CUNNINGHAM**, Bridget, and James Shields, int. Apr. 10, 1842.

Bridget, and Thomas Curly, int. Jan. 5, 1847.

Catherine, and Thomas Mulhearn, int. Jan. 25, 1848.

Ellen W., and John Richardson, int. Feb. 27, 1846.

Henry, and Mary L. Williams, May 22, 1822.*

Henry, and Mrs. Ceselia Dix, int. Feb. 5, 1837.

Joseph Lewis, and Catharine Greene Amory, int. May 11, 1828.

Josiah, and Lois Fillebrown, Mar. 12, 1782.

Lois, Mrs., and Stephen Williams [jr. c. R. 3.], July 2, 1805.*

Mary, and Joshua Winship, June 2, 1772.

Mary, and John Ward, June 23, 1847.*

Michael, and Bridget Donnily, int. Aug. 10, 1845.

Nath[anie]l [resident. int.], and Susanna [Susana. int.] Wilton of Cambridge, at Cambridge, Feb. 9, 1786.*

Patrick, and Catherine Killerly, int. July 11, 1848.

Patrick, [of Pawtucket, R. I. int.], and Rosanna Carroll, Sept. 19, 1848.*

Sarah, and Daniel Saunders, July 9, 1778.

Sarah, and Luther Newell, Jan. 7, 1810.*

Thomas, and Rosannah Harney, int. Jan. 21, 1844.

William, and Mrs. Abigail Cheney, Feb. 7, 1782.

William, and Catherine Kenny, int. Nov. 9, 1847.

**CURLEY** (see also Corley, Curly), Barney, and Catharine Tracy, int. June 14, 1840.

Bridget, and Patrick Glinn, int. Apr. 16, 1837.

Bridget, and Patrick O'Horo, int. Aug. 15, 1848.

Bridget, and William Dewick, int. Oct. 30, 1848.

Bridget, and Patrick Cawley, int. July 19, 1849.

Bridget [of Boston. int.], b. Ireland, and James Cone, b. Ireland, Oct. 12, 1849.*

Caroline, and William Brooks, int. Apr. 21, 1844.

Catherine, and Michael Gately, int. Jan. 10, 1841.

Catherine, and James Fallon, int. Aug. 2, 1847.

Deranda, and James Glynn, int. Aug. 31, 1845.

Elizabeth, and John Dolan, int. Nov. 11, 1848.

* Intention also recorded.

CURLEY, James, and Hanna Downey, int. May 5, 1844.

James, and Winneford Garaty, int. May 21, 1846.

John, and Catherine Donlavey, int. Dec. 23, 1848.

Martin, and Mary McCue, int. Feb. 20, 1849.

Margarett, and John Erskine, jr., int. Oct. 16, 1847.

Mary, and John Flinn, int. Sept. 26, 1841.

Mary, and Martin Connilly, int. Sept. 15, 1847.

Mary, b. Ireland, and James Miley, b. Ireland, Mar. 11, 1849.

Mary Ann, and Hubert Kelly, int. June 16, 1844.

Michael, b. Ireland, and Ann Cruffy [Cruffey. int.], b. Ireland, July 25, 1849.*

Patrick, and Margarett Carr, int. Nov. 23, 1847.

Patrick, and Mary Haith, int. Jan. 31, 1848.

Patrick, and Bridget Lines, int. Dec. 19, 1848.

Patrick, and Matilda Cook, int. Dec. 17, 1849.

Thomas, and Catherine Good, int. Jan. 25, 1849.

**CURLY** (see also Curley), Bridget, and John Curly, int. Mar. 1, 1848.

Catherine, and Michael Daily, int. Aug. 7, 1847.

John, and Bridget Waters, int. Jan. 12, 1848.

John, and Bridget Curly, int. Mar. 1, 1848.

Mary, and Patrick Rallikin, int. Dec. 29, 1844.

Rosana [Rosanna. dup.], and Michael McGann, int. Oct. 29, 1847. [Nov. 9, 1847. dup.]

Thomas, and Bridget Cunningham, int. Jan. 5, 1847.

William, and Ann Finneran, int. Feb. 5, 1849.

**CURRIER,** Adaline K. [Currer. int.], and Graham Hall, carpenter, May 6, 1846.*

Dolly, of Amesbury, and William C. Bonney, int. Jan. 5, 1848.

Hannah, of South Hampton, and Nathaniel Currier, int. Feb. 18, 1810.

Joseph [of Boston. c. r. 3.], and Sarah N[iles. c. r. 3.] Gray, Apr. 3, 1833.*

Lois, of South Hampton, N. H., and Samuel Doggett, Nov. 28, 1816.*

Martha Jane, of Methuen, and Henry May, int. Nov. 11, 1846.

Nathaniel, and Hannah Currier of South Hampton, int. Feb. 18, 1810.

**CURSON** (see also Carson), Elizabeth, and John A. Hoxie, int. July 21, 1847.

* Intention also recorded.

**CURTICE** (see also Curtis), Experience [Curtis. c. r. 2.], and
   Benjamin Smith, Mar. 21, 1716-17.
Sarah, and John Harkness, Aug. 18, 1709.

**CURTIS** (see also Curtice, Curtiss), Abigail B., and John
   Wild [Weld. int.] of Cambridge, May 12, 1807.*
Abby R., of Stoughton, and David I. Cross, int. Feb. 9, 1847.
Anna, and Samuel Blaney, June 12, 1791.*
Anna, and Amory Bell, Apr. 13, 1823.*
Benjamin, and Mrs. Abigail Bridge, Oct. 17, 1751.
Benjamin B., and Dolly B. Jones, Nov. 21, 1821.*
Betsy [Eustis. int.], and Legrand Lucus, Mar. 24, 1831.*
Daniel, and Sarah Wild of Randolph, int. Nov. 13, 1848.
Elizabeth, and Isaac Newell, Dec. 14, 1659.
Elizabeth, Mrs., and Samuel Mellish, jr. of Dorchester, at
   Dorchester, July 17, 1775.
Elizabeth, and Nathaniel Brewer, Nov. 6, 1788.*
Elizabeth, and Edward J. Robbins, int. Sept. 29, 1822.
Elizabeth, and Samuel S. Chase, June 4, 1840.*
George J. [Capt. int.], and Matilda C. Cooledge [Coolidge.
   c. r. 3.], Nov. 4, 1834. [Nov. 11, 1835. c. r. 3.]*
George, and Martha Ann Upton of Fitchburg, int. Aug. 24,
   1845.
George, a. 25 y., painter, s. W[illia]m and Hannah, and Har-
   riet E. Hood, a. 19 y., d. Abraham and Eliza, Apr. 23,
   1848.*
Hanna, and William Gary, Aug. 25, 1651.
Hannah, and Jeremiah Gore, Jan. 7, 1768.
Harriet, and [Capt. int.] William H[eath. int.] Spooner, Oct.
   19, 1825.*
Harriet, and Willard A. Humphrey, int. Mar. 17, 1833.
Henry, of Quincy, a. 21 y., boot maker, s. Samuel and Jerusha,
   and Harriet A. Seaver, a. 20 y., d. John C. and Mary,
   June 5, 1849.*
Isaac, and Mehitabel Craft, Apr. 13, 1727.
Isaac, and Anna Heath, Nov. 15, 1758.
Isaac, and Sally Heath, Feb. 27, 1805.*
Isaac, and Margaret Bell, Aug. 31, 1809.*
Isaac, and Sarah Rebecca Pierce, Jan. 21, 1841.*
Isack, and Hannah Poly, May 10, 1670.
Jared B., and Mary Ann C. Doggett, June 27, 1839.*
John, and Anna Craft, Sept. 9, 1804. c. r. 2.
John, and Sarah W. Pearson, int. Nov. 27, 1831.

* Intention also recorded.

CURTIS, Joseph, and Katherine Parker, July 3, 1771.
Joseph [Capt. int.], and Bethiah [Allen. different ink. int.]
    Parker, May 27, 1800. C. R. 3.*
Joseph, jr., and Mary Ellis Hartshorn, Sept. 25 [22. C. R. 3.],
    1825.*
Joseph H., and Maria Curtis, Mar. 20, 1832.*
Maria, and Joseph H. Curtis, Mar. 20, 1832.*
Martha A. [of Boston. C. R. 3.], and Thomas [M. C. R. 3.]
    Andrews of Hollowell [Hallowell. C. R. 3.], Me., Apr.
    14, 1831.
Martha C., and Henry W. Carr, int. Nov. 6, 1836.
Mary H., and Edward J. Robbins, Mar. 5, 1805.*
Mary Jane, and Andrew Chase, jr., int. Oct. 6, 1833.
Nathaniel [Esq. int.], and [Mrs. int.] Abigail B. Leeds, Jan.
    18, 1842.*
Nelson, and Mary S. Hyde, Aug. 30 [May 23. C. R. 3.], 1843.*
Patience, and Peleg Heath, Dec. 22, 1768.
Penuel, and EstherPearce of Hopkinton, int. Feb. 12, 1809.
Philip, and Obedience Holland, Oct. 20, 1658.
Polly [resident. int.], and Joshua Gore, Oct. 1, 1784.*
Rebeckah, and Joseph Ruggles, Oct. 20, 1748.
Ruth, Mrs., of Dorchester, and William Bosson, at Dorches-
    ter, July 9, 1767.
Salley [Sally. dup.], and Ebenezer Goddard, Oct. 1, 1777.
    [Sept. 30, 1778. dup.]
Samuel, and Mrs. Sarah Partridge, Dec. 12, 1784.*
Sarah, and Moses Richards of Charlestown, Nov. 24, 1825.*
Sarah H., and William Croome of Lancaster, Dec. 26, 1833.*
Susan W., and Charles Greenleaf Batchelder of Hollowell
    [Hallowell. C. R. 3.], Me., Dec. 9, 1841.
Susanna, and William McCarty, Feb. 12, 1805.*
Thomas, and Eleanor Warren, int. Aug. 17, 1806.
William, and Mehitabel P. Corson, int. Feb. 17, 1849.

CURTISS (see also Curtis), Abiel, and John Beacon, Nov. 21,
    1693.
Hannah, and Samuel Blake, May 15, 1712.
John, and Anna Craft of Newton, int. Aug. 26, 1804.
Obedience, and Benjamin Gamblin, Feb. 11, 1677-8.
Samuel, and Hannah Gore, June 6, 1711.
Sarah, and Joseph Daviss of Woodstock, Jan. 31, 1722-3.
Sarah, and James Hering, June 14, 1722.
[Susannah, and Daniel Whitney. T. C.] —, 1704.

* Intention also recorded.

**CUSHING,** Beza, and Hannah Boilston, Feb. 15, 1753.

Charles, Esq., and Elisabeth Sumner, Aug. 25, 1768.

Deborah J., a. 21 y., d. John and Sarah, and Joshua Briggs, a. 24 y., cabinet maker, s. Cornelius and Mary, May 8, 1849.*

James, Rev., of Haverhill, and Mrs. Ann Wainwright, Oct. 15, 1735.

James W., a. 23 y., clerk, s. John and Sarah, and Sarah H. Briggs, a. 21 y., d. Cornelius and Mary, Jan. 3, 1849.*

Lucy, of Dorchester, and James Bryant, int. Apr. 16, 1837.

Sarah, of Scituate, and Ebenezer Perpoint, at Scituate, Aug. 16, 1750.

**CUSHMAN,** George H., and Rachel B. Jones of North Bridgewater, int. Sept. 14, 1845.

J. H., and Rebecca Reed of Taunton, int. Aug. 24, 1845.

Martha, and Moses Lyon, Feb. 5, 1828.*

Mehitable C., of Kingston, and James H. Stetson, Oct. 13, 1844.

**CUSICH** (see also Cusick), Hannah [Cusick. int.], and Michael Gleason, Oct. 26, 1845.*

**CUSICK** (see also Cusich), Jane, and Michael Mahan, int. Sept. 16, 1848.

**CUTLER** (see also Cutter), Gershom [Gersham Cutter. int.], jr., and Catherine Sumner, at Cambridge, June 23, 1786.*

Julia Ruth, and Samuel Ward, jr. of New York, int. Sept. 22, 1812.

**CUTTER** (see also Cutler), Edith P., of Jaffrey, N. H., and John W. Pool, int. Aug. 16, 1835.

Elinor, of Medford, and Jonathan Hall, at Medford, Aug. 20, 1761.

Ezekiel W., and Eliza S. Richards, Nov. 28, 1841.*

Marion M., of Lowell, and George W. Corbett, int. Jan. 5, 1847.

**CUTTING,** Ephraim, and Theoda Pratt, int. June 20, 1802.

**DABNEY,** Emely Gardner, and Oliver Mills [of Boston, May 16, C. R. 3.], Apr. 16, 1813.*

**DACY,** Mary, and Michael Kly, int. Sept. 23, 1836.

* Intention also recorded.

**DAGER** (see also Dagur), Lucy Ann, and John Sanford, July 3, 1834.*

**DAGUR** (see also Dager), Sarah [Ann. int.], and Erastus Lord, ——, 1832. [Sept. 25, 1831. int.]*

**DAILEY** (see also Daily), Mary Ann, and Dennis O'Brien, int. July 16, 1837.

**DAILY** (see also Daley, Daly), Mary, and Thomas Knee, int. May 6, 1838.
Mary, and Patrick McKoene, int. May 12, 1849.
Michael, and Catherine Curly, int. Aug. 7, 1847.
Timothy, and Mary Glynn, Oct. 3, 1848.

**DALAN,** John, and Catharine Kenny, int. Feb. 1, 1835.

**DALE,** Harriet S., and H. B. Foster of Concord, N. H., Oct. 22, 1844.
John C., and Caroline J. Darling of Cambridge, int. Apr. 22, 1838.

**DALRIMPLE** (see also Dalrymple), Henry, of Cambridge, and Catherine Tilestone, Sept. 13, 1807.*

**DALRYMPLE** (see also Dalrimple), William H., Rev., of Arlington, and Elizabeth Adams, July 9, 1835.

**DALTON,** Edwin W., and Antoinett J. Rackleff of Bath, Mar. 19, 1843.*
George W., and Lucy Frye of Danvers, int. Oct. 25, 1840.
Jeremiah, jr., and Lucretia Sims, May 19, 1831.*

**DALY** (see also Daily), Patrick, and Bridget Horan, int. Mar. 26, 1849.

**DAMAN** (see also Damon), Temperance Cushing, of Scituate, and John Penny, int. Dec. 7, 1806.

**DAMMON** (see also Damon), Lydia, and Thomas Beals, int. Apr. 30, 1809.

**DAMON** (see also Daman, Dammon), Ann, of Milton, and George Gerrish, int. Feb. 8, 1824.
Jonathan, and Rachel French of Weymouth, at Weymouth, Apr. —, 1781.
Mary, of Scituate, and Joshua Farrington, int. Jan. 15, 1809.

* Intention also recorded.

DAMON, Mary [of Dedham. int.], and Thomas Glover, May 26, 1822.*

Mary Ann, of Reading, and William Welsh, int. Feb. 8, 1846.

Rebecca, and Allen Farrow, May 31, 1812.*

DANA, Anna [Nancy. dup.], and Thaddeus Bruce, June 1, 1786.*

Elizabeth, Mrs., and Thomas Pearson, Jan. 2, 1820.*

Elizabeth M., a. 23 y., d. Francis and Lochada, and John Muncks of Baltimore, a. 30 y., merchant, s. Andrew and Margarett, Oct. 18, 1849.*

Francis, and Eleaner Foster, Jan. 14, 1768.

Francis, and Lochada Davis, Oct. 27, 1822.*

George, and Sarah W. Billings, Nov. 30, 1820. C. R. 2.*

Hannah, Mrs., of Dedham, and John Ayers of Needham, July 5, 1757.

Hannah, Mrs., and Lt. Nathaniel Griggs, May 21, 1793.

Harriot, and Riley Hayford, int. Nov. 10, 1822.

Henrietta B., of Marblehead, and Augustus A. Hayes, int. June 26, 1836.

James B., of Brighton, a. 23 y., gardener, s. Charles and Esther, of Brighton, and Lucy B. Peck, a. 20 y., d. Sam-[ue]l and Hannah, May 19, 1847.*

Jonathan, of Brookline, and Elizabeth Shed, int. Feb. 11, 1797.*

Joseph, and Joa Loud, Jan. 13, 1791.*

Rachel, of Brookline, and Increase Davis, int. Mar. 12, 1786.

Rebeckah, and Caleb Child [of New Medfield.C. R. 2.], Oct. 19, 1738.

Sarah, and Ezekiel Williams, Nov. 20, 1777.

Susannah, and Thomas Williams, jr., Nov. 20, 1777.

Thankful, Mrs., and William Upham of Weston, Nov. 9, 1727.

Thomas, and Martha Williams, Nov. 1, 1750.

Thomas, jr., and Hannah Williams, Nov. 20, 1777.

DANDLEY, Mary M. P., d. James and Sarah, and Charles W. Newell, a. 25 y., painter, s. Willard and Sarah, Dec. 3, 1846.*

DANE, Annis, and John Parmenter [Parminter. CT. R.], Aug. 9, 1660. [1661. CT. R.]

John, and Ann Chandler, July 2, 1643.

Joseph, of Cambridge, and Ann Mary Gore, Mar. 1, 1818.*

Owen, and Jane Drum, int. Aug. 14, 1836.

* Intention also recorded.

**DANFORD** (see also Danforth), Ann, and Samuel Jones, Sept. 5, 1679.

**DANFORTH** (see also Danford), Ellen, and Josiah Snelling, Nov. 27, 1833.*
Harriot, and Daniel W. Gliddens, Nov. 13, 1834.*
Louisa, and Robert W. Ames, July 2, 1835.*
Mary J[ane. dup.], and Cha[rle]s W. [C. W. dup.] Matthews, May 1, 1842.*
Rhoda A., and Edward Hatch, int. Feb. 6, 1842.
Samuel Adams, and Cordelia Roseline Gragg, May 20, 1842.*
Samuell, and Mrs. Mary Wilson, Nov. 5, 1651.
Sarah, of Billerica, and Varnum Waugh, int. Feb. 15, 1829.
Susan C., and Nathaniel W. Hastings, Nov. 4, 1843.*
Thomas, and Mary D. Weston, Nov. 10, 1842.*
Thomas S., and Mary Jane Glidden of Parsonsfield, Me., int. Apr. 9, 1837.

**DANIEL** (see also Daniels), Dennis O., and Mary Ann Fagen, int. Jan. 1, 1837.
John, and Henrietta Wells, int. Oct. 21, 1832.

**DANIELS** (see also Daniel), Abigail [Mrs. int.], and Daniel Turner, Apr. 6, 1845.*
Mary C., and Francis R. Trow, int. Aug. 28, 1842.
Richard, and Sarah Chamberlain, May 20, 1829. c. r. 2.*
Rufus, and Mary Ann Mears, Nov. 22, 1827.*
Sarah, and Ira Canterbury of Medfield, Apr. 6, 1820.*
Susannah, and Sampson Packard, Sept. 28, 1808. c. r. 2.*

**DARAGH,** Margarett, and Henry Russell, int. Feb. 6, 1847.

**DARBY** (see also Derby), Rebecca, and Martin Morse of Natick, Nov. 21, 1819.*

**DARLING,** Caroline J., of Cambridge, and John C. Dale, int. Apr. 22, 1838.
Charles [Charles B. Durling. int.], a. 21 y., carpenter, s. Luther and Isabella, and Caroline S[ophia. int.] Pineo, a. 21 y., housewife, d. Peter B. and Alveia, June 15, 1845.*
John H., of Oxford, N. H., and Relief D. Willis, May 2, 1837.
Lydia, of Marlborough, and Edward Savery, int. Dec. 24, 1809.
Person, of Jaffrey, N. H., and Caroline Poole, Sept. 30, 1832.*

* Intention also recorded.

**DASCOMBE,** William, and Ruth Kelley, June 14, 1791.*

**DAVEN,** Elizabeth C., and George Dixen, Feb. 8, 1849.

**DAVENPORT** (see also Devenport), Abigail, and Thomas
   Addams of Canterbury, at Dorchester, Feb. 23, 1714-15.
Abigail B., of Dorchester, and Amos Morse, int. Sept. 18, 1825.
Catharine, and Jones Howe, May 12, 1844.*
Elijah L., and Martha O. Sweat, int. Dec. 6, 1829.
Elizabeth, and John Willson, Jan. 25, 1720-21.
Enoch, and Nancy Newman, Apr. 25, 1813.*
James, and Sarah A. A. Wiswall, Sept. 11, 1845.
Jonathan, of Dorchester, and Susanna White, at Dorchester,
   Sept. 14, 1758.
Joseph, and Mrs. Susana Brewer, Apr. 3, 1783.*
Josiah, of Warwick, and Anne Payson, Jan. 28, 1782.
Mehitabl[e], of Milton, and James Mears, at Milton, Dec. 15,
   1726.
Nancy, Mrs., and Joshua Sampson, int. Aug. 23, 1829.
Oliver, and Mary Ellis Gay of Canton, int. Apr. 1, 1824.
Peggy, of Milton, and Peleg Heath, jr., int. Nov. 1, 1807.

**DAVICE** (see also Davis), William, and Dorithy Mixer of
   Watertown, at Watertown, Jan. 12, 1709-10.

**DAVIDSON,** Esther A., and James Sanderson, int. July 28,
   1849.

**DAVIE,** Ellen, and Issac Sprague, int. Aug. 6, 1843.

**DAVIS** (see also Davice, Daviss), Aaron, and Mary Perrin,
   Jan. 25, 1732-3.
Aaron, and Susannah Craft, Nov. 20, 1760.
Aaron, and Hannah Richards, Oct. 17 [18. c. r. 2.], 1763.
Aaron, [jr. int.], and Theoda Williams, Jan. 24, 1793.*
Aaron, jr., and Catharine Gay, Apr. 10, 1811. c. r. 2.*
Abba A., and Josiah Nute, Oct. 1, 1837.*
Abigail ,and Peter Colamer, at Scituate, Nov. 8, 1694.
Abigail, and Joseph Williams, May 22, 1706.
Abigail, and William Cheny, Apr. 7, 1715.
Abigail, and Lemuel May, Dec. 15, 1768.
Abigail, and William Heath, Jan. 28, 1779.
Abigail, and William Harden, Dec. 4, 1780.
Abigail, and Joel Gay, Dec. 2, 1790.*
Abigail, and Jeremiah Richards, Oct. 31, 1792.*

* Intention also recorded.

DAVIS, Adeline, and Charles [J. int.] Hendee, Aug. 30, 1836.*
Amasa, and Martha Searl, Nov. 7, 1782. C. R. 2.*
Amy [Amey. int.], and Thomas Mayo, Aug. 19, 1792.*
Ann, and Henry Swift, Nov. 30, 1843.*
Ann, and Franklin Clark, at Danvers, Mar. 7, 184- [1847. int.]*
Ann L. [Ann L. E. int.], a. 20 y., d. John and E., and Archibald Esilman, a. 29 y,, Oct. 15, 1848.*
Anna, and Moses Pond, Nov. 13, 1788.*
Anne, and Thomas Mayo, jr., June 30, 1763. [Jan. 27. C. R. 2.]
Benjamin Baker, of Brookline, and Susannah Robinson Clap, July 8, 1818.*
Benj[ami]n B., of Brookline, and Elizabeth Seaver, Jan. 24, 1839.*
Bethia, and Joshua Child of Brooklyn [of Brookline. C. R. 2.], Jan. 31, 1732-3.
Bridget, and James Ruddy, int. Oct. 23, 1842.
Caleb, and Loisa [Louisa. C. R. 3.] M. Packard, July 19, 1807.*
Caroline M., and Lemuel Little, Apr. 2, 1823.*
Caroline, and William Fellowes of Louisville, Ky., June 9, 1829.*
Catharine [Mrs. int.], and Matthias Hiler, July 31, 1785.*
Catharine, and David Talbot, Oct. 19, 1806. C. R. 2.*
Cecelia, and Stephen Augustus Dix, Dec. 12, 1822.*
Charity, and Ehpraim Murdock, May 26, 1768.
Charles, and Mrs. Harriott Fellows, Sept. 8, 1799.*
Charles [2d. int.], and Lucy H. Gould, May 21 [31. C. R. 3.], 1818.*
Charles, and Mary Vila Ball, int. Aug. 24, 1845.
Charles, jr., and Eliza S. Dorr, Nov. 24, 1829.*
David C., and Euphemia Murray, int. June 14, 1835.
Deborah, and Joshua Richards, Feb. 18, 1796.*
Dorothy, of Brooklyn, and Eleazer May, Jan. 29, 1735. [1736. C. R. 2.]
Ebenezer, and Hannah White, Apr. 18, 1700.
Ebenezer, and Sarah Sumner, Aug. 19, 1756.
Elener Maria, and Israel Little [of Boston. C. R. 3.], Nov. 22, 1826.*
Elisabeth, and Isaac Williams, Nov. 12, 1767.
Elisabeth, and John Newell, Nov. 19, 1767.
Eliza, and Adin Ayers, June 30, 1802.*
Elizabeth, and Thomas Mayo, May 4, 1699.

* Intention also recorded.

Davis, Eliza[beth, and Joseph Holland of Brookline, at Boston, Dec. 17, 1717.

Eliz[abe]th, and John Taylor of Medway, July 10, 1732.

Elizabeth, and Jesse Richards [of Portland. int.], Nov. 18, 1792.*

Elizabeth, and Lemuel Crane of Dorchester, Oct 2 [20. c. r. 2.], 1793.

Elsey E., and Abiel S[mith. int.] Lewis, Apr. 17, 1842.*

Elsey Fellowes, and Supply C. Thwing, May 18, 1824.*

Emeline, and Thomas C. Dorsey, both of Lowell, Jan. 25, 1845.

Eunis, Mrs., and Ebenezer Wales, Jan. 18, 1770.

Ezra, and Sarah Child of Brooklyn [Brookline. c. r. 2.], Dec. 1, 1737.

Ezra, jr., and Sarah Mayo, Dec. 21, 1769.

George B., and Nancy G. Davis, int. Dec. 8, 1833.

Gershom, and Sarah Pirepont, June 24, 1708.

Gilman, and Sarah Homans Leeds, int. May 19, 1822.

Hanah, and John Healy, July 29, 1725.

Hanna, and Joseph Grigs [Griggs. ct. r.], Nov. 8, 1654.

Hannah, of Muddy River, and Daniel Allin, Oct. 26, 1705.

Hannah, and Ebenezer White of Brookline, Apr. 21, 1766.

Hannah, and John Davis Williams, Dec. 15, 1768.

Hannah, and Bartholomew White, Nov. 29, 1798. c. r. 2.*

Hannah, and Ebenezer Murdock, May 25, 1803. c. r. 2.*

Hannah, and David Dudley, Oct. 23, 1814.*

Harriot, and Daniel A. Sigourney, Oct. 16, 1823.*

Increase, and Rachel Dana of Brookline, int. Mar. 12, 1786.

Increase Sumner, and Nancy Cook, May 14, 1818. c. r. 2.*

Isaac, and Deborah Johnson, Dec. 19, 1705.

Isaac, and Elizabeth White, Mar. 23, 1795.*

Isaac, and Lydia Clapp of Walpole, int. Sept. 28, 1806.

Isaac, and Salome White, Dec. 9, 1813.*

Isaac, 3d, and Jerusha Nash of Holden, int. Dec. 14, 1817.

Isaac G., and Almira Bullock of Lowell, int. July 24, 1843.

Jacob, and Dorothy Baker, Oct. 30, 1764.

Jacob, and Harriet Humphries, Nov. 26, 1840.*

James M., and Betsey T. Whittemore, June 12, 1836.

Jane, and Sam[ue]ll Corbin [Corban. c. r. 2.] of Dudley, Jan. 6, 1735. [1736. c. r. 2.]

Jemima, and John Healey, Sept. 8, 1761.

* Intention also recorded.

Davis, Job, a. 35 y., laborer, s. Eben and Mary, and Caroline
    Hate, a. 30 y., Mar. 14, 1848.*
Joel, and Sophia R. Abbott, int. Mar. 15, 1818.
Joel G., and Sara Bogle of Brighton, int. Nov. 8, 1840.
John, and Marie Devotion, Feb. 5, 1667.
John, and Mary Torrey, at Dorchester, Jan. 14, 1673.
John, and Mrs. Sarah Weld, Apr. 7, 1737.
John, and Mary White, Sept. 30, 1742.
John, of Oxford, and Deborah Weld, Oct. 27, 1751.
John, and Mary Scott, May 20, 1762.
John, and Locada Davis, Nov. 26, 1795.*
John, and Ann Murphy, int. Jan. 13, 1848.
John, jr., and Polly [Polley. int.] Thayer, at Weymouth, Nov.
    5, 1786.*
John A., and Charity M. Dudley, Nov. 24, 1825. c. r. 2.*
John B. Esq., and Laura M. Gay, int. Sept. 17, 1826.
John C., and Elizabeth Kenrick of Newton, int. Aug. 10,
    1823.
John F., and Mary Ann Cracklin, Nov. 6, 1842.*
John H., and Caroline M. White, Jan. 15, 1804. c. r. 3.
Jon[atha]n, and Sarah Williams, Oct. 31, 1781. c. r. 2.
Jonathan, Dr., and Sarah Williams, May 1, 1797.
Jonathan H. [John. int.], and Caroline M. White, Jan. 15,
    1804.*
Joseph, and Sarah Camberlin, Oct. 28, 1670.
Joseph [of Brookline. c. r. 2.], and Elizabeth Lane, Dec. 8,
    [3. c. r. 2.], 1715.
Joseph, and Experience Willis [Mills. c. r. 2.], May 11, 1726.
Joseph, and Elsy Fellowes, July 27, 1800.*
Joseph E., and Hepzibah Alger of North Bridgwater, int.
    Dec. 23, 1827.
Joseph N., a. 26 y., tinman, s. Eli and Asenath, and Caroline
    S. Hoit, a. 27 y., d. John T. and Betsey T., Feb. 9, 1848.*
Joshua, and Sarah Pierpont of Brooklyn, Dec. 15, 1731.
Julia A. M., and Dr. William Ingalls, jr. of Laurell Hill,
    Louisiana, int. Nov. 8, 1840.
Lemuel, and Elizabeth Pond of Newton, at Newton, Jan. 27,
    1791.*
Lemuel Baker, and Releif [Relief. int.] Holland Tilestone of
    Dorchester, at Dorchester, Nov. 14, 1797.*
Levi, and Eliza Towl, July 9, 1820.*
Locada, and John Davis, Nov. 26, 1795.*

* Intention also recorded.

DAVIS, Lochada, and Francis Dana, Oct. 27, 1822.*

Lucy, and Chenery Clark [Clarke. int.], Oct. 3, 1805. c. R. 2.*

Lydia S., a. 37 y., d. John and Lydia S., and Horace Scudder, widr. of Dorchester, a. 44 y., merchant, s. David and Desire, of Barnstable, June 9, 1847.*

Lydia, of Bradford, N. H., and David E. Washburn, int. June 16, 1849.

Maria, and W[illia]m Davis, jr., Oct. 24, 1839.*

Marietta, and John Mills, Oct. 15, 1820.*

Martha, and Benja[min] Tucker, jr. [of Leicester. c. R. 2.], Dec. 14, 1760.

Martha Ann, and John Hatch, int. Sept. 22, 1844.

Mary, and Isaack Heath, jr., Dec. 16, 1650.

Mary, and George Bacon, May 4, 1699.

Mary, and Samuel Warner, June 16, 1708.

Mary, and William Carter, Oct. 26, 1726.

Mary, and Ephraim Jackson, Nov. 29, 1753.

Mary, Mrs., of Brookline, and William Pierpont, at Brookline, Oct. 29, 1761.

Mary, and Jesse Dunton, Sept. 12, 1771.

Mary, and Henry Whiting, int. Apr. 4, 1784.

Mary, of Brookline, and James Mears, jr., int. Nov. 21, 1784.

Mary, and Paul Gore, Dec. 14, 1793.*

Mary, and Isaiah Dunster, May 5, 1796.*

Mary, and Mark Craffy, June 22, 1848.*

Mary Ann, and John Williams, July 17, 1823.*

Mary E., and Jacob B. Morse, Oct. 9, 1839.*

Mary W., and John L. De Wolf of Brighton, May 24, 1841.*

Mercy of Brookline, and Capt. Jos[ep]h Williams, int. Oct. 17, 1784.

Moses, and Mrs. Rebecca Sabin, May 13, 1731.

Moses, and Sarah Bartlett of Newton, at Newton, Apr. 28, 1768.

Moses, and Hannah Pierpont, Mar. 13, 1770.

Moses, and Rebecah Sharp of Brookline, int. Oct. 30, 1791.

Nancy, and Elisha Hathaway, Sept. 6, 1801.*

Nancy B., and William Jones, Aug. 3, 1840.*

Nancy Fellowes, and William Whiting, July 17, 1823.*

Nancy G., and George B. Davis, int. Dec. 8, 1833.

Nancy W[illiams. int.], and Ralph S[mith. int.] Dorr of Buenos Ayres [Feb. 24. int], 1833.*

Nathanael, and Abigail Lyon, Nov. 4, 1736.

* Intention also recorded.

Davis, Nathan[ie]l, and Lidia Richards, Oct. 15, 1761.
Nehemiah, and Katharine Dudley, Dec. 27, 1779.
Nehemiah, and Hannah Hall of Newton, int. Dec. 25, 1803.
Noah, and Elisabeth Weld, Sept. 19, 1765.
Noah, and Sarah Chardon Pitts, int. Nov. 6, 1814.
Obadiah, and Sarah Williams, Sept. 13, 1744. c. r. 2.
Patience, and John Capen, jr., Dec. 17, 1772.
Paul, and Anna Voss of Milton, Nov. 26, 1723.
Paul, and Martha Pond, Apr. 1, 1760.
Polly S., and William Heath, jr., Dec. 26, 1816.*
Rachel [Rachael. int.], and Edward Richards, June 5, 1800.
    c. r. 2.*
Rebecca, and Timothy Hide of Newton, at Boston, Aug. 14,
    1718.
Rebecca, and John White of Charlestown, Oct. 6, 1805.*
Rebecca S., and William A. Hayde, int. Oct. 11, 1840.
Relief H., and Moses B. McIntosh, int. Mar. 17, 1833.
Reuben, and Charlotte Richards[on. in pencil], Feb. 18, 1819.*
Ruthy, and Capt. William Wyman [jr. int.], Sept. 4, 1806.
    c. r. 2.*
Sally, and Apollos Field of Charlestown, Sept. 28, 1806.*
Samuel, and Mary Chamberlaine, June 23, 1709.
Samuel, and Polly Weaton, Dec. 4, 1794.*
Samuel, and Nancy Harding, Oct. 20, 1835.*
Samuell, of Oxford, and Mary Weld, Oct. 13, 1731.
Sarah, and Timothy Stevens, Mar. 12, 1664.
Sarah, and Joseph Scott, Feb. 8, 1704-5.
Sarah, Mrs., and Obadiah Coolidge, July 30, 1750.
Sarah, and David Weld, July 11, 1756.
Sarah, Mrs., and Paul Hencock, May 23, 1771.
Sarah, and [Ens. int.], John Cluley Jones, July 5, 1792.*
Sarah, and Edward W. Bradley, Apr. 4, 1826.*
Sarah, and William H. Loring, Aug. 22, 1841.*
Sarah H., a. 20 y., d. Gilman and Sarah H., and George A.
    Chapin, a. 22 y., clerk, s. Aaron and Lucy W., June 2,
    1846.*
Stephen, and Ann Allen of Brookline, at Brookline, Nov. 12,
    1761.
Stephen, and Martha Tileston, at Dorchester, July 1, 1787.*
Susannah, and Moses White, Jan. 18, 1776.
Susan[na]h, and William Dudley, int. Apr. 22, 1804.
Suse, and William Dudley, June 17, 1804. c. r. 2.

* Intention also recorded.

DAVIS, Theoda, Mrs., and Hon. Jonathan Hunewell, Feb. 1,
    1820.*
Thomas, Capt., and Rena Armsby of Sutton, int. Oct. 6, 1816.
Tobias, and Bridget Kinman, Dec. 13, 1649.
William, and Allice Thorpe, Oct. 21, 1658.
William, of Brooklyn, and Jemima Woods, Dec. 29, 1743.
William, and Mary Smith, Sept. 19, 1797.*
William, and Sally Smith, Sept. 7, 1800.*
William, of Milton, and Unice [Eunice. int.] Vose, Apr. —,
    [Mar. 9. int], 1823. C. R. 3.*
William, and Lucy D. Mayo, Jan. 6, 1825.*
William, jr., and Jane Ann Hutchings, int. Feb. 26, 1832.
W[illia]m, jr., and Maria Davis, Oct. 24, 1839.*
William H., and Elizabeth H. Bassett of Bridgewater, int. July
    15, 1838.
Zibiah, and Isaiah Dunster Swallow, May 30, 1813. C. R. 2.*

**DAVISS** (see also Davis), Elizabeth, and Thomas Bugbe,
    Nov. 1, 1722.
Hanah, and Nathaniell Craft, May 24, 1722.
John, and Martha Griggs, June 8, 1721.
Jonathan, and Sarah Baker, Feb. 14, 1721-2.
Joseph, of Woodstock, and Sarah Curtiss, Jan. 31, 1722-3.
Sarah, and Joshua Healey of Newton, June 21, 1722.

**DAWSON,** Jamese, and Margaret Ryan, int. Sept. 18, 1847.

**DAY,** Eliza, and Michael Hickey, int. May 23, 1848.
Erasmus, of Webster, and Sarah Newton, int. Apr. 14, 1839.
James, and Catharine E. Capen, June 9, 1833.*
John C., of Cambridge, and Phebe Priest, Mar. 3, 1849.
Josiah F., of Newton, and Mary A. Savage, int. Mar. 17,
    1822.
Martha, Mrs., of Needham, and Nath[anie]l Talbot, int. Nov.
    26, 1807.
Mary A. P., a. 23 y., d. Moses and Sarah, and William Ling-
    ham, jr., a. 21 y., grocer, s. William and Lucy, Mar. 3,
    1848.*
Mary R. [N. int.], and Joshua G. Rich, Sept. 28, 1842.*
Moses, and Sarah G. Sessions, July 26, 1831.*
Sarah, of Dover, and Aaron D. Mayo, int. Apr. 6, 1820.
Susan, Mrs., of Walpole, and Willard Bullard, int. Oct. 11,
    1835.
Thomas, and Mary L. Smith, Aug. 21, 1843.*

* Intention also recorded.

**DEAL,** Catherine, and Patrick Gafney, int. Nov. 15, 1847.

**DEAN** (see also Deane), Alfred E., and Love Waldron
  [Waldren. int.], Aug. 17, 1845.*
Angenette, and Frederick I. Frost, int. Apr. 25, 1841.
Eliza A., and Joseph W. Palmer, int. Aug. 11, 1839.
George, and Caroline Allen, Apr. 27, 1845.*
Israel, and Katharine Bird, Mar. 27, 1704-5.
Lazel, and Jane Frost, int. Jan. 18, 1835.
Louisa, and Nehemiah Mc Kecknie, int. Mar. 27, 1843.
Martha A., and George M. Adler, int. Oct. 8, 1843.
Rhoda, and William Hattan, int. Mar. 4, 1832.
William Henry, and Louisa Richardson, int. Mar. 25, 1832.

**DEANE** (see also Dean), Enos [W. int.], and Hepzibah P.
  Eaton, Sept. 25, 1837.*

**DEARBORN,** Julia M., and [Col. int.] A. W. H. Clapp of
  Portland, Me., June 24, 1834.*

**DEBUKE,** Jemima, and Isaac Winslow, at Boston, Nov. 25,
  1770.

**DECILVEE,** Joseph [a Portuguese. c. r. 2.], and Mary Niles,
  Aug. 15, 1754.

**DECKER,** William C., of Boston, and Sarah C. Clifford, int.
  Oct. 28, 1848.

**DECOSTER,** John, and Betsey Harris of Stoughton, int. Sept.
  15, 1805.

**DEFLY,** Bridget, and Michael McVale, int. Jan. 18, 1848.

**DELANO,** Emeline, and George Delano, both of Dorchester,
  Dec. 27, 1843.
George, and Emeline Delano, both of Dorchester, Dec. 27,
  1843.

**DELIA,** Hannah, and Patrick Finnegan, int. Feb. 17, 1848.

**DEMERITT,** Ruth, Mrs., and John Emerson, Jan. 6, 1833.

**DEMPSEY,** John, and Mary White, int. Oct. 30, 1848.

**DEMPSTER,** John, and Jane Garrick, int. Aug. 8, 1849.

* Intention also recorded.

**DENIO,** Patience, and Eben[eze]r Harrington, int. Aug. 14, 1808.

**DENISON** (see also Dennerson), Dorothy, Mrs., and Samuel Williams, Apr. 28, 1720.
Edward, and Elizabeth Weld, Mar. 30, 1641.
George, and Bridget Tomson, Mar. —, 1640.
William, and Dorothy Weld, May 12, 1686.

**DENMON,** Anna Wilhelmina, and William Waters, jr., July 19, 1812.*

**DENNERSON** (see also Denison), James, of Brookline, and Calinda W. Richards, int. Mar. 27, 1842.

**DENNIS,** Joshua, a. 24 y., carpenter, s. Abijah and Rachel, and Cordelia C. Morse, a. 23 y., d. Barnet and Sarah, July 25, 1848.*
Louisa H., a. 19 y., and Lorenzo F. Lennell [Linnell. int.], a. 24 y., carpenter, s. Enoch and Elizabeth of Portland, Me., Feb. 28, 1847.*
Polly, of Marblehead, and Nathan Bartlett, int. May 18, 1817.

**DENSSDELL** (see also Dinsdell), Robert [Dinsdell. int.], and Salla [Salley. int.] Tucker of Walpole, at Walpole, Oct. 28, 1787.*

**DERBY** (see also Darby, Dorby), Meranda, and Asa Hunt of Weymouth, July 7, 1824.*
Sarah, of Brookline, and Lemuel Bradlee, int. Apr. 30, 1820.
Sherman, of Dublin, N. H., and Dorothy C. Broad, Nov. 14, 1837.*

**DERICK,** Hugh, and Eliza Flynn, int. May 29, 1848.

**DEVATION** (see also Devotion), Elisabeth, and Joseph Weld, Sept. 2, 1674.

**DEVENPORT** (see also Davenport), Lydia, and Daniel Pierce, both of Dorchester, May 10, 1803.

**DEVINE,** Ann, and Patrick McDonnell, int. Oct. 21, 1838.
Ellen, b. Ireland, and Timothy Mulray, b. Ireland, Nov. 16, 1849.

* Intention also recorded.

**DEVOTION** (see also Devation), Hannah, and John Ruggles, jr., May 1, 1679.

Marie, and John Davis, Feb. 5, 1667.

Martha, and John Ruggles, jr., Sept. 2, 1674.

**DEWICK,** William, and Bridget Curley, int. Oct. 30, 1848.

**DEWING,** Eben[eze]r, and Sarah Richards of Dedham, int. Apr. 30, 1809.

Joseph [resident. int.], of Brookline, and Mrs. Dorothy Holbrook, May 5, 1784.*

Lucy, of Needham, and Stephen Loud, June 22, 1806.*

**DE WOLF,** John L., of Brighton, and Mary W. Davis, May 24, 1841.*

Nathan [of Dorchester. int.], and Hannah Talbot [Talbott. int.], July 31, 1808. c. R. 2.*

**DEXTER,** Anson, and Lucy Richards, Nov. 19, 1834.*

Charlotte A., and John Wade, int. Nov. 24, 1849.

Francis, and Richard Woody, Dec. 29, 1646.

Samuel D., a. 22 y., clergyman, s. Sam[ue]l and Eliza, and Mary [Maria. int.] G. Rea, a. 26 y., d. Archilaus and Maria, Nov. 29, 1847.*

Sarah L., a. 22 y., d. Anson and Sarah, and William E. James, a. 24 y., clerk, s. John and Mary E., May 10, 1848.*

William P., of Brookline, and Margarett Austin, int. Mar. 26, 1847.

**DICKERMAN,** Caleb, and Sally Knower, Oct. —, 1807.*

Hannah, and John Tucker, Dec. 22, 1805. c. R. 3.*

John, and Lydia Leach of Bridgewater, at Bridgewater, Nov. 8, 1770.

Lemuel, and Elizabeth Payson, Dec. 1, 1772.

Nancy, and John Richards, May 17, 1801. c. R. 3.*

Rebeca, and Charles Belknap, jr., Oct. 1, 1803*

Sally, and Jesse Stutson, Jan. 13, 1801.*

**DICKEY,** Adam, and Meriam Abbott Jones of Dedham, Feb. 12, 1829.*

William, and Phebe Webster of Manchester, N. H., int. Nov. 30, 1834.

**DICKSON** (see also Dixon), Alexander [Dixon. c. R. 3.], and Susannah May, Sept. 6, 1842.*

* Intention also recorded.

DIER, John, and Mary Tucker, Sept. 2, 1725.

DIKE, Paulina A., of Pittsford, Vt., and John W. Griggs, int. May 7, 1843.

DILL, Jane, of Lowell, and David Huntington, int. May 26, 1844.

DILLAWAY, Charles K., and Martha R[uggles. int.] Portor, Aug. 27, 1835.*

DILLINGHAM (see also Dillinham), Lois F., of Turner, Me., and Atwell Richardson, int. Oct. 31, 1841.

DILLINHAM (see also Dillingham), Lilley, and James Peabody, int. July 26, 1818.

DILLION (see also Dillon), Bridgett, and William Kannavan, int. Oct. 1, 1846.

DILLON (see also Dillion), Catherine, and John Kian, int. Nov. 21, 1848.
John, and Bridgett Mulakin, int. Nov. 7, 1846.
Thomas, and Mary Gleason, int. Sept. 14, 1845.

DIMAN, Daniel, of Plymouth, and Rebecca Muncrief, Dec. 15, 1830.*

DINGAM, Henry, and Elizabeth Alcock, Apr. —, 1641.

DINN, Ellen, and Timothy Mulrey, int. Oct. 29, 1849.

DINSDELL (see also Denssdell, Dinsdill), Charles, and [Mrs. int.] Ally Loud, resident, June 14, 1785.*
Clarissa, and Eben[eze]r Poole, jr., Dec. 15, 1833.*
Joanna, and Amos Fisk, Jan. 19 [17. C. R. 3.], 1810.*
Lucy, and Timothy [A. int.] Crosfield of New York, Aug. —, 1796.*
Olive, and Henry Fessenden, Mar. 3, 1791.*
Theoda, and James W. Vose, int. June 12, 1808.

DINSDILL (see also Dinsdell), William, and Lucy Lee, Feb. 18, 1754.

DIVOLL, James W., and Jane O'Neal, int. Oct. 13, 1847.

* Intention also recorded.

[**DIX**. int.], Catharine H., and John A. Bolles, Esq., Nov. 11, 1834.*

Ceselia, Mrs., and Henry Cunningham, int. Feb. 5, 1837.

Stephen Augustus, and Cecelia Davis, Dec. 12, 1822.*

**DIXON** (see also Dickson), George, and Elizabeth C. Daven, Feb. 8, 1849.

**DOANE,** John, and Percis Crafts, int. Mar. 16, 1794.

**DOARY,** James, and Winefred Kearhin, int. Nov. 12, 1843.

**DODD,** John A., and Mary P. Adams, June 16, 1842.*

John A., widr., a. 36 y., merchant, s. John and Harriet, and Theoda H. Adams, a. 24 y., d. James and Mary, Sept. 9, 1847.*

**DODGE** (see also Dodgeman), Andrew V., and Sarah A. Milikin, int. May 5, 1847.

Augusta L., of Shirley, and Robert Somerby, int. June 7, 1847.

Daniel, and Caroline Clark of Amherst, N. H., int. Nov. 27, 1834.

Ebenezer, jr., and Anne [Ann. int.] Bennett, Aug. 3, 1845.*

Hannah C., 2d m., a. 37 y., b. N. H., d. George Blanchard, and Harry Allen, 2d m., a. 55 y., pianoforte maker, b. Leominster, s. Silas, Oct. 6, 1849.

Harriet, a. 20 y., d. Ebenezer and Mary, and Edward Lang, jr., a. 23 y., carpenter, s. Edward and Eliza, Jan. 23, 1848.*

Sarah F., d. Eben[eze]r and Mary, and John McInnes, overseer in carpet factory, s. John and Nancy, Jan. 23, 1849.*

Solomon, and Jane F. Clarke, May 20, 1840.*

**DODGEMAN** (see also Dodge), Sophia, and Thomas Byrom, Sept. 25, 1832.

**DOGGETT,** Elizabeth Sumner, and Elijah Lewis, Aug. 5, 1819.*

Jesse, Lt., and Elizabeth Sumner, Dec. 1, 1790.*

John, and Sophia Miller of Charlestown, int. Feb. 26, 1804.

John, and Mary Holland, int. Aug. 7, 1847.

Lemuel [Daggett. c. r. 3.], and [Mrs. c. r. 3.] Nancy Tuttle, Oct. 8, 1807.

Mary, and Samuel Jackson, int. Oct. 20, 1833.

Mary Ann C., and Jared B. Curtis, June 27, 1839.*

* Intention also recorded.

DOGGETT, Samuel, and Lois Currier of South Hampton, N. H., Nov. 28, 1816.*

Samuel, and Electa Webster of Stockbridge, int. Aug. 14, 1842.

Sophia, and Jonathan Holmes Cobb, Esq. of Dedham, Sept. 26, 1822.*

**DOHERTY** (see also Dorathy, Dorety, Dorherty), Ann, and John Mulhern, int. Aug. 9, 1840.

Cornelius, and Bridget Whelen, int. May 9, 1841.

Daniel, and Catherine McGinness, int. Aug. 14, 1849.

George, and Bridget McLaughlin, int. July 4, 1841.

Isabella, and Patrick Doherty, int. Nov. 3, 1849.

James, and Ellen Hoar, int. June 7, 1841.

James, and Anna King, int. Nov. 26, 1849.

Margarett [Margerie. int.], b. Ireland, and William Young, b. Ireland, July 19, 1849.*

Patrick, and Margarett Gibbons, int. June 25, 1849.

Patrick, and Isabella Doherty, int. Nov. 3, 1849.

**DOLAN** (see also Doland, Dolin, Dollon), Bridget, and John Cain, int. Jan. 22, 1847.

Elizabeth, and Michael Dolan, int. May 1, 1849.

John, and Bridget Broderick, int. Jan. 1, 1843.

John, and Bridget Branan, int. July 3, 1846.

John, and Elizabeth Curley, int. Nov. 11, 1848.

John, and Mary Kelly, int. Mar. 31, 1849.

Larkin, and Catharine Cornelius, int. Jan. 7, 1845.

Margarett, and Hugh McDonnell, int. May 3, 1849.

Mary, and Thomas Hyland, int. May 20, 1848.

Mary, b. Ireland, and Patrick Laynard [Leynard. int.], b. Ireland, Dec. 16, 1849.*

Michael, and Maria Veledge, int. Jan. 29, 1843.

Michael, and Bridget Bryan, int. Jan. 18, 1848.

Michael, and Elizabeth Dolan, int. May 1, 1849.

Patrick, and Bridget Kenney, int. Jan. 6, 1833.

Patrick, and Mary Glynn, int. Mar. 28, 1841.

Patrick, and Ellen Hubbard, int. Apr. 10, 1847.

Patrick, and Mary Coyen, int. June 5, 1848.

Simon, and Bridget Thompson, int. Dec. 31, 1847.

Thokas, and Mary Spalman, int. Apr. 6, 1845.

Thomas, and Hannah Foya, int. Apr. 15, 1838.

* Intention also recorded.

DOLAN, Thomas, and Winnefred Henry, int. July 21, 1844.

Thomas, b. Ireland, and Mary Costolo [Costly. int.], b. Ireland, Feb. 16, 1849.*

**DOLAND** (see also Dolan), Bridgett, and Michael Mitchell, int. Oct. 11, 1848.

Mary, and Lemuel Burnham, int. July 24, 1836.

Michael, and Catherine McElroy, int. June 1, 1847.

Michael, and Catherine Brine, int. Jan. 17, 1848.

**DOLE**, Harriet Salome, and Henry B. Foster of Concord, N. H., int. Sept. 29, 1844.

**DOLIN** (see also Dolan), Bridget, and Owin Donnelly, int. July 14, 1845.

Ellen, and Peter Dolin, int. Dec. 31, 1844.

Mary, and Edward Gurhy, int. May 20, 1837.

Peter, and Ellen Dolin, int. Dec. 31, 1844.

Thomas, and Margaret Regan, int. Sept. 3, 1843.

**DOLLON** (see also Dolan), Winefred, and David Brodrick, int. Sept. 20, 1845.

**DONAGAON** (see also Donegan), Mary, and Cornelius Rigan, int. Aug. 28, 1847.

**DONAHOE**, Mary, and Michael Donovan, int. Jan. 26, 1848.

Mary, and Michael Hickey, int. Jan. 8, 1849.

**DONALD** (see also Donneld), John, of Chelsea, and Dorcas A. Thornton, July 25, 1842.

**DONALLEN** (see also Donnellan), Mary F., and John J. Overen of Charlestown, int. May 22, 1849.

**DONALLY** (see also Donnelly), Margarett, and John Bonar, int. Dec. 27, 1849.

**DONAVAN** (see also Donovan), Catherine, and John Mullin, int. May 30, 1848.

Jeremiah, and Ellen Sheehy, int. Dec. 18, 1849.

Mary, and John Collins, int. Sept. 17, 1843.

Michael, and Mary Donahoe, int. Jan. 26, 1848.

**DONEGAN** (see also Donagaon, Donnogan, Dunnigan), James [Donagan. int.], and Mary McCarty, June 10, 1848.*

* Intention also recorded.

**DONELAN** (see also Donnellan), Ellen, and John English, int. Jan. 1, 1843.

**DONELON** (see also Donnellan), Bridget, and Bernard Minton, int. Dec. 30, 1846.

**DONHAM,** Mary Ann, and Senir Hosford, Sept. 25, 1835.

**DONIVAN** (see also Donovan), Hanora, and William Sullivan, int. Sept. 25, 1847.

**DONLAN** (see also Donlin), Bridget, and Michael Killean, int. July 5, 1840.
James, and Sarah Lines, int. Sept. 11, 1842.

**DONLAVEY** (see also Dunlary), Catherine, and John Curley, int. Dec. 23, 1848.

**DONLIN** (see also Donlan), Mary, and John Kilduff, int. Aug. 4, 1839.
Michael, and Catherine Cary, int. Dec. 8, 1849.
Thomas [Donlan. int.], b. Ireland, and Sara [Sarah. int.] McCafty, b. Ireland, Aug. 3, 1849.*

**DONNALLON** (see also Donnellan), Michael, and Margarett Gill, int. May 27, 1848.

**DONNAVAN** (see also Donovan), Ellen, and Timothy Sullivan, int. Mar. 22, 1847.
Julia, and James Walsh, int. Dec. 29, 1849.
Mary, and John Mahony, int. Feb. 8, 1846.

**DONNELD** (see also Donald), Mary, and Johannes Fattler, int. Sept. 9, 1838.

**DONNELLAN** (see also Donallen, Donallon, Donelon, Donnelon), Bridget, and Florence Donnellan, int. Aug. 31, 1846.
Florence, and Bridget Donnellan, int. Aug. 31, 1846.

**DONNELLY** (see also Donally, Donnely, Donnily), Bridget, b. Ireland, and Edward Gaylard, b. Ireland, Nov. 14, 1849.*
Catharine, and Michael Matthews, int. Apr. 29, 1828.
Catherine, and William Mulhern, int. Jan. 25, 1847.
Elizabeth, and John Brady, int. Jan. 13, 1846.

* Intention also recorded.

DONNELLY, Margarett [Donnally. int.], b. Ireland, and James [Thomas. int.], Gilligan, b. Ireland, Nov. 8, 1849.*
Mary A., spinster, and Robert G. Westacott, cabinet maker, Dec. 6, 1845.*
Michael, and Anne Carberry, int. May 2, 1845.
Michael, and Bridget McMark, int. Sept. 1, 1847.
Owin, and Bridget Dolin, int. July 14, 1845.

**DONNELON** (see also Donnellan), Thomas, and Bridgett Follen, int. Oct. 21, 1846.

**DONNELY** (see also Donnelly), Catharine, and Nicholas Dunnigan, int. Feb. 11, 1844.
Catharine, and Martin Glynn, int. Sept. 29, 1844.

**DONNILY** (see also Donnelly), Bridget, and Michael Cunningham, int. Aug. 10, 1845.

**DONNOGAN** (see also Donegan), Patrick, b. Ireland, and Hannah Bouge, b. Ireland, Sept. 11, 1849.

**DONOVAN** (see also Donavan, Donivan, Donnavan, Dunavin), Mary, and Daniel Lovett, int. Sept. 22, 1849.
Mary, and Patrick Boyle, int. Oct. 11, 1849.
Michael, and Johannah Buckley, int. Dec. 29, 1848.
Patrick, and Mary O'Neil, int. Mar. 4, 1848.

**DOOLEY,** Ellen, and John Murphy, int. Nov. 13, 1849.
Michael, and Johana Pomphret, int. Sept. 3, 1844.

**DOOLILAN,** Ellen, of Boston, and James Doonigan, int. May 24, 1847.

**DOONACON** (see also Doonigan), Nicholas, and Rose Harney, int. July 16, 1843.

**DOONIGAN** (see also Doonacon), James, and Ellen Doolilan of Boston, int. May 24, 1847.

**DOR** (see also Dorr), Abraham, and Susanna Winchester, Nov. 5, 1747.
Moses, and Eloner Gerald, Oct. 2, 1760.

**DORAN,** Daniel, b. Ireland, and Hannah McCarty, b. Ireland, Mar. 3, 1849.*

**DORATHY** (see also Doherty), Ann, and John Duffy, int. Feb. 2, 1840.

* Intention also recorded.

DORBY (see also Derby), Anne, and Sam[ue]l Whittemore, Nov. 13, 1771.

DORE (see also Dorr), Jonathan, and Mary R. [A. int.] Goldsmith, Aug. 28, 1831.*

DORETY (see also Doherty), James, and Mary O'Flaherity, int. June 15, 1849.

DORHERTY (see also Doherty), Catharine, and Patrick Read, int. Apr. 27, 1845.

DORN, Mary, and Edwin Macavoy, int. May 13, 1848.

DORNBACH (see also Dornback), Sophia, and Frederick Messenger, int. Aug. 21, 1846.

DORNBACK (see also Dornbach), Jacob, and Caroline Frederick, int. Apr. 1, 1848.

DORR (see also Dor, Dore), Abraham, and Rebecca Bill, Sept. 10, 1786.*
Charles, and Ann Morse, May 20, 1821. c. r. 2.*
Clemence, and Edmund Weld, July 8, 1725.
Ebeneser, and Clarissa Badlam of Dorchester, int. Oct. 1, 1815.
Ebenez[e]r, and Mary Boardman of Cambridge, at Cambridge, Feb. 16, 1709-10.
Ebenezer, Capt., and Mary Bridge, at Boston, Sept. 25, 1749.
Edward, and Abigail Loring, Apr. 25, 1734.
Edward, and Abigail Ruggles, Aug. 9, 1744.
Edward, and Abigail Gridley, Apr. 3, 1746. [1747?]
Eliza S., and Charles Davis, jr., Nov. 24, 1829.*
Elizabeth, and James Scott, Feb. 18, 1719-20.
Elizabeth, and Mark Keith of Easton, at Easton, Feb. 17, 1762.
Harbottle, and Dorothy Weld, Apr. 8, 1725.
Helen Augusta, a. 31 y., d. A. C. and Charlotte, and Amos Cotting, widr., of Brookline, a. 49 y., clerk, s. Amos and Dinah, Nov. 12, 1846.*
Jonathan, and Betsey Smith, Aug. 30, 1802.*
Joseph, and Nancy Ruggles, Feb. 16, 1769.
Lucretia, and Joshua Child, Aug. 5, 1816.*
Mary, and Jonathan [Josiah. c. r. 2.] Pierce [of Woburn. c. r. 2.], Mar. 15, 1753.

* Intention also recorded.

DORR, Mary, and Enock Hide, Apr. 29, 1772.

Mary, and Benj[ami]n Gates of Dorchester, int. Dec. 6, 1829.

Moses, and Mrs. Catharine Weld, Aug. 29, 1784.*

Nancy, and Jeremiah P. Smith, Feb. 17, 1805.*

Nancy, and William Mayo [of Brighton. int.], Mar. 18, 1827. C. R. 2.*

Nath[anie]l, and Susan Lambert, int. Nov. 29, 1807.

Ralph S[mith. int.], of Buenos Ayres, and Nancy W[illiams. int.] Davis, [Feb. 24. int.], 1833.*

Sarah, and James Pierpont, May 8, 1744.

Susan Ann, and John Phillips of Newburyport, Nov. 24, 1829.*

William, and Jane Partridge, Mar. 31, 1779.

W[illia]m B., and Mary Hickling, Sept. 15, 1834.*

DORSEY, Bridget, and Michael Follen, int. Oct. 23, 1848.

Nathaniel, and Louisa Perry, Oct. 18, 1838.*

Thomas C., and Emeline Davis, both of Lowell, Jan. 25, 1845.

DOUBLEDAY, John [G. of Boston. C. R. 3.], and Lydia Weld, Jan. 3, 1796.*

DOUBT, Sarah, and Thomas Wyman, Apr. 19, 1757.

DOUDLE, Jacob, a. 29 y., laborer, b. Germany, s. Jacob and Mary, and Ann Gleanor, a. 21 y., b. Ireland, d. Thomas and Ann, Nov. 5, 1849.*

DOUGLASS (see also Dugglas), Robert J., and Elizabeth Cox, Jan. 1, 1843.

DOVE, George, and Elizabeth Hayward, Nov. 30, 1823.*

George, jr., and Susan [L. int.] Nicholas, Dec. 14, 1845.*

John, and Sarah Muncrief [both residents. int.], July 3, 1786.*

John, and Mary Thwing of Cambridge, int. Jan. 23, 1803.

John, and Mary Hopkins, int. Oct. 1, 1820.

John, and Maria Mirick, int. July 24, 1836.

William, and Mary Read, Dec. 4, 1808.*

William, and Mrs. Susan Newman, Nov. 12, 1818.*

William, jr., and Mary Mirick, int. May 10, 1835.

DOW, Mary E., a. 23 y., d. Alfred and Sarah, and John S. Richardson, a. 27 y., laborer, s. W[illia]m and Mary, Feb. 19, 1848.*

Mary H., and Benjamin H. Welch, int. Aug. 2, 1846.

Sidney R., and Matilda E. Mayo, Dec. 28, 1843.*

* Intention also recorded.

**DOWED,** Mary, and Barnard Dunn, int. Feb. 1, 1849.

**DOWELL,** Elizabeth, and Giles Pason, Apr. —, 1637.

**DOWNE** (see also Downer), Sally, and Caleb Keith, Oct. 8, 1812.*

**DOWNER** (see also Downe), Catharine, and William Hancock, int. June 24, 1838.
Cutler, and Elizabeth S. Tyler, Dec. 1, 1845.*
Elizabeth A., and Jacob Clapp, Oct. 17, 1819.*
John, and Catharine Wyman, Nov. 9, 1800.*
Mary, and Loring Tiffany, int. Dec. 15, 1822.

**DOWNES** (see also Downs), John [Stephen. int.], and Bridget Condren [Condrin. int.], May 15, 1842. c. r. 5.

**DOWNEY** (see also Downy), Eliza[beth. int.], and John Good [Goold], Aug. 11, 1847.*
Hanna, and James Curley, int. May 5, 1844.
Mary, and John Mulhern, int. Feb. 7, 1848.
Patrick, and Hannah Bouge, int. Aug. 27, 1849.

**DOWNING,** Angelina [Dowing. int.], a. 22 y., d. John and Jane, and David Erskine, a. 27 y., carpenter, s. Joseph, Sept. 3, 1848.
Margret, and Thomas Pope, Jan. 2, 1705-6.
Mary, and Stephen Gulliver of Dorchester, Nov. 26, 1843.
Patience, and James Ward, July 5, 1829.*
Temperance A., a. 52 y., and Joseph Winsor, widr., a. 37 y., merchant, s. Joshua and Olive, of Duxbury, Feb. 28, 1847.*

**DOWNS** (see also Downes), Nancy, Mrs., of Salem, and Ebenezer Fox, Mar. 20, 1785.*
Nancy Guild, and William Thompson Symmes, Aug. 24, 1823.
Sarah, and Elijah Sever, Dec. 10, 1771.

**DOWNY** (see also Downey), Catharine, and Patrick Kelley, int. Jan. 6, 1839.

**DOWS** (see also Dowse), Benjamin, and Mary Huen, Apr. 7, 1680.
Benjamin, and Tabitha Brookes, May 11, 1709.
John, and Mehetabel Payson of Dorchester, at Dorchester, Nov. 7, 1751.

* Intention also recorded.

**DOWSE** (see also Dows), John, jr., and Mrs., Hannah Molton
of Dorchester, at Dorchester, Oct. 3, 1776.
Mary, and John Androws, Oct. 2, 1781.
Nath[anie]l, of Sherburne, and Mary A. Clarke, Apr. 12,
1838.*

**DOYLE,** Bridget, and James Harney, int. July 9, 1843.
Catharine, and Dennis Doyle, int. May 18, 1845.
Dennis, and Catharine Doyle, int. May 18, 1845.
Esther, and William Bracken, int. Oct. 7, 1848.
Joanna, and Thomas Joice, int. Aug. 31, 1848.
John, and Bridget Kelly, int. Oct. 28, 1848.
Mary, and John Cary, int. July 31, 1848.
Mary Trumbull, and John Richardson, Oct. 19, 1818.*
Phillip, and Mary Bennett, Apr. 9, 1767.
Polly, and Ezekiel [Hezek[ia]h. int.] Brown, Dec. 12, 1799.*
Sarah, and James Finaughty, int. Nov. 7, 1846.

**DRAKE,** Andrew P., and Dorinda Tufts, int. July 29, 1832.
Julia T. [of Newton. int.], a. 24 y., and James T. White, a. 32
y., carpenter, s. James and Abba, Jan. 9, 1848.*
Laurena R., and James Orrall, a. 24 y., daguerrotype painter,
s. Sophia, Dec. 29, 1847.*
Martha Ann, and Charles W. Munroe, June 6, 1847.*
Samuel T., and Elizabeth A. Hyland of Manchester, N. H.,
int. Sept. 14, 1845.

**DRAPER,** Aaron, and Mrs. Mary Fisher of Dedham, at Ded-
ham, Feb. 21, 1760.
Aaron, and Polly Wild [Weld. int.], Oct. 16, 1800. c. r. 2.*
Abigail, and Ens. John Baker, Feb. 23, 1762.
Abigail, and David Lyon, Feb. 19 [9. c. r. 2.], 1764.
Abijah, Dr., and Lavina Tyler of Attleborough, int. Dec. 7,
1806.
Abijah W., resident of Philadelphia, physician, a. abt. 31 y., s.
Abijah, M. D. and Lavina (Tyler), and Lydia Frances
Swain of Nantucket, resident of Philadelphia, a. abt. 27 y.,
b. Nantucket, d. Hezekiah and Lydia, of the Society of
Friends, at Philadelphia, Jan. 20, 1839.
Abijah W., 2d. m. a. 40 y., physician, s. Abijah and Lavina
(Tyler), and Sarah H. Reynolds, d. Abel and Anna
Hewins, Apr. 26, 1848.*
Augusta, and Chauncey Woodward of Brookline, farmer, Nov.
25, 1847.*

* Intention also recorded.

DRAPER, Benjamin, and Mary Parker, Aug. 23, 1738.

Benj[ami]n J. G., and Hannah Burrill of Dedham, int. Apr. 10, 1825.

Betsey, and Nath[anie]l Fisher, int. Oct. 7, 1838.

Charles R., and Mary A. Burke of Eaton, N. H., int. Apr. 20, 1845.

David M., and Mary Ann C. Ruggles of Wrentham, int. Mar. 19, 1837.

Ebenezer, and Dorothy Child of Brookline, May 2, 1723.

Eunice, and Nathan Aldis, June 24, 1708.

Elizabeh, and Jacob Robinson, Jan. 21 [Feb. 23. C. R. 2.], 1764.

Elizabeth, and Nathaniel Tileston, Nov. 9, 1790*

Gideon, and Abigail Aldis, Apr. 22, 1713.

Grace, Mrs., and Joseph Babcock, Esq., of Dorchester, int. Oct. 26, 1800.

James, and Abigail Whiting, Feb. 18, 1680.

James, and Rachel Aldis, May 2, 1716.

James, and Abigail Child [of Brookline. C. R. 2.], Nov. 12, 1719.

James, and Margarett M. Ross, int. Mar. 5, 1849.

John, and Elizebeth Lyon, Feb. 29, 1768.

Jonathan, and Tiley Coplin of Stoughton, at Stoughton, May 11, 1775.

Katherine, and Ezekiel Whitney of Watertown, at Watertown, Dec. 6, 1763.

Kesiah [Mrs. C. R. 2.], and Oliver Vose, Feb. 5, 1778.

Margaret, and Joshua Weld, Dec. 14, 1756.

Mary, and Joseph Tyler, Sept. 23, 1756.

Mary, and Sam[ue]l Heath, Dec. 3, 1767.

Mary, and William Foster, June 11, 1778.

Mary, and Zenas White, May 16, 1822. C. R. 2.*

Mary Ann, and Joseph Priest, int. June 4, 1837.

Moses, and Hannah Chandler, July 7, 1685.

Moses [John. C. R. 2.], and Anna Worthy Leek [both residents. C. R. 2.], Apr. 8 [28. C. R. 2.], 1757.

Moses, jr., and Sally Gurney, May 1, 1796.*

Nathanael, and Abigail Lyon, Jan. 22, 1705-6.

Nathaniel, and Mehetabel Weld, May 25, 1732.

Nathaniel, and Anne Jones, July 3, 1780.

Patience, and Ebenezer Case, Mar. 13, 1689-90.

Paul, of Brookfield, and Nancy Mann, June 13, 1816. C. R. 2.*

* Intention also recorded.

DRAPER, Sally, and Ebenezer Turner of Dedham, int. Mar. 17, 1816.

Samuel, and Sarah Jackson of Newton, at Newton, June 27, 1771.

Sarah, and James Hadlock, May 19, 1669.

Sarah, and Josiah Sumner of Milton, Dec. 8, 1737.

Sarah, and Nathaniel Whiting, jr., at Boston, Sept. 23, 1767.

Sarah, Mrs., and Simeon Pratt, Feb. 5, 1795.*

Thomas, and Elizabeth Gardner of Sherborn, at Sherborn, May 4, 1768.

William, and Kesiah Whiting, Sept. 24, 1767.

William, and Rebecca [Rebekah. int.] Richards, Aug. 13, 1782. C. R. 2.*

William, jr., and Nancy Murdock, May 22, 1806. C. R. 2.*

DRESSER, Richard M., and Sarah S. Page, int. Sept. 22, 1833.

Susan, of Dedham, and Ebenezer Paul, Apr. 15, 1847. C. R. 7.

DREW (see also Drue), Andrew B., and Betsy D. Edgerly, int. June 3, 1832.

Angeline, and Samuel W. Bodge, int. Oct. 16, 1836.

John A., and Hannah J. Traip, int. Nov. 2, 1845.

Louisa, and Moses Hemenway, int. June 19, 1842.

Lucretia, and Nathaniel H. Randall, June 1, 1815.*

Mary E., and John F. Estabrook of Westborough, Nov. 30, 1843.*

Nathaniel, and Elizabeth Toby, May 24, 1829.*

Sophronia, of Plymouth, and William Clarke, int. Aug. 14, 1842.

DRICOLL (see also Driscoll), Cornelious, and Julia Clouney, int. Sept. 11, 1844.

DRINAN, Catharine, and John Murphy, int. Sept. 8, 1844.

DRINKWATER, William, of Merrimac, N. H., a. 24 y., s. William and Sarah, and Agnes Brown, a. 22 y., Oct. 21, 1847.*

DRISCALL (see also Driscoll), Margaret, and Dennis O'Leary, int. July 19, 1846.

* Intention also recorded.

DRISCOLL (see also Dricoll, Driscall), Bridget, and Patrick McCormick, int. July 24, 1848.

Jane [Jean Drischal. int.], b. Ireland, and Ignatus Byrne [Ignutious Burns. int.], b. Ireland, Nov. 14, 1849.*

DROWN, Sarah, and Joseph Shepherd of Boston [Oct. 15, 1804. different ink.]*

Susan, and Arthur F. Anderson, int. Dec. 13, 1829.

DRUCE (see also Druse), Elizabeth, and Elisha Fuller, July 6, 1780.

John, and Elizabeth Bishop, May 23, 1700.

Obadiah [of Brookline. c. r. 2.], and Mary Bridge, Feb. 1, 1750. [1749-50. c. r. 2.]

DRUE (see also Drew), Rosemund, [sic.] and Marie Druse, Feb. 18, 1677.

DRUM, Jane, and Owen Dane, int. Aug. 14, 1836.

DRURY, David, and Ruth Parker, July 3, 1818.*

Ruth, and William Coon, int. Aug. 24, 1828.

DRUSE (see also Druce), Marie, and Rosemund [sic.] Drue, Feb. 18, 1677.

DUDLEY, Abigail H., and John Brown of Charlestown, Oct. 13, 1835.*

Anne, Mrs., and John Winthrop, Dec. 16, 1707.

Betsey, and John Seaver, Apr. 19, 1798.*

Catharine, Mrs., and William Dummer, Apr. 28, 1714.

Charity M., and John A. Davis, Nov. 24, 1825. c. r. 2.*

David, and Hannah Davis, Oct. 23, 1814.*

Ebenezer, and Nabby Murdock, Jan. 3, 1799. c. r. 2.*

Ebenezer, jr., and Elizabeth F. Richards, June 18, 1826. c. r. 2.*

Elijah, and Isabel Weld, Oct. 30, 1791.*

Elisabeth Child, and Nathan Griggs, Dec. 27, 1812.*

Elizabeth, and Joseph Richards, Esq., [of Dedham. different ink.], Mar. 24, 1748-9.

Ephraim, and Elmira Swallow, May 7, 1835.*

Hannah, and Joseph Williams, Esq., Apr. 5, 1770.

Isabel, Mrs., and Moses Whiting of Dedham, Nov. 24, 1816.*

Joseph and Pedy Whitney, June 14, 1801.*

Joseph W., and Lucy R. Gay, Mar. 11, 1827.*

* Intention also recorded.

DUDLEY, Katharine, and Nehemiah Davis, Dec. 27, 1779.

Levi P., of Dedham, and Sarah Jane Brown, int. Nov. 9, 1845.

Lucy, and Simon Tufts [of Medford. C. R. 2.], Feb. 23, 1748-9.

Lucy, Mrs., and Seth Tucker Whiting, Sept. 11, 1783.*

Mary, Mrs., and Francis Wainwright, Jan. 1, 1712.

Mary, and Capt. Henry H. Williams, int. Mar. 24, 1833.

Mary Ann D., and W[illa]m G. Lewis, Oct. 13, 1841.*

Nathan A. M. [N. A. Monroe. int.], and Elizabeth G[ray. int.] Jewett, Nov. 12, 1845.*

Paul, and Martha Foster, Apr. 27, 1779.

Pedy, and Lewis Slack, June 2, 1833.*

Rebecca, Mrs., and Samuel Sewall, Sept. 15, 1702.

Rebecca, Mrs., and Benj[ami]n Gerrish, May 10, 1744. C. R. 2.

Rebecca, and Nathaniel Parker, June 1, 1788.*

Sally, and John W. Fellows, Mar. 29, 1795.*

Samuel, and Susan Davenport Brewer, Nov. 18, 1810.*

Samuel, and Mary E. Gray, int. Dec. 3, 1837.

Sarah M., and Mottrom [Motram. C. R. 2.] V. Arnold of Quincy, Jan. 15, 1835.*

Thomas, Esq., and Katherin Hagburne, Apr. 14, 1644.

Thomas, and Mrs. Hannah Whiting, Apr. 26, 1753.

Thomas and Abigail Weld, May 14, 1778.

Tho[ma]s, and Eliza Mylod, May —, [Apr. 21. C. R. 3.], 1805.*

Thomas, and Mary Burril, Feb. 8, 1807.*

William, and Sarah Williams, Feb. 22, 1774.

William, and Suse [Susan[na]h. int.] Davis, June 17, 1804. C. R. 2.*

**DUFF**, James, and Sarah Burnett, May 28, 1753.

James, and Mrs. Abigail Stoel of Dedham, at Dedham, July 8, 1760.

**DUFFY** (see also Durfee, Durfy, Dufly), Ann, and Patrick Savage, int. Apr. 30, 1843.

Jane, and Patrick Clinton, int. Feb. 22, 1848.

John, and Ann Dorathy, int. Feb. 2, 1840.

Mary, and John Mullen, int. Feb. 8, 1846.

Michael, and Ellen Kenard, int. Sept. 25, 1847.

Patrick, and Mary Lamay, int. Apr. 2, 1849.

Thomas, and Mary Hanner, int. Apr. 14, 1844.

William, and Mary Anne Kelly, int Nov. 11, 1846.

* Intention also recorded.

DUFLY (see also Duffy), Lawrence, and Bridget Farrington, int. Sept. 16, 1838.

DUGAN (see also Duignin, Durgan, Durgin), James, and Sophia Atherton, int. Mar. 29, 1818.

Margarett [Dugen. int.], b. Ireland, and Patrick Boyde, b. Ireland, Dec. 18, 1849.*

DUGGLAS (see also Douglass), Ann, and Nathannaell Gary, Oct. 14, 1658.

Elizabeth, and John Chandler, Feb. 16, 1658.

DUICK, Benjamin, and Hannah Gay, int. May 3, 1795.

Benjamin, and Mary Pierpont, int. Feb. 2, 1800.

DUIGNIN (see also Dugan), Ann, and Andrew Kildry, int. Jan. 18, 1846.

DUKE, James, and Bridget McGuire, int. Jan. 1, 1843.

DUMMER, William, and Mrs. Catherine Dudley, Apr. 28, 1714.

DUMPHY, Harriet, of Quincy, and William Enslin, int. June 9, 1839.

DUNAVIN (see also Donovan), Cornelius, and Joanna Callehan, int. Jan. 29, 1843.

DUNBAR (see also Dunborr), Calvin C., and Adeline A. Lunt, June 10, 1840.*

DUNBORR (see also Dunbar), Hannah [Dunbar. int.], of Hingham, and Thomas Seaver, at Hingham, Jan. 19, 1783.*

DUNCAM (see also Duncan), Jonas L., and Mary Ann W. Stevens, Aug. 21, 1842.*

DUNCAN (see also Duncam), John L., and Sarah L. Cassell of Dorchester, int. Jan. 4, 1848.

DUNFEE, Mary, and Patrick Murlhaugh, int. Apr. 7, 1848.

DUNHAM, Lydia, and Nathaniel B. Harlow, 2d., both of Bridgewater, Nov. 30, 1848.

* Intention also recorded.

**DUNKIN,** Deliverance, and Titus Jones, Feb. 11, 1724-5.
Hannah, and John Scot, May 29, 1672.
Jane F., and William Bowen, int. Aug. 7, 1848.
Mary, and Bernard Nash, int. Aug. 13, 1846.
Sarah, and W[illia]m Lyon, s. William, Sept. —, 1675.

**DUNLAP,** Matilda, and Giles Pease, both of Springfield, Jan. 7, 1847.
William, and Frances A. Webster, Nov. 14, 1843.*

**DUNLARY** (see also Donlavey), Ann, and Patrick Conrey, int. Sept. 29, 1845.

**DUNMEDY,** Elizabeth, and Joseph Yendley, int. Oct. 16, 1842.

**DUNN,** Barnard, and Mary Dowed, int. Feb. 1, 1849.
Bridget, and John Gallagher, int. Aug. 4, 1849.

**DUNNAN,** Ellen, and Michael Egan, int. May 28, 1843.

**DUNNELL,** Lydia, and Joseph Stedman, int. Mar. 13, 1803.

**DUNNIGAN** (see also Donegan), Nicholas, and Catharine Donnely, int. Feb. 11, 1844.

**DUNNING,** Alice J. C. [Alice Jane E. int.], and Daniel M. Brown, Apr. 22, 1846.*
Elizabeth [Elisabeth. int.], a. 24 y., and John D. Mead, a. 25 y., carpenter, s. Levi and Polly of Deerfield, N. H., July 22, 1846.*
Sarah Ann [Duning. int.], and David McDaniel [McDonold. int.], Nov. 30, 1843.*

**DUNSTER,** Isaiah, and Mary Davis, May 5, 1796.*
Mary [Mrs. int.], and Maj. Ebenezer McIntosh of Needham, Jan. 11, 1821. c. r. 2.*

**DUNTEN** (see also Dunton), Sam[ue]l, and Elisabeth Tucker, July 11, 1765.

**DUNTON** (see also Dunten), Charlotte, and Nath[anie]l Tolman, int. Apr. 20, 1834.
Jesse, and Mary Davis, Sept. 12, 1771.

**DURAND** (see also Durant), Bridget, and Thomas Mc Guire, int. Jan. 9, 1842.

* Intention also recorded.

**DURANT** (see also Durand), Charles, and Nabby L. Williams, Apr. 6, 1806.*

Margarett, of Boston, and Martin Mullen, int. Jan. 1, 1849.

Maria, and Payson Williams of Watertown, int. May 12, 1811.

Maria Cornelia, and Andrew Ritchie of Boston, Mar. 27, 1807.*

William, and Susannah L. Marsh, int. May 11, 1828.

**DURFEE** (see also Duffy), Hannah V., of Fall River, and T. Lewis Robinson, int. Oct. 28, 1848.

Sarah B., of Fall River, and Franklin H. Lewis, int. Dec. 7, 1848.

**DURFY** (see also Duffy), Patrick, and Bridget Hanon, int. May 13, 1848.

**DURGAN** (see also Dugan), James, and Cyrene Hagar, int. Sept. 22, 1822.

**DURGIN** (see also Dugan), Mehitabel, and Timothy L. Marshall, Apr. 4, 1824.*

**DURNIN,** Ann, and Hugh Killean, int. Apr. 17, 1842.

**DURNINGER,** Daniell, and Huldah Lamb, Jan. 24, 1722-3.

**DURST,** Louisa Margaret, and Michael Ham of Dorchester, int. Nov. 3, 1833.

**DUSEY,** Peter, and Mary Ball, Sept. 3, 1718.

**DWIGHT** (see also Wright), Anne, of Dedham, and Benjamin Lyon, Dec. 21, 1742.

George [Wright. int.], and Roxanna Besse, Feb. 22, 1846.*

John, Dr., and Mary Corey, May 18, 1812. c. r. 2.*

Marianne, a. 30 y., d. John and Mary, and John Orvis, a. 30 y., yeoman, s. Soren and Sillis of Ferrisburg, Vt., Dec. 24, 1846.*

**DWINE,** James, and Rosanna Kelly, int. Sept. 15, 1846.

Mary, and Michael Follen, int. July 8, 1847.

**DWINELL,** Samuel, and Catharine Owens, int. Sept. 11, 1825.

**DWIR** (see also Dyer), Michael, and Margaret Butler, int. Oct. 15, 1845.

* Intention also recorded.

**DWYER** (see also Dyer), William T., and Harriet N. Jackson, int. Aug. 25, 1844.

**DWYRE** (see also Dyer), Catherine, and Patrick Henesy, int. Oct. 30, 1847.

Francis, and Hannah Burns, int. July 14, 1844.

**DYER** (see also Dwir, Dwyer, Dwyre), Ezekiel D., and Mrs. Rebecca Morse, May 29, 1828.*

Jareb [of Canterbury. int.], and Sasanna [Susanna. int.] Pierpont Newell, Nov. 6, 1784.*

John A., a. 22 y., carpenter, s. William and Sally, and Esther J. Benjamin, of Athens, Me., a. 19 y., d. John and Esther, Sept. 13, 1846.*

Maragrett, and Henry Ames, int. July 20, 1848.

Mary E., a. 22 y., d. Asa and Hannah, and James C. Farmer, a. 23 y., fireman on railroad, s. David and Betsey, Apr. 16, 1848.*

Nehemiah F., of Braintree, and Joanna B. Ward, Nov. 4, 1835.*

Peter, and Eunice Penniman, both of Braintree, [Apr. ?], 1797.

Sarah, of Weymouth, and John Ruggles, sr., Mar. 15, 1674-5.

Susan S., and Chester M. Gay [a. 24 y. in pencil], int. Mar. 17, 1844.

Thankful V., and Warren Hall of Bennington, N. H., int. July 29, 1847.

**EAGEN** (see also Egan), Elizabeth, and Edward Butler, Nov. 6, 1743.

**EAGER,** Catherine, and Mark Lynch, int. May 15, 1848.

**EAGLES,** Elizabeth, and Samuel S. Littlefield, Apr. 4, 1837.*

Rebecca, and Cha[rle]s R. Shattuck, June 29, 1840.*

**EAMES,** Amanda M. F., of Providence, and Charles E. Elliot, int. Sept. 7, 1845.

Anna, of Framingham, and Amasa Fobes, int. July 4, 1802.

Cutler, and Abigail Francis Paiths, int. Feb. 3, 1833.

**EARLAY,** Thomas, and Mary Carney, int. Aug. 9, 1849.

**EAST,** Mary Ann, and Jacob Priest, int. Dec. 15, 1833.

* Intention also recorded.

**ESTABROOKS** (see also Estabrook), Samuel, of Brookline, and Mary Crease, Aug. 22, 1791.*

**EASTBURN,** John H[enry. int.], and Susan F[osdick. int.] Simmons [Jan. 20. int.], 1833.*

**EASTEY** (see also Esty), Elijah, and Salley Williams, Oct. 22, 1791.*

**EASTHAM,** Emily, and Henry P. Baker of New Bedford, Apr. 14, 1839.

**EASTMAN,** Francis S., and Sally Patten, May 1, 1833.*
Lycurgus, and Eliosa B. Simmons, Sept. 26, 1832.*

**EASTY** (see also Esty), Oliver, Lt., of Orange, and Elizabeth Gay, Feb. 22, 1794.*

**EATON,** Abigail [Abiel. c. r. 2.], and John Ward [of Newton. c. r. 2.], Nov. 28, 1751.
Benjamin, and Sarah Bordman, Apr. 17, 1735.
Cordelia, and Nehemiah Mack, int. May 19, 1849.
Ellen E., of Needham, and John F. J. Mayo, int. Mar. 29, 1848.
Hepzibah P., and Enos [W. int.] Deane, Sept. 25, 1837.*
Jasper H., and Elizabeth Tuttle, May 7, 1837.*
Jeremiah, and Eunice Hitchings, Feb. 26, 1826.*
John, of Stoughton, and Eliz[abe]th Lovering, Apr. 23, 1729.
John, and Eliza Pike, Feb. 13, 1842.*
Mary, of Dedham, and James Herring, at Dedham, Apr. 12, 1733.
Nathaniel, and Martha Gridley, Apr. —, 1770.
Salome, and Abraham S. Parker, Dec. 31, 1844.*

**EAYRES** (see also Ayers), Ebenezer, and Mrs. Clemency Weld, Nov. 25, 1784.

**ECKART,** Joseph, and Mary Ann King, int. Nov. 26, 1847.

**EDDS** (see also Edes), Elizabeth, of Needham, and Luther Ware, int. Apr. 3, 1800.

**EDDY,** Daniel B., and Elizabeth Clough, int. Oct. 13, 1844.
Martin, and Elizabeth W. Clough, Oct. 28, 1845.*

**EDES** (see also Edds), Elizabeth, Mrs., and Calvin Burt of Longmeadow, Oct. 16, 1835.*

* Intention also recorded.

EDES, Sally, and Abner Austin, Dec. 1, 1825.*
Sarah, and Thomas Lillie, Dec. 15, 1822.

**EDGERLY,** Betsy D., and Andrew B. Drew, int. June 3,
1832.
Sarah, and Levi Hussey, int. July 21, 1822.
Sylvester, and Catharine Munroe of Charlestown, int. Oct. 4,
1840.

**EDLAND,** Mary G. P., of Bedford, and Lorenso Stevens, int.
Dec. 6, 1845.

**EDMUNDS,** Ebenezer, and Elizabeth Beacon, Sept. 12, 1717.
Joseph, and Nancy Shepherd, Apr. 25, 1793.*
Joseph [Edmonds. int.], and Sarah Goodwin, Oct. 17, 1844.*
William, and Margaret Connell, Mar. 27, 1835. [Apr. 5. int.]*

**EDSALL,** Sarah, and William Pecock, s. W[illia]m, Aug. 3,
1681.

**EDWARD** (see also Edwards), James [Edwards. int.], b. Ireland, and Bridget Connerty, b. Ireland, Aug. 12, 1849.*

**EDWARDS** (see also Edward), Charles W. [Edward. int.], of
Portland, Me., and Lydia S. Homan, May 23, 1845.*
Daniel M., and Ellen Maria Flinn, int. Apr. 4, 1824.
John, and Emily B. Manning of Boston, int. Jan. 29, 1847.
Robert, and Susanna C. Phillips of Dorchester, int. Mar. 5,
1809.
Robert, and Cynthia Litchfield of Scituate, int. Apr. 10, 1814.
Thomas, and Catherine Kenny, int. Nov. 20, 1844.

**EGAN** (see also Eagen, Egen), John, and Louisa A. Corporal,
June 9, 1838.*
John, and Rosanna Madan, int. Jan. 8, 1843.
Maria, and Matthew McCauley, int. Aug. 31, 1848.
Michael, and Ellen Dunnan, int. May 28, 1843.
Timothy, and Catharine Gurry, int. Oct. 18, 1845.

**EGEN** (see also Egan), James, and Mary Ann Myers, int.
Sept. 30, 1846.

**EIVES,** John, and Hannah Johnson, both residents, Aug. 31,
1786.*

* Intention also recorded.

**ELDRIDGE** (see also Aldridge), Gideon, and Phebe Anne White, Aug. 11, 1834.*

R. R. S. [Rhoda Rebecca Spencer. int.], and Thomas C. Wilson of Salem, Oct. 12, 1837.*

**ELIOT** (see also Elliot), Sarah, and John Bowles, Nov. 16, 1681.

**ELISHA,** George, and Mary Freeman, Jan. 1, 1844. C. R. 7.*

Polly, and John White, July 22, 1801.*

**ELLEN,** Catherine, and Francis J. Brehin, int. Oct. 7, 1848.

**ELLIOT** (see also Eliot), Albert T., of Providence, and Sarah E. Wetherbee, int. Nov. 21, 1841.

C. E., and Sarah A. Loker of Brookline, int. Jan. 20, 1849.

Charles E., and Amanda M. F. Eames of Providence, int. Sept. 7, 1845.

John [Rev. John Eliot. C. R. 1.], and Hanna Mumford, Sept. 4, 1632.

John, and Mrs. Harriet Langley, int. June 10, 1827.

Mary, and Edward Pason, Jan. 1, 1642.

**ELLIS,** Beulah A., of Dorchester, and James F. Twombly of Woburn, Apr. 14, 1842.

Charles, of Dorchester, and Maria Mayo, Mar. 7, 1816. C. R. 2.*

Charles M., and Harriet L. Lewis of Pepperell, int. Jan. 21, 1844.

David [of Boston. C. R. 3.], and Nancy Weld, Jan. 1, 1818.*

Elizabeth Marion, and Franklin Copeland, int. Dec. 27, 1849.

Elloner, of Dedham, and Noah Weld, at Dedham, Apr. 4, 1751.

Hannah, and Philip Searle, May 29, 1690.

Hannah, Mrs., and Benjamin Tompson, jr., July 2, 1730.

Hannah [Coney. int.], and George Henry Williams, Sept. 27, 1838.*

Isaiah M., and Mary A. Welch, of Chelsea, int. Jan. 6, 1846.

Nathaniel, and Sarah Robbins, Dec. 9, 1804.*

Olive, Mrs., of Dedham, and Jason Hartshorn, int. Mar. 30, 1817.

Royal [of Boston. C. R. 3.], and Matilda White, Feb. 23, 1817.*

Sarah, and John Baker, Apr. 6, 1748.

Sarah, and Thomas Kindrick, May 23, 1790.*

Sarah R., and Matthew Binney, Sept. 13, 1827.*

Timothy, and Beulah Pond, June 30, 1776.

* Intention also recorded.

**ELLISON,** John, and Eliza Kenney of Milton, int. Aug. 28, 1842.

**ELLSWORTH,** Thomas, and Milly Farrington, Apr. 23, 1797.*

**ELVILL** (see also Elwell), Rebecca, and Isaac Belknap, at Boston, July 17, 1781.

**ELWELL** (see also Elvill, Ewell), Lot, and Sarah Jones, July 23, 1838.*

**EMERSON,** Charles F., a. 21 y., dyer, s. Leonard and Alice, and Emma L. Nichols, a. 18 y., d. Issac and Esther, Mar. 13, 1848.*

John, and Mary Pease, Feb. 26, 1818.*

John, and Mrs. Ruth Demeritt, Jan. 6, 1833.

Sophronia, of Candia, N. H., and Daniel Atherton, int. Nov. 15, 1835.

William, a. 24 y., provision dealer, s. Oliver and Elizabeth, and Caroline L. Bryant of Medford, a. 22 y., d. Nathan and Mary, Nov. 26, 1847.*

**EMERY,** Francis W. R., and Sophronia Faulkner, int. June 14, 1829.

Joseph W., of Philadelphia, and Nancy [L. int.] Faulkner, July 1, 1832.*

Mary Ann L., and James E. Macey, July 4, 1833.

**EMMLEN,** Rica, and Jacob Nagman, int. June 25, 1849.

**EMMONS,** Nahum, and Eliza Littlefield, Oct. 17, 1830.

**ENGLESBIE,** Sarah, and Caleb Savor, at Charlestown, Dec. 15, 1671.

**ENGLISH,** John, and Ellen Donelan, int. Jan. 1, 1843.

Sarah, and Sam[ue]l Lovering, Nov. 28, 1775.

**ENSLIN,** Caroline, and Henry Blackman, July 9, 1822.*

William, and Harriet Dumphy of Quincy, int. June 9, 1839.

**ERSKINE,** David, a. 27 y., carpenter. s. Joseph, and Angelina Downing [Angeline Dowing. int.], a. 22 y., d. John and Jane, Sept. 3, 1848.*

John, of Abington, and Hannah Sturtevant, Sept 15, 1813.*

John, and Jane E. Adams of Dorchester, int. June 11, 1847.

John, jr., and Margarett Curley, int. Oct. 16, 1847.

ERVIN (see also Irving), Michael, of Dedham, and Ruth May, Dec. 18, 1803.*

ERVING (see also Irving), George, Esq., and Lucy Winslow, Oct. 25, 1768.

ESILMAN, Archibald, a. 29 y., and Ann L. [L. E. int.] Davis, a. 20 y., d. John and E., Oct. 15, 1848.*

ESSER, Caspar, and Elizabeth Bliss, int. Nov. 7, 1848.

ESTABROOK (see also Estabrooks), Elizabeth S., of Rutland, and Alden Graham, int. Mar. 30, 1845.
Harriet, and Lewis Carlton of Brooksville, Me., int. Aug. 1, 1847.
John F., of Westborough, and Mary E. Drew, Nov. 30, 1843.*
Silas, and Sarah J. Burton, Dec. 5, 1846.

ESTERS, Rosanna, of Rome, Me., and Nelson Coburn of Charlestown, Dec. 11, 1848.

ESTEY (see also Esty), John, and Betsey Littlefield of Braintree, int. Dec. 8, 1793.

ESTY (see also Eastey, Easty, Estey), Edward P. W., and Elizabeth Whitemore, May 20, 1827. C. R. 2.*
Jacob [Estey, resident. int.], and Lucy Williams, July 16, 1782. C. R. 2.*

EUSTIS (see also Curtis), Anna, of Needham, and Josiah Foster, int. Dec. 11, 1808.
Betsy, and Legrand Lucas, Mar. 24, 1831. C. R. 3.

EVANS (see also Evens), Edwin, and Susan E. Fairbanks of Dedham, int. Jan. 12, 1845.
Eliza A. W., a. 18 y., d. Cha[rle]s and Emeline, and Jeremiah Blake, a. 23 y., engraver, s. Jeremiah and Lucy, Nov. 9, 1847.*
Jeremiah, and Sally Bellows, Feb. 18, 1827.*
William, and Hannah Shannon, int. Mar. 9, 1823.
William, and Hepzibah [C. int.] Weld, Sept. 30, 1834.*
William, and Mary Adams, May 30, 1844.*

EVENS (see also Evans), Hannah, of Bedford, and Jonas Putman, int. Feb. 17, 1811.
Johannah, and Joshuea Hemenway, Jan. 16, 1667.

* Intention also recorded.

**EVERETT,** Eliza M., and Benjamin F. Campbell, int. Apr. 26, 1829.

Ellen L., a. 20 y., d. Eliphalet and Eliza, and Cushing Webber, a. 24 y., dentist, s. James H. and Rebecca, Jan. 1, 1849.*

Hannah, and Richard Seaver, Nov. 30, 1748.

Hannah, of Dorchester, and Henry Bartlett, M. D., int. Mar. 23, 1828.

Hannah B. [of Dorchester. int], and Charles Griggs, Aug. 12, 1827. c. r. 2.*

Harriet A. [Everill. int.], and William Barton, May 17, 1844.*

Isabell, and Dudley Williams, int. Aug. 26, 1832.

Joanna B., of Dorchester, and Dr. Henry Gardner, June 9, 1803.

Mary, and Ephraim Blancher, May 5, 1752.

Mary A., of Cambridge, and Elisha James, int. Oct. 27, 1848.

Milley G., of Dedham, and Joseph Clapp, int. Oct. 16, 1825.

Nathaniel, and Sally Baker, Apr. 12, 1801. c. r. 2.*

Sally, Mrs., and Thomas Lagatty [Lagallee. int.], Mar. 19, 1809. c. r. 2.*

William, and Rachel M. Ford of Dover, int. May 16, 1846.

**EVERTON,** Jane, and Ebenezer Bacon, Nov. 13, 1729.

**EVLETH,** Henry P., and Rachel A. Lyon, int. Dec. 2, 1824.

**EWELL** (see also Elwell), Gardner, of Dorchester, and Abby White, int. Oct. 4, 1840.

Perez, and Nancy Williams, Aug. 26, 1804.*

Sally W., and Ebenezer D. Morrison, May 4, 1826.*

William, a. 27 y., farmer, s. Perez, and Lovey Gowell, a. 26 y., d. Benj[amin], Dec. 26, 1847.*

**FADDEN,** James, of Dedham, and Polley Pond, int. Feb. 8, 1801.

**FAGEN** (see also Fagin), Mary Ann, and Dennis O. Daniel, int. Jan. 1, 1837.

**FAGENCLER** (see also Faulkner), W[illia]m [Faulkner. c. r. 5.], and Catharine Cochran [Coughran. int.], Dec. 26, 1844.*

**FAGIN** (see also Fagen), Eliza, and John Welch, int. Oct. 10, 1846.

* Intention also recorded.

**FAHAY** (see also Fahey), Patrick [Fahey. int.], and Ann Kelly, Oct. 16, 1847.*

**FAHEY** (see also Fahay, Fahy, Fuhey), Bridget, and Thomas Griffin, int. Oct. 2, 1847.

**FAHY** (see also Fahey), Michael, and Anne Campbell, int. Feb. 2, 1845.

**FAIRBANKS,** Aaron D., a. 26 y., gentleman, s. Aaron and Nancy, and Jennet Munroe, May 2, 1848.*
Gerry, and Polly Sumner, May 20, 1806.*
Harriot S., of Needham, a. 23 y., d. Joshua and Clarissa, and Rufus H. Mills of Needham, a. 21 y., silk manufacturer, s. Rufus and Sarah E., of Needham, Mar. 3, 1847.
John [of Dedham. C. R. 2.], and Sarah Amos, ——, 1749. [Jan. 3, 1749-50. C. R. 2.]
Lewis, and Jane Walker, Jan. 1, 1811.*
Susan E., of Dedham, and Edwin Evans, int. Jan. 12, 1845.
Susan F., and William Claffin [jr. int.], Feb. 9, 1823.*

**FAIRBROTHER,** Nancy Brown, and Ebenezer Hearsey, Apr. 6, 1815.*

**FAIRFIELD,** John, Rev., of Pepperelborough, and [Mrs. int.] Martha Ruggles, Sept. 15, 1785.*
Sarah G., and John Choate, Nov. 9, 1819.*

**FALES,** Clarissa, of Dedham, and Benjamin Wait, int. Sept. 29, 1799.
Mary Ann, of Lowell, and Edwin A. Nurse, int. Nov. 27, 1842.
Sally, of Dedham, and Asa Penniman, at Dedham, Sept. 24, 1795.*
Sarah, and Samuel Lethbridge, jr., of Wrentham, Nov. 16, 1773.

**FALL,** Elizabeth M., of Ossipee, N. H., and Matthew Harris, int. Feb. 15, 1846.

**FALLEN** (see also Fallon, Fullon), Bridget, and Michael Mullen, int. Feb. 16, 1845.
Bridget, and Michael O'Brien, int. Mar. 23, 1845.
Catharine, and Michael Harney, int. Apr. 7, 1839.

* Intention also recorded.

**FALLEY,** Ellen, b. Ireland, and Burnet Scanlan, b. Ireland, May 25, 1849.

**FALLON** (see also Fallen), James, and Catherine Curley, int. Aug. 2, 1847.

John, and Catharine McKearnan, int. Nov. 3, 1839.

**FARL,** Eleanor, and Samuel Gates, Mar. 12, 1838.*

**FARLAND,** Catherine, and Patrick McDaniel, int. Dec. 15, 1847.

**FARLEY,** Eliz[abe]th, and Thomas Mayo, jr., July 25, 1734.
Enoch, and Elizabeth Pike, Feb. 13, 1711.
Henry W., and Sarah E. Chamberlain, int. Dec. 22, 1849.

**FARLING,** Bridget, and William Gately, int. Apr. 21, 1844.

**FARMER,** Caleb S., and Mary Small of Dedham, int. Dec. 1, 1839.
James C., a. 23 y., fireman on railroad, s. David and Betsey, and Mary E. Dyer, a. 22 y., d. Asa and Hannah, Apr. 16, 1848.*
Samuel R., and Betsey Abbott, both of Ossipee, N. H., Jan. 17, 1849.*

**FARNHAM** (see also Farnum), Lucy J., and William R. Sinclair, Apr. 5, 1843.*

**FARNSWORTH,** Edmund, a. 21 y., leather dresser, s. William and Catherine, and Lydia H. Glines, a. 20 y., d. Nathan H. and Sarah H., May 24, 1846.*
Franklin, and Frances Ann Page of Walpole, int. Nov. 27, 1847.
Mary E[llen. int.], a. 22 y., d. Asa and Elizabeth, and Gordon F. Tucker of Lowell, merchant, Nov. 18, 1847.*
Mary Elizabeth, and Joseph Henry Meredith of Baltimore, int. Sept. 22, 1847.

**FARNUM** (see also Farnham), Charlotte, and [Capt. int.] Henry Oxnard [of Boston. c. R. 3.], May 5, 1819.*
Julia A., of Amherst, N. H., and Jerahmeel C. Pratt, int. May 23, 1841.
Paul, and Mrs. Mary G. Tiffany, int. Nov. 27, 1831.

**FARR,** Abigail [H. int.], and James Pierce, Jan. 1, 1816.*
Nancy, and William Waters, Feb. 26, 1834.*

* Intention also recorded.

**FARREL** (see also Farrell), Joseph, and Catharine Kelly, int. Oct. 19, 1845.

**FARRELL** (see also Farrel, Farrelly), Ambrose, and Mrs. Lois Burbank, Aug. 17, 1828.*
Ann, and Thomas Scelly, int. May 31, 1848.
Ellen Maria, and John McDermott, int. June 30, 1849.
Patrick, and Ann Hurly, int. Nov. 9, 1847.
Patrick, b. Ireland, and Sarah Wise, b. Ireland, Nov. 16, 1849.*
Thomas, and Bridget Broderick, int. Sept. 25, 1842.

**FARRELLY** (see also Farrell), Catherine, and John Holland, int. Feb. 20, 1847.
Mary, and John Watson, int. Nov. 16, 1846.

**FARREN,** Nathan, of Brookline, and Mrs. Abigail Foster, at Brookline, Apr. 7, 1763.

**FARRENTON** (see also Farrington), Judith, and Abiel Lyon of Woodstock, Nov. 24, 1703.

**FARRER** (see also Farrow), Mary Ann, and William Briggs, Mar. 19, 1838.*

**FARRINGTON** (see also Farrenton), Abby J. B., and William M. Oliver, Nov. 17, 1842.*
Benjamin, Capt., and Betsey Ockington, Jan. 11, 1816. c. R. 2.
Ben[jami]n, Dea., and Hannah Kingsbury, Sept. 27, 1827. C. R. 2.*
Bridget, and Lawrence Dufly, int. Sept. 16, 1838.
Bridget, and John Gilligan, int. June 16, 1839.
Clarissa, and Ebenezer Parsons, May 20, 1804. c. R. 2.*
George L., and Rhoda Baker, Oct. 10, 1805.*
James, and Desire Whitney, Apr. 3, 1828. c. R. 2.
Joshua, and Mary Damon of Scituate, int. Jan. 15, 1809.
Leonard, of Walden [Vt. int.], and Mary W. Gay, Nov. 5, 1815.*
Lucy, and Daniel Pomroy, Jan. 24, 1802. c. R. 2.*
Margaret, and Isaac S. Walker, int. Mar. 29, 1846.
Mary Adeline, and Francis Stone, Feb. 20, 1827.*
Melatiah, and David Richards, Dec. 1, 1772.
Milley, and Thomas Ellsworth, Apr. 23, 1797.*

* Intention also recorded.

FARRINGTON, Silas, and Elizabeth W. Kelley, int. May 25, 1828.

Sophia M., and George H. Blendell, Aug. 9, 1827.*

Sukey, and Reuben Wallis, Jan. 30, 1805.*

Washington, and Martha P. Hill, int. Oct. 19, 1834.

**FARROW** (see also Farrer), Allen, and Rebecca Damon, May 31, 1812.*

**FARWELL,** Edwin F., and Susan Barney of Newton, int. Apr. 4, 1844.

John, and Lucy Stratton of Foxborough, int. Jan. 12, 1823.

**FATTLER,** Johannes, and Mary Donneld, int. Sept. 9, 1838.

**FAULKNER** (see also Fagencler), George, M. D., and Mary Ann Spalding of Billerica, int. Aug. 7, 1847.

Nancy [L. int.], and Joseph W. Emery of Philadelphia, July 1, 1832.*

Sophronia, and Francis W. R. Emery, int. June 14, 1829.

**FAUNCE,** Calvin B., and Elizabeth R. Richards, Apr. 27, 1836.*

James B., and Ann P. Langley of Newton, Nov. 29, 1838.*

Stephen, jr., and Rebecca W. Langley, May 16, 1832.*

**FAXON,** Abigail B. [a. 21 y. in pencil], of Quincy, and James M. Munroe [a. 21 y. in pencil], int. Mar. 3, 1844.

Henrietta, a. 18 y., b. Abington, d. Elisha and Hannah W., and Sylvanus H Whorf [of Boston, int.], a. 24 y., merchant, s. Samuel and Joanna R., Sept. 2, 1849.*

Isiah, and Katherine Fitz Jerrald, Oct. 11, 1757.

Mary, of Brookline, and Charles O. Howe, int. Oct. 26, 1848.

Nancy, of Quincy, and John S. Salmon, int. Feb. 4, 1847.

Rebecca, and Benjamin Munroe, Sept. 17, 1826.*

Sarah, and Joseph Weld, s. John, Nov. 27, 1679.

Seymour, and Lydia Morse Marshall of Brookline, int. Nov. 21, 1819.

Thomas, and Areminta Bradlee, int. Dec. 13, 1829.

**FAY,** Ellen, and Martin Carroll, int. Jan. 15, 1837.

Elsy, and William Trask, int. Apr. 26, 1818.

James, and Mary Barrit, int. June 4, 1847.

Lucy Mariah, of Lebanon, N. H., and Charles Marsh, int. Sept. 18, 1842.

* Intention also recorded.

**FEALY** (see also Feeley), Patrick, and Margarett Glynn, int. Nov. 24, 1847.

**FEARING,** Lincoln, and Harriot A. Williams, int. Dec. 25, 1831.
——, wid., and Robert Williams, at Hingham, Nov. 3, 1675.

**FECHEM** (see also Feecham), Lampetia, and Pardon Albee of Sutton, Jan. 4, 1825.*

**FEECHAM** (see also Fechem), Samuel, and Lydia Talbutt [Talbot. c. r. 2.], Aug. 10, 1794.*

**FEELEY** (see also Fealy, Feely), Michael, and Mary Rafferty, int. Oct. 27, 1844.

**FEELY** (see also Feeley), Julia, and John Burns, int. Dec. 10, 1837.

**FEENEY,** Ellen, and Matthew Ragin, int. June 12, 1849.

**FEHITY,** Martin, and Ann Kelly, int. Nov. 2, 1847.

**FEIGELLY,** Ferona, and John Hankey, int. Oct. 22, 1847.

**FEILDER** Mary, and John Searle, Oct. 21, 1713.
Sarah, and John Ruggles, May 24, 1704.

**FELKER,** James W., of Nottingham, N. H., and Lydia J. Bird of Dorchester, Oct. 9, 1846.

**FELLOWES** (see also Fellows), Cornelius, Capt., and Hannah Parker, int. Jan. 4, 1795.
Elsy, and Joseph Davis, July 27, 1800.*
Hannah Pierpont, and Joseph Bancroft, May 12, 1811.*
Josephine M., and William H. Simmons [Esq. int.], June 24, 1840.*
Nancy, and Charles Hunt of Watertown, Dec. 22, 1804.*
Nathaniel Esq., of Havana, and Lucy Lambert, Oct. 9, 1825.*
Sarah, Mrs., and Thomas Rumrill, Aug. —, 1803.*
William of Louisville, Ky., and Caroline Davis, June 9, 1829.*

**FELLOWS** (see also Fellowes), Cornelius, and Sarah Williams, Dec. 20, 1763.
Harriott, Mrs., and Charles Davis, Sept. 8, 1799.*
John W., and Sally Dudley, Mar. 29, 1795.*
Salley, and Nathaniel Ruggles, int. Sept. 10, 1786.

* Intention also recorded.

**FELTON,** Abigail, and Joseph Richardson, Jan. 27, 1774.

Edward Jackson, and Tamesin [Tamerin. int.] Baker, Sept. 19, 1782. c. r. 2.*

Horace, and Charlottee Lewis of Dedham, int. Oct. 14, 1838.

Joshua, and Mary Wardell, Jan. 28, 1766.

Joshua, and Mrs. Lois Pattee, Oct. 31, 1780.

Lucy, and David Lincoln of Hingham, Nov. 10, 1793.*

Mary, Mrs., and Samuel Wait, May 7, 1786.*

Mary Ann, and James B. Tolman, Jan. 15, 1835.*

Mary E., and Benj[amin] G. Pigeon, Jan. 1, 1844.*

Nathan[ie]l, jr., and Mary Williams, Dec. 21, 1769.

Samuel, and Sarah A. Skinner, int. Sept. 30, 1832.

**FENNELTON,** Hannah, and Patrick Cayle, int. Dec. 2, 1848.

**FENNO** (see also Fennoe), Elizabeth, of Quincy, and Thomas Weld, jr., int. Oct. 13, 1816.

James, resident, and Mary Corey, int. Jan. 11, 1784.

Joseph, and Elisabeth Dupee Lillie, June 30, 1822.

Mary, of Dorchester, and Ebenezer Glover of Stoughton, Sept. 21, 1797.

**FENNOE** (see also Fenno), Jonathan, and Esther Hunt, Oct. 24, 1749.

**FERGUSON** (see also Furguson), George, and Susan Herbert of Portland, Me., int. June 11, 1847.

John, and Ellenor Reynolds, int. Aug. 20, 1843.

Mary Ann, and William M. Tegert, int. Sept. 28, 1845.

Robert [Furguson. int.], and Julia A. Wyman, Sept. 8, 1844.*

**FERNALD,** Mary Louisa, and Robert M. Pollock, Dec. 22, 1844.

**FERRY,** Elizabeth, a. 21 y. b. Ireland, d. John and Elizabeth, and David Crowley, a. 34 y., laborer, b. Ireland, s. Charles and Julia, Dec. 8, 1849.*

**FERSONS,** William McDole, of Bedford, N. H., a. 24 y., yeoman, s. William and Polly, and Hannah B. Maloon, a. 24 y., d. Josiah and Sally, Nov. 29, 1846.*

**FESENDEN** (see also Fessenden), Nathan, of Lexington, and Jane Goodridge, June 21, 1801.*

* Intention also recorded.

**FESSENDEN** (see also Fesenden), Henry, and Olive Dinsdell, Mar. 3, 1791.*

Mary Ann, and Aaron D. Field both of Dorchester, Dec. 22, 1824.

Oliva P., and Arthur Somerby, Oct. 21, 1827.

**FEX** (see also Fox), Joseph, and Geartant Coller, int. Apr. 11, 1848.

**FICKET,** James H., of Portland [Me. int.], and Emeline Webber, Sept. 21, 1848.*

**FIELD,** Aaron D., and Mary Ann Fessenden both of Dorchester, Dec. 22, 1824.

Apollos [Appollas. c. R. 3.], of Charlestown, and Sally Davis, Sept. 28, 1806.*

Catharine [F. int.], and Daniel Niles, Mar. 10, 1836.*

Charles D., and Mary M. Randall, Sept. 15, 1830.*

Elijah, and Mrs. Polly Gridley, Feb. 22, 1784.*

Elizabeth, and Samuel Barret [Barrett. c. R. 3.] of Windsor, Vt., Nov. 15, 1814.*

Frederick W., of Quincy, and Susannah M. Goddard, int. Apr. 26, 1829.

Frederick W., of Quincy, and Elizabeth Mirick, int. May 13, 1832.

Harriet N., and Charles H. Gosam of Portland, Feb. 16, 1840.*

Joseph, Rev., of Weston, and Charlotte Maria Leatham, Oct. 15, 1816.*

Ozias, and Charlotte E. Whiting, Feb. 16, 1837.*

Serena, of Abington, a. 40 y., d. William and Jemima, and Consider A. Southworth, widr. of Stoughton, a. 42 y., manufacturer, s. Consider and Mary, July 22, 1847.

William, of Dedham, a. 24 y., trader, b. North Bridgewater, s. Jabez and Mary, and Mary F. P. Whiting, a. 22 y., b. Southborough, d. Moses and Pesis R., Sept. 19, 1849.*

**FILLEBROWN,** Abigail, and Joseph Muncreif, jr., Nov. 24, 1791.*

Anna, and Amasa May of Woodstock, int. Jan. 15, 1792.

Jonas, and Mary W. Goddard, int. May 20, 1832.

Lois, and Josiah Cunningham, Mar. 12, 1782.

Thomas, jr., of Washington, D. C., and Mary F. [T. int.] Sumner, Aug. 19, 1819.*

* Intention also recorded.

FILLMORE, Benj[ami]n D., and [Mrs. int.] Sarah Stodder, Aug. 11, 1833.*

FINAGHTY (see also Finaughty), Peter, and Ellen Shay, int. Sept. 22, 1839.

FINATY (see also Finaughty), Mary, and James Murtagh, int. Nov. 19, 1843.

FINAUGHTY (see also Finaghty, Finaty, Finity), James, and Sarah Doyle, int. Nov. 7, 1846.

FINCH, Samuell, and Judith [Judeth. CT. R.] Potter, Dec. 13, 1654.

FINEGAN (see also Finnegan), Colman, and Hannah Shaughnessey, int. May 19, 1844.

FINITY (see also Finaughty), Ann, and Lawrence Gately, int. Dec. 21, 1845.

FINN, Catharine, and Michael Killan, int. Sept. 27, 1840.
Elizabeth, and Patrick Clinton, int. May 5, 1849.
Maria, and Patrick McDaniel, int. May 20, 1837.
Maria, and Lawrence Watson, May 15, 1848.*
Mary Ann, and James Carney, June 8, 1848.

FINNEGAN (see also Finegan), Ellen, and John Gately, int. July 21, 1844.
Patrick, and Hannah Delia, int. Feb. 17, 1848.

FINNERAN (see also Finneron), Ann, and William Curly, int. Feb. 5, 1849.

FINNERON (see also Finneran), William, and Abigail Louisa Trask, int. Apr. 3, 1825.

FINTON, Elizabeth, and John Collins, int. Jan. 8, 1843.

FISH, Nathaniel, and Mary Weld Ward, Mar. 9, 1815.*

FISHER, Abigail, and Peter Bachi, Feb. 14, 1826.*
Amos, and Eliza Gore, Dec. 8, 1805.*
Anna, and Isaac Heath, s. Isaac, Feb. 2, 1680.
Cynthia, of Newton, and Lemuel Richards, July 20, 1806.
Edmund, and Isabella Savage, Apr. 24, 1844.*
Enoch H., and Ann Parrot, Mar. 4, 1829.*

* Intention also recorded.

FISHER, Experience, of Dedham, and Moses Richardson, at Dedham, Oct. 4, 1770.

George, and Magdalena Kraft of Dorchester, int. Nov. 3, 1833.

Jacob, and Mary Withington, Jan. 13, 1799.*

John, and Mrs. Sarah Newhall, Jan. 6, 1822.*

Lewis, and Polly Randall of Sharon, int. Mar. 26, 1797.

Mary, Mrs., of Dedham, and Aaron Draper, at Dedham, Feb. 21, 1760.

Molley, of Dedham, and John Allen Frizzel of Walpole, May 23, 1792.

Nathaniel, of Providence, and Abigail F. Muncrief, July 23, 1810.*

Nath[anie]l, and Betsey Draper, int. Oct. 7, 1838.

Oliver, and Betsy Child, May 5, 1803. C. R. 2.

Roxana, and Ebenezer Wale, jr., of Dorchester, int. Nov. 20, 1823.

Susanna, of Needham, and Joseph Richards, int. Oct. 30, 1808.

Warren, and Nancy D. Simmons, Dec. 17, 1833.*

William D., and Martha Bartlett of Norway, Me., July 8, 1848.

FISK (see also Fiske), Amos, and Joanna Dinsdell, Jan. 19, 1810.*

Anna, of Groton, and Theop F. Bisby, int. Feb. 10, 1805.

Harriot, and Chester Guild, June 5, 1822.*

Luther, of Concord, N. H., and Sally Wait, Oct. 14, 1795.*

Maria, and William Fowle, ——, 1833.

Mary, and Joseph Mills of Newton, int. May 5, 1811.

Sally, and Jonathan Webster of Salisbury, Oct. 10, 1802.*

Sam[ue]l, and Abba S. H. Clapp, June 20, 1833.*

FISKE (see also Fisk), Emily W., and John I. Brown, int. Nov. 30, 1837.

FITCH, Amos, [of Boston. C. R. 3.], and Martha Star [Starr. C. R. 3.], Apr. 7, 1813.*

Charles, and Nancy Jackson Adams of Pepperell, int. Sept. 15, 1833.

Martha L., and Joseph W. Page of South Reading, June 10, 1841.*

FITTS, Ephr[ai]m, and Rachel Goodwin, of South Hampton, int. Sept. 7, 1806.

* Intention also recorded.

**FITZGERALD** (see also Fitzjerald, Fitz Jerrald), John, b. Ireland, and Margarett [Mary. int.] Campbell, b. Ireland, Dec. 28, 1849.*

Mary Ann, and Matthew Hogan, int. June 5, 1848

Morris, and Ann Sullivan, int. Apr. 26, 1840.

Stpehen [Fitzgeral, of Boston. c. R. 3.], and Sarah F. James, Sept. 27, 1843.*

Timothy, and Mary Hars of Boston, Nov. 13, 1846.

**FITZJERALD** (see also Fitzgerald),William [Fitzgerald. dup.], and Elizabeth Spur [Spare, 2d. dup.], of Stoughton, at Stoughton [at Canton, Jan. 30. dup.], Jan. 5, 1795.

**FITZ JERRALD** (see also Fitzgerald), Katherine, and Isiah Faxon, Oct. 11, 1757.

**FITZMORRIS,** Bridget, and Hugh Mee, int. Nov. 11, 1847.

Bridget, and Francis May, int. Apr. 17, 1848.

John, and Margarett Good, int. May 4, 1849.

**FITZPATRICK,** Mary, and William Lynch, int. Nov. 15, 1840.

**FLAGG,** Mary, of Newton, and John Peller, at Newton, Mar. 31, 1771.

**FLANAGAN** (see also Flannagan), Ann, and Hugh Murphy, int. Jan. 20, 1839.

Edward, and Elizabeth Larkin, int. Oct. 1, 1837.

**FLANNAGAN** (see also Flanagan), Thomas, and Ann Gately, int. July 16, 1839.

**FLEMING** (see also Flemming), Michael, and Catharine Leonard, int. Oct. 8, 1843.

Robert, and Eliza Todd, Nov. 12, 1848.

Thomas, and Ame Jeffries, Nov. 26, 1845.*

**FLEMMING** (see also Fleming), James, and Catharine Rogers, int. Apr. 9, 1843.

**FLETCHER,** Elizabeth, and John B. Cochran, both of Lowell, at Lowell, Sept. 1, 1839.

Emeline, of Northbridge, and Judson Chapin, int. May 5, 1839.

* Intention also recorded.

FLETCHER, Hannah J., and Elbridge G. Scott, int. Nov. 1, 1835.

Harriet, and William E. Hicks, of Charlestown, July 21, 1844.*

Jeremy, and Huldah P. Jacobs of Portland, Me., int. Nov. 3, 1844.

Oliver, Esq., of Chelmsford, and Grace Weld, Nov. 13, 1766.

Rufus F., a. 32 y., farmer, s. Alpheus and Ruth, and Mary S. Atkins, a. 32 y., seamstress, d. Charles and Rebecca, Oct. 27, 1845.*

FLINN (see also Flynn), Blandena, and John Larkin, int. Dec. 31, 1837.

Bridget, and John Kelly, int. Nov. 9, 1847.

Daniel Findley, and Margaret Conner, int. Apr. 27, 1791.

Ellen Maria, and Daniel M. Edwards, int. Apr. 4, 1824.

Honora, and Thomas O'Connor, int. Nov. 7, 1846.

John, and Mercy Jordan, Dec. 26, 1826.

John, and Mary Curley, int. Sept. 26, 1841.

Michael, and Mary Tracy, int. Oct. 2, 1842.

FLINT, Austin [Dr. int.], of Northampton, and Anne Skillings, Apr. 24, 1835.*

David B., and Elizabeth L. Fuller, Aug. 21, 1844.*

Eliphilet, of Weathersfield, and Sarah Burdin, Mar. 21, 1776.

Lorenzo, and Mrs. Sarah F. Tuttle, June 23, 1840.*

FLITCHING, Florindina, and Francis Phillip, int. Aug. 23, 1840.

FLOOD, Bridget, and Bernard Ronney, int. May 4, 1845.

Catherine, and James Runey, int. Oct. 14, 1847.

James, and Elizabeth Mallard, Dec. 25, 1845.*

Michael, and Eliza Burns, int. Jan. 13, 1849.

FLOWER, Mary Ann, of Andover, and [Capt. int.] Lewis Stark, Jan. 13, 1842.*

FLOYD, Andrew, and Elizabeth Bradshaw of Medford, at Medford, Oct. 31, 1765.

James M., and Mary Stevens, June 10, 1849.

Marshall, and Eliza Hill, Mar. 26, 1818.*

FLYNN (see also Flinn), Catherine, and James Cary, int. Dec. 1, 1848.

Eliza, and Hugh Derick, int. May 29, 1848.

* Intention also recorded.

FLYNN, Lawrence, and Bridget Kenny, int. Dec. 28, 1845.
Margret, and Michael Connelly, int. Nov. 3, 1844.
Michael, and Margarett Murphy, int. Mar. 3, 1848.
Thomas, and Sarah Hall, int. Sept. 7, 1846.

**FOARREST** (see also Forest), John, and Elisabeth Lusk, June 4, 1747.

**FOBES** (see also Forbes), Amasa, and Anna Eames of Framingham, int. July 4, 1802.
Cassandra A., of Bridgewater, and Capt. George King, int. Aug. 28, 1831.

**FOGERTY,** Ann, and George McCloud, Oct. 2, 1839.

**FOGG,** Francis A., of Salem, and Abigail Prentiss, int. Nov. 6, 1842.

**FOLAN** (see also Follen), Bridget, and Owen Quigly, int. Sept. 22, 1848.

**FOLEY,** Andrew, and Mary Ann Seaver, int. June 9, 1849.
Bernard, and Anne Ball, int. Oct. 10, 1846.
James, and Mary Hays, int. Dec. 25, 1847.
Margaret, and Henry Lynch, int. Apr. 24, 1836.
Margaret, and John Mullens, int. Sept. 16, 1838.
Maurice, and Bridget Gallagher, int. Jan. 6, 1848.

**FOLIETT,** Louis, and Mehitable S. Savens, Apr. 1, 1839.*

**FOLLAN** (see also Follen), Mary, and Patrick Glinnon, int. Dec. 31, 1849.

**FOLLEN** (see also Folan, Follan), Benjamin, and Sarah Wadleigh, Sept. 15, 1833.
Bridgett, and Thomas Donnelon, int. Oct. 21, 1846.
Ellen, and Thomas Garrity of Boston, int. Jan. 9, 1847.
Hanna, and John Clougher, int. Mar. 31, 1844.
John, and Eliza Casbury, int. Apr. 2, 1846.
Margaret, and John P. Stumpf, int. Dec. 1, 1844.
Mary, and Samuel Whittemore, int. Nov. 24, 1848.
Michael, and Mary Dwine, int. July 8, 1847.
Michael, and Bridget Dorsey, int. Oct. 23, 1848.
Winefred, and Luke Mee, int. Mar. 16, 1845.

* Intention also recorded.

**FOLSOM** (see also Foslom), Alonzo W., and Harriet Soden of Saxonville, int. Oct. 29, 1843.

Eben H., and Harriet Bell, Mar. 26, 1843.*

Hawley, of Acton, Me., blacksmith, s. Benjamin and Sarah, and Lucy S. Corporal, a. 18 y., Nov. 24, 1847.*

Henry A., a. 24 y., carpenter, and Elizabeth R. C. [C. R. int.] Clark, a. 23 y., Dec. 14, 1847.*

Levi B., and Frances C. Webb, int. June 15, 1849.

**FOOT** (see also Foote), David, of Bath, Me., and Caroline R. Rumrill, int. Sept. 3, 1837.

Sarah A., and Henry W. Miller, int. Apr. 3, 1842.

**FOOTE** (see also Foot), Emerson, of Cold Springs, N. Y., and Maria H. Shepherd, int. Sept. 9, 1838.

**FORBES** (see also Fobes), Elisha, and Nancy Burrell, Dec. 29, 1799.*

Mary, and Tilson Williams, int. Mar. 26, 1826.

Mary B., and William Carlyle [of Dorchester. int.], Mar. 8, 1845.*

Sarah, and George Williams, int. June 19, 1842.

**FORBUSH,** Elijah [Furbush. c. r. 3.], and Sally Packard, Aug. 28, 1808.*

**FORD,** Charles N., and Sylvia Ann Morrison of Brookline, int. Mar. 1, 1835.

Eliza, of Dorchester, and Robert Martin, int. Dec. 10, 1837.

Eunice, and Thomas M. Murdock of Brookline, int. Sept. 29, 1833.

Honora, and Patrick Kenedy, int. Dec. 17, 1847.

Joseph, and Sarah Foster, both of Dorchester, Apr. 28, 1803.

Julia, and Jeremiah Crowley, int. Sept. 2, 1846.

Mary Ann, and Ebenezer N. Lord, Mar. 11, 1844.*

Rachel M., of Dover, and William Everett, int. May 16, 1846.

Sarah, of Brookline, and Lemuel Foster, int. Jan. 4, 1818.

Sylvia W., a. 23 y., d. Asa and Nancy, and Oliver B. Marsh, a. 24 y., machinist, s. Jason and Sarah, Apr. 18, 1848.*

**FOREN,** Thomas, and Margarett Cloughe, int. June 13, 1846.

**FOREST** (see also Foarrest), Eleanor, and William C. Andrews of Dedham, May 10, 1845.

* Intention also recorded.

**FORGAR,** Elizabeth, and John P. Lausterer of Boston, int. Sept. 6, 1849.

**FOSGAT,** see Tosgaterf.

**FOSGATE,** Rosilla, of Brookline, and Reuben Lawrence, int. Aug. 12, 1832.

**FOSLOM** (see also Folsom), Robinson, and Sarah R. Pierce of Quincy, int. Mar. 22, 1835.

**FOSS,** Charles, and Caroline F. Willey, int. Sept. 18, 1831.
Huldah B., and Benj[ami]n Huff, int. Aug. 13, 1837.
Ivory H., and Harriet Quimby, Mar. 29, 1846.*
Samuel A., widr. a. 26 y., coachman, s. James and Abigail, and Nancy P. Silsbee, a. 28 y., d. Joseph and Elizabeth Park, June 24, 1849.*
William, and Jarusha Brooks, int. Jan. 17, 1819.

**FOSTER,** Abigail, Mrs., and Nathan Farren of Brookline, at Brookline, Apr. 7, 1763.
David K., a. 27 y., omnibus driver, s. Jos[eph] S. and Susan, and Lucy W. Tucker, a. 24 y., d. Seth and Hannah, Sept. 29, 1847.*
Edmund, Col., of Dorchester, and Ann H. Baker, Oct. 20, 1825.*
Edward [of Boston. c. r. 3.], and Deborah Richards, June 20, 1830.*
Eleaner, and Francis Dana, Jan. 14, 1768.
Eliza Jane, and Ezra Morse, int. Dec. 2, 1827.
Elizabeth, and Ebenezer Barnard, at Dorchester, Sept. 29, 1715.
Enoch P. P., of Lynn, a. 33 y., cordwainer, s. Enoch and Susanna of Lynn, and Sarah Kellogg, a. 38 y., Dec. 1, 1846.*
H. B. [Henry B. int.], of Concord, N. H., and Harriet S[alome. int.] Dole, Oct. 22, 1844.*
Hannah B[arret. int.], a. 23 y., d. John S. and Theoda W., and Elliott E. Kellogg of Burlington, Vt., a. 28 y., attorney at law, s. Alpheus and Augusta of Jamaica, Vt., Nov. 7, 1848.*
Hopestill, eldest s. Capt. Hopestill, of Dorchester, and —— Pason, at Dorchester, 15 : 12 m : 1666.
Jane, and Thomas Cheney, Apr. 6, 1780.

* Intention also recorded.

FOSTER, John, and Margaret Ware, Dec. 7, 1704.

John, and Ruth Phillips, Oct. 3, 1771.

John [jr. int.], and Rhoda Thayer, June 10, 1804.*

John S., and Theoda Williams Bartlett, June 23, 1811.*

John S., of Quincy, and Sarah W. Hendley, int. Sept. 17, 1837.

Joseph W., and Rebecca W. McLane , Sept. 1, 1844.*

Josiah, and Anna Eustis of Needham, int. Dec. 11, 1808.

Lemuel, and Sarah Ford of Brookline, int. Jan. 4, 1818.

Martha, and Paul Dudley, Apr. 27, 1779.

Mary, and Thomas Thompson, Oct. 28, 1765.

Mary, and Ebenezer Brewer, Dec. 24, 1794.*

Rufus, and Sally Goddard, Jan. 10, 1796.

Sarah, and Joseph Ford, both of Dorchester, Apr. 28, 1803.

Sarah, Mrs., and Tilla Chaffin [jr. int.] of Holden, May 20, 1829.*

Sarah F., and Harriman Smith, Aug. 7, 1842.*

Susanna, and Ames Hide, Apr. 4, 1765.

Theoda D., a. 37 y., d. John S. and Theoda W., and Rev. Solon W. Bush of Burlington, Vt., a. 31 y., clergyman, s. Thomas and Mary B., June 28, 1849.*

Thomas, and Sarah Parker, Oct. 15, 1662.

Timothy, of Dorchester, and Abiell Williams, Mar. 3, 1742-3.

William, and Mary Draper, June 11, 1778.

**FOUR,** Nicholas, and Catharine Sane, int. Jan. 5, 1845.

**FOURACRESS,** Mary, resident, and John Herring, Nov. 24, 1774.

**FOWLE** (see also Fowles), Anna, and [Capt. int.] Nathaniel Colburn, Dec. 2, 1830.*

Elizabeth J., a. 24 y., d. John and Prudence, and Daniel Le-Better, a. 26 y., clerk, s. Daniel and Eliza, May 27, 1847.*

John, and Prudence W. Jones, Nov. 29, 1818.*

John D. [Fowel. int.], a. 25 y., upholsterer, s. John and Prudence, and Eliza J. Baker, a. 20 y., d. Theodore and Ann, July 19, 1849.*

Lucy, and Nath[anie]l Stone, June 8, 1809.*

Susanna [Sukey Fowl. int.], and Giles Alexander, at Boston, Apr. 2, 1797.*

William, and Maria Fisk, ———, 1833.

**FOWLER,** Alfred N., and Mary Ann Nash, Nov. 10, 1847.

Edmund M. jr., and Pamelia C. Houghton, int. Aug. 29, 1841.

* Intention also recorded.

FOWLER, Hannah, of Dorchester, and Seth Tucker, int. Mar. 1, 1807.

Nancy D., and Asa F. Onion, Sept. 29, 1842.*

Susannah W., and Daniel Herring, Apr. 23, 1828.*

FOWLES (see also Fowle), Hanna, and Samuell Ruggles, Jan. 10, 1654.

FOX (see also Fex), Ann, and Michael Hologhan, int. June 12, 1848.

Caroline M., and David R. Nash, ———, 1832. [Aug. 21, 1831. int.]*

Ebenezer, and Mrs. Nancy Downs of Salem, Mar. 20, 1785.*

James, and Mrs. Hannah Howard, June 26, 1783.*

Richard, and Elizabeth Bird, Nov. 6, 1760.

FOXCROFT, Phebe Anne [Ann. c. r. 5.], and Rev. George Waters of Lynn, May 3, 1838. [1837. c. r. 5.]*

FOY (see also Foya, Foye), Andrew, and Ann McEvoy of Eastport, Me., int. Mar. 27, 1847.

FOYA (see also Foy), Hannah, and Thomas Dolan, int. Apr. 15, 1838.

FOYE (see also Foy), John W., and Susan Gay, int. Oct. 11, 1840.

FRACKER, George, and Frances L. Richardson, int. Oct. 26, 1828.

FRAIZER, Peter, and Flora Cummins, int. Sept. 24, 1809.

FRANCES (see also Francis), Jane, and Jonathan Bennet, Nov. 9, 1763.

FRANCIS (see also Frances), Daniel S., a. 20 y., merchant, s. Thomas D. and Martha E., and Sarah F. Sampson of Weymouth, a. 18 y., d. Sarah, Nov. 15, 1846.*

Eliza A., and Warren W. Stone, Sept. 18, 1842.*

Elizabeth A., a. 19 y., d. Joseph and Mary, and George Sherive, a. 23 y., currier, s. John and Sarah, Dec. 10, 1848.*

FRANK, John, and Sarah Weld, July 23, 1663.

FRAWLEY, William, and Bridget Sheehan, int. June 11, 1849.

* Intention also recorded.

**FREDERICK** (see also Friedricks), Caroline, and Jacob Dornback, int. Apr. 1, 1848.

**FREELAND,** Jerusha, of Hopkinton, and Isaiah Warren, int. Sept. 6, 1807.

Patty, of Hopkinton, and John Jones, Sept. 21, 1801.*

**FREEMAN,** Betsey, Mrs., and Caleb Aspinwall, resident, int. Mar. 13, 1785.

Charles, and Mary E. Nason, int. Sept. 3, 1843.

Elizabeth R., and John Hall, June 12, 1842.*

Emily, and Daniel E. Page, Nov. 28, 1837.*

Francis, and Rhoda E. Chadwick, Aug. 25, 1844.*

Leonard, and Betsy Horton, Oct. 16, 1808.*

Lucy H., and Henry S. Loud, Feb. 5, 1843.*

Mary [Polly. int.], and Nathaniel Winship, at Boston, July 16, 1786.*

Mary, and George Elisha, Jan. 1, 1844. C. R. 7.*

Mary Ann, and Reuben Hunting [jr. int.], Apr. 15, 1832.*

Mary Ann, and Willim E. Johnson, int. July 16, 1837.

Samuel, and Rebecca Newton, July 27, 1794.*

Samuel, and Esther Crawford, in Brewster, Sept. 6, 1841.*

**FRENCH,** Amos W., and Eliza Sprowl, int. Oct. 27, 1844.

Benjamin B., and Eliza D. Orcutt, both of Braintree, Aug. 22, 1837.

Catharine J., of Chester, N. H., and Dr. Phenehas P. Wells, int. Mar. 27, 1836.

Dorcas, and Christopher Peake, Jan. 3, 1636.

Eunice, of Braintree, and James Collins, Jan. 5, 1804.*

Jonathan, and Ann Weld, Feb. 18, 1802. C. R .2.*

Lucy, of Dedham, and Samuel S. Williams, int. June 5, 1814.

Moses, and Hannah Wheeler of Concord, int. Nov. 24, 1811.

Naomi, of Andover, and Henry L. Goldsmith, int. Mar. 21, 1830.

Rachel, of Weymouth, and Jonathan Damon, at Weymouth, Apr. —, 1781.

Sarah, and Jonnathan Peake, Aug. 15, 1660.

Susan E., of Weymouth, and Joseph Stevens, Mar. 21, 1841. C. R. 7.

Theodore, and Mary Maria Rand, Sept. 8, 1833.

**FRIARY,** Mary, and Michael Smith, int. Feb. 8, 1846.

* Intention also recorded.

**FRIEDRICKS** (see also Frederick), Hennretta, and Jacob Schneider, int. Aug. 17, 1845.

**FRIETZ,** Lenora, and Godfrey Shuls, int. Sept. 18, 1848.

**FRIEZE,** Isaac, and Elisabeth Kerworth, Sept. 28, 1843.*
Sarah, and Richard Lloyd, Dec. 26, 1819.*

**FRINK,** Anthony, and Christian Ciaginln, int. Apr. 2, 1843.

**FRIROL,** Isaac, and Susannah Pike of Dedham, at Dedham, May 18, 1738.

**FRISELL** (see also Frizell, Frizzel), John, and Mary Tatman, May 8, 1734.
Susannah, and Thomas Bentley, int. Feb. 25, 1827.

**FRIZELL** (see also Frisell), Sally M., and William H. Lord, int. May 26, 1844.

**FRIZZELL** (see also Frisell), Allen John, of Walpole, and Molley Fisher of Dedham, May 23, 1792.

**FROST,** Frederick I., and Angenette Dean, int. Apr. 25, 1841.
George, of Charlestown, a. 29 y., baker, s. Joseph and Caroline, and Elizabeth [Elisabeth. int.] A. Pearson, a. 23 y., d. Susan, June 4, 1848.*
Henry, and Hannah K. Hastings, int. Oct. 5, 1845.
Jane, and Lazel Dean, int. Jan. 18, 1835.
Samuel, and Hannah Mascraft, July 15, 1701.
Sarah B., of Charlestown, and Samuel F. Lucas, int. Feb. 3, 1839.
Sarah E. S., of Dorchester, a. 23 y., d. Joseph and Caroline of Dorchester, and Samuel Maxfield, jr., a. 25 y., painter, s. Samuel and Mary, May 20, 1846.*
Thomas, and Louisa J. Homan, int. May 8, 1836.
Thomas M., and Martha Cummings, int. Nov. 12, 1843.
William O., a. 21 y., laborer, s. Benj[amin] and Eliza, and Caroline A. Boulton, a. 18 y., d. Leonard and Mary Ann, Jan. 14, 1847.*

**FROTHINGHAM,** Mary Eliza, and Rev. Chandler Robbins, int. Nov. 28, 1833.

**FRUEAN,** Sarah, and Rufus Ball, int. Apr. 5, 1835.

* Intention also recorded.

**FRUMENTO,** Augostino, and Lucy O. Richardson [residents. int.], Sept. 12, 1804.*

**FRYE,** Lucy, of Danvers, and George W. Dalton, int. Oct. 25, 1840.

**FUHEY,** (see also Fahey), Jeremiah, and Ellen Burns, int. July 27, 1848.

**FULLER,** Aaron, and Elizabeth Legallees, Nov. 29, 1827. c. r. 2.

Anna, of Newton, and Benjamin Williams, at Newton, Apr. 29, 1766.

Anna, of Newton, and Capt. Willliam Winchester, int. Sept. 28, 1800.

Daniel, of Marlborough, and Lucy Brown, Apr. 17, 1814.*

Daniel, and Juliet Haven, int. Apr. 6, 1823.

David, and Harriet Herring [Harring. int], Feb. 13, 1820. c. r. 2.*

Ebeneser, resident, and Mary Brown of Needham, int. Apr. 11, 1784.

Ebenezer [resident. int.], and Lydia Goddard, May 5, 1793.*

Edwin, and Mary Ann Pond of Dorchester, int. Nov. 23, 1846.

Elisha, and Elizabeth Druce, July 6, 1780.

Elisha, and Esther Hartshorn of Boylston, int. Dec. 13, 1812.

Elizabeth, and John Osgood of Andover, Nov. 21, 1810.*

Elizabeth A., and Reuben Weeks, int. Nov. 23, 1845.

Elizabeth L., and David B. Flint, Aug. 21, 1844.*

Francis A., of Hartford, Conn., and Elis[abeth] R. Wells [Wills. int.], June 4, 1844.*

Hannah, [Mrs. int.], and Joseph Glasson of Jersey City, July 29, 1846.*

Lucy H., and Freeman Simpson, Sept. 26, 1834.*

Luther, and Abigail Smith, Mar. 23, 1794.*

Margarett [Margaret. int.] J. W., and Edwin Hatch of Acton, May 11, 1845.*

Mary, and Joseph Hartwell, Jan. 13, 1799.*

Mary E., and John Chamberlain, int. June 16, 1844.

Olive, and Winthrop Guptill, int. Aug. 23, 1829.

Perez, of Medway, and Elizabeth A. Newman, Apr. 5, 1827.*

Thankfull, and Thomas Weld, Feb. 13, 1769.

Timothy, of Needham, and Abigail Smith, int. Sept. 4, 1796.

Waldin, and Mary Muncreif, Dec. 6, 1790.*

William, and Mrs. Elisabeth Alderchurch, Aug. 2, 1759.

* Intention also recorded.

**FULLON** (see also Fallen), Eliza J., and John R. Kelley, int. Jan. 10, 1848.

**FULLUGHAN,** Catherine, and Andrew Lalley, int. Sept. 1, 1849.

**FULLUM,** Boylston, and Bulah Campbell, int. May 29, 1825.

**FULTON,** Elizabeth, and Robert Black, Feb. 15, 1844.*

**FURGUSON** (see also Ferguson), Rebecca, and John Polsey, Feb. 6, 1840.*

**GAFFEY** (see also Gaffy), Luke, and Margarett Kelly, int. Dec. 13, 1848.

**GAFFIELD** (see also Garfield), Maranda, and Asher Taylor, Dec. 30, 1844.*

**GAFFIGAN,** Margarett, and Martin Connors, int. Jan. 19, 1849.

**GAFFY** (see also Gaffey), Ellen, and James Claffy, int. Jan. 23, 1842.
Patrick, and Ann Kelley, int. Sept. 10, 1848.

**GAFNEY,** Patrick, and Hannah Clougher, int. Oct. 28, 1845.
Patrick, and Catherine Deal, int. Nov. 15, 1847.
Peter, and Mary Brady, int. May 18, 1847.
Thomas, and Honora Mullin, int. Jan. 26, 1848.
Thomas, and Bridget Killian, int. Mar. 3, 1848.

**GAINES,** John, and Susanna Pottle, Jan. 25, 1807.*

**GAIRY,** John, and Ellen Walsh, int. Nov. 22, 1849.

**GAITLY** (see also Gately), Michael, and Rosana Ranahan, int. Aug. 27, 1847.
Timothy, and Margarett McNamara, int. Oct. 29, 1847.

**GALAGHER** (see also Gallagher), James, and Mary Hartigan, int. July 8, 1838.
Margarett, and Joseph Lamb, int. July 17, 1846.

**GALE,** Benjamin, and Olive Young, int. June 1, 1828.
Betsey, Mrs., and Maj. Isaac Gale, July 16, 1815.*
Clarissa, and Samuel Rumrill, Dec. 2, 1810. c. r. 2.*

* Intention also recorded.

GALE, Elisha, and Eliza Pond, Jan. 25, 1807.*

Hannah, and Ebenezer Maynard of Westborough, June 22, 1814.*

Isaac ,and Anna Norcross of Newton, int. Apr. 27, 1806.

Isaac, Maj., and Mrs. Betsey Gale, July 16, 1815.*

Louisa, and John Whittemore, int. Feb. 14, 1830.*

Olive [Mrs. int.], and James D. Bullock, June 8, 1845.*

Reuben, and Tamzin G. Crosby, Sept. 12, 1839.*

William, and Lydia Gartret, Dec. 16, 1821.*

**GALEUCIA,** Hannah, and Ralph Bradhurst, Mar. 28, 1716.

**GALHER** (see also Gallagher), Patrick, and Catherine Birmingham, int. Jan. 9, 1847.

**GALLAGHAR** (see also Gallagher), Andrew, and Hannah Lynch, int. Apr. 18, 1841.

**GALLAGHER** (see also Galagher, Galher, Gallaghar, Gallayher, Gallergher), Bridget, and John Burns, int. Nov. 3, 1844.

Bridget, and Maurice Foley, int. Jan. 6, 1848.

Catherine, and Michael Hickory, int. Aug. 26, 1846.

Ellen, and Daniel Shea, int. Jan. 13, 1849.

John, and Ann Kelly, int. Oct. 5, 1848.

John, and Bridget Dunn, int. Aug. 4, 1849.

**GALLAYHER** (see also Gallagher), Michael, and Catherine McGarry, int. Oct. 27, 1844.

**GALLERGHER** (see also Gallagher), James, and Catharine Lamb, int. Feb. 8, 1846.

**GALLIGAN** (see also Gallighan), Sarah, and Cormick Sharkey, int. Apr. 14, 1839.

**GALLIGHAN** (see also Galligan), Elizab[eth], and James Willey, Aug. 23, 1843.*

**GALLUP,** J. Henry E. [John H. E. int.], and Susan H. Crafts, Jan. 11, 1844.*

**GALVIN,** Catherine, and Daniel Lahy, int. Sept. 22, 1849.

Mary, and John Charlton, int. Jan. 6, 1833.

* Intention also recorded.

**GAMBLIN** (see also Gambling), Benjamin, and Obedience Curtiss, Feb. 11, 1677-8.

Hannah, and Caleb Sever, May 3, 1704.

**GAMBLING** (see also Gamblin), Marie, and Thomas Baker, May 27, 1663.

**GANNETT,** Patience, of Sharon, and Seth Gay, int. June 21, 1812.

**GANNON,** Matthew, and Maria Garity, int. Oct. 5, 1845.

Peter, and Bridget Cain, int. Oct. 1, 1843.

Thomas, and Ellen Blake, int. Apr. 4, 1841.

**GARATY** (see also Garrity), Lawrence, and Mary Lydon, int. July 7, 1847.

Winneford, and James Curley, int. May 21, 1846.

**GARBETT,** Elizabeth, a. 26 y., d. Richard and Elizabeth, and Charles H. Smith, a. 26 y., clerk, s. William H. and Rebecca S., May 3, 1849.*

**GARD,** John, of Lynn, a. 22 y., tinplate worker, b. Ireland, s. John, and Mary Ann Weir, a. 21 y., b. Ireland, d. Thomas, Dec. 24, 1849.*

**GARDINER** (see also Gardner), Dorcas [of Brookline. c. r. 2.], and Nathanael Woodward, June 23, 1715.

Isaac [of Brookline. c. r. 2.], and Susanna Heath, June 3, 1715.

Thomas, and Rebecca Mayo, Mar. 14, 1710.

**GARDNER** (see also Gardiner), Abby M., and John H. Griggs, June 25, 1848.

Addington, of Brookline, and Mary Allen, at Brookline, ——, 1718.

Andrew, and Mrs. Mary Swan, Nov. 12, 1702.

Charlotte, and Hon. David Perham of Brewer, Me., Oct. 13, 1830.*

Elizabeth, of Sherborn, and Thomas Draper, at Sherborn, May 4, 1768.

George W., and Sarah Jane S. Marder, Feb. 16, 1846.

Harriet, of Dorchester, and Andrew Robertson, int. May 7, 1826.

Harriet A., and Frederic W. Smith, July 2, 1837.*

* Intention also recorded.

GARDNER, Henry, Dr., and Joanna B. Everett of Dorchester, June 9, 1803.

Isaac, Col., of Brookline, and Mrs. Sarah Spooner, June 3, 1801.*

Joseph, and Mary Wilson, May 11, 1732.

Joseph E., and Mary B. Jones, July 15, 1849.

Joseph H., and Mrs. Harriet Robertson, Oct. 4, 1835.*

Joshuah, and Mary Weld, Mar. 22, 1681-2.

Martha E., and Charles W. Woodbury, int. June 2, 1846.

Mary, and Thomas Tilestone, —— 30, 1700.

Mary, Mrs., and John Prentice of Lancaster, Dec. 4, 1705.

Mary, and Adam Sylvester, Dec. 4, 1828.

Myra Vinal, a. 24 y., and James Mason, a. 30 y., weaver, Oct. 12, 1846.*

Peter, and Rebecca Crooke, May 9, 1646.

Rebecca, and Eliphalett Carpenter, June 31, 1702.

Rebecca, and Robert Lovering, Mar. 12, 1735. C. R. 2.

Rebeccah, and Moses Crafts, June 24, 1667.

Robert, and Abigail B. Noyes, Aug. 12, 1827.

Samuel J., Esq., and Mary B. Kingsley of Hampton, Me., int. Oct. 1, 1820.

Samuel Pickering, and Rebecca Russell Lowell, Sept. 19, 1797.*

Sarah, and John Gore, May 31, 1683.

Sarah, of Muddy River, and Thomas Stedman, Sept. 10, 1705.

Sarah A., and William H[enry. C. R. 3.] Severance [both of Boston. C. R. 3.], Sept. 10, 1848.

Thomas, and Mary Bowls, Nov. 17, 1673.

Thomas, and Lucey Smith, July 4, 1641.

GARETY (see also Garrity), Mary [Garrety. int.], and Sumner Smith, Oct. 28, 1848.*

Patrick, and Ann Stanford, int. Jan. 13, 1848.

GARFIELD (see also Gaffield), Edwin, and Ellen H. Barlow, July 2, 1837.*

Elinor, and Cyrus S. Merrill, int. Sept. 25, 1847.

GARGIN, Terrance, and Jane Prior, Feb. 4, 1849.

GARISH, Noah R., and Mary C. Wilson, int. May 1, 1842.

GARITY (see also Garrity), Maria, and Matthew Gannon, int. Oct. 5, 1845.

* Intention also recorded.

**GARLAND,** Hiram R., and Lucinda Smith, May 12, 1816.
C. R. 2.*

Thomas, and Mary Williams of New Market, N. H., int. Feb.
15, 1843.

**GARNSOY,** Henry, and Sarah Wheelock of Medfield, at Dedham, Nov. 7, 1700.

**GARRATHY** (see also Garrity), Patrick [Gerratty. dup.],
and Bridget Kelly, int. Aug. 17, 1845.

**GARRICK,** Jane, and John Dempster, int. Aug. 8, 1849.

**GARRITY** (see also Garaty, Garety, Garity, Garrathy), Patrick, and Bridget Gately, int. Jan. 13, 1849.

Thomas, of Boston, and Ellen Follen, int. Jan. 9, 1847.

**GARY,** Anne, and Thomas Bishop, June 7, 1683.
Elisabeth, and William Abbot, s. George, June 19, 1682.
Hannah, and Caleb Philips, Aug. 2, 1703.
Nathanael, and Anne Rice, Nov. 12, 1685.
Nathannaell, and Ann Dugglas, Oct. 14, 1658.
Samuell, and Elizabeth Parker, Dec. 6, 1669.
William, and Hanna Curtis, Aug. 25, 1651.

**GASIN** (see also Gason), Catherine, and Thomas Mullen, int.
Mar. 1, 1848.

**GASON** (see also Gasin), Benjamin [Geysen. int.], and
Susanna P. Sloan, Mar. 13, 1831.*

Benjamin, and Mrs. Elizabeth Hood, int. Apr. 19, 1840.

**GATELEY** (see also Gately), Catharine, and James Hickey,
int. Jan. 3, 1830.
James, and Mary Lynch, int. June 7, 1840.
John, and Elizabeth L. Grant, int. Sept. 11, 1825.
Mary, and Michael Kelly, int. Apr. 14, 1833.

**GATELY** (see also Gaitly, Gateley), Ann, and John Carty,
int. June 22, 1849.
Ann, and Thomas Flannagan, int. July 16, 1849.
Bridget, and Patrick Gately, int. July 24, 1842.
Bridget, and Patrick Garrity, int. Jan. 13, 1849.
Catharine, and John Norton, int. Dec. 31, 1843.
Ellen, and Michael Noughton, int. Jan. 19, 1845.
John, and Ellen Finnegan, int. July 21, 1844.

* Intention also recorded.

GATELY, John, and Mary Gurhy, int. Dec. 22, 1844.

Lawrence, and Ann Finity, int. Dec. 21, 1845.

Mary, and Thomas Norton, int. Jan. 14, 1844.

Michael, and Catherine Curley, int. Jan. 10, 1841.

Michael, and Catharine Kenedy, int. Nov. 19, 1843.

Patrick, and Bridget Gately, int. July 24, 1842.

Sarah, and Luke Mulkern, int. Oct. 23, 1842.

William, and Bridget Farling, int. Apr. 21, 1844.

**GATES,** Benj[ami]n, of Dorchester, and Mary Dorr, int. Dec. 6, 1829.

Catharine, Mrs., and Aaron Willard [both residents. int.], Mar. 6, 1783.*

Nancy, and William Gossom, int. Nov. 10, 1845.

Samuel, and Eleanor Farl, Mar. 12, 1838.*

**GAUTT,** James, of Sandwich, and Elizabeth C. Russell, Feb. 3, 1830.

**GAVIN,** John, and Bridget Harrison, int. June 11, 1837.

**GAY,** Aaron, and Hannah Healy of Newton, at Newton, May 17, 1753.

Aaron [of Cambridge. int.], and Louisa Seaverns, July 15, 1804. C. R. 2.*

Abigail, and Ebenezer Lyon [of Rehoboth. C. R. 2.], Nov. 6, 1718.

Abigail, Mrs., and Moses Whiting of Dedham, Mar. 27, 1809.*

Asahel, of Norwich, Conn., and Mary Read, Sept. 29, 1822.*

Betsy, and Elisha Horton [of Boston. C. R. 3.], May 2, 1818.*

Catharine, and Aaron Davis, jr., Apr. 10, 1811. C. R. 2.*

Chester M. [a. 24 y. in pencil], and Susan S. Dyer, int. Mar. 17, 1844.

Elizabeth, and Lt. Oliver Easty of Orange, Feb. 22, 1794.*

Hannah, and Benjamin Duick, int. May 3, 1795.

Jane H., a. 20 y., instructress, d. Timothy and Mary, and Daniel H. Parker, a. 20 y., cabinet maker, s. Abraham and Mary, May 11, 1844.*

Joel, and Abigail Davis, Dec. 2, 1790.*

Joel W., and Nancy Gay of Canton, int. Apr. 11, 1824.

Laura M., and John B. Davis, Esq., int. Sept. 17, 1826.

Lemuel, and Abigail H. Whitney, Feb. 28, 1832.*

Louisa S., and James S. Brown, May 29, 1825.*

Lucy, of Sharon, and Hartford Morse, int. Apr. 12, 1812.

* Intention also recorded.

GAY, Lucy R., and Joseph W. Dudley, Mar. 11, 1827.*
Luther, and Salley Coney, both residents, int. Mar. 12, 1786.
Mary, and Phineas Hammond [Phinehas Hammon. int.], Dec.
    29, 1782. C. R. 2.*
Mary, and Solomon Howe Hudson, June 12, 1821. C. R. 2.*
Mary, of Walpole, and Jacob Marshall, Sept. 12, 1827.*
Mary Ann, and John M. A. Hering, int. Aug. 2, 1849.
Mary Ellis, of Canton, and Oliver Davenport, int. Apr. 1,
    1824.
Mary W., and Leonard Farrington of Walden [Vt. int.], Nov.
    5, 1815.*
Nancy, of Canton, and Joel W. Gay, int. Apr. 11, 1824.
Olive, and Jonas Lewes, Mar. 12, 1769.
Olive, and Eben[eze]r Ward Vose, Oct. 21, 1810. C. R. 2.
Olive Draper, and Joel Seaverns, Jan. 20, 1811.*
Sarah, and Daniel Whitney, Mar. 7, 1769.
Seth, and Elizabeth [Betsey. int.] Hoogs of Newton, at New-
    ton, Feb. 10, 1785.*
Seth, and Patience Gannett of Sharon, int. June 21, 1812.
Susan, and John W. Foye, int. Oct. 11, 1840.
Tabitha, of Newton, and Jeremiah Richards, 3d, at Newton,
    Dec. 7, 1752.
Timothy, and Mary W. Smith, May 23, 1824.*
Willard, and Mary B. Pratt, May 11, 1818.*

GAYLARD, Edward, b. Ireland, and Bridget Donnelly, b.
    Ireland, Nov. 14, 1849.*

GEDDINGS (see also Giddens), John, and Nancy Weld, Jan.
    16, 1803.*

GEISLER, Jacob, and Eustena Kinter, int. May 16, 1849.

GEMMING, Margarett, and John McGee, int. Jan. 4, 1848.

GEORGE, Abigail, and Samuel Heley, June 6, 1744.
Elisabeth, and Eleazer Kingsbury of Needham, Oct. 22, 1747.
Freelove, and John Swaine, Jan. 16, 1757.
Gilbert B., and Helen C. Kingsbury of Franklin, int. Oct. 7,
    1846.
Greenleaf C., a. 21 y., clerk, s. Jacob and Abigail, and Mary
    B. Callander, a. 20 y., d. Joseph and Mary, Dec. 17,
    1846.*
J. Phillips, and Caroline Bond [Boid. C. R. 5.], Oct. 13, 1844.*

* Intention also recorded.

GEORGE, Jacob, widr., a. 54 y., blacksmith, s. Benj[amin] and Hannah, and Judith Payne, a. 39 y., d. Walter and Betsey, Nov. 4, 1847.*

Mary, and Samuel Gridley, Jan. 5, 1744.

Sarah, and Edward Kelton [Kilton. c. r. 2.], June 7, 1750.

GERALD, Eloner, and Moses Dor, Oct. 2, 1760.

John W., of Charlestown, and Catherine Green, int. July 9, 1847.

GERHARDSLEIN, Joseph, and Louisa Miller, int. May 18, 1848.

GERISH (see also Gerrish), Maria T., and Samuel C. Morison, int. Feb. 15, 1829.

GERRISH (see also Gerish), Amos, and Sarah [Mary. int; Mrs. Mary. c. r. 3.] Lynch, Apr. 3, 1822.*

Benj[ami]n, and Mrs. Rebecca Dudley, May 10, 1744. c. r. 2.

George, and Ann Damon of Milton, int. Feb. 8, 1824.

James, and Elizabeth Medah, int. Nov. 16, 1823.

GETCHEL, Phebe Jane, and Mark E. Hodgdon, Jan. 9, 1845.

GIBBENS (see also Gibbons), Daniel L., Maj., and Mary R. Howe, June 3, 1819.*

GIBBINS (see also Gibbons), Thomas, and Bridget White, int. Jan. 7, 1838.

GIBBON (see also Gibbons), Samuel, and Lydia Pond, at Boston, Sept. —, 1756.

GIBBONS (see also Gibbens, Gibbins, Gibbon), Ann, and Dominick Bradley, int. Apr. 25, 1849.

Margarett, and Patrick Doherty, int. June 25, 1849.

Owen, and Catherine Connill, int. May 13, 1848.

GIBBS, Alexander Hamilton [of Boston. c. r. 3.], and Ellen Mary [Maria M. int.] Hatch, Nov. 25, 1816.*

GIBSON (see also Gipson), Alexander C., and Lucy Harrison, int. Feb. 22, 1835.

Elizabeth B., and Elijah E. Lawrence, int. Nov. 13, 1831.

Frances, and George White, int. Oct. 31, 1846.

Martha, and Jacob Newell, Nov. 7 [3. ct. r.], 1657.

Mary, and John Ruggle, jr., Apr. 3, 1655.

* Intention also recorded.

GIBSON, Mary [Mercy. int.], and John Armstrong, Jan. 6, 1834.*

Mary Ann, and Norman M. Littleton, int. Nov. 15, 1849.

Timothy, from State of North Carolina, and Mary Lisher of Stoughton, int. Jan. 28, 1798.

**GIDDENS** (see also Geddings), Joseph R., and Mary H. Monroe, Jan. 17, 1842.*

**GILBERT** (see also Gilburd), John, and Mary W. Lee of Waltham, int. Nov. 29, 1848.

Jonathan, and Mary Reed, Nov. 19, 1761.

Samuel Shepard, and Mrs. Sarah Devereux Colman, int. Sept. 25, 1836.

**GILBURD** (see also Gilbert), Sarah, and Richard Retlon, Jan. 31, 1721-2.

**GILCREAS,** David A., and Hannah Maria Teuck, Apr. 28, 1845.

**GILES** (see also Gyles), Bethia, and James Wiley of Charlestown, int. Sept. 5, 1841.

John, Capt., of Brunswick, and Hanah Heath, Nov. 6 [Feb. 6. c. r. 2.], 1721.

**GILFORD,** Hannah, and Richard White, int. May 25, 1823.

**GILL,** Margarett, and Michael Donnallon, int. May 27, 1848.

Maria, and John Payson, Apr. 1, 1813.*

Mary, of Dorchester, and Nicholas Bonemort, int. Mar. 18, 1832.

Moses, A. M., and Mary Baldwin of Shrewsbury, int. Sept. 16, 1810.

William, and Isabella Richardson, int. Apr. 12, 1846.

**GILLAGAN** (see also Gilligan), Ellen, and John Tamoney, int. Oct. 15, 1846.

Michael, and Mary Murray, int. Jan. 5, 1845.

**GILLEN,** Delia H., and William D. Wheeler, Oct. 4, 1847.

**GILLIGAN** (see also Gillagan, Gilligin), Ann, and John Quillan, int. Apr. 9, 1843.

Catharine, and John Kelly, int. May 7, 1843.

James, b. Ireland, and Margarett Donnelly, b. Ireland, Nov. 8, 1849.

John, and Bridget Farrington, int. June 16, 1839.

* Intention also recorded.

GILLIGAN, Michael, and Ann Conaty, int. Sept. 6, 1847.
Thomas, and Margarett Donnally, int. Nov. 19, 1849.

GILLIGIN (see also Gilligan), Michael, and Bridget Killian, int. Dec. 22, 1848.

GILLISPIE, Margarett, b. Ireland. and John Brady [Bradley. int.], b. Ireland, Nov. 19, 1849.*

GILMAN, Hannah, and Eliphalet Sias, int. Sept. 16, 1832.
William, and Rhoda Lyon, May 18, 1800. c. r. 2.*
William, and Betsey O. Webb of Taunton, int. Dec. 15, 1833.

GILMARTIN, Mary, and John Lynch, int. June 22, 1848.

GILMORE, Angeline, and William C. Trow of Taunton, Apr. 1, 1831.*
John, and Susan Hews, int. Oct. 19, 1849.

GILSON, Jonas, and Elizabeth P. Ripley, Oct. 7, 1813.*

GINES, Sophia, and Thomas Hussy, int. Jan. 22, 1849.

GIPSON (see also Gibson), Abraham, of Burlington, and Polly Herring, July —, 1806.*

GLADHILL, Abraham, a. 22 y., carpet weaver, s. John and Betsey, and Anne Whitaker, a. 23 y., d. Samuel and Sarah, Aug. 18, 1849.*

GLASSON, Joseph, of Jersey City, and [Mrs. int.] Hannah Fuller, July 29, 1846.*

GLAZIER, Marshall, of Brookline, and Emily Kingsbury, int. Sept. 14, 1845.
Mary E., and George S. Norris, Nov. 24, 1842.*

GLEANOR, Ann, a. 21 y., b. Ireland, d. Thomas and Ann, and Jacob Doudle, a. 29 y., laborer, b. Germany, s. Jacob and Mary, Nov. 5, 1849.*

GLEASON (see also Glezen, Glezin), Charles, Rev., and Mrs. Bethiah Scarbrough, Nov. 5, 1747.
Mary, and Thomas Dillon, int. Sept. 14, 1845.
Michael, and Hannah Cusich [Cusick. int.], Oct. 26, 1845.*

GLENNING, Mary, and John Hanning, int. Oct. 6, 1847.

* Intention also recorded.

**GLENON** (see also Glinnon), Bridget, and James Kelly, int. Nov. 16, 1847.

**GLEZEN** (see also Gleason), Mary, and Jacob Pepper, Apr. 15, 1714.

**GLEZIN** (see also Gleason), Joyce, and Jacob Newel [May ?], 1700.
William, and Thankfull Trowbridge, May 16, 1705.

**GLIDDEN** (see also Gliddens, Gliddon), Mary Jane, of Parsonsfield, Me., and Thomas S. Danforth, int. Apr. 9, 1837.

**GLIDDENS** (see also Glidden), Daniel W., and Harriot Danforth, Nov. 13, 1834.*

**GLIDDON** (see also Glidden), Sarah, and James C. Hodgdon, Dec. 22, 1842.*

**GLINES,** Clarissa, and John W. Taylor, Dec. 5, 1831.*
Frances, and Josiah Weeks, Apr. 11, 1833.*
Hiram, and Eunice Knox, Nov. 24, 1825.*
Lydia, and Jesse Leonard, Nov. 4, 1827.*
Lydia H., a. 20 y., d. Nathan H. and Sarah H., and Edmund Farnsworth, a. 21 y., leather dresser, s. William and Catherine, May 24, 1846.*
Nahum M., and Ann G. Morse, Sept. 7, 1831.*
Nathan H., and Sarah Rowell, Apr. 16, 1820.*
Sarah A. [C. int.], and Melzar C. Waterman, Oct. 27, 1844.*

**GLINN** (see also Glynn), Patrick, and Bridget Curley, int. Apr. 16, 1837.

**GLINNEN** (see also Glinnon), Margarett, and James Connerty, int. Nov. 21, 1848.

**GLINNON** (see also Glenon, Glinnen, Glynnen), Patrick, and Mary Follan, int. Dec. 31, 1849.

**GLOVER,** Anna, and Stephen Wales, both of Dorchester, Apr. 7, 1793.
Ebenezer, of Stoughton, and Mary Fenno of Dorchester, Sept. 21, 1797.
Edward [of Brookline int.], and Hannah Brown, Jan. 1, 1805. C. R. 2.*

* Intention also recorded.

GLOVER, Elmira S., and Joseph Porter of Brighton, May 27, 1838.*

Frances G., and Samuel F. Train, Nov. 20, 1839.*

George S., and Helen M. Paul of Sherburne, int. Sept. 5, 1841.

Israel E., and Harriet Burditt, int. July 31, 1820.

Mary, of Dorchester, and James Lewis, jr., int. Nov. 11, 1821.

Mary, and John Shackford, Sept. 13, 1835.*

Mary Lee, of Dorchester, and John Pearson, int. Sept. 17, 1820.

Mehitabell, and Ezekiel Tileston, Jan. 10, 1774.

Samuel, and Lois Kilton, both of Dorchester, Mar. 7, 1793.

Theodore R., and Mary Ann Thomas Malbon of Hingham, int. Apr. 29, 1846.

Thomas, and Mary Damon [of Dedham. int.], May 26, 1822.*

Thomas, and Bethia [F. int.] Thompson, Mar. 24, 1842.*

**GLYN** (see also Glynn), John, and Susan S. Broadrick, int. Aug. 18, 1839.

**GLYNN** (see also Glinn, Glyn), Henry, and Abigail Cobb, May 28, 1839.*

James, and Deranda Curley, int. Aug. 31, 1845.

Margarett, and Patrick Fealy, int. Nov. 24, 1847.

Margarett E., of Boston, and George Coyle, int. Oct. 9, 1847.

Martin, and Catharine Donnely, int. Sept. 29, 1844.

Mary, and John Glynnen, int. June 9, 1839.

Mary, and Patrick Dolan, int. Mar. 28, 1841.

Mary, and Timothy Daily, Oct. 3, 1848.

Patrick, and Margaret Mulvy, int. Jan. 6, 1848.

**GLYNNEN** (see also Glinnon). John, and Mary Glynn, int. June 9, 1839.

**GOAD** (see also Goard, Gord), Mary, and John Williams, Jan. 15, 1712.

Sarah, and John Willson, Dec. 13, 1711.

**GOARD** (see also Goad), Richard, and Phebe Hewes, Nov. 30, 1639.

**GODDARD** (see also Goodard, Godward), Caroline, and Francis O. Watts, May 1, 1826.*

Catherine, and Samuel Crease, Oct. 18, 1807.*

* Intention also recorded.

GODDARD, Deborah, of Brookline, and William Child, at Brookline, Jan. 16, 1723.

Ebenezer, and Salley [Sally. dup.] Curtis, Oct. 1, 1777. [Sept. 30, 1778. dup.]

Ebenezer, and Vashti Colson, May 18, 1800.*

Elizabeth, and John Adams of Framingham, at Framingham, June 27, 1706.

Hannah, Mrs., and John Reed, Nov. 23, or 24, 1751.

Hannah R., and Henry Kellogg of Walpole, N. H., int. Nov. 15, 1840.

James, and Mary Woodward, Nov. 27, 1713.

John, and Mary Sprague of Malden, at Malden, Nov. 15, 1732.

John [of Brookline. c. r. 2.], and Sarah Brewer, June 30, 1753.

Joseph, and Mary Bugbee, May 29, 1716.

Lucinda, and James Warren of Attleborough, Apr. 2, 1816.*

Lucinda W., and Sullivan Carpenter, int. Oct. 27, 1833.

Lucretia, and Isaac Hyde of Cambridge, Sept. 22, 1805.*

Lucy, of Brookline, and Lewis Withington, int. Apr. 30, 1820

Lydia, and Ebenezer Fuller [resident. int.], May 5, 1793.*

Mary, Mrs., and John Stone, Oct. 23, 1729.

Mary W., and Jonas Fillebrown, int. May 20, 1832.

Sally, and Rufus Foster, Jan. 10, 1796.

Sally, and Theodore Tuttle, May 4, 1826.*

Samuel, and Joanna Brewer, May 28, 1782.

Sarah, and Andrew Bordman, Oct. 20, 1715.

Sarah, and James Baylie, at Boston, Apr. 13, 1720.

Sarah, and Isaac Wendall, Nov. 26, 1771.

Sarah, and John B. Witherbee, int. May 16, 1841.

Stephen, and Charlotte Hawes of Canton, int. Sept. 25, 1801.

Susannah, of Brookline and James Jones, int. Mar. 24, 1822.

Susannah M., and Frederick W. Field of Quincy, int. Apr. 26, 1829.

William, and Mrs. Elizabeth White of Brookline, at Brookline, Dec. 23, 1761.

GODDING (see also Goding), Hannah, and John Livermore, Mar. 22, 1815.*

Jane [Goulding. int.], and John S. Hubbard of Charlestown, Dec. 25, 1837.*

GODELL (see also Goodale), Mary, and Samuel B. Alker of Cambridge, int. Mar. 28, 1830.

* Intention also recorded.

**GODFREY,** Eliza, and Edward C. Lang, int. Dec. 14, 1823.

Henry A. M., a. 24 y., carpenter, s. Abram and Lydia, and Caroline Thompson, a. 23 y., dressmaker, d. Asa and Sarah, Sept. 21, 1845.

**GODING** (see also Godding), Margarett, and George Clap, Oct. 18, 1821.*

Martha, and John Boman, Mar. 4, 1821.*

**GODWARD** (see also Goddard), John, Capt., and Susanna Lincoln, at Hingham, Nov. 16, 1738.

**GOFF** (see also Goffe), Samuel, and Anna Williams, Sept. 16, 1784.*

**GOFFE** (see also Goff), Mary, and John Keyes, Dec. 14, 1772.

**GOLAVER,** Robert, and Catharine Rice, resident, int. Aug. 23, 1795.

**GOLD** (see also Gould), Abigail, and Thomas Lyon, Mar. 10, 1669.

Thomas, and Rebecca Lyon, Dec. 18 [4. c. r. 2.], 1716.

**GOLDEN** (see also Goolding, Goulding), Hannah, and Patrick Conlan, int. Jan. 18, 1848.

Mary Ann, and Alexander Ambush of Quincy, int. Sept. 15, 1849.

**GOLDSMITH,** Benjamin, and Mary Smith of Hamilton, int. Mar. 13, 1825.

George, and Lucinda Hutchings [of Boston. c. r. 3.], Dec. 23, 1832.*

Henry L., and Naomi French of Andover, int. Mar. 21, 1830.

John, of Andover, and Hannah Lowder, May 26, 1796.*

John, and Mary H. Sumner, both of Brookline, May 26, 1825.*

Mary R. [A. int.], and Jonathan Dore, Aug. 28, 1831.*

Mercy L., and Thomas Nutter, Jan. 8, 1832.*

Solomon, and Ruth Blasdel, int. Aug. 23, 1829.

**GOLDSTON** (see also Gould), Mary [Gould. c. r. 1.], and Josuah Hewes [Hues. c. r. 1.], Oct. 8, 1634.

**GOOCH,** Elizabeth, and Leonard Fisher Lethbridge, Dec. 22, 1774.

George W., and Claraetta Priest of Providence, R. I., int. June 5, 1846.

* Intention also recorded.

**GOOD,** Catherine, and Thomas Curley, int. Jan. 25, 1849.
John, and Eliza Downey, Aug. 11, 1847.
Margarett, and John Fitzmorris, int. May 4, 1849.
Margarett, and Edward McDonough, int. July 2, 1849.
Thomas, and Mary Sullivan, int. Oct. 7, 1848.

**GOODALE** (see also Godell), Aaron, and Mehetable Blake of
Holden, int. Dec. 23, 1804.

**GOODARD** (see also Goddard), Mary, and James Bucknan
of Malden, Sept. 17, 1747.

**GOODENOW** (see also Goodnough), Jesse, and Caroline A.
[M. int.] Parker, Sept. 8, 1823. c, r. 2.*

**GOODHUE,** Benjamin S., and Mary E. Bell, Mar. 12, 1835.
Margaret B., and George Noyes, Apr. 5, 1837.*
Mary E. [G. int.], and John C. Palfrey, May 25, 1837.*
Sarah, and William Johnson, int. Nov. 13, 1836.

**GOODMAN,** Mary F., and John Conneff, int. July 13, 1845.

**GOODNOUGH** (see also Goodenow, Goodnow), Betsy, and
Alvan Howe, Apr. 2, 1822. c. r. 2.*
Ephraim, and Elizabeth Herring, Mar. 6, 1796.*
Stephen, and Lucy Withington, Sept. 15, 1796.*

**GOODNOW** (see also Goodnough), Samuel H., of Sudbury,
and Sally Guptil, int. July 8, 1811.

**GOODRICH** (see also Goodridge), David, Dr., of Templeton,
and Susan Wait, Nov. 18, 1813.*
Mary E., and Charles M. Walcot [Walcott, of Philadelphia.
int.], Nov. 1, 1843.*

**GOODRIDGE** (see also Goodrich), Elizabeth, and Robert
Smith of Boston, Sept. 26, 1802.
Jane, and Nathan Fesenden of Lexington, June 21, 1801.*
Mary, Mrs., and Benjamin Lynde, jr., Esq. of Salem, Nov.
1, 1731.
Walter, and Mrs. Mary Bowles, Feb. 8, 1727-8.

**GOODWIN,** Cynthia, of Kennebunkport, Me., and Lyman B.
Hanaford, int. Sept. 15, 1844.
George K., a. 22 y., carriage painter, s. Jeremiah and Caroline,
and Sarah Louisa Winslow, a. 18 y., d. Reuben and Harriet, Nov. 18, 1847.*

* Intention also recorded.

GOODWIN, Lucy, and Joseph Thurston, Dec. 22, 1805.*

Mary [Nancy, of Cambridge. int.], and Aaron Rummerill, at Cambridge, June 23, 1799.*

Mary, and Oliver Rouse, Nov. 4, 1810.*

Mary, and Philip Adams, Sept. 30, 1827.

Mehitable [Mehitabel. int.], a. 21 y., d. Nahum and Mehitable, and Benjamin Gowell [Gowel. int.] of Lebanon, Me., a. 21 y., yeoman, s. Benjamin and Olive of Lebanon, Me., June 28, 1846.*

Rachel, of South Hampton, and Ephr[ai]m Fitts, int. Sept. 7, 1806.

Sarah, and Joseph Edmunds [Edmonds. int.], Oct. 17, 1844.*

Serena, and Reuben Wentworth, Sept. 28, 1834.*

Thomas I., of Charlestown, and Abby Dennison Rhodes, Dec. 7, 1820.*

GOOGINS (see also Gookin), Hannah, and David Baker, July 23 [28. C. R. 2.], 1778.

GOOKIN (see also Googins), Edmund [Daniel. C. R. 2.], and Deborah Whiting, Jan. 3, 1760.

Mary, and Joseph Billings of Stoughton, int. Jan. 3, 1790.

GOOLD (see also Gould), John, and Elizabeth Downey, int. July 28, 1847.

Thomas, and Hannah Woods, Dec. 16, 1736.

GOOLDING (see also Golden), Bridget [Golden. dup.], and Michael McCormick, int. Aug. 8, 1848. [Sept. 20. 1849. dup.]

GORD (see also Goad), Joseph [Gorde. dup.], and Ann Chaplin, Mar. 23, 1680-81.

GORDON, Bridget, and Thomas Gurry, int. Nov. 5, 1849.

Rebecca, and Dandridge Taft, Oct. 26, 1824.*

Sarah W., of Portland, Me., and Amos T. Maxwell, int. Oct. 9, 1842.

GORE, Abigail, Mrs., and Benjamin May, Oct. 31, 1751.

Adeline B., and Calvin Whiting [of Boston. C. R. 3.], Oct. 29, 1829.*

Ann Mary, and Joseph Dane of Cambridge, Mar. 1, 1818.*

Charles F., and Mary Richards of Dedham, int. Sept. 27, 1829.

Ebenezer, and Susanna Paul, Nov. 20, 1712.

* Intention also recorded.

GORE, Eben[eze]r, and Susannah Richardson, Feb. 21, 1745.
C. R. 2.
Ebenezer, Capt., and Hannah Seaver, May 15, 1777.
Eliza, and Amos Fisher, Dec. 8, 1805.*
Hannah, and Ralph Bradhers, June 13, 1677.
Hannah, and Samuel Curtiss, June 6, 1711.
Hannah, Mrs., and Jonathan Brown of Cambridge, Nov. 4,
1731.
Hannah V., and Elias Miller, Oct. 28, 1821.*
Jeremiah, and Hannah Curtis, Jan. 7, 1768.
Jeremiah, jr., and Susanna Billings, Oct. 16, 1819. C. R. 2.*
John, and Sarah Gardner, May 31, 1683.
John, and Mary Thorering, Nov. 15, 1744. C. R. 2.
John, jr., and Abigail Parker, June 26, 1744. C. R. 2.
John C., and Mary James, May 27, 1838.*
Joshua, and Polly Curtis [resident. int.], Oct. 1, 1784.*
Joshua, and Mrs. Lucy Ward of Weston, int. Apr. 25, 1802.
Mary, and Joseph Hammond of Newton, at Newton, Apr. 3,
1744.
Mary, and Benjamin Bass, Dec. 7, 1757.
Mary, Mrs., and Thomas Mayo, Oct. 26, 1784.*
Mary, and John Graham, Feb. 16, 1817.*
Nancy D., and Jonathan A. Richards, Nov. 23, 1820.*
Paul, and Mary Kenney, Jan. 21, 1764.
Paul, and Mary Davis, Dec. 14, 1793.*
Priscilla, and Joseph Winchester, Mar. 1, 1758.
Samuel, and Mary Williams, Feb. 23, 1727.
Samuel, and Hannah Heath, Feb. 15, 1770.
Samuel, and Abagail White of Brookline, int. June 22, 1800.
Samuell, and Elisebeth Weld, Aug. 28, 1672.
Sarah, and James Pirepont, June 3, 1709.
Sarah, and Daniel Bugbee, Oct. 29, 1765.
Susanna, and Jonathan Craft, Apr. 22, 1736.

GORMAN, John, b. Ireland, and Jane Rodgers, b. Ireland,
Sept. 6, 1849.*
Mary O., and Tary McGrath, int. Sept. 3, 1846.
Michael, and Catherine Rourk, int. Aug. 13, 1849.
Patrick, and Catherine Carney, int. Apr. 26, 1848.

GORTON, Abraham, and Mary Sumner, May 31, 1683.
Avis, of Charleston, and James Riley, int. June 15, 1823.
Independence W., and Maria Haynes, Apr. 30, 1826.*
Mary, and Daniel Mascroft, May 23, 1665.

* Intention also recorded.

GOSAM (see also Gossom), Charles H., of Portland, and Harriet N. Field, Feb. 16, 1840.*

GOSS, Abigail, of Northborough, and Hollis Johnson, int. Sept. 10, 1809.

Elizabeth, and Thomas Lynch, int. Aug. 15, 1841.

George S., and Eliza B. Maxfield, int. Mar. 27, 1836.

Mary N., of Newton, and James H. Barnard of Waterbury, Conn., Dec. 5, 1844.

GOSSOM (see also Gosam), Oliver C., a. 32 y., currier, s. Oliver C. and Catherine, of Ohio, and Frances Holland, a. 20 y., Dec. 27, 1846.*

William, and Nancy Gates, int. Nov. 10, 1845.

GOST, John, of Hatfield, and Hanah Griggs, Oct. 16, 1722.

GOULD (see also Gold, Goldston, Goold), Ann M., and Thomas L. Williams, July 17, 1844.

Charles P., and Naomi P. Burbank, Dec. 19, 1830.*

Daniel, and Eunice Brown, int. May 6, 1792.

Eliza, and James O. Ward of New York, Nov. 21, 1838. [1837. C. R. 3.]*

Elizabeth, and Edmund Chepman [Chipman. int.; Chessman of Boston. C. R. 3.], Jan. 30, 1820.*

Hannah, Mrs., and Thomas Bentley, int. Dec. 25, 1825.

Jacob, and Lucy Ruggles, May 26, 1796.*

John, and Elizabeth Sumner, Feb. —, 1795.*

Joseph D., and Sarah P. Seaverns, June 2, 1833.*

Lucy H., and Charles Davis [2d. int.], May 21 [31. C. R. 3.], 1818.*

Mary Ann, of Andover, and William White, int. July 16, 1839.

Mary R., and Dwight Prouty [of Boston. C. R. 3.], Dec. 4, 1828.*

Otis, and Ruth White, Oct. 13, 1793.*

Otis, and Mrs. Asenath Bacon, Dec. 1, 1814.*

Patty, and Daniel Brown, Nov. 24, 1802.*

Sophia, and Capt. John Perkins Prentiss, int. Nov. 14, 1824.

Tryphena, and Solomon Prentiss Pond, both of Franklin, Feb. 4, 1791.

GOULDING (see also Golden), John, and Ann Meugla [Nengla. int.], May 27, 1848.*

* Intention also recorded.

**GOVE,** Sarah Ann, of Cambridge, and Augustus C. Swasey, June 9, 1844.*

**GOWELL,** Benjamin [Gowel. int.], of Lebanon, Me., a. 21 y., yeoman, s. Benjamin and Olive of Lebanon, Me., and Mehitable Goodwin, a. 21 y., d. Nahum and Mehitable, June 28, 1846.*

Caroline, and Andrew Hayes, int. Dec. 12, 1841.

Esther, and Horatio Wentworth, Sept. 5, 1839.*

Lovey, a. 26 y., d. Benj[amin], and William Ewell, a. 27 y., farmer, s. Perez, Dec. 26, 1847.*

Susan, and George W. Grant, Jan. 10, 1842.*

**GOWITH,** Eleanor, and J. Bryant Hill, int. Sept. 17, 1843.

**GRACE,** John. b. Ireland, and Joanna Cleary, b. Ireland, Oct. 22, 1849.

**GRADY** (see also Gready), Mary, and John Harney, int. Apr. 25, 1841.

Thomas, and Ann McKelley, int. Jan. 5, 1845.

**GRAFTON,** Joseph, Rev., of Newton, and Hannah Parker [Barker. int.], Nov. 12, 1805.*

**GRAGG,** Cordelia Roseline, and Samuel Adams Danforth, May 20, 1842.*

Elisabeth B., and Joseph Palmer [M. D. int.], Dec. 7, 1843.*

Harriet A., and Jonathan Moore Taylor of New York, int. Mar. 27, 1842.

**GRAHAM** (see also Greahan, Greham), Alden, and Elizabeth S. Estabrook of Rutland, int. Mar. 30, 1845.

Caroline, and John C. Hobbs, May 2, 1833.*

John, and Mary Gore, Feb. 16, 1817.*

Louisa, and Joseph W. Sweat, int. Nov. 7, 1830.

Mary A., and Robert L. Hobbs, Apr. 7, 1837.*

Patrick, and Ellen Connally of Brookline, int. May 25, 1846.

**GRALY** (see also Greely), Lydia, and Benjamin Smith, June 14, 1733.

**GRANDISON,** Harriet [Harriot. int.], of Scituate, and Benja[min] Brooker [Broker. int.], at Scituate, Jan. 27, 1791.*

* Intention also recorded.

**GRANGER,** Calvin, and Mrs. Hannah Williams, int. Aug. 26, 1810.

Maria D., and Mark Bills, both of Cambridge, Aug. 18, 1835.

**GRANT,** Charles E., and Eliza A. H. Bacon, June 26, 1839.*
Cyrus, and Charlotte W. Baker, int. Nov. 8, 1840.
Elizabeth L., and John Gateley, int. Sept. 11, 1825.
George W., and Susan Gowell, Jan. 10, 1842.*
Lydia F., and Henry McIntire, Mar. 1, 1838.
Moses C., and Mary N. Baker, Feb. 4, 1839.*

**GRAVES** (see also Greaves), Hanna, and John Mayo [Mahoe. CT. R.], May 24, 1654.
John, and Judith Alward [maid servant. C. R. 1.], Dec. —, 1635.
Thomas, and Ursilla Wilson, Feb. 5, 1707.

**GRAY,** Ann Greenough, and George Whitney of Quincy, Dec. 15, 1829.*
Catherine, and Phillip Whealan, int. May 15, 1847.
George H., and Ann Wakefield, at Boston, May 9, 1844. C. R. 3.
Hugh, and Ann Carr, int. Dec. 24, 1847.
Mary E., and Samuel Dudley, int. Dec. 3, 1837.
Mary Woodward, a. 20 y., d. Alfred T. and Mary W., and Joseph Willet Robbins, a. 23 y., clerk, s. Edward J. and Elizabeth, Apr. 7, 1847.*
Olive, and Eben[eze]r Ward, int. Sept. 9, 1810.
Peter, and Relief Ripley, Apr. 24, 1806.*
Sarah, and James Kilduff, int. July 10, 1842.
Sarah N[iles. C. R. 3.], and Joseph Currier [of Boston. C. R. 3.], Apr. 3, 1833.*

**GREADY** (see also Grady), Michael, and Mary Ann Kenny, int. Oct. 24, 1847.

**GREAHAN** (see also Graham), Patrick [a. 27 y. in pencil.], and Mary Kelly [a. 27 y. in pencil], int. Feb. 11, 1844.

**GREALY** (see also Greely), Patrick, and Ann McDermott, int. Oct. 17, 1841.

**GREATON,** Anne. and Sam[ue]l Heath, jr., int. Nov. 9, 1783.
Nancy, Mrs., and Samuel Heath, Feb. 3, 1784.
Richard Humphry, Lt., and Sarah Bourn, Feb. 6, 1787.*

* Intention also recorded.

**GREAVES** (see also Graves), Judith, and William Potter, June 2, 1646.

**GREELY** (see also Graly, Grealy, Grely), Hannah, and Michael Bronly, int. July 31, 1848.
Lydia, and John Richards, Apr. 10, 1750. c. r. 2.

**GREEN** (see also Greene), Abel, and Betsey Jackson, int. June 22, 1823.
Catherine, and Thomas White, int. Jan. 16, 1847.
Catherine, and John W. Gerald of Charlestown, int. July 9, 1847.
Charlotte [Greene. int.], a. 23 y., d. Lemuel and Dorcas, and Matthew J. Ramsey, a. 27 y., laborer, s. Thomas and Dorothy, Aug. 15, 1847.*
Daniel B., and Rebeccah Cobb, Mar. 10, 1825.*
Harriet, and Amasa Murdock of Newton, int. Nov. 27, 1834.
Jacob, and Mrs. Sarah Champney of Dorchester, at Dorchester, Mar. 14, 1771.
Jane, and George Lord, Nov. 19, 1833.*
John jr., and Eliza L. Bird, May 23, 1813.*
Mary, and Thomas Griggs, Aug. 26, 1640.
Mary Ann E., and Frederick A. Stone of Brookline, int. Jan. 15, 1848.
Milo, of Stoneham, and Ann Noyes Stodder, int. July 10, 1846.
Peter, and Mary Ann Kelly [Kelley. int.], Sept. 25, 1848.*
Ransom, and Sally [Sarah Cobb. int.] of Taunton, Aug. 30, 1827.*
Rebecca F., and Warren Thayer of New York, int. June 8, 1845.
Sarah E., of Dedham, and Frederick L. Bickford, Nov. 29, 1832.
Sophia, and Thomas Reading, June 25, 1837.*
Walter H., and Margaret Watson, Oct. 27, 1837.*
William, and Hannah Livermore, Aug. 20, 1835.*
William, and Ellen Raynolds, int. June 1, 1845.
William, and Bridget Kenney, int. Dec. 25, 1845.

**GREENE** (see also Green), Augusta P., and Thomas Hassard of Baltimore, int. Nov. 1, 1835.
Henry W., and Mary Hoxie Sands of New Shoreham, R. I., int. June 17, 1848.
Jane, and Martin Stebbin, Dec. 25, 1639.

* Intention also recorded.

**GREENOUGH** (see also Greenwood), Anna [Anne. c. r. 3.], and Henry [K. int.] Burgwyn [Henry King Burgynen. c. r. 3.] of Newbern, N. C., Nov. 28, 1838.*

Maria F., and William H. Sumner of Dorchester [of Boston. c. r. 3.], Dec. 13, 1835. [Nov. 20, 1836. int.]*

Newman, and Phebe Capen, int. Apr. 14, 1822.

**GREENWOOD** (see also Greenough, Grenewood), Alice, of Newton, and James Shedd, at Newton, Sept. 28, 1743.

Angeline, and Richard Warren of New York, int. Sept. 4, 1836.

Catharine Amelia, and Dr. George Bartlett, int. Oct. 23, 1834.

Ethan A., Esq., and Mrs. Caroline Warren, Feb. 1, 1829.*

John, of Newton, and Mrs. Alice Lyon, July 24, 1729.

John [Greenough. dup.], and Eliza [abeth. dup.] Payson, Nov. 2 [16. dup.], 1806.*

**GREGORY,** Marshall, and Grace Vose, both of Milton, May 28, 1795.

Mary B., a. 22 y., d. Charles and Betsey, and David Talbot, a. 26 y., painter, s. Nathaniel and Nancy, Mar. 20, 1845.*

**GREGSON,** Isaac, and Nancy Nevens, int. Jan. 15, 1815.

**GREHAM** (see also Graham), Margarett, and John Staunton, int. June 13, 1848.

**GRELY** (see also Greely), Elizabeth, and Thomas Seaver, Mar. 26, 1713.

**GRENEWOOD** (see also Greenwood), Elizabeth, Mrs., and Sam[ue]ll White, Nov. 8, 1721.

**GRIDLEY,** Abigail, and Edward Dorr, Apr. 3, 1746. [1747 ?.]

Anne, and John Swift, Nov. 18, 1779.

Charles H., and Mary B. Morrisson of Dresden, Me., int. Dec. 9, 1846.

Elizabeth, Mrs., and Solomon Ayers, Mar. 18, 1752.

Elizabeth, and Charles Nolen, Aug. 4, 1793.*

Esther, and Thomas Parker, Apr. 29, 1777.

Hannah, and Ebenezer Pierpont, June 1, 1749.

James W. L., and ·Joanna B. Bowman of Boston, int. July 9, 1847.

Lois, and Adam Pattia, May 12, 1774.

Martha, and Nathaniel Eaton, Apr. —, 1770.

* Intention also recorded.

GRIDLEY, Mary, and William Blaney, Feb. 17, 1755.

Polly, Mrs., and Elijah Field, Feb. 22, 1784.*

Rebecca, and Ephraim Mills [Mille. int.], at Boston, Nov. 10, 1793.*

Rebeckah, of Brookline, and Edw[ar]d Bridge, Sept. 16, 1759.

Samuel, and Mary George, Jan. 5, 1744-5.

Samuel, and Abigail Baker, Apr. 23, 1747.

Sarah, and Lt. Moses Scott, Sept. 26, 1763.

Sarah, Mrs., and Thaddeus Partridge, Oct. 3, 1782.*

Susanna, and Aaron Child, Nov. 9, 1769.

Thomas M., of Westboro, and Henrietta H. Webber, d. John, May 14, 1846.*

William, and Lidia Blaney, Dec. 4, 1755.

William, and Mrs. Elizabeth Woods, Jan. 4, 1785.*

**GRIFFEN** (see also Griffin), Catherine, and Michael Coyle, int. Feb. 16, 1848.

**GRIFFIN** (see also Griffen), Catharine, and Thomas Kenny, int. Apr. 16, 1843.

Elizabeth, and Samuel Sumner of Pomfret, Nov. 20, 1723.

Elizabeth M., and Ichabod Sampson, Jan. 4, 1845.*

George W., and Lydia L. Smith, Mar. 13, 1844. c. r. 7.*

L. H., and Eliza J. Torrey of Deer Isle, Me., int. Aug. 18, 1847.

Lydia L., wid., of Dedham, a. 47 y., d. Richard, of Benson, Vt., and Asa Kidder, widr. of Wardsborough, Vt., a. 53 y., farmer, s. Richard and Rebecca, Mar. 1, 1848.

Margarett, b. Ireland, and John McGrath, b. Ireland, Oct. 22, 1849.

Martin, and Bridget Kelly, int. June 12, 1846.

Mary, b. Ireland, and Patrick Cosgrove, b. Ireland, Dec. 11, 1849.*

Sarah, and Thomas Hammond [of Newton. c. r. 2.], Dec. 30, [Feb. 30. c. r. 2.], 1714.

Thomas, and Bridget Fahey, int. Oct. 2, 1847.

**GRIFFITH,** Margarett, and John McGrath, int. Oct. 8, 1849.

**GRIGGS** (see also Grigs), Abigail, and Isaac Newel, Dec. 14, 1715.

Abigail, and Lemuel Baker, Nov. 17, 1785.*

Abigail, and Paul Pratt of Weston [of Newton. c. r. 2.], Aug. 29, 1822. c. r. 2.*

* Intention also recorded.

GRIGGS, Charles, and Hannah B. Everett [of Dorchester. int.], Aug. 12, 1827. C. R. 2.*

Elizabeth, and Ephram Bacon, at Dedham, Aug. 28, 1700.

Ester, and Sam[ue]l Levet of Beverly, at Boston, Jan. 5, 1726.

George [of Brookline. C. R. 2.], and Susanna Baker, Sept. 3, 1747.

Hanah, and John Gost of Hatfield, Oct. 16, 1722.

Hannah, and David Southwick "Adjacent to ye Town of Woodstock," Apr. 15, 1726.

Hannah, and Asa Mors, May 14, 1778.

James, of Brookline, and Mary Mayo, Mar. 29, 1744. C. R. 2.

Jemima, and John White, at Needham, Sept. 12, 1775.

John, jr., and Elisabeth Casse, [June ?], 1682.

John, and Sarah Davies Williams, Nov. 23, 1820. P. R. 3.

John H., and Abby M. Gardner, June 25, 1848.

John W., and Paulina A. Dike of Pittsford, Vt., int. May 7, 1843.

Julia Ann, a. 38 y., d. Lemuel and Ruth, and Abraham G. Parker, widr., a. 62 y., s. Caleb and Hannah, Mar. 11, 1849.*

Keziah, and Stephen York, Aug. 31, 1834.*

Lemuel, and Ruth Smith. June 14, 1805.*

Maria, and Hazen Stanniels, int. Oct. 5, 1834.

Martha, and John Daviss, June 8, 1721.

Mary, and John Cory, May 13, 1713.

Mary, and Aaron Heley, June 16, 1766.

Mary [Mrs. int.], and Alexander Hodgon Jennings, Nov. 27, 1806. C. R. 2.*

Moses, of Cambridge, and [Mrs. int.] Meletiah Richards, Aug. 18, 1785.*

Moses, and Peggy Connelly, Apr. 30, 1797. C. R. 2.*

Nathan, and Elisabeth Child Dudley, Dec. 27, 1812.*

Nathanael [of Brookline. C. R. 2.], and Mary Jones, Apr. 17, 1746.

Nathaniel, Lt., and Mrs. Hannah Dana, May 21, 1793.

Samuel, and Mercy Burrill, both residents, Aug. 5, 1788.*

Sarah, and Stephen McIntosh, Dec. 10, 1781. C. R. 2.

Sarah, of Brookline, and John Holbrook, int. Aug. 31, 1783.

Sarah D. [of Boston, int.], a. 18 y., d. John and Sarah, and Horatio G. Morse, a. 29 y., physician, s. Amos and Irena, Apr. 22 [23. P. R. 3.], 1847.*

Stephen, and Mary Ann Cabot, int. Aug. 11, 1822.

* Intention also recorded.

GRIGGS, Thankful, Mrs., and Joshua Wyman of Woburn, Sept. 11, 1798.*

Thomas, and Mary Green, Aug. 26, 1640.

Thomas, and Margaret Williams, Sept. 1, 1743.

Tho[ma]s, and Prudence Richards, int. Oct. 19, 1783.

William H., and Martha E. Scruton of Dover, N. H., int. Jan. 9, 1847.

————, wid., and Jasper Rawlins, June 8, 1651.

**GRIGS** (see also Griggs), John, and Mary Pattin, Nov. 11, 1652.

Joseph [Griggs. CT. R.], and Hanna Davis, Nov. 8, 1654.

**GRIM,** John, and Elizabeth Weeks, int. June 25, 1837.

**GRIMES,** Mary J. W., and William S. Morton of Milton, int. Sept. 1, 1839.

**GRINGE,** Elizabeth, of Dorchester, and Henry Smith, int. Apr. 17, 1825.

**GRISWOLD** (see also Griswould), Maria, of Walpole, and John Hayes, int. Oct. 24, 1841.

**GRISWOULD** (see also Griswold), Susannah, and Ebenezer Warren, Dec. 6, 1739.

**GROOMS,** Elijah [Groomes. int.], and Elisabeth Stevenson [Elizabeth Stevinson. int.], July 7, 1844.*

**GROOSVENAUR** (see also Grosvenor), Thomas, and Elizabeth Pepper, May 22, 1718.

**GROSVENOR** (see also Groosvenaur), Aurelia T., and Joseph P. Chick, Dec. 22, 1845.*

Elizabeth H., of Paxton, and Isaac D. White, int. Apr. 18, 1841.

**GROVER,** Stephen, and Polly Miles, int. Oct. 26, 1806.

**GROZER,** Elizabeth, and Geo[rge] C. Hurter of Zenia, Ohio, Oct. 22, 1839.

Marcia, and Zacheus Atkins of New Sharon, Me., June 23, 1840.*

**GRUSH,** Abby [Gruch. int.], and Charles Wells, July 29, 1844.*

* Intention also recorded.

GRUSH, Job T., and Abigail F. Badger, int. Oct. 6, 1822.

Job T., widr., a. 47 y., currier, s. Thomas and Esther, and Mary B. Badger, a. 49 y., d. John and Sarah, Feb. 23, 1848.*

Martha, and Samuel Ward, July 16, 1845.*

GRYNORD, Barnard, and Rachel McDonough, int. May 8, 1847.

GUDWORTH, Samuel S. [Cudworth. c. r. 3.], and Almira Jaines, May 19, 1842.*

GUILD (see also Guile), Benj[ami]n, and Electa Ann Keith, int. Apr. 25, 1830.

Chester, and Harriot Fisk, June 5, 1822.*

George A., and Nancy E. Jones of Newton, int. Jan. 7, 1844.

Harriet, and E. Foster Briggs, Nov. 13, 1845.*

James, and Sophia B. Child, int. Aug. 28, 1842.

Mary D., and Daniel F. Child, Nov. 14, 1839.*

Samuel, and Sarah Mears, Nov. 23, 1806.*

Samuel, jr., and Elizabeth B. D. Thayer of Brookline, int. Dec. 17, 1843.

Warren, of Dedham, and Julia A. Woodward of Newton, Mar. 1, 1843. c. r. 7.

GUILE (see also Guild), Sam[ue]l [Guild. c. r. 2.], of Dedham, and Sarah Smith, [Apr. 24. c. r. 2.], 1766.

GULLIVER, Mary H., and Calvin Bird, both of Dorchester, June 13, 1848.

Stephen, of Dorchester, and Mary Downing, Nov. 26, 1843.

GUNNISON, Sarah Ann, of Dorchester, and Charles Bugbee, int. Nov. 25, 1827.

GUPTIL (see also Guptill), Sally, and Samuel H. Goodnow of Sudbury, int. July 8, 1811.

GUPTILL (see also Guptil), Winthrop, and Olive Fuller, int. Aug. 23, 1829.

GURHY (see also Gurry), Edward, and Mary Dolin, int. May 20, 1837.

Mary, and John Gately, int. Dec. 22, 1844.

Thomas, and Bridget Logue, int. Jan. 23, 1842.

* Intention also recorded.

**GURIGH** (see also Gurry), Margaret, and James Calvin, int. Oct. 21, 1838.

**GURKY,** Barnard, and Ann Hannan, int. July 3, 1842.

**GURNEY,** James H., and Susan Mallard, Apr. 3, 1810.*
James H., and Delpha Stetson of Bridgewater, int. May 2, 1813.
Joseph, and Lois Hopkin, Mar. 30, 1815.*
Josephine, and William B. Cann, int. Dec. 28, 1845.
Ruth S., and Nahum Ward, Feb. 26, 1845.*
Sally, and Moses Draper, jr., May 1, 1796.*
Susan, and Nahum Ward, Sept. 13, 1829.*

**GURREY** (see also Gurry), James, and Catharine Brian, int. Oct. 21, 1845.

**GURRY** (see also Gurhy, Gurigh, Gurrey), Bridget, and William McGann, int. Nov. 9, 1849.
Catharine, and Timothy Egan, int. Oct. 18, 1845.
Thomas, and Bridget Gordon, int. Nov. 5, 1849.

**GUSHEE,** Artemas D., and Abby Leonard of Taunton, int. Oct. 16, 1836.

**GYLES** (see also Giles), Mary, and Nathaniel Loring, June 18, 1747.

**HAAS,** Augusta Elizabeth, and John George Schwarzwalder, int. July 6, 1848.
John, and Ketren Smeht, int. Aug. 4, 1833.

**HACKEY,** Margarett, and Michael Cochran of Boston, int. Apr. 7, 1849.

**HACKNEY,** Margaret, and Michael Collins, int. July 9, 1837.

**HADLOCK,** James, and Sarah Draper, May 19, 1669.

**HAGAR** (see also Hager), Charlotte A., of Charlestown, and Isaac F. Nute, July 13, 1847.
Cyrene, and James Durgan, int. Sept. 22, 1822.
Samuel, and Cyrene Smith, Apr. 7, 1816. C. R. 2.*

**HAGBURNE,** Katherin, and Thomas Dudley, Esq., Apr. 14, 1644.

* Intention also recorded.

**HAGER** (see also Hagar), Cyrene [Hagar. int.], and Danforth Richards, Apr. 20, 1828. c. R. 2.*

Sarah Amelia, of Westminster, and Charles Upton, int. Nov.
23, 1845.

**HAGERTY,** William, and Catherine McDonough, int. Dec.
26, 1846.

**HAHEYE,** Patrick, and Catharine McCafferty, int. May 1,
1842.

**HAITH,** (see also Heath), Mary, and Patrick Curley, int.
Jan. 31, 1848.

**HAKE,** Thomas, of Boston, and Margaret Chandler, at Boston, Nov. 6, 1754.

**HALE,** Almira, of Newton, and Harvey Rice, int. Apr. 15,
1838.

Joanna, and William York, Dec. 8, 1828.

Thomas, and Jane Lord, — : 1 2 m : 1639. c. R. 1.

**HALEY** (see also Healey), Barbara, and Oliver Matthews of
Austerlitz, N. Y., Sept. 22, 1825.*

John, and Mary Cortlin, int. Aug. 19, 1838.

Michael, and Ellen Quinn, int. Nov. 28, 1846.

Peter, and Mary McDermot, int. Aug. 15, 1849.

**HALL,** David, and Mary M. Child, Jan. 28, 1829.*

David, and Mrs. Lucy Hartt, int. Sept. 3, 1844.

David P., and Margaret D. Cheney, Dec. 15, 1836.*

Eber W., and Deborah A. Potter of Needham, int. Apr. 3,
1845.

Elizabeth, of Dorchester, and James Webster, June 30, 1793.*

Ellen, and Martin Hobbs, int. Feb. 8, 1848.

Enoch, and Emeline Hosmer of Acton, int. Apr. 2, 1837.

Ephraim, and Thankful Craft, Sept. 23, 1731.

Ezra T., and Abigail J. Howe, int. Dec. 8, 1844.

Graham, carpenter, and Adaline K. Currier [Currer. int.],
May 6, 1846.*

Hannah, of Newton, and Nehemiah Davis, int. Dec. 25, 1803.

Hellen [Helen. c. R. 3.] Louisa, and Simon Davis Leavens,
Oct. 22, 1832.*

Hendrick, and Catharine Sanery, June 24, 1834.*

Hiram, and Rebecca D. Child, Dec. 18, 1836.*

* Intention also recorded.

HALL, Horace M., and Elizabeth H. Parker, Oct. 6, 1844.*

John, of Rehoboth, and Mary Newell, at Rehoboth, Nov. 18, 1684.

John, and Elizabeth R. Freeman, June 12, 1842.*

Jonathan, and Elinor Cutter of Medford, at Medford, Aug. 20, 1761.

Jonathan, and Mary [Howard. int.] Randall, May 11, 1807.*

Katharine, and Joseph Weld, Dec. 9, 1779.

Martha, and Thomas Paine, Mar. 22, 1735-6.

Mary, and Lemuel Child, Sept. 20, 1768.

Mary, of Needham, and John Smith, jr., at Needham, July 19, 1781.

Mary, of Boston, and John W. Norris, int. June 12, 1847.

Nancy, and Seth Leonard, Apr. 12, 1807. c. R. 2.

Oliver, and Clarissa D. Stone of Dorchester, int. Nov. 23, 1834.

Richard, and Elisebeth Holbroke, May 22, 1679.

Richard, and Mary Kneland, Apr. 21, 1720.

Richard, and Sobiah Weeks, Feb. 3, 1737-8.

Sally, of Newton, and Timothy Randall, int. Mar. 22, 1840.

Sarah, and Harvey Chandler, Dec. 26, 1821.

Sarah, and Thomas Flynn, int. Sept. 7, 1846.

Sarah H., and William Barnes, Apr. 21, 1840.*

Warren, of Bennington, N. H., and Thankful V. Dyer, int. July 29, 1847.

William, and Almira Stevens, Aug. 11, 1839.*

William Demeritt, and Arackzien S. Brown of Pittston, Me., int. Mar. 17, 1844.

HALLAGAN (see also Houlahin), Catherine, and James McLaughlin, int. Apr. 30, 1849.

HALLET, Frances, d. George and Eliza, and Joseph Andrews, widr., a. 40 y., engraver, s. Ephraim and Lucy, of Hingham, May 19, 1847.*

Maria, a. 25 y., d. George and Eliza, and Joseph W. Balch, a. 26 y., merchant, s. Jos[eph] and Caroline A. B., June 8, 1846.*

HALLOWELL, Emily W., and Granville W. Wilson, May 18, 1838.*

Harriet, of Framingham, and Thomas Maccarty, Jan. 3, 1830.*

Luther, and Mary Jane Newell, May 16, 1824.

* Intention also recorded.

HALLOWELL, Nancy, of Framingham, and Capt. Daniel Atwood, int. May 13, 1821.

Susan G., and Levi P. Haskell, Mar. 30, 1848.

HALLY (see also Healey), Mary, and Patrick McOuliffe, int. May 5, 1849.

HAM (see also Hamm), Michael, of Dorchester, and Louisa Margaret Durst, int. Nov. 3, 1833.

Susanna, a. 20 y., d. John and Jerusha, and Thomas White, a. 21 y., ropemaker, s. William and Mary, Sept. 9, 1847.*

HAMBURG, Benedict, and Maria Jeres, int. Oct. 2, 1848.

HAMDEN, Ameriah, and Lucinda Knapp, int. May 15, 1825.

HAMILTON, Alvin, and Lenity G. Hamlin, Nov. 10, 1835.*

Caroline, of Dorchester, and George W. Pond, int. Sept. 13, 1829.

Edward, of Lincoln, a. 24 y., examiner of drugs, s. Luther and Delia, and Eliza P. Kendrick, a. 24 y., d. John and Eliza, Sept. 20, 1848.*

Eliza, a. 20 y., b. Ireland, and Thomas Cobain, a. 22 y., engineer, b. Ireland, s. William and Betsey, Dec. 27, 1849.*

HAMLET, Jonathan, and Abigail Bancroft, int. Nov. 24, 1822.

HAMLIN, Lenity G., and Alvin Hamilton, Nov. 10, 1835.*

HAMM (see also Ham), Maria, and George Phillipp, int. June 6, 1841.

HAMMER, Lewis, and Anna A. [M. int.] Hooper, June 12, 1845.*

HAMMOND, Alexander, and Rose Logan, Nov. 26, 1835.*

Andrew J., and Mary H. Burley, Oct. 20, 1844.*

Daniel and Sally Stoddard, Oct. 14, 1810.*

Eunice, and Peter Seaver, Feb. 15, 1758.

Hannah, of Cambridge, and Zacharias Shed, int. Oct. 30, 1791.

Hannah, and John Sayward Trott, Dec. 2, 1813.*

John, and Pamelia Caldwell, Nov. 23, 1823.

Joseph, of Newton, and Mary Gore, at Newton, Apr. 3, 1744.

Phineas [Hammon. int.], and Mary Gay, Dec. 29, 1782. c. R. 2.*

Stephen, and Sarah M. Haskell, ——, 1832. [Sept. 18, 1831. int.]*

* Intention also recorded.

HAMMOND, Thomas, and Mary Bacon, Aug. 8, 1705.
Thomas [of Newton. c. R. 2.], and Sarah Griffin, Dec. 30 [Feb. 30. c. R. 2.], 1714.

HAMPSON, Abram, and Ann Cumsky, int. Feb. 17, 1849.

HANAFORD (see also Hannaford), Lyman B., and Cynthia P. Goodwin of Kennebunkport, Me., int. Sept. 15, 1844.

HANCHETT, Sarah, and Isaac Perry, Apr. 21, 1715.

HANCOCK (see also Hencock), Ann, and William Brackett of Newton, Feb. 21, 1813.*
Belcher, Capt., and Nancy Ackers of Brookline, int. Sept. 30, 1787.
Henry Kellam, and Mary Ann Slack, int. Nov. 8, 1829.
Sarah [Mrs. int.], and Capt. Jonathan Carrel [Carriel, of Groton. int.], May 22, 1783.*
William, and Catharine Downer, int. June 24, 1838.

HAND, Elisabeth, and Robert Lenahan, int. Aug. 12, 1846.
Mary, and John Lenahan, int. Aug. 3, 1845.
William, and Mary Mahoney, int. Feb. 16, 1840.

HANKEY, Anthony, and Nancy B. Young, int. Nov. 17, 1846.
John, and Ferona Feigelly, int. Oct. 22, 1847.

HANNAFORD (see also Hanaford), William, and Betsey Knower, Nov. 21, 1802.*

HANNAGAN, Catherine, and Dennis Maloney, int. Apr. 30, 1849.
James, and Mary Cady, int. May 30, 1841.

HANNAN, Ann, and Barnard Gurly, int. July 3, 1842.

HANNDEN, Helen, of Wilmington, and James P. Morton, int. June 1, 1845.

HANNER, Mary, and Thomas Duffy, int. Apr. 14, 1844.

HANNING, Bridgett, and James Kelley, int. Nov. 6, 1848.
John, and Mary Glenning, int. Oct. 6, 1847.

HANON, Bridget, and Patrick Durfy, int. May 13, 1848.

HANSCOM (see also Hanscomb), Sarah Ann, and Ivory Mc-Daniel, —— 16, 1842.*

* Intention also recorded.

HANSCOMB (see also Hanscom), James S., and Nancy Bellowes [Bellows, of Boston. c. r. 3.], Dec. 25, 1833.*

HANSET, John, and Elizabeth Perry, Apr. 2, 1644.

HANSON, Calvin W., and Maria Prienty, int. Oct. 1, 1849.
Hannah, Mrs., and Frederic Stevens, Nov. 11, 1838.
John L., and Charlotte E. Kelley of Saco, Me., int. Mar. 15, 1840.
John L., and Rowena P. Hillard of Kennebunk, Me., int. Dec. 1, 1849.
Moses, and Mary F. Kelly [Kelley. int.], May 28, 1844.*

HARADON, Joseph, and Abig[ai]l Whitney, May 30, 1781. c. r. 2.

HARBITTLE, Dorothy, and Thomas Lambe, July 16, 1640.

HARDEN, William, and Abigail Davis, Dec. 4, 1780.

HARDING, John, of Newton, and Tamor Belson, int. Mar. 30, 1806.
Joseph, and Sarah Mastriss, Sept. 14, 1754.
Nancy, and Samuel Davis, Oct. 20, 1835.*
Sally, and Nathaniel Wight [resident. int.], Nov. 1, 1801. c. r. 2.*

HARDY, Phebe, wid., of Dedham, a. 50 y., housewife, and Nathaniel Owen, widr. of Dedham, a. 66 y., tin manufacturer, Apr. 16, 1846.

HARKNESS, John, and Sarah Curtice, Aug. 18, 1709.
Mary, and John Stone, May 11, 1733.
Mary, and Daniel Richards, Jan. 29, 1734-5.

HARLEY, Margarett, a. 21 y., d. David and Jennette, and Matthew Lindsay, carpet weaver, s. Matthew and Elizabeth, Feb. 4, 1848.*
Nancy, and Thomas Maude, June 8, 1849.*

HARLIN, Thomas, and Catherine Shorley, int. Sept. 13, 1848.

HARLOW, George D., and Sarah F. Martin, int. Nov. 10, 1844.
Joseph, and Sally A. Bates of Weymouth, int. Feb. 6, 1847.
Nathaniel B. 2d, and Lydia Dunham, both of Bridgewater, Nov. 30, 1848.

* Intention also recorded.

HARLOW, William H., and Mary G. Hawes of Dorchester, int. Apr. 15, 1838.

William H., and Catharine R. Hawes, Feb. 16, 1845.*

**HARMON,** Ivory, and Louisa M. Merrill, int. Sept. 5, 1841.

Rosannah L., a. 20 y., tailoress, d. Daniel and Loratisha, and James Cook, a. 23 y., carpenter, s. Thomas and Nancy, Apr. 20, 1845.*

**HARNDEN,** Henry, of Wilmington, and Mary Ann Leightner, int. Nov. 30, 1847.

**HARNEY,** Bridget, and John Kelly, int. May 5, 1849.

Catherine, and Thomas Pickley, int. Dec. 22, 1845.

Ellen, and John Higgins, int. Apr. 6, 1849.

James, and Bridget Doyle, int. July 9, 1843.

John, and Mary Grady, int. Apr. 25, 1841.

Maria, and Bernard Harrington, int. Apr. 8, 1838.

Michael, and Catharine Fallen, int. Apr. 7, 1839.

Rosannah, and Thomas Cunningham, int. Jan. 21, 1844.

Rose, and Nicholas Doonacon, int. July 16, 1843.

Thomas, and Bridget Claffy, int. May 16, 1841.

**HARPER,** James, of Brighton, and Judith Carter, int. Aug. 24, 1828.

Joseph, and Abigail Bragg, int. Sept. 8, 1833.

**HARRIMAN,** Charles, and Sylvia Burrows, int. Aug. 17, 1834.

**HARRINGTON** (see also Herrington), Ann M., and George Hill, ——, 1833. [Aug. 19, 1832. int.]*

Bernard, and Maria Harney, int. Apr. 8, 1838.

Eben[eze]r, and Patience Denio, int. Aug. 14, 1808.

Ellen, and Thomas Spelman, int. Mar. 1, 1848.

Francis D., and Harriet P. Sharp of Watertown, Feb. 20, 1844.

George W., and Elizabeth Smith, int. June 26, 1831.

George W., and Lucy S. Harris, Feb. 24, 1833.*

James, and Margaret Miley, int. May 28, 1843.

Joseph, Esq., and Rebecca Smith, May 13, 1812.*

Leonard B., of Salem, and Margaret G. Hersey, int. Dec. 26, 1830.

Lucretia O., and Eliphalet Baker, Jan. 1, 1834.*

Mary, and Michael Hynds, int. June 20, 1848.

Mary, and Martin Rigney, int. June 26, 1848.

* Intention also recorded.

HARRINGTON, Polly, Mrs., and Dea. Jeremiah Wiswall of Newton, int. Dec. 17, 1809.

Sarah S. [B. int.], of Lexington, and Conrad H. Rosemeyer, Nov. 29, 1838.*

Stephen, and Mrs. Nancy Bruce, Apr. 18, 1804.*

**HARRIS** (see also Harriss), Abigail, of Brookline, and Isaiah Whiting, Feb. —, 1759.

Abigail, and Benjamin Meriam, Nov. 24, 1816.*

Betsey, of Stoughton, and John Decoster, int. Sept. 15, 1805.

Charlotte, and Hackabath [Hackaliah. int.] Chamberlain, Dec. 24, 1801.*

Charlotte, and Jesse Savage, int. Dec. 3, 1815.

Daniel, of Dudley, and Elizabeth Bridge, June 20, 1745.

Hannah, of Brookline, and Elijah Child, int. Feb. 2, 1783.

Hezekiah B., and Phebe Ann Churchill, Aug. 25, 1834.

James, a. 21 y., carpenter, s. John and Elizabeth, and Harriet L. Callender, a. 20 y., d. Joseph and Mary, Dec. 27, 1846.*

Jane N., and George J. Blaisdell, Apr. 27, 1841.*

John, jr., a. 24 y., painter, s. John and Elizabeth, and Mary Rhoades, a. 18 y., d. Daniel and Louisa, Jan. 2, 1848.*

Joseph, of Brookline, and Rebecca Adams, at Boston, June 10, 1731.

Lucy S., and George W. Harrington, Feb. 24, 1833.*

Matthew, and Elizabeth M. Fall of Ossipee, N. H., int. Feb. 15, 1846.

Mehitable, and Stephen Walker [of Rehoboth. c. r. 2.], July 20, 1738.

Robart, and Elizabeth Boffee, Jan. 24, 1642.

Sally, and Richard Potter, Sept. 15, 1808.*

Samuel, and Mary Andress [Andross. c. r. 3.], Nov. 11, 1753.

Sarah, Mrs., of Brooklyn, and John Hooper, Mar. 4, 1730-31.

William, a. 24 y., carpenter, s. John and Elizabeth, and Lucy Ann Rhoades, a. 20 y., June 20, 1847.*

William, and Joanna Cotter, int. Aug. 2, 1848.

**HARRISON,** Bridget, and John Gavin, int. June 11, 1837.

Hannah, and John Bancroft, int. Nov. 27, 1836.

Lucy, and Alexander C. Gibson, int. Feb. 22, 1835.

Patrick, and Bridget Havey, int. June 11, 1845.

* Intention also recorded.

**HARRISS** (see also Harris), Abigail, and Benjamin Craft, Jan. 10, 1704-5.

Daniel, s. Robert, and Johanna Brewer, Nov. 14, 1682.

Mary, and Isaac Johnson, jr., Oct. 26, 1669.

**HARROD,** Sarah A., of Dorchester, and George Rexford, at Dorchester, Apr. 28, 1842.

**HARS,** Mary, of Boston, and Timothy Fitzgerald, int. Nov. 13, 1846.

**HART** (see also Hartt), Ann, and James Spear, Apr. 27, 1845.*

Daniel, and Margaret O'Kryan, int. Sept. 22, 1844.

Nath[anie]l, of Dublin, N. H., and Clarissa Hill, int. Mar. 6, 1825.

**HARTIGAN,** Mary, and James Galagher, int. July 8, 1838.

**HARTSHORN,** (see also Hartshorne), Caroline, and William H. Spooner, Dec. 6, 1821.*

Charles P., and Lucinda J. Morse of Dedham, int. Dec. 18, 1836.

Esther, of Boylston, and Elisha Fuller, int. Dec. 13, 1812.

Jason, and Mrs. Olive Ellis of Dedham, int. Mar. 30, 1817.

John, and Mary Mann of Randolph, int. Nov. 6, 1808.

Mary Ellis, and Joseph Curtis, jr., Sept. 25, 1825.*

Warren, and Hannah Billings of Sharon, int. Nov. 17, 1805.

**HARTSHORNE** (see also Hartshorn), Hezekiah [Keziah Hartshorn. c. r. 3.], and Joseph Hewins [jr. c. r. 3.] of Sharon, Mar. 31, 1811.*

**HARTT** (see also Hart), Lucy, Mrs., and David Hall, int. Sept. 3, 1844.

**HARTWELL,** John Walker, widr., of Cincinnati, Ohio, a. 34 y., underwriter, s. Jonathan and Elizabeth B., and Elizabeth T. Oliver, a. 19 y., d. Nathaniel K. Greenwood and Anne Oliver, Feb. 18, 1847.*

Joseph, and Mary Fuller, Jan. 13, 1799.*

**HARVEY** (see also Harvy), Abigail G., and Charles Cole, May 15, 1831.*

Catherine, and Joseph H. Barden, Dec. 25, 1848.*

* Intention also recorded.

HARVEY, Hannah H., and Thomas Smith of Dedham, int. Nov. 27, 1831.

Lydia M., and John N. Tileston of Dorchester, int. Mar. 20, 1842.

Mary, and George B. Howard, Apr. 14, 1834. [1833. c. r. 2.]*

Samuel, and Catharine Herring [Hering. int.], Jan. 5, 1806. c. r. 2.*

Sarah, of Lowell, and Charles R. Kelton, int. Jan. 31, 1830.

Susan F., and James Webber, Apr. 20, 1837. c. r. 7.

Susan F., and George Lindall, int. Mar. 12, 1843.

William, and Sally Cain, Oct. 6, 1811. c. r. 2.*

William, and Eliza B. Holt, Dec. 7, 1845. c. r. 7.*

**HARVY** (see also Harvey), Sally A., and Ebben W. Whittemore, int. Mar. 18, 1838.

**HASE** (see also Hayes), Allas, and Thomas Hurly, int. Aug. 13, 1846.

Dennis, and Ann McClarc, int. Apr. 14, 1844.

Washington E., of Dover, N. H., a. 21 y., machinist, and Abigail Amanda Read, a. 17 y., d. Richard W. and Lois, June 8, 1846.*

**HASKELL,** Catherine P., and Charles Bicknell, int. May 22, 1825.

Levi P., and Susan G. Hallowell, Mar. 30, 1848.

Lydia, and Alexander Mitchell, May 1, 1830.

Sarah M., and Stephen Hammond, ——, 1832. [Sept. 18, 1831. int.]*

William, and Marilla P. Starkweather of Walpole, N. H., int. Aug. 25, 1844.

**HASKINS,** Jane, and George Stacy, int. Mar. 25, 1827.

Rebecca G., a. 24 y., d. Ralph and Rebecca G., and Charles C[offin. int.] Jewett of Providence, R. I., a. 32 y., professor, s. Paul and Eleanor P., Apr. 5, 1848.*

**HASLETT,** William W., of Claremont, N. H., and Mary W. [M. c. r. 3.] Wales, Oct. 6, 1814.*

**HASLIN,** Thomas, and Maria Stanton, int. July 16, 1846.

**HASSAM,** Johathan, widr., of Manchester, N. H., a. 64 y., gentleman, and Mary Smith, a. 56 y., d. Daniel E. and Lydia Proctor, Jan. 24, 1849.*

* Intention also recorded.

**HASSARD,** Thomas, of Baltimore, and Augusta P. Greene, int. Nov. 1, 1835.

**HASSION,** Margarett, b. Ireland, and Patrick Killard, b. Ireland, July 25, 1849.*

**HASSOLD,** John, and Johannah Woessner, int. May 5, 1844.

**HASTINGS,** Bridget, and Thomas Moracy, int. Jan. 13, 1849.
Charles F., and Eliza Paine, int. July 11, 1824.
Esther, resident, and Joseph Learned, int. Feb. 20, 1803.
Fanny L., and John L. [J. L. int.] Stanton, Mar. 30, 1845.*
Hannah K., and Henry Frost, int. Oct. 5, 1845.
Jacob, of Boston, and Sarah H. Weld, Jan. 26, 1804.*
John I., and Mary B. Scott, int. Nov. 1, 1835.
Joseph, and Sarah Ann B. Morey, int. Dec. 16, 1838.
Joseph, and Melinda Livermore, Sept. 13, 1812.*
Mary, of Marlborough, N. H., and John McElory, Mar. 13, 1823.*
Mary Ann, of Brighton, and Joseph Arnold, jr., int. Mar. 3, 1833.
Mary Jane, and Francis A. Newton, Mar. 6, 1845.
Michael, and Bridget Burk, int. Feb. 10, 1849.
Nathaniel W., and Susan C. Danforth, Nov. 4, 1843.*
Thomas, and Prudence Trott of Dorchester, at Dorchester, Feb. 11, 1761.
Thomas, and Maria Robbins of Brighton, int. Nov. 7, 1813.

**HASWELL,** Mary, Mrs., and John Lemist, int. Apr. 21, 1816.
Mary, and George Murdock [of Boston. c. r. 3.], May 20, 1819.*
Rebecca Cordia, and John Jones Clarke, Esq., May 25, 1830.*

**HATCH,** Cyrus M., a. 23 y., carpenter, s. John and Naomi, and Lydia P. Littlefield, a. 21 y., d. Oliver and Comfort, June 18, 1846.*
Edward, and Rhoda A. Danforth, int. Feb. 6, 1842.
Edwin, of Acton, and Margarett J. W. Fuller, May 11, 1845.*
Elisabeth Ann, and Benjamin Blagge, int. Aug. 6, 1815.
Ellen Mary [Maria M. int.], and Alexander Hamilton Gibbs [of Boston. c. r. 3.], Nov. 25, 1816.*
Henry, and Nancy Seaverns, Dec. 10, 1816.*
John, and Martha Ann Davis, int. Sept. 22, 1844.
Josephine Augusta, and Isaac Waters, May 29, 1815.*
Mary, and Eleazer Weld, at Boston, Apr. 23, 1761.

* Intention also recorded.

HATCH, Thankful H., of Dorchester, and Benjamin Capen.
Apr. 24, 1827.
Thomas, and Eliza Hersey, int. May 13, 1821.

HATE, Caroline, a. 30 y., and Job Davis, a. 35 y., laborer,
s. Eben and Mary, Mar. 14, 1848.*

HATHAWAY, Elisha, and Nancy Davis, Sept. 6, 1801.*
Elisha, and Mrs. Susannah Richardson, June 1, 1814.*

HATTAN (see also Hatton), William, and Rhoda Dean, int.
Mar. 4, 1832.

HATTON (see also Hattan), Mary, and Horatio N. Bragg,
int. July 29, 1832.

HAUS (see also Hawes), Mehittabel, of Dedham, and John
Aldeft, at Dedham, May 15, 1733.

HAVEN, Ann Shapley, of Philadelphia, and Supply Clap
Thwing, at Philadelphia, June 30, 1847. P. R. 1.
Juliet, and Daniel Fuller, int. Apr. 6, 1823.
Mary ,wid., a. 50 y., d. Andrew Cunningham, and Horatio
Leonard, widr. of Raynham, a. 60 y., gentleman, June
1, 1847.*
Moses, and Sophia Haven of Hopkinton, int. Sept. 20, 1807.
Sarah A. [Susan A. int.], and Charles B. Pevear, Jan. 1, 1845.*
Sophia, of Hopkinton, and Moses Haven, int. Sept. 20, 1807.

HAVERTY, John, and Bridget Mahon, int. Nov. 3, 1844.

HAVEY, Bridget, and Patrick Harrison, int. June 11, 1845.
Ellen, and John McDonald, int. Jan. 22, 1847.
Patrick, and Penney Marden, int. Sept. 20, 1845.
Thomas, and Catherine Huges of Boston, int. June 20, 1846.

HAVILAND, Thomas Philip [of Boston. int.], a. 22 y., clerk,
s. Thomas and Mary, and Kate Robinson [Robertson.
int.], a. 19 y., d. Andrew and Harriet, May 12, 1847.*

HAWES (see also Haus, Haws), Ann, Mrs., and John Clap,
May 22, 1823.*
Benjamin, and Mary Pilsbury Shannon, Nov. 6, 1814.*
Catharine R., and William H. Harlow, Feb. 16, 1845.*
Charlotte, of Canton, and Stephen Goddard, int. Sept. 25,
1801.

* Intention also recorded.

HAWES, Elisha, of Stoughton, and Hannah A. Tucker, int. Jan. 1, 1837.
Joanna, and Isaac Bradley, both residents, June 11, 1789.*
John, and Elisabeth L. Vose of Dorchester, int. Jan. 23, 1814.
John H., and Achsah Barber of Medway, int. Nov. 16, 1806.
Julia Ann, and Franklin Procter, Dec. 31, 1843.*
Maria Anna, and Otis Stevens, int. July 30, 1843.
Mary, and Reuben Randall, Apr. 22, 1813.*
Mary G., of Dorchester, and William H. Harlow, int. Apr. 15, 1838.
Sally, and David Burt, Feb. 23, 1812.*
Sarah, and William Bosson, Jan. 24, 1771.
Williard [Willard. int.], and Susan M. Withington, Jan. 24, 1844.*

HAWKINS, Lewis B., and Martha S. W. Sinclair, int. July 3, 1842.
Rebecah, and John Stebens, June 4, 1680.

HAWKS, James, and Louisa Travis of Natick, int. Mar. 2, 1828.

HAWLEY, Thomas, and Dorithy Lamb, Feb. 2, 1651.

HAWS (see also Hawes), Benjamin, and Elisabeth Holbrook, Dec. 3, 1770.
Jerimiah [Jeremiah. int.], and Anna Sanderson [Saunderson int.] of Weston, at Weston, Dec. 16, 1794.*
Josiah, of Needham, and Mary Smith, Aug. 27, 1740.
Lucy, and Ens. John Baker, Jan. 8, 1775.
Sarah, and Seth Clap, both of Dorchester, Sept. 10, 1793.
Zach [ens, of Dedham. c. R. 2.], and Mary Smith, Nov. 1, 1753.

HAY (see also Hayes), Henry W., and Catherine Shackley of Dracut, int. June 15, 1848.
Joseph, and Bathsheba Whiting, Apr. 4, 1815. c. R. 2.*
Joseph, and Lucy Whiting, int. Oct. 10, 1841.

HAYCLE, Mary, and Joseph Baker, July 14, 1822.*

HAYDEN, Elijah, of Quincy, and Nancy Croxford, int. Mar. 16, 1806.
John, and Judith Cole, Nov. 2, 1797.*
John, of Cambridge, and Abigail Crafts, July 10, 1811.*

* Intention also recorded.

HAYDEN, Hannah, and Henry Orcutt, Apr. 21, 1818.*

Harriet, and Oliver Blake, int. Apr. 5, 1835.

Louisa, and Simon F. Marshall, May 14, 1842.*

Sally Ruggles, of Quincy, and Nathaniel Scott, jr., int. June 23, 1793.

Sarah E., and Royal J. Barlow, Aug. 12, 1838.*

**HAYES** (see also Hase, Hay, Hays), Alvin, and Charlotte A. Carter, int. Mar. 22, 1849.

Andrew, and Caroline Gowell, int. Dec. 12, 1841.

Andrew C., and Abigail Rice Johnson, int. Aug. 10, 1834.

Ann, and Moses Chamberlain, Jan. 7, 1845.*

Augustus A., and Henrietta B. Dana of Marblehead, int. June 26, 1836.

Benjamin, a. 32 y., carpenter, s. John and Elizabeth of Nova Scotia, and Maria Reynolds, a. 23 y., d. Stephen and Mary, Aug. 13, 1846.*

Henry, and Lydia Pierce of Milton, int. Aug. 4, 1811.

James, and Hannah O'Bryan, int. Aug. 25, 1844.

John, and Maria Griswold of Walpole, int. Oct. 24, 1841.

John J. [I. int.], and Rebecca L. Tyler, Nov. 16, 1845.*

Joshua, and Martha W. Richards, Nov. 13, 1836.*

Thomas M., of Haverhill, and Sarah K. Bartlett, Jan. 16, 1844.*

**HAYFORD,** Melvina F., and Oscar E. Little, int. May 12, 1844.

Riley, and Harriot Dana, int. Nov. 10, 1822.

**HAYNES,** Benjamin, and Ruthy Porter, int. Dec. 15, 1793.

Benjamin, of Charlestown, and Betsy Hunting, int. Nov. 3, 1811.

Clark L., of Brookline, and Ann Pierce, int. Mar. 15, 1835.

Hannah, of Charlestown, and Abraham Rice, int. Sept. 27, 1818.

Harriet, and John Stevens, jr., int. Nov. 11, 1838.

Maria, and Independence W. Gorton, Apr. 30, 1826.*

Mary, of Sudbury, and Seth Lawrence, int. Apr. 14, 1800.

Mary H., and Willard A. Humphrey, June 6, 1830.*

Nathan, and Elizabeth H. Towne, int. Jan. 25, 1846.

Ophin [Opher. int.], and Harriot Mallard, Dec. 23, 1810.*

Peter, and Sally Rice of Sudbury, int. Feb. 8, 1807.

Sally, and Reuben Hunting, June 8, 1818.*

Sarah, and Benjamin F. James, Aug. 29, 1841.*

* Intention also recorded.

HAYNES, Sarah M., and John Clark, jr., both of Framingham, Nov. 19, 1848.

Susan M., and Josiah M. Russell, May 28, 1843.*

HAYS (see also Hayés), Mary, and James Foley, int. Dec. 25, 1847.

HAYT (see also Hoyt), Charles, and Sally Sampson, Sept. 23, 1807.*

HAYWARD, Caleb, and Martha Cotton, Dec. 9, 1773.

Elizabeth, and George Dove, Nov. 30, 1823.*

John, and Experience Peirpont, 12 : 12 m : 1678.

John, of Dublin, N. H., and Elizabeth C. Seaver, July 3, 1823.*

Lucy C., and Samuel J. Taft, int. Jan. 2, 1831.

Sally, and Joseph Stratton, June 21, 1801.*

Sukey, and Andrew Newman, Feb. 12, 1804.*

HAZELTINE (see also Hazelton, Heseltine), Merrill J., of Barnet, Vt., and Abigail S. Knights, int. Sept. 6, 1849.

HAZELTON (see also Hazeltine), George, and Ann Miller, Nov. 25, 1848.*

HAZELWOOD, Eliza, and Otis Ayers, Dec. 24, 1835.*

HAZEN, Enoch, of Rowley, and Martha Thompson, Feb. 9, 1797.*

Mary Ann, of Boston, and Rev. E. F. Slafter, int. July 24, 1849.

HAZLET (see also Hazlett), William, and Eliza Kingsbury, residents, Feb. 9, 1803.*

HAZLETT (see also Hazlet), Avis, and John Brooks, Oct. 5, 1823.*

Elizabeth, and Albert S. Burlingame of Brighton, int. Sept. 26, 1830.

William, and Sarah Walker, July 27, 1818.*

HEAD, George S., a. 24 y., mason, s. Richard and Abigail, and Susan B. Chase of Stratham, N. H., a. 20 y., d. Andrew and Sarah, Apr. 23, 1848.*

John, of Haverhill, and Laura Wyman, int. Mar. 8, 1835.

* Intention also recorded.

HEAD, Richard, and Abigail Hill, Dec. 27, 1821.*
Sarah A., a. 19 y., and Charles M. Clark, a. 21 y., laborer, s.
    Ezra and Amanda, of Amherst, N. H., Jan. 7, 1847.*

HEALD, Calvin, and Mary C. Ward, July 25, 1830.*

HEALEY (see also Haley, Hally, Healy, Heley), John, and
    Jemima Davis, Sept. 8, 1761.
Joshua, of Newton, and Sarah Daviss, June 21, 1722.
Margaret, Mrs., and Noah Perrin, Oct. 6, 1731.
Nehemiah, and Sarah Herring, Dec. 1, 1772.

HEALY (see also Healey), Bernard, and Margaret Mooney,
    int. May 18, 1845.
Ebenezer [of Newton. c. r. 2.], and Rachel Whiteing, Apr.
    20, 1715.
Hannah, of Newton, and Aaron Gay, at Newton, May 17,
    1753.
Jane, and Patrick Toule, int. Dec. 14, 1847.
John, and Hanah Davis, July 29, 1725.
Maurice, and Hannah Ryan, int. Feb. 17, 1848.
Thomas, and Mary Manahan, int. Nov. 17, 1844.

HEARSEY (see also Hersey), Ebeneser, and Nancy Brown
    Fairbrother, Apr. 6, 1815.*
Harriet, and Joshua Batchelder, int. Dec. 12, 1824.
Jane, and Robert P. [V. int.] Smith, Nov. 27, 1808. c. r. 3.*
Stephen, of Milton, and Jerusha Wares, Apr. 14, 1793.*
Tamien [Tamcien. int; Tamsen. c. r. 3.] Eliza [Hersey. c. r.
    3.], and Amos Smith Larrison [Larison. c. r. 3.], Oct.
    9, 1814.*
Zerubbabel, and Nancy Crafts, Sept. 21, 1820.*

HEATH (see also Haith), Anna, and Francis Youngman, Dec.
    2, 1685.
Anna, and Jonathan Seaver, Dec. 12, 1732.
Anna, and Isaac Curtis, Nov. 15, 1758.
Dan W., of Wrentham, and Lucy Ann Morse of Dedham,
    June 20, 1837. c. r. 7.
Ebenezer, of Brookline, and Hannah Williams, Jan. 11, 1791.*
Elizabeth, and John Bowles, Apr. 2, 1649.
Elizabeth, and James Noble, Esq., May 22, 1760.
Elizabeth, and Benjamin Weld, June 12, 1796.*
Hanah, and James Clarke, Apr. 27, 1681.

* Intention also recorded.

HEATH, Hannah, and Capt. John Giles of Brunswick, Nov. 6, 1721. [Feb. 6. C. R. 2.]

Hannah, and Samuel Gore, Feb. 15, 1770.

Isaac, s. Isaac, and Anna Fisher, Feb. 2, 1680.

Isaack, jr., and Mary Davis, Dec. 16, 1650.

John, and Susannah Craft, Jan. 12, 1758.

John, and Caroline Cory of Braintree, int. Jan. 14, 1827.

Joseph, and Christian Bridge, at Boston, June 18, 1732.

Joseph, Esq., and Mrs. Elizabeth Ruggles, June 9, 1743.

Joseph, and Rebeckah Cheney, Dec. 2, 1747.

Joseph, and Mary Newell, Nov. 29, 1774.

Joseph, and Naomi Vose of Milton, at Milton, Dec. 18, 1798.*

Joseph, and Hannah [Mrs. Sarah. int.] Murdock, Sept. 3, 1811. C. R. 2.*

Lucy, and William Seaver, jr., Dec. 1, 1796.*

Margarett, and Ebenezer Sever, Dec. 2 [12. C. R. 2.], 1714.

Mary, and Thomas Mayo [Nov. 15. C. R. 2.], 1749.

Mathew, and George Brand, July 24, 1643.

Peleg, and Patience Curtis, Dec. 22, 1768.

Peleg, jr., and Peggy Davenport of Milton, int. Nov. 1, 1807.

Polly S., Mrs., and Dearborn Blake, July 21, 1824.*

Prudence, and Ebenezer Richards, May 12, 1743. C. R. 2.

Salley [Sarah. int.], Mrs., and Maj. [Capt. int.] John Jones Spooner, Nov. 25, 1783.*

Sally, and Elisha Whitney, jr., Feb. 26, 1804. C. R. 2.*

Sally, and Isaac Curtis, Feb. 27, 1805.*

Sam[ue]l, and Mary Draper, Dec. 3, 1767.

Samuel [jr. int.], and Mrs. Nancy [Anne. int.] Greaton, Feb. 3, 1784.*

Samuell, and Elizabeth Payson, Dec. 3, 1733.

Sarah, and Capt. Nehemiah D. Williams, Dec 14, 1815.*

Sarah, and Joseph P. Shaw, ——, 1833. [Sept. 9, 1832. int.]*

Sarah E., and David A. Hills of [Westminster. int.], Vt., Dec. 19, 1839.*

Stephen [Hath, of Boston. int.], a. 24 y., carpenter, s. Timothy and Susan, and Susan B. Randall, a. 24 y., d. John and Sarah, June 18, 1846.*

Susanna, and Henry Bowen, Apr. 14, 1685.

Susanna, and Isaac Gardiner [of Brookline. C. R. 2.], June 3, 1715.

Susanna, and [Capt. int.] Benjamin Rich, [mariner. int.], resident, Mar. 31, 1800.*

* Intention also recorded.

HEATH, William, and Hannah Weld, Nov. 11, 1685.
William, and Prudence Bridge, Apr. 24, 1716.
William, and Prudence Williams, Oct. 20, 1748.
William, and Abigail Davis, Jan. 28, 1779.
William, jr., and Elizabeth Spooner, June 18, 1789.*
William, jr., and Polly S. Davis, Dec. 26, 1816.*

**HEAVY,** Bridget, and Lawrence Corbut, int. Apr. 24, 1842.

**HEEGAN,** Sabanna, and Patrick Timens, int. July 3, 1847.

**HEFRAN,** Margaret, and Morris Clancey, int. May 12, 1849.

**HELEY** (see also Healey), Aaron, and Mary Griggs, June 16, 1766.
Rachel, and John Adams [of Wrentham. c. r. 2.], Nov. 15, 1739.
Samuel, and Abigail George, June 6, 1744.
Sarah, and Pelatiah Lyon, May 27, 1760.

**HEMENWAY** (see also Hemingway), Joshuea, and Johannah Evens, Jan. 16, 1667.
Moses, and Louisa Drew, int. June 19, 1842.

**HEMINGWAY** (see also Hemenway, Henngway), Elizabeth, and Jeremiah Rogers, Jan. 7, 1702-3.
Elizabeth, and Isaac Stanhope, Feb. 15, 1703-4.
Ichabod, and Margaret Brown, Dec. 10, 1702.
Joanna, and Edward Ainsworth, Jan. 11, 1687-8.
Joshua, and Elizabeth Weeks, Apr. 5, 1704.
Thankfull, and Jacob Parker, May 3, 1687.

**HENCOCK** (see also Hancock), Paul, and Mrs. Sarah Davis, May 23, 1771.

**HENDEE,** Charles [J. int.], and Adeline Davis, Aug. 30, 1836.*

**HENDERSON,** Elizabeth Ann, and Benjamin Robbins, int. May 29, 1842.
John, jr., of St. Louis, Mo., a. 26 y., attorney at law, s. John and Theodoria, and Catharine Leland, a. 28 y., d. Sherman and Elizabeth [Betsey Adams. p. r. 4.], June 30, 1847.*

* Intention also recorded.

HENDERSON, Mary Ann, of Dover, N. H., and Peter R. Corson, May 29, 1838.*

Nathan, and Mrs. Lydia Bodge, Feb. 21, 1802.*

**HENDLEY,** Sarah W., and John S. Foster, int. Sept. 17, 1837.

**HENERY** (see also Henry), Nancy [Hennery. int.], and Jesse Blake, June 2, 1844.*

**HENESY** (see also Hennessy), Patrick, and Catherine Dwyre, int. Oct. 30, 1847.

**HENNESSY** (see also Henesy, Hennicy), Ann [Hennesssey. int.], b. Ireland, and John [Stephen. int.] B. Wing, b. Ireland, Oct. 11, 1849.*

Margarett, b. Ireland, and Michael Brodders [Broaders. int.], b. Ireland, Aug. 3, 1849.*

**HENNGWAY** (see also Hemingway), Ralph, and Elizabeth Hewes, July 5, 1634.

**HENNICY** (see also Hennessy), Catherine, and Michael Quigley, int. June 3, 1848.

**HENRY** (see also Henery), Harriet M., a. 19 y., d. Jon[atha]n and Mary, and Henry S. Whittemore, a. 27 y., stonelayer, s. Michael, jr. and Betsey, Dec. 8, 1848.*

Mary G., a. 27 y., d. Jona[than] and Mary, and John Rice, jr. of Cambridge, a. 26 y., organ pipe maker, s. John and Freelove, Jan. 31, 1848.*

Winnefred, and Thomas Dolan, int. July 21, 1844.

**HENSHAW,** Elizabeth, and Henery [Rev. Henry. int.] H. F. Sweet [of Palmer. int.], Jan. 18, 1826. c. r. 2.*

John, and Sarah Corey, Aug. 12, 1790.*

Sarah, and John T. Whittemore, int. Aug. 18, 1844.

**HERBERT,** Susan, of Portland, Me., and George Ferguson, int. June 11, 1847.

**HERING** (see also Herring), James, and Sarah Curtiss, June 14, 1722.

John M. A., and Mary Ann Gay, int. Aug. 2, 1849.

**HERR,** Francis A., and Cecilia Canck, int. Jan. 27, 1849.

**HERRING** (see also Hering), Catharine [Hering. int.], and Samuel Harvey, Jan. 5, 1806. c. r. 2.*

* Intention also recorded.

HERRING, Daniel, and Susannah W. Fowler, Apr. 23, 1828.*

Elizabeth, and Ephraim Goodnough, Mar. 6, 1796.*

Ezra T., and Frances L. Stevens, Oct. 1, 1843.*

Harriet [Herring. int.], and David Fuller, Feb. 13, 1820. c. r. 2.*

James, and Ann Lewis of Dorchester, at Dorchester, Aug. 11, 1725.

James, and Mary Eaton of Dedham, at Dedham, Apr. 12, 1733.

James, jr., and Thankful Perry, June 17, 1767.

Jesse [Jessee. int], and Hannah Whitney, May 13, 1798. c. r. 2.*

John, and Mary Fouracress, resident, Nov. 24, 1774.

Lydia, and Gersham Crocker, Nov. 14, 1802. c. r. 2.*

Mary, of Dedham, and John Lyon, Apr. 16, 1724.

Mary, and David Stone [of Newton. c. r. 2.], Feb. 13, 1755.

Mary, and Alden Jones, Mar. 6, 1796.*

Nancy, and Thaddeus Smith, at Dedham, Oct. 2, 1796.*

Polly, and Abraham Gipson of Burlington, July —, 1806.*

Sally, and Edward Richards [Richard. int.], Nov. 5, 1798. c. r. 2.*

Sarah, and Nehemiah Healey, Dec. 1, 1772.

Wyatt, and Susanna Austin, Oct. 5, 1794.*

**HERRINGTON** (see also Harrington), Hannah, and Isaiah Coolige, Mar. 27, 1759.

**HERSEY** (see also Hearsey), Charles S. [Hearsey. c. r. 3.], and Sally G. Coney, Jan. 24, 1828.*

Eliza, and Thomas Hatch, int. May 13, 1821.

Hannah W., and Frederick F. Thayer, int. Nov. 20, 1842.

Joseph, of Providence, and Sarah A. Hersey, int. Nov. 20, 1836.

Margaret G., and Leonard B. Harrington of Salem, int. Dec. 26, 1830.

Mary Ann G., a. 34 y., d. Zerubbabel and Betsey, and Levi Levitt of Hull, a. 38 y., gentleman, May 28, 1846.*

Samuel M., and Harriot Ames, int. Nov. 23, 1828.

Sarah A., and Joseph Hersey of Providence, int. Nov. 20, 1836.

Sarah Elizabeth, and Benjamin Callender, int. May 24, 1835.

Sears, and Mrs. Ann Chittenden, Apr. 15, 1827.*

**HESELTINE** (see also Hazeltine), Jeremiah, and Mariah Prince, Mar. 27, 1836.

* Intention also recorded.

**HESILRIGE,** Hannah, and Rev. Thomas Abbot, July 18, 1776.

**HETLER,** Emeline, and George H. L. Rehm, int. Nov. 9, 1849.

**HEWENS** (see also Hewins), Sarah H., and George T. Raynolds, int. Mar. 31, 1839.

**HEWES** (see also Hews), Elizabeth, and Ralph Henngway, July 5, 1634.
George, and Mrs. Abigail Seaver, Nov. 14, 1728.
James E., and Elizabeth Bradlee, Mar. 30, 1828.*
John, and Catherine Bird, Sept. 8, 1848.
Josuah [Hues. c. r. 1.], and Mary Goldston [Gould. c. r. 1.], Oct. 8, 1634.
Lucy Ann, and George Coffin Richards, Dec. 24, 1847.*
Mary Ann [Hewse int.], a. 21 y., and Thomas T. Mason, jr., a. 22 y., upholsterer, s. Thomas and Mary T., Apr. 30, 1848.*
Mary Harriet, of Dorchester, and Edmund Jackson, int. Oct. 22, 1826.
Phebe, and Richard Goard, Nov. 30, 1639.
Thomas, and Mary Collins, int. Jan. 5, 1848.

**HEWET** (see also Hewett), Margaret, and Jonathan Stowell of Newton, Mar. 6, 1722-3.

**HEWETT** (see also Hewet, Hewit), Lloyd, and Margarett Hussey, Mar. 20, 1836.*

**HEWINS** (see also Hewens), Joseph [jr. c. r. 3.], of Sharon, and Hezekiah [Keziah. c. r. 3.] Hartshorne, Mar. 31, 1811.*
Mary, of Sharon, and George W. Johnson, int. Dec. 3, 1843.

**HEWIT** (see also Hewett), John, and Margaret Searl, Oct. 31, 1735.

**HEWS** (see also Hewes), Susan, and John Gilmore, int. Oct. 19, 1849.

**HICKEY** (see also Hickory), James, and Catharine Gateley, int. Jan. 3, 1830.
M. Anna, and Robert W. Amazeen, int. June 12, 1847.
Mary, and Joseph Sawyer, int. Dec. 4, 1849.

* Intention also recorded.

HICKEY, Michael, and Eliza Day, int. May 23, 1848.

Michael, and Mary Donahoe, int. Jan. 8, 1849.

**HICKLING,** Eliza E., and Charles F. Bradford, Nov. 15, 1843.*

Mary, and W[illia]m B. Dorr, Sept. 15, 1834.*

**HICKORY** (see also Hickey), Michael, and Catherine Gallagher, int. Aug. 26, 1846.

**HICKS,** Barrington, and Mary B. Page, int. Nov. 6, 1836.

Elias, of Rehoboth, and Eliza Weatherspoon, int. Sept. 9, 1821.

John, and Mrs. Rebecca Whittemore, int. Oct. 6, 1822.

William E., of Charlestown, and Harriet Fletcher, July 21, 1844.*

**HIDE** (see also Hyde), Amos, and Susannah Foster, Apr. 4, 1765.

Enock, and Mary Dorr, Apr. 29, 1772.

Mary, and Caleb Watson, Dec. 15, 1665.

Oliver, and [Mrs. int.] Hannah Whitten [Witing, both residents. int.], at Dorchester, Oct. 14, 1800.*

Timothy, of Newton, and Rebecca Davis, at Boston, Aug. 14, 1718.

**HIGGENS** (see also Higgins), Elizabeth, of Walpole, and Jabez Man, at Walpole, Mar. 2, 1778.

**HIGGINS** (see also Higgens), John, and Ellen Harney, int. Apr. 6, 1849.

Mary, and John McCarty [McCarthy. dup.], int. Dec. 28, 1845.*

**HIGNEY,** Mary, and James Coyle, int. May 9, 1849.

**HILBERT,** Athone, and Henrietta Kuhn, Dec. 25, 1838.*

**HILER** (see also Hiller), Matthias, and [Mrs. int.] Catharine Davis, July 31, 1785.*

**HILL** (see also Hills), Abagail, of Cambridge, and Edward Bradbury, int. Sept. 16, 1804.

Abigail, and Richard Head, Dec. 27, 1821.*

Caroline, and Patrick Wright [Jan. 20. int.], 1833.*

Charles, and Caroline L. Whitney of Quincy, int. July 21, 1833.

* Intention also recorded.

HILL, Clarissa, and Nath[anie]l Hart of Dublin, N. H., int. Mar. 6, 1825.

Eliza, and Marshall Floyd, Mar. 26, 1818.*

George, and Ann M. Harrington, ——, 1833. [Aug. 19, 1832. int.]*

J. Bryant, and Eleanor Gowith, int. Sept. 17, 1843.

Joanna C., of Waterborough, Me., and Nahum Smith, int. Oct. 16, 1847.

John, and Adeline Sweet, May 18, 1837.*

John G., and Usula Rieker, int. Apr. 25, 1841.

Libbe Adams, of Canton, and Isaac Smith Houghton, int. Nov. 30, 1809.

Margery, and James Morgaine, Aug. 6, 1640.

Martha P., and Washington Farrington, int. Oct. 19, 1834.

Mary, of Sherborn, and Joseph Payson, at Sherborn, Jan. 27, 1774.

Mary M., and William B. Clements, Oct. 18 [1. c. r. 5.], 1840.*

Nancy, and Francis Joy [residents. int.], Aug. 12, 1804.*

Nancy, and Seth Leonard, int. Feb. 15, 1807.

Noble H. [of Boston. int.], a. 27 y., merchent, s. David and Lucinda, and Elizabeth C. Conant, a. 21 y., d. Mrs. Elizabeth Thayer, July 5, 1849.*

Pamelia [C. c. r. 3.], and Rufus Bigelow [of Boston. c. r. 3.], Sept. 3, 1820.*

Samuel, and Hulda Ruggles, June 9, 1709.

Susan, of Waterford, Vt., and Lyman L. Parmalee, May 23, 1847.

Sylvester, and Mary Ann Kelly, int. Jan. 15, 1847.

Thomas, and Julia Bartlett, Sept. 27, 1825.*

HILLARD, Mary Robbins, and Archibald Laidlaw, int. May 7, 1826.

Rowena P., of Kennebunk, Me., and John L. Hanson, int. Dec. 1, 1849.

HILLER (see also Hiler), Lucy, and William Lambert, jr., int. June 8, 1806.

Thomas, a. 31 y., rope maker, s. Felix A. and Bethiah, and Mary S. Osgood, a. 22 y., d. David and Lydia, May 31, 1846.*

HILLS (see also Hill), Anne, of Boston, and Samuel Sutton, jr., int. Oct. 21, 1846.

* Intention also recorded.

HILLS, David A. of [Westminster. int.], Vt., and Sarah E. Heath, Dec. 19, 1839.*

Jonathan, and Sukey Bosson, Dec. 19, 1803.*

Joseph, and Harriet F. Robbins, Sept. 13, 1838.*

William H., of Cambridge, and Elizabeth Tenney of Monson, Me., July 25, 1846.

HILTON, Ann, Mrs., and Ebenezer Pierpont, Feb. 19, 1722-3.

Frances E., of Brentwood, N. H., and Joseph Wiggin, int. Dec. 4, 1842.

HINDS (see also Hynds, Hynes), George P., and Barbara Burikes, int. Mar. 22, 1835.

HINE, Marcia, of Livermore, Me., and David B. Smith, int. Oct. 31, 1846.

HISCOCK, Sarah, and Frederic Weld, int. Nov. 12, 1815.

HITCHCOCK, Thomas, and Margaret Stedman, residents, Nov. 12, 1788.*

HITCHINGS (see also Hitchins), Eunice, and Jeremiah Eaton, Feb. 26, 1826.*

HITCHINS (see also Hitchings), Lucy [Hitchings. int.], of Dorchester, and Gardner Mathews, at Dorchester, Nov. 28, 1797.*

HIXON, Ezra, and Eunice Ware of Wrentham, int. July 15, 1804.

HOAR, Ellen, and James Doherty, int. June 7, 1841.

HOBART, Caleb, Esq., of Milton, and Mary Willard, Mar. 31, 1830.*

Jane F. [Tatman. int.], and William Cobb of Wrentham, Oct. 12, 1837.*

HOBBS, Catharine, of Weston, and William D. Seaver, int. Oct. 22, 1826.

John C., and Caroline Graham, May 2, 1833.*

Martin, and Ellen Hall, int. Feb. 8, 1848.

Robert L., and Mary A. Graham, Apr. 7, 1837.*

HODGDEN (see also Hodgdon), Harriet A., and Freeman C. Morton, int. Aug. 3, 1845.

* Intention also recorded.

**HODGDON** (see also Hodgden), Abram [Abraham. int.], and
　　Emely Ayers, Dec. 25, 1825.*
Abram, widr., a. 44 y., housewright, s. Parker and Mary, and
　　[Mrs. int.] Ann Holmbert, wid., a. 49 y., housewife, d.
　　Amos and Martha Allen. Mar. 4, 1845.*
Almira, and Benj[amin] F. Ayers, Oct. 1, 1837.*
Henrietta D., and Charles A. Richards [Reckards. int.], Jan.
　　16, 1844.*
James C., and Sarah Gliddon, Dec. 22, 1842.*
Luther, and Mrs. Mary Ann Page, int. Oct. 3, 1841.
Mark E., and Phebe Jane Getchel, Jan. 9, 1845.
Roxanna A. [Hodsdon, a. 20 y. in pencil. int.], and Daniel S.
　　Pevear [a. 23 y. in pencil.], Apr. 4, 1844.*
Zilpha, and B[enj[ami]n. int.] F. Ayers, Sept. 4, 1842.*

**HODGE** (see also Hodges), Thomas S., and Mary A. McLane
　　of Lowell, int. Nov. 19, 1847.

**HODGES** (see also Hodge), Geo[rge] C., and Emely Childs,
　　May 2, 1833.*

**HOGAN** (see also Horgan), Matthew, and Mary Ann Fitz-
　　gerald, int. June 5, 1848.
Matthew, and Hannah Sullivan, int. Sept. 27, 1849.

**HOIT** (see also Hoyt), Caroline S., a. 27 y., d. John T. and
　　Betsey T., and Joseph N. Davis, a. 26 y., tinman, s.
　　Eli and Asenath, Feb. 9, 1848.*

**HOITS** (see also Hoyt), Hannah, and Abner Clap of Dor-
　　chester, at Dorchester, Nov. 2, 1757.

**HOLBROKE** (see also Holbrook), Elisabeth, and Richard
　　Hall, May 22, 1679.

**HOLBROOK** (see also Holbroke, Holbrooke), Abigail, and
　　Ichabod Woodward of Brookline, at Brookline, July 1,
　　1725.
Amos, and Betsey Craft, Nov. 16, 1806.*
Amos, jr., and Sophia Wait of Leicester, int. Oct. 7, 1832.
Daniel, and Elizabeth Paul, at Dorchester, Nov. 11, 1703.
Dorothy, Mrs., and Joseph Dewing [resident. int.], of Brook-
　　line, May 5, 1784.*
Elisabeth, and Benjamin Haws, Dec. 3, 1770.
Hanah, and Daniel Williams, June 25, 1724.

* Intention also recorded.

HOLBROOK Hepsibah C., and Ebenezer Rhoades [of Boston. C. R. 3.], Mar. 12, 1834.*

James, and Lucy Landers, Feb. 7, 1828.*

John, Ens., and Mrs. Mary Palmer of Middleborough, Jan. 26, 1737-8.

John, and Sarah Griggs of Brookline, int. Aug. 31, 1783.

Lucy Maria, d. Asa and Sarah, and Daniel C. Millett of New York, clergyman, s. Daniel and Elizabeth C., Aug. 24, 1847.*

Mary, and John Puffer, at Dorchester, 17 : 10 m : 1695.

Mary, and Samuel Aspinwall, Feb. 26, 1761.

Mehitabel, and Nehemiah May, Nov. 30, 1726.

Rachel R., Mrs., and Reuben Smith, int. Sept. 29, 1833.

Ralph, and Dorothy Williams, Jan. 9, 1739-40.

Richard G., and Ellen McCarty, int. Dec. 28, 1845.

Sabin, and Mary Whittemore, Jan. 10, 1813. C. R. 2.*

Samuel, and Elisabeth Williams, Sept. 1, 1755.

**HOLBROOKE** (see also Holbrook), Daniel, and Elizabeth Sever, May 29, 1696.

Daniel, and Abigail Craft, May 29, 1698.

Elizabeth, and Joseph Mayo, Mar. 10, 1692.

John, and Mary Cheiny, Sept. 24, 1684.

John, and Mrs. Sarah Ruggles, Aug. 19, 1714.

**HOLDEN** (see also Holdin), Eunice, and William M. Blackman, both of Dorchester, Oct. 15, 1823.

Francis, and Mary Ann J. Bicknell, ——, 1832. [May 9, 1831. int.]*

Pricilla, and John Clap, Nov. 6, 1803.*

**HOLDIN** (see also Holden), John, and Sarah Clap of Dorchester, Dec. 3, 1793.*

**HOLDRIDGE,** Hanah, and John Pepper of Woodstock, Mar. 1, 1721-2.

**HOLLAND** (see also Hollen), Frances, a. 20 y., and Oliver C. Gossom, a. 32 y., currier, s. Oliver C. and Catherine, of Ohio, Dec. 27, 1846.*

John, and Catherine Farrelly, int. Feb. 20, 1847.

Joseph, of Brookline, and Eliza[beth] Davis, at Boston, Dec. 17, 1717.

Mary, and John Doggett, int. Aug. 7, 1847.

* Intention also recorded.

HOLLAND, Obedience, and Philip Curtis, Oct. 20, 1658.
Sarah, of Cambridge, and Arthur Sumner, jr., int. Mar. 3,
1833.

**HOLLEN** (see also Holland), Margret, and William Cullinan, int. Apr. 15, 1838.

**HOLLINGER,** Catharine, and David How, June 9, 1839.*

**HOLLIS,** Ann Elizabeth, of Dorchester, and Joseph Lambert. int. Dec. 8, 1844.
John W., of Brighton, and Judith Bussey Ward, May 9, 1838.*

**HOLMAN,** Gilbert W., and Jane C. Bryant, Jan. 2, 1844.

**HOLMBERT,** Ann, wid. a. 49 y., housewife, d. Amos and
Martha Allen, and Abram Hodgdon, widr., a. 44 y., housewright, s. Parker and Mary, Mar. 4, 1845.*

**HOLMES** (see also Homes), Amelia Ann, of Plymouth, and
John Smith, int. Jan. 11, 1849.
Charlotte, and James A. White, Oct. 13, 1833.
David, of Oxford, and Mehitabel Mayo, June 30, 1743. c. r. 2.
Elizabeth F., and Samuel Nutter, Oct. 10, 1830.*
Ephraim, and Mary Corporal, int. May 11, 1845.
Ezra, and Alliece Jones of Concord, int. Feb. 24, 1811.
Ira, and Margaret Lee, int. Dec. 14, 1845.
John, and Hannah Newel, Apr. 9, 1690.
Jonathan, and Nancy Hall Sylvester, Aug. 20, 1809.
Mehitabel, and William Triscot, Oct. 25, 1705.
Martha Ann, of Provincetown, and Abraham W. Rand, int.
May 10, 1849.
Mary, and Joseph Williams, May 10, 1753.
Mary, of Marshfield, and Oliver Phillips, int. Dec. 15, 1833.
William, and Harriet Weld, Oct. 29, 1823.*
William H., and Charlotte H. Averill, Oct. 20, 1835.*

**HOLOGHAN** (see also Houlahin), Michael, and Ann Fox,
int. June 12, 1848.

**HOLROYD,** Sarah, of Providence, R. I., and Noah Kendall,
int. Nov. 8, 1812.

**HOLT,** Adeline L., and Jonathan Snow, Mar. 5, 1839.*
Eliza B., and William Harvey, Dec. 7, 1845. c. r. 7.*
Lucy A., and Amasa Howe of Worcester, int. Sept. 29, 1839.

* Intention also recorded.

HOLT, Mary D. [Halt. c. r. 3.], and Leonard Newton of Milton, Apr. 17, 1823.*

HOLY, Lucretia P., and William V. Thompson, int. Apr. 26, 1840.

HOMAGER, Thomas, and Sarah Mansfield, Oct. 18, 1807.*

HOMAN (see also Homans), Gilbert W., and James C. Bryant, int. Dec. 3, 1843.
Hannah R., a. 18 y., d. Milton and Ann, and George W. Arkerson of Cambridge, a. 29 y., carpenter, s. W[illia]m and Sarah, Dec. 25, 1846.*
Louisa J., and Thomas Frost, int. May 8, 1836.
Lydia S., and Charles W. Edwards [Edward. int.] of Portland, Me., May 23, 1845.*

HOMANS (see also Homan), Phebe W., and Tobias Stone, July 18, 1837.

HOMER, Eliza A., of Dorchester, a. 22 y., d. Joseph and Mary, and Willet C. Blemus of Dedham, a. 24 y., cabinet maker, s. Thomas and Pheby, July 8, 1849.
Samuel R., and Sarah A. Clark, int. Oct. 26, 1845.

HOMES (see also Holmes), George, of Dorchester, and Frances M. Withington, int. June 13, 1841.

HOMME, Nicholas, and Barbe Scearalf, int. Oct. 24, 1845.

HOOD, Elizabeth, Mrs., and Benjamin Gason, int. Apr. 19, 1840.
Harriet E., a. 19 y., d. Abraham and Eliza, and George Curtis, a. 25 y., painter, s. W[illia]m and Hannah, Apr. 23, 1848.*
Louisa, and George Roberts, July 14, 1844.*
Prudence J., and William Twombly, int. May 10, 1840.

HOOGS, Elizabeth [Betsey. int.], of Newton, and Seth Gay, at Newton, Feb. 10, 1785.*

HOOKER, Joseph, and Nancy Spurr, Dec. 6, 1789.*

HOOPER, Anna A. [M. int], and Lewis Hammer, June 12, 1845.*
Hannah H., and Pliny D. Parsons of Bangor, Me., Nov. 20, 1834.*

* Intention also recorded.

HOOPER, Irene P., and James Staniels, Sept. 17, 1820.*
John, and Mrs. Sarah Harris of Brooklyn, Mar. 4, 1730-31.
Louis, of Charlestown, and Samuel Woodward, int. Jan. 29,
    1786.
Mary L., and Samuel Staniels, Mar. 27, 1825.*
Phebe, of Wilmington, and Nicholas Stricker, at Woburn,
    Nov. 29, 1731.
Polly, Mrs., and Dr. Peter Gilman Robbins, Dec. 11, 1818.*
Robert, of Marblehead, and Polly Williams, Dec. 21, 1809.*
Robert, jr., of Marblehead, and Caroline Leatham, Oct. 15,
    1816.*
Sarah E., and Chauncy Jordan, Apr. 17, 1832.*

HOPKIN (see also Hopkins), Lois, and Joseph Gurney, Mar.
    30, 1815.*

HOPKINS (see also Hopkin), Mary, and John Dove, int. Oct.
    1, 1820.
Mary B., and James S. Young, int. Mar. 24, 1839.
Paulina, of Orleans, and John D. F. Wilcox, int. June 23,
    1848.

HOPSACK, Margaret [Margarett Hossack. int.], and An-
    drew Struthers, both of Scotland, July 14, 1849. C. R. 5.*

HORAN, Bridget, and Patrick Daly, int. Mar. 26, 1849.

HORGAN (see also Hogan), Cornelius, a. 39 y., laborer, and
    Elizabeth H. Colton, a. 33 y., Sept. 6, 1847.

HORN, Andrew, and Samantha Bills, Apr. 11, 1826.*
Maria, and James Claffee, int. Sept. 18, 1842.
Richard, and Cynthia W. Merrill of Parsonfield, Me., int.
    Dec. 26, 1841.

HORTON, Betsy, and Leonard Freeman, Oct. 16, 1808.*
Elisha [of Boston. C. R. 3.], and Betsy Gay, May 2, 1819.*
Mary, and John Waugh, jr., int. Jan. 12, 1840.
Mary, and Thomas McCradle, int. Sept. 17, 1849.
Mary A., of Canton, and Ephraim S. Mulloken, int. Apr. 14,
    1849.
Zenos, and Nancy Sever of Cambridge, int. May 6, 1798.

HOSFORD, Senir, and Mary Ann Donham, Sept. 25, 1835.

HOSMER, Emeline, of Acton, and Enoch Hall, int. Apr. 2,
    1837.

* Intention also recorded.

**HOUGHTON,** A. M., of Sterling, and Mary F. Quinnam, int. Sept. 30, 1849.

Isaac Smith, and Libbe Adams Hill of Canton, int. Nov. 20, 1809.

James, of Dorchester, and Merriam Carter, Dec. 11, 1834.*

John, and Nancy Williams of Dorchester, int. Aug. 18, 1805.

John H., and Elizabeth D. Bird, int. Mar. 27, 1831.

Joseph, and Anna Williams, Dec. 17, 1772.

Joseph, and Harriet [Maria. int.] Seaver, June 13, 1839.*

Lawson, and Mary Nightingale, May 13, 1827.*

Levi [Capt. int.], and Eliza Reed, Oct. 5, 1823.*

Pamelia C., and Edmund M. Fowler, jr., int. Aug. 29, 1841.

Patrick, and Bridget Killin, int. May 22, 1842.

Thomas, and Elizabeth Skinner of Warren District, Me., int. Oct. 31, 1819.

**HOULAHIN** (see also Hallagan, Hologhan), Mary, and Daniel O'Hare, int. Feb. 2, 1847.

**HOUSTON,** Francis, and Elizabeth R. Neal, int. May 4, 1849.

**HOUTHWAIT,** William, and Penelope Little, Apr. 8, 1819.*

**HOVEY,** Abigail, of Bradford, and Guy Carlton, int. Oct. 27, 1811.

Catherine, and Jonathan Smith, Aug. 21, 1760.

Ezekiel, and Katharine White, Nov. 12, 1747.

Freeman, of Cambridgeport, and Sophronia Walker, July 5, 1838.*

**HOW** (see also Howe), Abigail, and John Blackman, jr. of Dorchester, at Dorchester, Jan. 1, 1746.

Abig[ai]l, and Jason Winch, Dec. 13, 1777.

David, and Catharine Hallinger, June 9, 1839.*

Deborah, and Isaac How, May 11, 1685.

Elizabeth, and Edmund Parker, May 31, 1647.

Ezekiel, Capt., and Mrs. Rebecca Ruggles, Dec. 22, 1772.

Hannah, and Joshua Sever, May 9, 1768.

Isaac and Deborah How, May 11, 1685.

James, and Susannah Richardson, Dec. 28, 1773.

John, and Henrietta Sparhawk, Oct. 26, 1803.*

Mary, and Thomas Raymor, Mar. 29, 1758.

Polly, of Dorchester, and David Baker, int. Nov. 29, 1801

Sarah, and Samuel Knight, Oct. 16, 1685.

* Intention also recorded.

**HOWARD,** Ansel, of Taunton, and Louisa Wilbar, Oct. 22, 1826.*

Caleb, and Mary Morton, Jan. 8, 1761.

George B., and Mary Harvey, Apr. 14, 1834. [1833. c. r. 2.]*

Hannah, Mrs., and James Fox, June 26, 1783.*

John, and Clarissa H. Carter, int. Apr. 30, 1820.

John R., and Rebecca Noyes, Dec. 31, 1834.*

Reuben, and Lucy H. Burrill, int. Mar. 9, 1834.

Richard B., of Cayuga Falls, Ohio, a. 21 y., baker, s. John B. and Deborah, and Emily C. Brooks, a. 20 y., d. Benjamin and Louisa, Aug. 26, 1849.*

Sarah I. [J. int.], and Timothy W. Short, July 25, 1837.*

**HOWE** (see also How, Howes), Abigail G., and Thomas Vose of Baltimore, Maryland, Aug. 25, 1812.*

Abigail J., and Ezra T. Hall, int. Dec. 8, 1844.

Abraham F. [Esq. int.], and [Mrs. int.] Mary Crehore, Oct. 2, 1842.*

Alvan, and Betsy Goodnough,. Apr. 2, 1822. c. r. 2.*

Alvan, and Elizabeth Crane [of Dorchester. int.], Apr. 29, 1827. c. r. 2.*

Amasa, of Worcester, and Lucy A. Holt, int. Sept. 29, 1839.

Betsy, and Charles Shepherd of Northampton, June 1, 1809.*

Charles, of Dorchester, and Lucy Williams, Dec. 7, 1820.*

Charles, of Abington, and Lydia F. Josselyn, Oct. 31, 1839.

Charles O., and Mary Faxon of Brookline, int. Oct. 26, 1848.

Charlotte, and Guy Carleton, Dec. 23, 1841.*

David, and Elizabeth Chamberlain, May 16, 1780.

David, jr., and Elizabeth Tucker, Jan. 10, 1819.*

Edward, of Portland, and Suviah Marston, June 1, 1815.*

Eliza, of Sudbury, and Samuel Paine, jr., int. July 14, 1805.

Elizabeth, a. 23 y., d. Alvin and Betsey, and Lemuel Richards [jr. int.], a. 25 y., currier, s. Lemuel and Mary, Dec. 10, 1846.*

George L., and Caroline A. Parker of Milton, int. Nov. 7, 1846.

Harriet E., and James White, int. May 20, 1838.

Helen Matilda, and Elisha Crocker of Charleston, S. C., int. Aug. 5, 1827.

Isaac, 3d, of Dorchester, and Abigail Kelton of Dorchester, Dec. 10, 1810.

Jacob, and Mrs. Abigail Pheasea, both residents, int. Apr. 24, 1785.

* Intention also recorded.

HOWE, James, and Elizabeth Clap of Dorchester, June 30, 1803.

Jane, and William Williams, jr., int. Nov. 4, 1821.

John, and Hannah Niles [Hiles. int.], Apr. 14, 1805.*

John, and Clarissa Burrell, int. Dec. 25, 1808.

Jones, and Catharine Davenport, May 12, 1844.*

Joseph, and Charlotte Brown, Apr. 6, 1814. c. r. 2.*

Lydia, and John Champney, Mar. 11, 1804.*

Mark A. DeW. [Mark Anthony De Wolf. Rev. int.], and Julia Bowen Amory, Oct. 16, 1833. c. r. 5.*

Mary R., and Maj. Daniel L. Gibbens, June 3, 1819.*

Nathaniel S., of Jonesville, Mich., a. 29 y., lawyer, s. Isaac R. and Sarah S., and Sarah A. Bradley, a. 25 y., d. Charles and Sarah, May 26, 1846.*

Patience, Mrs., and Lemuel Bradley, Jan. 23, 1783.*

Rachel, jr., and Edward Robinson, both of Dorchester, Dec. 6, 1793.

Sarah, and Benjamin Cheesman [Dec. ?], 1778.

Susanna, Mrs., and Ralph Smith, Nov. 27, 1804.*

Thomas, and Esther Carter, Mar. 7, 1819.*

William B., widr., a. 29 y., machinist, s. Levi and Abigail, and Rebecca A. Woodbridge, a. 23 y., d. Thomas and Sophia, June 8, 1847.*

HOWES (see also Howe), Mary, and Benjamin Knower, Apr. 27, 1806.*

Phebe C., of Lynn, and D. N. St. Johns Browne, int. Sept. 16, 1847.

HOWGATE, William, of Lowell, a. 24 y., machinist, s. James and Hannah, and Ellen Maude, a. 22 y., d. David and Martha, June 9, 1848.*

HOWLAND, Charles, and Elizabeth Crease, July 8, 1793.*

Hepsibah, of Dover, and Daniel Lyon, May 14, 1835.*

HOXIE, John A., and Elizabeth Curson, int. July 21, 1847.

HOY, Mary, a. 20 y., carpet weaver, and Godfrey Billeg, a. 25 y., carpet weaver, s. Matthias and Mary, Jan. 19, 1848.*

HOYT (see also Hayt, Hoit, Hoits), William, and Sophia Perkins, int. Aug. 27, 1826.

* Intention also recorded.

**HUBBARD,** Ebenezer, and Nancy Yates, Dec. 28, 1848.*
Ellen, and Patrick Dolan, int. Apr. 10, 1847.
John S., of Charlestown,* and Jane Godding [Goulding. int.],
 Dec. 25, 1837.*
Mariah H., and William Waymouth [Weymouth. int.], Dec.
 26, 1843.*
Martha F., and Ebenezer [A. dup.] Murray, int. Apr. 30,
 1843. [Dec. 8, 1844. dup.]

**HUCKINS,** Francis, a. 22 y., merchant, s. James and Lucy, and
 Mary L. Walker, a. 20 y., d. Sam[ue]l and Mary L., Jan.
 11, 1849.*

**HUCKLINGS,** Sarah A., and Ward Wheeler, Aug. 6, 1843.*

**HUDSON** (see also Hudsonn), Mary S., and George G. North,
 int. Nov. 28, 1841.
Rachel, and Simon Johnson, Nov. 19, 1843.
Solomon Howe, and Mary Gay, June 12, 1821. c. r. 2.*

**HUDSONN** (see also Hudson), Mary, of Lynn, and John
 Crafts, Mar. 30, 1669.

**HUEN,** Mary, and Benjamin Dows, Apr. 7, 1680.

**HUFF,** Benj[ami]n, and Huldah B. Foss, int. Aug. 13, 1837.
Hannah, and Patrick Slany, int. Oct. 19, 1849.
Joseph, and Rhoda Seaverns, Apr 8, 1834.*

**HUGES** (see also Hughes), Catherine, of Boston, and Thomas
 Havey, int. June 20, 1846.

**HUGGINS,** Chester M., and Elizabeth S. Cotter, int. Oct.
 1, 1837.

**HUGHES** (see also Huges), Margaret, and John Lightmer,
 int. Jan. 1, 1843.
Mary, and Francis Roonijen, int. Sept. 22, 1848.

**HULTON,** Erick Magnus, and Eliza Ann Russell, Mar. 8,
 1840.

**HUMPHREY** (see also Humphreys, Humphries, Humphry),
 Mary, and Peter Newcomb of Braintree, Apr. 30, 1702.
Sarah Ann, of Brookline, and Charles Leroy, Sept. 8, 1841.*
Willard A., and Mary H. Haynes, June 6, 1830.*
Willard A., and Harriet Curtis, int. Mar. 17, 1833.

* Intention also recorded.

**HUMPHREYS** (see also Humphrey), William, of Dorchester, . and Elizabeth Loud, int. Oct. 3, 1824.

**HUMPHRIES** (see also Humphrey), Edward, and Rebecca Leeds, Aug. 30, 1801.*
Harriet, and Jacob Davis, Nov. 26, 1840.*

**HUMPHRY** (see also Humphrey), Sally, of Dorchester, and Elisha Toby, int. Apr. 5, 1801.

**HUNEWELL** (see also Hunnewell), Jonathan, Hon., and Mrs. Theoda Davis, Feb. 1, 1820.*

**HUNNEMAN,** Ann F. H., and Joseph F. Milner, int. Apr. 17, 1831.
Hannah H., and William W. Seaver of Philadelphia, int. Sept. 27, 1829.
Mary C., a. 33 y., d. William C. and Hannah, and William Bacon, jr., a. 34 y., trader, s. William and Elizabeth, June 10, 1849.*
Samuel Hewes, and Elizabeth Champney, June 30, 1825.*

**HUNNEWELL** (see also Hunewell), Louisa, of Charlestown, and George W. Pierce, int. Aug. 3, 1845.

**HUNSTABLE,** Susanna R. [Mrs. int.], and Albert Tolman of Worcester, Apr. 3, 1839.*

**HUNT,** Asa, of Weymouth, and Meranda Derby, July 7, 1824.*
Charles, of Watertown, and Nancy Fellowes, Dec. 22, 1804*
Elizabeth H., and James Brazier, int. Mar. 15, 1818.
Esther, and Jonathan Fennoe, Oct. 24, 1749.
Jane, and Richard Boyle, int. Jan. 30, 1847.
John, and S. Jane Symmes of Medford, int. Oct. 10, 1846.
Mary Parker, of Dorchester, and William Joy [jr. int.], Apr. 21, 1822.*
Myra, and William Pettes of Charleston, Va., Oct. 5, 1840.*
Nancy, Mrs., and John S. Williams, May 6, 1807.*
Rachel, of Milton, and Cotton Sparhawk, int. July 5, 1789.
Thomas, of Stockbridge, and Mary Pattin, Oct. 27, 1789.*
Thomas, and Elizabeth McNabo, int. Oct. 19, 1849.
Timothy, and Susan Sumner, Dec. 2, 1824.*
Timothy, and Angeline Bodge, Jan. 17, 1840.*

**HUNTER,** Nancy B., and Samuel James of Cambridge, int. Mar. 11, 1838.

* Intention also recorded.

**HUNTING,** Asa, and Abigail Blaney, Oct. 18, 1789.*
Betsy, and Benjamin Haynes of Charlestown, int. Nov. 3, 1811.
Mary Ann, and [Rev. int.] Lemuel Capen of Sterling, Oct.
    11, 1815.*
Reuben, and Sally Haynes, June 8, 1818.*
Reuben [jr. int.], and Mary Ann Freeman, Apr. 15, 1832.*

**HUNTINGTON,** David, and Jane Dill of Lowell, int. May 26,
    1844.
Lucy, Mrs., of Norwich, d. Col. Hezekiah, Esq. and Hannah,
    and Samuel Williams, May 31, 1762.

**HUNTOON,** Benjamin, widr. of Canton, a. 53 y., minister, s.
    Benj[ami]n and Mehitabel of Salisbury, N. H., and Ann
    Payson Lewis, a. 42 y., d. Elijah, July 30, 1846.*
Julia F., of Cambridge, and Milton Nelson, Jan. 1, 1837.

**HURD,** Almira, and Stephen Senter, Dec. 27, 1829.
Benjamin, and Prissilla Craft, Sept. 15, 1774
Dorcas B., of Acton, Me., and Charles Nutter, int. Oct. 17,
    1841.
James, and Elizabeth C. Newton, int. Nov. 11, 1838.

**HURLEY** (see also Hurly), Hannah, and Cornelius Sullivan,
    int. Aug. 20, 1849.
Mary H., and Andrew J. Hammond, int. Aug. 4, 1844.

**HURLY** (see also Hurley), Ann, and Patrick Farrell, int.
    Nov. 9, 1847.
John, and Susan Wren, int. May 4, 1849.
Thomas, and Allas Hase, int. Aug. 13, 1846.

**HURTER,** Geo[rge] C., of Zenia, Ohio, and Elizabeth Grozer,
    Oct. 22, 1839.*

**HUSSEY** (see also Hussy), James, and Ellen Landergin of
    Boston, int. Sept. 10, 1849.
Levi, and Sarah Edgerly, int. July 21, 1822.
Margarett, and Lloyd Hewett, Mar. 20, 1836.*
Ralph R., and Martha Lyon, int. Nov. 9, 1847.

**HUSSY** (see also Hussey), Thomas, and Sophia Gines, int.
    Jan. 22, 1849.

**HUSTON,** William R., of Dedham, a. 31 y., housewright, and
    Susan E. Lee of Charlestown, a. 24 y., Oct. 28, 1847.

* Intention also recorded.

**HUTCHINGS** (see also Hutchins), Jane Ann, and William Davis, jr., int. Feb. 26, 1832.

Lucinda [of Boston. c. R. 3.], and George Goldsmith, Dec. 23, 1832.*

Mary, and Lysander Stockwell, both of Boston, Sept. 7, 1836.

Simon, and Lucy Sanderson, int. Oct. 23, 1834.

**HUTCHINS** (see also Hutchings), Abel, of Concord, N. H., and Elizabeth Partridge, Jan. 22, 1786.*

Enoch, and Sally Child, Mar. 25, 1819.*

Mary E., and Henry W. Miller, Dec. 24, 1843. c. R. 7.*

Owen B., a. 27 y., carpenter, s. Amos and Abigail, and Sarah P. Johnson, a. 26 y., d. Daniel and Elizabeth H., June 20, 1849.*

Simon, and Caroline R. Rumrill, int. Nov. 3, 1833.

William, and Nancy Trow of Brookline, Apr. 7, 1819.*

**HUTCHINSON,** Charles, and Diantha Reckard, int. July 3, 1842.

**HUXFORD,** Thomas, of Boston, and Sally S[wift. int.] Roby, Dec. 13, 1801.*

**HYDE** (see also Hide), Hester, of Needham, and William Barnard, int. July 16, 1826.

Isaac, of Cambridge, and Lucretia Goddard, Sept. 22, 1805.*

Lavina, of Brookline, and Josiah Weatherby, Nov. 27, 1796.*

Leonard, and Jerusha Lethbridge of Franklin, int. June 14, 1812.

Mary S., and Nelson Curtis, Aug. 30 [May 23. c. R. 3.], 1843.*

Sarah E., of Newton, and Joseph Rider, int. Apr. 7, 1849.

William A., and Rebecca S. Davis, int. Oct. 11, 1840.

William J., of Brookline, a. 31 y., yeoman, s. Leonard and Jerusha, and Sarah W. Childs, a. 29 y., d. Stephen and Rebecca, June 1, 1848.*

**HYLAND,** Elizabeth A., of Manchester, N. H., and Samuel T. Drake, int. Sept. 14, 1845.

Lucy, and Edward Turner, May 15, 1781.

Thomas, and Mary Dolan, int. May 20, 1848.

**HYNDS** (see also Hinds), Michael, and Mary Harrington, int. June 20, 1848.

* Intention also recorded.

**HYNES** (see also Hinds), Catherine, and William Toomey, int. May 13, 1847.
Edward, and Mary McGennis, int. Jan. 6, 1849

**HYSLOP,** Elizabath, and Hon. Increase Sumner, Esq., Sept. 30, 1779.

**ILIG,** Catherine, and Charles Bleesz, int. Dec. 23, 1846.

**INCHES,** Henderson, of Boston, and Susan Brimmer, Sept. 15, 1802.*

**INGALLS** William, jr., Dr., of Laurell Hill, Louisiana, and Julia A. M. Davis, int. Nov. 8, 1840.

**INGLESBY,** Sarah, and Caleb Sever, Dec. 15, 1671.

**INGULDEN,** Elizabeth, and Phillip Meadows, Apr. —, 1641.
Elizabeth, and Joseph Patching, Apr. 18, 1642

**IOYKEL,** Jacob, and Barbere Keslern, May 7, 1833.*

**IRELAND** Jonathan, and Mrs., ——, Robinson, Mar. 6, 1745-6.

**IRVING** (see also Ervin, Erving), Eliza P., and Samuel N. Burbeck, int. Mar. 20, 1831.

**IRWIN,** Hannah, and Clement Moriarty, int. June 5, 1848.

**IVERS,** William H., and Lucy Jane Allen, Apr. 22, 1845.*

**IVES,** Robert, of Providence, R. I., and Harriet Bowen Amory, int. Sept. 16, 1827.

**IVRY,** Ellen, and William G. Pierson, int. Sept. 27, 1835.

**JACKSON,** Andrew, and Mary Elizabeth Randall, int. Apr. 29, 1838.
Antepas, jr., and Mary Clap, Dec. 10, 1823.*
Betsey, and Abel Green, int. June 22, 1823.
Daniel, and Lauraette Richardson, int. Oct. 18, 1835.
Edmund, and Mary Harriet Hewes of Dorchester, int. Oct. 22, 1826.
Ephraim, and Mary Davis, Nov. 29, 1753.
Esther, of Newton, and Abner Whitney, at Newton, Mar. 21, 1768.
Harriet N., and William T. Dwyer, int. Aug. 25, 1844.
Jemima, and Humphry Bicknell, July 19, 1789.*

* Intention also recorded.

JACKSON, Joseph, and Susanna Ruggles, Dec. 11, 1755.

Martha, and Jonathan Tucker, jr., Jan. 13, 1731-2.

Mary Ann, and William Burrage [of Boston. C. R. 3.], May 14, 1835.*

Mary L., and James L. Sims, June 9, 1833.

Patty, and James Burdekin, at Boston, June 6, 1791.*

Rebeccah, and Luther White, Dec. 18, 1798. C. R. 2.*

Samuel, and Mary Doggett, int. Oct. 20, 1833.

Sarah, of Newton, and Samuel Draper, at Newton, June 27, 1771.

William, and Maria Moulton, Feb. 11, 1821.*

JACOBS, Huldah P., of Portland, Me., and Jeremy Fletcher, int. Nov. 3, 1844.

Richard G., and Jane L. Robins, Mar. 26, 1846.*

JAMES, Almira, and Samuel S. Gudworth [Cudworth. C. R. 3.], May 19, 1842.*

Benjamin F., and Sarah Haynes, Aug. 29, 1841.*

Charles, Ens., and Hannah Clap of Scituate, int. Sept. 22, 1799.

Elisha, and Sarah White, Dec. 23, 1817.*

Elisha, and Mary A. Everett of Cambridge, int. Oct. 27, 1848.

George, and Dorothy P. Richards of Newton, May 19, 1836.

Harvey, and Abigail Norcross, int. Mar. 26, 1826.

John, and Mary C. White, Apr. [5. C. R. 3.], 1808.*

Lydia H., and Josiah H. Moore, Sept. 21, 1828.*

Mary, and John C. Gore, May 27, 1838.*

Milton, and Harriet Leeds of Dorchester, Oct. 18, 1827.*

Samuel, of Cambridge, and Nancy B. Hunter, int. Mar. 11, 1838.

Sarah F., and Stephen Fitzgerald [Fitzgeral, of Boston. C. R. 3.], Sept. 27, 1843.*

Thomas, jr., and Polly Carlton, int. Oct. 30, 1808.

Titus, and Mary Whippy, Jan. 1, 1718.

William E., a. 24 y., clerk, s. John and Mary E., and Sarah L. Dexter, a. 22 y., d. Anson and Sarah, May 10, 1848.*

JAQUES, Isaac, and Mary Richardson, Mar. 1, 1812.*

JARVIS (see also Jervis), Mary Ann P., and Christopher M. Weld, M. D., int. Apr. 11, 1841.

JEFFRIES, Ame, and Thomas Fleming, Nov. 26, 1845.*

* Intention also recorded.

**JEFTS,** Mary, and Joseph Payson, Oct. 25, 1758.

**JEMERSON** (see also Jennison), Mary L., and Charles D. Perry of Brookline, int. May 28, 1837.*

**JENKINS,** Martha, and George Corporal, July 8, 1838.*
Mary Ann, of Dorchester, and Isaac C. Abbot of Groton, Oct. 23, 1834.
Sally, and Thomas D. Sloan [residents. int.], Apr. 24, 1808.*

**JENNESS,** Anna Y., of Rye, N. H., and Obed Rand, int. Feb. 1, 1835.
Josiah D., and Mary Ann Allen, Apr. 29, 1841.*
Lucy M., and S. S. [J. Smith. int.] Jenness of Detroit, Sept. 6, 1842.*
S. S. [J. Smith. int.], of Detroit, and Lucy M. Jenness, Sept. 6, 1842.*
Sarah A., of Rye, N. H., and Yeaton Jenness, int. Apr. 17, 1847.
Yeaton, and Sarah A. Jenness of Rye, N. H., int. Apr. 17, 1847.

**JENNINGS,** Alexander Hodgon [Hodgdon, and Mrs. int.], Mary Griggs, Nov. 27, 1806. C. R. 2.*
Anna, and Jonathan Robinson, Nov. 25, 1795.*
Nathaniel, and Sarah Wharff [of Gloucester. int.], Dec. 9, 1816. C. R. 2.*
Stephen, and Mary Croxford, Apr. 23, 1772.
Thomas, and Mary McDonnell, int. Feb. 5, 1849.

**JENNISON** (see also Jemerson). Nathaniel, and Mehetable Shirley, Aug. 4, 1774.
Sarah, and Asa Whitemore, Mar. 21, 1811.*

**JERES,** Maria, and Benedict Hamburg, int. Oct. 2, 1848.

**JERVIS** (see also Jarvis), James, and Abigail Saunders, both resident, Aug. 14, 1732.

**JEWELL,** Elcedania S., and Nathaniel Roberts, int. Aug. 26, 1832.
Mary, and Lewis Mores, June 28, 1807. C. R. 2.*
Sarah, and Nathan Ballcom, Jan. 12, 1768.

* Intention also recorded.

**JEWETT,** Charles C[offin. c. r. 5.], of Providence, R. I., a. 32 y., professor, s. Paul and Eleanor P., and Rebecca G. Haskins, a. 24 y., d. Ralph and Rebecca G., Apr. 5, 1848.*

Daniel T., and Sarah J. Wilson, both of Bangor, Dec. 1, 1848.

Elizabeth G[ray. int.], and Nathan A. M. [N. A. Monroe. int.] Dudley, Nov. 12, 1845.*

Elizabeth S., of Pepperell, and George W. Bradlee, int. Oct. 11, 1840.

Luke, and Julia Ann Trask, Aug. 17, 1826.*

**JOHNS** (see also Jones), Henrietta, and Sanford Libby, Oct. 15, 1840.*

**JOHNSON** (see also Johnston, Johnstone), Abigail Rice, and Andrew C. Hayes, int. Aug. 10, 1834.

Alfred, and Ann Kennicut, int. Dec. 10, 1843.

Betsy, and Prince Jones, Apr. 29, 1806.*

Deborah, and Isaac Davis, Dec. 19, 1705.

Elisha, and Abigail Weld, May 25, 1709.

Eliza, of Holliston, and Henry C. Adams, int. Mar. 11, 1832.

Eliza B. [S. int.], and Clement Pinkham, Nov. 16, 1830.*

Elizabeth, and Robart Pepper, Mar. 14, 1642.

Elizabeth, and Henry Bowen, Dec. 20, 1658.

Elizabeth, and James Burril, Dec. 7, 1775.

George W., and Mary Hewins of Sharon, int. Dec. 3, 1843.

Hannah, and John Eives, both residents, Aug. 31, 1786.*

Hannah E., of Sharon, and Gilbert S. May, int. Mar. 18, 1838.

Hollis, and Abigail Goss of Northborough, int. Sept. 10, 1809.

Humpherey, and Abigail May, Dec. 6, 1678.

Isaac, and Elizabeth Piper, int. June 28, 1848.

Isaack, and Elizabeth Porter, Jan. 20, 1636.

Issac, jr., and Mary Harriss, Oct. 26, 1669.

John, and Margaret Morriss, Apr. 4, 1689.

John, and Mary Ramsey, May 26, 1702.

John, and Eleanor Middleton [both residents. int.], July 9, 1786.*

Joseph, and Hannah Pike, Mar. 9, 1779.

Josiah E., and Mrs. Harriet Tillton, int. Sept. 11, 1842.

Kendal, and Anne Woodward, Oct. 23, 1770.

Lawrance, and Hannah Preston, both residents, Mar. 15, 1785.*

Lawrence, of Boston, and Margarett Riley, int. Oct. 29, 1846.

Lydia, and James Ball, int. Oct. 13, 1844.

* Intention also recorded.

JOHNSON, Mary, and Willyam Bartholmew, Dec. 17, 1663.

Mary Ann, a. 26 y., d. William and Sarah, and Rufus King, a. 24 y., laborer, s. Elijah and Hannah, Apr. 18, 1847.*

Moses, and Anna C. B. Brewer, Aug. 8, 1824.*

Nancy Burt, and Samuel Kneeland, Oct. 5, 1820.*

Nathaniell, and Marie Smith, Apr. 29, 1667.

Obadiah, and Sarah Loring of Lexington, at Lexington, Oct. 21, 1776.

Peter, and Mary Jones, Nov. 22, 1832.*

Sarah Osgood, and Robert Morgan, Apr. 23, 1845.*

Sarah P., a. 26 y., d. Daniel and Elizabeth H., and Owen B. Hutchins, a. 27 y., carpenter, s. Amos and Abigail, June 20, 1849.*

Simon, and Rachel Hudson, Nov. 19, 1843.

Stephen, Rev., of Lime, Conn., and Abigail Leveritt, May 28, 1776.

Umphry, and Ellen Cheaney, Mar. 20, 1642.

William, and Sarah Goodhue, int. Nov. 13, 1836.

William E., and Mary Ann Freeman, int. July 16, 1837.

**JOHNSTON** (see also Johnson), Levina, and Thomas McCormick [of Boston. int.], Mar. 28, 1849.*

William C., a. 19 y., glassblower, s. William, and Ellen C. Costello, [both of Boston. c. r. 5.], a. 19 y., July 30, 1849.

**JOHNSTONE** (see also Johnson), Archibald, and Mary S. Watts, Sept. 24, 1848.

**JOICE,** Mary, and Thomas Cannon, int. July 24, 1845.

Mary Ann, and John Spelman, int. Jan. 4, 1846.

Thomas, and Johnna Doyle, int. Aug. 31, 1848.

**JOLLY,** Dennis, and Bridget Carberry, int. May 2, 1846.

**JONES** (see also Johns, Jons), Alden, and Mary Herring, Mar. 6, 1796.*

Alliece, of Concord, and Ezra Holmes, int. Feb. 24, 1811.

Ann M., and James S. Brackett of Portland, int. Dec. 16, 1838.

Anne, and Nathaniel Draper, July 3, 1780.

Antoinette S., and Joseph L. Moffat, int. Apr. 7, 1833.

Charles, and Abigail Seaverns, int. Dec. 3, 1809.

Daniel, a. 29 y., and Eliza P. Cass, a. 20 y., d. Benj[amin] and Roxana, July 31, 1848.*

* Intention also recorded.

JONES, Dolly B., and Benjamin B. Curtis, Nov. 21, 1821.*

Edmund, and Charlotte Kingsbury of Dorchester, Apr. 16, 1817.*

Eliza M., and J. H. Coggeshall, Oct. 13, 1842.*

George, and Rebecca Orne, int. Jan. 16, 1831.

Hannah, and Eliphaz [Eliphas. c. R. 3.] Clap, Apr. 27, 1817.*

Harriet A., of Lowell, and Jacob Lovejoy, June 5, 1842. c. R. 7.

Harriot H., and Ammi C. Lombard, int. Jan. 15, 1837.

Ichabod, of Dorchester, and Rebecca Perry, at Dorchester, Feb. 22, 1741

Isaac, of Guilford, N. H., a. 32 y., clerk, s. Simpson and Mary, and S. Elliot Newton, d. Antipas and Elizabeth, June 17, 1849.*

James, and Susannah Goddard of Brookline, int. Mar. 24, 1822.

John, and Elizabeth Bacon, Feb. 4, 1713.

John Cluley, [Ens. int.], and Sarah Davis, July 5, 1792.*

John, and Hannah Payson, Dec. 17, 1795.*

John, and Patty Freeland of Hopkinton, Sept. 21, 1801.*

Lewis, an Prudence Whitney [Whiting. int.], Dec. 29, 1790.*

Lewis, and Martha Miles, Apr. 9, 1807. c. R. 2.*

Lucy, and Henry Pitts, Jan. 17, 1802.*

Martha Ann, and Joshua Batchelder, int. Sept. 9, 1827.

Mary, and Nathanael Griggs [of Brookline. c. R. 2.], Apr. 17, 1746.

Mary, and Jonathan Lyon, Feb. 21, 1748-9.

Mary, and Peter Johnson, Nov. 22, 1832.*

Mary B., and Joseph E. Gardner, July 15, 1849.

Mary E. [Glines. int.]. and W[illia]m Whitney, June 4, 1840.*

Meriam Abbott, of Dedham, and Adam Dickey, Feb. 12, 1829.*

Nancy E., of Newton, and George A. Guild, int. Jan. 7, 1844.

Philander, and Emily Wheeler, July 4, 1841.

Prince, and Betsy Johnson, Apr. 29, 1806.*

Prudence W., and John Fowle, Nov. 29, 1818.*

Rachel B., of North Bridgewater, and George H. Cushman, int. Sept. 14, 1845.

Salley, and Peter Seaver, Nov. 28, 1776.

Samuel, and Ann Danford, Sept. 5, 1679.

Sarah, and Lot Elwell, July 23, 1838.*

Solomon, and Nabby Baker, Apr. 11, 1799.*

* Intention also recorded.

JONES, Susan H., and George B. Cordwell, int. Dec. 20, 1835.
Titus, and Deliverance Dunkin, Feb. 11, 1724-5.
William, and Nancy B. Davis, Aug. 3, 1840.*
William, and Emily Barnard, int. Feb. 26, 1849.
W[illia]m B., and Maria A. Blaisdell, Oct. 13, 1844.*
William Henry, and Catharine Brigham, int. Apr. 7, 1833.

JONS (see also Jones), Amelia, and Jacob Schneider, int. Mar. 16, 1845.

JORDAN (see also Jorden), Chauncy, and Sarah E. Hooper, Apr. 17, 1832.*
Elizabeth, and Eilphalet Lyon, Jan. 1, 1712.
Jesse, and Ann B. Mirick, Apr. 13, 1826.*
Joseph P, and Deborah D. Causens, both of Dorchester, Sept. 29, 1822.
Maria, of Dorchester. and David L. Morse, int. Apr. 3, 1836.
Mary, and Cyrus Stedman, int. Sept. 23, 1832.
Mary, and Brine Kelly, int. Jan. 30, 1849.
Mercy, and John Flinn, Dec. 26, 1826.
Sylvanus, and Cordelia C. Austin, Aug. 23, 1831.*

JORDEN (see also Jordan), Patrick, and Margaret Killacky, int. Feb. 15, 1846.
Royal C., and Lucretia McMichael, int. Dec. 14, 1845.

JOSELYN (see also Josselyn), Mary Jane, and Charles B. Pelton, Nov. 5, 1848.

JOSLYN (see also Josselyn), Hannah M., and Ira Burnham, int. Sept. 13, 1835.
JOSSELYN (see also Joselyn, Joslyn), Alonzo, a. 28 y., moulder, s. Charles and Lucy, and Caroline A. Morse, a. 21 y., d. Harford and Lucy, Dec. 24, 1846.*
Charles C., and Luretta Ryan, Mar. 19, 1838.*
Lydia F., and Charles Howe of Abington, Oct. 31, 1839.

JOY, Caleb. and Nancy Woodbury, int. Jan. 1, 1815.
Ellen R., a. 17 y., and Jeremiah Pearson, a. 24 y., Mar. 1, 1849.*
Francis, and Nancy Hill [residents. int.], Aug. 12, 1804.*
William [jr. int.], and Mary Parker Hunt of Dorchester, Apr. 21, 1822.*
William H., and Hetty Leonard, Nov. 26, 1826.*

* Intention also recorded.

JOYAL, Teophile, and Mary Coyle, int. Dec. 21, 1845.

KAIME (see also Cain, Caine, Kane), William W. [Kaine. c. r. 3.], and Rebecca G. Roby of Chichester, N. H., Dec. 3, 1835.*

KALBFUS, John, and Elizabeth Clark, int. Dec. 5, 1841.

KALLOCK, George, Rev., of Chester, N. H., and Rebecca B. Stetson of Brookline, Oct. 27, 1829.

KANE (see also Kaime), Mary, and James McGonacle, int. Sept. 12, 1841.

KANNAVAN, William, and Bridgett Dillion, int. Oct. 1, 1846.

KAOG, William, and Bridgett Spellman, int. July 16, 1847.

KARENCE, Lawrence, and Elizabeth Mibey, int. Mar. 19, 1837.

KATURN, John, and Mary Sullivan, Apr. 2, 1835.*

KAVANAH (see also Cavanagh), Patrick, b. Ireland, and Sarah Colton, b. Ireland, July 24, 1849.

KEAGAN (see also Keegan, Kegin), Michael, and Hannah Brennon [Brennan. int.], May 15, 1848.*

KEARHIN (see also Kearin), Winefred, and James Doary, int. Nov. 12, 1843.

KEARIN (see also Kearhin), Charles, and Ellen Brady, int. July 21, 1849.

KEARNAN, Bridget, and Cornelius Murphy, int. Sept. 29, 1844.

KEEGAN (see also Keagan), Patrick, and Maria Morgan, int. Nov. 12, 1849.

KEEGEE, James, and Mary Lally, int. Mar. 31, 1844.

KEEN, Augustus B., and Prudence Woods of Dedham, int. Aug. 17, 1834.

KEGERY, Mary, and Nathaniel P. Standish, int. July 26, 1848.

* Intention also recorded.

**KEGIN** (see also Keagan), Mary, and Michael Lally, int. Apr. 5, 1848.

**KEIFFE,** Bridget, and Michael Walsh, int. Sept. 19, 1848.

**KEITH,** Amelia, of Taunton, and George Crossman, June 11, 1797.*
Caleb [Kieth. c. R. 3.], and Sally Downe, Oct. 8, 1812.*
Electa Ann, and Benj[ami]n Guild, int. Apr. 25, 1830.
James M., a. 30 y., attorney-at-law, s. Bethuel and Mary, and Adeline Wetherbee, a. 28 y., d. John and Sarah, Aug. 20, 1849.*
Joseph L., and Achsah Sawyer, int. Sept. 13, 1812.
Joshua and Grace Underwood, May 11, 1806.*
Mark, of Easton, and Elizabeth Dorr, at Easton, Feb. 17, 1762.
Mary Eliz[abet]h, a. 25 y., d. W[illia]m and Sally, and Benj[ami]n S. Proctor of Worcester, a. 27 y., clerk, s. Geo[rge] B. and Mary B. of Pembroke, N. H., Aug. 16, 1846.*
Sarah, and Joseph H. Billings, Oct. 22, 1835.*
Susan, and George W. Mann, int. Sept. 9, 1838.
William S., and Harriet Whittemore, May 30, 1830.*

**KELLAN,** Mary, and John Kenney, int. Dec. 22, 1839.

**KELLER,** Orinda J., of Lowell, a. 19 y., d. Matthew and Hannah, and Samuel L. White, a. 22 y., s. Joseph and Elizabeth, Oct. 17, 1847.

**KELLEY** (see also Kelly), Ann, and Joseph Anderson, int. Aug. 4, 1848.
Ann, and Patrick Gaffy, int. Sept. 10, 1848.
Ann, and James McBride, int. Aug. 16, 1849.
Bridget, and Martin Welch, int. Jan. 8, 1843.
Bridget, and John Kenney, int. June 16, 1844.
Catharine, and Patrick Kelley, int. July 21, 1839.
Catharine, and William Moran of Watertown, int. Aug. 28, 1842.
Catherine, and Thomas Riley, int. Apr. 24, 1848.
Charlotte E., of Saco, Me., and John L. Hanson, int. Mar. 15, 1840.
Daniel, and Bridget Kenny, int. Oct. 24, 1824.
Edward, and Margaret Malcy, int. July 12, 1835.

* Intention also recorded.

KELLEY, Elener, and Patrick Kelley, int. Oct. 25, 1842.

Elizabeth W., and Silas Farrington, int. May 25, 1828.

James, and Bridget Condra, int. Oct. 31, 1837.

James, and Hannah Brown, int. Oct. 1, 1843.

James, and Bridgett Hanning, int. Nov. 6, 1848.

Jane, and Thomas Caughlay, int. May 3, 1849.

John, and Winnefred Cunniff of Dorchester, int. Dec. 31, 1843.

John R., and Eliza J. Fullon, int. Jan. 10, 1848.

Luke, and Mary Kelley, int. July 25, 1841.

Maria, and Martin Shene, int. May 16, 1841.

Mary, and Luke Kelley, int. July 25, 1841.

Mary, and Henry Maloon, int. Aug. 25, 1849.

Mary F., and Moses Hason, int. May 5, 1844.

Michael, and Mary Young, int. Feb. 14, 1849.

Patrick, and Catharine Downy, int. Jan. 6, 1839.

Patrick, and Catharine Kelley, int. July 21, 1839.

Patrick, and Mary Kilduff, int. Nov. 10, 1839.

Patrick, and Catharine Lee, int. May 2, 1841.

Patrick, and Elener Kelley, int. Oct. 25, 1842.

Rody, and Margaret Kenny, int. Mar. 27, 1842.

Ruth, and William Dascombe, June 14, 1791.*

Timothy, and Hannah Murphy, int. Apr. 23, 1848.

Timothy, and Celia Cosgrave, int. Oct. 11, 1848.

W[illia]m H., and Sophronia Ann Cleaveland, Jan. 18, 1842.

**KELLHAM,** Frances, Mrs., and John E. Warner, June 11, 1829.*

**KELLOGG,** Elliott E., of Burlington, Vt., a. 28 y., attorney-at-law, s. Alpheus and Augusta, of Jamaica, Vt., and Hannah B[arret. int.] Foster, a. 23 y., d. John S. and Theoda W., Nov. 7, 1848.*

Henry, of Walpole, N. H., and Hannah R. Goddard, int. Nov. 15, 1840.

Sarah, a. 38 y., and Enoch P. P. Foster of Lynn, a. 33 y., cordwainer, s. Enoch and Susanna, of Lynn, Dec. 1, 1846.*

**KELLY** (see also Kelley), Ann, and Martin Fehity, int. Nov. 2, 1847.

Ann, and John Gallagher, int. Oct. 5, 1848.

Ann, and Patrick Fahay [Fahey. int.], Oct. 16, 1848.*

Bartholomew, and Margaret Rogers, int. May 5, 1844.

* Intention also recorded.

KELLY, Bridget, and Patrick Garrathy [Gerratty. dup.], int. Aug. 17, 1845.

Bridget, and John Doyle, int. Oct. 28, 1848.

Bridgett, and Martin Griffin, int. June 12, 1846.

Brine, and Mary Jordan, int. Jan. 30, 1849.

Catharine, and Joseph Farrel, int. Oct. 19, 1845.

Catherine, and Peter Carney of Brookline, int. July 25, 1846.

Catherine, and Martin Kilroy, int. July 3, 1847.

Catherine, and James Skerry, int. Feb. 18, 1848.

Francis [Frances. int.] P. D., a. 26 y., visor maker, d. Joseph and Betsey, and William Blake, a. 27 y., patent leather dresser, s. William and Abigail, Feb. 4, 1846.*

Hannah, and Thomas Coan, int. Apr. 29, 1846.

Hubert, and Mary Ann Curley, int. June 16, 1844.

James, and Susan Proctor of Carlisle, int. Oct. 6, 1833.

James, and Bridgett McCarty, int. Aug. 27, 1847.

James, and Bridget Glenon, int. Nov. 16, 1847.

John, and Catharine Gilligan, int. May 7, 1843

John, and Ann Corbett, int. Dec. 18, 1846.

John, and Bridget Flinn, int. Nov. 9, 1847.

John, and Mary Martin, int. Feb. 7, 1848.

John, and Bridget Harney, int. May 5, 1849.

Luke [Kelley. int.], b. Ireland, and Margaret Aigin [Aigen. int.], b. Ireland, Sept. 30, 1849.*

Margarett, and Luke Gaffey, int. Dec. 13, 1848.

Mary, and Charles Procter, Feb. 8, 1807.*

Mary, [a. 27 y. in pencil.], and Patrick Greaham, [a. 27 y. in pencil.], int. Feb. 11, 1844.

Mary, and James Collins, int. Apr. 26, 1845. [1846. dup.]

Mary, and Samuel Champion, int. Sept. 19, 1846.

Mary, and Patrick Bannon, int. Apr. 27, 1848.

Mary, and Patricy, Kelly, int. Oct. 17, 1848.

Mary, and John Dolan, int. Mar. 31, 1849.

Mary, b. Ireland, and Michael Malone, b. Ireland, Sept. 8, 1849.

Mary Ann, and Sylvester Hill, int. Jan. 15, 1847.

Mary Ann [Kelley. int.], and Peter Green, Sept. 25, 1848.*

Mary Anne, and William Duffy, int. Nov. 11, 1846.

Mary F., and Moses Hanson, May 28, 1844.

Michael, and Mary Gateley, int. Apr. 14, 1833.

Patrick, and Elizabeth Commerford, int. Aug. 28, 1847.

Patrick, and Mary Kelly, int. Oct. 17, 1848.

* Intention also recorded.

KELLY, Peter, and Bridget Morgan, int. Jan. 1, 1848.
Rosanna, and James Dwine, int. Sept. 15, 1846.
Thomas, and Mary Trumbell, int. May 13, 1846.
Thomas, and Ellen Corley, int. Apr. 24, 1847.
Thomas, and Bridgett Cuniff, int. Nov. 4, 1848.

KELSEY, Martha A., of Dracut, and David S. McLane, July 31, 1842. C. R. 7.

KELTON, Abigail, of Dorchester, and Alexander Lear, int Nov. 30, 1794.
Abigail, of Dorchester, and Isaac Howe, 3d, of Dorchester, Dec. 10, 1810.
Charles R., and Sarah Harvey of Lowell, int. Jan. 31, 1830.
Edward [Kilton. C. R. 2.], and Sarah George, June 7, 1750.
Elizabeth, and Henry Whealer [Wheeler. C. R. 2.], Dec. 28, 1773.
Rufus, and Margaret Seaver, Dec. 11, 1804.*

KEMPIS, Kazienna, and John Beltman, int. Aug. 11, 1849.

KENAN (see also Kennan), Catherine, and Hugh Tughey, int. May 1, 1849.

KENARD, Ellen, and Michael Duffy, int. Sept. 25, 1847.

KENCHEN, William, resident, and Bethiah Ramsdill, May 13, 1742.

KENDALL, Hugh R. jr., and Ann Frances Seaver, May 17, 1826.*
Noah, and Sarah Holroyd of Providence, R. I., int. Nov. 8, 1812.
Sewall, and Sarah Wyman, Feb. 22, 1820.*

KENDRICK (see also Kenrick, Kindrick), Elijah, and Mary Stevens, June 9, 1709.
Eliza P., a. 24 y., d. John and Eliza, and Edward Hamilton, of Lincoln, a. 24 y., examiner of drugs, s. Luther and Delia, Sept. 20, 1848.*
John A., and Mary E. Crosby of Nashua, N. H., int. Aug. 13, 1843.
Margarett W., a. 21 y., and William A. Norton [of Boston. int.], a. 23 y., type founder, s. William and Seba, July 14, 1847.*

* Intention also recorded.

**KENEDY** (see also Kennedy), Catharine, and Michael Gately, int, Nov. 19, 1843.
Mary, and Thomas Canniff, int. Jan. 15, 1848.
Mary, and John Morgan, int. Jan. 16, 1848.
Patrick, and Honora Ford, int. Dec. 17, 1847.

**KENNA** (see also Kenney), P. M., and Elen Tolen, int. Oct. 26, 1841.

**KENNAN** (see also Kenan, Kennon), Susan E., and Lewis Baxter, jr., of Quincy, int. Dec. 25, 1842.

**KENNEDY** (see also Kenedy), Anna E. T., and Ephraim W. Stanton, int. Aug. 20, 1846.
James, and Catherine McCurry, int. May 18, 1847.
Maria, and John Minchin, Jan. 5, 1846.*

**KENNEY** (see also Kenna, Kennie, Kenny), Ann, and John Wild, int. Aug. 26, 1848.
Bridget, and Daniel Kelley, int. Oct. 24, 1824.
Bridget, and Patrick Dolan, int. Jan. 6, 1833.
Bridget, and Adam Allendoff, int. May 13, 1838.
Bridget, and William Green, int. Dec. 25. 1845.
Bridget, and James Waters, int. Mar. 4, 1848.
Bridget, and Patrick Kenney, int. July 21, 1849.
Bridget, b. Ireland, and John Byrne [Byron. int.], b. Ireland, Nov. 29, 1849.*
Catharine, and Patrick Maker, int. Feb. 2, 1840.
Eliza, of Milton, and John Ellison, int. Aug. 28, 1842.
Jane, and James Leonard, int. Oct. 13, 1844.
John, and Mary Kellan, int. Dec. 22, 1839.
John, and Bridget Kelley, int. June 16, 1844.
Josiah, and Catherine Twing, Oct. 28, 1775.
Maria, and Peter Tracy, int. Aug. 17, 1849.
Mary, and Paul Gore, Jan. 21, 1764.
Mary, and Hugh Naughton, int. May 18, 1845.
Michael, and Sarah Killian, int. Dec. 22, 1845.
Otis, and Mrs. Ann Beals both of Canton, June 12, 1826.
Patrick, and Bridget Kenney, int. July 21, 1849.
Timothy, and Mary Conitee, int. Mar. 27, 1842.

**KENNICUT,** Ann, and Alfred Johnson, int. Dec. 10, 1843.

**KENNIE** (see also Kenney), Nathan, and Clarissa Cheny of Hopkinton, int. July 28, 1805.

* Intention also recorded.

**KENNINGTON,** Mary, and John Stone, jr., Feb. 25, 1849.*

**KENNISTON,** Benjamin C. [Kenneston. int.], and Sarah Taylor, May 12, 1844.*

**KENNON** (see also Kennan), Ann Augusta, of Quincy, and Gustavus Bills, int. May 7, 1843.

**KENNY** (see also Kenney), Bridget, and Patrick Ward, int. Aug. 10, 1845.
Bridget, and Lawrence Flynn, int. Dec. 28, 1845.
Catharine, and John Dalan, int. Feb. 1, 1835.
Catherine, and Thomas Edwards, int. Nov. 20, 1844.
Catherine, and William Cunningham, int. Nov. 9, 1847.
Eliza, and Thomas Sullivan, int. Dec. 11, 1849.
Ellen, and John Moran, int. Dec. 28, 1845.
Jonah, of Preston, Conn., and Elizabeth Lowder, May 22, 1803.*
Margaret, and Rody Kelley, int. Mar. 27, 1842.
Mary Ann, and Michael Gready, int. Oct. 24, 1847.
Thomas, and Catharine Griffin, int. Apr. 16, 1843.

**KENRICK** (see also Kendrick), Elizabeth, of Newton, and John C. Davis, int. Aug. 10, 1823.
Mary [Kendrick. c. r. 3.], and Reuben Smith, Dec. 1, 1811.*

**KENT,** G. N., and A. J. Newton, int. May 7, 1843.
Hepsy Elizabeth, and George Mock, int. Nov. 2, 1823.
James D., and Ann M. Bourne, Mar. 24, 1841.
Lucy Ann, of Readfield, Me., a. 22 y., and Lemuel May, a. 32 y., omnibus driver, s. Benj[amin] and Mary, Jan. 12, 1847.*
Polly, and Jabez Porter of Malden, at Malden, Mar. 20, 1777.
William A. Esq., of Concord, N. H., and Mrs. Margaret Tucker, July 5, 1821.*

**KER** (see also Kerr), John, and Isabella Walker of Londonderry, July 9, 1724.

**KERR,** see Berr.

**KERWORTH,** Elisabeth, and Isaac Frieze, Sept. 28, 1843.*

**KESLERN,** Barbere, and Jacob Ioykel, May 7, 1833.*

* Intention also recorded.

**KETTELL,** Sam[ue]l, and Mrs. Rebecca Ballard Randolf, Sept. 18, 1815.*

**KEYES** (see also Keys, Kyes), John, and Mary Goffe, Dec. 14, 1772.

Lewis, of Framingham, and Lucy S. Seaverns, Aug. 19, 1818.*

Mary, and Ebininzer Shedden, int. Nov. 25, 1804.

**KEYS** (see also Keyes), Simeon, and Ruthy Whitimore, Apr. 17, 1803.*

**KIAN,** John, and Catherine Dillon, int. Nov. 21, 1848.

**KIDDER,** Asa, widr., of Wardsborough, Vt., a. 53 y., farmer, s. Richard and Rebecca, and Lydia L. Griffin, wid. of Dedham, a. 47 y., d. Richard, of Benson, Vt., Mar. 1, 1848.

Sarah, of Medford, and Thompson Kidder, int. Dec. 31, 1843.

Thompson, and Sarah of Medford, int. Dec. 31, 1843.

**KIGGINS,** Michael, and Hannah Murphy, int. July 8, 1848.

**KILDERY** (see also Kildry), Eliza, and Alvan M. Newton, int. Nov. 10, 1844.

**KILDRY** (see also Kildery), Andrew, and Ann Duignin, int. Jan. 18, 1846.

**KILDUFF** (see also Killduff), Bridget, and Thomas Norton, int. Feb. 4, 1838.

James, and Sarah Gray, int. July 10, 1842.

John, and Mary Donlin, int. Aug. 4, 1839.

Mary, and Patrick Kelley, int. Nov. 10, 1839.

William, and Ann Ledwidge, int. Nov. 14, 1849.

**KILLACKY,** Margaret, and Patrick Jordan, int. Feb. 14, 1846.

**KILLAN,** Ann, and Thomas Shay, int. Apr. 9, 1837.

Catharine, and Robert Bradley, int. Apr. 12, 1846.

Michael, and Catharine Finn, int. Sept. 27, 1840.

**KILLARD,** Patrick, b. Ireland, and Margaret Hassion, b. Ire-land, July 25, 1849.*

**KILLDAY,** Andrew, and Ann Mulry, int. Sept. 1, 1849.

**KILLDUFF** (see also Kilduff), Margarett [Kilduff. int.], b. Ireland, and Peter Shea, b. Ireland, Apr. 30, 1849.*

* Intention also recorded.

KILLDUFF, Mary, and Michael Reynolds, int. Aug. 29, 1849.
Sabina, b. Ireland, and William Newsome, b. Ireland, Oct. 29, 1849.*

KILLEA, John, and Bridget Martin, int. Nov. 27, 1847.

KILLEAN (see also Killian), Catharine, and Martin McDonnell, int. Oct. 29, 1843.
Hugh, and Ann Durnin, int. Apr. 17, 1842.
Michael, and Bridget Donlan, int. July 5, 1840.

KILLEREN, Ann, and James McQueeny, int. Jan. 4, 1846.

KILLERLY, Catherine, and Patrick Cunningham, int. July 11, 1848.

KILLIAN (see also Killean, Killin, Killion), Bridget, and Thomas Gafney, int. Mar. 3, 1848.
Bridget, and Michael Gilligin, int. Dec. 22, 1848.
John, and Ann Costerly, int. May 4, 1847.
John, and Bridget Carrol, int. May 16, 1849.
John, b. Ireland, and Mary Connor [Comer. int.], b. Ireland, Aug. 4, 1849.*
Sarah, and Michael Kenney, int. Dec. 22, 1845.
Thomas, and Mary Morgan, int. Sept. 7, 1845.

KILLILLIN, Matthew [Killillea. int.], b. Ireland, and Mary Murray, b. Ireland, Aug. 7, 1849.*

KILLIN (see also Killian), Bridget, and Patrick Houghton, int. May 22, 1842.

KILLION (see also Killian), Michael, and Bridget Coghnanton, int. Jan. 12, 1845.

KILLROY (see also Kilroy), Mary, and John Morgan, Oct. 24, 1848.
Michael, and Eliza Lester, int. June 29, 1845.

KILROY (see also Killroy), John, and Mary Turles, int. Dec. 24, 1843.
Martin, and Catherine Kelly, int. July 3, 1847.
Mary, and John Morgan, int. Sept. 19, 1848.

KILTON, Abigail [Kelton. int.], of Dorchester, and Alexand [Alexander. int.] Lear, at Dorchester, Jan. 22, 1795.
Lois, and Samuel Glover, both of Dorchester, Mar. 7, 1793.

* Intention also recorded.

**KILTS,** Patrick, and Mary Walsh, int. Aug. 11, 1848.

**KIMBALL,** Betsey A. G., a. 20 y., d. Richard and Eliza, and William G. Lavers, a. 23 y., blacksmith, s. John W. and Catherine, Nov 21, 1847.*

Betsey Brown, a. 27 y., d. Truman and Hannah, and John Lewis of Lowell, machinist, Sept. 22, 1846.*

George, and Matilda J. Moore, Mar. 5, 1837.*

Israel, and Sarah Rhoades, int. Sept. 4, 1836.

Mark, and Mary Jane Perkins of Kennebunkport, Me., int. Sept. 16, 1838.

Mary Ann [Mrs. int.], wid., a. 38 y., tailoress, d. Eben[eze]r and Polly Leach, and Abraham Parker, widr., a. 56 y., mason, s. Francis and Mary, Sept. 7, 1845.*

Nancy C., of Hallowell, Me., and Israel D. Russell, int. Oct. 9, 1847.

Nath[anie]l, and Caroline Mayo, int. Apr. 12, 1840.

**KINDRICK** (see also Kendrick), Caleb, of Newton, and Abigail Bowin, Sept. 14, 1721.

Esther, of Newton, and Joseph Mayo, at Newton, Nov. 14, 1745.

Thomas, and Sarah Ellis, May 23, 1790.*

**KING,** Ann, and Thomas Barane, int. Sept. 20, 1845.

Ann, and Patrick Magee, int. June 27, 1848.

Anna, and James Doherty, int. Nov. 26, 1849.

Daniel E., and Emeline Rice of Cambridge, int. Nov. 11, 1838.

Edward [William. c. R. 2.], and Mary Colman, Apr. 19, 1750.

Elizabeth, and Joseph Bacon, resident, int. Apr. 14, 1793.

George, Capt., and Cassandra A. Fobes of Bridgewater, int. Aug. 28, 1831.

Horace, and Catharine A. Mead of Rutland, May 20, 1837.

Mary Ann, and Joseph Eckart, int. Nov. 26, 1847.

Rufus, a. 24 y., laborer, s. Elijah and Hannah, and Mary Ann Johnson, a. 26 y., d. William and Sarah, Apr. 18, 1847.*

Rufus T., and Emeline E. Stone of Framingham, int. Aug. 8, 1841.

Rufus T., and Chloe W. Smith, int. July 13, 1848.

Sarah, and Edward Voy, int. Sept. 4, 1847.

**KINGSBERRY** (see also Kingsbury), Noah [of Dedham. c. R. 2.], and Mehittabell Morey, Sept. 30, 1718.

* Intention also recorded.

**KINGSBURY** (see also Kingsberry), Albert, and Sarah W. Smith, int. Apr. 5, 1849.

Charlotte, of Dorchester, and Edmund Jones, Apr. 16, 1817.*

Eleazer, of Needham, and Elisabeth George, Oct. 22, 1774.

Eliza, and William Hazlet, residents, Feb. 9, 1803.*

Elizabeth, and John Marston, Apr. 16, 1837.*

Emily, and Marshall Glazier of Brookline, int. Sept. 14, 1845.

Hannah, and Dea. Ben[jami]n Farrington, Sept. 27, 1827.
C. R. 2.*

Helen C., of Franklin, and Gilbert B. George, int. Oct. 7, 1846.

John W., and Elizabeth Ann Upham of Newton, Apr. 25, 1840. C. R. 7.

Josiah, and Susanna Mory, Jan. 16, 1704-5.

Moses G., and Mary Butler of Malden, int. Jan 6, 1839.

Rachel, of Walpole, and Samuel Thompson, int. June 21, 1829.

Sarah, of Needham, and John Stedman, int. July 26, 1795.

Theodore, and Jerusha Burrel, May 25, 1806.*

**KINGSLEY** (see also Kinsley), Mary B., of Hampden, Me., and Samuel J. Gardner, Esq., int. Oct. 1, 1820.

**KINMAN,** Bridget, and Tobias Davis, Dec. 13, 1649.

**KINSLEY** (see also Kingsley), Adam, Esq., and Martha Willis both of Canton, Dec. 31, 1823.

**KINTER,** Eustena, and Jacob Geisler, int. May 16, 1849.

**KIRK,** Joseph, and Mary Cain, int. July 16, 1849.

**KIRKWOOD** Sarah, of Concord. N. H., and Hugh K. Prentiss, int. Nov. 2, 1834.

**KITCH,** Mary, and Michael Cochran of Boston, int. Sept. 27, 1849.

**KITE,** Mary, and John Brough, Sept. 24, 1847.

**KITTREDGE,** Eliza H., a. 19 y., d. Alvah and Mehitable, and Andrew B. Lawrie, a. 23 y., merchant, s. Andrew and Margarett, Apr. 4, 1848.*

John S., and Mary Marshall of Bradford, N. H., int. Nov. 6, 1847.

* Intention also recorded.

KITTREDGE, Joseph, of Andover, a. 26 y., physician, s. Jos[eph]
and Hannah, and Henrietta F[rances. int.] Watson, a. 25
y., d. Geo[rge] and Eliza, Dec. 15, 1847.*
Martha Osgood, of Andover, and Dr. Lemuel Barron, int.
Sept. 17, 1809.

KLY, Michael, and Mary Dacy, int. Sept. 25, 1836.

KNAPP, Lucinda, and Ameriah Hamden, int. May 15, 1825.

KNEE, Thomas, and Mary Daily, int. May 6, 1838.

KNEELAND (see also Kneland), Abigail [Mrs. int.], and
Josiah Newell [of Newton. int.], Jan. 29, 1783. C. R. 2.*
Salley, and Benjamin Bronsdel [Bronsdon. int.] of Milton,
Jan. 15, 1786.*
Samuel, and Nancy Burt Johnson, Oct. 5, 1820.*

KNELAND (see also Kneeland), Mary, and Richard Hall,
Apr. 21, 1720.

KNIGHT (see also Knights), Albert, and Chloe Robbins of
Dorchester, Apr. 2, 1840.*
Betsy, of Bolton, and John V. Stevens, at Lancaster, Jan. 31,
1797.*
Sally, and William Lawrence, May 2, 1802.*
Samuel, and Sarah How, Oct. 16, 1685.
William A., of Providence, R. I., and Ellen P. Webber, Aug.
27, 1841.*

KNIGHTS (see also Knight), Abigail S., and Merrill J. Hazeltine of Barnet, Vt., int. Sept. 6, 1849.
Pametia, and John W. Allen, Sept. 4, 1821.*

KNOWER, Benjamin, and Elizabeth Weld, July 26, 1773.
Benjamin, and Mary Howes, Apr. 27, 1806.*
Betsey, and William Hannaford, Nov. 21, 1802.*
Hannah, and Nathan Watson, Oct. 1, 1797. C. R. 3.*
Mary, and Jonas Randall, Nov. 24, 1805.*
Sally, and Caleb Dickerman, Oct. —, 1807.*
Samuel, and Sauannah Stratton, Dec. 1, 1822.*

KNOWLS, Wesley, and Lydia Tolman, Apr. —, 1834.

KNOWLTON, Sirus, and Mary Whittemore, int. May 22,
1808. (banns forbidden by Mary Whittemore.)

* Intention also recorded.

**KNOX,** Daniel, and Sarah D. Robbins, June 14, 1818.*
Eunice, and Hiram Glines, Nov. 24, 1825.*
Robert, and Margaret Mackashlin, resident, Nov. 26, 1728.

**KOCH,** Barbara, of Milton, and John Vogelsang, Jan. 8, 1837.*

**KOERKEL,** Ann Maria, and H. L. George Rehm, int. Oct. 26, 1849.

**KORKLING,** Daniel, and Ellen Mee, int. July 16, 1846.

**KRAFT** (see also Craft), Magdalena, of Dorchester, and George Fisher, int. Nov. 3, 1833.

**KRAMER,** Matthew, and Polly Webber, Mar. 20, 1831.*
Sebastion, and Mary Ann Webber, Feb. 4, 1832.*

**KRAUS,** Elizabeth, and Lewis Schwenn, int. Aug. 5, 1838.

**KUEBLER,** Matthew F., and Louisa E. Pierce, Feb. 3, 1842.

**KUHN,** Henrietta, and Athone Hilbert, Dec. 25, 1838.*

**KYBURZ,** Daniel, and Louisa Bossuet, int. May 6, 1832.

**KYES** (see also Keyes), Caroline, and Alvin M. Robbins, int. Oct. 18, 1840.

**LACY,** Patrick, and Electious Percle, int. May 10, 1849.

**LADD,** Mary M., a. 22 y., b. Holderness, N. H., d. Asa and Betsey, and Wyman Brooks, a. 36 y., carpenter, b. Robbinston, Me., s. Abel and Mary, Nov. 4, 1849.*

**LAGATTY** (see also Legallees), Thomas [Lagallee. int.], and Mrs. Sally Everett, Mar. 19, 1809. c. r. 2.*

**LAHY** (see also Leahy), Daniel, and Catherine Galvin, int. Sept. 22, 1849.

**LAIDLAW,** Archibald, and Mary Robbins Hillard, int. May 7, 1826.

**LAITHBRIDGE** (see also Lethbridge), Abagail, of Franklin, and Elisha Seaverns, int. Oct. 30, 1808.

**LAKEMAN,** Sarah, and George B. Wellman, int. Jan. 13, 1839.

* Intention also recorded.

**LALLEY** (see also Lally), Andrew, and Catherine Fullughan, int. Sept. 1, 1849.

**LALLY** (see also Lalley), Ellen, and William Carl, int. Oct. 11, 1848.
Hannah, and Richard McLaughlin, int. Aug. 18, 1846.
James, and Alice Lynch, int. Feb. 19, 1849.
Mary, and James Keegee, int. Mar. 31, 1844.
Michael, and Ellen McCarty, int. Nov. 23, 1845.
Michael, and Mary Kegin, int. Apr. 5, 1848.

**LAMAY,** Mary, and Patrick Duffy, int. Apr. 2, 1849.

**LAMB** (see also Lambe), Caleb, and Marie Wise, June 30, 1669.
Catharine, and James Gallergher, int. Feb. 8, 1846.
Dorithy, and Thomas Hawley, Feb. 2, 1651.
Huldah, and Daniell Durninger, Jan. 24, 1722-3.
Joseph, and Margarett Galagher, int. July 17, 1846.
Joshua, and Susanna Cary, Oct. 1, 1702.
Mary, and Atherton Mather, Oct. 24, 1705.

**LAMBE** (see also Lamb), Thomas, and Dorothy Harbittle, July 16, 1640.

**LAMBERT,** Charlotte, and Peter Wainwright, jr., Nov. 11, 1825.*
Harriet, and Capt. William Blanchard of Dorchester, int. Sept. 8, 1816.
Henry L., and Abba E. Morse, both of Salem, May 17, 1848.
Joseph, and Ann Elizabeth Hollis of Dorchester, int. Dec. 8, 1844.
Lucy, and Nathaniel Fellowes, Esq. of Havana, Oct. 9, 1825.*
Mary, and Charles Stimpson, July 21, 1799.*
Patrick. and Ann McDaniel, int. Apr. 23, 1849.
Susan, and Nath[anie]l Dorr, int. Nov. 29, 1807.
William, jr., and Lucy Hiller, int. June 8, 1806.

**LAMSON,** Susan, and Leonard Butterfield, int. Sept. 2, 1832.

**LANDERGIN,** Ellen, of Boston, and James Hussey, int. Sept. 10, 1849.

**LANDERS,** Lucy, and James Holbrook, Feb. 7, 1828.*

* Intention also recorded.

**LANE,** Eliza A., of Boston, and Lyman Locke, int. Apr. 8, 1848.
Elizabeth, and Joseph Davis [of Brookline. c. r. 2.], Dec. 8 [3. c. r. 2.], 1715.
Job, and Mrs. Martha Ruggles, at Billerica, Dec. 16 [17. dup.], 1713.
John, and Margrett Robinson, Mar. 30, 1767.
John, and Anne Sarchfield, int. May 19, 1844.
Margarett, and Patrick Reilly, int. Sept. 3, 1847.

**LANG,** Charles E., a. 22 y., painter, s. Edward and Eliza, and Sarah F. Sancy [Sanery. int.], a. 18 y., d. Francis and Elizabeth, Nov. 23, 1848.*
Edward, jr., a. 23 y., carpenter, s. Edward and Eliza, and Harriet Dodge, a. 20 y., d. Ebenezer and Mary, Jan. 23, 1848.*
Edward C., and Eliza Godfrey, int. Dec. 14, 1823.

**LANGDON,** Mary, and Stephen Williams, Dec. 12, 1771.

**LANGLEY,** (see also Longley), Ann P., of Newton, and James B. Faunce, Nov. 29, 1838.*
Esther, and George Nolin, Feb. 16, 1794.*
Harriet, Mrs., and John Elliot, int. June 10, 1827.
Rebecca W., and Stephen Faunce, jr., May 16, 1832.*
Samuel, and Esther Mayo, Feb. 7, 1771.
Samuel, and Emely Pierpont, Dec. 1, 1805.*
Susan S., and W[illia]m Cummings, May 27, 1830.
Susanna, and Samuel Silsby, July 3, 1806.*
W[illia]m, and Mona Clark of Medfield, int. Sept. 18, 1808.

**LANGMAID,** Margarett A., of Nottingham, N. H., a. 20 y., d. John and Ann, and Isaiah Palmer, a. 23 y., carpenter, s. Truworthy and Betsey M., Nov. 4, 1848.*

**LANGSTAFF,** Grace O[livia. int.], a. 20 y., d. Thomas and Thankful, and John Robinson, a. 22 y., cabinet maker, s. Robert and Lilias, Nov. 26, 1848.*

**LARABEE** (see also Larrabee), Thomas, and Mary Bowden, Nov. 30, 1828.*

**LARKIN,** Elizabeth, and Edward Flanagan, int. Oct. 1, 1837.
Hannah, and Mark Lynsky, int. May 3, 1847.
John, and Blandena Flinn, int. Dec. 31, 1837.

* Intention also recorded.

**LARRABEE** (see also Larabee, Larrobee), Lucy A., and Joseph F. Sinclair, int. Feb. 28, 1836.

**LARRISON,** Amos Smith [Larison. c. R. 3.], and Tamien [Tamcien. int; Tamsen. c. R. 3.], Eliza Hearsey [Hersey. c. R. 3.], Oct. 9, 1814.*

**LARROBEE** (see also Larrabee), John, and Elizabeth Williams of Cambridge, int. Nov. 22, 1829.

**LARY** (see also Leary), Bathsheba, and David Shaw, int. Sept. 29, 1847.
Margaret, and Patrick Connin, int. July 29, 1838.

**LASKIN,** Mary, and Timothy Welch, int. Feb. 20, 1849.

**LATHBRIDGE** (see also Lethbridge), Richard, and Mary Willson, Dec. 22, 1772.

**LAUGHLIN** (see also McLaughlin), Mary, of Boston, and Joseph W. Tracy, int. June 28, 1848.
Patrick, and Ellen Tracy, int. Jan. 4, 1847.

**LAUGHTON,** Charles H., and Pamelia G. Rich, Aug. 8, 1844.*
George, and Mehet[ab]le Cudlis, at Boston, July 29, 1725.
Jane, of Brookline, and William H. Brown, int. Aug. 27, 1820.
Sarah E., and Christopher S. Mills, Aug. 31, 1845.*

**LAURIATT,** Elizabeth B., and Francis G. Caffin, Oct. 8, 1826.

**LAUSTERER,** John P., of Boston, and Elizabeth Forgar, int. Sept. 6, 1849.

**LAVERS,** William G., a. 23 y., blacksmith, s. John W., and Catherine, and Betsey A. G. Kimball, a. 20 y., d. Richard and Eliza, Nov. 21, 1847.*

**LAW,** Thomas T., and Betsey Shirley of Chatham, N. H., Nov. 14, 1830.

**LAWLEY,** Ann, and Michael Mulray, int. Dec. 30, 1848.

**LAWRANCE** (see also Lawrence), Seth, and Mary Haynes of Sudbury, int. Apr. 14, 1800.

* Intention also recorded.

LAWRENCE (see also Lawrance), Byrem, Rev., of Indianapolis, Ind., and Elizabeth Prentiss, Sept. 23, 1832.*

Elijah E., and Elizabeth B. Gibson, int. Nov. 13, 1831.

Fanny, Mrs., and Jacob Walker of Brookline, Sept. 6, 1827.*

Issac, and Mary Ann Montgomery, May 3, 1820.*

Mary, of Waltham, and Chester Lyman, int. Sept. 2, 1810.

Nath[anie]l, and Matilda Rumrill, June 22, 1823.*

Peggy, of Dedham, and James Clap, jr., int. Mar. 10, 1805.

Reuben, and Rosilla Fasgate of Brookline, int. Aug. 12, 1832.

Reuben, and Nancy Turner [of Boston. c. r. 3.], Mar. 23 [22. c. r. 3.], 1843.*

Samuel, and Fanny McCumber, Sept. 7, 1818.*

William, and Sally Knight, May 2, 1802.*

LAWRIE, Andrew B., a. 23 y., merchant, s. Andrew and Margarett, and Eliza H. Kittredge, a. 19 y., d. Alvah and Mehitable, Apr. 4, 1848.*

LAWSON, Catherine, and Thomas Cochran, int. Sept. 11, 1846.

LAYNARD (see also Linard), Patrick[Leynard. int.], b. Ireland, and Mary Dolan, b. Ireland, Dec. 16, 1849.*

LAZARUS, Ellen, of Wilmington, N. C., a. 23 y., d. Aaron and Rachel, and John Allen, a. 34 y., reformer, s. Solomon and Abigail, Oct. 4, 1848.*

LEACH, Lydia, of Bridgewater, and John Dickerman, at Bridgewater, Nov. 8, 1770.

Mary [Leech. c. r. 5.], and Thomas Craige [Crigue. int; Craig. c. r. 5.], Dec. 4, 1845.*

Mary Ann, and George Adams, int. Aug. 28, 1836.

Nathaniel, and Nancy Little, May 23, 1839.*

Patrick, b. Ireland, and Rosa O'Brine, b. Ireland, Aug. 5, 1849.*

Sally, and John Sole, Aug. 9, 1807.*

Sam[ue]l, and Mary E. White of Dedham, int. Apr. 6, 1828.

LEAHY (see also Lahy), Mary, and Stephen Recorden, int. July 22, 1848.

LEAMY, Mary, and Robert Riordin, int. Nov. 2, 1848.

LEAR (see also Leear), Alexand [Alexander. int.] and Abigail Kilton [Kelton. int.] of Dorchester, at Dorchester, Jan. 22, 1795.*

* Intention also recorded.

**LEARNED** (see also Leonard), Elijah, of Watertown, and Sarah Pond, May 19, 1796.*
Jonas, and Hannah Titterton, both residents, Aug. 16, 1787.*
Joseph, and Esther Hastings, resident, int. Feb. 20, 1803.
Susan, and John Perry [of Boston. c. r. 3.], June 4, 1818.*

**LEAROCK,** Hannah, and Benja[min] S. Noyes, June 5, 1832.*

**LEARY** (see also Lary, O'Leary), Cornelius, and Julia Coughlin, int. July 31, 1846.
Dennis, and Catharine Long, int. June 23, 1844.
Jane, and Daniel McCarty, int. Sept. 7, 1846.

**LEATHAM,** Caroline, and Robert Hooper, jr. of Marblehead, Oct. 15, 1816.*
Charlotte Maria, and Rev. Joseph Field of Weston, Oct. 15, 1816.*

**LEAVENS** (see also Levens), Simon Davis, and Hellen Louisa Hall, Oct. 22, 1832.*

**LEAVIT** (see also Leavitt), Israel, and Elizabeth Mory, Dec. 27, 1710.

**LEAVITT** (see also Leavit, Levet, Levitt), Jonathan, and Angelina Towle of Exeter, N. H., int. June 9, 1833.

**LE BARON,** W[illia]m [Dr. int.], of Andover, and Sarah J[arvis. int.] Carr, June 7, 1841.*

**LE BETTER,** Daniel, a. 26 y., clerk, s. Daniel and Eliza, and Elizabeth J. Fowle, a. 24 y., d. John and Prudence, May 27, 1847.*

**LEDEVIDGE** (see also Ledwidge), Ann, b. Ireland, and William Ledevidge, b. Ireland, Nov. 22, 1849.
William, b. Ireland, and Ann Ledevidge, b. Ireland, Nov. 22, 1849.

**LEDWIDGE** (see also Ledevidge), Ann, and William Kilduff, int. Nov. 14, 1849.

**LEE** (see also Lees), Catharine, and Patrick Kelley, int. May 2, 1841.
Geo[rge] C., and Susan Pratt, Oct. 13, 1834.*

* Intention also recorded.

Lee, Henry, of Worcester, and Katha[rine] Payson, at Boston, Dec. 25, 1725.

John, of Freetown, and Mary Mather, at Boston, May 3, 1722.

Lucy, and William Dinsdill, Feb. 18, 1754.

Margaret, and Ira Holmas, int. Dec. 14, 1845.

Mary, and John Spear of Braintree, Mar. 26, 1742.

Mary W., of Waltham, and John Gilbert, int. Nov. 29, 1848.

Stephen D., of Brighton, and Catharine E. Pratt, Nov, 15. 1836.*

Susan E., of Charlestown, a. 24 y., and William R. Huston of Dedham, a. 31 y., housewright, Oct. 28, 1847.

W[illia]m Raymond, and Helen M. Amory, July 7, 1842.*

**LEEAR**(see also Lear), Henry, and Mary Lynch, int. Apr. 16, 1843.

**LEEDS,** Abigail B. [Mrs. int.], and Nathaniel Curtis, [Esq. int.], Jan. 18, 1842.*

Harriet, of Dorchester, and Milton James, Oct. 18, 1827.*

James B., and Abigail B. Cook of Brighton, Feb. 7, 1822.*

James M., and Betsy Putnam, int. Apr. 29, 1838.

Mary, Mrs., and Simon Willard, Jan. 23, 1788.*

Rebecca, and Edward Humphries, Aug. 30, 1801.*

Sarah, and Dana Baker, Feb. 3, 1822.*

Sarah Homans, and Gilman Davis, int. May 19, 1822.

Susanna, Mrs., of Dorchester, and Abel Chamberlain, at Dorchester, Apr. 11, 1775.

**LEEK,** Anna Worthy, and Moses Draper, Apr. 8, 1757.

**LEES** (see also Lee), Jane A., of Lowell, and Nathaniel R. Cochran, May 4, 1841.*

**LEFAVOUR,** Daniel, and Lucy P. Leonard of Cambridge, int. Apr. 17, 1842.

**LEFSTROM,** Magnus, and Susan White, Sept. 21, 1845.*

**LEGALLEES** (see also Lagatty), Elizabeth, and Aaron Fuller, Nov. 29, 1827. c. r. 2.

**LEHMAN,** Henry, and Elizabeth Bauer, Oct. 12, 1834.*

**LEIGHTNER,** Mary Ann, and Henry Harnden of Wilmington, int. Nov. 30, 1847.

* Intention also recorded.

**LEIGHTON,** Emily A., and Benjamin F. Perry, Dec. 20, 1845.*

James L., and Sarah Jane Thayer of Gray, Me., int. Nov. 6, 1846.

**LELAND,** Anna, of Sherburne, and Draper Smith, int. Apr. 2, 1809.

Catharine, a. 28 y., d. Sherman and Elizabeth [Betsey (Adams). P. R. 4.], and John Henderson, jr. of St. Louis, Mo., a. 26 y., attorney-at-law, s. John and Theodoria, June 30, 1847.*

Ebenezer, and Mrs. Sukey Wilson, Aug. 4, 1793.*

Edwin S., s. Sherman and Betsey (Adams), and Margaret B. Miles, Apr. 20, 1840. P. R. 4.

Sherman, and Betsey Adams, Oct. 13, 1811. P. R. 4.

**LEMIST,** Frances C., and Manlius S. Clarke, Dec. 1, 1841.

John, and Eliza Warner [Warren. int.] of Medford, at Medford, Oct. 8, 1809.*

John, and Mrs. Mary Haswell, int. Apr. 21, 1816.

Stephen, Capt., and Catharine S. Clark of Gilmanton, N. H., int. Jan. 20, 1839.

**LENAHAN,** John, and Mary Hand, int. Aug. 3, 1845.

Robert, and Elisabeth Hand, int. Aug. 12, 1846.

**LENNON,** William, and Ellen G. Conboy, int. Nov. 5, 1843.

**LEONARD** (see also Learned), Abby, of Taunton, and Artemas D. Gushee, int. Oct. 16, 1836.

Anna, and Kimball Whitney, int. Oct. 3, 1802.

Catharine, and Michael Fleming, int. Oct. 8, 1843.

Eliza, b. Ireland, and Patrick McMorris [McMorrow. int.], b. Ireland, July 19, 1849.*

Elizabeth, and Gilman Clough, Aug. 19, 1827.*

Elizabeth, and John Adler of Dorchester, int. Oct. 6, 1844.

Eunice, and Simeon Stearns, May 1, 1808.*

George, and Sarah F. Leverett of Brookline, May 1, 1825.*

Hetty, and William H. Joy, Nov. 26, 1826.*

Horatio, widr., of Raynham, a. 60 y., gentleman, and Mary Haven, wid., a. 50 y., d. Andrew Cunningham, June 1, 1847.*

James, and Jane Kenney, int. Oct. 13, 1844.

Jesse, and Lydia Glines, Nov. 4, 1827.*

* Intention also recorded.

LEONARD, Lucy P., of Cambridge, and Daniel Lefavour, int. Apr. 17, 1842.

Mary B., of Foxborough, and Enoch Tibbets, int. May 30, 1849.

Mary R., and William Nash, Dec. 21, 1826.*

Michael, and Ellen Castolane, int. Nov. 10, 1844.

Seth, and Nancy Hall [Hill. int.], Apr. 12, 1807. c. r. 2.*

Squire, of Dorchester, and Elizabeth White, Nov. 24, 1799.*

Susan, and Lemuel Bradlee, July 4, 1824.*

LEROY, Charles, and Sarah Ann Humphrey of Brookline, Sept. 8, 1841.*

Frances M., of Sterling, and Thomas Bryant, int. Aug. 8, 1846.

LESTER, Eliza, and Michael Killroy, int. June 29, 1845.

LETHBRIDGE (see also Laithbridge, Lathbridge), Hebsibah, of Franklin, and Calvin Sampson, int. May 31, 1818.

Jerusha, of Franklin, and Leonard Hyde, int. June 14, 1812.

Leonard Fisher, and Elizabeth Gooch, Dec. 22, 1774.

Richard, and Hopestill Monk, June 7, 1742.

Richard [Leathbridge. c. r. 3.], and Mary Mayo, Apr. 6, 1813.*

Richard, and Mary Harris Shattuck, Sept. 17, 1835.*

Samuel, jr., of Wrentham, and Sarah Fales, Nov. 16, 1773.

Sarah, and John Clark, both residents, July 21, 1735.

Sarah, and Abraham Woodward, jr., June 23, 1743.

LEVANSELLER, Austin, a. 24 y., pianoforte manufacturer, s. Peter and Elizabeth, and Mary E. McCure [McClure. int.], of Waldo, Me., a. 22 y., d. Thomas, Dec. 1, 1847.*

LEVENS (see also Leavens, Levins), John, and Rachell Wright, July 5, 1639.

LEVERETT (see also Leveritt), Francis Baker, and John Shays of Danvers, Aug. 18, 1816. c. r. 2.*

Sarah F., of Brookline, and George Leonard, May 1, 1825.*

William, and Charlottee Whiting, Nov. 7, 1793.*

William, Rev., and Mary A. Cole of Providence, R. I., int. Mar. 13, 1825.

LEVERITT (see also Leverett), Abigail, and Rev. Stephen Johnson of Lyme, Conn., May 28, 1776.

* Intention also recorded.

**LEVET** (see also Leavitt), Sam[ue]l, of Beverly, and Ester Griggs, at Boston, Jan. 5, 1726.

**LEVINS** (see also Levens), John, and Hannah Woods, June 7, 1665.

**LEVITT** (see also Leavitt), Levi, of Hull, a. 38 y., gentleman, and Mary Ann G. Hersey, a. 34 y., d. Zerubbabel and Betsey, May 28, 1846.*

**LEWES** (see also Lewis), John [Lewis. c. r. 2.], and Abigail Stone, Jan. 20, 1763.
Jonas, and Olive Gay, Mar. 12, 1769.

**LEWIS** (see also Lewes), Abiel S[mith. int.], and Elsey E. Davis, Apr. 17, 1842.*
Andrew, of Dedham, and Mrs. Mary Pond, int. Aug. 28, 1796.
Ann, of Dorchester, and James Herring, at Dorchester, Aug. 11, 1725.
Ann, and Philemon.R. Russell of Charlestown, Dec. 30, 1822.*
Ann Payson, a. 42 y., d. Elijah, and Benjamin Huntoon of Canton, a. 53 y., minister, s. Benj[ami]n and Mehitabel of Salisbury, N. H., July 30, 1846.*
Barachiah, and wid. Susanna Octinton of Needham, at Needham, Dec. 15, 1756.
Barachias, and Hannah Adams of Watertown, at Watertown, Dec. 4, 1734.
Beulah, of Dedham, and John Whiting, at Dedham, Dec. 1, 1789.
Charlottee, of Dedham, and Horace Felton, int. Oct. 14, 1838.
Charlotte C., and Horatio G. Simpson, int. Nov. 1, 1840.
Elijah, and Fanny Sumner, Nov. 14, 1803.*
Elijah, and Elizabeth Sumner Doggett, Aug. 5, 1819.*
Elizabeth, and John Webber, jr., int. May 8, 1836.
Francies M. P., and John L. Wilson of Philadelphia, Oct. 26, 1837.*
Franklin H., and Sarah B. Durfee of Fall River, int. Dec. 7, 1848.
Harriet L., of Pepperell, and Charles M. Ellis, int. Jan. 21, 1844.
Jabez, and Lucretia Winchester, Feb. 8, 1807.*
James, and Hannah Seaver, May 24, 1787.*
James, jr., and Mary Glover of Dorchester, int. Nov. 11, 1821.

* Intention also recorded.

LEWIS, John, of Lowell, machinist, and Betsy Brown Kimball,
a. 27 y., d. Truman and Hannah, Sept. 22, 1846.*
John G., and Mary Z. Cook, int. Apr. 7, 1833.
Jonas, and Lucy Child of Newton, at Newton, Apr. 9, 1766.
Joseph, and Lydia Crain, Sept. 7, 1806. C. R. 2.
Joshua, and Mary Lyon, Sept. 26, 1776.
Joshua, Capt., and Mrs. Lydia H. Barnett of Dorchester, Apr.
19, 1827.*
Mary S., and William Caswell, Nov. 27, 1806.*
Sarah, of Dedham, and Thomas Clark, at Dedham, Dec. 21,
1775.
Tabitha R., and David Simpson, jr., int. Nov. 8, 1835.
Thomas M., and Hannah Campbell, int. Jan. 2, 1842.
Timothy, and Mrs. [wid. int.] Abigail Whitney, Aug. 7, 1785.*
William, of Walpole, and Judith Ann Whittemore, int. Sept.
1, 1833.
W[illia]m G., and Mary Ann D. Dudley, Oct. 13, 1841.*

LIBBEY (see also Libby), Joseph, and Mary Whitney, Dec.
14, 1843.

LIBBY (see also Libbey), Alfred I., and Elizabeth I. Mitchell,
int. Mar. 15, 1846.
Sanford, and Henrietta Johns, Oct. 15, 1840.*

LIGHTMER, John, and Margaret Hughes, int. Jan. 1, 1843.

LILLIE, Elisabeth Dupee, and Joseph Fenno, June 30, 1822.
Lucinda, and George W. Redfield, Jan. 30, 1842.*
Thomas, and Sarah Edes, Dec. 15, 1822.

LINARD (see also Laynard), Michael, and Mary Smyth, int.
May 6, 1848.
Patrick, and Catharine Canrey, int. Jan. 19, 1845.

LINCOLN, Charles, and Nancy [Coney. int.; Mary Coney.
C. R. 3.] Lincoln, Feb. —, 1805.*
David, of Hingham, and Lucy Felton, Nov. 10, 1793.*
Irene H., and George H. Richards, June 22, 1842.*
Martha W., and Edward L. Balch [of Boston. C. R. 3.], Dec.
1, 1844.*
Nancy [Coney. int.; Mary Coney. C. R. 3.], and Charles Lin-
coln, Feb. —, 1805.*
Paul, and Roxanna T. Pierce, int. Apr. 24, 1846.*
Prudence, and Samuel Payson, Mar. 31, 1677.

* Intention also recorded.

LINCOLN, Susanna, and Capt. John Godward, at Hingham, Nov. 16, 1738.

Susanna M., and George A. Stephenson, int. Sept. 30, 1846.

**LINDALL,** George, and Susan F. Harvey, int. Mar. 12, 1843.

Sylvanus, and Abigail Chamberlain, Apr. 5, 1819. c. r. 2.*

**LINDSAY** (see also Lindsey), Matthew, a. 25 y., carpet weaver, s. Matthew and Elizabeth, and Margarett Harley, a. 21 y., d. David and Jennette, Feb. 4, 1848.*

**LINDSEY** (see also Lindsay), George [Lindsay. c. r. 5.], of St. Stevens, New Brunswick, and Sarah E. Bugbee, int. Aug. 11, 1844.*

**LINEN** (see also Linnen), Peter, and Mary Bray, int. Oct. 2, 1836.

**LINES** (see also Lynds), Bridget, and Patrick Curley, int. Dec. 19, 1848.

Bridgett, and Michael Pinder, int. Feb. 5, 1847.

Sarah, and James Dohlan, int. Sept. 11, 1842.

**LINGHAM,** Aurilla, of Quincy, and James H. Snow, int. May 21, 1843.

William, Capt., and Lucy Allen, Apr. 3, 1825.*

William, jr , a. 21 y., grocer, s. William and Lucy, and Mary A. P. Day, a. 23 y., d. Moses and Sarah, Mar. 3, 1848.*

**LINNELL,** Eliza A. C., a. 25 y., d. Enoch and Elizabeth, of Portland, Me., and Matthew Oliver, a. 22 y., currier, s. Francis and Elizabeth of Cape Breton, Feb. 28, 1847.*

Lorenzo F., a. 24 y., carpenter, s. Enoch and Elizabeth, of Portland, Me., and Louisa H. Dennis, a. 19 y., Feb. 28, 1847.*

**LINNEN** (see also Linen), Michael, and Sarah Cady, int. July 9, 1843.

**LION** (see also Lyon), Deborah, of Dedham, and Joshua Lion, at Dedham, Oct. 3, 1733.

John, and Abigall Polly, May 10, 1670.

Joshua, and Deborah Lion of Dedham, at Dedham, Oct. 3, 1733.

Lewis, and Louisa Woessnor, int. Nov. 14, 1841.

* Intention also recorded.

LION, Samuel, and Elizabeth Capen of Dorchester, at Dorchester, Dec. 1, 1703.

William, and Sarah Ruggles, June 17, 1646.

**LISHER,** Mary, of Stoughton, and Timothy Gibson, from State of North Carolina, int. Jan. 28, 1798.

**LITCHFIELD,** Charles, and Deborah Tolman, int. May 15, 1836.

Cynthia, of Scituate, and Robert Edwards, int. Apr. 10, 1814.

Edwin, and Mary E. Pearson, Apr. 1, 1845.*

Elizabeth, and Jean Joseph Taunjans [Tarenjans. int.], Jan. 7, 1793.*

Emily, and Theodore A. Sampson, Feb. 6, 1845.*

Rachel, of Cohasset, and Mark P. Sweat, Oct. 11, 1829.*

Simeon, and Hannah Richards of Dorchester, int. May 7, 1820.

Varsel Edward, and Nancy Parsley, int. Nov. 30, 1845.

**LITTLE,** Israel [of Boston. c. r. 3.], and Elener Maria Davis, Nov. 22, 1826.*

Lemuel, and Caroline M. Davis, Apr. 2, 1823.*

Margarett, of Goffstown, N. H., and Jonathan J. Caldwell, int. Dec. 29, 1847.

Mary, and Jonathan F. Cook, Sept. 21, 1806.*

Nancy, and Nathaniel Leach, May 23, 1839.*

Oscar E., and Melvina F. Hayford, int. May 12, 1844.

Penelope, and William Houthwait, Apr. 8, 1819.*

William G., and Elisabeth [Elizabeth. int.] R. Welch, Feb. 1, 1846.*

**LITTLEFIELD,** Abner, and Sarah Ann Chase, int. Apr. 5, 1829.

Betsy, of Braintree, and John Estey, int. Dec. 8, 1793.

Eliza, and Nahum Emmons, Oct. 17, 1830.

Emeline, of Medway, and Reuben Breck, int. Oct. 30, 1825.

Horase, of Lebanon, Me.. and Mary E. Chase, int. Oct. 21, 1832.

John, and Olivia Morse, Apr. 5, 1837.*

Lydia P., a. 21 y., d. Oliver and Comfort, and Cyrus M. Hatch, a. 23 y., carpenter, s. John and Naomi, June 18, 1846.*

Mary P., and Henry Read, int. May 24, 1835.

Otho H., and Clarissa W. Rumrill, int. Aug. 17, 1834.

Samuel S., and Elizabeth Eagles, Apr. 4, 1837.*

* **Intention also recorded.**

**LITTLETON,** Norman M., and Mary Ann Gibson, int. Nov. 15, 1849.

**LIVERMORE,** Abigail, and Elisha Williams of Hartford, Aug. 30, 1780.
Hannah, and William Green, Aug. 20, 1835.*
John, and Hannah Godding, Mar. 22, 1815.*
Mary, and Charles Rumrill, Nov. 22, 1821.*
Melinda, and Joseph Hastings, Sept. 13, 1812.*
Nathaniel, and Rebecca Richardson, July 14, 1814.*
Rachel, Mrs., and James Burrill, Nov. 26, 1812.*
Sarah, and Robert Pierpont, Mar. 30, 1797.*

**LIVINGSTON,** Edward, and Bridget Welch, int. July 9, 1846.

**LLOYD,** Richard, and Sarah Frieze, Dec. 26, 1819.*
Sarah, and James Richards, Mar. 24 [4.c. r. 3.], 1822.*

**LOAN,** Marks, and Julia Creohen, int. Nov. 15, 1847.

**LOCKE,** Hollis S., and Henrietta McGraw, int. Mar. 2, 1849.
Jeremiah, of Wakefield, N. H., and Elizabeth D. Seaver, int. Apr. 6, 1834.
Lyman, and Eliza A. Lane of Boston, int. Apr. 8, 1848.
Stephen H., and Abigail Wight of Dedham, int. Mar. 6, 1831.

**LODGE,** John, and Elizabeth Norris of Cambridge, Nov. 12, 1848.

**LOGAN,** Mary, and Alexander McConal, int. Jan. 1, 1848.
Rose, and Alexander Hammond, Nov. 26, 1835.*

**LOGUE,** Bridget, and Thomas Gurhy, int. Jan. 23, 1842.

**LOKER,** Sarah A., of Brookline, and C. E. Elliot, int. Jan. 20, 1849.

**LOMBARD,** Ammi C., and Harriot H. Jones, int. Jan. 15, 1837.
Elizabeth [S. int.], of Dedham, and John Robinson, May 9, 1827.*

**LONG,** Caleb, and Phebe Caswell of Berkley, int. Feb. 26, 1809.
Catharine, and Dennis Leary, int. June 23, 1844.
Mary, and James Adams, int. Aug. 7, 1847.
Sarah S., a. 22 y., d. Enoch and Mary, and John A. Scott, a. 21 y., blacksmith, s. John and Elizabeth, Sept. 17, 1848.*

* Intention also recorded.

**LONGAN,** Ann, and David Powers, int. Oct. 9, 1842.

**LONGER,** Robert, of Quincy, and Elmiria Robbins, Apr. 7, 1835.

**LONGLEY,** (see also Langley), Anna [Langley. int.], and Isaac Silsby, Dec. 10, 1807.*

**LOOLEY,** Catherine, and Michael Turley, Oct. 15, 1848.*

**LOONEY,** Ellen, and James Walley, Apr. 30, 1845.

**LORD,** David H., Rev., of Burrillville, R. I., and Annette Merrill of Parsonsfield, Me., Nov. 9, 1848.
Ebenezer N., and Mary Ann Ford, Mar. 11, 1844.*
Erastus, and Sarah [Ann. int.] Dagur, ———, 1832. [Sept. 25, 1831. int.]*
George, and Jane Green, Nov. 19, 1833.*
Jane. and Thomas Hale, 12m: 1639. C. R. 1.
William H., and Sally M. Frizell, int. May 26, 1844.

**LORING,** Abigail, and Edward Dorr, Apr. 25, 1734.
Nathaniel, and Mary Gyles, June 18, 1747.
Sally, of Quincy, and Amos W. Mellen, int. Aug. 24, 1823.
Sarah, of Lexington, and Obadiah Johnson, at Lexington, Oct. 21, 1776.
William H., and Sarah Davis, Aug. 22, 1841.*

**LOTHROP,** Charles D., and Mary E. Richardson of Acton, int. Aug. 11, 1839.
Hannah, and William Miller, Feb. 7, 1805.*

**LOUD** (see also Lowd), Ally [Mrs. int.], resident, and Charles Dinsdell, June 14, 1785.*
Debby, and Benjamin Seaver, May 25, 1794.*
Elizabeth, and William Humphreys of Dorchester, int. Oct. 3, 1824.
Henry S., and Lucy H. Freeman, Feb. 5, 1843.*
Joa, and Joseph Dana, Jan. 13, 1791.*
John, and Harriet Ricker, int. Sept. 12, 1841.
Lucy, and Caleb Thomas, June 27, 1790.*
Stephen, and Lucy Dewing of Needham, June 22, 1806.*

**LOUDER** (see also Lowder). Henry, and Polly Searls, int. Dec. 8, 1799.

* Intention also recorded.

**LOUGEE** (see also Louger), Greenleaf F. [T. int.], and Mary A. Parsons, June 29, 1845.*

**LOUGER** (see also Lougee), Sylvester G. [T. Lougee. int.], and Reuamah Burley, Dec. 31, 1844.*

**LOVEJOY**, Jacob, and Harriet A. Jones of Lowell, June 5, 1842. c. r. 7.
Joseph, of Dorchester, a. 20 y., laborer, s. Jacob and Betsey, of Enfield, N. H., and Sarah Skinner, a. 22 y., d. Jedediah and Anne, Nov. 26, 1846.*
Sophia J., and George E. Webber, int. Jan. 9, 1849.

**LOVERAIN** (see also Lovering), Robert, and Allis Craft, Jan. 3, 1704-5.

**LOVERIN** (see also Lovering), Alice, and Ephraim Lyon, July 4, 1723.

**LOVERING** (see also Loverain, Loverin), Eliz[abe]th, and John Eaton of Stoughton, Apr. 23, 1729.
Robert, and Rebecca Gardner, Mar. 12, 1735. c. r. 2.
Ruhamey, of Exeter, N. H., and Joshua Blanchard, int. Oct. 28, 1792.
Sam[ue]l, and Sarah English, Nov. 28, 1775.

**LOVETT**, Daniel, and Mary Donovan, int. Sept. 22, 1849.
Deborah, and John Campbell, int. Jan. 11, 1829.

**LOVEWELL**, Hannah, and Joseph Baker, May 31, 1739.

**LOW**, Caroline M., and Jacob W. Pollard, July 14, 1846.
Caroline A., of Springvale, Me., and George L. Parker, int. Oct. 26, 1847.

**LOWD** (see also Loud), Rebecca, and John Meriam, Jan. 9, 1802.*

**LOWDENBECK**, Margarett, and Frederick Miller, int. Apr. 22, 1846.

**LOWDER** (see also Louder), Charlotte, and George Titcomb [of Boston. c. r. 3.], Oct. 18, 1829.*
Elizabeth, Mrs., of Dorchester, and Capt. Stephen Williams, at Dorchester, Dec. 14, 1738.

* Intention also recorded.

LOWDER, Elizabeth, and Jonah Kenny of Preston, Conn., May 22, 1803.*

Hannah, and John Goldsmith of Andover, May 26, 1796.*

Harriet, and [Capt. int.] George R. M. Weld, June 2, 1833.*

John, and Mary Chandler, Mar. 12, 1744-5.

John, jr., and Elizabeth Chandler of Andover, at Andover, May 4, 1769.

LOWELL, Asa B., and Prsula A. Blake of Wrentham, int. Mar. 4, 1838.

John, jr., and Rebecca Amory, int. May 26, 1793.

Rebecca Russell, and Samuel Pickering Gardner, Sept. 19, 1797.*

Susan C., d. John A., and William Sohier, Oct. 13, 1846.

LUCAS (see also Lucus), Mary T., resident, and Ephraim Capen of Dorchester, May 4, 1842.

Samuel F., and Sarah B. Frost of Charlestown, int. Feb. 3, 1839.

LUCE, Abby A., of Tisbury. a. 21 y., d. Richard and Hepsabeth, and William C. West of Chilmark, a. 27 y., mariner, s. George and Prudence, June 13, 1849.

LUCUS (see also Lucas), Legrand [Lucas. c. r. 3.], and Betsy Curtis [Eustis. int.], Mar. 24, 1831.*

LULY, Mary, and Thomas Meder, int. Nov. 27, 1848.

LUNT, Adeline A., and Calvin C. Dunbar, June 10, 1840.*

James H., and Louisa A[ugusta. int.] Williams, Apr. 29, 1833.*

LUSK, Elizabeth, and John Foarrest, June 4, 1747.

LYDON, Mary, and Lawrence Garaty, int. July 7, 1847.

LYDSTON, Alfred H., a. 27 y., carpenter, and Mary J. Simpson, a. 22 y., Oct. 26, 1847.*

LYMAN, Annie Jean, of Greenfield, and Charles Short, int. Sept. 22, 1849.

Chester, and Mary Lawrence of Waltham, int. Sept. 2, 1810.

LYNCH, Alice, and James Lally, int. Feb. 19, 1849.

Bridgett, and James Lynch, int. Oct. 30, 1848.

* Intention also recorded.

LYNCH, Henry, and Margaret Foley, int. Apr. 24, 1836.
Hannah, and Andrew Gallaghar, int. Apr. 18, 1841.
James, and Bridgett Lynch, int. Oct. 30, 1848.
John, and Mary Gilmartin, int. June 22, 1848.
Mark, and Catherine Eager, int. May 15, 1848.
Mary, and James Gateley, int. June 7, 1840.
Mary, and Henry Leear, int. Apr. 16, 1843.
Sarah [Mary. int.; Mrs. Mary. c. r. 3.], and Amos Gerrish,
　　Apr. 3, 1822.*
Thomas, and Elizabeth Goss, int. Aug. 15, 1841.
Thomas, and Ellen Mulkaky, int. Feb. 7, 1848.
William, and Mary Fitzpatrick, int. Nov. 15, 1840.

LYNDE, Benjamin, jr., Esq., of Salem, and Mrs. Mary Good-
　　ridge, Nov. 1, 1731.
Joseph, of Malden, and Hannah Wait, Oct. 10, 1802.*

LYNDS (see also Lines), Bridget, b. Ireland, and Michael
　　Tulley, b. Ireland, Oct. 30, 1849.

LYNSKY, Mark, and Hannah Larkin, int. May 3, 1847.

LYON (see also Lion, Lyons), Abiel, of Woodstock, and
　　Judith Farrenton, Nov. 24, 1703.
Abigail, and Nathanael Draper, Jan. 22, 1705-6.
Abigail, and Nathanael Davis, Nov. 4, 1736.
Alice, Mrs., and John Greenwood of Newton, July 24, 1729.
Ann, and Isaac Barlett, int. Oct. 3, 1824.
Anne, and Obadiah Lyon, Jan. 26, 1740.
Benjamin, and Hannah Polley, Feb. 1, 1731-2.
Benjamin, and Anne Dwight of Dedham, Dec. 21, 1742.
Benjamin, and Elisabeth Man, Mar. 12, 1770.
Benjamin, and Elizabeth Allen, Oct. 16, 1796.*
Benjamin D., and Mary Arnold, int. Feb. 23, 1823.
Daniel, and Elizabeth Bird, May 9, 1771.
Daniel, and Hepsibah Howland of Dover, May 14, 1835.*
David, and Mary Perry [Terry. c. r. 2.], Mar. 11, 1715.
　　[1714-15. c. r. 2.]
David, and Abigail Draper, Feb. 19, 1764. [Feb. 9. c. r. 2.]
Deborah, and Benjamin Sever, Oct. 4, 1739.
Ebenezer, and Elizabeth Torbot, at Dedham, July 15, 1700.
Ebenezer [of Rehoboth. c. r. 2.], and Abigail Gay, Nov. 6,
　　1718.
Eliphalet, and Elizabeth Jordan, Jan. 1, 1712.

* Intention also recorded.

Lyon, Eliza, and Lemuel Richards of Concord, int. Mar. 17, 1822.

Elizabeth, and Caleb Pond of Dedham, at Dorchester, July 28, 1721.

Elizabeth, wid., and Lemuel Tucker, June 29, 1786.*

Elizabeth A., and Cephas Manning, int. Oct. 5, 1845.

Elizebeth, and John Draper, Feb. 29, 1760.

Ephraim, and Abigail Crosbee, June 13, 1709.

Ephraim, and Alice Loverin, July 4, 1723.

Esther, and Benjamin Willson, July 2, 1706.

Esther, and Samuel White, Dec. 13, 1739.

Hannah, and Nathaniel Whiting, May 1, 1729.

Harriet [Hannah. int.], and John T. Whittemore, Apr. [28. c. r. 3.], 1822.*

Hulda, and Ebenezer Whiting, Oct. 30, 1748.

Jeremiah, and Eliza Ann Willard, Aug. 13, 1820.*

John, and Mary Herring of Dedham, Apr. 16, 1724.

John, and Mary Spring, int. Dec. 9, 1792.

John Adams, of Brookline and Charlotte Barrett, int. Dec. 15, 1800.

Jonathan, and Mary Jones, Feb. 21, 1748-9.

Joseph, s. William, and Mary Bridge, d. John, Mar. 23, 1680-81.

Joseph, and Mary Aldridge of Braintree, Dec. 5, 1701.

Joseph, and Elizabeth Philleps, May 30, 1710.

Joseph, and Huldah Smith, Oct. 28, 1735.

Martha, and Ralph R. Hussey, int. Nov. 9, 1847.

Mary, and Ebenezer Philips [of Woodstock. c. r. 2.], Dec. 17, 1719.

Mary, and Nathanael Lyon, Sept. 17, 1734.

Mary, and Joseph Richards, May 16, 1740.

Mary, and Joshua Lewis, Sept. 26, 1776.

Mary, and John Bird of Needham, at Needham, May 21, 1785.

Mary, and George Snell, May 7, 1820. c. r. 2.*

Mary Jane, and Roger S. Mackintosh, int. May 11, 1845.

Moses, and Martha Cushman, Feb. 5, 1828.*

Nathanael, and Mary Lyon, Sept. 17, 1734.

Nathanael, and Margaret Topham, Jan. 23, 1738-9.

Obadiah, and Anne Lyon, Jan. 26, 1740.

Olive, and Thomas Beeton of Westborough, int. Dec. 1, 1816.

Paul, and Mrs. Elizabeth Sumner of Milton, int. May 27, 1821.

Pelatiah, and Rachel Lyon, Apr. 16, 1745.

* Intention also recorded.

Lyon, Pelatiah, and Sarah Heley, May 27, 1760.
Rachel, and Pelatiah Lyon, Apr. 16, 1745.
Rachel, and Zebdiel Adams, int, May 6, 1792.
Rachel A., and Henry P. Evleth, int. Dec. 2, 1824.
Rebecca, and Thomas Gold, Dec 18. [4. c. r. 2.], 1716.
Rhoda, and William Gilman, May 18, 1800. c. r. 2.*
Samuel, and Joanna Weld, Dec. 20, 1705.
Samuel, and Mary Robbins, at Cambridge, Nov. 24, 1742.
Samuel S., of Bethel, and Rebecca A. Wilson, Nov. 23, 1848.
Sarah, and Asa Pason, Dec. 31, 1772.
Sarah, and Robert Posthill, Oct. 17, 1790.*
Thomas, and Abigail Gold, Mar. 10, 1669.
Thomas, jr., and Anne Case, Nov. 1, 1692.
Thomas, and Abigail Clark, at Dedham, July 8, 1698.
Thomas, and Abigail Weld, Jan. 24, 1738-9.
Thomas, and Hannah Weld, Nov. 3, 1748.
Thomas, and Rhoda Whiting, Jan. 12, 1758.
W[illia]m, s. William, and Sarah Dunkin, Sept. —, 1775.

LYONS (see also Lyon), Patrick, and Mary Cavanough, int.
July 24, 1836.
Roger, and Catherine Conners, int. Sept. 25, 1847.

McALEER, Susan, and Michael McCullin, int. Feb. 4, 1844.

McANATTIN, Mary, and Patrick Sharkey, int. July 7, 1849.

McANDREWS, Thomas, and Margarett Sweeney, int. July 3,
1847.

MACAVOY (see also McAvoy), Edwin, and Mary Dorn, int.
May 13, 1848.

McAVOY (se also Macavoy), William, and Catherine Slane
of Boston, int. July 13, 1847.

McBRIDE, Felix, and Catharine McGuire, int. Oct. 29, 1837
James, and Ann Kelley, int. Aug. 16, 1849.

McCAFFERTY (see also McCafty), Catharine, and Patrick
Haheye, int. May 1, 1842.

McCAFTY (see also Cafferty), Sara [Sarah. int.], b. Ireland,
and Thomas Donlin [Donlan. int.], b. Ireland, Aug. 3,
1849.*

* Intention also recorded.

**McCAINE** (see also McCairn), Adeline D., wid., a. 37 y., dressmaker, d. Reuben and Ruth More, and Joseph W. Mathes, a. 23 y., painter, s. Benj[amin] and Anna, Dec. 14, 1845.*

**McCAIRN** (see also McCaine), Ellen, and John C. Batie, int. Sept. 22, 1847.

**McCART** (see also McCarty), Elizabeth, and Richard Parks. int. Oct. 5, 1845.

**McCARTHY** (see also McCarty), Anne, and Thomas Prince, Apr. 22, 1779.
Elizabeth, and Thomas Williams, jr., int. Sept. 18, 1791.

**MACCARTY** (see also McCarty), Martha S., and Francis S. Salmon, Apr. 1, 1831.*
Thomas, and Sarah Cotterell, Dec. 16, 1772.
Thomas, and Harriet Hallowell of Framingham, Jan. 3, 1830.*
William, and Martha Jane M. Salmon, int. Mar. 4, 1832.

**McCARTY** (see also Carthy, Carty, McCart, McCarthy, Maccarty), Bridget, and Michael Mitchell, int. Feb. 14, 1849.
Bridgett, and James Kelly, int. Aug. 27, 1847.
Catherine, and John Cain, int. May 28, 1847.
Dan, and Catharine Barry, int. Aug. 17, 1845.
Daniel, and Jane Leary, int. Sept. 7, 1846.
Ellen, and Michael Lally, int. Nov. 23, 1845.
Ellen, and Richard G. Holbrook, int. Dec. 28, 1845.
Hannah, b. Ireland, and Daniel Doran, b. Ireland, Mar. 3, 1849.*
John, and Mary Higgins, int. Sept. 8, 1844. [Dec. 28, 1845. dup.]
Mary, and James Donegan, June 10, 1848.*
Mary J., and Stephen J. Rogers of Boston, int. May 18, 1849.
Patrick, and Eliza Barry, int. Dec. 1, 1848.
William, and Martha Nolen, Nov. 21, 1799.*
William, and Susanna Curtis, Feb. 12, 1805.*
William, and Catherine McDaniel, int. July 6, 1847.

**McCARY,** Elizabeth, and Edward McElroy, int. Apr. 3, 1849.

**McCAULEY** (see also McCawley), Matthew, and Maria Egan, int. Aug. 31, 1848.

* Intention also recorded.

**McCAWLEY** (see also McCauley), Bridget, and Michael O'Hara, int. May 26, 1849.

**McCLARC,** Ann, and Dennis Hase, int. Apr. 14, 1844.

**McCLAREN,** James, and Mary Campbell, int. June 8, 1817.

**McCLEALAN** (see also McLellan), Esther, and Thomas Weld, Apr. 12, 1781.

**McCLOUD,** Alexander, and Mary Welch, Oct. 15, 1838.*
George, and Ann Fogerty, Oct. 2, 1839.
William, and Mary Bride, int. Apr. 18, 1830.

**MACCLURE** (see also McClure), Richard, jr., and Ann Matthus, June 4, 1751.

**McCLURE** (see also Macclure), Elisa, and Joseph Blake, May, 29, 1814.*
Rosannah, and Peter Connelly, int. Sept. 22, 1849.

**McCOEN,** Ann [McCuen. int.], b. Ireland, and John Connor. b. Ireland, Feb. 24, 1849.*
John, and Ellen Cavanagh, int. July 11, 1848.

**McCOLFE,** Francis, and Catherine Tague, int. Dec. 5, 1848.

**McCONAHY,** Peter, and Catherine Reilly, int. Apr. 2, 1849.

**McCONAL,** Alexander, and Mary Logan, int. Jan. 1, 1848.

**McCOOMBS,** Esther, and Sam[ue]l Crooks, June 8, 1845.

**McCORMIC** (see also McCormick), Patrick, and Catherine Ambrook, int. Oct. 12, 1846.

**McCORMICK** (see also McCormic), Ann, and James McCormick, int. Aug. 4, 1847.
James, and Ann McCormick, int. Aug. 4, 1847.
James, and Catherine Smith, int. July 20, 1849.
John, of Norton, and Eliza V. Robertson, int. Jan. 13,1849.
Michael, and Bridget Golden [Goolding. dup.], int. Sept. 20, 1849. [Aug. 8, 1848. dup.]
Patrick, and Bridget Driscoll, int. July 24, 1848.
Thomas [of Boston. int.], and Levina Johnston, Mar. 28, 1849.*

**McCOY,** Emeline L., a. 24 y., seamstress, and Edward H. Tileston, a. 24 y., carpenter, Sept. 22, 1845.*

* Intention also recorded.

**McCRADLE,** Thomas, and Mary Horton, int. Sept. 17, 1849.

**McCUBRY,** Andrew, and Elizabeth Crimbel, Sept. 7, 1835.

**McCUE,** James, and Mary Sullivan, int. June 9, 1849.
Mary, and Martin Curley, int. Feb. 20, 1849.
Peter, and Hannah O'Bryan, int. Apr. 3, 1842.

**McCULLIN,** Michael, and Susan McAleer, int. Feb. 4, 1844.

**McCUMBER,** Fanny, and Samuel Lawrence, Sept. 7, 1818.*

**McCURE,** Mary E. [McClure. int.], of Waldo, Me., a. 22 y.,
d. Thomas, and Austin Levanseller, a. 24 y., pianoforte
manufacturer, s. Peter and Elizabeth, Dec. 1, 1847.*

**McCURRY,** Catherine, and James Kennedy, int. May 18,
1847.

**McCUSKY,** Ann, and William O'Neil, int. July 6, 1849.

**McDANIEL,** Ann, and Patrick Lambert, int. Apr. 23, 1849.
Catherine, and William McCarty, int. July 6, 1847.
David, and Sarah Ann Dunning, Nov. 30, 1843.
Elizabeth, and Thomas O'Brien, int. Apr. 30, 1846.
Ivory, and Sarah Ann Hanscom, —— 16, 1842.*
John, and Mary Black, int. Oct. 19, 1848.
Michael, and Mary Connaway, int. June 12, 1846.
Michael, and Bridget Mee, int. Sept. 28, 1846.
Patrick, and Maria Finn, int. May 20, 1837.
Patrick, and Catherine Farland, int. Dec. 15, 1847.
Thomas, and Catherine Cary, Sept. 30, 1848.*

**McDERMOT** (see also McDermott), Frances H. [McDermott.
int.], of Thomaston, Me., a. 19 y., d. John and Mary, and
William H. White, a. 23 y., carpenter, s. James and Abigail, June 1, 1845.*
Mary, and Peter Haley, int. Aug. 15, 1849.

**McDERMOTT** (see also McDermot), Ann, and Patrick
Grealy, int. Oct. 17, 1841.
Bridget, and Henry McGinis, int. Nov. 2, 1845.
John, and Ellen Maria Farrell, int. June 30, 1849.
Patrick, and Mary McDevitt, int. Feb. 2, 1840.

**McDEVITT,** Mary, and Patrick McDermott, int. Feb. 2, 1840.

* Intention also recorded.

**McDONALD** (see also McDonold), George W. B., a. 25 y., stairbuilder, s. Elisabeth, and Ellen Crane, a. 29 y., housewife, d. John T. G. and Abigail, Apr. 30, 1846.*

John, and Ellen Havey, int. Jan. 22, 1847.

William, s. W[illia]m and Sarah, and Margarett Cogswell, a. 24 y., Apr. 5, 1848.*

**McDONNELL** (see also McDonnill), Hugh, and Margarett Dolan, int. May 3, 1849.

Martin, and Catharine Killean, int. Oct. 29, 1843.

Mary, and Thomas Jennings, int. Feb. 5, 1849.

Michael, and Ellice Meiley, int. May 3, 1835.

Patrick, and Ann Devine, int. Oct. 21, 1838.

**McDONNILL** (see also McDonnell), Peter, and Mary Mahan, int. Apr. 9, 1843.

**McDONOLD** (see also McDonald), David, and Sarah Ann Duning, int. Nov. 12, 1843.

**McDONOUGH** Catharine, and Patrick McManus, int. June 18, 1843.

Catherine, and William Hagerty, int. Dec. 26, 1846.

Dormick, and Mary O'Neil, int. Dec. 30, 1847.

Edward, and Margarett Good, int. July 2, 1849.

Elizabeth, and John Murray, int. Apr. 9, 1843.

Francis, and Margarett Cuddy, int. Feb. 1, 1847.

Margarett, and JohnMcLaughlin, int. June 18, 1847.

Patrick, and Mary Roney, int. Nov. 15, 1849.

Rachel, and Barnard Grynord, int. May 8, 1847.

**McDUFFIE,** Julia A., of Manchester, N. H., a. 20 y., d. John and Elizabeth, and Joseph Cracklin, a. 31 y., painter, s. W[illia]m and Frances, Apr. 27, 1848.*

**McELOREN,** Ellen, and Charles Smith, int. May 13, 1847.

**McELROY,** Catharine, and Michael Doland, int. June 1, 1847.

Edward, and Elizabeth McCary, int. Apr. 3, 1849.

John, and Mary Hastings of Marlborough, N. H., Mar. 13, 1823.*

**McEVOY,** Ann, of Eastport, Me., and Andrew Foy, int. Mar. 27, 1847.

**McEWIN,** John, and Lydia Brown, Apr. 19, 1811.*

* Intention also recorded.

MACEY, James E., and Mary Ann L. Emery, July 4, 1833.

McFALL, John, and Mary Care, May 9, 1844.*

McGAN (see also McGann), Andrew, and Mary Stanhford, int. Dec. 16, 1847.

McGANN (see also McGan), Michael, and Rosanna [Rosana. dup.] Curly, int. Nov. 9, 1847. [Oct. 29, dup.]
William, and Bridget Gurry, int. Nov. 9, 1849.

McGARRY, Catherine, and Michael Gallayher, int. Oct. 27, 1844.

McGAUGEN (see also McGukin), Ann, and James Campbell, int. Aug. 3, 1848.

McGEE (see also Magee, MaGee), John, and Margarett Gemming, int. Jan. 4, 1848.

McGENNIS (see also McGinness), Mary, and Edward Hynes, int. Jan. 6, 1849.
Winneford, and Adam Allendorf, int. Dec. 14, 1848.

McGETTRICK, Andrew, and Bridget Rock, int. May 3, 1848.

McGINIS (see also McGinness), Henry, and Bridget McDermott, int. Nov. 2, 1845.

McGINLEY, Catherine, and Edward O'Brien of Boston, int. Sept. 15, 1849.

McGINNESS (see also McGennis, McGinis, McInnes), Catherine, and Daniel Doherty, int. Aug. 14, 1849.

McGLAFFLING, Polly, and Enos Brook, Dec. 25, 1800. c. r. 2.*

McGLINN, James, and Ann Maria Clark, int. July 11, 1830.

McGONAGLE, James, and Mary Kane, int. Sept. 12, 1841.

McGOVERIN (see also McGovern), James, and Margarett Cook, int. Aug. 6, 1849.

McGOVERN (see also McGoverin), Patrick, b. Ireland, and Catherine Clenton, b. Ireland, Dec. 30, 1849.

* Intention also recorded.

**McGOWAN** (see also McGown), Thomas, and Catherine Cullin, int. Sept. 10, 1847.

**McGOWN** (see also McGowan), Patrick, and Catherine Clenton, int. Nov. 24, 1849.

**McGRATH** (see also McGraw), John, b. Ireland, and Margarett Griffin [Griffith. int.], b. Ireland, Oct. 22, 1849.*
Tary, and Mary O. Gorman, int. Sept. 3, 1846.

**McGRAW** (see also McGrath), Henrietta, and Hollis S. Locke, int. Mar. 2, 1849.

**McGUIRE,** Ann, b. Ireland, and James Mitchell, b. Ireland, July 30, 1849.*
Bridget, and James Duke, int. Jan. 1, 1843.
Catharine, and Felix McBride, int. Oct. 29, 1837.
Rebecca, and Daniel Burk of Providence, R. I., int. Oct. 15, 1849.
Thomas, and Bridget Durand, int. Jan. 9, 1842.

**McGUKIN** (see also McGaugen), Mary [Mcguken. int.], and Benjamin Owens, Apr. 5, 1846.*

**MACHEES,** Daniel, and Sarah Wilson, Mar. 18, 1662.

**McINNES** (see also McGinness), John, overseer in carpet factory, s. John and Nancy, and Sarah F. Dodge, d. Eben-[eze]r and Mary, Jan. 23, 1849.*

**McINTIER** (see also McIntire), Timothy, and Polly Weld, July 9, 1786.*

**McINTIRE** (see also McIntier), Hannah, and James West of Randolph, Jan. 1, 1827.*
Henry, and Lydia F. Grant, Mar. 1, 1838.
Malinda, and Lorenzo W. Tucker, int. May 24, 1835.
Samuel, and Adaline Williams, int. Sept. 9, 1827.
Sarah A., and Albert O. Tucker, Nov. 26, 1840.*

**MACINTOSH** (see also McIntosh), William, and Adeline Arnold, int. Mar. 14, 1841.

**McINTOSH** (see also Macintosh, Mackintash, Mackintosh), Ebenezer, Maj., of Needham, and [Mrs. int.] Mary Dunster, Jan. 11, 1821. C. R. 2.*
Lucinda, and Abel Allen, int. Mar. 6, 1842.
Moses B., and Relief H. Davis, int. Mar. 17, 1833.

* Intention also recorded.

McIntosh, Priscilla, of Needham, and Calvin Broad, int. Mar. 6, 1814.

Stephen, and Sarah Griggs, Dec. 10, 1781. C. R. 2.

W[illia]m H., a. 25 y., provision dealer, s. Sam[ue]l and Priscilla, and Lavina [Levina. int.] M. Palmer, a. 23 y., milliner, d. W[illia]m and Charlotte, Nov. 12, 1845.*

**MACK,** Nehemiah, and Cordelia Eaton, int. May 19, 1849.

Patrick, and Bridget Purcel, int. Mar. 22, 1849.

**MACKASHLIN,** Margaret, resident, and Robert Knox, Nov. 26, 1728.

**McKAY,** John J., a. 39 y., clerk, s. Angus and Barbara, and Eunice H. Woodforth, a. 30 y., d. James, Mar. 15, 1849.*

**McKEARNAN,** Catharine, and John Fallon, int. Nov. 3, 1839.

**McKECKNIE,** Nehemiah, and Louisa Dean, int. Mar. 27, 1843.

**McKELLEY,** Ann, and Thomas Grady, int. Jan. 5, 1845.

**McKENNA** (see also McKenney), John, and Ann Brady, int. Oct. 28, 1848.

Sarah, b. Ireland, and Michael Ackin [Achinson. int.], b. Ireland, Nov. 6, 1849.*

**McKENNEY** (see also McKenna), Peter, and Bridget Carey, int. July 10, 1847.

**MACKINTASH** (see also McIntosh), William, and Abigail Whiting, Aug. 15, 1745.

**MACKINTOSH** (see also McIntosh), Eliza Ann, a. 19 y., d. John and Maria, and Andrew Jackson Cobb, a. 27 y., s. W[illia]m and Sarah, Nov. 5, 1846.*

Roger S., and Mary Jane Lyon, int. May 11, 1845.

**MACKNEY,** Mary, and Alexander Naughton, int. Nov. 20, 1846.

**McKOENE,** Patrick, and Mary Daily, int. May 12, 1849.

**McLANE,** David S., and Martha A. Kelsey of Dracut, July 31, 1842. C. R. 7.

* Intention also recorded.

McLANE, Mary A., of Lowell, and Thomas S. Hodge, int. Nov. 19, 1847.

Rebecca W., and Joseph W. Foster, Sept. 1, 1844.*

**McLAUGHLIN** (see also Laughlin), Barnard, and Mary J. Campbell, int. Jan. 14, 1838.

Bridget, and George Doherty, int. July 4, 1841.

Bridget, and Patrick Walsh, int. June 8, 1845.

Bridget, b. Ireland, and John Wood, b. Ireland, Dec. 14, 1849.

James, and Catherine Hallagan, int. Apr. 30, 1849.

John, and Sabrana Sprague, int. July 10, 1846.

John, and Margarett McDonough, int. June 18, 1847.

John, b. Ireland, and Margarett O'Beirne [O'Burne. int.], b. Ireland, Oct. 20, 1849.*

Malcom, and Ann Norton, int. Sept. 22, 1844.

Mary, and Patrick Scale, int. June 5, 1848.

Patrick, and Mary Ann O'Brien, int. Sept. 3, 1849.

Richard, and Hannah Lally, int. Aug. 18, 1846.

Thomas, and Sarah Quigley, int. Apr. 5, 1840.

Thomas, b. Ireland, and Bridget Cone, b. Ireland, Nov. 24, 1849.*

**McLELLAN** (see also McClealan), James S. [Capt. c. r. 3.], of Richmond [Bath. c. r. 3.], Me., a. 29 y., seaman, s. Alexander and Rachel, and Ann F. Seaverns, a. 21 y., d. Joel and Ann T., Oct. 21 [22. c. r. 3.], 1846.*

**McMAHAN,** Daniel, and Mary Munagle, int. June 14, 1840.

**McMANUS,** Bernard, and Bridget McGuire, int. Apr. 27, 1848.

Patrick, and Catharine McDonough, int. June 18, 1843.

**McMARK,** Bridget, and Michael Donnelly, int. Sept. 1, 1847.

**McMICHAEL,** Lucretia, and Royal C. Jorden, int. Dec. 14, 1845.

**McMORRIS,** Patrick [McMorrow. int.], b. Ireland, and Eliza Leonard, b. Ireland, July 19, 1849.*

**McNABO,** Elizabeth, and Thomas Hunt, int. Oct. 19, 1849.

**McNAMARA** (see also McNamarra), Margarett, and Timothy Gaitly, int. Oct. 29, 1847.

* Intention also recorded.

**McNAMARRA** (see also McNamara), Thomas, and Ann Clara, int. Sept. 11, 1848.

**McNEAL** (see also McNeil), Anthony, and Ellen Claffe, int. Jan. 9, 1842.

**McNEIL** (see also McNeal), Michael, and Ann Craffy, int. Jan. 10, 1848.

**MACOMBER,** Albert, and Sarah Pratt of Hingham, int. Aug. 7, 1842.

**MACONEY,** Timothy, and Ann Riley, Oct. 16, 1848.

**McCULIFFE,** Patrick, and Mary Hally, int. May 5, 1849.

**McQUEENY,** James, and Ann Killeren, int. Jan. 4, 1846.

**McROBERT,** William E., a. 23 y., carpenter, s. Edward and Abigail, and Elizabeth Corbett [Corbell. int.], a. 23 y., tailoress, d. Robert and Catharine, Sept. 16, 1845.*

**McSORSEY,** John, and Bridget Conniff, int. Apr. 27, 1849.

**McSWEENY,** Ellen, and John Mahony, int. Jan. 17, 1848.

**McVALE,** Michael, and Bridget Defly, int. Jan. 18, 1848.

**McVAY,** Mary, and Thomas Shea, int. Feb. 20, 1849.

**MADAN** (see also Maddan), Rosanna, and John Egan, int. Jan. 8, 1843.

**MADDAN** (see also Madan), Martin, and Margarett Whalen, int. July 26, 1849.

**MAGEE** (see also McGee), Patrick, and Ann King, int. June 27, 1848.

**MaGEE** (see also McGee), Catherine, and James Staunton, int. Nov. 8, 1848.
Michael, and Caroline Rigbey, int. Apr. 17, 1842.

**MaGEVEREY,** Luke, and Elizabeth Carrall, int. Dec. 12, 1846.

**MAGIN,** Catharine, and Michael Minton, int. Oct. 22, 1843.

**MAGUIRE,** Bridget, and Lewis Brown, Mar. 3 [24. c. r. 3.], 1844.*
Bridget, and Bernard McManus, int. Apr. 27, 1848.

* Intention also recorded.

**MAHAN** (see also Mahon), Margaret, and Thomas Caine, int. Dec. 29, 1844.

Mary, and Peter McDonnill, int. Apr. 9, 1843.

Michael, and Jane Cusick, int. Sept. 16, 1848.

**MAHER,** John, and Catherine Mulligan, int. May 23, 1846.

**MAHON** (see also Mahan), Bridget, and John Haverty, int. Nov. 3, 1844.

Francis, and Sarah Brooks, int. Dec. 29, 1844.

Edward, and Bridgett Mulvay, int. Oct. 19, 1846.

Mary Ann, and Patrick Brooks, int. Apr. 16, 1843.

**MAHONEY** (see also Mahony, Mehoney), Ann, and Patrick O'Keeffe, int. Jan. 14, 1844.

John, and Ann Cuddy, int. Feb. 14, 1848.

Mary, and William Hand, int. Feb. 16, 1840.

**MAHONY** (see also Mahoney), Elizabeth, and Jeremiah Sexton, int. Nov. 4, 1838.

John, and Mary Quinn, int. Aug. 31, 1845.

John, and Mary Donnovan, int. Feb. 8, 1846.

John, and Ellen McSweeny, int. 17, 1848.

Margaret, and John Nortin, int. Jan. 20, 1848.

Timothy, and Charlotte Swany, int. Aug. 4, 1848.

**MAILLET,** John, and Eliza Makerwhit, at Boston, Dec. 29, 1729.

**MAKEPIECE,** Augustus, of West Brookfield, and Harriette A. Newton, int. Jan. 7, 1849.

**MAKER,** Nancy, and Nathaniel Patten, Feb. 8, 1807.*

Patrick, and Catharine Kenney, int. Feb. 2, 1840.

**MAKERWHIT,** Eliza, and John Maillet, at Boston, Dec. 29, 1729.

**MALBON,** Mary Ann Thomas, of Hingham, and Theodore R. Glover, int. Apr. 29, 1846.

**MALCY,** Margaret, and Edward Kelley, int. July 12, 1835.

**MALEY** (see also Maloy), John, and Sarah Conry, int. Jan. 19, 1849.

* Intention also recorded.

**MALLARD,** Catharine Williams, and Lorey Pease, June 8, 1823.*

David, and Keziah Watson, June 20, 1824.*

Elizabeth, and James Flood, Dec. 25, 1845.*

Harriot, and Ophin [Opher. int.] Haynes, Dec. 23, 1810.*

Mary W., and George Whitney, Nov. 8, 1827.*

Susan, and James B. Gurney, Apr. 3, 1810.*

**MALONE** (see also Maloney), Mary, and James Victory, int. Dec. 28, 1849. (null.)

Michael, b. Ireland, and Mary Kelly, b. Ireland, Sept. 8, 1849.

Thomas, and Bridget Conner, int. May 25, 1845.

**MALONEY** (see also Malone, Maloon), Dennis, and Catherine Hannagan, int. Apr. 30, 1849.

Margaret, and Cornelius Slattery, Feb. 7, 1846.

**MALOON** (see also Malony), Hannah B., a. 24 y., d. Josiah and Sally, and William McDole Fersons of Bedford, N. H., a. 24 y., yeoman, s. William and Polly, Nov. 29, 1846.*

Henry, and Mary Kelley, int. Aug. 25, 1849.

**MALOY** (see also Maley), Mary [Malay. int.], b. Ireland, and Richard Collins, b. Ireland, Sept. 6, 1849.*

**MAN** (see also Mann), Elisabeth, and Benjamin Lyon, Mar. 12, 1770.

Jabez, and Elizabeth Higgens of Walpole, at Walpole, Mar. 2, 1778.

Margaret, and John Cheever [both residents. c. r. 2.], July 1, 1736.

Robert, and Sarah Butcher, Oct. 18, 1705.

Timothy, and Elisabeth Parker, Dec. 6, 1770.

**MANAGHAN** (see also Manahan), James, and Ann Young, int. Apr. 11, 1841.

**MANAHAN** (see laso Managhan), John, and Sarah Colman, int. May 4, 1845.

Mary, and Thomas Healy, int. Nov. 17, 1844.

William, of Deering, N. H., and Mary Bowers, May 16, 1830.*

**MANN** (see also Man), Aaron, and Eliza Pratt, int. Mar. 19, 1837.

* Intention also recorded.

MANN, George W., and Susan Keith, int. Sept. 9, 1838.

Mary, of Randolph, and John Hartshorn, int. Nov. 6, 1808.

Moses, Col. [of Needham. int.], and Mrs. Anna Corey, Jan. 1, 1804. C. R. 2.*

Nancy, and Paul Draper of Brookfield, June 13, 1816. C. R. 2.*

**MANNING,** Cephas. and Elizabeth A. Lyon, int. Oct. 5, 1845.

Emily B., of Boston, and John Edwards, int. Jan. 29, 1847.

James C., and Ann Connelly, June 14, 1848.*

Michael, b. Ireland, and Ann Tracy, b. Ireland, June 26, 1849.*

Patrick, and Catharine Byrns, int. Jan. 19, 1845.

**MANNION,** Bridget, and Martin Carney of Boston, int. May 8, 1847.

Patrick, and Rosanna Menton. int. Aug. 6, 1846.

**MANSFIELD,** George, and Susanna Tuckerman, Oct. 22, 1770.

Mary B., of Dorchester, and Charles Maxwell, int. Feb. 17, 1822.

Sarah, and Thomas Homager, Oct. 18, 1807.*

Sarah E., of Camden, Me., and Charles Perkins, Mar. 26, 1843.*

Stephen, and Nancy Crosby, Oct. 10, 1786.*

**MANSOR,** Sarah, and Daniel Rogers, Nov. 16, 1741.

**MARBLE,** James S., and Emiley Ayers of Ossipee, N. H., int. Aug. 9, 1829.

Nelson, and Sarah Richards, Feb. 21, 1826. C. R. 2.*

**MARDEN,** Elizabeth, and William W. Colman, int. Apr. 2, 1837.

Olive, and Samuel Whittemore, Mar. 11, 1834.*

Penney, and Patrick Havey, int. Sept. 20, 1845.

William, of Franklin, boat builder, and Eliza Boyden, Oct. 24, 1847.*

**MARDER,** Sarah Jane S., and George W. Gardner, Feb. 16, 1846.

**MAREAN,** William, and Elizabeth Clarke, Jan. 7, 1701-2.

William, and Lucy Colby both of Brookline, Aug. 3, 1823. C. R. 3.

* Intention also recorded.

**MARONEY,** Timothy, and Ann Riley, int. Oct. 2, 1848.

**MARSH,** Celia F., and Henry H. Richardson, June 14, 1842.*

Charles, and Lucy Mariah Fay, of Lebanon, N. H., int. Sept. 18, 1842.

Edmund S., of Quincy, and Lucy Smith, int. Oct. 31, 1846.

Louisa L., and William White, int. Jan. 20, 1833.

Oliver B., a. 24 y., machinist, s. Jason and Sarah, and Sylvia W. Ford, a. 23 y., d. Asa and Nancy, Apr. 18, 1848.*

Susannah L., and William Durant, int. May 11, 1828.

Warren, and Hannah Withington, Apr. 13, 1806.*

**MARSHALL,** Cyrus, and Sally Brown, Nov. 26, 1826.*

Esther, and George Bent of East Sudbury, Jan. 17, 1821.*

Jacob, and Mary Gay of Walpole, Sept. 12, 1827.*

John, of North Yarmouth, Me., and Mary E. Woodward, Nov. 6, 1833.*

John I. [J. int.], of Framingham, and Elizabeth B. Taber, Jan. 11, 1838.*

Lydia Morse, of Brookline, and Seymour Faxon, int. Nov. 21, 1819.

Mary, of Bradford, N. H., and John S. Kittredge, int. Nov. 6, 1847.

Rebecca, of Brookline, and Samuel Barry, int. Oct. 17, 1802.

Simon F., and Louisa Hayden, May 14, 1842.*

Timothy L., and Mehitabel Durgin, Apr. 4, 1824.*

**MARSTON,** John, and Elizabeth Kingsbury, Apr. 16, 1837.*

John M., a. 28 y., carpenter, s. John and Jerusha, of Portland, Me., and Ellen M. Richardson, a. 18 y., d. Josiah and Martha, Nov. 19, 1846.*

Suviah, and Edward Howe of Portland, June 1, 1815.*

**MARTIN,** Ann, and Joseph Muncrief, jr., Mar. 25, 1823.*

Bartlett F. [J. int.], and Eunice R. Pray, Aug. 24, 1845.*

Bridget, and John Killea, int. Nov. 27, 1847.

Henry A., and Frances C. Crosby of Lowell, int. July 24, 1848.

John, and Elizabeth Mason, int. Sept. 19, 1809.

John D., of Candia, N. H., and Mary J. Mead, Aug. 4, 1845.*

Mary, and Tho[ma]s Tileston [Timothy Tillson. c. r. 3.], June 18, 1809.*

Mary, and John Kelly, int. Feb. 7, 1848.

Robert, and Eliza Ford of Dorchester, int. Dec. 10, 1837.

* Intention also recorded.

MARTIN, Sarah, of Newburyport, and James M. Southwick, int. Feb. 2, 1845.

Sarah F., and George D. Harlow, int. Nov. 10, 1844.

Willard, and Catharine Cowley [Calder. int; of Boston. c. R. 3.], Jan. 5, 1817.*

**MASCRAFT** (see also Mascroft), Elizabeth, and Samuel Spencer, Mar. 18, 1700-1701.

Hannah, and Samuel Frost, July 15, 1701.

**MASCROFT** (see also Mascraft), Daniel, and Mary Gorton, May 23, 1665.

**MASON,** Aaron, of Watertown, and Sally Pratt, Aug. 28, 1796.*

Abby W., of Attleboro, and James T. Atwood, May 16, 1843. c. R. 7.

Charles, and Clementina Bonnmort, Dec. 25, 1817. c. R. 2.*

Charlotte T., and George H. Webster, June 20, 1843.*

Elizabeth, and John Martin, int. Sept. 19, 1809.

James, a. 30 y., weaver, and Myra Vinal Gardner, a. 24 y., Oct. 12, 1846.*

Lydia, and Caleb Bates of Concord, Nov. 13, 1823.*

Mary, and Timothy Sullivan, int. Jan. 17, 1849.

Nicholas, and Sarah D. Ransom, int. Nov. 30, 1849.

Robert, and Elisabeth Chandler, Nov. 18, 1680.

Sarah, and Charles H. Billings, Apr. 1, 1841.*

Thomas T., jr., a. 22 y., upholsterer, s. Thomas and Mary T. and Mary Ann Hewes [Hewse. int.], a. 21 y., Apr. 30, 1848.*

William, widr., a. 30 y., cabinet maker, s. Thomas and Mary, and Harriet L. Brooks, a. 18 y., dressmaker, d. Benj[a-min] and Louisa, Aug. 3, 1845.*

**MASSEY,** Sarah W., and George B. Munroe [Monroe. int.], May 11, 1843.*

**MASTRISS,** Sarah, and Joseph Harding, Sept. 14, 1754.

**MATHER** (see also Mathers), Atherton, and Mary Lamb, Oct. 24, 1705.

Mary, and John Lee of Freetown, at Boston, May 3, 1722.

Susannah, and William Warren of Brookline, at Boston, June 26, 1727.

* Intention also recorded.

**MATHERS** (see also Mather), John, and Catherine Richards, Nov. 14, 1775.

**MATHES,** Joseph W., a. 23 y., painter, s. Benj[amin] and Anna, and Adeline D. McCaine, wid., a. 37 y., dressmaker, d. Reuben and Ruth More, Dec. 14, 1845.*

**MATHEWS** (see also Matthews), Gardener, and Lucy Hitchins [Hitchings. int.], of Dorchester, at Dorchester, Nov. 28, 1797.*

**MATTHEWS** (see also Mathews, Matthus), C. W. [Cha]rle]s W. dup.], and Mary Jane [Mary J. dup.] Danforth, May 1, 1842.*
Michael, and Catharine Donnelly, int. Apr. 29, 1828.
Oliver, of Austerlitz, N. Y., and Barbara Haley, Sept. 22, 1825.*
Polly, and John Mayo, Sept. 11, 1794.*

**MATTHEWSON,** Noel [Mathewson. int.], widr., of Barrington, R. I., a. 37 y., brickmaker, s. Noel and Susannah, and Mary Ann Webb, a. 35 y., d. Walter and Sally, June 7, 1847.*

**MATTHUS** (see also Matthews), Ann, and Richard Macclure, jr., June 4, 1751.

**MAUD** (see also Maude), Henry, a. 25 y., carpet weaver, s. David, and Jane Williams, a. 21 y., d. Thomas and Mary, Aug. 31, 1849.*

**MAUDE** (see also Maud), Ellen, a. 22 y., d. David and Martha, and William Howgate of Lowell, a. 24 y., machinist, s. James and Hannah, June 9, 1848.*
Thomas, and Nancy Harley, June 8, 1849.*

**MAXFIELD,** Eliza B., and George S. Goss, int. Mar. 27, 1836.
Hannah, and William Bugbee, Nov. —, 1766.
John, and Mary Bugbee, May 12, 1767.
Samuel, jr., a. 25 y., painter, s. Samuel and Mary, and Sarah E. S. Frost of Dorchester, a. 23 y., d. Joseph and Caroline of Dorchester, May 20, 1846.*
Sarah B., and John Munroe, Sept. 21, 1837.*

* Intention also recorded.

**MAXWELL,** Alexander, and Betsy Nolen, int. Nov. 20, 1785.
Amos T., and Sarah W. Gordon of Portland, Me., int. Oct. 9, 1842.
Anne, and William Williams, Dec. 2, 1762.
Charles, and Mary B. Mansfield of Dorchester, int. Feb. 17, 1822.
Clement P., of Westbrook, Me., .a 27 y., merchant, s. Eben-[eze]r and Esther, of Gray, Me., and Mary Ann Reckard, a. 18 y., June 21, 1846.*
Elizabeth Ann, and Jabez Nason, Dec. 16, 1813.*

**MAY** (see also Mayes), Abby, of Beverly, and John Adams, int. Aug. 24, 1828.
Abigail [Mrs. c. r. 2.], and Sam[ue]ll Williams, jr., Feb. 10, 1746-7.
Abigail, and Joseph Brewer, Apr. 15, 1798.*
Abigail, and Moses Brewer, Dec. 23, 1798.*
Abigal, and Humpherey Johnson, Dec. 6, 1678.
Amasa, of Woodstock, and Anna Fillebrown, int. Jan. 15, 1792.
Benjamin, and Mary Williams, May 4, 1738.
Benjamin, and Mrs. Abigail Gore, Oct. 31, 1751.
Benjamin, and Mary Star [Starr. c. r. 3.], Dec. 1, 1811.*
Benjamin, and Sarah C. Randall, Jan. 4, 1838. c. r. 3.*
Catherine, and Dr. Charles Winship, int. Feb. 28, 1808.
Dinah, and Ezekiel Smith of Marshfield, at Marshfield, June 29, 1714.
Ebenezer, jr., and Mrs. Susannah Parker, Mar. 6, 1752.
Eleazer, and Dorothy Davis of Brooklyn, Jan. 29, 1735. [1736. c. r. 2.]
Fanny, of Warwick, and Henry Pomroy, int. Dec. 28, 1806.
Francis, and Bridget Fitzmorris, int. Apr. 17, 1848.
Gilbert S., and Hannah E. Johnson of Sharon, int. Mar. 18, 1838.
Henry, and Martha Jane Currier of Methuen, int. Nov. 11, 1846.
John, and Prudence Bridge, June 2, 1684.
Katharine [Catharine. c. r. 3.], and Tho[ma]s Avis [of Boston. c. r. 3.], Oct. 17, 1799.*
Lemuel, and Abigail Davis, Dec. 15, 1768.
Lemuel, a. 32 y., omnibus driver, s. Benj[amin] and Mary, and Lucy Ann Kent of Readfield, Me., a. 22 y., Jan. 12, 1847.*

* Intention also recorded.

MAY, Mary, d. John, and Joseph Pepper, Nov. 4, 1675.
Mary, and William Wales, Mar. 13, 1794.*
Mehetabell, and John Bowen, June 6, 1734.
Moses, and Mary Perrin, Mar. 13, 1760.
Prudence, and Benjamin Winchester, Dec. 31, 1719.
Prudence, and John Parker, Nov. 24, 1785.*
Ruth, and Michael Ervin of Dedham, Dec. 18, 1803.*
Samuel, and Katherine Mears, Nov. 3, 1748.
Samuel, and Abigail Williams, Oct. 4, 1753.
Sarah, and Samuell Williams, s. Sam[uel], Feb. 24, 1679.
Sarah, and William Williams, Sept. 4, 1755. C. R. 2.
Sarah, and Stephen Nute of Milton, N. H., June 22, 1823.*
Susanna, and Joseph Williams, Dec. 15, 1763.
Susanna, and Daniel Starr, June 30, 1793.*
Susannah, and Alexander Dickson [Dixon. C. R. 3.], Sept. 6,
    1842.*

MAYES (see also May), John, and Sarah Bruer, Nov. 19,
    1656.
Samuell, and Abigaile [Abigail. CT. R.] Stanffull, Jan. 7,
    1657.

MAYNARD, Ebenezer, of Westborough, and Hannah Gale,
    June 22, 1814.*

MAYO, Aaron D., and Sarah Day of Dover, int. Apr. 6, 1820.
Abigail, and John Willson, jr., Dec. 22, 1737.
Abig[ai]l, Mrs., and Joseph Richards, jr., Jan. 1, 1777.
Anna, and Paul Dudley Richards, June 20, 1776.
Caleb, and Polly Richards, Oct. 17, 1776.
Caroline, and Nath[anie]l Kimball, int. Apr. 12, 1840.
Elizabeth, and Nathanael Brewer, Apr. 10, 1717.
Elizabeth, and John Bridge, Apr. 6, 1727.
Esther, and Samuel Langley, Feb. 7, 1771.
Hannah, and Isaac Morise, Mar. 2, 1680.
Hannah, and Samuel Weld, June 18, 1765.
Hannah, and Jeremiah Richards, jr., May 23, 1728.
Hannah Davis, and Samuel Wyman of Baltimore, Oct. 19,
    1820.*
Henrietta H., and Elisha Tolman, jr., Sept. 16, 1824.*
John [Mahoe. CT. R.], and Hanna [Hannah. CT. R.] Graves,
    May 24, 1654.
John, and Sarah Burden, July 8, 1685.
John, and Polly Mathews, Sept. 11, 1794.*

* Intention also recorded.

MAYO, John F. J., and Ellen E. Eaton of Needham, int. Mar. 29, 1848.

Joseph, and Elizabeth Holbrooke, Mar. 10, 1692.

Joseph, and Esther Kindrick of Newton, at Newton, Nov. 14, 1745.

Joseph, jr., of Warwick, and Mrs. Lucy Richards, Mar. 12, 1772.

Lucy, and Solomon Whiting, Nov. 22, 1781. c. R. 2.

Lucy D., and William Davis, Jan. 6, 1825.*

Lucy R., a. 28 y., d. Seth and Charity, and Preserved Smith of Troy, Ohio, a. 27 y., merchant, s. Preserved and Bebe M., Sept. 10, 1846.*

Maria, and Charles Ellis of Dorchester, Mar. 7, 1816. c. R. 2.*

Mary, and James Griggs of Brookline, Mar. 29, 1744. c. R. 2.

Mary, and Eliakim Richards of Dedham, at Dedham, Jan. 7, 1765.

Mary, and Elias Cook, Jan. 27, 1793.*

Mary, and Richard Lethbridge [Leathbridge. c. R. 3.], Apr. 6, 1813.*

Matilda E., and Sidney R. Dow, Dec. 28, 1843.*

Mehitabel, and David Holmes of Oxford, June 30, 1743. c. R. 2.

Nehemiah, and Mehitabel Holbrook, Nov. 30, 1726.

Polly, Mrs., and William Cummings, Mar. 10, 1793.

Prudence, and William Bosson, jr., Sept. 18, 1777.

Rebecca, and Thomas Gardiner, Mar. 14, 1710.

Rebecca, and Ebenezer Weld, Sept. 6, 1768.

Roxana, and Calvin Baker, Sept. 21, 1815.*

Sarah, Mrs., and Samuell Scarboro, Feb. 10, 1730-31.

Sarah, and Ezra Davis jr., Dec. 21, 1769.

Susanna, and William Bosson, jr., int. Oct. 31, 1784.

Thomas, and Elizabeth Davis, May 4, 1699.

Thomas, jr., and Eliz[abe]th Farley, July 25, 1734.

Thomas, and Mary Heath [Nov. 15. c. R. 2.], 1749.

Thomas, jr., and Anne Davis, June 30, 1763. [Jan. 27. c. R. 2.]

Thomas, Lt., and Catherine Williams, Apr. 27, 1773.

Thomas, and Mrs. Mary Gore, Oct. 26, 1784.*

Thomas, and Amy [Amey. int.] Davis, Aug. 19, 1792.*

William, and Nancy Dorr, Mar. 18, 1827. c. R. 2.*

MAZEKER, Ellen, and Herman Shoemaker, int. Feb. 14, 1849.

* Intention also recorded.

**MEAD** (see also Meades, Meed), Catharine A., of Rutland, and Horace King, int. May 20, 1837.
Eliza S., and William D. Clark, int. Apr. 16, 1837.
George R., and Mary Ann P. Ball, int. Nov. 12, 1837.
Jacob, of Waltham, and Polly Murdock, May 19, 1796.*
John D., a. 25 y., carpenter, s. Levi and Polly, of Deerfield, N. H., and Elizabeth Dunning, a. 24 y., July 22, 1846.*
Mary J., and John D Martin of Candia, N. H., Aug. 4, 1845.*

**MEADER** (see also Medah, Meder), Ann Maria, of Nantucket, and John Howland Swain, int. Sept. 25, 1847.

**MEADES** (see also Mead), Richard, and Marie Benit, Nov. 6, 1678.

**MEADOWS,** Phillip, and Elizabeth Ingulden, Apr. —, 1641.

**MEAKINS,** Thomas, and Elizabeth Tulston, Feb. 14, 1650.

**MEARS,** Abigail, Mrs., and Rev. Amos Addams, Feb. 15, 1770.
Amos Adams, and Mary Whitemore, Nov. 7, 1805.*
Catharine, Mrs., and William Blaney, May 8, 1783.*
James, and Mehitabl[e] Davenport of Milton, at Milton, Dec. 15, 1726.
James, and Hannah Wardell, Aug. 1, 1754.
James, jr., and Mary Davis of Brookline, int. Nov. 21, 1784.
John, and Abagail Minot of Milton, at Milton, ——, 1757.
John, jr., and Mary Parker, Apr. 16, 1789.*
John, and Sarah Robinson of Dorchester, int. Aug. 17, 1794.
Katherine, and Samuel May, Nov. 3, 1748.
Mary Ann, and Rufus Daniels, Nov. 22, 1827.*
Nabby, Mrs., and John Jones Spooner of Dorchester, at Dorchester, Dec. 7, 1778.
Sarah, and Samuel Guild, Nov. 23, 1806.*

**MECUEN,** Edward F., and Jane P. Wilbar [Wilbur. int.], May 1, 1842.*
John, and Lois Whittemore of Dorchester, int. Apr. 26, 1812.
Margaret, and Edward Brown, Nov. 17, 1839.*

**MEDAH** (see also Meader), Elizabeth, and James Gerrish, int. Nov. 16, 1823.

**MEDCALF** (see also Metcalf), John, and Grace Williams, Oct. 29, 1718.

* Intention also recorded.

**MEDCALFE** (see also Metcalf), Sarah, and Timothy Clarke of Medfield, Nov. 22, 1705.

**MEDER** (see also Meader), John L., and Jane Arnold, Mar. 17, 1831.*
Nathaniel R. [of Boston. c. R. 3.], and Maria F. Arnold, Nov. 18, 1830.*
Thomas, and Mary Luly, int. Nov. 27, 1848.

**MEE,** Bridgett, and Michael McDaniel, int. Sept. 28, 1846.
Ellen, and Daniel Korkling, int. July 16, 1846.
Hugh, and Bridget Fitzmorris, int. Nov. 11, 1847.
Luke, and Winefred Follen, int. Mar. 16, 1845.

**MEED** (see also Mead), Bethiah R., and Simeon Rundlet, int. Apr. 12, 1835.

**MEHONEY** (see also Mahoney), Mary Ann Crane, and Payne Wiswall, Sept. 5, 1824.*

**MEILEY,** Ellice, and Michael McDonnell, int. May 3, 1835.

**MEILZ,** Mary, and Patrick Moore, int. Nov. 7, 1841.

**MELCHER,** Esther, and John W. Noyes, int. Nov. 28, 1824.
Pamelia, of Kensington, N. H., and Arno Bettues, int. Jan. 25, 1818.

**MELLEN,** Amos W., and Sally Loring of Quincy, int. Aug. 24, 1823.
Isaac M., and Lucy Clarke, June 5, 1825.*

**MELLISH,** Betsey, and Joseph Craft, Jan. 1, 1801.*
Betsy, and James Blackman, both of Dorchester, Sept. 28, 1797. c. R. 3.
Clarinda, and John Cliflin, Jan. 13, 1805.*
Lucretia, of Dorchester, and Abel Reed of Milton, Apr. 19, 1824.
Samuel, jr., of Dorchester, and Mrs. Elizabeth Curtis, at Dorchester, July 17, 1775.

**MELLUS,** I. P., and E. B. Phiney, int. Feb. 22, 1846.
Mary S., a. 19 y., d. John and Mary, and William F. Bran, a. 23 y., carpenter, s. William, May 31, 1848.*
William C., and Emily A. Averill, Jan. 1, 1845.*

**MELODY,** John, and Margarett Broderick, int. Feb. 8, 1849.

* Intention also recorded.

MELVILLE, William, and Rhoda Powers of Petersham, int. Feb. 24, 1799.

MENTON, Rosanna, and Patrick Mannion, int. Aug. 6, 1846.

MEREDITH, Joseph Henry, of Baltimore, and Mary Elizabeth Farnsworth, int. Sept. 22, 1847.

MERIAM (see also Merriam), Abijah, and Caty Coburn, Nov. 21, 1805.*
Benjamin, and Abigail Harris, Nov. 24, 1816.*
John, and Rebecca Lowd, Jan. 9, 1803.*

MERIUM (see also Merriam), Emeline T., and John H. Plumer, int. Nov. 23, 1845.

MERRIAM (see also Meriam, Merium), Joseph W. [of Boston. c. R. 3.], and Sarah Wilhelmia Seaverns, Oct. 9, 1834.*
Sarah, Mrs., and John Poad, Dec. 26, 1781. c. R. 2.

MERRIFIELD, Mary Ann, a. 26 y., d. Stephen and Lydia, and Horace B. Swan, a. 35 y., laborer, s. Jonah and Elizabeth, June 7, 1848.*

MERRILL, Annette, of Parsonfield, Me., and Rev. David H. Lord of Burrillville, R. I., Nov. 9, 1848.
Cynthia, of Parsonfield, Me., and Richard Horn, int. Dec. 26, 1841.
Cyrus S., and Elinor Garfield, int. Sept. 25, 1847.
Ezekiel, of Lowell, and Hannah C. Poole of Watertown, Dec. 1, 1831.
Gyles, a. 33 y., manufacturer, b. Haverhill, s. Moses and Miriam, and Eliza W. Newbury of Middletown, Conn., a. 33 y., b. England, d. Leonard and Grace, Nov. 28, 1849.*
Louisa M., and Ivory Harmon, int. Sept. 5, 1841.
Lydia Jane, and Thomas Murphy [of Dorchester. int.], Nov. 3, 1844.*
Nathan, of Watertown, and Amanda Brown of Brighton, Oct. 31, 1847.

MERRY, Mary, of Lynn, and Edmund Wild, at Lynn, Nov. 25, 1779.

MESERVE (see also Meservey), Isaac H., and Mary W. Shackford of Barrington, N. H., int. Dec. 4, 1848.
Louisa, and Ezra Young, int. Apr. 12, 1846.

* Intention also recorded.

**MESERVEY** (see also Meserve), Abigil, and George Terrill of Quincy, Aug. 22, 1819.*

**MESSENGER,** Frederick, and Sophia Dornbach, int. Aug. 21, 1846.

**MESSILER,** Jacob, and Phillipina Weigel, int. June 21, 1849.

**METCALF** (see also Medcalf, Medcalfe), Joseph, of Dedham, and Ruth Adis, at Dedham, Feb. 21, 1764.
Rebecca, of Royalston, and Hervey Woods, int. Oct. 11, 1807.
Sarah, of Medway, and Samuel White, jr., at Medway, Apr. 29, 1766.

**MEUGLA,** Ann, and John Goulding, May 27, 1848.

**MIBEY,** Elizabeth, and Lawrence Karence, int. Mar. 19, 1837.

**MICKLES,** James, and Rebeccah Pendor, Dec. 11, 1746.

**MICUNA,** Catharine, and Patrick Murry, int. June 2, 1844.

**MIDDLETON,** Eleanor, and John Johnson [both residents. int.], July 9, 1786.*

**MIGHELL,** Thomas, and Mrs. Bethula Weld, Nov. 8, 1669.

**MIGNAULT,** Pierre Bazile, M. D., of Worcester, and Elizabeth A. Sullivan, int. Aug. 12, 1848.

**MILAN,** John, and Elizabeth Camell, int. Apr. 10, 1848.

**MILBERRY,** Elizabeth, and Job Walker, at Gloucester, Mar. 20, 1755.

**MILES,** Harriet H., of Stowe, and Charles Crane, int. Nov. 3, 1833.
James W[ilson. int.], and Matilda Paine, Apr. 13, 1848.*
Margaret B., and Edwin S. Leland, s. Sherman and Betsey (Adams), Apr. 20, 1840. P. R. 4.
Martha, and Lewis Jones, Apr. 9, 1807. C. R. 2.*
Polly, and Stephen Grover, int. Oct. 26, 1806.
Tho[ma]s, and Mehit[a]ble Parmeter, int. Nov. 26, 1807.

**MILEY,** James, b. Ireland, and Mary Curley, b. Ireland, Mar. 11, 1849.
Margaret, and James Harrington, int. May 28, 1843.

* Intention also recorded.

**MILIKIN** (see also Mulliken), Sarah A., and Andrew V. Dodge, int. May 5, 1847.

**MILLER,** Ann, and George Hazelton, Nov. 25, 1848.*

Elias P., and Hannah V. Gore, Oct. 28, 1821.*

Frederick, and Margarett Lowdenbeck, int. Apr. 22, 1846.

George, of Dorchester, and Hannah T. Todd, Oct. 30, 1836.*

George, and Catharine Newenvings, int. Aug. 7, 1846.

George H., and Caroline L Shepard, int. June 12, 1847.

Hannah, and Amasa Sessions of Pomfret, Oct. 25, 1744. c. R. 2.

Henry W., and Sarah A. Foot, int. Apr. 3, 1842.

Henry W., and Mary E. Hutchins, Dec. 24, 1843. c. R. 7.*

Jacob [resident. int.], and Lydia Pierce, Oct. 6, 1811.*

Jane, a. 21 y., d. John, and William Burns, a. 25 y., shoemaker, s. George and Martha of Ireland, Nov. 5, 1846.*

John F., and Harriet L. Smith, int. Sept. 4, 1842.

Letita [Leticia. int.] A., and Henry G. Rafley [Rufley. int.], Sept. 15, 1844.*

Louisa, and Joseph Gerhardslein, int. May 18, 1848.

Mary, of Charlestown, and John B. Butterfield, int. Sept. 1, 1811.

Sophia, of Charlestown, and John Doggett, int. Feb 26, 1804.

Victoria, and Francis Bowmaster, int. Aug. 25, 1847.

William, and Hannah Lothrop, Feb. 7, 1805.*

**MILLERD,** Hannah, of Rehoboth, and John Morey, at Rehoboth, Aug. 17, 1730.

**MILLES** (see also Mills), John F., and Harriet L. Smith, Oct. 2, 1842.

**MILLETT,** Daniel C., of New York, clergyman, s. Daniel and Elizabeth C., and Lucy Maria Holbrook, d. Asa and Sarah, Aug. 24, 1847.*

**MILLS** (see also Milles), Christopher S., and Sarah E. Laughton, Aug. 31, 1845.*

Elizabeth, of Needham, and Joseph Corey, at Needham, May 25, 1758.

Ephraim [Mille. int.], and Rebecca Gridley, at Boston, Nov. 10, 1793.*

James, and Emily D. Snell, May 7, 1843.*

* Intention also recorded.

MILLS, Jemima, of Needham, and Samuel Perry, at Needham, Dec. 6, 1781.

John, and Marietta Davis, Oct. 15, 1820.*

Joseph, of Newton, and Mary Fisk, int. May 5, 1811.

Nathaniell, and Ann Baker, Oct. 29, 1718.

Oliver [of Boston. c. r. 3.], and Emely Gardner Dabney, Apr. 16, 1813.*

Philip, and Ann Wight of Needham, at Needham, Dec. 22, 1774.

Rufus H., of Needham, a. 21 y., silk manufacturer, s. Rufus and Sarah E., of Needham, and Harriot S. Fairbanks of Needham, a. 23 y., d. Joshua and Clarissa, Mar. 3, 1847.

Stephen, and Martha Allesson, Aug. 4, 1768.

William ,of Needham, and Mary Watson, June 17, 1724.

MILNER, Joseph F., and Ann F. H. Hunneman, int. Apr. 17, 1831.

MILNES, John, of Lowell, and Eliza Townsend, Mar. 31, 1847. c. r. 5.

MINCHIN, John, and Maria Kennedy, Jan. 5, 1846.*

MINER, Philana, and Samuel Belding [jr. int.], June 5, 1828.*

MINNS, George W., and Elizabeth F. Woodward of Brookline, int. Aug. 29, 1849.

MINON, Michael G., of Boston, and Ann Cawley, int. May 13, 1848.

MINOT (see also Minott) Abagail, of Milton, and John Mears, at Milton, ——, 1757.

Catharine [E. int.], and W[illia]m W. Pratt, Feb. 16, 1843.*

Sophia, and Valentine Boos, Aug. 21, 1834.

MINOTT (see also Minot), John [of Dorchester. int.], and Catta [Calla. int.] Smith, Nov. 27, 1806. c. r. 2.*

MINTON, Bernard, and Bridget Donelon, int. Dec. 30, 1846.

Michael, and Catharine Magin, int. Oct. 22, 1843

MIRICK, Abner, and Eliza Nightingale, Oct. 27, 1829.*

Ann B., and Jesse Jordan, Apr. 13, 1826.*

Benjamin, and Mrs. Charlotte Brown, Nov. 2, 1826.*

* Intention also recorded.

MIRICK, Elizabeth, and Frederick W. Field of Quincy, int. May 13, 1832.

Emily, and Joseph D. Williams, Aug. 16, 1826.*

George, and Joan Brown, int. June 16, 1833.

Maria, and John Dove, int. July 24, 1836.

Mary, and William Dove, jr., int. May 10, 1835.

Sarah, and Hosea B. Stiles, Aug. 15, 1841.*

MITCHELL, Albert F., of Brookline, and Mary Ann Whittemore, int. Nov. 28, 1833.

Alexander, and Lydia Haskell, May 1, 1830.

Asenath, and Nathaniel W. Crossman, Dec. 25, 1836.*

Elizabeth I., and Alfred I. Libby, int. Mar. 15, 1846.

James, and Margaret Tracy, int. Aug. 14, 1842.

James, b. Ireland, and Ann McGuire, b. Ireland, July 30, 1849.*

Michael, and Bridgett Doland, int. Oct. 11, 1848.

Michael, and Bridget McCarty, int. Feb. 14, 1849.

Octavia S., and David Cornell, int. June 5, 1836.

Rebecca, of Boxford, and John Blodget, int. Aug. 4, 1833.

Sarah E., and Cyrus Munroe [Monroe. int.], Feb. 27, 1845.*

Terrence, and Ann Murray, int. June 14, 1847.

MIXER, Dorithy, of Watertown, and William Davice, at Watertown, Jan. 12, 1709-10.

MOCK, George, and Hepsy Elizabeth Kent, int. Nov. 2, 1823.

MOFFAT, Joseph L., and Antoinette S. Jones, int. Apr. 7, 1833.

MOLTON (see also Moulton), Hannah, Mrs., of Dorchester, and John Dowse, jr., at Dorchester, Oct. 3, 1776.

MONK (see also Monks, Muncks, Munk, Munke), Dorothy, and Samuell Stone of Stoughton, Apr. 1, 1734.

Elisa, and Dorothy Boson, Aug. 5, 1714.

Hopestill, and Richard Lethbridge, June 7, 1742.

MONKS (see also Monk), Mathew, and Ellen Ryan, int. Nov. 4, 1846.

* Intention also recorded.

**MONROE** (see also Munroe), Catharine [Munroe. dup.], and
John Ross, Feb. 7. 1833.*

Margaret Cooledge [Coolidge. c. r. 5.], and Benj[ami]n Mor-
ril [jr. int.], Dec. 1, 1836.*

Mary H., and Joseph R. Giddens, Jan. 17, 1842.*

**MONTGOMERY,** John, resident, and Mary Cotterill, Mar. 27,
1788.*

Mary Ann, and Issac Lawrence, May 3, 1820.*

**MOODY,** Henry H., and Sarah M. Stetson of Dorchester,
Apr. 12, 1845.*

**MOONEY,** Elizabeth, and Patrick Cummins, int. Aug. 2, 1840.

James [of Eaton, N. H. int.], and Lizey Shannon, Mar. 4,
1819.*

John, and Mary Clark, int. Jan. 1, 1849.

Margaret, and Bernard Healy, int. May 18, 1845.

**MOORE** (see also Moors, More, Mowear), Alpheus, and Mary
R. Taylor, Sept. 9, 1827.*

Catharine, and Thomas S[amuel. int.] Sommers, Dec. 1, 1845.*

Charles H., and Emily A. Stafford of Munroe, Me., int. Feb.
6, 1847.

Eusebia, and Samuel Parker, Nov. 20, 1808.*

Henry, and Catherine Scott, int. Feb. 7, 1848.

John, of Brookline, and Sarah Seaverns, int. Mar. 24, 1833.

Joseph, of Malden, and Betsey Collins, int. Oct. 27, 1805.

Joseph, and Rebecca Peabody, Jan. [21. c. r. 3.], 1816.*

Josiah H., and Lydia H. James, Sept. 21, 1828.*

Matilda J., and George Kimball, Mar. 5, 1837.*

Nancy ,and Ebenezer Pratt, int. Feb. 17, 1833.

Nathan, and Charlotte P. Nutting, int. Oct. 17, 1841.

Page, a. 34 y., operative, s. James and Nancy, and Emily A.
Burnham, a. 27 y., upholstress, d. Enoch and Judith, Feb.
6, 1845.

Patrick, and Mary Meilz, int. Nov. 7, 1841.

Patrick, and Bridget Burns, int. May 12, 1848.

Sarah, and Thomas P. Williams, Oct. 29, 1845.*

Sarah Jane, and William B. Cook, int. July 25, 1814.

William C., and Mary Ann Ames, May 22, 1823.*

**MOORS** (see also Moore), Josiah, and Louisa Sevens of
Brookline, Nov. 12, 1827.

* Intention also recorded.

**MORACY,** Thomas, and Bridget Hastings, int. Jan. 13, 1849.

**MORAN,** John, and Ellen Kenny, int. Dec. 28, 1845.
William, of Watertown, and Catharine Kelley, int. Aug. 28, 1842.

**MORE** (see also Moore), Thomas, and Susanna Newel, at Dorchester, Oct. 3 [Sept. 6. dup.], 1673.

**MOREY** (see also Mory), Francis F., and Hannah Bird, int. Nov. 6, 1848.
John, and Hannah Millerd of Rehoboth, at Rehoboth, Aug. 17, 1830.
John W., of Boston, and Daphne C. Barker of Cambridge, Oct. 11, 1840. c. r. 3.
Mehittabell, and Noah Kingsbury [of Dedham. c. r. 2.], Sept. 30, 1718.
Sarah Ann B., and Joseph Hastings, int. Dec. 16, 1838.
Susannah, and Robert Pierpont, Mar. 12, 1752.
Susannah, and Aaron D. Weld, int. Aug. 28, 1808.

**MORGAINE** (see also Morgan), James, and Margery Hill, Aug. 6, 1640.

**MORGAN** (see also Morgaine), Bridget, and Peter Kelly, int. Jan. 1, 1848.
James H., and Polly W. White, int. Nov. 3, 1837.
John, and Mary Kenedy, int. Jan. 16, 1848.
John, and Mary Killroy [Kilroy. int.], Oct. 24, 1848.*
Maria, and Patrick Keegan, int. Nov. 12, 1849.
Mary, and Thomas Killian, int. Sept. 7, 1845.
Robert, and Sarah Osgood Johnson, Apr. 23, 1845.*

**MORGRIDGE** (see also Mugridge), John, of Calais, Me., and Mary Ellery Bugbee, Apr. 8, 1830.*

**MORIARTY,** Clement, and Hannah Irwin, int. June 5, 1848.

**MORISE** (see also Morris), Isaac, and Hannah Mayo, Mar. 2, 1680.

**MORISON** (see also Morrison), Samuel C., and Maria T. Gerish, int. Feb. 15, 1829.

**MORONEY,** Catharine, and Cornelius Regan, int. July 2, 1843.

* Intention also recorded.

**MORRELL** (see also Morrill), Hanna, and Daniel Bruer, Nov. 5, 1652.

**MORRILL** (see also Morrell, Morrol), Benj[ami]n [jr. int.], and Margaret Cooledge [Coolidge. c. r. 3.] Monroe, Dec. 1, 1836.*
Gregory T., and Martha B. Trefry, Oct. 30, 1844.
Joseph, jr., and Helen E. Brooks of Boston, int. Dec. 13, 1849.
Lydia Swift, and Anthony Ness, June 16, 1835.
Sarah, a. 20 y., d. Joseph and Nancy, and Thomas F. Wells, a. 25 y., merchant, s. Thomas and Anna Maria, Oct. 31, 1849.*

**MORRIS** (see also Morise, Morriss), Ellen, and Michael Quingley, int. Apr. 30, 1849.
Isaac, and Mary Pirepont, Nov. 3, 1702.
James, of Nova Scotia, 2d m., a. 28 y., master mariner, b. Nova Scotia, s. Henry and Jane, and Mary Ann Cogswell, a. 24 y., b. Nova Scotia, Dec. 4, 1849.*
Mary, and Timothy Norton, int. Sept. 24, 1849.
Sarah F., of Wilbraham, and Daniel D. Chaffee, int. Apr. 21, 1833.

**MORRISON** (see also Morison, Morrisson), Ebenezer D., and Sally W. Ewell, May 4, 1826.*
John [Morrisson. int.], and Julia Sullivan, Feb. 25, 1847.*
Jonathan Holmes, and Nancy Hall Silvester, Aug. 20, 1809. c. r. 3.*
Nancy, and Samuel Wentworth, June 12, 1831.*
Sylvia Ann, of Brookline, and Charles N. Ford, int. Mar. 1, 1835.

**MORRISS** (see also Morris), Edward, and Elisabeth Bowen, May 24, 1683.
Elisabeth, and Joshua Childe, Mar. 9, 1685.
Grace, and Benjamin Childe, Mar. 7, 1682-3.
Margaret, and John Johnson, Apr. 4, 1689.

**MORRISSON** (see also Morrison), Mary B., of Dresden, Me., and Charles H. Gridley, int. Dec. 9, 1846.

**MORROL** (see also Morrill), Katherine, and John Smith, Aug. 1, 1647.

* Intention also recorded.

**MORROW,** Ann Eleanor [Ann E. int.], a. 19 y., d. Thomas and Ellen, and John Whitford, a. 21 y., miner, s. W[illia]m and Jane, June 7, 1848.*

**MORS** (see also Morse), Asa, and Hannah Griggs, May 14, 1778.

**MORSE** (see also Mors), Abba E., and Henry L. Lambert both of Salem, May 17, 1848.

Adam, and Martha Rumril, Dec. 1, 1811. C. R. 2.*

Amos, and Abigail B. Davenport of Dorchester, int. Sept. 18, 1825.

Ann, and Charles Dorr, May 20, 1821. C. R. 2.*

Ann G., and Nahum M. Glines, Sept. 7, 1831.*

Caroline A., a. 21 y., d. Harford and Lucy, and Alonzo Josselyn, a. 28 y., moulder, s. Charles and Lucy, Dec. 24, 1846.*

Charles, and Louisa Cole of Watertown, int. Dec. 2, 1832.

Chester H., and Abigail S. Stevens, of Randolph, int. Dec, 23, 1832.

Clarissa, and Samuel Pool, Oct. 8, 1828.*

Cordelia C., a. 23 y., d. Barnet and Sarah, and Joshua Dennis, a. 24 y., carpenter, s. Abijah and Rachel, July 25, 1848.*

Cynthia, of Falmouth, and David Swift [resident. int.], at Falmouth, Sept. 24, 1786.*

David, of Cambridge, and Mary Bell, int. Nov. 17, 1822.

David L., and Maria Jordan of Dorchester, int. Apr. 3, 1836.

Elizabeth H., of Dorchester, and Samuel Vickery, Apr. 13, 1831.*

Emeline, and Joshua Seaver , int. Nov. 23, 1846.

Ezra, and Rebecca Thomas, Nov. 8, 1821.*

Ezra, and Eliza Jane Foster, int. Dec. 2, 1827.

George, and Mary Ann Wheeler, int. Aug. 28, 1831.

Harriet, and John Champney, jr., at Brookline, May 28, 1843

Harriet A., and Robert C. Nichols, int. July 3, 1846.

Harriet E., and Benj[ami]n H. Burrill, int. Sept. 4, 1836.

Hartford, and Lucy Gay of Sharon, int. Apr. 12, 1812.

Horatio G., a. 29 y., physician, s. Amos and Irena, and Sarah D. Griggs [3d. P. R. 3; of Boston. int.], a. 18 y., d. John and Sarah, Apr. 22 [23. P. R. 3.], 1847.*

Isaac, and Ester Woodward, Oct. —, 1807.*

Isaac, and Lucy Coverly, int. July 17, 1831.

Jacob B., and Mary E. Davis, Oct. 9, 1839.*

* Intention also recorded.

MORSE, James, and Lucy Whiting of Dedham, int. Mar. 24, 1805.

Lewis, and Olive Richards, Jan. 2, 1803.*

Lewis, and Mary Jewell, June 28, 1807. C. R. 2.*

Lewis, and Susan Whitaker, July 16, 1820.*

Lucinda J., of Dedham, and Charles P. Hartshorn, int. Dec. 18, 1836.

Lucy Ann, of Dedham, and Dan W. Heath of Wrentham, June 20, 1837. C. R. 7.

Lucy G., and James Card, int. June 14, 1835.

Martha, and Timothy Bacon, Dec. 16, 1714.

Martha T., and Ebenezer Tucker, Mar. 6, 1834.*

Martin, of Natick, and Rebecca Darby, Nov. 21, 1819.*

Mary, and Stephen Sampson, Oct. 11, 1805.*

Mary Ann, of Dorchester, and Stephen Chamberlain, jr., int. May 4, 1823.

Mary Holmes, and Amos Cheney of Cambridge, May 8, 1823.*

Mary S., of Lowell, and Francis B. Smilie, int. Feb. 4, 1848.

Narcissa, late of Cambridge, and Isaac Stearns of Waltham, Nov. 15, 1810.

Nathaniel A., and Mary W. Perkins, Nov. 6, 1836.*

Olivia, and John Littlefield, Apr. 5, 1837.*

P., of Natick, and Elisha Robbins, int. Dec. 30, 1804.

Patty, of Walpole, and Joseph Tucker, int. Dec. 29, 1799.

Perley, and Sarah Brewer, May 1, 1817.*

Rebecca, Mrs., and Ezekiel D. Dyer, May 29, 1828.*

Unity, of Walpole, and Abraham Rice, int. Sept. 15, 1816.

William, and Phebe A. Spofford, Apr. 23, 1848.*

MORTO, Sarah, and John Chase, int. Feb. 21, 1819.

MORTON, Amanda, a. 21 y., d. William, and George Carson, a. 24 y., carpenter, s. George and Margarett, Oct. 4, 1846.*

Elizabeth, and James Orr, June 20, 1756.

Freeman C., and Harriet A. Hodgden, int. Aug. 3, 1845.

Hannah Adelia, a. 28 y., d. John and Bethia, and George Smith, a. 26 y., carpenter, s. Elisha and Clarissa, of Sudbury, Apr. 25, 1847.*

James, and Abigail Seaver, Feb. 15, 1769.

James P., and Helen Hannden of Wilmington, int. June 1, 1845.

* Intention also recorded.

MORTON, Jane L., a. 18 y., d. William and Mary, and Alfred C. Murray, a. 25 y., upholsterer, s. William and Eliza H., Apr. 29, 1849.*

Mary, and Caleb Howard, Jan. 8, 1761.

Mary H., of Milton, and George Thompson of Charlestown, Nov. 11, 1833. C. R. 3.

Susan E., and James L. Smith, int. Dec. 3, 1837.

William S., of Milton, and Mary J. W. Grimes, int. Sept. 1, 1839.

**MORY** (see also Morey), Elizabeth, and Israel Leavit, Dec. 27, 1710.

John, and Mary Cheney, Sept. 9, 1768.

Mary, and Charles Watson, Nov. 26, 1711.

Susanna, and Josiah Kingsbury, Jan. 16, 1704-5.

Thomas, and Susanna Newell, Sept. 6, 1673.

**MOSELY,** Ann R., and Edward T. Talbot, both of Dorchester, Feb. 2, 1835.

**MOSES,** T. B., and Frances L. Bouve, int. June 9, 1844.

**MOSHER,** Jeremiah, and Mrs. Hannah Craft, Nov. 29, 1750.

Jeremiah, and Isabella Shippe [Shippy. c. R. 2.], Aug. 20, 1752.

**MOSMAN,** Elisabeth, and Joseph Walcot of Needham, July 14, 1725.

**MOSS,** Benjamin, of Medfield, and Rachel Bullard, Sept. 28, 1702.

**MOTT,** Augusta, and John Brucher, int. Nov. 27, 1847.

Celestinah, and John Smith, int. Sept. 9, 1847.

**MOULTON** (see also Molton), Elizabeth, and Charles G. Colbeth [Colbath. c. R. 3.], May 6, 1840.*

John M., and Elizabeth Ann Woods, int. July 3, 1825.

Jonathan, widr., a. 30 y., laborer, s. Cha[rle]s and Rebecca, of Wakefield, N. H., and Olive Rand, a. 30 y., d. Sam-[ue]l and Polly, of Rye, N. H., Jan. 12, 1847.*

Maria, and William Jackson, Feb. 11, 1821.*

Mary, and Henry Shurtlief, June 3, 1753.

**MOUNTJOY,** Mary, Mrs., and Philip Thomson, June 4, 1714.

* Intention also recorded.

**MOWEAR** (see also Moore), Richard, and Thankfull Sever, Mar. 29, 1705.

**MUDGE,** Harriet, and Ashly Parmlee, Oct. 6, 1842.

**MUGRIDGE** (see also Morgridge), William, and Eliza Ann Stevens, June 19, 1841.*

**MULAKIN** (see also Mulliken), Bridgett, and John Dillon, int. Nov. 7, 1846.

**MULHEARN** (see also Mulhern), Thomas, and Catherine Cunningham, int. Jan. 25, 1848.

**MULHERN** (see also Mullhearn, Mulkern), John, and Ann Doherty, int. Aug. 9, 1840.
John, and Mary Downey, int. Feb. 7, 1848.
William, and Catherine Donelly, int. Jan. 25, 1847.

**MULKAKY,** Ellen, and Thomas Lynch, int. Feb. 7, 1848.

**MULKERN** (see also Mulhern), Luke, and Sarah Gately, int. Oct. 23, 1842.

**MULLAIN** (see also Mullen), Bridget, and Thomas Norton, int. June 6, 1848.

**MULLEANY,** Thomas, and Bridget Tobin, int. May 26, 1849.

**MULLEN** (see also Mullain. Mullens, Mullin), Catherine, and Michael Staunton, int. July 3, 1847.
John, and Mary Duffy, int. Feb. 8, 1846.
Martin, and Margarett Durant of Boston, int. Jan. 1, 1849.
Mary, and Patrick Roark, int. Dec. 30, 1847.
Mary Ann C., and John Walker of Boston, int. Apr. 28, 1849.
Michael, and Bridget Fallen, int. Feb. 16, 1845.
Thomas, and Catherine Gasin, int. Mar. 1, 1848.
William, and Bridget Rourke, int. Sept. 27, 1848.

**MULLENS** (see also Mullen), John, and Margaret Foley, int. Sept. 16, 1838.

**MULLIGAN,** Ann, and James Coyne, int. June 18, 1849.
Catherine, and John Maher, int. 23, 1846.

**MULLIKEN** (see also Milikin, Mulakin), Ephraim S., and Mary A. Horton of Canton, int. Apr. 14, 1849.

* Intention also recorded.

**MULLIN** (see also Mullen), Honora, and Thomas Gafney, int. Jan. 26, 1848.

John, and Catherine Donavan, int. May 30, 1848.

**MULRAY** (see also Mulry), Ann [Mulry. int.], b. Ireland, and Patrick Collins, b. Ireland, Oct. 20, 1849.*

Honora [Mulrey. int.], b. Ireland, and James Cavanah [Cavno. int.], b. Ireland, Nov. 27, 1849.*

Michael, and Ann Lawley, int. Dec. 30, 1848.

Timothy [Mulrey. int.], b. Ireland, and Ellen Devine [Dinn. int.], b. Ireland, Nov. 16, 1849.*

**MULRY** (see also Mulray), Ann, and Andrew Killday, int. Sept. 1, 1849.

**MULVAY** (see also Mulvy), Bridgett, and Edward Mahon, int. Oct. 19, 1846.

**MULVY** (see also Mulvay), Margaret, and Patrick Glynn, int. Jan. 6, 1848.

**MUMFORD**, Hanna, and [Rev. C. R. 1.], John Elliot [Eliot. C. R. 1.], Sept. 4, 1632.

**MUNAGLE**, Mary, and Daniel McMahan, int. June 14, 1840.

**MUNCKS** (see also Monk), John, of Baltimore, [Md. int.], a. 30 y., merchant, s. Andrew and Margarett, and Elizabeth M. Dana, a. 23 y., d. Francis and Lochada, Oct. 18, 1849.*

**MUNCREAF** (see also Muncreif), Joseph, and Mary Pierpont, Dec. 24, 1766.

**MUNCREIF** (see also Muncreaf), Abigail F., and Nathaniel Fisher of Providence, July 23, 1810.*

Joseph, jr., and Abigail Fillebrown, Nov. 24, 1791.*

Joseph, and Sarah Baker of Dorchester, Aug. 8, 1793.

Joseph, jr., and Ann Martin, Mar. 25, 1823.*

Mary, and Waldin Fuller, Dec. 6, 1790.*

Mary, and James Pitty of Hingham, Jan. 14, 1819.*

Nancy Young, and Elisha Turner, jr., Sept. 6, 1818.*

Rebecca, and Daniel Diman of Plymouth, Dec. 15, 1830.*

Sarah, and John Dove [both residents. int.], July 3, 1786.*

**MUNK** (see also Monk), Hannah, and John Bugbee, jr., Oct. 29, 1741.

* Intention also recorded.

**MUNKE** (see also Monk), Ann, and John Stebbin, Apr. 17, 1644.

**MUNROE** (see also Monroe), Benjamin, and Rebecca Faxon, Sept. 17, 1826.*

Catharine, of Charlestown, and Sylvester Edgerly, int. Oct. 4, 1840.

Charles W., and Martha Ann Drake, June 6, 1847.*

Charlotte, and Charles Winship, July 10, 1808.*

Cyrus [Monroe. int.], and Sarah E. Mitchell, Feb. 27, 1845.*

Daniel, and Abigail Parker, Sept. 15, 1774.

Francis, of Framingham, and Abigail L. Trask, int. Oct. 23, 1843.

George B., and Sarah W. Massey, May 11, 1843.*

James M. [a. 21 y. in pencil.], and Abigail B. Faxon [a. 21 y. in pencil.] of Quincy, int. Mar. 3, 1844.

Jedediah, and Sarah Parker, May 30, 1782.

Jennet, and Aaron D. Fairbanks, a. 26 y., gentleman, s. Aaron and Nancy, May 2, 1848.*

John, and Sarah B. Maxfield, Sept. 21, 1837.*

Lucy Ann, and Kendall Brooks, 2d, int. Apr. 23, 1843.

Nehemiah Dea., and Thankful Stratton of Fitzwilliam, N. H., int. July 25, 1819.

Rhoda P[arker. Monroe. c. r. 3.], and John Windship [Winship of Boston. c. r. 3.], Apr. 21, 1805.*

Sally, and John W. Smith, Dec. 23, 1804.*

**MUNSAY** (see also Munsey), Martha, of Wiscasset, Me., and John Withers, Nov. 12, 1845.

**MUNSEY** (see also Munsay), Mary Jane, and Charles Thomas, int. Feb. 26, 1843.

**MURDOCK,** Abel, and Margarette Passenger, int. Sept. 4, 1825.

Amasa, of Newton, and Harriet Green, int. Nov. 27, 1834.

Betsy [Betsey. int.], and Edward Sparhawk [of Cambridge. int.], July 22, 1804. c. r. 2.*

Charity, and Ebenezer Murdock, Apr. 23, 1797. c. r. 2.*

Cornelia M., of Lowell, and Charles W. Brown, int. Nov. 6, 1836.

Ebenezer, and Charity Murdock, Apr. 23, 1797. c. r. 2.*

Ebenezer, and Hannah Davis, May 25, 1803. c. r. 2.*

* Intention also recorded.

MURDOCK, Ephraim [of Brookline. c. r. 2.], and Sarah Sever, Mar. 26, 1761.

Ephraim, and Charity Davis, May 26, 1768.

George [of Boston. c. r. 3.], and Mary Haswell, May 20, 1819.*

Hannah, and David Weld, jr., May 15, 1783.*

Hannah, and Joseph Heath, Sept. 3, 1811. c. r. 2.

Mary, and Nathaniel Richards, June 9, 1814. c. r. 2.*

Nabby, and Ebenezer Dudley, Jan. 3, 1799. c. r. 2.*

Nancy, and William Draper, jr., May 22, 1806. c. r. 2.*

Polly, and Jacob Mead of Waltham, May 19, 1796.*

Robert, and Hannah Stedman, Apr. 28, 1692.

Sarah, and David Cory, May 22, 1791.*

Sarah, Mrs., and Joseph Heath, int. Aug. 10, 1811.

Samuel, and Elizabeth Newell, Mar. 26, 1786.*

Thomas M., of Brookline, and Eunice Ford, int. Sept. 29, 1833.

**MURLHAUGH,** Patrick, and Mary Dunfee, int. Apr. 7, 1848.

**MURPHY** (see also Murply), Andrew, and Julia Sweeney, int. Sept. 26, 1846.

Ann, and John Davis, int. Jan. 13, 1848.

Christopher, and Margarett Neenan, int. Oct. 16, 1847.

Cornelius, and Bridget Kearnan, int. Sept. 29, 1844.

Edward D., and Charlotte A. Noyes, Mar. 16, 1848.*

Hannah, and Timothy Kelley, int. Apr. 23, 1848.

Hannah, and Michael Kiggins, int. July 8, 1848.

Hugh, and Ann Flanagan, int. Jan. 20, 1839.

John, and Margaret Cummings, int. Apr. 25, 1841.

John, and Catharine Drinan, int. Sept. 8, 1844.

John, and Catharine Cady, int. May 13, 1845.

John, of Brookline, and Hannah Rhine, int. Apr. 13, 1847.

John, a. 21 y., shoemaker, s. Edward and Lucy, and Eliza Beachman, a. 19 y., d. Anthony and Catherine, Feb. 15, 1849.*

John, and Ellen Dooley, int. Nov. 13, 1849.

Margarett, and Henry Brawley, int. Oct. 23, 1847.

Margarett, and Michael Flynn, int. Mar. 3, 1848.

Michael, and Mary Sullivan, June 24, 1848.*

Thomas [of Dorchester. int.], and Lydia Jane Merrill, Nov. 3, 1844.*

William, and Hannah Sullivan. int. Apr. 6, 1846.

* Intention also recorded.

**MURPLY** (see also Murphy), Hannah, and John Collins, int. Apr. 4, 1844.

**MURRAY** (see also Murrey, Murry), Alfred C., a. 25 y., up-holsterer, s. William and Eliza H., and Jane L. Morton, a. 18 y., d. William and Mary, Apr. 29, 1849.*
Ann, and Terrence Mitchell, int. June 14, 1847.
Ebenezer [A. dup.], and Martha F. Hubbard, int. Apr. 30, 1843. [Dec. 8, 1844. dup.]
Euphemia, and David C. Davis, int. June 14, 1835.
Hubbard G., and Eliza Ann Wilby, Mar. 1, 1843.*
John, and Elizabeth McDonough, int. Apr. 9, 1843.
John, and Sarah Winn, int. Mar. 7, 1849.
Mary, and Michael Gillagan, int. Jan. 5, 1845.
Mary, b. Ireland, and Matthew Killillin [Killillea. int.], b. Ireland, Aug. 7, 1849.*

**MURREY** (see also Murray), Catharine, and Patrick Rodgers, int. July 29, 1827.

**MURRY** (see also Murray), Bridget, and Richard O'Burne, int. Aug. 11, 1849.
Margaret, and Nath[anie]l Sweeny, int. Oct. 22, 1837.
Patrick, and Catharine Micuna, int. June 2, 1844.

**MURTAGH,** James, and Mary Finaty, int. Nov. 19, 1843.

**MYERS,** Mary Ann, and James Egen, int. Sept. 30, 1846.

**MYLAY,** Mary, and Bryan Byrnes, int. Dec. 21, 1847.

**MYLOD,** Eliza, and Tho[ma]s Dudley, May —, 1805. [Apr. 21, C. R. 3.]*

**NAGMAN,** Jacob, and Rica Emmlen, int. June 25, 1849.

**NASH,** Bernard, and Mary Dunkin, int. Aug. 13, 1846.
David R., and Caroline M. Fox, ——, 1832. [Aug. 21, 1831. int.]*
Jerusha, of Holden, and Isaac Davis, 3d, int. Dec. 14, 1817.
Mary, and Mears Orcutt, Aug. 21, 1849. C. R. 3.
Mary Ann, and Alfred N. Fowler, Nov. 10, 1847.
William, and Mary R. Leonard, Dec. 21, 1826.*

**NASON,** Andrew, and Lucretia W. Shed, Nov. 23, 1836.*
Jabez, and Elizabeth Ann Maxwell, Dec. 16, 1813.*
Mary E., and Charles Freeman, int. Sept. 3, 1843.

* Intention also recorded.

**NAUGHTON** (see also Norton), Alexander, and Mary Mackney, int. Nov. 20, 1846.
Catharine, and Thomas Nolan, int. June 4, 1846.
Hugh, and Mary Kenney, int. May 18, 1845.
Patrick, and Catharine Shaily, int. Feb. 1, 1846.

**NAVAN,** W[illia]m, and Ann Noland, int. May 12, 1839.

**NEAL,** Elizabeth R., and Francis Houston, int. May 4, 1849.
John [of Boston. C. R. 3.], and Caroline M. Sanborn [Sanborne. C. R. 3.], Jan. 19, 1843.

**NEALEY,** Joseph, and Susan Chamberlain, Feb. 7, 1828. C. R. 2.*

**NEEDHAM,** Ezekiel, and Dorothy Stevens, May 4, 1738.

**NEENAN,** Margarett, and Christopher Murphy, int. Oct. 16, 1847.

**NEILEN,** Hannah, and Dennis Coyle, int. Nov. 29, 1849.

**NELSON,** George W., and Ellen Coyle, int. Sept. 27, 1847.
Milton, and Julia F. Huntoon of Cambridge, Jan. 1, 1837.

**NENGLA,** Ann, and John Goulding, int. May 13, 1848.

**NESS** (see also Nuss), Anthony, and Lydia Swift Morrill, June 16, 1835.

**NEVENS,** Nancy, and Isaac Gregson, int. Jan. 15, 1815.

**NEWBURY,** Eliza W., of Middletown, Conn., a. 33 y., b. England, d. Leonard and Grace, and Gyles Merrill, a. 33 y., manufacturer, b. Haverhill, s. Moses and Miriam, Nov. 28, 1849.*

**NEWCOMB,** Joseph, and Sarah Bennett, int. Feb. 16, 1848.
Peter, of Braintree, and Mary Humphrey, Apr. 30, 1702.

**NEWEL** (see also Newell), Abram, and Susan Rand [d. Rob[er]t in pencil], Feb. 8, 1651.
Benjamin, and Sarah Polley, May 4, 1726.
Elizabeth, and ——, ——, Apr. 9, 1690.
Experience, and Samuel Willis, May 23, 1700.
Hannah, and John Holmes, Apr. 9, 1690.
Isaac, and Abigail Griggs, Dec. 14, 1715.

*Intention also recorded.

NEWEL, Jacob, and Joyce Glezin [May ?], 1700.
Martha, Mrs., and Elisha Townsend, July 24, 1729.
Mary, and Frances Richee, May 25, 1727.
Rebecca, and William Cheny, May 24, 1686.
Sarah, and Isaac Child [of Brookline. c. r. 2.], Nov. 4, 1713.
Susanna [Newell. dup.], and Thomas More [Mory. dup.], at
    Dorchester, Oct. 3 [Sept. 6. dup.], 1673.

NEWELL (see also Newel), Abraham, s. Abraham, and Abi-
    gail Roder, July 21, 1681.
Allen, of Brookline, and Harriet Wood, June 28, 1827.*
Caroline, and James T. Bicknell [Bicknall. int.], May 23,
    1841.*
Catherine R., of Ashland, a. 25 y., d. Willard and Sarah, and
    Henry Baylies of Ashland, a. 28 y., tailor, s. Daniel and
    Lucy, Apr. 4, 1849.
Charles W., a. 35 y., painter, s. Willard and Sarah, and
    Mary M. P. Dandley, d. James and Sarah, Dec. 3, 1846.*
Daniel, and Clarissa, Stickney of Jeffrey, int. Sept. 14, 1800.
Ebenezer, and Mrs. Susannah Sanders, Feb. 25, 1741-2.
Ebenez[e]r, jr., and Abigail Pierpont, Aug. 4, 1742.
Elizabeth, and Samuel Murdock, Mar. 26, 1786.*
George H., a. 21 y., cabinet manufacturer, s. Willard and
    Sarah, and Rosetta A. Boutelle of Antrim, N. H., d.
    Charles and Betsey, July 12, 1849.*
Grace, and William Toy, Sept. 14, 1644.
Isaac, and Elizabeth Curtis, Dec. 14, 1659.
Jacob, and Martha Gibson, Nov. 7 [3. ct. r.], 1657.
John, of Brookline, and Sarah Seaver, at Brookline, Oct. 15,
    1741.
John, and Elisabeth Davis, Nov. 19, 1767.
Josiah, and [Mrs. int.] Abigail Kneeland, Jan. 29, 1783.
    c. r. 2.*
Luther, and Sarah Cunningham, Jan. 7, 1810.*
Maria A., d. Luther and Sarah, and Isaac S. Burrell [Buriell.
    int.], a. 27 y., wheelwright, s. Benj[amin] and Lucy, Jan.
    23, 1848.*
Mary, and John Hall of Rehoboth, at Rehoboth, Nov. 18,
    1684.
Mary, and Joseph Heath, Nov. 29, 1774.
Mary Jane, and Luther Hallowell, May 16, 1824.
Sally, and Timothy Batts, Oct. 19, 1800.*

* Intention also recorded.

NEWELL, Sarah, and Capt. Peter Perit, Nov. 22, 1778.
Sarah, and George Southhack, int. Dec. 2, 1832.
Sasanna [Susanna. int.] Pierpont, and Jareb Dyer [of Canterbury. int.], Nov. 6, 1784.*
Susan, Mrs., and Andrew Whittemore, Aug. 3, 1841.*

**NEWENVINGS,** Catharine, and George Miller, int. Aug. 7, 1846.

**NEWHALL,** Elizabeth, and Nathan Burditt, Oct. 4, 1791.*
Sarah, Mrs., and John Fisher, Jan. 6, 1822.*

**NEWLAND,** John, and Mary Child, Sept. 5, 1770.

**NEWMAN,** Andrew, and Sukey Hayward, Feb. 12, 1804.*
Andrew, and Elizabeth Wheeler, May 19, 1826.*
Andrew W., and Caroline Cole of Watertown, int. Nov. 15, 1835.
Eliza S., a. 25 y., d. W[illia]m J. and Sarah B., and Charles D. Swain, a. 25 y., grocer, s. Joseph and Elizabeth, June 4, 1848.*
Elizabeth A., and Perez Fuller of Medway, Apr. 5, 1827.*
John, Rev., and Mrs. Hannah Sumner, Oct. 27, 1748.
Mary Ann, and John Wyeth of Cambridge, Nov. 12, 1839.*
Nancy, and Enoch Davenport, Apr. 25, 1813.*
Sarah J., a. 29 y., d. W[illia]m J. and Sarah, and Thaddeus C. Craft of Baltimore, Md., a. 30 y., merchant, s. George and Eleanor, June 27, 1847.*
Susan, Mrs., and William Dove, Nov. 12, 1818.*
William J., and Sally Babcock of Milton, int. Feb. 24, 1810.

**NEWSOME,** William, b. Ireland, and Sabina Killduff, b. Ireland, Oct. 29, 1849.*

**NEWTON,** A. J., and G. N. Kent. int. May 7, 1843.
Alvan, and Jerusha Child, int. Mar. 9, 1817.
Alvan M., and Eliza Kildery, int. Nov. 10, 1844.
Antepas, jr., and Sarah A. Winsor, Nov. 8, 1840.*
Antipas, and Elizabeth Carter [Newton. int.], Apr. 4, 1808.*
Elizabeth C., and James Hurd, int. Nov. 11, 1838.
Francis A., and Mary Jane Hastings, Mar. 6, 1845.
Harriette A., and Augustus Makepiece of West Brookfield, int. Jan. 7, 1849.
Isaac S., victualler, s. Antipas, and Caroline A. Parker, d. Charles, May 6, 1847.

* Intention also recorded.

NEWTON, Leonard, of Milton, and Mary D. Holt, [Halt. c. r. 3.], Apr. 17, 1823.*

Leonard, and Louisa Child [Childs. c. r. 3.], Apr. 28, 1831.*

Louisa, and Freeman Phillips of Dedham, int. Nov. 17, 1849.

Mary Ann, and Samuel Wiswall, Apr. 14, 1836.*

Rebecca, and Samuel Freeman, July 27, 1794.*

S. Elliot, d. Antipas and Elizabeth, and Isaac Jones of Guilford, N. H., a. 32 y., clerk, s. Simpson and Mary, June 17, 1849.*

Sarah, and Erasmus Day of Webster, int. Apr. 14, 1839.

**NIBRONT,** Catharine, and Louis Nuff, int. July 19, 1840.

**NICHOLLS** (see also Nichols), Frederick G., of Kingston, N. H., and Sarah Williams, Jan. 29, 1823.*

**NICHOLS** (see also Nicholls), Charles C., and Betsey F. M. Ripley, Nov. 3, 1845.*

Charles S[aunders. int.], of Salem, and Amelia [Amilia. int.] A. Ainsworth, Apr. 21, 1845.*

Emma L., a. 18 y., d. Isaac and Esther, and Charles F. Emerson, a. 21 y., dyer, s. Leonard and Alice, Mar. 13, 1848.*

Jane, a. 27 y., d. Isaac and Esther, and William Robinson, a. 21 y., bricklayer, s. James and Jane, June 30, 1849.

Joanna G., of New Hampton, N. H., and Edward C. Cochran, int. Sept. 13, 1835.

John, and Hannah Tucker, May 7, 1736.

Joseph B., and Emily W. Chenery, Nov. 20, 1823.*

Mary, of Cohasset, and George Sampson, int. Nov. 6, 1814. [Aug. 22. 1813. dup.]

Mary, and Capt. Ammon Rodgers, Mar. 25, 1827.*

Mary, of Nashua, N. H., and Edward Prescott, int. Sept. 22, 1844.

Reuben, and Joanna Bullard, Jan. 20, 1830. c. r. 2.*

Robert C., and Harriet A. Morse, int. July 3, 1846.

Susan [L. int.], and George Dove, jr., Dec. 14, 1845.*

**NIELAN,** Edward, and Mary Cochran, int. June 26, 1849.

**NIGHTINGALE,** Abraham, of Quincy, and Betsy Trask, Nov. 28, 1805.*

Eliza, and Abner Mirick, Oct. 27, 1829.*

Frances A., and John B. Thomas, Aug. 30, 1842.

Mary, and Lawson Houghton, May 13, 1827.*

* Intention also recorded.

**NILES,** Daniel, and Catharine [F. int.] Field, Mar. 10, 1836.*
Hannah, [Hiles. int.], and John Howe, Apr. 14, 1805.*
Mary, and Joseph Decilvee [a Portuguese. c. R. 2.], Aug. 15, 1754.

**NISSBIT,** Eleanour, and John Bosson, Sept. 3, 1747.

**NIXON,** George, and Sarah F. Austin, Feb. 18, 1836.*

**NOBLE,** James, Esq., and Mrs. Elizabeth Heath, May 22, 1760.
Rachel, and William Carver, Aug. 2, 1804.*

**NOLAN** (see also Nolen), Thomas, and Elizabeth Blaney, Feb. 20, 1762.
Thomas, and Catharine Naughton, int. June 4, 1846.

**NOLAND** (see also Nolen), Ann, and W[illia]m Navan, int. May 12, 1839.

**NOLEN** (see also Nolan, Noland, Nolin), Betcy, and Alexander Maxwell, int. Nov. 20, 1785.
Charles, and Elizabeth Gridley, Aug. 4, 1793.*
Hannah, b. Ireland, and Dennis Coyle, b. Ireland, Dec. 14, 1849.
Martha, and William McCarty, Nov. 21, 1799.*
Polly, and Benjamin Bolter, Dec. 21, 1794.*
Thomas, and Mehitable Pratt, Mar. 17, 1789.*

**NOLIN** (see also Nolen), George, and Esther Langley, Feb. 16, 1794.*

**NORCROSS,** Abigail, and Harvey James, int. Mar. 26, 1826.
Adelaide C., and John W. Boss of Eastport, Me., Nov. 26, 1844.*
Anna, of Newton, and Isaac Gale, int. Apr. 27, 1806.
Caroline, of Newton, and James Whittemore, int. Mar. 10, 1839.
Nehemiah, and Ruth Bugbee, June 26, 1764.

**NORRIS,** Elizabeth, of Cambridge, and John Lodge, Nov. 12, 1848.
George S., and Mary E. Glazier, Nov. 24, 1842.*
John W., and Mary Hall of Boston, int. June 12, 1847.
Maria, and Abraham North, int. Nov. 30, 1849.

* Intention also recorded.

**NORTH**, Abraham, and Maria Norris, int. Nov. 30, 1849.
George G., and Mary S. Hudson, int. Nov. 28, 1841.

**NORTIN** (see also Norton), John, and Margaret Mahony, int. Jan. 20, 1848.

**NORTON** (see also Naughton, Nortin, Noughton), Ann, and Malcom McLaughlin, int. Sept. 22, 1844.
Frances S., and Joseph E. Andrews, int. May 20, 1837.
John, and Catharine Gately, int. Dec. 3l, 1843.
Maria, and John Coffey, int. June 8, 1849.
Patrick, and Mary O'Brine, int. Oct. 30, 1848.
Patrick, b. Ireland, and Mary Creelan [Crehan. int.], b. Ireland, Oct. 18, 1849.*
Roger, and Elizabeth Plunket, int. June 2, 1844.
Thomas, and Bridget Kilduff, int. Feb. 4, 1838.
Thomas, and Mary Gately, int. Jan. 14, 1844.
Thomas, and Bridget Mullain, int. June 6, 1848.
Timothy, and Mary Morris, int. Sept. 24, 1849.
William A. [of Boston. int.], a. 23 y., type founder, s. William and Seba, and Margarett W. Kendrick, a. 21 y., July 14, 1847.*
Winefred, and Thomas Connors, int. Dec. 20, 1845.

**NOUGHTON** (see also Norton), Michael, and Ellen Gately, int. Jan. 19, 1845.

**NOYES** (see also Noyse), Abigail B., and Robert Gardner, Aug. 12, 1827.
Benj[ami]n S., and Hannah Learock, June 5, 1832.*
Charlotte A., and Edward D. Murphy, Mar. 16, 1848.*
Esther S., and Stephen Whitmore, jr., of Salem, Sept. 17, 1832.*
George, and Margaret B. Goodhue, Apr. 5, 1837.*
John W., and Esther Melcher, int. Nov. 28, 1824.
Lydia, and Daniel P. Upton, [Jan. 6. int.], 1833.*
Mary Ann, and Joshua B. Rew [Ray. int.] of Charlestown, Apr. 24, 1834.*
Rebecca, and John R. Howard, Dec. 31, 1834.*
Salome, and Thomas D[avis. c. r. 2.] Richards, Apr. 24, 1831.*
Sarah [S. int.], and Nathan Oakes, Aug. 30, 1842.*
Sarah Ann, and William B. Barker, Apr. 24, 1836.*
Simeon, jr., and Eunice Blake, Sept. 21, 1841.*

* Intention also recorded.

**NOYSE** (see also Noyes), William, and Hannah Ruggles, Dec. 17, 1712.

**NUDD,** Stephen W., and Hannah D. Piper of Stratham, N. H., int. Aug. 22, 1846.

**NUFF,** Louis, and Catharine Nibront, int. July 19, 1840.

**NUGENT,** George, and Ellen Ragin, int. Nov. 6, 1846.

**NURSE,** Edwin A., and Mary Ann Fales of Lowell, int. Nov. 27, 1842.

**NUSS** (see also Ness), Anthony, and Lydia Smeidt, int. May 24, 1835.

**NUTE,** Enoch, and Hannah Trull, int. Mar. 27, 1831.
Hannah, and Matthew L. Clogston, Aug. 12, 1832.*
Isaac F., and Charlotte A. Hagar of Charlestown, July 13, 1847.
Josiah, and Abba A. Davis, Oct. 1, 1837.*
Jotham, and Clarissa G. Stevens, Sept. 28, 1844.*
Stephen, of Milton, N. H., and Sarah May, June 22, 1823.*

**NUTTER,** Charles, and Dorcas B. Hurd of Acton, Me., int. Oct. 17, 1841.
Samuel, and ElizabethF. Holmes, Oct. 10, 1830.*
Thomas, and Mercy L. Goldsmith, Jan. 8, 1832.*

**NUTTING,** Charlotte P., and Nathan Moore, int. Oct. 17, 1841.

**NYE,** Achsah B., of Falmouth, and George P. Burnham, int. May 6, 1838.

**OAKES,** Nathan, and Sarah [S. int.] Noyes, Aug. 30, 1842.*

**OATISS** (see also Otis), Mary, and Samuel Clark, Mar. 28, 1743.

**O'BEIRNE** (see also O'Burne), Margarett [O'Burne. int.], b. Ireland, and John McLaughlin, b. Ireland, Oct. 20, 1849.*

**O'BRIEN** (see also O'Brine, O'Bryan, O'Kryan), Dennis, and Mary Ann Dailey, int. July 16, 1837.

* Intention also recorded.

O'BRIEN, Edward, of Boston, and Catherine McGinley, int. Sept. 15, 1849.

Margaret, and John O'Connell, int. May 19, 1844.

Mary, and James Boylan, int. May 9, 1848.

Mary Ann, and Patrick McLaughlin, int. Sept. 3, 1849.

Michael, and Bridget Fallen, int. Mar. 23, 1845.

Thomas, and Elizabeth McDaniel, int. Apr. 30, 1846.

O'BRINE (see also O'Brien), Mary, and Patrick Norton, int. Oct. 30, 1848.

Rosa, b. Ireland, and Patrick Leach, b. Ireland. Aug. 5, 1849.

O'BRYAN (see also O'Brien), Eliza, and John Behan, int. Nov. 17, 1844.

Hannah, and Peter McCue, int. Apr. 3, 1842.

Hannah, and James Hayes, int. Aug. 25, 1844.

O'BURNE (see also O'Beirne), Richard, and Bridget Murry, int. Aug. 11, 1849.

OCKINGTON (see also Octinton), Betsey, and Capt. Benjamin Farrington, Jan. 11, 1816. c. r. 2

O'CONNELL, John, and Margaret O'Brien, int. May 19, 1844.

Mary, and John Powers, int. Apr. 9, 1837.

O'CONNER (see also Connors), Margarett, and Patrick Quinlan, int. June 4, 1846.

O'CONNOR (see also Connors), Thomas O., and Honora Flinn, int. Nov. 7, 1846.

OCTINTON (see also Ockington), Susanna, wid., of Needham, and Barachiah Lewis, at Needham, Dec. 15, 1756.

ODALL, Charles and Maria I. [J. int.] Roberts, July 13, 1834.*

O'DAY, Dennis, and Margarett O'Day, Oct. 28, 1848.*

Margarett, and Dennis O'Day, Oct. 28, 1848.*

ODIORNE, Direxa P., and Rufus S. Allen, int. Apr. 19, 1840.

O'FLAHERITY (see also O'Flaherty), Mary, and James Dorety, int. June 15, 1849.

O'FLAHERTY (see also O'Flaherity), Mary, and James Bulger of Beverly, int. June 4, 1843.

* Intention also recorded.

**O'HARA** (see also O'Hare, O'Horo), Michael, and Bridget McCawley, int. May 26, 1849.

**O'HARE** (see also O'Hara), Daniel, and Mary Houlahin, int. Feb. 2, 1847.

**O'HORO** (see also O'Hara), John, and Ellen Causgrive, int. Aug. 8, 1848.
Patrick, and Bridget Curley, int. Aug. 15, 1848.

**O'KEEFE** (see also O'Keefee, O'Keeffe), Deborah, and James Tracey, int. Sept. 28, 1845.

**O'KEEFEE** (see also O'Keefe), Michael, and Mary Conoly, int. Feb. 5, 1843.

**O'KEEFFE** (see also O'Keefe), Patrick, and Ann Mahoney, int. Jan. 14, 1844.

**O'KRYAN** (see also O'Brien), Margaret, and Daniel Hart, int. Sept. 22, 1844.

**OLDMAN,** Elizabeth, Mrs., and Samuel Blackman, jr. of Dorchester, at Dorchester, Feb. 28, 1780.

**O'LEARY** (see also Leary), Dennis, and Margaret Driscall, int. July 19, 1846.

**OLIVER,** Elizabeth, and Dr. Benjamin Waterhouse of Cambridge, June 1, 1788.*
Elizabeth T., a. 19 y., d. Nathaniel K. Greenwood and Anne Oliver, and John Walker Hartwell, widr., of Cincinnati, Ohio, a. 34 y., underwriter, s. Jonathan and Elizabeth B., Feb. 18, 1847.*
Mary, and Horatio Weld [both of Boston. c. r. 3.], Jan. 21, 1810.
Mary F[rances. c. r. 5.], and Pierre [Peter. c. r. 5.] S. M. Andrews of Lynnfield, June 17, 1841.*
Matthew, a. 22 y., currier, s. Francis and Elizabeth of Cape Breton, and Eliza A. C. Linnell, a. 25 y., d. Enoch and Elizabeth of Portland, Me., Feb. 28, 1847.*
William M., and Abby J. B. Farrington, Nov. 17, 1842.*

**O'NEAL** (see also O'Neil), Jane, and James W. Divoll, int. Oct. 13, 1847.

* Intention also recorded.

**O'NEIL** (see also O'Neal), Mary, and Dormick McDonough, int. Dec. 30, 1847.

Mary, and Patrick Donovan, int. Mar. 4, 1848.

William, and Ann McCusky, int. July 6, 1849.

**ONION** (see also Onions), Asa F., and Nancy D. Fowler, Sept 29, 1842.*

Hannah, and Stephen T. Skinner of Woburn, Nov. 24, 1842.*

Henry [a. 25 y. in pencil. int.], and Harriet Jane Bills [a. 27 y. in pencil. int.], Apr. 11, 1844.*

Willard, and Mary Wheeler of Dorchester, int. May 19, 1833.

**ONIONS** (see also Onion), Willard, and Catharine C. Cheney, June 14, 1823.*

**ORANGE,** Thomas J., and Lucy Smith, int. Dec. 20, 1840.

**ORCUTT,** Eliza D., and Benjamin B. French both of Braintree, Aug. 22, 1837.

Henry, and Hannah Hayden, Apr. 21, 1818.*

Henry, and Mary Patrick, int. Mar. 23, 1845.

Mears, and Mary Nash, Aug. 21, 1849. c. r. 3.

**O'REILLY,** Gilbert H., of Augusta, Me., and Catherine H. Wells, int. June 19, 1847.

Thomas, and Mary Briady, int. Sept. 1, 1844.

**ORNE,** Rebecca, and George Jones, int. Jan. 16, 1831.

**ORR,** James, and Elizabeth Morton, June 20, 1756.

**ORRALL,** James, a. 24 y., daguerreotype painter, s. Sophia, and Laurena R. Drake, Dec. 29, 1847.*

**ORROK,** James L. P., and Mary Anne Tower Sweat, int. Feb. 14, 1830.

**ORTMAN** (see also Ortmans), Elizabeth, and Daniel Bamboer, int. Nov. 23, 1848.

Hammond H., and Anna M. Weterau, int. Nov. 23, 1848.

**ORTMANS** (see also Ortman), Anna Maria, and Simon Withero, int. Mar. 4, 1847.

**ORTON,** Mary Ann, and Henry W. Coltman, int. Feb. 4, 1847.

* Intention also recorded.

**ORVIS** John, a. 30 y., yeoman, s. Soren and Sillis, of Ferris-burg, Vt., and Marianne Dwight, a. 30 y., d. John and Mary, Dec. 24, 1846.*

**OSGOOD,** John, of Andover, and Elizabeth Fuller, Nov. 21, 1810.*
Mary, and Lemuel Richards, May 6, 1819. c. r. 2.*
Mary S., a. 22 y., d. David and Lydia, and Thomas Hiller, a. 31 y., rope maker, s. Felix and Bethiah, May 31, 1846.*

**OTIS** (see also Oatiss), George Lane, and Sarah Jane Rich-ards, int. July 5, 1848.
Joseph, Esq., and Mariah Walter, Feb. 22, 1770.
Margarett, and James Cartnall, int. Oct. 23, 1847.
Sally, and Robert G. Babcock, Aug. 3, 1818.*
Theodore, and Harriot Blanchard, Dec. 1, 1841.

**OVEREN,** John J., of Charlestown, and Mary F. Donallen, int. May 22, 1849.

**OWEN** (see also Owens), Mary [Owens. c. r. 3.], and Amos Whittemore, Oct. 7, 1821.*
Nathaniel, widr., of Dedham, a. 66 y., tin manufacturer, and Phebe Hardy, wid., of Dedham, a. 50 y., housewife, Apr. 16, 1846.

**OWENS** (see also Owen), Benjamin, and Mary McGukin [McGuken. int.], Apr. 5, 1846.*
Catharine, and Samuel Dwinell, int. Sept. 11, 1825.

**OXNARD,** Henry [Capt. int; of Boston. c. r. 3.], and Char-lotte Farnum, May 5, 1819.*

**PACKARD,** Charles, and Nancy T. Page, May 28, 1839.*
Loisa [Louisa. c. r. 3.] M., and Caleb Davis, July 19, 1807.
Rhoda, and Joseph Weatherby [Wetherby. int.], Aug. 17, 1797. c. r. 3.*
Sally, and Elijah Forbush [Furbush. c. r. 3.], Aug. 28, 1808.*
Sampson, and Susannah Daniels, Sept. 28, 1808. c. r. 2.*

**PACON** (see also Payson), Prudence, and Benjamin Thomson, at Dedham, Dec 13, 1698.

**PAGE,** Charles, and Elizabeth R. Warren, int. Feb. 22, 1818.
Daniel E., and Emily Freeman, Nov. 28, 1837.*
Emily H., and Thaddeus Bullen [Bullin. int.], May 5, 1844.*

* Intention also recorded.

PAGE, Frances Ann, of Walpole, and Franklin Farnsworth, int. Nov. 27, 1847.

Gilman, of Cambridge, and Hannah A. Blaney, May 20, 1835.*

Holman, and Elizabeth Cobb, int. Sept. 8, 1833.

John, of Stoughton, and Sarah S. Phillips, int. May 22, 1831.

Joseph W., of South Reading, and Martha L. Fitch, June 10, 1841.*

Mary Ann Mrs., and Luther Hodgdon, int. Oct. 3, 1841.

Mary B., and Barrington Hicks, int. Nov. 6, 1836.

Nancy T., and Charles Packard, May 28, 1839.*

Polly, and John Bodge, Sept. 3, 1821.*

Sarah Ann, of Raymond, N. H., and James W. Wason, int. Sept. 3, 1843.

Sarah S., and Richard M. Dresser, int. Sept. 22, 1833.

Sylvanus, and Abby F. Bowen, int. Feb. 5, 1843.

PAIN (see also Paine), Moses, and Mrs. Jane Bates, June 18, 1679.

PAINE (see also Pain, Payn, Payne), Elisabeth, and Jacob Pepper, Feb. 10, 1684-5.

Eliza, and Charles F. Hastings, int. July 11, 1824.

Elizabeth, of Rehoboth, and Jacob Pepper, at Rehoboth, Feb. 16, 1684.

John, of Dedham, and Mary Ruggles, at Dedham, Apr. 21, 1704.

Martha, and Jacob Commenges, July 15, 1740.

Mary Ann, and Thomas Culligin, int. Sept. 3, 1843.

Matilda, and James W[ilson. int.] Miles, Apr. 13, 1848.*

Samuel, jr., and Eliza Howe of Sudbury, int. July 14, 1805.

Thomas, and Martha Hall, Mar. 22, 1735-6.

PAITHS, Abigail Francis, and Cutler Eames, int. Feb. 3, 1833.

PALFREY, John C., and Mary E. [G. int.] Goodhue, May 25, 1837.*

PALMER, Catherine E., and Olis R. Bacheler, int. Apr. 26, 1840.

Elis[abe]th, Mrs., of Middlebury, and Ebenez[e]r Cheney, Dec. 25, 1729.

* Intention also recorded.

PALMER, Isaiah, a. 23 y., carpenter, d. Truworthy and Betsey M., and Margarett A. Langmaid of Nottingham, N. H., a. 20 y., d. John and Ann, Nov. 4, 1848.*

John, and Nancy Brobston, May 21, 1825.

Joseph [M. D. int.], and Elisabeth [Elizabeth. int.] B. Gragg, Dec. 7, 1843.*

Joseph W., and Elizabeth A. Dean, int. Aug. 11, 1839.

Kathrine [Catharine. c. r. 3.] H., and Henry Putman [Putnam. c. r. 3.] of Brunswick, Sept. 13, 1807.*

Lavina [Levina. int.] M., a. 23 y., milliner, d. W[illia]m and Charlotte, and W[illia]m H. McIntosh, a. 25 y., provision dealer, s. Sam[ue]l and Priscilla, Nov. 12, 1845.*

Louisa, of Somersett, and Stephen Williams, 4th, Jan. 25, 1807.*

Mary, Mrs., of Middleborough, and Ens. John Holbrook, Jan. 26, 1737-8.

Thomas K. [of Boston. int.], and Sarah Richard [Richards. int.], wid., Jan. 20, 1847.*

William H., and Sarah C. Wiswall, Nov. 28, 1839.*

PARK (see also Parks), Hannah, of Newton, and Thomas Baker, at Watertown, Aug. 2, 1722.

Hezekiah, and Elizabeth M. Cook of Lexington, int. Mar. 11, 1832.

PARKER, Abigail, and John Gore, jr., June 26, 1744. c. r. 2.

Abigail, and Daniel Munroe, Sept. 15, 1774.

Abigail, Mrs., and Joseph Smith, May 2, 1782.

Abigail, and William Shepherd, July 19, 1792.*

Abraham, widr., a. 56 y., mason, s. Francis and Mary, and [Mrs. int.] Mary Ann Kimball, wid., a. 38 y., tailoress, d. Eben[eze]r and Polly Leach, Sept. 7, 1845.*

Abraham G., widr., a. 62 y., s. Caleb and Hannah, and Julia Ann Griggs, a. 38 y., d. Lemuel and Ruth, Mar. 11, 1849.*

Abraham S., and Salome Eaton, Dec. 31, 1844.*

Anne, of Needham, and Benjamin Baker, at Needham, July 23, 1766.

Benjamin May [of Baltimore. int.], and Ann Parker Child, Oct. 1, 1823.*

Bethiah, and Caleb Stedman, jr., Sept. 22, 1743.

Bethiah [Allen. different ink. int.], and [Capt. int.] Joseph Curtis, May 27, 1800. c. r. 3.*

Caleb, and Fanny Scott, July 5, 1795.*

* Intention also recorded.

PARKER, Caleb, jr., and Susan Richard of Newton, int. Mar. 5, 1826.

Caroline A. [M. int.], and Jesse Goodenow, Sept. 8, 1823. C. R. 2.*

Caroline A., of Milton, and George L. Howe, int. Nov. 7, 1846.

Caroline A., d. Charles, and Isaac S. Newton, victualler, s. Antipas, May 6, 1847.

Catharine, and Maj. Ebenezer Brown of Lenox, int. June 8, 1788.

Daniel H., a. 20 y., cabinet maker, s. Abraham and Mary, and Jane H. Gay, a. 20 y., instructress, d. Timothy and Mary, May 11, 1844.*

Deborah [Mrs. C. R. 2.], and Thomas Cheney, Mar. 25, 1747.

Edmund, and Elizabeth How, May 31, 1647.

Edward W., and Mary Ann Rogers, Oct. 16, 1825.*

Elisabeth, and Timothy Man, Dec. 6, 1770.

Eliza, and William Shimmin, Sept. 24, 1811.*

Elizabeth, and Samuell Gary, Dec. 6, 1669.

Elizabeth H., and Horace M. Hall, Oct. 6, 1844.*

George L., and Caroline A. Low of Springvale, Me., int. Oct. 26, 1847.

Hannah, and Capt. Cornelius Fellowes, int. Jan. 4, 1795.

Hannah [Barker. int.], and Rev. Joseph Grafton of Newton, Nov. 12, 1805.*

Hannah G., and Henry S. Ward, Apr. 15, 1828.*

Harriet G., and Geo[rge] W. Stearns both of Brookline, Mar. 9, 1837.

Isaac, and Deborah Williams, June 27, 1776.

Jacob, and Thankfull Hemingway, May 3, 1687.

Jeremiah, and Mary Williams, June 16, 1743.

Jeremiah, and Mrs. Martha White, Nov. 15, 1750.

Jerem[ia]h, jr., and Abigail Peale of Salem, at Salem, Nov. 27, 1766.

John, and Prudence May, Nov. 24, 1785.*

John, and Rebecca Young, June 18, 1843.*

John A., and Frances Warren of Hardwick, int. Nov. 30, 1800.

Jonathan, and Abigail Baker, Feb. 11, 1752.

Jonathan, and Hannah Weld, Dec. 6, 1774.

Joseph W., and Nancy G. Wales of Dorchester, int. Nov. 11, 1821.

* Intention also recorded.

PARKER, Katherine, and Joseph Curtis, July 3, 1771.

Lucy E., and George Billings, Dec. 26, 1843.*

Luther, and Sally Buckman [Putman. int.], Jan. 7, 1807.*

Martha, and Charles Seaverns, Nov. 2, 1806. c. R. 3.*

Mary, and Benjamin Draper, Aug. 23, 1738.

Mary, and John Mears, jr., Apr. 16, 1789.*

Mary, and Luther Seaverns, Nov. 25, 1802.*

Mehitable T., and Thomas Cummings, Jan. 19, 1830.*

Nathan[ie]l, and Sarah Cheney, Apr. 12, 1753.

Nathaniel, and Rebecca Dudley, June 1, 1788.*

Nathaniel, and Lydia Brown of Brimfield, int. Oct. 4, 1818.

Nath[anie]ll, and Hannah Chamberlain, Jan. 1, 1756. c. R. 2.

Nicholas, and Mary Barrett, int. Oct. 11, 1849.

Noah, and Eleanor Whittemore, Dec. 10, 1772.

Oliver, and Lydia O. Smith, int. Sept. 10, 1837.

Peter [of Brookline. c. R. 2.] and Sarah Payson, July 24, 1751.

Ruth, and David Drury, July 3, 1818.*

Samuel, and Eusebia Moore, Nov. 20, 1808.*

Sarah, and Thomas Foster, Oct. 15, 1662.

Sarah, and Benjamin Sabin, July 5, 1678.

Sarah, and Jedediah Munroe, May 30, 1782.

Sarah, wid., and Eliakim Blackman of Dorchester, Oct. 18, 1789.*

Susannah, Mrs., and Ebenezer May, jr., Mar. 6, 1752.

Thomas, and Esther Gridley, Apr. 29, 1777.

Thomas, and Sarah Seaver, July 27, 1820.*

Timothy, and Mary Scarbrough, Sept. 8, 1718.

Timothy, and Mary Williams, Jan. 10, 1764.

Timothy, and Sarah Payson, June 25, 1778.

William, and Hannah Weld, June 9, 1793.*

William C., of Billerica, and Mary L. Pearson, Oct. 5, 1841.*

PARKES (see also Parks), Theoda, and Samuel Williams, Mar. 2, 1653.

PARKHURST, John M., of Milford, a. 27 y., merchant, s. Alexander and Mary, and Emeline K. Colburn, a. 23 y., d. Jonathan and Betsey, May 28, 1846.*

PARKMAN, Elias, and Elizabeth Weld, Oct. 29, 1718.

PARKS (see also Park, Parkes), Ann, and Edward Pason, Aug. 20, 1640.

Hannah, and Stephen Tucker, May 31, 1739.

* Intention also recorded.

PARKS, James H., and Margarett R. Smart of Portsmouth, N. H., int. Jan. 27, 1849.
Lydia, and George Pittis, July 5, 1726.
Richard, and Elizabeth McCart, int. Oct. 5, 1845.

PARMALEE (see also Parmelee, Parmlee), Lyman L., and Susan Hill of Waterford, Vt., May 23, 1847.

PARMELEE (see also Parmalee), Diana P., and Geo[rge] W. C. Washburn of Livermore, Me., Oct. 17, 1845.

PARMENTER (see also Parmeter), Dorcas, of Sudbury, and Abel Swallow, int. May 22, 1814.
Horace, and Mary F. Richards, Jan. 1, 1832.
John [Parminter CT. R.], and Annis Dane, Aug. 9, 1660. [1661. CT. R.]

PARMETER (see also Parmenter), Mehitable, and Tho[ma]s Miles, int. Nov. 26, 1807.
Welcome, and Sarah H. Tobey, int. Aug. 17, 1823.

PARMLEE (see also Parmalee), Ashly, and Harriet Mudge, Oct. 6, 1842.
Gilbert, and Mary E. Richardson, Oct. 13, 1844.

PARROT (see also Parrott), Ann, and Enoch H. Fisher, Mar. 4, 1829.*

PARROTT (see also Parrot), Frances Pamelia, of Marblehead, and Robert L. Corbett, Nov. 10, 1847.

PARRY (see also Perry), William, and Ann Williams, both residents, Oct. 16, 1731.

PARSLEY, Nancy, and Varsel Edward Litchfield, int. Nov. 30, 1845.

PARSONS, Ebenezer, and Clarissa [Clarisa. int.] Farrington, May 20, 1804. C. R. 2.*
Mary A., and Greenleaf F. [T. int.] Lougee, June 29, 1845.*
Pliny D., of Bangor, Me., and Hannah H. Hooper, Nov. 20, 1834.*

PARTRIDGE (see also Patridge), Abigail, and William Bosson, jr., Aug. 15, 1745.
Abigail, and John Pierce Sawin, Dec. 16, 1798.*
Catharine, and Elnathan Taber, Jan. 8, 1797.*

* Intention also recorded.

PARTRIDGE, Elizabeth, and Abel Hutchins of Concord, N. H., Jan. 22, 1786.*

Jane, and William Dorr, Mar. 31, 1779.

Sarah, Mrs., and Samuel Curtis, Dec. 12, 1784.*

Thaddeus, and Mrs. Sarah Gridley, Oct. 3, 1782.*

Thad[deu]s [jr. int.], and Mary [Peggy. int.] Smith of Dedham, June 1, 1786.*

PASON (see also Payson), Asa, and Sarah Lyon, Dec. 31, 1772.

Bathsheba, and Benjamin Thwing, Aug. 12, 1719.

Benjamin, and Mary Williams, Nov. 25, 1713.

Edward, and Ann Parks, Aug. 20, 1640.

Edward, and Mary Elliot, Jan. 1, 1642.

Edward, of Dorchester, and Katherine Scarbrough, July 14, 1720.

Giles, and Elizabeth Dowell, Apr. —, 1637.

Jacob, and Martha Williams, Nov. 14, 1716.

Joseph, and Mehitabel Winchester, Mar. 4, 1713.

Prudence, and Richard Wheeler, Dec. 2, 1702.

Sarah, and Stephen Williams, jr., Apr. 8, 1725.

——, and Hopestill Foster, eldest s. Capt. Hopestill of Dorchester, at Dorchester, 15 : 1 2 m : 1666.

PASSENGER, Margaretta, and Abel Murdock, int. Sept. 4, 1825.

PATCH, Abigail [of Boston. c. R. 3.], and Robert Seaver, Nov. 20, 1834.*

PATCHING, Joseph, and Elizabeth Ingulden, Apr. 18, 1642.

PATEE (see also Pattee, Pattia, Pattie), Mary, of Dedham, and Kendall Brooks, int. Nov. 8, 1818.

Susan, and Asa Clark, int. Sept. 13, 1818.

PATERSON (see also Patterson), Jane, and John Brown of Rutland, July 27, 1720.

PATRICK, Elizabeth, and Charles Watson of New York, int. Mar. 29, 1840.

Mary [Partrick. int.], Mrs., and Thomas Wilson of Cambridge, May 6, 1784.*

Mary, and Henry Orcutt, int. Mar. 23, 1845.

Mary W., and James Wharf, Oct. 1, 1820.*

William, and Sarah Bosson, May 3, 1758.

* Intention also recorded.

**PATRIDGE** (see also Partridge), Elihu K., and Mary A. Smith, Sept. 22, 1840.*

**PATTEE** (see also Patee), Lois, Mrs., and Joshua Felton, Oct. 31, 1780.

**PATTEN** (see also Pattin), Nathaniel, and Nancy Maker, Feb. 8, 1807.*
Polly H., and Sam[ue]l N. Clark of Illinois, July 26, 1844.*
Sally, and Francis S. Eastman, May 1, 1833.*
William, and Sally Williams, Apr. 29, 1799.*

**PATTERSON** (see also Paterson, Pattison), Anna, of Cambridge, and Jacob Cromel, at Sudbury, May 30, 1769.
Helen, and William Thomas, int. Dec. 19, 1841.
Sarah, and Ebenezer G. Burbank, int. Dec. 7, 1828.
Sophia, and James Barry, jr., int. Sept. 30, 1821.

**PATTIA** (see also Patee), Adam, and Lois Gridley, May 12, 1774.

**PATTIE** (see also Patee), Lois, and Joshua Snow of New York, Mar. 23, 1794.*

**PATTIN** (see also Patten), Mary, and John Grigs, Nov. 11, 1652.
Mary, and Thomas Hunt of Stockbridge, Oct. 27, 1789.*

**PATTISON** (see also Patterson), John, and Kezia Bracket, June 11, 1706.

**PAUL,** Ebenezer, and Susan Dresser of Dedham, Apr. 15, 1847. C. R. 7.
Elizabeth, and Daniel Holbrook, at Dorchester, Nov. 11, 1703.
Elizabeth, of Dedham, and Charles Bullard, int. Nov. 10, 1822.
Helen M., of Sherburne, and George S. Glover, int. Sept. 5, 1841.
Ruth, of Dorchester, and John Bugbee, at Dorchester, Nov. 15, 1721.
Susanna, and Ebenezer Gore, Nov. 20, 1712.

**PAYN** (see also Paine), Samuel, of Pomfret, and Mary Sever, May 30, 1728.

**PAYNE** (see also Paine), Aaron, and Hannah Pond [of Dedham. int.], Aug. 27, 1798. C. R. 2.*

* Intention also recorded.

PAYNE, Eliza Ann, and Joseph Beagley, int. July 7, 1846.
Elizabeth, and Isaac Vergoose, Dec. 16, 1731.
Freeborn, and Louisa Borden, Apr. 3, 1836.*
Judith, a. 39 y., d. Walter and Betsey, and Jacob George, widr.,
    a. 54 y., blacksmith, d. Benj[amin] and Hannah, Nov. 4,
    1847.*

**PAYSON** (see also Pacon, Pason), Ann, of Dorchester, and
    Samuel Payson, at Dorchester, Feb. 21, 1750.
Ann, of East Sudbury, and John Wyman, at East Sudbury,
    Oct. 18, 1795.*
Anne, and Josiah Davenport of Warwick, Jan. 28, 1782.
Ebenezer, and Sarah Seaver, Aug. 20, 1734.
Eliza[beth. dup.], and John Greenwood [Greenough. dup],
    Nov. 2 [16. dup.], 1806.*
Elizabeth, and Samuell Heath, Dec. 3, 1733.
Elizabeth, and Lemuel Dickerman, Dec. 1, 1772.
Elizabeth, and Edward Russell, May 20, 1809. C. R. 2.*
Hannah, and John Jones, Dec. 17, 1795.*
Henry, and Abigail Brown, June 15, 1789.*
John, and Elizabeth Child [of Brookline. C. R. 2.], June 16,
    1738. [June 15. C. R. 2.]
John, and Maria Gill, Apr. 1, 1813.*
Joseph, and Mary Jefts, Oct. 25, 1758.
Joseph, and Abigail Pierpont, Jan. 1, 1761.
Joseph, and Mary Hill of Sherborn, at Sherborn, Jan. 27, 1774.
Katha[rine], and Henry Lee of Worcester, at Boston, Dec. 25,
    1725.
Katherine, and Jeremiah Williams, Sept. 15, 1743.
Leonard S., and Sarah Tarbox, int. May 20, 1827.
Martha, and Benjamin Weld, Nov. 21, 1745.
Mary, and Henry Williams, May 13, 1736.
Mary, and John Whitney, Apr. 22, 1773.
Mehetabel, of Dorchester, and John Dows, at Dorchester, Nov.
    7, 1751.
Rebecca [Mrs. int.], and Edward Sumner, July 4, 1785.*
Sally, of Sudbury, and Benjamin Wilson, Dec. 5, 1802.*
Samuel, and Prudence Lincoln, Mar. 31, 1677.
Samuel, and Ann Payson of Dorchester, at Dorchester, Feb.
    21, 1750.
Samuel, and Lydia Pierce, int. Dec. 4, 1825.
Sarah, and Robert Sharp of Brooklyn [Brookline. C. R. 2.],
    July 15, 1742.

* Intention also recorded.

PAYSON, Sarah, and Peter Parker [of Brookline. c. r. 2.], July 24, 1751.

Sarah, of Dorchester, and William Williams, at Dorchester, May 28, 1752.

Sarah, and Timothy Parker, June 25, 1778.

Sarah [Sally. c. r. 3.], and John Bisby [Bisbe. int; Bisbey of Boston. c. r. 3.], Apr. 11, 1797.*

Stephen, and Sarah Trowbridge, May 21, 1769. c. r. 2.

Waitstill, and Thomas Trott, Jan. 10, 1727-8.

**PEABODY,** James, and Billey Dillinham, int. July 26, 1818.

Rebecca, and Joseph Moore, Jan. [21. c. r. 3.], 1816.*

**PEACOCK** (see also Pecock), William, and Mary Willis, Apr. 12, 1653.

**PEAKE,** Christopher, and Dorcas French, Jan. 3, 1636.

Hannah, and Samuel Wales, Dec. 19, 1700.

Jonnathan, and Sarah French, Aug. 15, 1660.

Sarah, and Thomas Bugbee, June 4, 1701.

**PEALE,** Abigail, of Salem, and Jerem[ia]h Parker, jr., at Salem, Nov. 27, 1766.

**PEARCE** (see also Pierce), Esther, of Hopkinton, and Penuel Curtis, int. Feb. 12, 1809.

Rebecca, Mrs., of Dorchester, and Joseph Ruggles, int. Oct. 6, 1811.

**PEARSON** (see also Person, Pierson), Abigail, and Jesse Brown, Dec. 4, 1816.*

Elizabeth A., a. 23 y., d. Susan, and George Frost of Charlestown, a. 29 y., baker, s. Joseph and Caroline, June 4, 1848.*

Elizabeth S. W., and Joseph Swain, June 27, 1819.*

Jeremiah, a. 24 y., and Ellen R. Joy, a. 17 y., Mar. 1, 1849.*

John, and Mary Lee Glover of Dorchester, int. Sept. 17, 1820.

Julia, and James Child, int. Dec. 25, 1836.

Mary, and Charles Brown, Dec. 2, 1821.*

Mary, E., and Edwin Litchfield, Apr. 1, 1845.*

Mary L., and William C. Parker of Billerica, Oct. 5, 1841.*

Samuel, jr., and Mary P. Small of Cornish, Me., int. Oct. 15, 1837.

Sarah W., and John Curtis, int. Nov. 27, 1831.

Thomas, and Mrs. Elizabeth Dana, Jan. 2, 1820.*

Thomas, jr., and Nancy Pierce, Oct. 30, 1814.*

* Intention also recorded.

**PEARY,** John R., and Olive N. Bunker, Sept. 10, 1844.

**PEASE,** Giles, and Matilda Dunlap, both of Springfield, Jan. 7, 1847.

Lorey, and Catharine Williams Mallard, June 8, 1823.*

Mary, and John Emerson, Feb. 26, 1818.*

Samuel, of Dedham, and Hannah Reed [Read. c. r. 3.], Sept. 20, 1818.*

**PEASLEY,** Laura A., of Weare, N. H., and Theodore W. Pierce, int. Oct. 8, 1847.

**PECK** (see also Pike), Cascamer [Cascamier Beck. c. r. 3.; Pike. int.] of Dorchester, and Rebecca Coburn [Mrs. Rebecca Colburn. c. r. 3.], Aug. 17 [15. c. r. 3.], 1802.*

George B., and Ann P. Smith, of Providence, R. I., int. Apr. 7, 1842.

Lucy B., a. 20 y., d. Sam[ue]l and Hannah, and James B. Dana, of Brighton, a. 23 y., gardener, s. Charles and Esther, of Brighton, May 19, 1847.*

Oren, and Eliza Williams, Dec. 6, 1821.*

Samuel, and Hannah Baker, June 11, 1809. c. r. 2.*

**PECOCK** (see also Peacock), William, s. W[illia]m, and Sarah Edsall, Aug. 3, 1681.

**PEET,** Susannah, and John Crawley, at Boston, Nov. 25, 1756.

**PEIRCE** (see also Pierce), Ebene[ze]r S., and Nancy C. Rice of Brookline, int. Apr. 17, 1808.

Lucretia E., of Boston, and Solomon Wildes, int. Oct. 17, 1849.

Timothy, and Hannah Brodhurst, Oct. 12, 1709.

**PELLER,** John, and Mary Flagg of Newton, at Newton, Mar. 31, 1771.

**PELTON,** Charles B., and Mary Jane Joselyn, Nov. 5, 1848.

Joel W., b. Ireland, and Mary Ann G. Combs [Coombs. int.], b. Ireland, Dec. 16, 1849.*

Mary, of Dorchester, and John Sanders, Mar. 12, 1704-5.

**PENDERGAST,** Catharine, and Thomas Bradlee, int. Oct. 10, 1830.

**PENDOR,** Rebeckah, and James Mickles, Dec. 11, 1746.

* Intention also recorded.

**PENNELL,** Elizabeth G., and Melvin Vining, Mar. 12, 1849.
Nancy W., and Edward C. Thaxter, int. Aug. 10, 1834.

**PENNIMAN,** Asa, and Sally Fales of Dedham, at Dedham,
Sept. 24, 1795.*
Eunice, and Peter Dyer. both of Braintree [Apr. ?.], 1797.
Mary Jane, of Brookline, and Moses B. Williams, int. Feb. 26,
1843.

**PENNY,** Arabella, and Dr. Moses Willard [both residents.
int.], Oct. 4, 1785.*
George, of Hingham, and Sarah P. Beals, ——, 1832. [Dec.
11, 1831. int.]*
John, and Temperance Cushing Daman of Scituate, int. Dec.
7, 1806.

**PEPPER,** Ann, and Philip White of Newton, at Boston, Dec.
2, 1730.
Elizabeth, and Thomas Groosvenaur, May 22, 1718.
Jacob, and Elizabeth Paine, of Rehoboth, at Rehoboth, Feb.
16, 1684. [Feb. 10, 1684-5. dup]
Jacob, and Mary Glezen, Apr. 15, 1714.
John, of Woodstock, and Hanah Holdridge, Mar. 1, 1721-2.
Joseph, and Mary May, d. John, Nov. 4, 1675.
Joseph, and Anna Youngman, Dec. 15, 1720.
Mary, wid. Joseph, and Joshuah Sever, Feb. 28, 1677.
Rebecca, and Joseph Bill, at Boston, Nov. 5, 1736.
Robart, and Elizabeth Johnson, Mar. 14, 1642.
Stephen, and Sarah Crocket, at Boston, Feb. 12, 1728.

**PERCLE,** Electious, and Patrick Lacy, int. May 10, 1849.

**PERHAM,** David, Hon., of Brewer, Me., and Charlotte Gardner, Oct. 13, 1830.*

**PERIGOE,** John, and Eliz[abe]th Wilson, Jan. 4, 1727-8.

**PERIT,** Peter, Capt., and Sarah Newell, Nov. 22, 1778.

**PERKINS,** Charles, and Sarah E. Mansfield of Camden, Me.,
Mar. 26, 1843.*
Clarissa H. [K. int; of Boston. c. r. 3.], and Samuel Craigge,
[Craige. c. r. 3.], Sept. 14, 1826.*
Edward N., and Mary Spring of Boston, int. May 7, 1846.
Eliza, and Andrew C. Thompson, Oct. 8, 1833.*

* Intention also recorded.

PERKINS, Job H., and Susannah R. Averill, Jan. 1, 1846.*

Mary Jane, of Kennebunkport, Me., and Mark Kimball, int. Sept. 16, 1838.

Mary W., and Nathaniel A. Morse, Nov. 6, 1836.*

Mehitable, of Topsfield, and Samuel Smith, int. Dec. 12, 1824.

Reuben, and Hannah Clements of Hopkinton, at Hopkinton, Feb. 26, 1795.

Sally, of Rochester, N. H., and Thomas A. Clark, int. July 25, 1824.

Sophia, and William Hoyt, int. Aug. 27, 1826.

Susan L., and Russell S. Smith, int. Dec. 26, 1846.

**PERPOINT** (see also Pierpont), Ebenezer, and Sarah Cushing of Scituate, at Scituate, Aug. 16, 1750.

**PERRIN**, Abraham, and Mrs. Rachel Williams, Apr. 29, 1779.

Augustus [of Boston. c. R. 3.], and Harriet Child, Mar. 10, 1817.*

Elizabeth, and Ambrose Searl, Dec. 19, 1738.

Martha, and Benjamin Smith, Mar. 26, 1747.

Mary, and Aaron Davis, Jan. 25, 1732-3.

Mary, and Moses May, Mar. 13, 1760.

Nath[anie]ll, and Mary Seaver, int. Mar. 16, 1783.

Noah, and Patience Walker of Rehoboth, at Rehoboth, June 14, 1705.

Noah, and Mrs. Margaret Healey, Oct. 6, 1731.

Noah, and Joanna Ruggles, June 4, 1745.

Samuel, and Elizabeth Ruggles, Mar. 21, 1744-5.

Susannah, and John Richardson, Apr. 25, 1745.

Theoda, and Stephen Williams, Dec. 4, 1763.

**PERRY** (see also Parry), Benjamin F., and Emily A. Leighton, Dec. 20, 1845.*

Charles D., of Brookline, and Mary L. Jemerson, June 21, 1837.*

Eliza, of Dover, and Otis Travis, int. Mar. 17, 1822.

Elizabeth, and John Hanset, Apr. 2, 1644.

Elizabeth, and Nath[anie]l Blanchard, May 24, 1759.

Elizabeth, and William Crombie, int. Oct. 20, 1847.

Isaac, and Sarah Hanchett, Apr. 21, 1715.

Janett, and Sarah Ball of Dedham, at Dedham, Apr. 4, 1732.

John, jr., and Thankfull Ball, Apr. 24, 1740.

John [of Boston. c. R. 3.], and Susan Learned, June 4, 1818.*

Louisa, and Nathaniel Dorsey, Oct. 18, 1838.*

* Intention also recorded.

PERRY, Martin, of Ludlow, Vt., and Elizabeth Arnold, June 1,
1831.*

Mary [Terry. c. R. 2.], and David Lyon, Mar. 11, 1715.
[1714-5. c. R. 2.]

Mary, and John Blancher, Nov. 14, 1737.

Nathan F., and Eliza Brown, Oct. 3, 1821.*

Nathan F., and Mrs. Mary Rouse, Sept. 12, 1824.*

Rebecca, and Ichabod Jones of Dorchester, at Dorchester, Feb.
22, 1741.

Samuell, and Sarah Stedman, Jan. 28, 1668.

Samuel, and Jemima Mills of Needham, at Needham, Dec. 6,
1781.

Sarah, and Elnathan Whitney, Sept. 24, 1729.

Sarah, and Jonas Whitney, May 8, 1735.

Sarah, and Ezekiel Tolman, Nov. 20, 1764.

Thankfull, and James Herring, jr., June 17, 1767.

Thomas, and Sarah Aldis, May 30, 1710.

Thomas, and Elizabeth Smith, Mar. 21, 1716-17.

William G., and Mary E. Stillman, int. Sept. 21, 1845.

PERSON (see also Pearson). John, and Elizabeth Tucker of
Milton, at Milton, Jan. 14, 1701-2.

PETERS, George S., and Mary Ann Blair, int. May 18, 1828.

PETERSON, Frederick, and Sarah Christeen, int. June 14,
1837.

PETTEE (see also Pettes), Elizabeth, and John D. Young,
June 6, 1832.*

PETTES, (see also Pettee), George W., and Mary R. Balch,
Dec. 8, 1846.

William, of Charleston, Va., and Myra Hunt, Oct. 5, 1840.*

PEVEAR (see also Peveare, Pevere), Charles B., and Sarah
[Susan. int.] A. Haven, Jan. 1, 1845.*

Daniel S. [a. 23 y. in pencil. int.], and Roxanna A. Hodgdon
[Hodsdon. a. 20 y. in pencil. int.], Apr. 4, 1844.*

PEVEARE (see also Pevear), Burnham, and Mary Ann Stetson, May 5, 1825.*

PEVERE (see also Pevear), Bradbury, of Dedham, and Elizabeth P. Stetson, Mar. 28, 1819.*

* Intention also recorded.

**PHEASEA,** Abigail, Mrs., and Jacob Howe, both residents, int. Apr. 24, 1785.

**PHILBRICK** (see also Prilbrook), Charles G., and Eliza M. Pinkham, Oct. 6, 1844.
John D., and Julia A. Putman of Danvers, int. Aug. 13, 1843.

**PHILBROOK** (see also Philbrick), Levi, a. 27 y., sash and blind maker, s. Henry and Betsey, and Mary Ann Averill, a. 21 y., d. James and Elizabeth, Jan. 23, 1848.*

**PHILIPS** (see also Phillips), Caleb, and Elisabeth Polley, Oct. 16, 1681.
Caleb, and Hannah Gary, Aug. 2, 1703.
Ebenezer [of Woodstock. c. r. 2.], and Mary Lyon, Dec. 17, 1719.
Hannah, and Benjamin Smith, Apr. 23, 1724.
Ruth, and John Foster, Oct. 3, 1771.

**PHILLEPS** (see also Phillips), Elizabeth, and Joseph Lyon, May 30, 1710.
William, and Margarett Biscon, Sept. 16, 1713.

**PHILLIP** (see also Phillips), Francis, and Florindina Flitching, int. Aug. 23, 1840.

**PHILLIPP** (see also Phillips), George, and Maria Hamm, int. June 6, 1841.

**PHILLIPS** (see also Philips, Philleps, Phillip, Phillipp, Pilleps), Benjamin, of Charlestown, and Luce Boilstone, Mar. 10, 1702-3.
Elijah B., and Maria R. Ayling, int. Dec. 29, 1844.
Elizabeth, and Zacharia Whiting of Dedham, at Dedham, June 26, 1729.
Freeman, of Dedham, and Louisa Newton, int. Nov. 17, 1849.
John, of Newburyport, and Susan Ann Dorr, Nov. 24, 1829.*
Joshua, and Rebecca Smith, Mar. 24, 1805. c. r. 2.*
Lydia, and Roswel Pomroy, int. July 7, 1804.
Mary, and Daniel Benjamin, Apr. 13, 1746. (sic) [1756 ?.]
Mary O., of Easton, and William Bartlett, int. June 11, 1837.
Oliver, and Mary Holmes of Marshfield, int. Dec. 15, 1833.
Polly, and Richard Waitt of Marblehead, int. Aug. 24, 1800.
Polly, and John Wait of Marblehead, Oct. 17, 1802.*
Samuel M., and Rebecca C. Simmons, July 27, 1823.*

* Intention also recorded.

PHILLIPS, Sarah S., and John Page of Stoughton, int. May 22, 1831.

Susanna C., of Dorchester, and Robert Edwards, int. Mar. 5, 1809.

**PHINEY,** E. B., and I. P. Mellus, int. Feb. 22, 1846.

**PHIPPS,** Abner J., of Andover, and Elizabeth F. Abbe, int. Nov. 20, 1842.

David, of Hopkinton, and Elizabeth Stymes [Stymer. int. May 22, 1800.*

John S., and Clarissa Ann Stockman, Oct. 5, 1837.*

Mary E., a. 21 y., d. William and Elizabeth V., and William G. Train, a. 23 y., merchant, s. Samuel and Hannah P., Apr. 4, 1849.*

Samuel, and Elizabeth Stevens, Dec. 26, 1700.

Sarah, and Jesseniah Crosby, Dec. 29, 1774.

William [of Boston. c. r. 3.], and Elizabeth Vinton Staniford, June 2, 1826.*

**PICKET,** Christopher, and Elizabeth Stone, June —, 1647.

**PICKLEY,** Thomas, and Catherine Harney, int. Dec. 22, 1845.

**PICO,** Abagail, and Dr. Nathaniel S. Prentis, int. May 10, 1807.

**PIERCE** (see also Pearce, Peirce), Abby D., and Harvey S. Cooledge, int. Sept. 20, 1849.

Ann, and Clark L. Haynes of Brookline, int. Mar. 15, 1835.

Daniel, and Lydia Devenport, both of Dorchester, May 10, 1803.

Elizabeth, Mrs., jr., of Dorchester, and Jonathan Champney, at Dorchester, Mar. 2, 1773.

Emily R., and Alfred Williams [of Boston. c. r. 3.], Nov. 13, 1842.*

George W., and Cynthia Richards, Mar. 31, 1840.*

George W., and Louisa Hunnewell of Charlestown, int. Aug. 3, 1845.

Hannah, and James Tucker, Aug. 5, 1731.

Hannah Clap, and Capt. Charles Stearns of Brookline, int. Feb. 12, 1832.

Hannah D., a. 19 y., d. Levi and Hannah, and George H. Burton, a. 24 y., carpenter, s. Thomas and Mary, Oct. 15, 1848.*

* Intention also recorded.

PIERCE, Horace W., a. 27 y., provision dealer, s. Horace and
 Sarah, of Brighton, and Louisa H. Swallow, a. 27 y., d.
 Ezra and Nancy E., Dec. 24, 1848.*

James, and Lydia Clap of Dorchester, at Dorchester, June
 20, 1796.*

James, and Abigail [H. int.], Farr, Jan. 1, 1816.*

Joanna, and Baalis Bullard of Dorchester, May 27, 1804.*

John, and Rachel Blake, both of Dorchester, June 13, 1793.

John, and [Mrs. int.] Lydia Beals, Mar. 20, 1818.*

John A., of Dorchester, and Phebe A. Warner, Apr. 2, 1840.*

John H., and Sophia Sanderson of Brighton, int. June 8, 1828.

Jonas, jr., and Mary A. Whittemore, int. June 5, 1842.

Jonathan [Josiah, of Woburn. c. r. 2.], and Mary Dorr, Mar.
 15, 1753.

Jonathan M., and Frances Stetson, int. Mar. 24, 1833.

Keziah, and Lot [Lott. p. r. 5.] Young, Apr. 23, 1807.*

Lemuel, and Hannah Richards, int. Mar. 30, 1794.

Lemuel, and Sally [Sarah. int.] White of Newton, at Newton, July 3, 1795.*

Louisa E., and Matthew F. Kuebler, Feb. 3, 1842.

Lucy, and Dan S. Smally [Dan[iel] S. Smalley. c. r. 3.], June
 1, 1842.*

Lydia, of Milton, and Henry Hayes, int. Aug. 4, 1811.

Lydia, and Jacob Miller [resident. int.], Oct. 6, 1811.*

Lydia, and Samuel Payson, int. Dec. 4, 1825.

Mary, and Turell [Tirrell. int.] Tuttle, July 22, 1810. c. r. 2.*

Mary, and Baker Bryant, Jan. 1, 1827.*

Mason, of Stoughton, and Lucinda Prescott, Oct. 14, 1821.*

Nancy, and Thomas Pearson, jr., Oct. 30, 1814.*

Nancy, of Dorchester, and Jonathan Brooks, int. Jan. 19, 1840.

Roxanna T., and Paul Lincoln, int. Apr. 24, 1846.

Sally, of Warwick, and Hervey Woods, int. Mar. 21, 1819.

Sarah R., of Quincy, and Robinson Foslom, int. Mar. 22,
 1835.

Sarah Rebecca, and Isaac Curtis, Jan. 21, 1841.*

Theodore W., and Laura A. Peasley of Weare, N. H., int.
 Oct. 8, 1847.

William P., and Phidelia A. Booth, int. Feb. 10, 1849.

PIERPOINT (see also Pierpont), Ebenezer, and Mary Ruggles, Oct. 20, 1692.

Experiance, and John Hayward, 12 : 12 m : 1678.

* Intention also recorded.

**PIERPONT** (see also Perpoint, Pierpoint, Pirepont), Abigail, and Ebenez[e]r Newell, jr., Aug. 4, 1742.

Abigail, and Joseph Payson, Jan. 1, 1761.

Anne, and Robert Pierpont, Jan. 13, 1761.

Ebenezer, and Mrs. Ann Hilton, Feb. 19, 1722-3.

Ebenezer, and Mrs. Hannah Wiswell of Dorchester, at Dorchester, Sept 10, 1746.

Ebenezer, and Hanah Gridley, June 1, 1749.

Ebenezer, and Rebecca Wait, Apr. 24, 1786.*

Emely, and Samuel Langley, Dec. 1, 1805.*

Hannah, Mrs., and Sam[ue]l Williams, Feb. 22, 1770.

Hannah, and Moses Davis, Mar. 13, 1770.

James, and Sarah Dorr, May 8, 1744.

Mary, and Isaac Morris, Nov. 3, 1702.

Mary, and Joseph Muncreaf, Dec. 24, 1766.

Mary, and Nath[anie]l Sparhawk, Oct. 13, 1778.

Mary, and Benjamin Duick, int. Feb. 2, 1800.

Robert, and Hannah Ruggles, May 25, 1738.

Robert, and Susanah Morey, Mar. 12, 1752.

Robert, and Anne Pierpont, Jan. 13, 1761.

Robert, Esq., and Mrs. Hannah Potter of Waltham, at Waltham, Sept. 6, 1775.

Robert, and Sarah Livermore, Mar. 30, 1797.*

Sarah, and Abraham Woodward of Brookline, June 4, 1728.

Sarah, of Brooklyn, and Joshua Davis, Dec. 15, 1731.

William, and Mrs. Mary Davis of Brookline, at Brookline, Oct. 29, 1761.

**PIERSON** (see also Pearson), William G., and Ellen Ivry, int. Sept. 27, 1835.

**PIGEON,** Benj[amin] G. [Pidgeon. int.], and Mary E. Felton, Jan. 1, 1844.*

**PIKE** (see Peck), Eliza, and John Eaton, Feb. 13, 1842.*

Eliza Ann, and Amory F. Sherman, Jan. 1, 1838.*

Elizabeth, and Enoch Farley, Feb. 13, 1711.

George H., and Mary Baker of Shapleigh, Me., int. Aug. 4, 1848.

Hannah, and Joseph Johnson, Mar. 9, 1779.

Ja[m]es, and Abigail Story [May or June ?], 1708.

Katharine, and Francis Wood, Dec. 28, 1780.

Lucretia, of Dorchester, and Elisha Tolman of Lincoln, Sept. 18, 1797.

* Intention also recorded.

PIKE, Michal, of Framingham, and Mehetabell Brown, at Framingham, May 28, 1706.

Sarah, and Thomas Baker, May 28, 1702.

Susannah, of Dedham, and Isaac Frirol, at Dedham, May 18, 1738.

Thomas, and Harriet Waters, Dec. 4, 1837.*

Timothy, and Abigail Randell, int. June 13, 1802.

W[illia]m G., of Newton, and Mianda Clark, Mar. 23, 1841.*

PILLEPS (see also Phillips), Frederick, and Elisabeth Ryder of Boston, int. July 23, 1846.

PINDER, Michael, and Bridgett Lines, int. Feb. 5, 1847.

PINEO, Caroline S., a. 21 y., housewife, d. Peter B. and Alveia, and Charles Darling [Durling. int.], a. 21 y., carpenter, s. Luther and Isabella, June 15, 1845.*

PINKHAM, Clement, and Eliza B. [G. int.] Johnson, Nov. 16, 1830.*

Eliza M., and Charles G. Philbrick, Oct. 6, 1844.

Thomas B., and Julia D. Thomas, Oct. 24, 1848.*

PIPER, Elizabeth, and Isaac Johnson, int. June 28, 1848.

Hannah D., of Stratham, N. H., and Stephen W. Nudd, int. Aug. 22, 1846.

PIREPONT (see also Pierpont), James, and Sarah Gore, June 3, 1709.

Sarah, and Gershom Davis ,June 24, 1708.

PITCHER, Samuel, of Milton, and Elizabeth Worth, Jan. 6, 1703-4.

PITTIS, George, and Lydia Parks, July 5, 1726.

PITTS, Eliza, and Henry Seeva of Brookline, int. Feb. 13, 1825.

Henry, and Lucy Jones, Jan. 17, 1802.*

Lucy, Mrs., and Jacob Saunderson of Charlestown, int. May 19, 1805.

Sarah Chardon, and Noah Davis, int. Nov. 6, 1814.

PITTY, James, of Hingham, and Mary Muncrief, Jan. 14, 1819.*

* Intention also recorded.

**PLANT,** Samuel, and Delicia Mary Poignand, int. Aug. 26, 1809.

**PLATT,** George, of New York City, and Mary C. Russell, Nov. 19, 1839.*

**PLUMER** (see also Plummer), John H., and Emeline T. Merium, int. Nov. 23, 1845.
Leonard, a. 26 y., stairbuilder, and Isabella M. Crawford, a. 30 y., Aug. —, 1846.*

**PLUMMER** (see also Plumer), John M[arden. int.], and Harriet Carr, Sept. 26, 1833.*

**PLUNKET,** Elizabeth, and Roger Norton, int. June 2, 1844.
George, and Ellen Cary, int. Apr. 11, 1841.

**POAD,** John, and Mrs. Sarah Merriam, Dec. 26, 1781. c. r. 2.

**POIGNAND,** Delicia Mary, and Samuel Plant, int. Aug. 26, 1809.

**POLLARD,** Anna, and Isaac Rand, Oct. 30, 1814.*
Jacob W., and Caroline M. Low, July 14, 1846.

**POLLEY** (see also Polly, Poly), Elisabeth, and Caleb Philips, Oct. 16, 1681.
Hannah, and Benjamin Lyon, Feb. 1, 1731-2.
John, and Jane Walker, June 2, 1684.
John, and Sarah Williams, Jan. 1, 1704-5.
Mary, and Ezekiel Carver [Cheever. c. r. 2.], Jan. 26, 1738.
Sarah, and Caleb Sever, Nov. 26, 1723.
Sarah, and Benjamin Newel, May 4, 1726.
Susanna, and Samuel Weld, June 28, 1683.

**POLLOCK,** Robert M., and Mary Louisa Fernald, Dec. 22, 1844.

**POLLY** (see also Polley), Abigall, and John Lion, May 10, 1670.

**POLSEY,** John, and Rebecca Furguson, Feb. 6, 1840.*

**POLY** (see also Polley), Hannah, and Isack Curtis, May 10, 1670.

**POMPHRET,** Johana, and Michael Dooley, int. Sept. 3, 1844.

* Intention also recorded.

**POMROY,** Aaron, and Abigail Burrell, Oct. 25, 1801.*
Daniel, and Lucy Farrington, Jan. 24, 1802. c. r. 2.*
Henry, and Fanny May of Warwick, int. Dec. 28, 1806.
Roswel, and Lydia Phillips, int. July 7, 1804.
Titus, and Nancy Woodard [Woodward. residents. int.], Feb.
26, 1804. c. r. 2.*

**POND,** Abigail, and Isaac Whitiney, Oct. 19, 1758.
Beulah, and Timothy Ellis, June 30, 1776.
Caleb, of Dedham, and Elizabeth Lyon, at Dorchester, July 28,
1721.
Caleb, and Sally Belcher of Randolph, int. Nov. 30, 1806.
Eliza, and Elisha Gale, Jan. 25, 1807.*
Elizabeth, of Newton, and Lemuel Davis, at Newton, Jan. 27,
1791.*
Enoch, Rev.. of Ashford, Conn., and Mrs. Mary Baker, Nov.
12, 1801.*
George W., and Caroline Hamilton of Dorchester, int. Sept. 13,
1829.
Hannah [of Dedham. int.], and Aaron Payne, Aug. 27, 1798.
c. r. 2.*
John, of Portsmouth, N. H., and Hannah Willard, Dec. 31,
1809.*
Joshua, of Dedham, and Jane Ball, June 21, 1744. c. r. 2.
Lydia, and Samuel Gibbon, at Boston, Sept. —, 1756.
Lydia, and William Smith, Apr. 26, 1798. c. r. 2.*
Martha, and Paul Davis, Apr. 1, 1760.
Mary, Mrs., and Andrew Lewis of Dedham, int. Aug. 28, 1796.
Mary Ann, of Dorchester, and Edwin Fuller, int. Nov. 23,
1846.
Moses, and Anna Davis, Nov. 13, 1788.*
Nancy, and Warner [Warren. int.] Claflin, Nov. 8, 1801.
c. r. 2.*
Nath[anie]ll, and Sarah White, May —, 1756. c. r. 2.
Polley, and James Fadden of Dedham, int. Feb. 8, 1801.
Rebeccah, and Solomon Chenery, Mar. 29, 1798. c. r. 2.*
Sarah, and Elijah Learned of Watertown, May 19, 1796.*
Sarah B., and Job Sumner, June 9, 1825. c. r. 2.*
Simeon, and Esther [Sarah. c. r. 2.] White, Nov. 30, 1763.
[Dec. 1. c. r. 2.]
Solomon Prentiss, and Tryphena Gould, both of Franklin, Feb.
4, 1791.

* Intention also recorded.

**POOL** (see also Poole), Ebenezer, and Olive Ward, Feb. 14, 1802.*

John W., and Edith P. Cutter of Jaffrey, N. H., int. Aug. 16, 1835.

Samuel, and Clarissa Morse, Oct. 8, 1828.*

**POOLE** (see also Pool), Caroline, and Person Darling of Jaffrey, N. H., Sept. 30, 1832.*

Eben[eze]r, jr., and Clarissa Dinsdell, Dec. 15, 1833.*

Elizabeth B., and John H. Butler of Moultonborough, N. H., Sept. 1, 1844.*

Hannah C., of Watertown, and Ezekiel Merrill of Lowell, Dec. 1, 1831.

William M., and Emeline Saunder of Livermore, Me., int. Nov. 1, 1840.

**POOR,** Elizabeth, and Henry Rich, Oct. 1, 1705.

**POPE,** Edmund F., and Mrs. Elizabeth Bradford, June 6, 1836.*

Lucy P., of South Reading, and Royal M. Barlow, int. Apr. 30, 1837.

Thomas, and Margret Downing, Jan. 2, 1705-6.

**PORSTARE,** Aif, and Frederick Young, int. Mar. 8, 1846.

**PORTER,** Eliphalet, Rev., and Patty Ruggles, Oct. 1, 1801. C. R. 2.*

Elizabeth, and Isaack Johnson, Jan. 20, 1636.

Elvina, and Charles M. Weeks of Greenland, N. H., Dec. 5, 1839.*

Jabez, of Malden, and Polly Kent, at Malden, Mar. 20, 1777.

Jacob, and Sarah Hall Cooper, Dec. 6, 1789.

James, a. 26 y., carpenter, s. Alexander and Margarett, and Maria Williams, a. 24 y., d. Sam[ue]l S. and Lucy, June 1, 1848.*

Joseph, of Brighton, and Elmira S. Glover, May 27, 1838.*

Letitia, and William Bell, int. Aug. 6, 1849.

Martha R[uggles. int.], and Charles K. Dillaway, Aug. 27, 1835.*

Naomi, and Henry Atherton, Jan. 30, 1804.*

Ruthy, and Benjamin Haynes, int. Dec. 15, 1793.

**PORTISE,** Hannah, and John Weld, Jan. 22, 1678.

* Intention also recorded.

**POST,** Laura H., of Boston, and John Waters, int. Dec. 12, 1846.

**POST HILL,** Betsy, and Rufus Converse, May 17, 1809.*
Robert, and Sarah Lyon, Oct. 17, 1790.*

**POTTER,** Deborah A., of Needham, and Eber W. Hall, int. Apr. 3, 1845.
Hannah, Mrs., of Waltham, and Robert Pierpont, Esq., at Waltham, Sept. 6, 1775.
Judith, [Judeth. CT. R.], and Samuel Finch, Dec. 13, 1654.
Richard, and Sally Harris, Sept. 15, 1808.*
William, and Judith Greaves, June 2, 1646.

**POTTLE,** Susanna, and John Gaines, Jan. 25, 1807.*

**POWERS,** David, and Ann Longan, int. Oct. 9, 1842.
John, and Mary O'Connell, int. Apr. 9, 1837.
Rhoda, of Petersham, and William Melville, int. Feb. 24, 1799.

**PRATT,** Catharine E., and Stephen D. Lee of Brighton, Nov. 15, 1836.*
Charles, and Sarah Cobb, int. Apr. 8, 1841.
Ebenezer, and Nancy Moore, int. Feb. 17, 1833.
Eliza, and Aaron Mann, int. Mar. 19, 1837.
George, 2d m, a. 34 y., cabinet maker, s. Thomas and Mary, and Margarett Jane Corbett, a. 19 y., d. David and Margarett, Sept. 19, 1849.*
Jerahmeel C., and Julia A. Farnum of Amherst, N. H., int. May 23, 1841.
John, of Portland, and Betsy Wyman, Jan. 30, 1810.*
Levi, and Mary Seaver, Mar. 31, 1796.*
Martha, and Eliphalet Brown of Dorchester, Oct. 18, 1821.*
Martha, and William J. Reynolds, [Esq. int.], Aug. 15, 1843.*
Mary, and Nathaniel W. Williams, Mar. 1, 1796.*
Mary Ann, and Joseph G. Chambers, Jan. 5, 1840.*
Mary B., and Willard Gay, May 11, 1818.*
Mehitable, and Thomas Nolen, Mar. 17, 1789.*
Olive B., and Nathan W. Brooks, int. May 26, 1822.
Patty W., and David Pulsifer, Nov. 13, 1803.*
Paul, of Weston, and Abigail Griggs, Aug. 29, 1822. C. R. 2.*
Phebe P., and Isaac H. Cary, ———, 1832. [Sept. 4, 1831. int.]*
Sally, and Aaron Mason of Watertown, Aug. 28, 1796.*

* Intention also recorded.

PRATT, Sally, and Hezekiah Turner [jr. int.], Dec. 27, 1820.*

Sarah, of Hingham, and Albert Macomber, int. Aug. 7, 1842.

Simeon, and Mrs. Sarah Draper, Feb. 5, 1795.*

Susan, and Geo[rge] C. Lee, Oct. 13, 1834.*

Susan, of North Yarmouth, Me., and True Russell, int. Jan. 1, 1849.

Theoda, and Ephraim Cutting, int. June 20, 1802.

William, and Mary Wyman, Feb. 7, 1799.*

W[illia]m W., and Catharine [E. int.] Minot, Feb. 16, 1843.*

PRAY, Eunice R., and Bartlett F. [J. int.] Martin, Aug. 24, 1845.*

PREDIGER, Eliza [Bredeger. int.], a. 18 y., b. Germany, d. Adam and Barbara, and John Vittveatt [Veatt. int.], a. 29 y., musician, b. Germany, s. Frederick and Malwina, Dec. 26, 1849.*

PRENTICE (see also Prentiss), James, of Sutton, and Mrs. Sarah Whiting, at Sutton, Dec. 24, 1770.

John, of Lancaster, and Mrs. Mary Garner, Dec. 4, 1705.

John, of Lancaster, and Anna Bayley, Oct. 11, 1728.

PRENTIS (see also Prentiss), Allice, and John Watson, Apr. 3, 1634.

Nathaniel S. Dr., and Abagail Pico, int. May 10, 1807.

PRENTISS (see also Prentice, Prentis), Abigail, and Erastus Champney of Brookline, int. Apr. 13, 1823.

Abigail, and Francis A. Fogg of Salem, int. Nov. 6, 1842.

Elizabeth, and Rev. Byrem Lawrence of Indianapolis, Ind., Sept. 23, 1832.*

Henry [M. D. int.], of Gloucester, and Caroline H. Staniford, June 18, 1825.*

Hugh K., and Sarah Kirkwood of Concord, N. H., int. Nov. 2, 1834.

John Parkins, Capt., and Sophia Gould, int. Nov. 14, 1824.

Martha R[uggles. int.], and Rev. Joseph Barnard of Salem [of New York. int.], Sept. 2, 1835.*

Sophia G., and Joseph H. Converse, int. May 30, 1849.

PRESCOTT, Benj[ami]n T., Dr., and Emeline Webber, int. Dec. 30, 1838.

Edward, and Mary Nichols of Nashua, N. H., int. Sept. 22, 1844.

* Intention also recorded.

PRESCOTT, Jerome, and Mary Ann Blanchard, May 30, 1835.

Lucinda, and Mason Pierce of Stoughton, Oct. 14, 1821.*

Martha A.. of Candia, N. H., and Moses D. Tucker, int. Oct. 14, 1821.*

Mary S., a. 22 y., d. Joseph O., and Jonathan R. Weld, a. 25 y., work on railroad, s. Joseph and Lucy S., Jan. 25, 1849.*

PRESTON, Cornelius, and Margarit Reynolds, int. Aug. 10, 1845.

Edward, resident, and Hanna Carpenter of Rehoboth, at Rehoboth, May 15, 1746.

Edward, [jr. int.], of Dorchester, and Rebecca Weld, June 11, 1793.*

Hannah, and Lawrance Johnson, both residents, Mar. 15, 1785.*

Mary W., of Dorchester, and Isaac H. White, int. Jan. 11, 1835.

PRICE, Augustus E., and Ann Maria Symonds both of Salem, Apr. 29, 1849.

Nelson, and [Mrs. int.] Caroline Putnam, Mar. 25, 1832.*

PRICHARD, Jeremiah, jr., of Porto Rico, a. 34 y., merchant, b. New Ipswich, s. Jeremiah and Nancy, and Helen Vila, a. 22 y., d. Joseph and Lydia, Dec. 11, 1849.*

PRIENTY, Maria, and Calvin W. Hanson, int. Oct. 1, 1849.

PRIER (see also Prior), Hannah, and Joseph Scott, May 17, 1708.

PRIEST, Claraetta, of Providence, R. I., and George W. Gooch, int. June 5, 1846.

Jacob, and Mary Ann East, int. Dec. 15, 1833.

Joseph, and Mary Ann Draper, int. June 4, 1837.

Phebe, and John C. Day of Cambridge, Mar. 3, 1849.

PRINCE, Daniel McC., and Nancy Thayer, July 4, 1804.*

John, Esq., and Harriet Warren, int. July 31, 1836.

Mariah, and Jeremiah Heseltine, int. Mar. 27, 1836.

Martha Anne, and Isaac F. Coffin, int. Apr. 6, 1845.

Sarah, and Joseph Worsley, Apr. 26, 1758.

Thomas, and Anne McCarthy, Apr. 22, 1779.

* Intention also recorded.

**PRIOR** (see also Prier), Jane, and Terrence Gargin, Feb. 4, 1849.

**PROCTER** (see also Proctor), Charles, and Mary Kelly, Feb. 8, 1807.*

Franklin [Proctor. int.], and Julia Ann Hawes, Dec. 31, 1843.*

**PROCTOR** (see also Procter), Benj[ami]n S. [Procter. int.], of Worcester, a. 27 y., clerk, s. Geo[rge] B. and Mary B. of Pembroke, N. H., and Mary Eliz[abet]h Keith, a. 25 y., d. W[illia]m and Sally, Aug. 16, 1846.*

Maria, a. 23 y., d. Abijah and Sarah, and James Taylor of Carlisle, a. 27 y., s. Abel and Sarah, Apr. 8, 1847.*

Susan, of Carlisle, and James Kelly, int. Oct. 6, 1833.

**PROUTY,** Dwight, [of Boston. c. r. 3.], and Mary R. Gould, Dec. 4, 1828.*

Frances H., and Moses Cornson, both of Newton, Sept. 2, 1847.

Henry H., and Delia C. Blossom of West Barnstable, int. Mar. 22, 1835.

**PUFFER,** Benjaman, of Stoughtonham, and Nancy Whitney, resident, at Sharon, Oct. 20, 1778.

John, and Mary Holbrook, at Dorchester, 17: 10m: 1695.

Jonathan [of Dorchester. c. r. 2.], and Abiel Beacon, July 18, 1717.

**PULSIFER,** David, and Patty W. Pratt, Nov. 13, 1803.*

**PURCEL,** Bridget, and Patrick Mack, int. Mar. 22, 1849.

**PUTMAN** (see also Putnam), Allen [Esq. int.], of Hamilton, and Hannah D. Williams, June 8, 1843.*

Allen [Putnam. int.], widr., a. 43 y., merchant, s. Daniel and Susannah, of Danvers, and Sarah Bass Bartlett, a. 40 y., d. Enoch and Sarah, June 10, 1846.*

Caroline [Mrs. int.], and Nelson Price, Mar. 25, 1832.*

George, Rev., and Elizabeth Ann Ware of Cambridge, int. July 31, 1831.

Henry [Putnam. c. r. 3.], of Brunswick, and Kathrine [Catharine. c. r. 3.] H. Palmer, Sept. 13, 1807.*

Julia A., of Danvers, and John D. Philbrick, int. Aug. 13, 1843.

* Intention also recorded.

**PUTNAM** (see also Putman), Ansel W., and Delia F.
Chandler of Boston, int. Sept. 7, 1846.
Betsy, and James M. Leeds, int. Apr. 29, 1838.
Jonas, and Hannah Evens of Bedford, int. Feb. 17, 1811.
Mary Ann, and Calvin Smith of Waltham, int. Mar. 13, 1842.
Sarah F., of Waltham, and George W. Butters, int. Apr. 17,
1842.

**PUTNEY,** Mary, of Dudley, and Nicholas Seaver, at Dudley,
Apr. 3, 1759.

**QUACKENBUSH,** Daniel P., of Landsing, Mich., a. 24 y.,
artist, and Ruth A. Brewster of Medford, a. 20 y., d.
John and Elizabeth, Oct. 15, 1848.

**QUIGLEY** (see also Quigly, Quingly), Michael, and Catherine
Hennicy, int. June 3, 1848.
Sarah, and Thomas McLaughlin, int. Apr. 5, 1840.

**QUIGLY** (see also Quigley), Michael, and Bridget Shrugnasy,
int. Feb. 28, 1848.
Owen, and Bridget Folan, int. Sept. 22, 1848.
Patrick, and Ellen Shoughnassy, int. Dec. 1, 1844.

**QUILLAN,** John, and Ann Gilligan, int. Apr. 9, 1843.

**QUIMBY,** Harriet, and Ivory H. Foss, Mar. 29, 1846.*

**QUINGLY** (see also Quigley), Michael, and Ellen Morris,
int. Apr. 30, 1849.

**QUINLAN,** Patrick, and Margarett O'Conner, int. June 4,
1846.

**QUINN,** Bridget, and George Carter, int. Feb. 14, 1848.
Ellen, and Michael Haley, int. Nov. 28, 1846.
Mary, and John Mahony, int. Aug. 31, 1845.

**QUINNAM,** Mary F., and A. M. Houghton of Sterling, int.
Sept. 30, 1849.

**QUOE,** Patrick, and Rosana Cary, int. Sept. 14, 1845.

**RACKLEFF,** Antoinett J., of Bath, and Edwin W. Dalton,
Mar. 19, 1843.*

**RAFFERTY,** Felix, of Lowell, and Mary Cochran, int. Dec.
29, 1849.
Mary, and Michael Feeley, int. Oct. 27, 1844.

* Intention also recorded.

**RAFLEY,** Henry G., and Letita A. Miller, Sept. 15, 1844.

**RAGIN** (see also Regan), Ellen, and George Nugent, int. Nov. 6, 1846.
Matthew, and Ellen Feeney, int. June 12, 1849.

**RALLIKIN,** Patrick, and Mary Curly, int. Dec. 29, 1844.

**RAMSDELL** (see also Ramsdill), Sarah, Mrs., and Elisha Vose, int. May 17, 1801.

**RAMSDILL** (see also Ramsdell), Bethiah, and William Kenchen, resident, May 13, 1742.

**RAMSEY,** Martha, and Isaac Coe, Sept. 11, 1706.
Mary, and John Johnson, May 26, 1702.
Matthew J., a. 27 y., laborer, s. Thomas and Dorothy, and Charlotte Green, a. 23 y., d. Lemuel and Dorcas, Aug. 15, 1847.*

**RANAHAN,** Rosana, and Michael Gaitly, int. Aug. 27, 1847.

**RAND** (see also Rands), Abraham W., and Martha Ann Holmes of Provincetown, int. May 10, 1849.
Clarissa, of Weston, and Henry Robbins, int. Feb. 26, 1826.
Elizabeth, and Nathaniel Brewer, Dec. 6, 1661.
Isaac, and Anna Pollard, Oct. 30, 1814.*
Juliet Eliza, and Samuel Trask, jr., int. Nov. 2, 1823.
Mary Maria, and Theodore French, Sept. 8, 1833.
Nahum, and Dolly Bristor, Feb. 11, 1842.*
Nathan, of Taunton, and Mary D. Whiting, int. Oct. 28, 1832.
Obed, and Anna Y. Jenness of Rye, N. H., int. Feb. 1, 1835.
Olive, a. 30 y., d. Sam[ue]l and Polly, of Rye, N. H., and Jonathan [Jonathon. int.] Moulton, widr., a. 30 y., laborer, s. Cha[rle]s and Rebecca, of Wakefield, N. H., Jan. 12, 1847.*
Susan [d. Rob[er]t. in pencil.], and Abram Newel, Feb. 8, 1651.

**RANDAL** (see also Randall), Thomas, of Dorchester, and Mrs. Katharine Tucker, Dec. 30, 1730.

**RANDALL** (see also Randal, Randell), Alice F., and James W. Ratbray of Framingham, int. Aug. 3, 1845.
Andrew W., and Cordelia W. Reccord, int. Mar. 3, 1844.
Catharine, and John Towl, May 13, 1825.*

* Intention also recorded.

RANDALL, John, and Sarah Abrams of Brookline, int. Apr. 9, 1812.*

Jonas, and Mary Knower, Nov. 24, 1805.*

Mary [Howard. int.], and Jonathan Hall, May 11, 1807.*

Mary Elizabeth, and Andrew Jackson, int. Apr. 29, 1838.

Mary M., and Charles D. Field, Sept. 15, 1830.*

Nathaniel H., and Lucretia Drew, June 1, 1815.*

Polly, of Sharon, and Lewis Fisher, int. Mar. 26, 1797.

Reuben, and Mary Hawes, Apr. 22, 1813.*

Robert, and Rebecca Spur, both of Dorchester, Sept. 8, 1793

Sally and William Cobb, Jan. 6, 1811.*

Sarah C., and Benjamin May, Jan. 4, 1838. C. R. 3.*

Stephen, and Sarah Ann Warren, Sept. 2, 1810.*

Stephen, and Rachel Tirrel, May 12, 1816.*

Susan B., a. 24 y., d. John and Sarah, and Stephen Heath, [Hath of Boston. int.], a. 24 y., carpenter, s. Timothy and Susan, June 18, 1846.*

Timothy, and Sally Hall of Newton, int. Mar. 22, 1840.

William H., and Elizabeth Colburn, Oct. 19, 1828.*

RANDELL (see also Randall). Abigail, and Timothy Pike, int. June 13, 1802.

RANDOLF, Rebecca Ballard, Mrs., and Sam[ue]l Kettell, Sept. 18, 1815.*

RANDS (see also Rand), Nancy, and Thomas L. Williams, int. Apr. 13, 1845.

RANKIN, Eliza M., a. 20 y., d. John M. and Harriet, and John T. Smith, a. 26 y., s. Caleb and Amy, Feb. 11, 1849.*

RANSFORD, Thomas, and Experience Smith, May 4, 1758.

RANSOM, Sarah D., and Nicholas Mason, int. Nov. 30, 1849.

RATBRAY, James W., of Framingham, and Alice F. Randall, int. Aug. 3, 1845.

RAWLINS (see also Rollins), Jasper, and wid. Griggs, June 8, 1651.

RAWSON, Jonathan, and Susannah Stone, ———, 1761. [bef. Mar. 26. C. R. 2.]

RAYMOND, Francis, and Mrs. Lydia D. Ross, May 3, 1830.*

Samuel, of Charlestown, and Mary L. Wheeler, Dec. 7, 1809.*

* Intention also recorded.

**RAYMOR,** Thomas, and Mary How, Mar. 29, 1758.

**RAYNOLDS** (see also Reynolds), Ellen, and William Green, int. June 1, 1845.
George T., and Sarah H. Hewens, int. Mar. 31, 1839.

**REA,** Mary [Maria. int.] G., a. 26 y., d. Archilaus and Maria, and Samuel D. Dexter, a. 22 y., clergyman, s. Sam[ue]l and Eliza, Nov. 29, 1847.*

**READ** (see also Reade, Reed), Abigail Amanda, a. 17 y., d. Richard W. and Lois, and Washington E. Hase of Dover, N. H., a. 21 y., machinist, June 8, 1846.*
Alfred T., and Lydia A. Story, int. Aug. 29, 1841.
Daniel, and Bridget Crown, both of Dorchester, May 16, 1803.
Henry, and Mary P. Littlefield, int. May 24, 1835.
Malinda, of Charlestown, and John Souther, int. June 6, 1819.
Mary, and William Dove, Dec. 4, 1808.*
Mary, and Asahel Gay of Norwich, Conn., Sept. 29, 1822.*
MaryE., a. 24 y., d. George and Rebecca, and George Weld, a. 25 y., gentleman, s. Sam[ue]l W. and Nancy, Dec. 14, 1848.*
Nancy P., and Nathan Viles, June 19, 1816.*
Patrick, and Catharine Dorherty, int. Apr. 27, 1845.
Thomas, and Ruth Wait, Mar. 9, 1788.*
William N., and Lucy M. Stevens, Sept. 4, 1839.*

**READE** (see also Read), Israel, of Rehoboth, and Rebeka Rigells, at Rehoboth, Nov. 5, 1684.

**READING,** Thomas, and Sopia Green, June 25, 1837.*

**REALEN,** Catharine, and Jacob Stefin, int. Sept. 23, 1838.

**RECCORD** (see also Reckard), Cordelia W., and Andrew W. Randall, int. Mar. 3, 1844.

**RECKARD** (see also Reccord, Reckards), Diantha, and Charles Hutchinson, int. July 3, 1842.
Mary Ann, a. 18 y., and Clement P. Maxwell of Westbrook, Me., a. 27 y., merchant, s. Eben[eze]r and Esther, of Gray, Me., June 21, 1846.*
Samuel T., a. 19 y., laborer, s. Perez T. and Zenith E., and Rosannah [Rosanna. int.] Bryant, a. 20 y., d. Ichabod and Betsey, Nov. 8, 1846.*

* Intention also recorded.

**RECKARDS** (see also Reckard), Charles A., and Henrietta D. Hodgdon, int. Dec. 31, 1843.

**RECORDEN,** Stephen, and Mary Leahy, int. July 22, 1848.

**REDDAHAN,** Rosanna, and James Cannaway, int. Dec. 11, 1849.

**REDDISH,** Thomas, and Maria Watson, int. Apr. 18, 1848.

**REDFIELD,** George W., and Lucinda Lillie, Jan. 30, 1842.*

**REED** (see also Read), Abel, of Milton, and Lucretia Mellish of Dorchester, Apr. 19, 1824.
Eliza, and [Capt. int.] Levi Houghton, Oct. 5, 1823.*
Eliza Ann, of Framingham, and Prince Chapman, int. Sept. 15, 1846.
George, of Newton, and Tabitha Rich, July 3, 1842.*
Hannah [Read. dup.], of Chelmsford, and Ephraim Craft, at Chelmsford, May 15, 1699.
Hannah [Read. c. r. 3.], and Samuel Pease of Dedham, Sept. 20, 1818.*
James, and Betsey Carlton, Feb. 2, 1812.*
John, and Mrs. Hannah Goddard, Nov. 23 or 24, 1751.
John, and Charlotte Terrill, int. Apr. 16, 1837.
John, jr., and Harriet [H. int.] White, Mar. 1, 1846.*
Mary, and Jonathan Gilbert, Nov. 19, 1761.
Rebecca, of Taunton, and J. H. Cushman, int. Aug. 24, 1845.
Rebecca T., and James W. Bracklin, int. Apr. 28, 1848.

**REES,** Dorothy J., and Moody White, Aug. 13, 1843.

**REEVE,** Thomas, and Hanna Roe, Apr. 15, 1645.

**REGAN** (see also Ragin, Rigan), Cornelius, and Catharine Moroney, int. July 2, 1843.
Margaret, and Thomas Dolin, int. Sept. 3, 1843.

**REHM,** George H. L., and Ann Maria Koerkel, int. Oct. 26, 1849.
George H. L., and Emeline Hetler, int. Nov. 9, 1849.

**REILLY** (see also Riley), Catherine, and Peter McConahy, int. Apr. 2, 1849.
Patrick, and Margarett Lane, int. Sept. 3, 1847.
Phillip O., and Ann Brady, int. Sept. 24, 1846.

* Intention also recorded.

**REMICK,** William [F. int.], of Dorchester, and Helen Frances Conckling, Jan. 1, 1843.*

**RETLON,** Richard, and Sarah Gilburd, Jan. 31, 1721-2.

**REW,** Joshua B. [Ray. int.], of Charlestown, and Mary Ann Noyes, Apr. 24, 1834.*

**REXFORD,** George, and Sarah A. Harrod of Dorchester, at Dorchester, Apr. 28, 1842.

**REYNOLDS** (see also Raynolds), Ann, and Lawrence Reynolds, int. Aug. 4, 1844.

Charles Green, and Charlotte Potter Staniford, int. Apr. 3, 1831.

Ellenor, and John Ferguson, int. Aug. 20, 1843.

John [of Bristol. c. r. 2.], and Dorothy Weld, May 5 [3. c. r. 2.], 1753.

Lawrence, and Ann Reynolds, int. Aug. 4, 1844.

Margarit, and Cornelius Preston, int. Aug. 10, 1845.

Maria, a. 23 y., d. Stephen and Mary, and Benjamin Hayes, a. 32 y., carpenter, s. John and Elizabeth, of Nova Scotia, Aug. 13, 1846.*

Michael, and Mary Killduff, int. Aug. 29, 1849.

Rebecca [W. Raynolds. int.], a. 24 y., domestic, d. John and Ann, and Marcus Trueman, a. 23 y., carpenter, s. John and Ann, Jan. 19, 1845.*

Sarah H., d. Abel and Anna Hewins, and Abijah W. Draper, 2d. m, a. 40 y., physician, s. Abijah and Lavina (Tyler), Apr. 26, 1848.*

William [Renalds. c. r. 2.], and Sarah Clewley, Mar. 31, 1748.

William J. [Esq. int.], and Martha Pratt, Aug. 15, 1843.*

**RHINE,** Hannah, and John Murphy of Brookline, int. Apr. 13, 1847.

**RHOADES** (see also Rhoads, Rhodes), Aaron [Rhodes. c. r. 3.], and Betsey Child, Nov. 8, 1812.*

Ebenezer [of Boston. c. r. 3.], and Hepsibah C. Holbrook, Mar. 12, 1834.*

Lucy, of Dedham, and Jonathan Smith, int. Jan. 22, 1809.

Lucy Ann, a. 20 y., and William Harris, a. 24 y., carpenter, s. John and Elizabeth, June 20, 1847.*

Mary, a. 18 y., d. Daniel and Louisa, and John Harris, jr., a. 24 y., painter, s. John and Elizabeth, Jan. 2, 1848.*

Sarah, and Israel, Kimball, int. Sept. 4, 1836.

* Intention also recorded.

**RHOADS** (see also Rhoades), Betsey [Rhoades. int.], and
Thomas Baker, Dec. 25, 1814. c. r. 2.*
Catherine, of Sharon, and Abner Willet, Feb. 17, 1814.*

**RHODES** (see also Rhoades), Abby Dennison, and Thomas
I. Goodwin of Charlestown, Dec. 7, 1820.*

**RICE,** Abigail, and Daniel Bugbee, June 21, 1733.
Abraham, and Unity Morse of Walpole, int. Sept. 15, 1816.
Abraham, and Hannah Haynes of Charlestown, int. Sept. 27,
1818.
Anne, and Nathanael Gary, Nov. 12, 1685.
Catharine, resident, and Robert Golaver, int. Aug. 23, 1795.
Daniel, and Elizabeth Winchester of Brookline, int. Apr. 8,
1787.
Emeline of Cambridge, and Daniel E. King, int. Nov. 11,
1838.
Harvey, and Almina Hale of Newton, int. Apr. 15, 1838.
John, jr., of Cambridge, a. 26 y., organ pipe maker, s. John
and Freelove, and Mary G. Henry, a. 27 y., d. Jona[than]
and Mary, Jan. 31, 1848.*
Louisa, a. 29 y., d. Henry, and Edward C. Weed [of Boston.
int.], a. 31 y., accountant, s. Samuel, Nov. 1, 1849.*
Nancy, of Dorchester, a. 17 y., d. Adam and Margaret, and
Thomas Boyd of Dorchester, a. 25 y., s. Sam[ue]l and
Sarah, Apr. 8, 1847.
Nancy C., of Brookline, and Ebene[ze]r S. Peirce, int. Apr.
17, 1808.
Olive, and Roswell Barret, Dec. 12, 1810.*
Sally, of Sudbury, and Peter Haynes, int. Feb. 8, 1807.
Sarah, and Thomas Cheney, Feb. 18, 1810.*

**RICH,** Benjamin [Capt., mariner. int.], resident, and Susanna
Heath, Mar. 31, 1800.*
Henry, and Elizabeth Poor, Oct. 1, 1705.
Joshua G., and Mary R. [N. int.] Day, Sept. 28, 1842.*
Pamelia G., and Charles H. Laughton, Aug. 8, 1844.*
Philip, and Joanna Bugbee, Oct. 4, 1710.
Priscilla A. [Precilla A. int.], and Reuben Rich, Nov. 2,
1845.*
Reuben, and Priscilla A. [Precilla A. int.] Rich, Nov. 2,
1845.*
Tabitha, and George Reed of Newton, July 3, 1842.*

* Intention also recorded.

**RICHARD** (see also Richards), Sarah, wid., and Thomas K. Palmer [of Boston. int.], Jan. 20, 1847.*

Susan, of Newton, and Caleb Parker, jr., int. Mar. 5, 1826.

**RICHARDS** (see also Richard), Abigail [Mrs. int.], and Calvin Allen, Apr. 16, 1801. c. r. 2.*

Anna, and Eben[eze]r Corey, int. Sept. 21, 1783.

Anny [Amelia Richard, of Cambridge. int.], and Levi Richards, at Cambridge, Aug. 1, 1799.*

Augusta B., and Thomas R. Whittemore, int. Nov. 19, 1843.

Catherine, and John Mathers, Nov. 14, 1775.

Catherine, wid., a. 32 y., d. Eliakim, and Eli M. Whitney, widr., a. 35 y., merchant, Feb. 9, 1845.*

Charles A., and Henrietta D. Hodgdon, Jan. 16, 1844.

Cynthia, and George W. Pierce, Mar. 31, 1840.*

Danforth, and Cyrene Hager, Apr. 20, 1828. c. r. 2.*

Daniel, and Mary Harkness, Jan. 29, 1734-5.

David, and Melatiah Farrington, Dec. 1, 1772.

Deborah, and Edward Foster [of Boston. c. r. 3.], June 20, 1830.*

Dorothy P., of Newton, and George James, May 19, 1836.

Ebenezer, and Prudence Heath, May 12, 1743. c. r. 2.

Ebenezer, and Elizabeth ——, Oct. —, 1769.

Edward, and Sally Herring, Nov. 5, 1798. c. r. 2.*

Edward, and Rachel Davis, June 5, 1800. c. r. 2.*

Edward, jr., and Annette Wallace of Henniker, N. H., Sept. 14, 1845.

Eleanor, and Ebenezer Ayers, Jan. 3, 1803. c. r. 2.*

Eliakim, of Dedham, and Mary Mayo, at Dedham, Jan. 7, 1765.

Eliza S., and Ezekiel W. Cutter, Nov. 28, 1841.*

Elizabeth, Mrs., of Dedham, and William Scarborough, at Dedham, June 19, 1765.

Eliz[abet]h, of Dedham, and Abner Child, int. Feb. 9, 1800.

Elizabeth F., and Ebenezer Dudley, jr., June 18, 1826. c. r. 2.*

Elizabeth R., and Calvin B. Faunce, Apr. 27, 1836.*

Emily G., and David Abbott of Charlestown, int. Dec. 11, 1847.

George Coffin, and Lucy Ann Hewes, Dec. 24, 1847.*

George H., and Irene H. Lincoln, June 22, 1842.*

Hannah, Mrs., and Rev. Ebenezer White [of Norton. c. r. 2.], July 6, 1749.

Hannah, and Aaron Davis, Oct. 17 [18. c. r. 2.], 1763.

* Intention also recorded.

RICHARDS, Hannah, and Lemuel Pierce, int. Mar. 30, 1794.

Hannah, of Dorchester, and Simeon Litchfield, int. May 7, 1820.

Hannah, and John R. Child, June 4, 1820. C. R. 2.*

Hepzibah C., of Dedham, and Stephen Child, 3d, int. Sept. 5, 1813.

James, and Sarah Lloyd, Mar. 24 [4. C. R. 3.], 1822.*

Jeremiah, jr., and Hannah Mayo, May 23, 1728.

Jeremiah, 3d, and Tabitha Gay of Newton, at Newton, Dec. 7, 1752.

Jeremiah, and Abigail Davis, Oct. 31, 1792.*

Jesse [of Portland. int.], and Elizabeth Davis, Nov. 18, 1792.*

John, and Lydia Greely, Apr. 10, 1750. C. R. 2.

John, and Nancy Dickerman, May 17, 1801. C. R. 3.*

Jonathan A., and Nancy D. Gore, Nov. 23, 1820.*

Joseph, and Mary Lyon, May 16, 1740.

Joseph, Esq. [of Dedham. different ink], and Elizabeth Dudley, Mar. 24, 1748-9.

Joseph, jr., and Mrs. Abig[ai]l Mayo, Jan. 1, 1777.

Joseph, and Susanna Fisher of Needham, int. Oct. 30, 1808.

Joseph G., and Mary A. Brown of Brunswick, Me., Aug. 10, 1844.*

Joshua, and Lois Scott, Sept. 11, 1763. C. R. 2.

Joshua, and Deborah Davis, Feb. 18, 1796.*

Lawrence, of Charlestown, and Eliza Turner, Nov. 22, 1821.*

Lemuel, and Cynthia Fisher of Newton, int. July 20, 1806.

Lemuel, and Beulah Stone of Newton, int. May 29, 1814.

Lemuel, and Mary Osgood, May 6. 1819. C. R. 2.*

Lemuel, of Concord, and Eliza Lyon, int. Mar. 17, 1822.

Lemuel [jr. int.], a. 25 y., currier, s. Lemuel and Mary, and Elizabeth Howe, a. 23 y., d. Alvin and Betsey, Dec. 10, 1846.*

Levi, and Anny Richards [Amelia Richard of Cambridge. int.], at Cambridge, Aug. 1, 1799.*

Lidia, and Nathan[ie]l Davis, Oct. 15, 1761.

Lucy, Mrs., and Joseph Mayo, jr. of Warwick, Mar. 12, 1772.

Lucy, and Anson Dexter, Nov. 19, 1834.*

Lucy S., of Dedham, and Joseph M. Weld, int. Apr. 30, 1809.

Martha W., and Joshua Hayes, Nov. 13, 1836.*

Mary, of Dedham, and John Talman, at Dedham, Jan. 5, 1709-10.

Mary, and Nathaniel Stearns of Warwick, May 27, 1773.

* Intention also recorded.

RICHARDS, Mary, and John Broad, Sept. 30, 1801. c. r. 2.*
Mary, of Dedham, and Charles F. Gore, int. Sept. 27, 1829.
Mary F., and Horace Parmenter, Jan. 1, 1832.
Mary P., and Charles Clap of Dorchester, int. Sept. 19, 1846.
Meletiah [Mrs. int.], and Moses Griggs of Cambridge, Aug.
    18, 1785.*
Molly, and Nathan[ie]l Wheeton, Oct. 7, 1759.
Moses, of Charlestown, and Sarah Curtis, Nov. 24, 1825.*
Nathaniel, and Sally Wilson [Salley Willson. int.] of New-
    ton, at Newton, Sept. 5, 1790.*
Nathaniel, and Mary Murdock, June 9, 1814. c. r. 2.*
Natha[nae]ll, and Mary Colburn, Aug. 12, 1736.
Nathan[ie]ll, and Mary Whiting, Jan. 19, 1748-9.
Olive, and Lewis Morse, Jan. 2, 1803.*
Paul Dudley, and Anna Mayo, June 20, 1776.
Polly, and Caleb Mayo, Oct. 17, 1776.
Prudence, and Tho[ma]s Griggs, int. Oct. 19, 1783.
Rebecca [Rebekah. int.], and William Draper, Aug. 13, 1782.
    c. r. 2.*
Rebecca, and William Cheney, July 14, 1811. c. r. 2.*
Sally, of Dedham, and John W. Child, int. Mar. 9, 1817.
Sarah, of Dedham, and Eben[eze]r Dewing, int. Apr. 30,
    1809.
Sarah, and Nelson Marble, Feb. 21, 1826. c. r. 2.*
Sarah Jane, and George Lane Otis, int. July 5, 1848.
Thomas D[avis. c. r. 2.], and Salome Noyes, Apr. 24, 1831.*
William, and Elizabeth Baker, May 30, 1733.
——, and Mr. —— Whitney, of Boston, Feb. 9, 1845. c. r. 3.

**RICHARDSON,** Abigail, and Thomas Rumrill, Nov. 9, 1793.*
Abijah, of Turner, Me., a. 24 y., s. Cornelius T. and Sarah
    R., and Caroline Williams, a. 27 y., d. Sam[ue]l S. and
    Lucy, Jan. 23, 1848.*
Amos H., and Susan S. Blodgett of Lexington, int. Aug. 18,
    1844.
Anna, Mrs., and Samuell Bayley, Dec. 17, 1730.
Atwell, and Lois F. Dillingham of Turner, Me., int. Oct. 31,
    1841.
Charlotte, and Reuben Davis, Feb. 18, 1819.*
Ellen M., a. 18 y., d. Josiah and Martha, and John M. Mar-
    ston, a. 28 y., carpenter, s. John and Jerusha, of Portland,
    Me., Nov. 19, 1846.*
Frances L., and George Fracker, int. Oct. 26, 1828.

* Intention also recorded.

RICHARDSON, George W., and Ann Croak, int. Nov. 9, 1828.

Harriet, of Medford, and Edward L. Staniels, int. Dec. 4, 1825.

Henry H., and Celia F. Marsh, June 14, 1842.*

Isabella, and William Gill, int. Apr. 12, 1846.

John, and Susannah Perrin, Apr. 25, 1745.

John, and Mary Trumbull Doyle, Oct. 19, 1818.*

John, and Ellen W. Cunningham, int. Feb. 27, 1846.

John, and Mercy Maria Ames of Belfast, Me., int. Nov. 5, 1846.

John S., a. 27 y., laborer, s. W[illia]m and Mary, and Mary E. Dow, a. 23 y., d. Alfred and Sarah, Feb. 19, 1848.*

Joseph, and Abigail Felton, Jan. 27, 1774.

Josiah, and Martha Wentworth, Apr. 26, 1812.*

Josiah, widr., gentleman, and Hannah M. Wentworth, wid., Jan. 9, 1848.*

Lauraette, and Daniel Jackson, int. Oct. 18, 1835.

Louisa, and William Henry Dean, int. Mar. 25, 1832.

Lucy O., and Augostino Frumento [residents. int.], Sept. 12, 1804.*

Luther, and Susanna Craft, Aug. 3, 1803.*

Manley, and Rebeccah Trask, int. Nov. 9, 1828.

Mary, and Isaac Jaques, Mar. 1, 1812.*

Mary E., of Acton, and Charles D. Lothrop, int. Aug. 11, 1839.

Mary E., and Gilbert Parmlee, Oct. 13, 1844.

Moses, and Experience Fisher of Dedham, at Dedham, Oct. 4, 1770.

Nabby [Heath. int.], and Zabdiel Adams, May 23, 1813.*

Nathanael, and Abigail Stevens, Oct. 6, 1741.

Oliver A., of Lowell, and Mary R. Brigham, Jan. 23, 1834.

Philander [Phylindia. int.], and James W. Averill, Dec. 3, 1843.*

Rebecca, and Nathaniel Livermore, July 14, 1814.*

Ruby A., and Charles Clark, Aug. 9, 1840.*

Susannah, and Eben[eze]r Gore, Feb. 21, 1745. C. R. 2.

Susannah, and James How, Dec. 28, 1773.

Susannah, Mrs., and Elisha Hathaway, June 1, 1814.*

Theodore S., and Anna S. Cole of Lynn, int. Mar. 25, 1848.

RICHEE (see also Ritchie), Frances, and Mary Newel, May 25, 1727.

* Intention also recorded.

**RICHMOND,** Andrew [jr. int.], of Halifax, and Harriet J. Waterman of Halifax, Dec. 1, 1836.*

**RICKER** (see also Rieker), George W., farmer, s. Henry and Margarett, and Cynthia Coburn [Colburn. int.], d. Phineas and Cynthia, Dec. 11, 1848.*

**RIDER** (see also Ryder), Ann Maria, and Hervey D. Allen, Dec. 22, 1844.
Joseph, and Sarah E. Hyde of Newton, int. Apr. 7, 1849.

**RIDING,** Sophia, and Benj[ami]n Swain, Aug. 8, 1841.*

**RIEKER** (see also Ricker), Harriet, and John Loud, int. Sept. 12, 1841.
Usula, and John G. Hill, int. Apr. 25, 1841.

**RIGAN** (see also Regan), Cornelius, and Mary Donagan, int. Aug. 28, 1847.

**RIGBEY,** Caroline, and Michael McGee, int. Apr. 17, 1842.

**RIGELLS,** Rebeka, and Israel Reade of Rehoboth, at Rehoboth, Nov. 5, 1684.

**RIGGS,** Edward, and Elizabeth Roosa, Apr. 5, 1635.

**RIGNEY,** Martin, and Mary Harrington, int. June 26, 1848.

**RILEY** (see also Reilly), Ann, and Timothy Maconey [Maroney. int.], Oct. 16, 1848.*
Elizabeth, and Samuel Carroll [Caroll. int.], Sept. 18, 1806. C. R. 2.*
James, and Avis Gorton of Charleston, int. June 15, 1823.
Margaret, and Andrew Allen, Mar. 12, 1806.*
Margarett, and Lawrence Johnson of Boston, int. Oct. 29, 1846.
Thomas, and Catherine Kelley, int. Apr. 24, 1848.

**RIORDIN,** Robert, and Mary Leamy, int. Nov. 2, 1848.

**RIPLEY,** Betsey F. M., and Charles C. Nichols, Nov. 3, 1845.*
Elizabeth P., and Jonas Gilson, Oct. 7, 1813.*
Relief, and Peter Gray, Apr. 24, 1806.*

**RITCHIE** (see also Richee), Andrew, of Boston, and Maria Durant, Mar. 27, 1807.*

* Intention also recorded.

ROACH, Catherine, and James Bradley, int. Apr. 18, 1848.

ROAN, John, and Ann Brady, int. Feb. 7, 1848.

ROARK (see also Rourke), Patrick, and Mary Mullen, int. Dec. 30, 1847.

ROBBINS (see also Robins), Aaron, and Sarah Beard, Feb. 9, 1817.*
Alvin M., and Caroline Kyes, int. Oct. 18, 1840.
Benjamin, and Elizabeth Ann Henderson, int. May 29, 1842.
Betsy, and Daniel Vaughan, Feb. 11, 1808.*
Chandler, Rev., and Mary Eliza Frothingham, int. Nov. 28, 1833.
Chloe, of Dorchester, and Albert Knight, Apr. 2, 1840.*
Clarissa A., and Charles Southworth, int. Dec. 6, 1835.
Edward J., and Mary H. Curtis, Mar. 5, 1805.*
Edward J., and Elizabeth Curtis, int. Sept. 29, 1822.
Elisha, and P. Morse of Natick, int. Dec. 30, 1804.
Elmira, and Robert Louger of Quincy, Apr. 7, 1835.
Harriet F., and Joseph Hills, Sept. 13, 1838.*
Henry, and Clarissa Rand of Weston, int. Feb. 26, 1826.
Jeremiah [Robbens. int.], and Rebekah Stratten, Oct. 8, 1798.
    C. R. 2.*
Joseph Willet, a. 23 y., clerk, s. Edward J. and Elizabeth, and Mary Woodward Gray, a. 20 y., d. Alfred T. and Mary W., Apr. 7, 1847.*
Lydia, and Wyman Wakefield, int. Mar. 4, 1810.
Maria, of Brighton, and Thomas Hastings, int. Nov. 7, 1813.
Mary, and Samuel Lyon, at Cambridge, Nov. 24, 1742.
Mary, of Lowell, and Aaron D. Vose, int. Apr. 25, 1841.
Nancy, and Abraham Sanborn of Lower Canada, Dec. 16, 1835.*
Peter Gilman, Dr., and Mrs. Polly Hooper, Dec. 11, 1818.*
Sally, and Robert Bancroft, July 20, 1818.*
Sarah, of Cambridge, and John Williams, int. May 22, 1804.
Sarah, and Nathaniel Ellis, Dec. 9, 1804.*
Sarah D., and Daniel Knox, June 14, 1818.*
Sarah W., and Henry J. Williams. Oct. 25, 1838.*
Williams, and Sarah Burrill [Burrell. int.], May 14, 1797.
    C. R. 3.*

ROBERTS, Abigail, and James H. Bean, int. Aug. 26, 1832.
George, and Louisa Hood, July 14, 1844.*

* Intention also recorded.

ROBERTS, Georgette Augusta, and James Robinson of New York, int. May 29, 1842.
Maria I. [J. int.], and Charles Odall, July 13, 1834.*
Nathaniel, and Elcedania S. Jewell, int. Aug. 26, 1832.
Samuel, of Quincy, and Olive A. Stetson, int. Oct. 5, 1845.

**ROBERTSON,** Andrew, and Harriet Gardner of Dorchester, int. May 7, 1826.
Eliza V., and John McCormick of Norton, int. Jan. 13, 1849.
Harriet, Mrs., and Joseph H. Gardner, Oct. 4, 1835.*

**ROBEY** (see also Roby), Betsey C., of Chichester, N. H., and Thomas W. Tucker, int. Dec. 14, 1834.

**ROBINS** (see also Robbins), Jane L. [Robbins. int.], and Richard G. Jacobs, Mar. 26, 1846.*

**ROBINSON** (see also Robison), Edward, and Rachel Howe, jr., both of Dorchester, Dec. 6, 1793.
Elisabeth, and John Stevens, ——, 1749. [Jan. 11, 1749-50. C. R. 2.]
George, a. 24 y., carpenter, s. Stephen and G., and Susan Jane Averill, a. 18 y., d. Nathaniel and Ann, Aug. 9, 1846.*
Henry, and Sarah Dudley Rumrill, int. Apr. 24, 1831.
Henry A., and Rebecca F. Anderson, Oct. 26, 1845.*
Henry W., a. 24 y., clerk, s. Jon[atha]n P. and Catherine, and Sarah R. Ward, a. 23 y., d. Richard and Lucy, July 22, 1846.*
Jacob, and Elizabeth Draper, Jan. 21 [Feb. 23. C. R. 2.], 1764.
James, and Patience Ruggles, July 3, 1711.
James, Capt., and Mary Withington, both of Dorchester, Dec. 5, 1793.
James, of New York, and Georgette Augusta Roberts, int. May 29, 1842.
Jane K., of Brookline, and Asa Bugbee, int. Apr. 23, 1820.
John, of Dorchester, and Mrs. Susanna Williams, May 11, 1727.
John, and Elizabeth [S. int.] Lombard of Dedham, May 9, 1827.*
John, a. 23 y., blacksmith, s. John and Lucy, and Emeline A. Bowman, a. 19 y., d. Brooks and A., July 21, 1847.*
John, a. 22 y., cabinet maker, s. Robert and Lilias, and Grace O[livia. int.] Langstaff, a. 20 y., d. Thomas and Thankful, Nov. 26, 1848.*

* Intention also recorded.

Robinson, Jonathan, and Anna Jennings, Nov. 25, 1795.*

Kate, [Robertson. int.], a. 19 y., d. Andrew and Harriet, and Thomas Philip Haviland [of Boston. int.], a. 22 y., clerk, s. Thomas and Mary, May 12, 1847.*

Margrett, and John Lane, Mar. 30, 1767.

Sarah, of Dorchester, and John Mears, int. Aug. 17, 1794.

Sarah Breck [Brick. int.], of Dorchester, and Lewis Withington, at Dorchester, Nov. 12, 1795.*

Sarah S., of Hartford, Me., and John Thomas, int. Apr. 13, 1847.

Susanna [Sukey. int.], of Dorchester, and John Clap, at Dorchester, Nov. 20, 1794.*

T. Lewis, and Hannah V. Durfee of Fall River, int. Oct. 28, 1848.

William, a. 21 y., bricklayer, s. James and Jane, and Jane Nichols, a. 27 y., d. Isaac and Esther, June 30, 1849.

——, Mrs., and Jonathan Ireland, Mar. 6, 1745-6.

**ROBISON** (see also Robinson), Robert, and Katharine Clark, at Boston, May 17, 1764.

——, wid., and Griffin Craft, at Dorchester, 15 : 5 m : 1673.

**ROBY** (see also Robey), Ann, of East Sudbury, and John Brown, at East Sudbury, Apr. 15, 1798.*

Rebecca [Rebekah. c. r. 3.] G., of Chichester, N. H., and William W. Kaime [Kaine. c. r. 3.], Dec. 3, 1835.*

Sally S[wift. int.], and Thomas Huxford of Boston, Dec. 13, 1801.*

**ROCK,** Bridget, and Andrew McGettrick, int. May 3, 1848.

**ROCKFORT,** Anna, and John Young, Oct. 12, 1848.*

**RODER,** Abigail, and Abraham Newell, s. Abraham, July 21 1681.

**RODGERS** (see also Rogers), Ammon, Capt., and Mary Nichols, Mar. 25, 1827.*

Jane, b. Ireland, and John Gorman, b. Ireland, Sept. 6, 1849.*

Patrick, and Catharine Murrey, int. July 29, 1827.

**ROE** (see also Rowe), Hanna, and Thomas Reeve, Apr. 15, 1645.

Hannah, Mrs., and Simon Brigham, int. ——, 1804.

* Intention also recorded.

**ROGERS** (see also Rodgers), Catharine, and James Flemming, int. Apr. 9, 1843.
Daniel, and Sarah Mansor, Nov. 16, 1741.
Dorcas, and Joseph Simpson, Oct. 11, 1728.
Hannah, and Samuel Weld, June 22, 1749.
Jeremiah, and Elizabeth Hemingway, Jan. 7, 1702-3.
Margaret, and John Brewer, at Boston, June 30, 1737.
Margaret, and Bartholomew Kelly, int. May 5, 1844.
Martha M., and George F. Bartlett, Sept. 2, 1824.*
Mary, and Shubal Sever, jr., July 4, 1734.
Mary Ann, and Edward W. Parker, Oct. 16, 1825.*
Shubael G., jr., and Susan G. Snow, Sept. 4, 1834.*
Simon, and Mrs. Elizabeth Bowen, July 10, 1728.
Simon, and Martha Ruggles, Dec. 22, 1737.
Stephen J., of Boston, and Mary J. McCarty, int. May 18, 1849.

**ROGOSKI,** Theodore, and Elisa Jane Tucker, int. May 8, 1846.

**ROLLINS** (see also Rawlins), Maria F., and William Watts, int. June 19, 1831.
Mary B., and William Sloan, Oct. 25, 1830.*

**RONEY** (see also Rooney), Mary, and Patrick McDonough, int. Nov. 15, 1849.

**RONNEY** (see also Rooney), Bernard, and Bridget Flood, int. May 4, 1845.

**ROOK,** William H., and Sarah C. Butler of Pelham, N. H., int. Sept. 16, 1848.

**ROONEY** (see also Roney, Ronney, Runey), Edward, and Bridget Brinnen, int. Dec. 29, 1846.

**ROONIJEN,** Francis, and Mary Hughes, int. Sept. 22, 1848.

**ROOSA,** Elizabeth, and Edward Riggs, Apr. 5, 1635.

**ROPES,** Benjamin H., and Amanda P. Bowers, int. June 3, 1838.
Charles B., and Rebecca Stevens, Nov. 21, 1839.*

**ROSEMEYER,** Conrad H., and Sarah B. Harrington of Lexington, Nov. 29, 1838.*

* Intention also recorded.

**ROSS** (see also Rouse, Ruse), Alice, and Josiah Crosby, int.
Dec. 11, 1842.
Elizabeth, of Deering, N. H., and Luther Sumner, int. Sept.
27, 1829.
John, and Catharine Monroe [Munroe. c. r. 3.], Feb. 7, 1833.*
Lydia D., Mrs., and Francis Raymond, May 3, 1830.*
Margarett M., and James Draper, int. Mar. 5, 1849.
Nabby, of Jaffrey, N. H., and Henry S. Ward, int. Aug. 1,
1830.
Nahum R., of Troy, N. Y., a. 30 y., machinist, and Emeline H.
Trask, a. 25 y., d. John and Sarah, May 26, 1847.*
Williamina, and Rainsford A. Cole of Utica, N. Y., int. Dec.
31, 1849.

**ROURK** (see also Rourke), Catherine, and Michael Gorman,
int. Aug. 13, 1849.

**ROURKE** (see also Roark, Rourk), Bridget, and William
Mullen, int. Sept. 27, 1848.

**ROUSE** (see also Ross), Mary, Mrs., and Nathan F. Perry,
Sept. 12, 1824.*
Oliver, and Mary Goodwin, Nov. 4, 1810.*

**ROWE** (see also Roe), David P., and Mary Worthen, July
26, 1837.*
John P., and Eliza S. Sanford [of Cambridge. int.], Jan. 1,
1844.*
Mary J., and Samuel S. [L. int.] Willard, May 4, 1845.*

**ROWELL,** Sarah, and Nathan H. Glines, Apr. 16, 1820.*

**RUDDY,** James, and Bridget Davis, int. Oct. 23, 1842.

**RUFLEY,** Henry G., and Leticia A. Miller, int. Sept. 1, 1844.

**RUGG,** Elizabeth A., of Charlestown, and Joseph L. Swift, int.
Apr. 23, 1837.

**RUGGLE** (see also Ruggles), John, jr., and Mary Gibson,
Apr. 3, 1655
Sam[ue]ll, and Hannah Fowles, 10 m : 11 m : 1654 CT. R.

**RUGGLES** (see also Ruggle), Abigail, and Edward Dorr,
Aug. 9, 1744.
Edward, and Hannah Craft, Jan. 24, 1715-16.

* Intention also recorded.

RUGGLES, Edward, and Mrs. Abigail Williams, Jan. 11, 1732-3.

Elizabeth, Mrs., and Joseph Heath, Esq., June 9, 1743.

Elizabeth, and Samuel Perrin, Mar. 21, 1744-5.

Elizabeth, and John Stack, Feb. 28, 1754.

Fanny, and [Dr. int.] James H. Sargent [of Fort Independence, Boston Harbor. int.], Feb. 26, 1812.*

Hannah, and William Noyse, Dec. 17, 1712.

Hannah, and John Ackers, May 26, 1715.

Hannah, and Robert Pierpont, May 25, 1738.

Hulda, and Samuel Hill, June 9, 1709.

Joanna, and Noah Perrin, June 4, 1745.

John, and Abigaile Crafts, Jan. 24, 1650.

John, jr., and Martha Devotion, Sept. 2, 1674.

John, jr., and Hannah Devotion, May 1, 1679.

John, sr., and Sarah Dyer of Weymouth, Mar. 15, 1674-5.

John, Sergt., and Elizabeth Verry, Feb. 12, 1700-1701.

John, and Sarah Feilder, May 24, 1704.

John, and Elisabeth Weld, Aug. 11, 1731.

John, and Mrs. Katherine Williams, Jan. 20, 1741-2.

Joseph, and Joanna White of Brookline, Oct. 20, 1720.

Joseph, and Rebeckah Curtis, Oct. 20, 1748.

Joseph, and Joanna Williams, Dec. 3, 1778.

Joseph, and Mrs. Rebecca Pearce of Dorchester, int. Oct. 6, 1811.

Julia F., and Benjamin F. Copeland, Nov. —, 1823.*

Katharine, and William Tucker of Milton, at Milton [Jan. 19. dup], 1758.

Luce, and Joseph Stevens, Feb. 15, 1715-16.

Lucy, and Jacob Gould, May 26, 1796.*

Martha, Mrs., and Job Lane, at Billerica, Dec. 16 [17. dup.], 1713.

Martha, and Simon Rogers, Dec. 22, 1737.

Martha [Mrs. int.], and Rev. John Fairfield of Pepperelborough, Sept. 15, 1785.*

Martha F., and David A. Simmons, Esq., June 27, 1820.*

Mary, d. John, sr., and John Searle, June 6, 1682.

Mary, and Ebenezer Pierpoint, Oct. 20, 1692.

Mary, and John Paine of Dedham, at Dedham, Apr. 21, 1704.

Mary, and Joseph Weld, Feb. 17, 1757.

Mary Ann C., of Wrentham, and David M. Draper, int. Mar. 19, 1837.

Nancy, and Joseph Dorr, Feb. 16, 1769.

* Intention also recorded.

RUGGLES, Nancy, and Obadiah Wright, Aug. 13, 1797.*
Nath[anie]l, and Martha Williams, Dec. 8, 1767.
Nathaniel, and Salley Fellows, int. Sept. 10, 1786.
Patience, and James Robinson, July 3, 1711.
Patty, and Rev. Eliphalet Porter, Oct. 1, 1801. C. R. 2.*
Rebecca, and John Bracket, Apr. 10, 1705.
Rebecca, Mrs., and Capt. Ezekiel How, Dec. 22, 1772.
Samuell, and Hanna Fowles, Jan. 10, 1654.
Samuell, and Anna Bright, May 26, 1670.
Samuell, jr., and Martha Woodbridge, July 8, 1680.
Sam[ue]ll, Rev., of Billerica, and Mrs. Eliz[abe]th Williams,
     Apr. 18, 1728.
Sarah, and William Lion, June 17, 1646.
Sarah, Mrs., and John Holbrooke, Aug. 19, 1714.
Sarah, and Samuel Smith, Nov. 23, 1715.
Sarah, and Hezekiah Turner, July 14, 1725.
Sarah, and Thomas Cole, Apr. 3, 1732.
Sarah, and Ralph Smith, Nov. 25, 1779.
Susanna, and Joseph Jackson, Dec. 11, 1755.

**RULLY,** Thomas, and Ann Tormey, int. June 19, 1845.

**RUMMERILL** (see also Rumrill), Aaron, and Mary Goodwin
     [Nancy, of Cambridge. int.], at Cambridge, June 23,
     1799.*

**RUMRIL** (see also Rumrill), Elisabeth C., and George Young,
     Oct. 17, 1844.
Martha, and Adam Morse, Dec. 1, 1811. C. R. 2.*

**RUMRILL** (see also Rummerill, Rumril), Caroline R., and
     Simon Hutchins, int. Nov. 3, 1833.
Caroline R., and David Foot of Bath, Me., int. Sept. 3, 1837.
Charles, and Mary Livermore, Nov. 22, 1821.*
Clarissa, Mrs., and Valentine Bunker, Jan. 29, 1826.*
Clarissa W., and Otho H. Littlefield, int. Aug. 17, 1834.
Elizabeth C., and George Young, int. Sept. 29, 1844.
Harriet G., and Nason P. Caswell, int. Nov. 12, 1837.
Louisa P., and John Burton, Nov. 10, 1812.*
Matilda, and Nath[anie]l Lawrence, June 22, 1823.*
Mary B., and John Watts, int. Mar. 14, 1830.
Samuel [Samuell. int.], and Clarissa Gale, Dec. 2, 1810. C.
     R. 2.*

* Intention also recorded.

RUMRILL, Samuel D., and Jane R. Atwood of Frankfort, Me.,
    int. July 25, 1846.
Sarah Dudley, and Henry Robinson, int. Apr. 24, 1831.
Thomas, and Abigail Richardson, Nov. 9, 1793.*
Thomas, and Mrs. Sarah Fellowes, Aug. —, 1803.*
William, and Nancy Young, June 13, 1841.*

RUMRY, Aaron, and Elizabeth Clap, Apr. 1, 1762.

RUNDLET, Lucinda, and Benjamin F. Wright, Oct. 22,
    1833.*
Simeon, and Bethiah R. Meed, int. Apr. 12, 1835.

RUNEY (see also Rooney), James, and Catherine Flood, int.
    Oct. 14, 1847.

RUSE (see also Ross), Henry, of Hartford, Conn., and Es-
    ther Spear of Boston, Oct. 21, 1831. c. r. 3.

RUSSELL, Edward, and Elizabeth Payson, May 20, 1809.
    c. r. 2.*
Eliza Ann, and Erick Magnus Hulton, Mar. 8, 1840.*
Elizabeth C., and James Gautt of Sandwich, Feb. 3, 1830.
Henry, and Margaret T. Daragh, int. Feb. 6, 1847.
Israel D., and Nancy C. Kimball of Hallowell, Me., int. Oct.
    9, 1847.
James W., and Maria B. Barker, int. Aug. 14, 1831.
Joanna F., of Dedham, and Simeon D. Butler, Aug. 31, 1843.
    c. r. 7.
John, and Sarah Symonds, Aug. 31, 1794.*
Josiah M., and Susan M. Haynes, May 28, 1843.*
Mary C., and George Platt of New York City, Nov. 19, 1839.*
Philemon R., of Charlestown, and Ann Lewis, Dec. 30, 1822.*
Sarah [Russel. dup; of Boston. c. r. 5.], and Simeon But-
    ler, of Chelsea, July 29, 1848.
True, and Abigail S. Thayer, int. Sept. 7, 1839.
True, and Susan Pratt of North Yarmouth, Me., int. Jan. 1,
    1849.

RUST, Hannah M., a. 21 y., d. Abednego and Hannah, and
    Charles Williams, a. 22 y., clerk, s. Sam[ue]l S. and Lucy,
    June 8, 1848.*
Nathaniel P., and Sarah A. Stodder of Lowell, int. Apr. 1,
    1848.

* Intention also recorded.

RYAN, Alice, and Thomas Savage, int. Oct. 1, 1843.
Charles H., a. 23 y., carpenter, and Mary E. Ward, a. 18 y.,
Jan. 17, 1847.*
Edward, and Bridget Stanton, int. Mar. 23, 1845.
Ellen, and Mathew Monks, int. Nov. 4, 1846.
Hannah, and Maurice Healy, int. Feb. 17, 1848.
James, and Margaret Chamberlain of Newton, at Newton,
June 6, 1771.
Luretta, and Charles C. Josselyn, Mar. 19, 1838.*
Margaret, and James Dawson, int. Sept. 18, 1847.
Mary, and Samuel Thompson, int. May 2, 1848.

RYDER (see also Rider), Elisabeth, of Boston, and Frederick Pilleps, int. July 23, 1846.

RYERSON, Louisa A., a. 1 8 y., d. Eben[eze]r and Mary, and
Asa Wyman, jr., a. 24 y., wood dealer, s. Asa and Esther,
Aug. 2, 1847.*
Lucy L., and Simeon Stubbs, int. Dec. 11, 1846.

SABIN, Benjamin, and Sarah Parker, July 5, 1678.
Benjamin, and Elizabeth. ———, ———, 1700.
Josiah, and Rebecca Cheny, June 18, 1701.
Rebecca, Mrs., and Moses Davis, May 13, 1731.

SABLES (see also Savell), Hannah, and Joseph Corey, Sept.
10, 1752.
John [Savels. int.], of Dorchester, and Esther Sumner, at
Dorchester, Mar. 1, 1798.*

SAFFORD (see also Stafford), Pliny, Dr., of Westminster,
Vt., and Sophia Smith, Feb. 25, 1824.*

SALLER, William, jr., and Elizabeth Capell of Newton, at
Newton, Apr. 20, 1773.

SALMON, Francis S., and Martha S. Maccarty, Apr. 1, 1831.*
John S., and Nancy Faxon of Quincy, int. Feb. 4, 1847.
Martha Jane M., and William Maccarty, int. Mar. 4, 1832.

SALTER, Mary, and Lemuel Wood, Mar. 31 [13. c. r. 2.],
1768.
Sally, of Watertown, and Daniel Skudder, Nov. 22, 1801.
William, and Mary Wilson, May 15, 1746.

* Intention also recorded.

SAMPSON, Betsey [resident. int.], and Samuel Tyler of Attleborough, Sept. 11, 1811.*

Calvin, and Hebsibah Lethbridge of Franklin, int. May 31, 1818.

George, and Mary Nichols of Cohasset, int. Aug. 22, 1813. [Nov. 6, 1814. dup.]

Hepza Dana, and Dudley Andrews, May 5, 1816.*

Ichabod, and Elizabeth M. Griffin, Jan. 4, 1845.*

Joshua, and Mrs. Nancy Davenport, int. Aug. 23, 1829.

Lephy, and Jesse Winch, int. Mar. 23, 1806.

Mary, and Jacob Skinner, Nov. 7, 1802.*

Sally, and Charles Hayt, Sept. 23, 1807.*

Sarah F., of Weymouth, a. 18 y., d. Sarah, and Daniel S. Francis. a. 20 y., merchant, s. Thomas D. and Martha E., Nov. 15, 1846.*

Stephen, and Mary Morse, Oct. 11, 1805.*

Theodore A., and Emily Litchfield, Feb. 6, 1845.*

SANBORN, (see also Sanburn), Abraham, of Lower Canada, and Nancy Robbins, Dec. 16, 1835.*

Abraham S., and Clarissa Buzzard, int. Oct. 5, 1817.

Caroline M. [Sanborne. c. r. 3.], and John Neal [of Boston. c. r. 3.], Jan. 19, 1843.

Charles, and Mary Ann Wilds, June 16, 1825.

Emma R., of Boston, and George W. Chamberlain, int. Dec. 8, 1847.

Jeremiah, and Caroline Basford, Jan. 11, 1831.*

Mary L., a. 17 y., d. Shubael and Mary, and Joseph Bailey, jr., a. 24 y., carpenter, s. Joseph and Sarah, Nov. 26, 1846.*

Shubael, and Mary Leeds Child, Mar. 23, 1828. c. r. 2.*

Solomon, and Elizabeth Wright, May 4, 1845.*

SANBURN (see also Sanborn), Abraham [Sanborn. int.], and Rebecca Swallow, Mar. 6, 1825. c. r. 2.*

SANCY (see also Sanery), Sarah F. [Sanery. int.], a. 18 y., d. Francis and Elizabeth, and Charles E. Lang, a. 22 y., painter, s. Edward and Eliza, Nov. 23, 1848.*

SANDERS (see also Saunders), John, and Mary Pelton of Dorchester, Mar. 12, 1704-5.

Susannah, Mrs., and Ebenezer Newell, Feb. 25, 1741-2.

* Intention also recorded.

**SANDERSON** (see also Saunderson), Anna [Saunderson. int.], of Weston, and Jerimiah Haws, at Weston, Dec. 16, 1794.*

Betsey, of Charlestown, and John White, jr., int. Feb. 13, 1814.

James, and Esther A. Davidson, int. July 28, 1849.

Lucy, and Simon Hutchings, int. Oct. 23, 1834.

Sophia, of Brighton, and John H. Pierce, int. June 8, 1828.

**SANDS,** Mary Hoxie, of New Shoreham, R. I., and Henry W. Greene, int. June 17, 1848.

**SANE,** Catharine, and Nicholas Four, int. Jan. 5, 1845.

**SANERY** (see also Sancy), Catharine, and Hendrick Hall, June 24, 1834.*

**SANFORD** (see also Stanford), Eliza S. [of Cambridge. int.], and John P. Rowe, Jan. 1, 1844.*

John, and Lucy Ann Dager, July 3, 1834.*

**SANGER,** Rebeckah, of Sherburne, and Benjamin Capen, int. Oct. 27, 1822.

**SARCHFIELD,** Anne, and John Lane, int. May 19, 1844.

**SARGENT** (see also Serjeant), Eliza Jane, and Charles Brown, int. Oct. 5, 1845.

Epes, jr., a. 34 y., editor of daily transcript, s. Epes and Hannah, and Elizabeth W. Weld, a. 28 y., d. Sam[ue]l H. and Nancy, May 10, 1848.*

James H. [Dr. of Fort Independence Boston Harbor. int.], and Fanny Ruggles, Feb. 26, 1812.*

Lucius Manlius, [jr. int.], a. 20 y., artist, s. L. M. and Sarah C., and Letitia Sullivan Amory, a. 17 y., d. Jon[atha]n and Letitia, Sept. 22, 1847.*

William P., and Sophia Sweet, int. Sept. 14, 1834.

**SAUNDER** (see also Saunders), Emeline, of Livermore, Me., and William M. Poole, int. Nov. 1, 1840.

**SAUNDERS** (see also Sanders, Saunder), Abigail, and James Jervis, both residents, Aug. 14, 1732.

Daniel, and Sarah Cunningham, July 9, 1778.

Sampson, and Catharine South, July 11, 1836.

**SAUNDERSON** (see also Sanderson), Jacob, of Charlestown, and Mrs. Lucy Pitts, int. May 19, 1805.

* Intention also recorded.

**SAVAGE,** Allis, and Richard Welsh, int. Oct. 6, 1844.
Isabella, and Edmund Fisher, Apr. 24, 1844.*
Jesse, and Charlotte Harris, int. Dec. 3, 1815.
John, and Anna Caswell of Berkley, int. Feb. 23, 1812.
Mary A., and Josiah F. Day, int. Mar. 17, 1822.
Patrick, and Ann Duffy, int. Apr. 30, 1843.
Thomas, and Alice Ryan, int. Oct. 1, 1843.

**SAVELL** (see also Sables, Savels), Benjamin, and Mary
Bridge. Jan. 10, 1716-17.

**SAVELS** (see also Savell), Sarah, and Joseph Coney of
Stoughton, at Stoughton, Sept. 1, 1748.

**SAVENS,** Mehitable S., and Louisa Foliett, Apr. 1, 1839.*

**SAVERY,** Edward, and Lydia Darling of Marlborough, int.
Dec. 24, 1809.
Minerva [Severy. int.], and John T. Sinclair, Dec. 27, 1843.*
Waitstill A., of Carver, and George P. Bowers, int. Sept. 29,
1844.

**SAVOR** (see also Seaver), Caleb [Sever. dup.], and Sarah
Englesbie [Inglesby. dup.], at Charlestown, Dec. 15,
1671.

**SAWIN,** John Pierce, and Abigail Patridge, Dec. 16, 1798.*

**SAWYER** (see also Sayer), Achsah, and Joseph L. Keith, int.
Sept. 13, 1812.
Eliza S., a. 38 y. tailoress, and William Stanley, widr. a. 48 y.,
engineer, s. Thomas and Mary. Apr. 29, 1844.*
Jane M., and Benjamin Celley, int. Feb. 19, 1837.
John, and Mary C. Clarke of Exeter, N. H., int. Feb. 16, 1845.
Joseph, and Mary Hickey, int. Dec. 4, 1849.
Ruth, and Thomas Cheney, Feb. 5, 1829.*

**SAXTON** (see also Sexton), J. P., and Nancy Burke, int. July
31, 1847.

**SAYER** (see also Swayer), Mary A. G., and Leonard J. Wilson of Milford, N. H., Nov. 26, 1849.*

**SCALE,** Patrick, and Mary McLaughlin, int. June 5, 1848.

**SCANDLIN** (see also Scanlan), Martin, and Ellen Carney,
int. Nov. 9, 1848.

* Intention also recorded.

**SCANLAN** (see also Scandlin), Burnet, b. Ireland, and Ellen
Falley, b. Ireland, May 25, 1849.

**SCARBOROUGH** (see also Scarbrough), William, and Mrs.
Elizabeth Richards of Dedham, at Dedham, June 19,
1765.

**SCARBOROW** (see also Scarbrough), Mary, and Phillip
Tory, Oct. 1, 1647.

**SCARBRO** (see also Scarbrough), Samuell, and Mrs. Sarah
Mayo, Feb. 10, 1730-31.

**SCARBROUGH** (see also Scarborough, Scarborow, Scarbro),
Bethiah, Mrs., and Rev. Charles Gleason, Nov. 5, 1747.
Katherine, and Edward Pason of Dorchester, July 14, 1720.
Mary, and Timothy Parker, Sept. 8, 1718.
Samuel, and Theoda Williams, Feb. 5, 1706.

**SCEARALF**, Barbe, and Nicholas Homme, int. Oct. 24, 1845.

**SCELLY**, Thomas, and Ann Farrell, int. May 31, 1848.

**SCHIELDS** (see also Shields), Catherine, of Boston, and
William Sullivan, int. Sept. 24, 1847.

**SCHNEIDER**, Jacob, and Amelia Jons, int. Mar. 16, 1845.
Jacob, and Hennretta Friedricks, int. Aug. 17, 1845.

**SCHUH**, John George, and Joanna Lizette Schulthers, int.
Sept. 21, 1846.

**SCHULTHERS**, Joanna Lizette, and John George Schuh, int.
Sept. 1, 1846.

**SCHWARZWALDER**, John George, and Augusta Elizabeth
Haas, int. July 6, 1848.

**SCHWAZ**, Charles, and V[irginia. int.] Catharine Baldner,
Aug. 8, 1839.*

**SCHWENN**, Lewis, and Elizabeth Kraus, int. Aug. 5, 1838.

**SCOT** (see also Scott), John, and Hannah Dunkin, May 29,
1672.
Samuell, and Mrs. Sarah Chamberlain, Nov. 4, 1730.

**SCOTT** (see also Scot), Catherine, and Henry Moore, int. Feb.
7, 1848.

* Intention also recorded.

SCOTT, Cynthia A., and Capt. Henry Conant, int. Dec. 21, 1823.
Ebenezer, [jr. int.], and Rachel Thayer [Mrs. Rebecca Thayo, resident. int.], May 9, 1785.*
Ebenezer, B. [jr. int.], and Adeline Bradlee, Oct. 9, 1825.*
Ebenezer W., and Sarepta White, July 21, 1842.
Elbridge G., and Hannah J. Fletcher, int. Nov. 1, 1835.
Fanny, and Caleb Parker, July 5, 1795.*
James, and Elizabeth Dorr, Feb. 18, 1719-20.
Jane, Mrs., and John Willson, July 9, 1740.
John A., a. 21 y., blacksmith, s. John and Elizabeth, and Sarah
    S. Long, a. 22 y., d. Enoch and Mary, Sept. 17, 1848.*
John W. A., and Alice Cook of New York, May 12, 1842.*
Joseph, and Sarah Davis, Feb. 8, 1704-5.
Joseph, and Hannah Prier, May 17, 1708.
Lois, and Joshua Richards, Sept. 11, 1763. c. r. 2.
Mary, and John Davis, May 20, 1762.
Mary B., and John I. Hastings, int. Nov. 1, 1835.
Moses, Lt., and Sarah Gridley, Sept. 26, 1763.
Nathaniel, jr., and Sally Ruggles Hayden of Quincy, int. June
    23, 1793.
Samuel, and Susana Tucker of Milton, int. Jan. 8, 1792.
Sarah, of Brookline, and Lott Thayer, int. Jan. 11, 1789.
Thomas W., and Susan C. Brewer, Sept. 28, 1818.*

**SCRUTON,** Martha E., of Dover, N. H., and William H.
    Griggs, int. Jan. 9, 1847.

**SCUDDER** (see also Skudder), Horace, widr., of Dorchester,
    a. 44 y., merchant, s. David and Desire, of Barnstable, and
    Lydia S. Davis, a. 37 y., d. John and Lydia S., June 9,
    1847.*

**SEAGER** (see also Seger), Eunice, and Aaron Blaney, Dec.
    6, 1770.

**SEALY,** Thomas, and Eliza Blanchard, Dec. 5, 1824.*

**SEARL** (see also Searle, Searls), Ambrose, and Elizabeth
    Perrin, Dec. 19, 1738.
Benjamin, and Margaret Angier, at Dorchester, Aug. 29, 1738.
Hannah, and William Clark, Oct. 1, 1723.
Margaret, and John Hewit, Oct. 31, 1735.
Martha, and Amasa Davis, Nov. 7, 1782. c. r. 2.*

* Intention also recorded.

**SEARLE** (see also Searl), Hannah, and Samuel Stone of Framingham, at Watertown, May 21, 1716.

John, and Mary Ruggles, d. John, sr., June 6, 1682.

John, and Mary Feilder, Oct. 21, 1713.

Philip, and Hannah Ellis, May 29, 1690.

**SEARLS** (see also Searl), Polly, and Henry Louder, int. Dec. 8, 1799.

**SEAVER** (see also Savor, Seeva, Sever), Abigail, Mrs., and George Hewes, Nov. 14, 1728.

Abigail, and James Morton, Feb. 15, 1769.

Ann F. [T. int.], and Joel Severns [Seaverns, jr. int.], Mar. 27, 1825. C. R. 2.*

Ann Francis, and Hugh R. Kendall, jr., May 17, 1826.*

Benjamin, and Debby Loud, May 25, 1794.*

Daniel, and Abiel Woodward, Oct. 15, 1747.

Ebenezer, jr., and Clarissa Weld, Jan. 19, 1817.*

Elizabeth, and Benj[ami]n B. Davis of Brookline, Jan. 24, 1839.*

Elizabeth C., and John Hayward of Dublin, N. H., July 3, 1823.*

Elizabeth D., and Jeremiah Locke of Wakefield, N. H., int. Apr. 6, 1834.

Elizabeth W., and George Seaver, June 29, 1823.*

George, and Elizabeth, W. Seaver, June 29, 1823.*

Hannah, and Peter Sever, Nov. 23, 1732.

Hannah, and Capt. Ebenezer Gore, May 15, 1777.

Hannah, and James Lewis, May 24, 1787.*

Harriet, and Joseph Houghton, June 13, 1839.

Harriet A., a. 20 y., d. John C. and Mary, and Henry Curtis of Quincy, a. 21 y., boot maker, s. Samuel and Jerusha, June 5, 1849.*

Jacob Weld. a. 29 y., merchant, s. Ebenezer and Clarissa, and Sarah A. Weld, a. 20 y., d. George F. and Lydia, July 10, [9. C. R. 3.], 1849.*

John, and Betsey Dudley, Apr. 19, 1798.*

John [2d. int.], and Abigail Lethbridge Seaverns, Nov. 24, 1833.*

John C., and Mary Shepherd, Mar. 12, 1823.*

Jonathan, and Anna Heath, Dec. 12, 1732.

Joseph, and Abigail Whitney, Nov. 17, 1799.*

Joshua, and Nancy Sumner, Apr. 6, 1803.*

* Intention also recorded.

SEAVER, Joshua, and Emeline Morse, int. Nov. 23, 1846.

Margaret, and Rufus Kelton, Dec. 11, 1804.*

Maria, and Joseph Houghton, int. May 26, 1839.

Mary, and Lemuell Boydon, Dec. 22, 1757.

Mary, and Nath[anie]l¹ Perrin, int. Mar. 16, 1783.

Mary, and Levi Pratt, Mar. 31, 1796.*

Mary Ann, and Andrew Foley, int. June 9, 1849.

Mary Elizabeth, a. 22 y., d. John C. and Mary, and Franklin
Williams, a. 23 y., gilder, s. Sam[ue]l S. and Lucy, Dec.
24, 1846.*

Nathanael, and Sarah Stevens, Oct. 23, 1746.

Nathaniel, and Lydia Wilson, Nov. 1, 1798.*

Nicholas, and Mary Putney of Dudley, at Dudley, Apr. 3,
1759.

Peter, and Eunice Hammond, Feb. 15, 1758.

Peter, and Mary Web, Apr. 9, 1758.

Peter, and Salley Jones, Nov. 28, 1776.

Richard, and Hannah Everett, Nov. 30, 1748.

Robert, and Abigail Patch [of Boston. c. r. 3.], Nov. 20,
1834.*

Sarah, and Ebenezer Payson, Aug. 20, 1734.

Sarah, and John Newell of Brookline, at Brookline, Oct. 15,
1741.

Sarah, and Thomas Parker, July 27, 1820.*

Sarah A., a. 24 y., d. John and Betsey, and Jeremiah Clement
[of Boston. int.], a. 30 y., grocer, s. Ebenezer and Sarah,
Sept. 16, 1847.*

Subal, and Hannah Wilson, Feb. 7, 1668.

Thomas, and Elizabeth Grely, Mar. 26, 1713.

Thomas, and Hannah Dunborr [Dunbar. int.] of Hingham, at
Hingham, Jan. 19, 1783.*

Tho[ma]s S., and Lydia Brown, Nov. 25, 1841.*

William, jr., and Lucy Heath, Dec. 1, 1796.*

William, and Martha P. Wentworth [Wanwright. int.], Mar.
2, 1843.*

William D., and Catharine Hobbs of Weston, int. Oct. 22,
1826.

William W., of Philadelphia, and Hannah H. Hunneman, int.
Sept. 27, 1829.

———— [of Wells. c. r. 2.], and Sarah Woods, Nov. —, 1752.

SEAVERN (see also Seaverns), Josiah, and Rebecca White,
Sept. 2, 1801.*

* Intention also recorded.

**SEAVERNS** (see also Seavern, Severance, Severns), Abigail, and Charles Jones, int. Dec. 3, 1809.

Abigail Lethbridge, and John Seaver [2d. int.], Nov. 24, 1833.*

Ann A., and W[illia]m Winchester, jr., Oct. 18, 1842.*

Ann F., a. 21 y., d. Joel and Ann T., and James S. [Capt. J. S. c. r. 3.] McLellan of Richmond [Bath. c. r. 3.], Me., a. 29 y., seaman, s. Alexander and Rachel, Oct. 21, [22. c. r. 3.], 1846.*

Charles, and Martha Parker, Nov. 2, 1806. c. r. 3.*

Elisha, and Abagail Laithbridge of Franklin, int. Oct. 30, 1808.

Joel, of Weston, and Deborah, Crosby, Oct. 15, 1797.*

Joel, and Olive Draper Gay, Jan. 20, 1811.*

Louisa, and Aaron Gay [of Cambridge. int.], July 15, 1804. c. r. 2.*

Lucy S., and Lewis Keyes of Framingham, Aug. 19, 1818.*

Luther, and Mary Parker, Nov. 25, 1802.*

Mary P., and William Winchester, jr., Nov. 30, 1826.*

Nancy, and Henry Hatch, Dec. 10, 1816.*

Rachel, of Weston, and William Spring, int. Nov. 10, 1805.

Rhoda, and Joseph Huff, Apr. 8, 1834.*

Samuel, and Charlotte Williams, Aug. 31, 1806.*

Sarah, and John Moore of Brookline, int. Mar. 24, 1833.

Sarah P., and Joseph D. Gould, June 2, 1833.*

Sarah Wilhelmia, and Joseph W. Merriam [of Boston. c. r. 3.], Oct. 9, 1834.*

**SEEVA** (see also Seaver), Henry, of Brookline, and Eliza Pitts, int. Feb. 13, 1825.

**SEGER** (see also Seager), Susan W., and Calvin Brown, int. May 6, 1838.

**SENTER** (see also Center), Stephen, and Almira Hurd, Dec. 27, 1829.

**SERJEANT** (see also Sargent), Thomas, and Elizabeth Bridge, May 11, 1765.

**SESSIONS,** Amasa, of Pomfret, and Hannah Miller, Oct. 25, 1744. c. r. 2.

Chester, and Catharine Smith, int. June 2, 1844.

Eben[eze]r, and Mary Allen and Sturbidge, int. Nov. 27, 1808.

Lucy, and William F. Stratton, Jan. 18, 1838.*

Sarah G., and Moses Day, July 26, 1831.*

* Intention also recorded.

**SEVENS** (see also Stevens), Louisa, of Brookline, and Josiah Moors, Nov. 12, 1827.

**SEVER** (see also Seaver), Abigail, and Edmund Cole, Mar. 29, 1705.

Benjamin, and Deborah Lyon, Oct. 4, 1739.

Caleb, and Hannah Gamblin, May 3, 1704.

Caleb, and Sarah Polley, Nov. 26, 1723.

Ebenezer, and Margarett Heath, Dec. 2 [12. c. r. 2.], 1714.

Ebenezer, jr., and Mary Weld, Nov. 5, 1755.

Elijah, and Sarah Downs, Dec. 10, 1771.

Elisebeth, and Samuel Craft, Oct. 16, 1661.

Elizabeth, and Daniel Holbrooke, May 29, 1696.

Jemima, and John Woods, Dec. 3, 1713.

Joshua, and Mercy Cooke, Feb. 27, 1706-7.

Joshua, and Hannah How, May 9, 1768.

Joshuah, and Mary Pepper, wid. Joseph, Feb. 28, 1677.

Mary, and Samuel Payn of Pomfret, May 30, 1728.

Nancy, of Cambridge, and Zenos Horton, int. May 6, 1798.

Peter, and Hannah Seaver, Nov. 23, 1732.

Richard, and Mary Bullard of Framingham, at Framingham, Nov. 13, 1745.

Robart, and Elizabeth Allard, Dec. 10, 1634.

Sarah, and Josiah Winchester, Mar. 25, 1707.

Sarah, and Ephraim Murdock [of Brookline. c. r. 2.], Mar. 26, 1761.

Shobaal, and Abigail Twelves, June 12, 1704.

Shubal, jr., and Mary Rogers, July 4, 1734.

Thankfull, and Richard Mowear, Mar. 29, 1705.

**SEVERANCE** (see also Seaverns), William H[enry. c. r. 3.], and Sarah A. Gardner [both of Boston. c. r. 3.], Sept. 10, 1848.

**SEVERNS** (see also Seaverns), Joel [Seaverns, jr. int.], and Ann F. [T. int.] Seaver, Mar. 27, 1825. c. r. 2.*

**SEWALL,** Samuel, and Mrs. Rebecca Dudley, Sept. 15, 1702.

**SEXTON** (see also Saxton), Jeremiah, and Elizabeth Mahony, int. Nov. 4, 1838.

**SHACKFORD,** Caroline E., and Lebbeus H. Varney, int. Dec. 1, 1844.

* Intention also recorded.

SHACKFORD, John, and Mary Glover, Sept. 13, 1835.*
Mary W., of Barrington, N. H., and Isaac H. Meserve, int.
Dec. 4, 1848.

SHACKLEY, Catherine, of Dracut, and Henry W. Hay, int.
June 15, 1848.

SHADDOCK (see also Shattuck), Hannah, and John Turner,
July 7, 1737.

SHAILY, Catharine, and Patrick Naughton, int. Feb. 1, 1846.

SHANNON, Hannah, and William Evans, int. Mar. 9, 1823.
Lizey, and James Mooney [of Eaton, N. H. int.], Mar. 4,
1819.*
Mary Pillsbury, and Benjamin Hawes, Nov. 6, 1814.*

SHAPLEIGH, Dependence, and Margarett Caldwell, int. Jan.
1, 1823.*
Jonathan, and Rebecca G. Ayres, Oct. 20, 1833.*

SHARKEY, Cormick, and Sarah Galligan, int. Apr. 14, 1839.
Patrick and Bridgett Thompson of Boston, int. Feb. 2, 1847.
Patrick, and Mary McAnattin, int. July 7, 1849.

SHARP, Elizabeth, and Samuel Craft, Dec. 25, 1693.
Harriet P., of Watertown, and Francis D. Harrington, Feb.
20, 1844.
James, and Susan Gray Thwing, Apr. 4, 1822.*
Martha, and Joseph Buckminster, May 12, 1686.
Rebecah, of Brookline, and Moses Davis, int. Oct. 30, 1791.
Robert, of Brooklyn [Brookline. c. r. 2.], and Sarah Payson,
July 15, 1742.

SHATTUCK (see also Shaddock), Cha[rle]s R., and Rebecca
Eagles, June 29, 1840.*
Christopher P., and Mary White, int. Apr. 12, 1835.
Deborah G., and Thomas Alker of Princeton, Dec. 13, 1827.*
Eliza B., and Samuel Smith, Apr. 7, 1830.*
Martha, and Daniel Starr, Dec. 12, 1784.*
Mary Harris, and Richard Lethbridge, Sept. 17, 1835.*
William, and Unice Blood, residents, July 16, 1788.*

SHAUGHNESSEY (see also Shoughnassy, Shrugnasy), Hannah, and Colman Finegan, int. May 19, 1844.

* Intention also recorded.

**SHAW,** David, and Bethsheba Lary, int. Sept. 29, 1847.

Isaac, and Nancy B. Bosson, Nov. 30, 1794.*

Isaac, and Polly Tyler, Aug. 18, 1811.*

Joseph P., and Sarah Heath, ———, 1833. [Sept. 9, 1832. int.]*

**SHAY** (see also Shea), Ellen, and Peter Finaghty, int. Sept. 22, 1839.

Thomas, and Ann Killan, int. Apr. 9, 1837.

**SHAYS** (see also Shea), John, of Danvers, and Francis Baker Leverett, Aug. 18, 1816. c. R. 2.*

**SHEA** (see also Shay, Shays), Daniel, and Ellen Gallagher, int. Jan. 13, 1849.

Mary, b. Ireland, and John H. Caball [Cahall. int.], b. Ireland, Nov. 10, 1849.*

Peter, b. Ireland, and Margarett Killduff [Kilduff. int.], b. Ireland, Apr. 30, 1849.*

Thomas, and Mary McVay, int. Feb. 20, 1849.

**SHEAD** (see also Shed), James [Shed. c. R. 2.], jr., and Mary Weld, May 29, 1740.

**SHEAFE,** John E., widr a. 28 y., woodturner, s. John and Joanna, and Sarah D. Bradley, a. 23 y., d. Lemuel and Sarah, May 31, 1846.*

**SHEALDS** (see also Shields), Mary, of Milton, and William G. Woods, int. Aug. 22, 1841.

**SHEARIN,** Edward [Shearer. c. R. 5.], and Mrs. Elizabeth Tomline [Tomlin. c. R. 5.], resident of Dorchester, Jan. 9, 1839.

**SHED** (see also Shead, Shedd), Elizabeth, and Jonathan Dana of Brookline, Mar. 2, 1797.*

James, of Brookline, and Mary Adams, at Brookline, June 12, 1712.

James, and Elizabeth Craft, May 8, 1718.

Joseph, and Mary Williams, Jan. 3, 1722-3.

Lucretia W., and Andrew Nason, Nov. 23, 1836.*

Martha, and John Ward, Dec. 29, 1771.

Oliver, and Grace Beal, July 17, 1787.*

Patty, of Brookline, and Amasa Smith, Dec. 16, 1810.*

* Intention also recorded.

SHED, Sarah, and Calvin Ware, Apr. 10, 1806.*
Thomas, and Hepzibah Winship, Dec. 26, 1771.
Zacharias, and Hannah Hammond of Cambridge, int. Oct. 30, 1791.

SHEDD (see also Shed), James, and Alice Greenwood of Newton, at Newton, Sept. 28, 1743.

SHEDDEN (see also Sheddon), Ebenezer, and Mary Keyes, int. Nov. 25, 1804.

SHEDDON (see also Shedden), William, and Sally Thompson of Walpole, int. Aug. 25, 1805.

SHEEHAN, Bridget, and William Frawley, int. June 11, 1849.

SHEEHY, Ellen, and Jeremiah Donavan, int. Dec. 18, 1849.

SHEFFIELD, Edmund, and Mary Wooddy, Apr. 17, 1644.

SHEING, Ellen, and Barnard Connell, int. July 10, 1849.

SHELDON, Richard, and Abag[ai]l Child of Sudbury, int. Nov. 27, 1808.

SHENE, Martin, and Maria Kelley, int. May 16, 1841.

SHEPARD (see also Shepherd, Sheppard), Alice, of Dorchester, and Abiel Winship, Oct. 16, 1793.
Caroline L., and George H. Miller, int. June 12, 1847.
Elvira W., of Canton, and Wilder Broad, int. Sept. 22, 1833.
Louisa, of Canton, and Elbridge G. Woodside, int. Oct. 4, 1835.
Mary, and Benjamin Bingham, Sept. 7, 1823.*

SHEPHERD (see also Shepard), Charles, of Northampton, and Betsy Howe, June 1, 1809.*
Joseph, of Boston, and Sarah Drown [Oct. 15, 1804. different ink.]*
Maria H., and Emerson Foote of Cold Springs, N. Y., int. Sept. 9, 1838.
Mary, and John C. Seaver, Mar. 12, 1823.*
Mehetable, of Dedham, and Isaiah Whiting, at Dedham, May 10, 1779.
Nancy, and Joseph Edmunds, Apr. 25, 1793.*
William, and Abigail Parker, July 19, 1792.*
William, and Adeline Brewer, Nov. 20, 1822.*

* Intention also recorded.

**SHEPPARD** (see also Shepard), Anne, and Daniel Coolidge, May 26, 1773.

**SHERIDAN,** Catharine, and Barnard Calahan, int. July 15, 1838.

Ellen, and James Corrigan, int. July 30, 1837.

**SHERIVE,** George, a. 23 y., currier, s. John and Sarah Ann, and Elizabeth A. Francis, a. 19 y., d. Joseph and Mary, Dec. 10, 1848.*

**SHERMAN,** Amory F., and Eliza Ann Pike, Jan. 1, 1838.

Beriah, and Elizabeth Brown, June 13, 1776.

**SHERRY,** James, and Catherine Kelly, int. Feb. 18, 1848.

**SHERTLIFF** (see also Shurtliff), Charlotte, and Obed[iah] A. [Abed A. int.] Boyden, July 1, 1828. c. r. 2.*

**SHIELD** (see also Shields), Catharine, and John Sullavan, int. Nov. 10, 1845.

**SHIELDS** (see also Schields, Shealds, Shield), James, and Bridget Cunningham, int. Apr. 10, 1842.

**SHIMMIN,** William, and Eliza Parker, Sept. 24, 1811.*

**SHINE** (see also Shiny), Michael, and Mary E. Claffy, int. July 16, 1843.

**SHINY** (see also Shine), Ellen, b. Ireland, and Bernard Connell, b. Ireland, July 10, 1849.

**SHIPPE,** Isabella [Shippy. c. r. 2.], and Jeremiah Mosher, Aug. 20, 1752.

**SHIRLEY** Betsey, of Chatham, N. H., and Thomas T. Law, int. Nov. 14, 1830.

John, and Mehitabel Williams, Nov. 13, 1760.

Mehetable, and Nathaniel Jennison, Aug. 4, 1774.

William W., and Elizabeth Walton, Mar. 7, 1825.*

**SHOEMAKER,** Herman, and Ellen Mazeker, int. Feb. 14, 1849.

**SHORLEY,** Catherine, and Thomas Harlin, int. Sept. 13, 1848.

* Intention also recorded.

**SHORT,** Charles, and Annie Jean Lyman of Greenfield, int. Sept. 22, 1849.

Submit, and Calvin Young, at Swansea, Sept. 18, 1842. P. R. 5.

Timothy W., and Sarah I. [J. int.] Howard, July 25, 1837.*

**SHOUGHNASSY** (see also Shaughnessey), Ellen, and Patrick Quigly, int. Dec. 1, 1844.

**SHOVE,** Mary S., and Dudley Whitney, int. Sept. 13, 1829.

**SHRUGNASY** (see also Shaughnessey), Bridget, and Michael Quigly, int. Feb. 28, 1848.

**SHULS,** Godfrey, and Lenora Frietz, int. Sept. 18, 1848.

**SHURTLIEF** (see also Shurtliff), Henry, and Mary Moulton, June 3, 1753.

**SHURTLIFF** (see also Shertliff, Shurtlief), Lucy W., of Carver, and William F. Tillson, int. May 8, 1849.

Mary [Shirtliff, of Brookline. int.], and Reed Taft, May 8, 1810. C. R. 2.*

Nancy E., and Ezra Swallaw, May 21, 1820. C. R. 2.*

**SHUTE,** Mary, of Malden, and John Trevalley, int. Feb. 17, 1793.

**SIAS,** Eliphalet, and Hannah Gilman, int. Sept. 16, 1832.

**SIDNEY,** Nath[anie]l, and Elisa Tuttle of Lynn, int. Jan. 24, 1813.

**SIGOURNEY,** Daniel A., and Harriot Davis, Oct. 16, 1823.*

Martha Ann, and Samuel Wales, jr., Oct. 7, 1829.*

**SILSBEE** (see also Silsby), Nancy P., a. 28 y., d. Joseph and Elizabeth Park, and Samuel A. Foss, widr., a. 26 y., coachman, s. James and Abigail, June 24, 1849.*

**SILSBY** (see also Silsbee), Isaac, and Anna Longley [Langley. int.], Dec. 10, 1807.*

Samuel, and Susanna Langley, July 3, 1806.*

**SILVESTER** (see also Sylvester), Nancy Hall, and Jonathan Holmes Morrison, Aug. 20, 1809. C. R. 3.*

**SIMMES** (see also Sims), Henry, and Jane Smith, int. Dec. 11, 1842.

* Intention also recorded.

**SIMMONS** (see also Symonds), Cornelia B., a. 23 y., d. David
A. and Martha, and William Wetherbee, a. 24 y., broker, s.
John and Sarah, June 10, 1847.*
David A., Esq., and Martha F. Ruggles, June 27, 1820.*
Eliosa B., and Lycurgus Eastman, Sept. 26, 1832.*
Lydia F., and Messer Barker of [Plymouth. int.], Ohio, Oct.
9, 1843.*
Nancy D., and Warren Fisher, Dec. 17, 1833.*
Rebecca C., and Samuel M. Phillips, July 27, 1823.*
Susan F[osdick. int.], and John H[enry. int.] Eastburn [Jan.
20. int.], 1833.*
Thomas, and S. H. Thwing, int. Oct. 2, 1825.
William H. [Esq. int.], and Josephine M. Fellowes, June 24,
1840.*

**SIMPSON,** Anna, and Benjamin Burnett, int. Oct. 18, 1789.
David, jr., and Tabitha R. Lewis, int. Nov. 8, 1835.
Elizabeth C., a. 25 y., d. Lewis and Mary, and Nathan D.
Conant, a. 25 y., s. Nathaniel and Rachel, Oct. 17, 1849.*
Freeman, and Lucy H. Fuller, Sept. 26, 1834.*
Horatio G., and Charlotte C. Lewis, int. Nov. 1, 1840.
Joseph, and Dorcas Rogers, Oct. 11, 1728.
Martha S., of Burnswick, Me., a. 22 y., d. Lewis and Mary,
and William H. Ward, jr., a. 23 y., teamster, s. W[illia]m
H. and Lucy L., Nov. 14, 1847.*
Mary J., a. 22 y., and Alfred H. Lydston, a. 27 y., carpenter,
Oct. 26, 1847.*

**SIMS** (see also Simmes, Symmes), James L., and Mary L.
Jackson, June 9, 1833.
Lucretia, and Jeremiah Dalton, jr., May 19, 1831.*
Samuel, of Dorchester, and Abigail Woods, Sept. 8, 1824.*
Stephen, and Hannah Webb, residents, Oct. 8, 1788.*
Stephen, and Charlotte Webb of Dedham, Oct. 7, 1823.*

**SINCLAIR,** John T., and Minerva Savery [Severy. int.], Dec.
27, 1843.*
Joseph F., and Lucy A. Larrabee, int. Feb. 28, 1836.
Martha S. W., and Lewis B. Hawkins, int. July 3, 1842.
William R., and Lucy J. Farnham, Apr. 5, 1843.*

**SKELLINS** (see also Skillings), Joseph, of Richmond, and
Eleanor Youngman, Aug. 19, 1731.

**SKIDMORE,** Nancy, and Preston Carpenter, June 26, 1823.*

* Intention also recorded.

**SKILLINGS** (see also Skellins), Anne, and [Dr. int.] Austin
  Flint of Northampton, Apr. 24, 1835.*

**SKINNER,** Caroline W., and Alpheus Trowbridge, Apr. 5,
  1838.*
Elizabeth, of Warren District, Me., and Thomas Houghton,
  int. Oct. 31, 1819.
Jacob, and Mary Sampson, Nov. 7, 1802.*
Sarah, and John H. Whitney, Jan. 30, 1834.*
Sarah, a. 22 y., d. Jedediah and Anne, and Joseph Lovejoy of
  Dorchester, a. 20 y., laborer, s. Jacob and Betsy of En-
  field, N. H., Nov. 26, 1846.*
Sarah A., and Samuel Felton, int. Sept. 30, 1832.
Stephen T., of Woburn, and Hannah Onion, Nov. 24, 1842.*
Susan, and Melzar Waterman, Sept. 11, 1831.*

**SKUDDER** (see also Scudder), Daniel, and Sally Salter of
  Watertown, Nov. 22, 1801.

**SLACK,** Lewis, and Pedy Dudley, June 2, 1833.*
Mary Ann, and Henry Kellam Hancock, int. Nov. 8, 1829.

**SLAFTER,** E. F., Rev., and Mary Ann Hazen of Boston,
  int. July 24, 1849.

**SLANE** (see also Slany), Catherine, of Boston, and William
  McAvoy, int. July 13, 1847.

**SLANY** (see also Slane), Patrick, and Hannah Huff, int. Oct.
  19, 1849.

**SLATTERRY,** Cornelius, and Margaret Maloney, Feb. 7,
  1846.

**SLENTON,** John [Slenten. int.], b. Ireland, and Catherine D.
  Carrigan [Corrigan. int.], b. Ireland, Nov. 18, 1849.*

**SLOAN,** Alice W., and Ephraim Walcott, int. Apr. 11, 1830.
David, and Elizabeth Whittemore, May 3, 1779.
Susanna P., and Benjamin Gason [Geysen. int.], Mar. 13,
  1831.*
Thomas, and Mary Ann Crocker, May 10, 1838.*
Thomas D., and Sally Jenkins [residents. int.], Apr. 24, 1808.*
William, and Mary B. Rollins, Oct. 25, 1830.*

* Intention also recorded.

**SLOCOMB,** Emmons, jr., of Cambridge, and Sarah Blanchard, Mar. 21, 1824.*

Samuel, of Cambridge, and Eliza Allen, int. Jan. 8, 1826.

**SLOMAN,** Mehitable, a. 26 y., d. John and Betsey, and William T. Chadwick, a. 24 y., provision dealer, s. W[illia]m and Betsey, May 14, 1848.*

**SLOPER,** Margaret, and David White, Nov. 16, 1775.

**SMAILES,** John, and Marcy Beetham, May 12, 1811.*

**SMALL** (see also Smally), Betsey, and Hewett Tolman of Marshfield, June 9, 1844.*

Mary, of Dedham, and Caleb S. Farmer, int. Dec. 1, 1839.

Mary P., of Cornish, Me., and Samuel Pearson, jr., int. Oct. 15, 1837.

Thomas, of Dedham, and Hannah Wheat, int. Nov. 20, 1842.

**SMALLY** (see also Small), Dan S. [Dan[iel] S. Smalley. c. R. 3.], and Lucy Pierce, June 1, 1842.*

**SMART,** Margarett R., of Portsmouth, N. H., and James H. Parks, int. Jan. 27, 1848.

**SMEHT** (see also Smith), Ketren, and John Haas, int. Aug. 4, 1833.

**SMEIDT** (see also Smith), Lydia, and Anthony Nuss, int. May 24, 1835.

**SMILIE,** Francis B., and Mary S. Morse of Lowell, int. Feb. 4, 1848.

**SMITH** (see also Smeht, Smeidt, Smyth), Abiel, and Hannah Clap, Feb. 23, 1817.*

Abigail, and Stephen Williams, 3d, Dec. 23, 1779.

Abigail, of Bridgewater, and Joshua Bowen, at Bridgewater, May 26, 1782.

Abigail, and Luther Fuller, Mar. 23, 1794.*

Abigail, and Timothy Fuller of Needham, int. Sept. 4, 1796.

Abigail [of Brookline. int.], and Adolphus Taft, Aug. 25, 1811. c. R. 2.*

Adeline, and Augustus Allen, Dec. 11, 1842.*

Almira L., and Spencer Cook, Jan. 12, 1842.*

Amasa, and Patty Shed of Brookline, Dec. 16, 1810.*

* Intention also recorded.

SMITH, Andrew H., and Caroline Colby, Apr. 13, 1845.*

Ann P., of Providence, R. I., and George B. Peck, int. Apr. 7, 1842.

Benjamin, and Experience Curtice [Curtis. c. r. 2.], Mar. 21, 1716-17.

Benjamin, and Hannah Philips, Apr. 23, 1724.

Benjamin, and Lydia Graly, June 14, 1733.

Benjamin, and Martha Perrin, Mar. 26, 1747.

Betsey, and Jonathan Dorr, Aug. 30, 1802.*

Calvin, of Waltham, and Mary Ann Putnam, int. Mar. 13, 1842.

Catharine M., and John Berry [Berg. int.], Nov. 27, 1843.*

Catharine, and Chester Sessions, int. June 2, 1844.

Catharine G. [Catherine. S. int.], and John C. Boyde [Boyd. int.], Oct. 7, 1845.*

Catherine, and James McCormick, int. July 20, 1849.

Catta [Calla. int.], and John Minott [of Dorchester. int.], Nov. 27, 1806. c. r. 2.*

Charles, and Ellen McEloren, int. May 13, 1847.

Charles H., a. 26 y., clerk, s. William H. and Rebecca S., and Elizabeth Garbett, a. 26 y., d. Richard and Elizabeth, May 3, 1849.*

Charlotte W., a. 19 y., d. Henry and Elizabeth, and Henry S. Crocker of Brooklyn, N. Y., a. 26 y., ropemaker, b. Brooklyn, N. Y., s. Warren and Olive P., Nov. 29, 1849.*

Chloe W., and Rufus T. King, int. July 13, 1848.

Cyrene, and Samuel Hagar, Apr. 7, 1816. c. r. 2*

David B., and Marcia Hine of Livermore, Me., int. Oct. 31, 1846.

Dorcas Levitt, and Manuel Swasey, jr., int. Nov. 14, 1824.

Draper, and Anna Leland of Sherburn, int. Apr. 2, 1809.

Ebenezer, and Anna Baldwin of Newton, at Newton, Dec. 22, 1767.

Ebenezer, and Abigail Whittemore, Nov. 15, 1774.

Ebenezer, and Abigail Williams, June 6, 1776.

Eliza S., and Thomas G. Bridgen of Middleborough, int. Mar. 28, 1841.

Elizabeth, and Thomas Perry, Mar. 21, 1716-17.

Elizabeth, and George W. Harrington, int. June 26, 1831.

Elizabeth J., and Thomas Blake, Oct. 2, 1839.*

Elizebeth, of Lexington, and William Tilestone, int. July 21, 1804.

* Intention also recorded.

SMITH, Enoch [A int.], of Newton, and Elizabeth Woods, June 16, 1793.*

Experience, and Thomas Ransford, May 4, 1758.

Ezekiel, of Marshfield, and Dinah May, at Marshfield, June 29, 1714.

Frederic W., and Harriet A. Gardner, July 2, 1837.*

George, a. 26 y., carpenter, s. Elisha and Clarissa of Sudbury, and Hannah Adelia Morton, a. 28 y., d. John and Bethia, Apr. 25, 1847.*

Gilman [jr. int.], of Sandwich, N. H., and Hannah Tasgaterf [Fosgat. C. R. 3.], Nov. 28, 1833.*

Hannah, and Daniel Chaddock [of Attleborough. C. R. 2.], May 25, 1738.

Hannah, and John Corey, Mar. 11, 1740-41.

Hannah, and Ebenezer Corey, Dec. 1, 1747.

Harriet L., and John F. Milles [Miller.int.], Oct. 2, 1842.*

Harriman, and Sarah F. Foster, Aug. 7, 1842.*

Henry, and Sarah Adams, May 26, 1713.

Henry, and Elizabeth Gringe of Dorchester, int. Apr. 17, 1825.

Henry W., and Julia A. Alden of West Randolph, int. Mar. 17, 1847.

Huldah, and Joseph Lyon, Oct. 28, 1735.

Humphrey, and Maria Smyth of Dedham, int. Dec. 17, 1843.

Isabella, and John Anan, int. Nov. 22, 1816.

James L., and Susan E. Morton, int. Dec. 3, 1837.

Jane, and Henry Simmes, int. Dec. 11, 1842.

Jeremiah P., and Nancy Dorr, Feb. 17, 1805.*

Jeremiah P., and Susannah Burrell, Nov. 27, 1808.*

John, and Katherine Morrol, Aug. 1, 1647.

John, and Elizabeth Walker, at Rehoboth, Apr. 22, 1714.

John, and Mrs. Elizabeth Tucker, Oct. 31, 1723.

John, and Mrs. Mary Smith, Nov. 9, 1725.

John, and Mary Williams, Dec. 9, 1779.

John, jr., and Mary Hall of Needham, at Needham, July 19, 1781.

John, and Celestinah Mott, int. Sept. 9, 1847.

John, and Amelia Ann Holmes of Plymouth, int. Jan. 11, 1849.

John T., a. 26 y., s. Caleb and Amy, and Eliza M. Rankin, a. 20 y., d. John M. and Harriet, Feb. 11, 1849.*

John W., and Sally Munroe, Dec. 23, 1804.*

* Intention also recorded.

Smith, Jonathan, and Mary Barnard [of Watertown. c. r. 2.], June 6, 1738.

Jonathan, and Catherine Hovey, Aug. 21, 1760.

Jonathan, and Lucy Rhoades of Dedham, int. Jan. 22, 1809.

Joseph, and Mary Brewer, Sept. 17, 1766.

Joseph, and Mrs. Abigail Parker, May 2, 1782.

Lemuel, and Hannah Turill of Weymouth, int. Sept. 15, 1782.

Lois, of Princeton, and Isaac Wellington, int. Jan. 4, 1829.

Lorenzo, and Helen Starr of Newton, int. Apr. 6, 1845.

Luce, and John Taylor, Mar. 12, 1721-2.

Lucey, and Thomas Gardner, July 4, 1641.

Lucinda, and Hiram R. Garland, May 12, 1816. c. r. 2.*

Lucy, and Thomas J. Orange, int. Dec. 20, 1840.

Lucy, and Edmund S. Marsh of Quincy, int. Oct. 31, 1846.

Luke, and Abigail Bellows, Dec. 1, 1765.

Lydia L., and George W. Griffin, Mar. 13, 1844. c. r. 7.*

Lydia O., and Oliver Parker, int. Sept. 10, 1837.

Marie, and Nathaniell Johnson, Apr. 29, 1667.

Mary, Mrs., and John Smith, Nov. 9, 1725.

Mary, and Josiah Haws of Needham, Aug. 27, 1740.

Mary, and Zach[eus. c. r. 2.], Haws [of Dedham. c. r. 2.], Nov. 1, 1753.

Mary [Peggy. int.], of Dedham, and Thad[deu]s [jr. int.], Partridge, at Dedham, June 1, 1786.*

Mary, and William Davis, Sept. 19, 1797.*

Mary, of Hamilton, and Benjamin Goldsmith, int. Mar. 13, 1825.

Mary, a. 56 y., d. Daniel E. and Lydia Proctor, and Jonathan Hassam, widr. of Manchester, N. H., a. 64 y., gentleman. Jan. 24, 1849.*

Mary, and Isaac Wentworth, int. June 2, 1849.

Mary A., and Elihu K. Patridge, Sept. 22, 1840.*

Mary Ann L., and William C. Appleton, int. Mar. 23, 1845.

Mary H., and John Wilson, int. Jan. 29, 1837.

Mary J., and Dennis Buckley, int. July 12, 1849.

Mary L., and Thomas Day, Aug. 21, 1843.*

Mary W., and Timothy Gay, May 23, 1824.*

Matilda B., and Benjamin P. Cashman, int. June 21, 1849.

Matthias H., Rev., of Guilford, Vt., and Mary Beath, int. Mar. 20, 1831.

Michael, and Mary Friary, int. Feb. 8, 1846.

* Intention also recorded.

SMITH, Nahum, and Joanna C. Hill of Waterborough, Me., int. Oct. 16, 1847.

Nancy, and Joseph Ware, Aug. 21, 1803.*

Nathan, jr., and Elizabeth Wellington of Waltham, int. Dec. 14, 1817.

Peter, and Mary A. Williams of Brooklyn, Nov. 2, 1837.*

Phinehas B., and Margaret S. Wiggen, int. Mar. 26, 1837.

Preserved, of Troy, Ohio, a. 27 y., merchant, s. Preserved and Bebe M., and Lucy R. Mayo, a. 28 y., d. Seth and Charity, Sept. 10, 1846.*

Ralph, and Mary Whittemore, Dec. 12, 1771.

Ralph, and Sarah Ruggles, Nov. 25, 1779.

Ralph, and Mrs. Susanna Howe, Nov. 27, 1804.*

Rebecca, and Joshua Phillips, Mar. 24, 1805. c. r. 2.*

Rebecca, and Joseph Harrington, Esq., May 13, 1812.*

Reuben, and Mary Kenrick [Kendrick. c. r. 3.], Dec. 1, 1811.*

Reuben, and Mrs. Rachel R. Holbrook, int. Sept. 29, 1833.

Reuben, and Mrs. Martha Tatchell, int. Dec. 27, 1835.

Reuben, jr., and Elizabeth F. Swain, int. Dec. 13, 1840.

Robert, of Boston, and Elizabeth Goodridge, Sept. 26, 1802.

Robert P. [V. int.], and Jane Hearsey, Nov. 27, 1808. c. r. 3.*

Russell S., and Susan L. Perkins, int. Dec. 26, 1846.

Ruth, and Lemuel Griggs, June 14, 1805.*

Sally, and William Davis, Sept. 7, 1800.*

Samuel, and Sarah Ruggles, Nov. 23, 1715.

Samuel, and Hannah Tirrell of Weymouth, at Weymouth, Nov. 21, 1782.

Samuel, and Mehitable Perkins, of Topsfield, int. Dec. 12, 1824.

Samuel, and Eliza B. Shattuck, Apr. 7, 1830.*

Sarah, and Sam[ue]l Guile [Guild. c. r. 2.] of Dedham [Apr. 24. c. r. 2.], 1766.

Sarah H., of Waltham, and Charles C. Bowman, June 3, 1847.

Sarah W., and Albert Kingsbury, int. Apr. 5, 1849.

Selina M., and Henry Trowbridge, Apr. 7, 1842.*

Sophia, and Henry Bacon, May 11, 1813.*

Sophia, and Dr. Pliny Safford of Westminster, Vt., Feb. 25, 1824.*

Sumner, and Mary Garety [Garrety. int.], Oct. 28, 1848.*

* Intention also recorded.

SMITH, Susannah, of Walpole, and Benjamin Wallace, int. Apr. 2, 1826.

Thaddeus, and Nancy Herring, at Dedham, Oct. 2, 1796.*

Thomas, of Dedham, and Hannah H. Harvey, int. Nov. 27, 1831.

Titus, and Abigail Burrill of Dedham, Mar. 22, 1832.*

William, and Lydia Pond, Apr. 26, 1798. C. R. 2.*

William, of Cambridge, and Polly Turner, Jan. 1, 1809.*

W[illia]m E., and Diana Ayer, Jan. 1, 1840.*

SMYTH (see also Smith), Maria, of Dedham, and Humphrey Smith, int. Dec. 17, 1843.

Mary, and Michael Linard, int. May 6, 1848.

SNELL, Emily D., and James Mills, May 7, 1843.*

Fanny, and Daniel Clapp, Aug. 14, 1845.*

George, and Mary Lyon, May 7, 1820. C. R. 2.*

Joseph D., and Jane G. Calder, Sept. 15, 1811.*

Julia D., and Sandrus H. Thomas, July 15, 1844.*

Mary A., of Dedham, and Artemas Berce, Mar. 18, 1847. C. R. 7.

Seth, and Frances Blanchard, Apr. 24, 1834.*

William, and Elizabeth Blanchard, June 28, 1827.*

SNELLING, Josiah, and Ellen Danforth, Nov. 27, 1833.*

SNOW, James H., and Aurilla Lingham of Quincy, int. May 21, 1843.

Jonathan, and Adeline L. Holt, Mar. 5, 1839.*

Joshua, of New York, and Lois Pattie, Mar. 23, 1794.*

Levi F., of Dorchester, and Abby L. Calder, Nov. 25, 1844.

Olive, and William Tucker, int. Mar. 7, 1830.

Susan G., and Shubael Rogers, jr., Sept. 4, 1834.*

SNOWDON (see also Soden, Sowden, Sowdon), Lydia R., and Stephen H. Bradlee, Dec. 15, 1844.*

Mary F. [Snowden. C. R. 5.], and John Beatty [Beaty. C. R. 5.], July 7, 1844.*

SODEN (see also Snowdon), Harriet, of Saxonville, and Alonzo W. Folsom, int. Oct. 29, 1843.

SOHIER, William, and Susan C. Lowell, d. John A., Oct. 13, 1846.

* Intention also recorded.

**SOLE,** John, and Sally Leach, Aug. 9, 1807.*

**SOLER,** George, and Eleanor Craft, July 28, 1835.*

**SOMERBY,** Arthur, and Oliva P. Fessenden, Oct. 21, 1827.
Robert, and Augusta L. Dodge of Shirley, int. June 7, 1847.

**SOMMERS** (see also Summers), Thomas S[amuel. int.], and
Catharine Moore, Dec. 1, 1845.*

**SOUNER,** George, and Mary Baldnor, int. Mar. 5, 1843.

**SOUSMAN,** Isaac I., and Lois M. Toby, int. May 1, 1842.

**SOUTH,** Catharine, and Sampson Saunders, July 11, 1836.

**SOUTHACK,** George, and Sarah Newell, int. Dec. 2, 1832.

**SOUTHER,** John, and Malinda Read of Charlestown, int.
June 6, 1819.
William H., and Caroline Taft, int. Oct. 11, 1840.

**SOUTHWICK,** David, "adjacent to ye town of Woodstock,"
and Hannah Griggs, Apr. 15, 1726.
James M., and Sarah Martin of Newburyport, int. Feb. 2,
1845.

**SOUTHWORTH,** Charles, and Clarissa A. Robbins, int. Dec.
6, 1835.
Consider A., widr., of Stoughton, a. 42 y., manufacturer, s.
Consider and Mary, and Serena Field of Abington, a. 40
y., d. William and Jemima, July 22, 1847.

**SOWDEN** (see also Snowdon), Phillip, jr., and Sarah Ann
Woodward, Mar. 27, 1838. c. r. 3.

**SOWDON** (see also Snowdon), Phillip, and Susan Stewart,
Mar. 19, 1838.*

**SPALDING** (see also Spauldin), Daniel, of Nashville, N. H.,
and Julia M. I. Williams, Oct. 1, 1842.*
Mary Ann, of Billerica, and George Faulkner, M. D., int. Aug.
7, 1847.

**SPALMAN** (see also Spellman), Mary, and Thomas Dolan,
int. Apr. 6, 1845.

**SPARE** (see also Spear), Elizabeth, 2d, and William Fitzgerald, at Canton, Jan. 30, 1795.

* Intention also recorded.

**SPARHAWK,** Cotton, and Rachel Hunt of Milton, int. July 5, 1789.

Edward [of Cambridge. int.], and Betsy [Betsey. int.] Murdock, July 22, 1804. c. R. 2.*

Henrietta, and John How, Oct. 26, 1803.*

Lydia, and Joseph Clark [Clarke. int.], at Boston, Aug. 12, 1788.*

Nath[anie]l, and Mary Pierpont, Oct. 13, 1778.

Nathaniel, and Frances Stone of Harwich, int. Oct. 19, 1788.

**SPAULDIN** (see also Spalding), Hepzibath, of Pepperell, and John A. Webber, int. Jan. 30, 1803.

**SPEAR** (see also Spare), Abraham, and Abigail Whitney, int. July 4, 1824.

Ebenezer, and Mrs. Elizabeth Ball of Dorchester, at Dorchester, Mar. 19, 1772.

Esther, of Boston, and Henry Ruse of Hartford, Conn., Oct. 31, 1831. c. R. 3.

James, and Ann Hart, Apr. 27, 1845.*

John, of Braintree, and Mary Lee, Mar. 26, 1742.

Joseph C., of New York City, and Susannah R. Champney, Aug. 3, 1837.*

Paul, and Clemence Weld, Aug. 25, 1756.

William Hervey, and Catharine Hinsdale Allen of Dedham, int. May 1, 1831.

**SPELLMAN** (see also Spalman, Spelman), Ann, and Patrick Clark, int. Dec. 31, 1847.

Bridgett, and William Kaog, int. July 16, 1847.

**SPELMAN** (see also Spellman), John, and Mary Ann Joice, int. Jan. 4, 1846.

Thomas, and Ellen Harrington, int. Mar. 1, 1848.

**SPENCER,** Ruth O., and Thomas Beal, July 31, 1842.*

Samuel, and Elizabeth Mascraft, Mar. 18, 1700-1701.

**SPENDLER,** Mary, and Frederick Bandlen, int. Dec. 22, 1847.

**SPLEEN,** Daniel, and Ellen Carin, int. May 29, 1849.

**SPOFFORD,** Phebe A., and William Morse, Apr. 23, 1848.*

* Intention also recorded.

**SPOONER,** Elizabeth, and William Heath, jr., June 18, 1789.*

John Jones, of Dorchester, and Mrs. Nabby Mears, at Dorchester, Dec. 7, 1778.

John Jones, Maj. [Capt. int.], and Mrs. Salley [Sarah. int.] Heath, Nov. 25, 1783.*

Sarah, Mrs., and Col. Isaac Gardner of Brookline, June 3, 1801.*

William H., and Caroline Hartshorn, Dec. 6, 1821.*

William H[eath. Capt. int.] and Harriet Curtis, Oct. 19, 1825.*

**SPRAGUE,** Isaac, and Ellen Davie, int. Aug. 6, 1843.

Mary, of Malden, and John Goddard, at Malden, Nov. 15, 1732.

Lucy A., a. 19 y., d. Hiram and Mary, and George S. Cheney, a. 22 y., tinplate worker, s. W[illia]m and Rebecca, Apr. 23, 1848.*

Sabrana, and John McLaughlin, int. July 10, 1846.

William, and Tryphene Blackman, Feb. 19 [9. c. r. 2.], 1764.

**SPRING,** Mary, and John Lyon, int. Dec. 9, 1792.

Mary, of Boston, and Edward N. Perkins, int. May 7, 1846.

Pebebena, and George Weber, June 9, 1839.*

William, and Rachel Seaverns of Weston, int. Nov. 10, 1805.

**SPROUL** (see also Sprowl), Hannah P., and William Wallace, int. Jan. 13, 1848.

**SPROWL** (see also Sproul), Eliza, and Amos W. French, int. Oct. 27, 1844.

**SPUR** (see also Spurr), Elizabeth, of Stoughton, and William Fitz Jerald, at Stoughton, Jan. 5, 1795.

Rebecca, and Robert Randall, both of Dorchester, Sept. 8, 1793.

Ruth, and Joseph Colman, Oct. 10, 1793.

**SPURR** (see also Spur), Eliphalet, and Sally Welson, int. Sept. 2, 1798.

Nancy, and Joseph Hooker, Dec. 6, 1789.*

Samuel, jr., and Elizabeth T. Brigham, int. May 30, 1841.

**SPURZHEIM,** Capen R., and Mary L. Atwood of Middleboro, int Oct. 18, 1849.

* Intention also recorded.

**STACK,** John, and Elizabeth Ruggles, Feb. 28, 1754.

**STACKPOLE,** Reuben M., and Rebecca W. Child, ——, 1833. [May 27, 1832. int.]*

**STACY,** George, and Jane Haskins, int. Mar. 25, 1827.

**STAFFORD** (see also Safford), Emily A., of Munroe, Me., and Charles H. Moore, int. Feb. 6, 1847.

**STANDDASH** (see also Standish), George, of Dorchester, and Lucy Williams, June 24, 1790.*

**STANDISH** (see also Standdash), Nathaniel P., and Mary Kegery, int. July 26, 1848.

**STANFFULL,** Abigaile [Abigail. CT. R.], and Samuel Mayes, Jan. 7, 1657.

**STANFORD** (see also Sanford, Stanhford, Staniford), Ann, and Patrick Garety, int. Jan. 13, 1848.
Ann, and Jeremiah Teeley, int. Mar. 1, 1848.

**STANHFORD** (see also Stanford), Mary, and Andrew Mc-Gan, int. Dec. 16, 1847.

**STANHOPE,** Isaac, and Elizabeth Hemingway, Feb. 15, 1703-4.

**STANIELS** (see also Stanniels), Edward L., and Harriet Richardson of Medford, int. Dec. 4, 1825.
Isaac M., and Martha E. Beach, Dec. 10, 1829.
James, and Irene P. Hooper, Sept. 17, 1820.*
Samuel, and Mary L. Hooper, Mar. 27, 1825.*

**STANIFORD** (see also Stanford), Caroline R. [H. C. R. 3.], and Henry Prentiss [M. D. int.] of Gloucester, June 18, 1825.*
Charlotte Potter, and Charles Green Reynolds, int. Apr. 3, 1831.
Elizabeth Vinton, and William Phipps [of Boston. C. R. 3.], June 2, 1826.*

**STANLEY,** William, widr., a. 48 y., engineer, s. Thomas and Mary, and Eliza S. Sawyer, a. 38 y., tailoress, Apr. 29, 1844.*

**STANNIELS** (see also Staniels), Hazen, and Maria Griggs, int. Oct. 5, 1834.

* Intention also recorded.

**STANTON** (see also Staunton), Bridget, and Edward Ryan, int. Mar. 23, 1845.

Ephraim W., and Anna E. T. Kennedy, int. Aug. 20, 1846.

Jacob C., and Nancy Cook of Wakefield, N. H., int. Nov. 4, 1832.

John L., and Fanny L. Hastings, Mar. 30, 1845.*

Lydia B., of Lebanon, Me., and John C. White, int. Feb. 15, 1846.

Maria, and Thomas Haslin, int. July 16, 1846.

Mary L., and George W. Cobb, May 9, 1845.*

**STAR** (see also Starr), Martha [Starr. c. R. 3.], and Amos Fitch [of Boston. c. R. 3.], Apr. 7, 1813.*

Mary [Starr. c. R. 3.], and Benjamin May, Dec. 1, 1811.*

**STARK,** Lewis [Capt. int.], and Mary Ann Flower of Andover, Jan. 13, 1842.*

**STARKWEATHER,** Marilla P., of Walpole, N. H., and William Haskell, int. Aug. 25, 1844.

**STARR** (see also Star), Daniel, and Martha Shattuck, Dec. 12, 1784.*

Daniel, and Susanna May, June 30, 1793.*

Helen, of Newton, and Lorenzo Smith, int. Apr. 6, 1845.

Sally, of Dedham, and George Clarke of Dorchester, Feb. 28, 1796.

**STAUNTON** (see also Stanton), James, and Catherine Ma-Gee, int. Nov. 8, 1848.

John, and Margarett Greham, int. June 13, 1848.

Michael, and Catherine Mullen, int. July 3, 1847.

**STAYNER,** Roger, and Susanna Besto, June 22, 1705.

**STEADMAN** (see also Stedman), Bethiah, Mrs., and Lt. John Williams, Sept. 12, 1749.

Sarah, and Nehemiah Chamberlain, Feb. 25, 1783. c. R. 2.*

**STEARNS,** Charles, Capt., of Brookline, and Hannah Clap Pierce, int. Feb. 12, 1832.

Geo[rge] W., and Harriet G. Parker, both of Brookline, Mar. 9, 1837.

Henry M., of Charlestown, and Caroline P. Beals, int. Dec. 28, 1834.

* Intention also recorded.

STEARNS, Isaac, of Waltham, and Narcissa Morse, late of Cambridge, Nov. 15, 1810.

Jacob, of Newton, and Mrs. Hannah M. Tucker, int. Apr. 23, 1843.

Nathaniel, of Warwick, and Mary Richards, May 27, 1773.

Simeon, and Eunice Leonard, May 1, 1808.*

William A., and Lydia B. Beals, int. May 31, 1835.

**STEBBIN** (see also Stebens), John, and Ann Munke, Apr. 17, 1644.

Martin, and Jane Greene, Dec. 25, 1639.

**STEBENS** (see also Stebbin), John, and Rebecah Hawkins, June 4, 1680.

**STEDMAN** (see also Steadman), Caleb, and Hannah Wiswel, ——, 1697.

Caleb, jr., and Bethiah Parker, Sept. 22, 1743.

Cyrus, and Mary Jordan, int. Sept. 23, 1832.

Hannah, and Robert Murdock, Apr. 28, 1692.

John, and Sarah Kingsbury of Needham, int. July 26, 1795.

Joseph, and Lydia Dunnell, int. Mar. 13, 1803.

Margaret, and Thomas Hitchcock, residents, Nov. 12, 1788.*

Sarah, and Samuell Perry, Jan. 28, 1668.

Thomas, and Sarah Gardner of Muddy River, Sept. 10, 1705.

**STEFIN,** Jacob, and Catharine Realen, int. Sept. 23, 1838.

**STELL,** Caroline Matilda, and James M. Thompson, int. May 24, 1835.

**STEPHENS** (see also Stevens) John, and Lucy Thomas, Jan. 28, 1810.*

Stephen, and Lucy Burrel, Jan. 1, 1809.*

**STEPHENSON** (see also Stevenson), George A., and Susanna M. Lincoln, int. Sept. 30, 1846.

Mary E., a. 19 y., d. Benj[ami]n and Mary, and Charles H. Blanchard, a. 24 y., merchant, s. Jedidiah and Sarah, Oct. 20, 1846.*

**STETSON** (see also Stutson), Cushing, of Baltimore, Md. [of Charlestown. int.], and Francis E. B. Bowles, Oct. 23, 1838.*

Delpha, of Bridgewater, and James H. Gurney, int. May 2, 1813.

* Intention also recorded.

STETSON, Ebenezer, and Ann Allen of Newton, at Newton, Sept. 11, 1755.

Elizabeth P., and Bradbury Pevere of Dedham, Mar. 28, 1819.*

Frances, and Jonathan M. Pierce, int. Mar. 24, 1833.

James H., and Mehitable C. Cushman of Kingston, int. Oct. 13, 1844.

Joseph, and Maria E. Brown, int. Jan. 19, 1845.

Mary Ann, and Burnham Peveare, May 5, 1825.*

Olive A., and Samuel Roberts of Quincy, int. Oct. 5, 1845.

Oren J., of Boston, and Mrs. Anna C. Upham of Newton, Oct. 14, 1847. C. R. 7.

Rebecca B., of Brookline, and Rev. George Kallock of Chester, N.H., Oct. 27, 1829.

Sarah M., of Dorchester, and Henry H. Moody, Apr. 12, 1845.*

**STEVENS** (see also Sevens, Stephens), Abigail S., and Nathanael Richardson, Oct. 6, 1741.

Abigail S., of Randolph, and Chester H. Morse, int. Dec. 23, 1832.

Almira, and William Hall, Aug. 11, 1839.*

Amos, and Elizabeth W. Baldwin of Grafton, int. Sept. 19, 1849.

Charlotte, a. 21 y., d. John and Lucy, and William Brock, a. 27 y., blacksmith, s. Luke and Jane, Oct. 29, 1848.*

Clarissa G., and Jotham Nute, Sept. 28, 1844.*

Dorothy, and Ezekiel Needham, May 4, 1738.

Ebenezer, and Mrs. Elizabeth Weld, July 9, 1750.

Eliza Ann, and William Mugridge, June 19, 1841.*

Elizabeth, and Samuel Phipps, Dec. 26, 1700.

Frances L., and Ezra T. Herring, Oct. 1, 1843.*

Frederic, and Mrs. Hannah Hanson, Nov. 11, 1838.

Hannah, and Capt. Jeremiah Tucker, Nov. 10, 1768.

Isaac, and Lydia Ann Brigham, Mar. 25, 1838.*

Jacob, and Adaline Williams, int. July 27, 1828.

John, and Elisabeth Robinson, ———, 1749. [Jan. 11, 1749-50. C. R. 2.]

John V., and Betsy Knight of Bolton, at Lancaster, Jan. 31, 1797.*

John, jr., and Harriet Haynes, int. Nov. 11, 1838.

Joseph, and Joanna Winchester, June 5, 1698.

Joseph, and Luce Ruggles, Feb. 15, 1715-16.

* Intention also recorded.

STEVENS, Joseph, and Susan E. French of Weymouth, Mar. 21 1841. C. R. 7.

Lorenso, and Mary G. P. Edland of Bedford, int. Dec. 6, 1845.

Louisa, and W[illia]m A. Colegate, Apr. 6, 1842.*

Lucy, and Samuel Chamberlain, Nov. 18, 1742.

Lucy M., and William N. Read, Sept. 4, 1839.*

Mable Jenners, of Concord, N. H., and David Wait, int. June 19, 1796.

Mary, and Elijah Kendrick, June 9, 1709.

Mary, Mrs., and Joseph Warren, May 29, 1740.

Mary, and James M. Floyd, June 10, 1849.

Mary Ann W., and Jonas L. Duncan, Aug. 21, 1842.*

Otis, and Maria Anna Hawes, int. July 30, 1843.

Rebecca, and Charles B. Ropes, Nov. 21, 1839.*

Samuel, and Dorothy Weld, May 25, 1708.

Samuel, and Mary Calfe, Oct. 9, 1712.

Sarah, and William Williams of Pomfret, Oct. 20, 1720.

Sarah, and Nathanael Seaver, Oct. 23, 1746.

Susan A., a. 24 y., d. Amos and Susan T., and Artemas W. Wilder, 2d m., of Montpelier, N. H. [Vt. int.], a. 30 y., merchant, b. Montpelier, s. Artemas and Sarah, Sept. 26, 1849.*

Susanna, Mrs, and John Sumner, Nov. 20, 1729.

Susannah [Jehannah. C. R. 2.], Mrs., and Rev. Sheerjashub Bourn of Scituate, Nov. 10, 1757.

Thankfull, of Braintree, and Francis Blanchard, resident, int. July 25, 1784.

Timothy, and Sarah Davis, Mar. 12, 1664.

**STEVENSON** (see also Stephenson), Elisabeth [Elizabeth Stevinson. int.], and Elijah Grooms [Groomes. int.], July 7, 1844.*

Nathaniel, and Lydia Abbot of Billerica, int. Mar. 7, 1819.

William, and Tabitha Eliza Banton, Oct. 23, 1814.

**STEWARD** (see also Stewart), Jane, and Samuel Thompson, June 30, 1747.

**STEWART** (see also Steward), Susan, and Phillip Sowdon, Mar. 19, 1838.*

**STICKNEY,** Clarissa, of Jeffrey. and Daniel Newell, int. Sept. 14, 1800.

William W. [of Boston. int.], a. 25 y., victualler, s. Charles and Lucy, of Grafton, N. H., and Lucy W. Cass, a. 24 y., d. Moses and Tanny, Nov. 26, 1846.*

* Intention also recorded.

**STILES,** Hosea B., and Sarah Mirick, Aug. 15, 1841.*
Tamar, of Boylston, and Dennis Andrews, int. Aug. 22, 1813.

**STILLMAN,** Mary E., and William G. Perry, int. Sept. 21, 1845.

**STIMPSON,** Charles, and Mary Lambert, July 21, 1799.*

**STOCKMAN,** Clarissa Ann, and John S. Phipps, Oct. 5, 1837.*
Silas, and Sarah E. Whittlesy of Litchfield, Conn., int. Nov. 12, 1847.

**STOCKWELL,** Lysander, and Mary Hutchings, both of Boston, Sept. 7, 1836.

**STODDARD,** Catharine G., and Nath[anie]l Brickett, jr., int. Aug. 9, 1840.
Sally, and Daniel Hammond, Oct. 14, 1810.*
Sally, and Samuel White, int. Jan. 13, 1822.

**STODDER,** Ann Noyes, and Milo Green of Stoneham, int. July 10, 1846.
Elisabeth, of Hingham, and John Burroughs, int. Mar. 24, 1816.
Samuel, and Susan Williams, Jan. 28, 1816.*
Sarah [Mrs. int.], and Benj[ami]n D. Fillmore, Aug. 11, 1833.*
Sarah A., of Lowell, and Nathaniel P. Rust, int. Apr. 1, 1848.
William H., and Sarah C. Barkman, int. May 4, 1848.
William L., and Almira Ames, Aug. 10, 1820.*

**STOEL** (see also Stowell), Abigail, Mrs., of Dedham, and James Duff, at Dedham, July 8, 1760.

**STONE,** Abigail, and John Lewes [Lewis. C. R. 2.], Jan. 20, 1763.
Abigail, Mrs., and Lt. Ebenezer Cheney, May 14, 1772.
Alanson, and Sarah E. Wales of Dorchester, int. Nov. 7, 1846.
Andrew, Dr., and Harriet C. Ward, int. Apr. 16, 1837.
Beulah, of Newton, and Lemuel Richards, int. May 29, 1814.
Clarissa D., of Dorchester, and Oliver Hall, int. Nov. 23, 1834.
Daniel, and Sophia Wadleigh, Dec. 1, 1822.*
David [of Newton. C. R. 2.], and Mary Herring, Feb. 13, 1755.

* Intention also recorded.

STONE, Eliza E., and Nathaniel R. Childs, Apr. 30, 1846.*
Elizabeth, and Christopher Picket, June —, 1647.
Emeline E., of Framingham, and Rufus T. King, int. Aug. 8, 1841.
Frances, of Harwich, and Nathaniel Sparhawk, int. Oct. 19, 1788.
Francis, and Mary Adeline Farrington, Feb. 20, 1827.*
Frederick A., of Brookline, and Mary Ann E. Green, int. Jan. 15, 1848.
John, and Mrs. Mary Goddard, Oct. 23, 1729.
John, and Mary Harkness, May 11, 1733.
John, jr., and Mary Kennington, Feb. 25, 1849.*
Mary, and Oliver [Charles. c. R. 2.] Baxter [of Braintree. c. R. 2.], Feb. 18, 1762.
Mary, Mrs., and Reuben Baldwin, int. Mar. 10, 1844.
Nath[anie]l, and Lucy Fowle, June 8, 1809.*
Peter, and Abigail Winchester, Dec. 5, 1749.
Samuel, of Framingham, and Hannah Searle, at Watertown, May 21, 1716.
Samuell, of Stoughton, and Dorothy Monk, Apr. 1, 1734.
Susannah, and Jonathan Rawson, ———, 1761. [bef. Mar. 26. c. R. 2.]
Thomas, and Mary Cragg, Dec. 4, 1639.
Tobias, and Phebe W. Homans, July 18, 1837.
Warren W., and Eliza A. Francis, Sept. 18, 1842.*

STORY, Abigail, and Ja[m]es Pike [May or June ?] 1708.
Lydia A., and Alfred T. Read, int. Aug. 29, 1841.
William, and Abigail Torrey, Dec. 3, 1707.

STOW, Elize[be]th, and Henry Archer, Dec. 4, 1639.

STOWELL (see also Stoel), Jesse, of Dedham, and Polly Talbott, int. Apr. 28, 1799.
Jonathan, of Newton, and Margaret Hewet, Mar. 6, 1722-3.
Mary Ann, and David Beck, int. Dec. 27, 1849.
Samuel, and Mrs. Lydia Calder of Dorchester, int. Nov. 3, 1805.

STOWERS, Susan, and John Ayers, int. May 4, 1845.

STRANGER, Joseph, and Sarah Watkins, int. Sept. 8, 1833.
Sarah, of Boston, and Cornelius Cowing, int. Dec. 3, 1849.

* Intention also recorded.

**STRATTEN** (see also Stratton), Rebekah, and Jeremiah Robbins [Robbens. int.], Oct. 8, 1798. C. R. 2.*

**STRATTON** (see also Stratten), Betsey, of Weston, and Jedediah Thayer, int. Feb. 22, 1801.

Hannah, of Foxborough, and Jedediah Carpenter, int. Feb. 12, 1809.

Jonathan, of Dorchester, and Waitstill Tolman, at Dorchester, July 21, 1800.*

Joseph, and Sally Hayward, June 21, 1801.*

Lucy, of Foxborough, and John Farwell, int. Jan. 12, 1823.

Susannah, and Samuel Knower, Dec. 1, 1822.*

Thankful, of Fitzwilliam, N. H., and Dea. Nehemiah Munroe, int. July 25, 1819.

William F., and Lucy Sessions, Jan. 18, 1838.*

**STREETER,** Mary, of Cambridge, and Andrew Watkin, at Charlestown, Dec. 10, 1701.

**STRICKER,** Nicholas, and Phebe Hooper of Wilmington, at Woburn, Nov. 29, 1731.

**STROBRIDGE** (see also Trowbridge), Rebeckah [Trowbridge. int.], and Levi Colburn of Needham, at Needham, Sept. 18, 1783.*

**STRONG,** Joseph, of South Hadley, and Harriot W. Whitney, Feb. 11, 1813.*

Sarah Jane, and Charles J. Anjema, int. May 19, 1844.

**STRUTHERS,** Andrew, and Margaret Hopsack [Margarett Hossack, int.], both of Scotland, July 14, 1849. C. R. 5.*

**STUBBS,** Simeon, and Lucy L. Ryerson, int. Dec. 11, 1846.

**STUMPF,** John P., and Margaret Follen, int. Dec. 1, 1844.

**STURGIS,** Harriet T., and William A. White of Watertown, int. Mar. 29, 1845.

James, and Mary Catherine Townsend, Oct. 8, 1845.*

**STURTEVANT** (see also Sturtevent), Hannah, and John Erskine of Abington, Sept. 15, 1813.*

**STURTEVENT** (see also Sturtevant), Isaac, Lt., and Rebecca Wyman, Apr. 18, 1782.

* Intention also recorded.

**STUTSON** (see also Stetson), Jesse, and Sally Dickerman, Jan. 13, 1801.*

**STYMES,** Elizabeth [Stymer. int.], and David Phipps of Hopkinton, May 22, 1800.*

**SULLAVAN** (see also Sullivan), John, and Catharine Shield, int. Nov. 10, 1845.

**SULLIVAN** (see also Sullavan), Ann, and Morris Fitzgerald, int. Apr. 26, 1840.
Cornelius, and Charlotte Wight, int. Apr. 1, 1847.
Cornelius, and Hannah Hurley, int. Aug. 20, 1849.
Elizabeth A., and Pierre Bazile Mignault, M. D. of Worcester, int. Aug. 12, 1848.
Hannah, and William Murphy, int. Apr. 6, 1846.
Hannah, and Matthew Hogan, int. Sept. 27, 1849.
John [of Boston. int.], b. Ireland, and Jane Talbot, b. Ireland, Feb. 20, 1849.*
Julia, and John Morrison [Morrisson. int.], Feb. 25, 1847.*
Margarett, and Patrick Clifford, int. Apr. 9, 1849.
Mary, and John Katurn, Apr. 2, 1835.*
Mary, and Michael Murphy, June 24, 1848.*
Mary, and Thomas Good, int. Oct. 7, 1848.
Mary, and James McCue, int. June 9, 1849.
Peter, and Ann Thompson, int. Feb. 8, 1849.
Thomas, and Eliza Kenny, int. Dec. 11, 1849.
Timothy, and Ellen Donnavan, int. Mar. 22, 1847.
Timothy, and Mary Mason, int. Jan. 17, 1849.
William, and Catherine Schields of Boston, int. Sept. 24, 1847.
William, and Hanora Donivan, int. Sept. 25, 1847.

**SUMMERS** (see also Sommers), Nicholas, and Sarah Swain, int. Apr. 25, 1841.

**SUMNER,** Arthur, jr., and Sarah Holland of Cambridge, int. Mar. 3, 1833.
Catherine, and Gershom Cutler [Gersham Cutter. int.], jr., at Cambridge, June 23, 1786.*
Edward, and Elizabeth Clap, Sept. 25, 1701.
Edward, and [Mrs. int.] Rebecca Payson, July 4, 1785.*
Edward, and Joanna Sumner of Shrewsbury, int. May 25, 1806.
Edward, and Philenia A. Tucker, int. Oct. 5, 1845.

* Intention also recorded.

SUMNER, Elisabeth, and Charles Cushing, Esq., Aug. 25, 1768.

Eliz[abe]th, Mrs., and Benjamin Boylston of Brookline, Nov. 30, 1727.

Elizabeth, and Lt. Jesse Doggett, Dec. 1, 1790.*

Elizabeth, and John Gould, Feb. —, 1795.*

Elizabeth, Mrs., of Milton, and Paul Lyon, int. May 27, 1821.

Esther, and John Sables [Savels. int.] of Dorchester, at Dorchester, Mar. 1, 1798.*

Fanny, and Elijah Lewis, Nov. 14, 1803.*

Hannah, Mrs., and Rev. John Newman, Oct. 27, 1748.

Increase, Hon., and Elizabath Hyslop, Sept. 30, 1779.

Joanna, of Shrewsbury, and Edward Sumner, int. May 25, 1806.

Job, and Sarah B. Pond, June 9, 1825. C. R. 2.*

John, and Mrs. Susanna Stevens, Nov. 20, 1729.

Josiah, of Milton, and Sarah Draper, Dec. 8, 1737.

Lucy, and William Bowman, June 5, 1777.

Luther, and Elizabeth Ross of Deering, N. H., int. Sept. 27, 1829.

Maria, and Timothy D. Brown, Apr. 25, 1813.*

Martha E[lizabeth. int.], and James Anderson, ———, 1832. [Oct. 23, 1831. int.]*

Mary, and Abraham Gorton, May 31, 1683.

Mary, Mrs., and Rev. Thomas Balch of Dedham, Oct. 11, 1737.

Mary and John Williams, May 5, 1768.

Mary F. [T. int.], and Thomas Fillebrown, jr. of Washington, D. C., Aug. 19, 1819.*

Mary H., and John Goldsmith, both of Brookline, May 26, 1825.*

Nancy, and Joshua Seaver, Apr. 6, 1803.*

Nancy, and Samuel W. Weld, May 27, 1818.*

Polly, and Gerry Fairbanks, May 20, 1806.*

Rebecca, and Dr. Samuel C. Williams of Shrewsbury, May 5, 1818.*

Samuel, of Pomfret, and Elizabeth Griffin, Nov. 20, 1723.

Samuel, and Susanna Boylston, Aug. 18, 1757.

Sam[ue]l, and Mary Weld, May 11, 1767.

Sam[ue]l, Dea., and Elizabeth Williams, July 19, 1781.

Sarah, and Ebenezer Davis, Aug. 19, 1756.

Sarah, and Samuel Churchill, Mar. 21, 1803.*

* Intention also recorded.

SUMNER, Sarah E., a. 16 y., d. Arthur and Mary, and Lucius B. Bodge, a. 23 y., gentleman, s. John and Mary, Nov. 26, 1847.*

Sarah F., of Charlestown, and Thomas S. Weld, int. Feb. 11, 1838.

Susan, and Timothy Hunt, Dec. 2, 1824.*

William, of Milton, and Mary Tucker, at Milton, ———, 1751.

William H., of Dorchester [of Boston C. R. 3.], and Maria F. Greenough, Dec. 13, 1835. [1836. C. R. 3.]*

SUNDERLAND, Elizabeth, and Nathanael Brewer, Dec. 26, 1705.

Margarett E., of Charlestown, and John D. Cooper, jr., June 27, 1849.

SUTTON, Samuel, jr., and Anne Hills of Boston, int. Oct. 21, 1846.

SWAIN (see also Swaine), Benj[ami]n, and Sophia Riding, Aug. 8, 1841.*

Charles D., a. 25 y., grocer, s. Joseph and Elizabeth, and Eliza S. Newman, a. 25 y., d. W[illia]m J. and Sarah B., June 4, 1848.*

Elizabeth F., and Reuben Smith, jr., int. Dec. 13, 1840.

John Howland, and Ann Maria Meader of Nantucket, int. Sept. 25, 1847.

Joseph, and Elizabeth S. W. Pearson, June 27, 1819.*

Lydia Frances, of Nantucket, resident of Philadelphia, a. abt. 27 y., b. Nantucket, d. Hezekiah and Lydia, of the Society of Friends, and Abijah W. Draper, resident of Philadelphia, physician, a. abt. 31 y., s. Abijah, M. D. and Lavina (Tyler), at Philadelphia, Jan. 20, 1839.

Sarah, and Nicholas Summers, int. Apr. 25, 1841.

SWAINE (see also Swain), John, and Freelove George, Jan. 16, 1757.

SWALLOW, Abel, and Dorcas Parmenter of Sudbury, int. May 22, 1814.

Elmira, and Ephraim Dudley, May 7, 1835.*

Ezra, and Nancy E. Shurtliff, May 21, 1820. C. R. 2.*

Isaiah Dunster, and Zibiah Davis, May 30, 1813. C. R. 2.*

Louisa H., a. 27 y., d. Ezra and Nancy E., and Horace W. Pierce, a. 27 y., provision dealer, s. Horace and Sarah, of Brighton, Dec. 24, 1848.*

* Intention also recorded.

SWALLOW, Rebecca, and Abraham Sanburn [Sanborn. int.],
Mar. 6, 1825. C. R. 2.*

**SWAN,** Ebenezer, and Sarah Whiston, Oct. 25, 1770.
Ebenezer, and [Mrs. C. R. 2.] Elizabeth Whiting, Oct. 31,
1780.
Horace B., a. 35 y., laborer, s. Jonah and Elizabeth, and Mary
Ann Merrifield, a. 26 y., d. Stephen and Lydia, June 7,
1848.*
Martha, and John Bender, int. Mar. 3, 1839.
Mary, Mrs., and Andrew Gardner, Nov. 12, 1702.
Thomas, and Mrs. Prudence Wade of Medford, at Charles-
town, Dec. 27, 1692.

**SWANY** (see also Sweeney), Charlotte, and Timothy Mahony,
int. Aug. 4, 1848.

**SWASEY** (see also Swazey), Augustus C., and Sarah Ann
Gove of Cambridge, June 9, 1844.*
Lydia, and William K. Cochran, ———, 1832. [Oct. 9, 1831.
int.]*
Manuel, jr., and Dorcas Levitt Smith, int. Nov. 14, 1824.
Rosalinda, and Joshua Tufts, Dec. 2, 1819.*

**SWAZEY** (see also Swasey), Mary Ann, a. 19 y., d. Emanuel
and Dorcas, and Isaac H. White, widr., a. 48 y., carpenter, s. Micah and Jane, Sept. 4, 1846.*

**SWEAT** (see also Sweet), Abagail, and John Bodge, int. Nov.
23, 1800.
Jeremiah M., and Lydia A. Caswell, int. Jan. 18, 1846.
Joseph W., and Louisa Graham, int. Nov. 7, 1830.
Mark P., and Rachel Litchfield of Cohasset, Oct. 11, 1829.*
Martha O., and Elijah L. Davenport, int. Dec. 6, 1829.
Mary Anne Tower, and James L. P. Orrok, int. Feb. 14, 1830.
Thacher, and Eliza M. Wentworth, int. Oct. 18, 1829.

**SWEENEY** (see also Swany, Sweeny), Ann, of Boston, and
John Boyle, int. Mar. 20, 1849.
Julia, and Andrew Murphy, int. Sept. 26, 1846.
Margarett, and Thomas McAndrews, int. July 3, 1847.
Miles, and Nancy Bowman, int. Feb. 17, 1849.

**SWEENY** (see also Sweeney), Nath[anie]l, and Margaret
Murry, int. Oct. 22, 1837.

* Intention also recorded.

**SWEET** (see also Sweat), Adeline, and John Hill, May 18, 1837.*

Henery H. F. [Rev. int.], and Elizabeth Henshaw, Jan. 18, 1826. c. r. 2.*

Sophia, and William P. Sargent, int. Sept. 14, 1834.

Thomas, and Nancy Brayley of Grafton, Dec. 27, 1840.*

**SWEETSER,** Eunice, of South Reading, and Timothy Bailey, int. Nov. 24, 1816.

Robert, and Caroline W. Bryant of Lynnfield, int. June 8, 1834.

**SWETNAM,** John, and Catherine Crowley, int. Aug. 30, 1847.

**SWIFT,** David [resident. int.], and Cynthia Morse of Falmouth, at Falmouth, Sept. 24, 1786.*

Henry, and Ann Davis, Nov. 30, 1843.*

John, and Anne Gridley, Nov. 18, 1779.

Joseph L., and Elizabeth A. Rugg of Charlestown, int. Apr. 23, 1837

Nancy, of Milton, and Samuel Barry, int. May 21, 1786.

Nancy, and Ezra Bourns [Baurns. int.] of Falmouth, Nov. 28, 1799.*

Samuel, and Polly Cheany, Nov. 2, 1806.*

**SWINNETON,** Joanna, and Benjamin West, June 19, 1718.

**SYLVESTER** (see also Silvester), Adam, and Mary Gardner, Dec. 4, 1828.

**SYMMES** (see also Sims), Elizabeth, and James Arkerson, Sept. 17, 1837.*

S. Jane, of Medford, and John Hunt, int. Oct. 10, 1846.

William Thompson, and Nancy Guild Downs, Aug. 24, 1823.

**SYMONDS** (see also Simmons), Ann Maria, and Augustus E. Price, both of Salem, Apr. 29, 1849.

Sarah, and John Russell, Aug. 31, 1794.*

**TABER,** Catharine, and Isaac Wyman, Dec. 8, 1822.*

Elizabeth B., and John I. [J. int.] Marshall of Framingham, Jan. 11, 1838.*

Elnathan, and Catharine Partridge, Jan. 8, 1797.*

Thomas, of New York, and Harriet Wyman, Apr. 15, 1824.*

* Intention also recorded.

**TAFT,** Adolphus, and Abigail Smith [of Brookline. int.], Aug. 25, 1811. C. R. 2.*

Caroline, and William H. Souther, int. Oct. 11, 1840.

Dandridge, and Rebecca Gordon, Oct. 26, 1824.*

Orray A., and Elizabeth White, int. Apr. 19, 1840.

Rebecca, Mrs., and John Tileston, Mar. 4, 1835.*

Reed, and Mary Shurtliff [Shirtliff. int.], May 9, 1810. C. R. 2.*

Samuel J., and Lucy C. Hayward, int. Jan. 2, 1831.

**TAGUE** (see also Teague), Catherine, and Francis McColfe, int. Dec. 5, 1848.

**TALBOT** (see also Talbott, Talbutt), David, and Catharine Davis, Oct. 19, 1806. C. R. 2.*

David, a. 26 y., painter, s. Nathaniel and Nancy, and [Mrs. int.] Mary B. Gregory, a. 22 y., d. Charles and Betsey, Mar. 20, 1845.*

Edward T., and Ann R. Mosely, both of Dorchester, Feb. 2, 1835.

Hannah [Talbott. int.], and Nathan DeWolf [of Dorchester. int.], July 31, 1808. C. R. 2.*

Jane, b. Ireland, and John Sullivan [of Boston. int.], b. Ireland, Feb. 20, 1849.*

Nathan, and Sarah Wilson of Newton, at Newton, June 12, 1770.

Nath[anie]l, and Mrs. Martha Day of Needham, int. Nov. 26, 1807.

**TALBOTT** (see also Talbot), Polly, and Jesse Stowell of Dedham, int. Apr. 28, 1799.

**TALBUTT** (see also Talbot), Lydia [Talbot. C. R. 2.], and Samuel Feecham, Aug. 10, 1794.*

**TALLANT,** Andrew, of Pelham, N. H., and Amealia Weld, Feb. 29, 1792.*

**TALMAN** (see also Tolman), John, and Mary Richards of Dedham, at Dedham, Jan. 5, 1709-10.

**TAMONEY,** John, and Ellen Gillagan, int. Oct. 15, 1846.

**TAPLEY,** Elvena S., of Danvers, and William O. Wallis of Chelsea, July 16, 1843.

* Intention also recorded.

**TAPPAN,** Mary Ann, of Boston, and Willard Bullard, jr., int. May 21, 1847.

**TARBELL,** Daniel, and Betsey Wheeler of Ashby, int. July 29, 1804.

**TARBOX,** Sarah, and Leonard S. Payson, int. May 20, 1827.

**TARR,** Mary, and Charles Bicknell, Sept. 13, 1827.*
David, and Louisa B. Varney, Jan. 5, 1837.*

**TARRALL,** Mary, of Cambridge, and Daniel Agin, int. May 25, 1846.

**TASGATERF,** Hannah [Fosgat. c. R. 3.], and Gilman Smith [jr. int] of Sandwich, N. H., Nov. 28, 1833.*

**TATCHELL,** Martha, Mrs., and Reuben Smith, int. Dec. 27, 1835.

**TATMAN,** Jabez. and Deborah Turner, Nov. 18, 1668.
Mary, and John Frisell, May 8, 1734.

**TAUNJANS,** Jean Joseph [Tarenjans. int.], and Elizabeth Litchfield, Jan. 7, 1793.*

**TAY,** Peter, b. Ireland, and Ann Blake, b. Ireland, Oct. 30, 1849.*

**TAYLOR,** Asher, and Maranda Gaffield, Dec. 30, 1844.*
James, of Carlisle, a. 27 y., s. Abel and Sarah, and Maria Proctor, a. 23 y., d. Abijah and Sarah, Apr. 8, 1847.*
Jonathan Moore, of New York, and Harriet A. Gragg, int. Mar. 27, 1842.
John, and Luce Smith, Mar. 12, 1721-2.
John, of Medway, and Eliz[abe]th Davis, July 10, 1732.
John W., and Clarissa Glines, Dec. 5, 1831.*
Mary R., and Alpheus Moore, Sept. 9, 1827.*
Obed, laborer, and Jerusha Bristor of Rumford, Me., a. 33 y., Sept. 7, 1846.*
Sarah, and Benjamin C. Kenniston [Kenneston. int.], May 12, 1844.*
Simeon, and Mary T. Trask, int. Oct. 12, 1834.

**TEAGUE** (see also Tague), Bani, and Sally White of Ossipee, N. H., int. Feb. 16, 1834.

* Intention also recorded.

**TEEL,** Lydia, and John Baker, int. May 4, 1806.

**TEELEY,** Jeremiah, and Ann Stanford, int. Mar. 1, 1848.

**TEGERT,** William M., and Mary Ann Ferguson, int. Sept. 28, 1845.

**TEMPLE,** Caroline, of Dorchester, and Samuel Blake, int. Nov. 30, 1828.

**TENNEY,** Elizabeth, of Monson, Me., and William H. Hills of Cambridge, July 25, 1846.

**TERRILL** (see also Tirrell), Charlotte, and John Reed, int. Apr. 16, 1837.
George, of Quincy, and Abigil Meservey, Aug. 22, 1819.*

**TEUCK,** Hannah Maria, and David A. Gilcreas, Apr. 28, 1845.

**THAIR** (see also Thayer), Benjamin, and Mrs. Jane Clark, both of Brookline, Mar. 9, 1769.

**THAXTER,** Edward C., and Nancy W. Pennell, int. Aug. 10, 1834.

**THAYER** (see also Thair), Abigail S., and True Russell, int. Sept. 22, 1839.
Elizabeth B. D., of Brookline, and Samuel Guild, jr., int. Dec. 17, 1843.
Ellen M., a. 25 y., d. Robert H. and Abigail, and Henry M. Barbour of Worcester, a. 25 y., s. Isaac R. and C. P., May 30, 1848.*
Esther, and Nathaniel Corey [Coney. int.], Apr. 9, 1801. c. R. 2.
Frederick F., and Hannah W. Hersey, int. Nov. 20, 1842.
Hannah, Mrs., and Richard Allen, int. May 29, 1791.
Jedediah, and Betsey Stratton of Weston, int. Feb. 22, 1801.
Lott, and Sarah Scott of Brookline, int. Jan. 11, 1789.
Lydia, of Braintree, and Samuel Croxford, at Braintree, Dec. 4, 1774.
Nancy, and Daniel McC. Prince, July 4, 1804.*
Polly [Polley. int.], and John Davis, jr., at Weymouth, Nov. 5, 1786.*

* Intention also recorded.

THAYER, Rachel [Mrs. Rebecca Thayo, resident. int.], and
Ebenezer Scott [jr. int.], May 9, 1785.*

Rachel, and Silas Cross, int. Sept. 30, 1798.

Rhoda, and John Foster [jr. int.], June 10, 1804.*

Sarah Jane, of Gray, Me., and James L. Leighton, int. Nov
6, 1846.

Thomas, and Rebecca White, Dec. 22, 1793.*

Warren, of New York, and Rebecca F. Green, int. June 8,
1845.

**THOMAS,** Adeline S., and Henry Brown, int. May 18, 1845.

Caleb, and Lucy Loud, June 27, 1790.*

Cha[rle]s H., of Hingham, and Louisa E. Bradford, Dec. 12,
1833.*

Charles, and Mary Jane Munsey, int. Feb. 26, 1843.

James, and Margarett Brown, Sept. 16, 1845.*

John, and Sarah S. Robinson of Hartford, Me., int. Apr. 13,
1847.

John B., and Frances A. Nightingale, Aug. 30, 1842.

Julia D., and Thomas B. Pinkham, Oct. 24, 1848.*

Lucy, and John Stephens, Jan. 28, 1810.*

Mary, of Middleboro, and Winslow Thomas, int. Mar. 10,
1848.

Rebecca and Ezra Morse, Nov. 8, 1821.*

Sandrus H., and Julia D. Snell, July 15, 1844.*

William, and Helen Patterson, int. Dec. 19, 1841.

Winslow, and Mary Thomas of Middleboro, int. Mar. 10, 1848.

**THOMPSON** (see also Thomson, Tompson, Tompsonn, Tomson), Abiel E., of Concord, N. H., and Margaret E.
Brazier, May 22, 1822.*

Andrew C., and Eliza Perkins, Oct. 8, 1833.*

Ann, and Peter Sullivan, int. Feb. 8, 1849.

Benja[min], and Sarah Bowman, at Boston, Sept. 22, 1724.

Benjamin, and Rebecca Wyman of Woburn, at Woburn, Aug.
18, 1730.

Bethia [F. int.], and Thomas Glover, Mar. 24, 1842.*

Bridget, and Simon Dolan, int. Dec. 31, 1847.

Bridgett, of Boston, and Patrick Sharkey, int. Feb. 2, 1847.

Caroline, a. 23 y., dressmaker, d. Asa and Sarah, and Henry
A. M. Godfrey, a. 24 y., carpenter, s. Abram and Lydia,
Sept 21, 1845

George, and Elizabeth Webb, Oct. 31, 1809.*

* Intention also recorded.

THOMPSON, George, of Charlestown, and Mary H. Morton of
Milton, Nov. 11, 1833. c. r. 3.

Geo[rge] M., of Southborough, and Eliz[abeth] F. Chucbuck,
Apr. 9, 1840.*

James M., and Caroline Matilda Stell, int. May 24, 1835.

Jane, and William Barnes [Barns. int.], Nov. 29, 1793.*

Martha [Tompson. int.], and Enoch Hazen of Rowley, Feb.
9, 1797.*

Mary E., and Micah Campbell, int. Aug. 7, 1842.

Sally, of Walpole, and William Sheddon, int. Aug. 25, 1805.

Samuel, and Jane Steward, June 30, 1747.

Samuel, and Rachel Kingsbury of Walpole, int. June 21, 1829.

Samuel, and Mary Ryan, int. May 2, 1848.

Thomas, and Mary Foster, Oct. 28, 1765.

William V., and Lucretia P. Holt, int. Apr. 26, 1840.

THOMSON (see also Thompson), Benjamin, and Prudence
Pacon, at Dedham, Dec. 13, 1698.

Philip, and Mrs. Mary Mountjoy, June 4, 1714.

William, and Mary Clark, Dec. 3, 1760.

THORERING, Mary, and John Gore, Nov. 15, 1744. c. r. 2.

THORNTON, Dorcas A., and John Donald of Chelsea, July
25, 1842.*

J. Wingate [of Boston. int.], a. 29 y., an attorney at law, s.
James B., of Saco, Me. and Eliza Gookin of Northampton, N. H., and Elizabeth [Elisabeth. int.] Wallace
Bowles, a. 19 y., d. Stephen J. and Elizabeth T., May
31, 1848.*

THORPE, Allice, and William Davis, Oct. 21, 1658.

THRASHER, Richard, and Mary Tileston, May 8, 1821.*

THURSTON, Eli, of Cambridge, and Frances Burrel, Apr. 27,
1806.*

Joseph, and Lucy Goodwin, Dec. 22, 1805.*

THWING (see also Twing), Benjamin, and Bathsheba Pason,
Aug. 12, 1719.

Isaac, of Dorchester, and Fanny Vose, int. Sept. 14, 1817.

Mary, of Cambridge, and John Dove, int. Jan. 23, 1803.

S. H., and Thomas Simmons, int. Oct. 2, 1825.

Supply C., and Elsey Fellowes Davis, May 18, 1824.*

* Intention also recorded.

THWING, Supply Clap, and Ann Shapley Haven, of Philadelphia, at Philadelphia, June 30, 1847. P. R. 1.
Susan Gray, and James Sharp, Apr. 4, 1822.*

TIBBETS, Enoch, and Mary B. Leonard of Foxborough, int. May 30, 1849.

TIFFANY, Loring, and Mary Downer, int. Dec. 15, 1822.
Mary G., Mrs., and Paul Farnum, int. Nov. 27, 1831.

TILDEN, Frances, and Robert W. Ames [a. 34 y. in pencil. int.], Mar. 4, 1844.*

TILESTON (see also Tilestone), Edward H., a. 24 y., carpenter, and Emeline L. McCoy, a. 24 y., seamstress, Sept. 22, 1845.*
Ezekiel, and Mehitabell Glover, Jan. 10, 1774.
John, of Dorchester, and Sarah Woods, Dec. 16, 1725.
John, and Mrs. Rebecca Taft, Mar. 4, 1835.*
John N., of Dorchester, and Lydia M. Harvey, int. Mar. 20, 1842.
Martha, and Stephen Davis, at Dorchester, July 1, 1787.*
Mary, and Richard Thrasher, May 8, 1821.*
Nancy, of Dorchester, and Jonathan Williams, int. Sept. 12, 1802.
Nathaniel, and Elizabeth Draper, Nov. 9, 1790.*
Thomas, Capt., of Dorchester, and Elizabeth Wait, July 8, 1790.*
Tho[ma]s, and Mary Martin, June 18, 1809.*

TILESTONE (see also Tileston), Catherine, and Henry Dalrimple of Cambridge, Sept. 13, 1807.*
Releif Holland [Tileston. int.], of Dorchester, and Lemuel Baker Davis, at Dorchester, Nov. 14, 1797.*
Thomas, and Mary Gardner, ——, 30, 1700.
William, and Elizebeth Smith of Lexington, int. July 21, 1804.

TILLSON, Maria L., and Thomas Q. Weston of Middleboro, int. Nov. 28, 1848.
Timothy, and Mary Martin, June 18, 1809. C. R. 3.
William F., and Lucy W. Shurtliff of Carver, int. May 8, 1849.

TILLTON, Harriet, Mrs., and Josiah E. Johnson, int. Sept. 11, 1842.

* Intention also recorded.

**TIMENS,** Patrick, and Sabanna Heegan, int. July 3, 1847.
John, jr., and Caroline B. Cook, Feb. 25, 1830.

**TINKHAM,** James, and Sarah R. Bell of Brookline, June 18, 1835. c. r. 7.
Luther, and Ann Jennette E. Braman of Providence, R. I., int. May 4, 1845.

**TIRREL** (see also Tirrell), Rachel, and Stephen Randall, May 12, 1816.*

**TIRRELL** (see also Terrill, Tirrel, Turill), Hanah, of Weymouth, and Samuel Smith, at Weymouth, Nov. 21, 1782.

**TITCOMB,** George [of Boston. c. r. 3.], and Charlotte Lowder, Oct. 18, 1829.*
Phebe, and Timothy W. Bennett of Brighton, Dec. 27, 1829.*

**TITTERTON,** Elizabeth, and Michael Whittemore [jr. int.], June 10, 1804. c. r. 2.*
Gabriel, and Fanny Child, both residents, Sept. 11, 1787.*
Hannah, and Jonas Learned, both residents, Aug. 16, 1787.*

**TOBEY** (see also Toby), Sarah H., and Welcome Parmeter, int. Aug. 17, 1823.

**TOBIN,** Bridget, and Thomas Mulleany, int. May 26, 1849.

**TOBY** (see also Tobey), Elisha, and Sally Humphry of Dorchester, int. Apr. 5, 1801.
Elisha, of Dorchester, and Betsey Whittemore, Dec. 5, 1802.*
Elizabeth, and Nathaniel Drew, May 24, 1829.*
Lois M., and Isaac I. Sousman, int. May 1, 1842.
Nancy, and William White, Sept. 1, 1825.*

**TODD,** Eliza, and Robert Fleming, Nov. 12, 1848.
Hannah T., and George Miller of Dorchester, Oct. 30, 1836.*

**TOLEMAN** (see also Tolman), Nancy, of Brookline, and John Woodward, int. May 7, 1786.

**TOLEN,** Elen, and P. M. Kenna, int. Oct. 26, 1841.

**TOLMAN** (see also Talman, Toleman), Albert, of Worcester, and [Mrs. int.] Susanna R. Hunstable, Apr. 3, 1839.*
Deborah, and Charles Litchfield, int. May 15, 1836.
Elisha, of Lincoln, and Lucretia Pike of Dorchester, Sept. 18, 1797.

* Intention also recorded.

TOLMAN, Elisha, jr., and Henrietta H. Mayo, Sept. 16, 1824.*

Ezekiel, and Sarah Perry, Nov. 20, 1764.

Hewett, of Marshfield, and Betsey Small, June 9, 1844.*

James B., and Mary Ann Felton, Jan. 15, 1835.*

Lydia, and Wesley Knowls, Apr. —, 1834.

Nath[anie]l, and Charlotte Dunton, int. Apr. 20, 1834.

Rebecca [Rebeccah. int.], and John Wetherbee [Weatherbee. int.], Feb. 12, 1797. c. r. 2.*

Waitstill, and Jonathan Stratton of Dorchester, at Dorchester, July 21, 1800.*

TOMLINE, Elizabeth, Mrs., resident of Dorchester, and Edward Shearin [Shearer. c. r. 5.], Jan. 9, 1839.*

TOMPSON (see also Thompson), Benjamin, jr., and Mrs. Hannah Ellis, July 2, 1730.

TOMPSONN (see also Thompson), Mary, and Joseph Wise, Dec. 3, 1641.

TOMSON (see also Thompson), Bridget, and George Denison, Mar. —, 1640.

TOOMEY (see also Tormey), William, and Catherine Hynes, int. May 13, 1847.

TOPHAM, Margaret, and Nathanael Lyon, Jan. 23, 1738-9.

TOPLIFF, Patience, of Dorchester, and Nathaniel Craft, at Dorchester, Nov. 26, 1701.

TORBOT, Elizabeth, and Ebenezer Lyon, at Dedham, July 15, 1700.

John, and Abigall Cass. at Dedham, Nov. 17, 1698.

TORMEY (see also Toomey), Ann, and Thomas Rully, int. June 19, 1845.

TORRANCE, Susanna Hardin, of Dedham, and John Cleveland, int. July 5, 1812.

TORREY (see also Tory), Abigail, and William Story, Dec. 3, 1707.

Daniel [Torsey. int.], of Lowell, and Roxanna Boothby, Dec. 22, 1844.

Eliza J., of Deer Isle, Me., and L. H. Griffin, int. Aug. 18, 1847.

Mary, and John Davis, at Dorchester, Jan. 14, 1673.

* Intention also recorded.

**TORY** (see also Torrey), Phillip, and Mary Scarborow, Oct. 1, 1647.

**TOULE** (see also Towle), Patrick, and Jane Healy, int. Dec. 14, 1847.

**TOWER,** Charles F., and Harriet N. Bisbee of Waterville, int. June 12, 1847.
Polly, and Benjamin Babbit, May 13, 1805.*

**TOWL** (see also Towle), Eliza, and Levi Davis, July 9, 1820.*
John, and Catharine Randall, May 13, 1825.*

**TOWLE** (see also Toule, Towl), Angelina, of Exeter, N. H., and Jonathan Leavitt, int. June 9, 1833.

**TOWNE,** Elizabeth H., and Nathan Haynes, int. Jan. 25, 1846.
William S., and Sarah J. Brown, int. July 2, 1846.

**TOWNSEND,** Elisha, and Mrs. Martha Newel, July 24, 1729.
Eliza, and John Milnes of Lowell, Mar. 31, 1847. c. r. 5.
Mary Catharine, and James Sturgis, Oct. 8, 1845.*

**TOY,** William, and Grace Newell, Sept. 14, 1644.

**TRACEY** (see also Tracy), James, and Deborah O'Keefe, int. Sept. 28, 1845.

**TRACY** (see also Tracey), Ann, b. Ireland, and Michael Manning, b. Ireland, June 26, 1849.*
Bridget, and Thomas Tracy, int. Dec. 5, 1849.
Catharine, and Barney Curley, int. June 14, 1840.
Ellen, and Patrick Laughlin, int. Jan. 4, 1847.
Francis, and Emily Branham, int. Jan. 15, 1848.
Joseph W., and Mary Laughlin of Boston, int. June 28, 1848.
Margaret, and James Mitchell, int. Aug. 14, 1842.
Mary, and Michael Flinn, int. Oct. 2, 1842.
Peter, and Maria Kenney, int. Aug. 17, 1849.
Thomas, and Bridget Tracy, int. Dec. 5, 1849.

**TRAIN,** Samuel F., and Francis G. Glover, Nov. 20, 1839.*
William G., a. 23 y., merchant, s. Samuel and Hannah P., and Mary E. Phipps, a. 21 y., d. William and Elizabeth V., Apr. 4, 1849.*

**TRAIP,** Hannah J., and John A. Drew, int. Nov. 2, 1845.

* Intention also recorded.

**TRASK,** Abigail L., and Francis Munroe of Framingham, int. Oct. 23, 1843.

Abigail Louisa, and William Finneron, int. Apr. 3, 1825.

Betsy, and Abraham Nightingale of Quincy, Nov. 28, 1805.*

Eliza [Else. c. r. 3.], and Jonathan W. Waldron, June 5, 1836.*

Emeline H., a. 25 y., d. John and Sarah, and Nahum R. Ross of Troy, N. Y., a. 30 y., machinist, May 26, 1847.*

Harriet S., a. 18 y., d. Lyman P. and Caroline, and William H. Allen, a. 22 y., carpenter, s. Oliver N. and Frances O., May 21, 1849.*

Julia Ann, and Luke Jewett, Aug. 17, 1826.*

Lyman, and Caroline Valentine, int. May 2, 1830.

Mary, and Lemuel Cox, int. Jan. 3, 1819.

Mary T., and Simeon Taylor, int. Oct. 12, 1834.

Penelope, of Munson, and Ezra Tupper, jr., int. Aug. 10, 1811.

Rebeccah, and Manley Richardson, int. Nov. 9, 1828.

Samuel, jr., and Juliet Eliza Rand, int. Nov. 2, 1823.

Susan F., a. 18 y., d. William and Elsey, and Joseph Q. Twombly, a. 21 y., painter, s. James H. and Abigail of Milton, N. H., Dec. 25, 1846.*

William, and Elsy Fay, int. Apr. 26, 1818.

**TRAVIS,** Clarke, and Ede Goulding [Goulder. int.] Bacon, of Natick, Apr. 15, 1824.*

Curtis, and Betsy Childs of Natick, int. Apr. 5, 1818.

Louisa, of Natick, and James Hawks, int. Mar. 2, 1828.

Otis, and Eliza Perry of Dover, int. Mar. 17, 1822.

**TREFETHEN,** Mary Ann Shaw, and James Williams, int. Dec. 24, 1843.

**TREFREY** (see also Trefry), Louisa, and Charles Bodge, int. July 12, 1829.

**TREFRY** (see also Trefrey), Martha B., and Gregory T. Morrill, Oct. 30, 1844.

**TREPEND,** Aristena, and Michael Casnar, int. July 10, 1846.

**TRESCOT** (see also Trescott), Joseph, and Abigail Bugbee, Feb. 19, 1718.

* Intention also recorded.

**TRESCOTT** (see also Trescot, Triscot), Ebenezer, of Dorchester, and Mrs. Deborah Bent, at Dorchester, June 19, 1776.
Elijah [of Boston. c. r. 3.], and Hannah Atwood, Dec. 3, 1835.*

**TREVALLEY,** John, and Mary Shute of Malden, int. Feb. 17, 1793.

**TREWORGY,** Eliza A., and Abiel Crosby, Nov. 26, 1848.

**TRISCOT** (see also Trescott), William, and Mehitabel Holmes, Oct. 25, 1705.

**TROBRIDGE** (see also Trowbridge), Caleb, Rev., of Groton, and Mrs. Hanah Walter, Sept. 18, 1718.

**TROTT,** John, of Dorchester, and Mary Chamberlaine, Jan. 23, 1733-4.
John Sayward, and Hannah Hammond, Dec. 2, 1813.*
Prudence, of Dorchester, and Thomas Hastings, at Dorchester, Feb. 11, 1761.
Sarah, 3d, Mrs., of Dorchester, and Edward Williams, at Dorchester, Feb. 19, 1740.
Sarah, and John Chamberlain [jr. c. r. 2.], Mar. 24, 1768.
Thomas, and Waitstill Payson, Jan. 10, 1727-8.

**TROW,** Francis R., and Mary C. Daniels, int. Aug. 28, 1842.
Nancy, of Brookline, and William Hutchins, Apr. 7, 1819.*
William C., of Taunton, and Angeline Gilmore, Apr. 1, 1831.*

**TROWBRIDGE** (see also Strobridge, Trobridge), Alpheus, and Caroline W. Skinner, Apr. 5, 1838.*
Henry, and Selina M. Smith, Apr. 7, 1842.*
Sarah, and Stephen Payson, May 21, 1769. c. r. 2.
Thankfull, and William Glezin, May 16, 1705.

**TRUEMAN,** Marcus, a. 23 y., carpenter, s. John and Ann, and Rebecca Reynolds [Rebecca W. Raynolds. int.], a. 24 y., domestic, d. John and Ann, Jan. 19, 1845.*

**TRULL,** Hannah, and Enoch Nute, int. Mar. 27, 1831.
John, and Sarah Whitney, Mar. [17. int.], 1799. [Apr. c. r. 3.]*
Sarah, and Amaziah Whitney of Brookline, Apr. 19, 1795.*

**TRUMBELL,** Mary, and Thomas Kelly, int. May 13, 1846.

* Intention also recorded.

**TUCK,** Addison P., and Nancy H. Bradeene of Dedham, int. May 8, 1836.

**TUCKER,** Albert O., and Sarah A. McIntire, Nov. 26, 1840.*
Bathsheba, and Levi Wilkerson, Apr. 23, 1776.
Benja[min], jr. [of Leicester. c. r. 2.], and Martha Davis, Dec. 14, 1760.
Betsey K., of South Bridgewater, and Joseph Batchelder, int. May 8, 1847.
Ebenezer, and Margarett Cheny, Jan. 10, 1711.
Eben[eze]r, and Eliza[beth] Clark, Nov. 22, 1743. c. r. 2.
Ebenezer, and Martha T. Morse, Mar. 6, 1834.*
Elijah, of Milton, and Elizabeth C. Tucker, Nov. 7, 1837. c. r. 3.*
Elisa Jane, and Theodore Rogoski, int. May 8, 1846.
Elisabeth, and Sam[ue]l Dunten, July 11, 1765.
Elizabeth, of Milton, and John Person, at Milton, Jan. 14, 1701-2.
Elizabeth, and Isaack Bowin, Apr. 15, 1720.
Elizabeth, and Daniel Weld, June 22, 1720.
Elizabeth, Mrs., and John Smith, Oct. 31, 1723.
Elizabeth, and David Howes, jr., Jan. 10, 1819.*
Elizabeth C., and Elijah Tucker of Milton, Nov. 7, 1837. c. r. 3.*
Gordon F., of Lowell, merchant, and Mary E[llen. int.] Farnsworth, a. 22 y., d. Asa and Elizabeth, Nov. 18, 1847.*
Hannah, and John Nichols, May 7, 1736.
Hannah A., and Elisha Hawes of Stoughton, int. Jan. 1, 1837.
Hannah M. Mrs., and Jacob Stearns of Newton, int. Apr. 23, 1843.
Henry, and Judith Cheaney of Newton, at Newton, Jan. 16, 1731-2.
James, and Hannah Pierce, Aug. 5, 1731.
Jemima, and Moses Whiting, May 26, 1764.
Jeremiah, Capt., and Hannah Stevens, Nov. 10, 1768.
John, and Hannah Dickerman, Nov. 28 [Dec. 22. c. r. 3.], 1805.*
Jonathan, jr., and Martha Jackson, Jan. 13, 1731-2.
Joseph, and Patty Morse of Walpole, int. Dec. 29, 1799.
Katharine, Mrs., and Thomas Randal of Dorchester, Dec. 30, 1730.
Lemuel, and Sarah Baker, Feb. 11, 1768.

* Intention also recorded.

TUCKER, Lemuel, and wid. Elizabeth Lyon, June 29, 1786.*

Lorenzo W., and Malinda McIntire, int. May 24, 1835.

Lucy W., a. 24 y.,d. Seth and Hannah, and David K. Foster, a. 27 y., omnibus driver, s. Jos[eph] S. and Susan, Sept. 29, 1847.*

Margaret, Mrs., and William A. Kent, Esq., of Concord, N. H., July 5, 1821.*

Mary, and John Clarke, Jan. 29, 1712.

Mary, and John Dier, Sept. 2, 1725.

Mary, and William Sumner of Milton, at Milton, ——, 1751.

Mary A., and James Bryant, int. Nov. 27, 1831.

Moses D., and Martha A. Prescott of Candia, N. H., int. Oct. 21, 1848.

Philenia A., and Edward Sumner, int. Oct. 5, 1845.

Rachel, and Ebenez[e]r Whiting, jr. [May 10, C. R. 2.], 1753.

Salla [Salley. int.], of Walpole, and Robert Denssdell [Dinsdell. int.], at Walpole, Oct. 28, 1787.*

Sarah, and John Weld, Dec. 30, 1719.

Seth, of Milton, and Hannah Whiting, at Milton, Oct. 26, 1732.

Seth, and Hannah Fowler of Dorchester, int. Mar. 1, 1807.

Sophia M., and Samuel S. Wallingford, Oct. 27, 1839.

Stephen, and Hannah Parks, May 31, 1739.

Susana, of Milton, and Samuel Scott, int. Jan. 8, 1792.

Thomas W., and Betsey C. Robey of Chichester, N. H., int. Dec. 14, 1834.

William, of Milton, and Katharine [Katherine. dup.] Ruggles, at Milton [Jan. 19, dup.], 1758.

William, and Olive Snow, int. Mar. 7, 1830.

**TUCKERMAN,** Susanna, and George Mansfield, Oct. 22, 1770.

**TUFTS,** Abby A., of Wilton, N. H., and John Bolin, int. Sept. 1, 1844.

Achsah, and Brooks Bowman, Aug. 6, 1826.*

Alfred, and Caroline M. Wright of Cambridge, int. Dec. 25, 1842.

Dorinda, and Andrew P. Drake, int. July 29, 1832.

Gorshom, and Elizabeth Child, Jan. 26, 1790.*

Joshua, and Rosalinda Swasey, Dec. 2, 1819.*

Simon [of Medford. C. R. 2.], and Lucy Dudley, Feb. 23, 1748-9.

* Intention also recorded.

TUGHEY, Hugh, and Catherine Kenan, int. May 1, 1849.

TULEY (see also Tulley), Jeremiah, and Ellen Burns, Aug. 10, 1848.

TULLEY (see also Tuley), Michael, b. Ireland, and Bridget Lynds, b. Ireland, Oct. 30, 1849.

TULSTON, Elizabeth, and Thomas Meakins, Feb. 14, 1650.

TUMBER, Peter, and Phillis Vaughan of Dedham, at Dedham, Feb. 24, 1780.

TUPPER, Ezra, jr., and Penelope Trask of Munson, int. Aug. 10, 1811.

TURILL (see also Tirrell), Hannah, of Weymouth, and Lemuel Smith, int. Sept. 15, 1782.

TURLES, Mary, and John Kilroy, int. Dec. 24, 1843.

TURLEY, Michael, and Catherine Looley, Oct. 15, 1848.*

TURNER (see also Turnor), Ann of Scituate, and Benjamin Woods, Mar. 28, 1723.
Daniel, and [Mrs. int.] Abigail Daniels, Apr. 6, 1845.*
Deborah, and Jabez Tatman, Nov. 18, 1668.
Dolly, and Robert Ayers, Nov. 28, 1801.
Ebeneser, of Dedham, and Sally Draper, int. Mar. 17, 1816.
Edward, and Lucy Hyland, May 15, 1781.
Elisha, jr., and Nancy Young Muncrief, Sept. 6, 1818.*
Eliza, and Lawrence Richards of Charlestown, Nov. 22, 1821.*
Greenleaf, and Lydia G. Crane, of Canton, int. Mar. 10, 1833.
Hezekiah, and Sarah Ruggles, July 14, 1725.
Hezekiah, jr., and Abigail Cole, Oct. 10, 1737.
Hezekiah [jr. int.], and Sally Pratt, Dec. 27, 1820.*
John, and Hannah Shaddock, July 7, 1737.
Nancy [of Boston. c. r. 3.], and Reuben Lawrence, Mar. 23, [22. c. r. 3.], 1843.*
Polly, and William Smith of Cambridge, Jan. 1, 1809.*

TURNOR (see also Turner), Mary, and Edward Chamberlin, Jan. 4, 1646.

TUTTLE, Ann, and Osgood Chase, Feb. 24, 1828.
Elisa, of Lynn, and Nath[anie]l Sidney, int. Jan. 24, 1813.
Elizabeth, and Jasper H. Eaton, May 7, 1837.*

* Intention also recorded.

TUTTLE, Hannah, and William White, June 26, 1827.

Nancy [Mrs. C. R. 3.], and Lemuel Doggett [Daggett. C. R. 3.], Oct. 8, 1807.*

Sarah F., Mrs., and Lorenzo Flint, June 23, 1840.*

Theodore, and Sally Goddard, May 4, 1826.*

Turell [Tirrell. int.], and Mary Pierce, July 22, 1810. C. R. 2.*

**TUXBURY,** Thomas L., and Sarah A. Burnap of Lowell, June 2, 1842. C. R. 7.

**TWELVES,** Abigail, and Shobaal Sever, June 12, 1704.

**TWIGG,** Margarett, and Michael Carney, int. Sept. 8, 1849.

**TWING** (see also Thwing), Catherine, and Josiah Kenney, Oct. 28, 1775.

**TWOMBLEY** (see also Twombly), Martin, and Dorathy Bunker of Cambridge, int. July 11, 1830.

**TWOMBLY** (see also Twombley, Twomley), Alexander H., and Caroline M. Williams, int. Oct. 14, 1846.

James F., of Woburn, and Beulah A. Ellis of Dorchester, Apr. 14, 1842.

Joseph Q., a. 21 y., painter, s. James H. and Abigail of Milton, N. H., and Susan F. Trask, a. 18 y., d. William and Elsey, Dec. 25, 1846.*

William, and Prudence J. Hood, int. May 10, 1840.

William C. [Thwombley. int.], and Phebe Bradbury, Aug. 26, 1844.*

**TWOMLEY** (see also Twombly), Samuel, and Jane Cowen, Mar. 25, 1828.

**TYLER,** Elizabeth S., and Cutler Downer, Dec. 1, 1845.*

Ellen W., a. 19 y., d. Abraham and Susan G., and George Cowles of Montgomery, Alabama, a. 34 y., merchant, s. Roswell and Laura, Sept. 7, 1848.*

Jane, and Capt. David Cook, Nov. 20, 1779.

John, and Sally [Salley. int.] Wales, at Boston, Jan. 29, 1786.*

Joseph, and Mary Draper, Sept. 23, 1756.

Lavina, of Attleborough, and Dr. Abijah Draper, int. Dec. 7, 1806.

Polly, and Isaac Shaw, Aug. 18, 1811.*

Rebecca L., and John J [I. int.] Hayes, Nov. 16, 1845.*

Samuel, of Attleborough, and Betsey Sampson [resident. int.], Sept. 11, 1811.*

* Intention also recorded.

**UNDERWOOD,** Grace, and Joshua Keith, May 11, 1806.*

**UPHAM,** Anna C., Mrs., of Newton, and Oren J. Stetson of Boston, Oct. 14, 1847. c. r. 7.
Elizabeth Ann, of Newton, and John W. Kingsbury, Apr. 23, 1840. c. r. 7.
William, of Weston, and Mrs. Thankful Dana, Nov. 9, 1727.

**UPTON,** Charles, and Sarah Amelia Hager of Westminster, int. Nov. 23, 1845.
Daniel P., and Lydia Noyes [Jan. 6. int.], 1833.*
Martha Ann, of Fitchburg, and George Curtis, int. Aug. 24, 1845.

**USHER,** Abijah [resident. int.], and Mrs. Mary Weld, Oct. 14, 1784.*

**VALENTINE,** Caroline, and Lyman Trask, int. May 2, 1830.

**VARERLY,** Sarah, and Thomas Waling, int. Nov. 9, 1846.

**VARNEY,** Lebbeus H., and Caroline E. Shackord, int. Dec. 1, 1844.
Louisa B., and David Tarr, Jan. 5, 1837.*

**VAUGHAN,** Daniel, and Betsy Robbins, Feb. 11, 1808.*
Phillis, of Dedham, and Peter Tumber, at Dedham, Feb. 24, 1780.

**VEAZY,** Lemuel, and Sarah Abbot of Sudbury, at Sudbury, Dec. 26, 1771.

**VELEDGE,** Maria, and Michael Dolan, int. Jan. 29, 1843.

**VERGOOSE,** Isaac, and Elizabeth Payne, Dec. 16, 1731.

**VERRY,** Elizabeth, and Sergt. John Ruggles, Feb. 12, 1700-1701.

**VICKERY,** Samuel, and Elizabeth H. Morse of Dorchester, Apr. 13, 1831.*

**VICTORY,** James, and Mary Malone, int. Dec. 28, 1849. (null.)

**VILA,** Helen, a. 22 y., d. Joseph and Lydia, and Jeremiah Prichard, jr. of Porto Rico, a. 34 y., merchant, b. New Ipswich, s. Jeremiah and Nancy, Dec. 11, 1849.*

* Intention also recorded.

**VILES,** Nathan, and Nancy P. Read, June 19, 1816.*

**VINAL,** John, and Susannah Adams, Apr. 18, 1793.

**VINING,** Melvin, and Elizabeth G. Pennell, Mar. 12, 1849.

**VITTVEATT,** John [Veatt. int.], a. 29 y., musician, b. Germany, s. Frederick and Malwina, and Eliza Prediger [Bredeger. int.], a. 18 y., b. Germany, d. Adam and Barbara, Dec. 26, 1849.*

**VOGELESANG,** John, and Barbara Koch of Milton, Jan. 8, 1837.*

**VOSE** (see also Voss), Aaron D., and Mary Robbins of Lowell, int. Apr. 25, 1841.
Eben[eze]r Ward, and Olive Gay [Gray. int.], Oct. 21, 1810. C. R. 2.*
Elisabeth, of Dorchester, and John Hawes, int. Jan. 23, 1814.
Elisha, and Mrs. Sarah Ramsdell, int. May 17, 1801.
Eliza[beth. int.] D., and Daniel Waters of Watertown, Mar. 30, 1820.*
Fanny, and Isaac Thwing of Dorchester, int. Sept. 14, 1817.
Grace, and Marshall Gregory, both of Milton, May 28, 1795.
James W., and Theoda Dinsdell, int. June 12, 1808.
Naomi, of Milton, and Joseph Heath, at Milton, Dec. 18, 1798.*
Oliver, and [Mrs. C. R. 2.] Kesiah Draper, Feb. 5, 1778.
Thomas, of Baltimore, Maryland, and Abigail G. Howe, Aug. 25, 1812.*
Unice [Eunice. int.], and William Davis of Milton, Apr. —, 1823. C. R. 3.*

**VOSS** (see also Vose), Anna, of Milton, and Paul Davis, Nov. 26, 1723.

**VOY,** Edward, and Sarah King, int. Sept. 4, 1847.

**WADE,** John, and Charlotte A. Dexter, int. Nov. 24, 1849.
Prudence, Mrs., of Medford, and Thomas Swan, at Charlestown, Dec. 27, 1692.

**WADLEIGH,** Sarah, and Benjamin Follen, Sept. 15, 1833.
Sophia, and Daniel Stone, Dec. 1, 1822.*

**WADSWORTH,** Thomas T., of Milton, and Mary Bradlee, June 3, 1829.*

* Intention also recorded.

**WAINWRIGHT,** Ann, Mrs., and Rev. James Cushing of Haverhill, Oct. 15, 1735.
Eliza, and Walter Channing, ———, 1832.
Francis, and Mrs. Mary Dudley, Jan. 1, 1712.
Peter, jr., and Charlotte Lambert, Nov. 11, 1825.*

**WAISNER,** J. G., and E. T. Wendemuth of Dorchester, int. June 1, 1848.

**WAIT** (see also Waitt), Benjamin, and Clarissa Fales of Dedham, int. Sept. 29, 1799.
David, and Mable Jenners Stevens of Concord, N. H., int. June 19, 1796.
Elizabeth, and Capt. Thomas Tileston of Dorchester, July 8, 1790.*
Hannah, and Joseph Lynds of Malden, Oct. 10, 1802.*
John, of Marblehead, and Polly Phillips, Oct. 17, 1802.*
Rebecca, and Ebenezer Pierpont, Apr. 24, 1786.*
Ruth, and Thomas Read, Mar. 9, 1788.*
Sally, and Luther Fisk of Concord, N. H., Oct. 14, 1795.*
Samuel, and Mrs. Mary Felton, May 7, 1786.*
Sophia, of Leicester, and Amos Holbrook, jr., int. Oct. 7, 1832.
Susan, and Dr. David Goodrich of Templeton, Nov. 18, 1813.*

**WAITT** (see also Wait), Richard, of Marblehead, and Polly Phillips, int. Aug. 24, 1800.

**WAKEFIELD,** Ann, and George H. Gray, at Boston, May 9, 1844. c. r. 3.
Wyman, and Lydia Robbins. int. Mar. 4, 1810.

**WALCOT** (see also Walcott), Charles M. [Walcott of Philadelphia. int.], and Mary E. Goodrich, Nov. 1, 1843.*

**WALCOTT** (see also Walcot, Walcutt), Ephraim, and Alice W. Sloan, int. Apr. 11, 1830.

**WALCUTT** (se also Walcott), Ephraim, and Susan Booth, int. June 21, 1829.

**WALDMIRE,** Pauline E., and Joseph Blank, int. Dec. 29, 1844.

**WALDRON,** Jonathan W., and Eliza [Else. c. r. 3.] Trask, June 5, 1836.*
Love [Waldren. int.], and Alfred E. Dean, Aug. 17, 1844.*

* Intention also recorded.

**WALE** (see also Wales), Mary W. [M. Wales. c. r. 3.], and William W. Haslett of Claremont, N. H., Oct. 6, 1814.*

**WALES** (see also Wale), Amasa [of Boston. c. r. 3.], and Martha Elizabeth Ward, Nov. 12, 1833.*

Ebenezer, and Mrs. Eunis Davis, Jan. 18, 1770.

Ebenezer, jr., of Dorchester, and Roxana Fisher, int. Nov. 20, 1823.

Elizabeth, of Dorchester, and John Andrews, jr., at Dorchester, Sept. 21, 1738.

Elizabeth, and Thomas Bigelow, Nov. 24, 1774.

Nancy G., of Dorchester, and Joseph W. Parker, int. Nov. 11, 1821.

Sally [Salley. int.], and John Tyler, at Boston, Jan. 29, 1786.*

Samuel, and Hannah Peake, Dec. 19, 1700.

Samuel, jr., and Martha Ann Sigourny, Oct. 7, 1829.*

Sarah E., of Dorchester, and Alanson Stone, int. Nov. 7, 1846.

Stephen, and Anna Glover, both of Dorchester, Apr. 7, 1793.

William, and Mary May, Mar. 13, 1794.*

**WALING,** Thomas, and Sarah Varerly, int. Nov. 9, 1846.

**WALKER,** Elizabeth, and Charles Bartlett of Concord, int. Sept. 11, 1842.

Elizebeth, and John Smith at Rehoboth, Apr. 22, 1714.

Frances, and George Brown, May 28, 1848.*

Gideon, and Isabella B. White, int. June 2, 1848.

Isaac S., and Margaret Farrington, int. Mar. 29, 1846.

Isabella, of Londonderry, and John Ker, July 9, 1724.

Jacob, of Brookline, and Mrs. Fanny Lawrence, Sept. 6, 1827.*

Jane, and John Polley, June 2, 1684.

Jane, and Lewis Fairbanks, Jan. 1, 1811.*

Job, and Elizabeth Milberry, at Gloucester, Mar. 20, 1755.

Job, and Mary Williams of Dorchester, at Dorchester, Aug. 22, 1765.

John, of New Ipswich, N. H., and Salley Brown, int. Mar. 18, 1787.

John, of Boston, and Mary Ann C. Mullen, int. Apr. 28, 1849.

Mary L., a. 20 y., d. Sam[ue]l and Mary L., and Francis Huckins, a. 22 y., merchant, s. James and Lucy, Jan. 11, 1849.*

Patience, of Rehoboth, and Noah Perrin, at Rehoboth, June 14, 1705.

* Intention also recorded.

WALKER, Peter [Walter of Rehoboth. c. r. 2.], and Mary Child, June 9, 1715.
Ruth T., and Ebenezer Whiting, 2d, Nov. 7, 1816.*
Sarah, and William Hazlett, July 27, 1818.*
Stephen [of Rehoboth. c. r. 2.], and Mehitable Harris, July 20, 1738.
Sophronia, and Freeman Hovey of Cambridgeport, July 5, 1838.*

WALLACE (see also Wallis), Annette, of Henniker, N. H., and Edward Richards, jr., int. Sept. 14, 1845.
Benjamin, and Susanah Smith of Walpole, int. Apr. 2, 1826.
Eliza, and John Coffee, int. Dec. 28, 1846.
Nancy, and John Beecher, int. Oct. 5, 1846.
William, and Hannah P. Sproul, int. Jan. 13, 1848.

WALLEY, James, and Ellen Looney, Apr. 30, 1845.
John, and Mrs. Sarah Walter, Sept. 25, 1723.

WALLINGFORD, Samuel S., and Sophia M. Tucker, Oct. 27, 1839.*

WALLIS (see also Wallace), David, and Anna Coursey, int. Mar. 3, 1844.
Reuben, and Sukey Farrington, Jan. 30, 1805.*
William O., of Chelsea, and Elvena S. Tapley of Danvers, July 16, 1843.

WALSH (see also Welch), Ellen, and John Gairy, int. Nov. 22, 1849.
James, and Julia Donnavan, int. Dec. 29, 1849.
Mary, and Patrick Kilts, int. Aug. 11, 1848.
Michael, and Bridget Keiffe, int. Sept. 19, 1848.
Patrick, and Bridget McLaughlin, int. June 8, 1845.

WALTER, Hanah, Mrs., and Rev. Caleb Trobridge of Groton, Sept. 18, 1718.
Mariah, and Joseph Otis, Esq., Feb. 22, 1770.
Natha[nae]ll, Rev., and Mrs. Rebecca Abbot, jr., Apr. 24, 1735.
Rebeckah, Mrs., and Rev. Mather Bils [Byles. c. r. 2.] of New London, May 12, 1761.
Samuel, Rev., and Susanna Willis, at Boston, Aug. 7, 1735.
Sarah, Mrs., and John Walley, Sept. 25, 1723.
Thomas and Mrs. Rebecca Belcher of Dedham, at Dedham. Dec. 25, 1718.

* Intention also recorded.

**WALTON,** Elizabeth, and William W. Shirley, Mar. 7, 1825.*

**WARD,** Edward, and Desire Whitney, Mar. 9, 1769.
Harriet C., and Dr. Andrew Stone, int. Apr. 16, 1837.
Henry S., and Hannah G. Parker, Apr. 15, 1828.*
Henry S., and Nabby Ross of Jaffrey, N. H., int. Aug. 1, 1830.
James, and Ann Allen, May 12, 1811.*
James, and Patience Downing, July 5, 1829.*
James O., of New York, and Eliza Gould, Nov. 21, 1838.
    [1837. c. r. 3.]*
Joanna B., and Nehemiah F. Dyer of Braintree, Nov. 4, 1835.*
John [of Newton. c. r. 2.], and Abigail [Abiel. c. r. 2.] Eaton,
    Nov. 28, 1751.
John, and Martha Shed, Dec. 29, 1771.
John, and Elizabeth Brewer, May 24, 1807.*
John, and Mary Cunningham, June 23, 1847.*
Judith Bussey, and John W. Hollis of Brighton, May 9, 1838.*
Lucy, Mrs., of Weston, and Joshua Gore, int. Apr. 25, 1802.
Lyman, and Harriet Crosby of Billerica, int. July 17, 1836.
Martha Elizabeth, and Amasa Wales [of Boston. c. r. 3.],
    Nov. 12, 1833.*
Mary, Mrs., and Benj[ami]n D. Baker of Salem, int. Oct. 16,
    1836. [Nov. 5, 1837. dup.]
Mary C., and Calvin Heald, July 25, 1830.*
Mary E., a. 18 y., and Charles H. Ryan, a. 23 y., carpenter,
    Jan. 17, 1847.*
Mary Weld, and Nathaniel Fish, Mar. 9, 1815.*
Michael, and Bridget Clogher, int. Jan. 3, 1841.
Nahum, and Susan Gurney, Sept. 13, 1829.*
Nahum, and Ruth S. Gurney, Feb. 26, 1845.*
Olive, and Ebenezer Pool, Feb. 14, 1802.*
Patrick, and Bridget Kenny, int. Aug. 10, 1845.
Samuel, and Joanna Bird of Dorchester, at Dorchester, Nov.
    20, 1799.*
Samuel, jr., of New York, and Julia Ruth Cutler, int. Sept.
    22, 1812.
Samuel, and Martha Grush, July 16, 1845.*
Sarah R., a. 23 y., d. Richard and Lucy, and Henry W. Robin-
    son, a. 24 y., clerk, s. Jon[atha]n P. and Catherine, Juiy
    22, 1846.*
Sylvester L., and Mary Ann Conant of Shapleigh, Me., int.
    Apr. 30, 1849.

* Intention also recorded.

WARD, William H., jr., a. 23 y., teamster, s. W[illia]m H. and
Lucy L., and Martha S. Simpson of Brunswick, Me., a. 22
y., d. Lewis and Mary, Nov. 14, 1847.*

WARDEL (see also Wardell), Mary, Mrs., and Ellis Baker,
Mar. 14, 1782. c. r. 2.

WARDELL (see also Wardel), Hannah, and James Mears,
Aug. 1, 1754.
Mary, and Joshua Felton, Jan. 28, 1766.

WARE( see also Wares), Calvin, and Sarah Shed, Apr. 10,
1806.*
Elizabeth Ann, of Cambridge, and Rev. George Putnam, int.
July 31, 1831.
Eunice, of Wrentham, and Ezra Hixon, int. July 15, 1804.
Hannah, and Ephraim Chaddock, both of Dorchester, June
23, 1845.
Joseph, and Nancy Smith, Aug. 21, 1803.*
Luther, and Elizebeth Edds of Needham, int. Apr. 3, 1800.
Margaret, and John Foster, Dec. 7, 1704.
Mary, and John Whittemore, June 27, 1822.*
William, of Needham, and Abigail Williams, Jan. 1, 1812.*

WARES (see also Ware), Jerusha, and Stephen Hearsey of
Milton, Apr. 14, 1793.*

WARNER, Eliza [Warren. int.], of Medford, and John
Lemist, at Medford, Oct. 8, 1809.*
John E., and Mrs. Frances Kellham, June 11, 1829.*
Mary C., of Townsend, and Asa Ames, int. Oct. 28, 1838.
Phebe A., and John A. Pierce of Dorchester, Apr. 2, 1840.*
Samuel, and Mary Davis, June 16, 1708

WARREN, Calvin, and Caroline Carter of Natick, int. Dec. 11,
1814.
Caroline, Mrs., and Ethan A. Greenwood, Esq., Feb. 1, 1829.*
Ebenezer, and Susannah Griswould, Dec. 6, 1739.
Ebenezer, and Sarah Cole, Aug. 22, 1746.
Eleanor, and Thomas Curtis, int. Aug. 17, 1806.
Elizabeth R., and Charles Page, int. Feb. 22, 1818.
Frances, of Hardwick, and John A. Parker, int. Nov. 30, 1800.
Hannah, Mrs., and Rev. John Chipman, Nov. 20, 1751.
Harriet, and John Prince, Esq., int. July 31, 1836.

* Intention also recorded.

WARREN, Isaiah, and Jerusha Freeland of Hopkington, int.
    Sept. 6, 1807.
James, of Attleborough, and Lucinda Goodard, Apr. 2, 1816.*
Joseph, and Mrs. Mary Stevens, May 29, 1740.
Richard, of New York, and Angeline Greenwood, int. Sept.
    4, 1836.
Sarah, and Ebenezer Weld, Oct. 24, 1764.
Sarah Ann, and Stephen Randall, Sept. 2, 1810.*
William, of Brookline, and Susannah Mather, at Boston, June
    26, 1727.

WASHBURN, Alexander C., a. 29 y., attorney-at-law, s. Cal-
    vin and Lydia, and Ellen M. Bailey, a. 22 y., d. John,
    May 7, 1849.*
David E., and Lydia Davis of Bradford, N. H., int. June 16,
    1849.
Geo[rge] W. C., of Livermore, Me., and Diana P. Parmelee,
    Oct. 17, 1845.

WASON (see also Watson), James W., and Sarah Ann Page
    of Raymond, N. H., int. Sept. 3, 1843.

WATERHOUSE, Benjamin M. D. "Professor of the Theory
    and practice of Phisic at the University in Cambridge,"
    and Elizabeth Oliver, int. May 11 [June 1. dup.], 1788.

WATERMAN, Harriet J., of Halifax, and Andrew Richmond
    [jr. int.] of Halifax, Dec. 1, 1836.*
Mary Jane, and Henry Basford, May 23, 1839.*
Melzar, and Susan Skinner, Sept. 11, 1831.*
Melzar C., and Sarah A. Glines, Oct. 27, 1844.*
Sarah S., of Sandwich, and Howard S. Williams, int. June 2,
    1849.

WATERS, Bridget, and John Curly, int. Jan. 12, 1848.
Daniel, of Watertown, and Eliza[beth. int.] D. Vose, Mar.
    30, 1820.*
George, Rev., of Lynn, and Phebe Anne Foxcroft, May 3,
    1838.*
Harriet, and Thomas Pike, Dec. 4, 1837.*
Isaac and Josephine Augusta Hatch, May 29, 1815.*
James, and Bridget Kenney, int. Mar. 4, 1848.
John, and Laura H. Post of Boston, int. Dec. 12, 1846.
Patrick, and Ann Burns, int. Apr. 13, 1849.

* Intention also recorded.

WATERS, William, jr., and Anna Wilhelmina Denmon, July 19, 1812.*

William, jr., and Eliza Wilson, July 11, 1815.*

William, and Nancy Farr, Feb. 26, 1834.*

WATKIN (see also Watkins). Andrew, and Mary Streeter of Cambridge, at Charlestown, Dec. 10, 1701.

WATKINS (see also Watkin), Sarah and Joseph Stranger, int. Sept. 8, 1833.

WATSON (see also Wason), Ann Priscilla, and Calvin Allen, Apr. 8, 1839.*

Caleb, and Mary Hide, Dec. 15, 1665.

Charles, and Mary Mory, Nov. 26, 1711.

Charles, of New York, and Elizabeth Patrick, int. Mar. 29, 1840.

Eliza P., a. 22 y., d. James and Mary Patricks, and Samuel R. Brown, a. 23 y., carpenter, s. Edward, July 4, 1847.*

Elizabeth M. S., and Joseph L. Cobb, June 7, 1826.*

Henrietta F., a. 25 y., d. Geo[rge] and Eliza, and Joseph Kittredge of Andover, a. 26 y., physician, s. Jos[eph] and Hannah, Dec. 15, 1847.*

James, of Boston, and Abigail Crocker, Dec. 1, 1811. c. r. 3.*

James, and Abigail Wheeler, Dec. 1, 1811.

John, and Allice Prentis, Apr. 3, 1634.

John, and Mary Farrelly, int. Nov. 16, 1846.

Keziah, and David Mallard, June 20, 1824.*

Lawrence, and Maria Finn, May 15, 1848.*

Margaret, and Walter H. Green, Oct. 27, 1837.*

Maria, and Thomas Reddish, int. Apr. 18, 1848.

Mary, and William Mills of Needham, June 17, 1724.

Nathan, and Hannah Knower, Oct. 1, 1797. c. r. 3.*

WATTS, Francis O., and Caroline Goddard, May 1, 1826.*

John, and Mary B. Rumrill, int. Mar. 14, 1830.

Maria, and Patrick Coffin, int. July 17, 1848.

Mary S., and Archibald Johnstone, Sept. 24, 1848.

William, and Maria F. Rollins, int. June 19, 1831.

WAUGH, Deborah, and Daniel T. Clark of Medford, int. Oct. 5, 1845.

John, jr., and Mary Horton, int. Jan. 12, 1840.

Varnum, and Sarah Danforth of Billerica, int. Feb. 15, 1829.

* Intention also recorded.

**WAYMOUTH,** William [Weymouth. int.], and Mariah H. Hubbard, Dec. 26, 1843.*

**WEARE,** Moses, and Clarissa Brown, Apr. 6, 1818.*

**WEATHERBEE** (see also Wetherbee), John, and Rebeccah Tolman, int. Jan 29, 1797.
Peggy, and William Whittemore, 2d, int. Feb. 18, 1816.

**WEATHERBY** (see also Wetherbee), Joseph, and Rhoda Packard, Aug. 17, 1797. c. r. 3.
Josiah, and Lavina Hyde of Brookline, Nov. 27, 1796.*

**WEATHERSPOON,** Eliza, and Levi H. Allen, int. Oct. 8, 1820.
Eliza, and Elias Hicks of Rehoboth, int. Sept. 9, 1821.

**WEATHERWAS,** Anna C., and Charles E. Allen, int. Apr. 26, 1835.

**WEB** (see also Webb), Mary, and Peter Seaver, Apr. 9, 1758.

**WEBB** (see also Web), Betsey O., of Taunton, and William Gilman, int. Dec. 15, 1833.
Charlotte, of Dedham, and Stephen Sims, Oct. 7, 1823.*
Ebenezer, and Rebecca Wood, Feb. 8, 1773.
Elizabeth, and George Thompson, Oct. 31, 1809.*
Frances C., and Levi B. Folsom, int. June 15, 1849.
Hannah, and Stephen Sims, residents, Oct. 8, 1788.*
John, and Mary Ashley of Braintree, Mar. 23, 1701-2.
Mary Ann, a. 35 y., d. Walter and Sally, and Noel Matthewson [Mathewson, int.], widr. of Barrington, R. I., a. 37 y., brickmaker, s. Noel and Susannah, June 7, 1847.*
Mercy, and Charles Belknap, Feb. 15, 1773.
William, and Sarah M. Brown, int. Apr. 7, 1839.

**WEBBER** (see also Weber), Cushing, a. 24 y., dentist, s. James H. and Rebecca, and Ellen L. Everett, a. 20 y., d. Eliphalet and Eliza, Jan. 1, 1849.*
Ellen P., and William A. Knight of Providence, R. I., Aug. 27, 1841.*
Emeline, and Dr. Benj[ami]n T. Prescott, int. Dec. 30, 1838.
Emeline, and James H. Ficket of Portland [Me. int.], Sept. 21, 1848.*
George E., and Sophia J. Lovejoy, int. Jan. 9, 1849.

* Intention also recorded.

WEBBER, Henrietta H., d. John, and Thomas M. Gridley of Westboro, May 14, 1846.*

James, and Susan F. Harvey, Apr. 20, 1837. C. R. 7.

John A., and Hepzibath Spauldin of Pepperell, int. Jan. 30, 1803.

John, jr., and Elizabeth Lewis, int. May 8, 1836.

John H., and Mary Breed, int. Sept. 16, 1838.

Mary Ann, and Sebastion Kramer, Feb. 4, 1832.*

Moses H., and Susan D. Burgess of Boston, int. May 20, 1846.

Polly, and Matthew Kramer, Mar. 20, 1831.*

WEBER (see also Webber), George, and Pebebena Spring, June 9, 1839.*

WEBSTER, Electa, of Stockbridge, and Samuel Doggett, int. Aug. 14, 1842.

Frances A., and William Dunlap, Nov. 14, 1843.*

George H., and Charlotte T. Mason, June 20, 1843.*

James, and Elizabeth Hall of Dorchester, June 30, 1793.*

Jonathan, of Salisbury, and Sally Fisk, Oct. 10, 1802.*

Phebe, of Manchester, N. H., and William Dickey, int. Nov. 30, 1834.

Susan P., of Manchester, and Lyman Andrews, int. Dec. 13, 1835.

WEED, Edward C. [of Boston. int.], a. 31 y. accountant, s. Samuel, and Louisa Rice, a. 29 y., d. Henry, Nov. 1, 1849.*

WEEKS, Charles M., of Greenland, N. H., and Elvina Porter, Dec. 5, 1839.*

Elizabeth, and Joshua Hemingway, Apr. 5, 1704.

Elizabeth, and John Grim, int. June 25, 1837.

Josiah, and Frances Glines, Apr. 11, 1833.*

Mindwell, and Abiel Bird of Dorchester, Jan. 29, 1704-5.

Reuben, and Elizabeth A. Fuller, int. Nov. 23, 1845.

Sobiah, and Richard Hall, Feb. 3, 1737-8.

WEIGEL, Phillipina, and Jacob Messiler, int. June 21, 1849.

WEING, Jacob, of Boston, and Elisabeth Baldner, int. Sept. 4, 1846.

WEIR, Mary Ann, a. 21 y., b. Ireland, d. Thomas, and John Gard of Lynn, a. 22 y., tinplate worker, b. Ireland, s. John, Dec. 24, 1849.*

* Intention also recorded.

**WELCH** (see also Walsh, Welsh), Abigail, Mrs., and Thomas Boyden, Sept. 28, 1780.

Benjamin H., and Mary H. Dow, int. Aug. 2, 1846.

Bridget, and Edward Livingston, int. July 9, 1846.

Elisabeth [Elizabeth. int.] R., and William G. Little, Feb. 1, 1846.*

Hannah, and William Brigney, int. Jan. 6 , 1848.

John, and Eliza Fagin, int. Oct. 10, 1846.

Martin, and Bridget Kelley, int. Jan. 8, 1843.

Mary, and William Coes [both residents. int.], Dec. 3, 1786.*

Mary, and Alexander McCloud, Oct. 15, 1838.*

Mary A., of Chelsea, and Isaiah M. Ellis, int. Jan. 6, 1846.

Timothy, and Mary Laskin, int. Feb. 20, 1849.

**WELD** (see also Wild, Wildes, Wilds), Aaron D., and Betsy Williams, Dec. 25, 1804.*

Aaron D., and Susannah Morey, int. Aug. 28, 1808.

Aaron D., and Martha Williams, May 27, 1819.*

Abigail, and Elisha Johnson, May 25, 1709.

Abigail, and Thomas Lyon, Jan. 24, 1738-9.

Abigail, and Thomas Dudley, May 14, 1778.

Amealia, and Andrew Tallant of Pelham, N. H., Feb. 29, 1792.*

Ann, and Jonathan French, Feb. 18, 1802. c. r. 2.*

Ann [Anna. int.] Minot, a. 25 y., d. William G., and [Rev. int.] Joseph Henry Allen, a. 25 y., clerk, s. Joseph and Lucy C., May 22, 1845.*

Benjamin, and Martha Payson, Nov. 21, 1745.

Benjamin, and Elizabeth Heath, June 12, 1796.*

Bethula, Mrs., and Thomas Mighell, Nov. 8, 1669.

Betsy, and Sam[ue]l H. Bradstreet of Charlestown, July 30, 1811. c. r. 3.

Catharine [Catherine. int.], Mrs., and Moses Dorr, Aug. 29, 1784.*

Christopher, M., M. D., and Mary Ann P. Jarvis, int. Apr. 11, 1841.

Clarissa, and Ebenezer Seaver, jr., Jan. 19, 1817.*

Clemence. and Paul Spear, Aug. 25, 1756.

Clemency [Clement. int.], Mrs., and Ebenezer Eayres [Cayrs. int.], Nov. 25, 1784.*

Daniel, and Elizabeth Tucker, June 22, 1720.

Daniel, and Hannah Williams, May 29, 1800.*

David, and Sarah Davis, July 11, 1756.

* Intention also recorded.

WELD, David, jr., and Hannah Murdock, May 15, 1783.*

Deborah, and Joshua Child, Sept. 6, 1715.

Deborah, and John Davis of Oxford, Oct. 27, 1757.

Dorothy, and William Denison, May 12, 1686.

Dorothy, and Samuel Stevens, May 25, 1708.

Dorothy, and Harbottle Dorr, Apr. 8, 1725.

Dorothy, and John Reynolds [of Bristol. C. R. 2.], May 5 [3. C. R. 2.], 1753.

Ebenezer, and Mary Craft, Nov. 18, 1725.

Ebenezer, and Sarah Warren, Oct. 24, 1764.

Ebenezer, and Rebecca Mayo, Sept. 6, 1768.

Ebenezer, jr., and Susannah Benjamin, ————, 1802.

Edmund, and Elizabeth White, Nov. 10, 1687.

Edmund, and Clemence Dorr, July 8. 1725.

Eleazer, and Mary Hatch, at Boston, Apr. 23, 1761.

Elijah [of Cambridge. int.], and Elizabeth Cotrell [Cotrill. int.], Oct. 17, 1782.*

Elisabeth, and John Ruggles, Aug. 11, 1731.

Elisabeth, and Isaac Child, jr. [of Brookline. C. R. 2.], Dec. 12, 1745.

Elisabeth, and Noah Davis, Sept. 19, 1765.

Elisebeth, and Samuell Gore, Aug. 28, 1672.

Elizabeth, and Edward Denison, Mar. 30, 1641.

Elizabeth, and Ebenezer Craft, Nov. 14, 1700.

Elizabeth, and Isaac Child, Apr. 18, 1716.

Elizabeth, and Elias Parkman, Oct. 29, 1718.

Elizabeth, Mrs., and Ebenezer Stevens, July 9, 1750.

Elizabeth, and Benjamin Knower, July 26, 1773.

Elizabeth, and Joseph Champney [resident. int.], Apr. 4, 1786.*

Elizabeth, and Benjamin Corey, Jan. 18, 1789.*

Elizabeth, and Samuel H. Bradstreet of Charlestown, July 30, 1811.*

Elizabeth, and William Williams, Aug. 25, 1822.*

Elizabeth W., a. 28 y., d. Sam[ue]l H. and Nancy, and Epes Sargent, jr., a. 34 y., editor of daily transcript, s. Epes and Hannah, May 10, 1848.*

Frederic, and Sarah Hiscock, int. Nov. 12, 1815.

Grace, and Oliver Fletcher, Esq. of Chelmsford, Nov. 13, 1766.

* Intention also recorded.

WELD, George, a. 25 y., gentleman, s. Sam[ue]l W. and Nancy, and Mary E. Read, a. 24 y., d. George and Rebecca, Dec. 14, 1848.*

George R. M. [Capt. int.], and Harriet Lowder, June 2, 1833.*

Hannah, and William Heath, Nov. 11, 1685.

Hannah, and Thomas Lyon, Nov. 3, 1748.

Hannah, and Jonathan Parker, Dec. 6, 1774.

Hannah [Mrs. c. r. 2.], and Abel [Abial. c. r. 2.] Withington, Dec. 14, 1774.

Hannah, and William Parker, June 9, 1793.*

Hannah, and John Davis Williams [jr. int.], May 16, 1798. c. r. 2.*

Harriet [Harriot. c. r. 3.], and William Holmes, Oct. 29, 1823.*

Hepzibah [C. int.], and William Evans, Sept. 30, 1834.*

Horatio, and Mary Oliver [both of Boston. c. r. 3.], Jan. 21, 1810.

Isabel, and Elijah Dudley, Oct. 30, 1791.*

Joanna, and Samuel Lyon, Dec. 20, 1705.

John, and Margret Bowen, Dec. 24, 1647.

John, and Hannah Portise, Jan. 22, 1678.

John, and Mehitabel Child, Dec. 3, 1712.

John, and Sarah Tucker, Dec. 30, 1719.

Jonathan R., a. 25 y., work on railroad, s. Joseph and Lucy S., and Mary S. Prescott, a. 22 y., d. Joseph O., Jan. 25, 1849.*

Joshua, and Margaret Draper, Dec. 14, 1756.

Joseph, and Barbary Clap, Apr. 20, 1639.

Joseph, and Elisabeth Devation, Sept. 2, 1674.

Joseph, s. John, and Sarah Faxon, Nov. 27, 1679.

Joseph, and Elizabeth Chamberlaine, May 22, 1711.

Joseph, and Mrs. Martha Child, June 4, 1729.

Joseph, and Mary Ruggles, Feb. 17, 1757.

Joseph, and Katherine Hall, Dec. 9, 1779.

Joseph, and Lois Baker, int. June 1, 1783.

Joseph M., and Lucy S. Richards of Dedham, int. Apr. 30, 1809.

Lucy A., and George Brown of Dedham, Nov. 15, 1838. c. r. 3.*

Lydia, and John [G. c. r. 3.] Doubleday [of Boston. c. r. 3.], Jan. 3, 1796.*

* Intention also recorded.

Weld, Margaret, and Nathaniel Brewer, Mar. 17, 1692.

Margaret, and Benjamin White, July 16, 1701.

Margarett, and Edward Child, June 2, 1712.

Mary, and Joshuah Gardner, Mar. 22, 1681-2.

Mary, and Samuell Davis of Oxford, Oct. 13, 1731.

Mary, and James Shead [Shed. c. r. 2.], jr., May 29, 1740.

Mary, and Ebenezer Sever, jr., Nov. 5, 1755.

Mary, and Sam[ue]l Sumner, May 11, 1767.

Mary, and Roland Clark, May 25, 1778.

Mary, Mrs., and Abijah Usher [resident. int.], Oct. 14, 1784.*

Mary, and Gardner Brewer, Apr. 1, 1831.*

Mehettabel, and Nathaniel Draper, May 25, 1732.

Nancy, and John Geddings, Jan. 16, 1803.*

Nancy, and David Ellis [of Boston. c. r. 3.], Jan. 1, 1818.*

Nathaniel, Dea., and Esther Child, Sept. 10, 1793.*

Noah, and Elloner Ellis of Dedham, at Dedham, Apr. 4, 1751.

Polly, and Timothy McIntier, July 9, 1786.*

Rebecca, and Edward Preston [jr. int.] of Dorchester, June 11, 1793.*

Rebeckah, and Joseph Brewer, Oct. 20, 1748.

Samuel, and Susanna Polley, June 28, 1683.

Samuel, and Elizabeth Brewer, Jan. 19, 1741-2.

Samuel, and Hannah Rogers, June 22, 1749.

Samuel, and Hannah Mayo, June 18, 1765.

Samuel, and Elizabeth Williams, Mar. 27, 1787.*

Samuel W., and Nancy Sumner, May 27, 1818.*

Sarah, and John Frank, July 23, 1663.

Sarah, and John Williams, June 1, 1709.

Sarah, and Jacob Chamberlain, Apr. 29, 1719.

Sarah, Mrs., and John Davis, Apr. 7, 1737.

Sarah, and Stephen Chamberlain, Aug. 7, 1755. c. r. 2.

Sarah, and Stephen Child, May 25, 1786.*

Sarah A., a. 20 y., d. George F. and Lydia, and Jacob Weld Seaver, a. 29 y., merchant, s. Ebenezer and Clarissa, July 10 [9. c. r. 3.], 1849.*

Sarah H., and Jacob Hastings of Boston, Jane. 26, 1804.*

Stephen M., and Sarah B. Balch, June 6, 1838.*

Susana, and Benjamin Billings, Apr. 18, 1890.*

Thomas, and Dorothy Whitinge, June 4, 1650.

Thomas, and Thankfull Fuller, Feb. 13, 1769.

Thomas, and Esther McClealan, Apr. 12, 1781.

* Intention also recorded.

WELD, Thomas, jr., and Elizabeth Fenno of Quincy, int. Oct. 13, 1816.

Thomas S., and Sarah F. Sumner of Charlestown, int. Feb. 11, 1838.

**WELLINGTON,** Isaac, and Lois Smith of Princeton, int. Jan. 4, 1829.

Elizabeth, of Waltham, and Nathan Smith, jr., int. Dec. 14, 1817.

**WELLMAN,** George B., and Sarah Lakeman, int. Jan. 13, 1839.

John, Dr., and Elizabeth Clewly, at Newton, Aug. 29, 1776.

**WELLS,** Catherine H., and Gilbert H. O'Reilly of Augusta, Me., int. June 19, 1847.

Charles, and Abby Grush [Gruch. int.], July 29, 1844.*

Elis[abeth] [Elizabeth. int.] R., and Francis A. Fuller of Hartford, Conn., June 4, 1844.*

Hannah, Mrs., and Nath[anie]l W. Williams, int. Nov. 27, 1808.

Henrietta, and John Daniel, int. Oct. 21, 1832.

Maria S., and John Champney, Aug. 28, 1837.

Phenehas P., Dr., and Catharine J. French of Chester, N. H., int. Mar. 27, 1836.

Thomas F., a. 25 y., merchant, s. Thomas and Anna Maria, and Sarah Morrill, a. 20 y., d. Joseph and Nancy, Oct. 31, 1849.*

**WELSH** (see also Welch), Richard, and Allis Savage, int. Oct. 6, 1844.

William, and Mary Ann Damon, of Reading, int. Feb. 8, 1846.

**WELSON,** Sally, and Eliphalet Spurr, int. Sept. 2, 1798.

**WENDALL,** Isaac, and Sarah Goddard, Nov. 26, 1771.

**WENDEMUTH,** E. T., of Dorchester, and J. G. Waisner, int. June 1, 1848.

**WENTWORTH,** Eliza M., and Thacher Sweat, int. Oct. 18, 1829.

Hannah M., wid., and Josiah Richardson, widr., gentleman, Jan. 9, 1848.*

Horatio, and Esther Gowell, Sept. 5, 1839.*

* Intention also recorded.

WENTWORTH, Isaac, and Mary Smith, int. June 2, 1849.

Jacob, and Ruth Champion, Apr. 23, 1843.*

Martha, and Josiah Richardson, Apr. 26, 1812.*

Martha P. [Wainwright. int.], and William Seaver, Mar. 2, 1843.*

Nancy, of Brookline, and Samuel S. Champion of Watertown, Nov. 26, 1829.

Reuben, and Serena Goodwin, Sept. 28, 1834.*

Samuel, and Nancy Morrison, June 12, 1831.*

Thomas M., and Ann M. Burnham, Oct. 31, 1839.*

WEST, Benjamin, and Joanna Swinneton, June 19, 1718.

Benjamin, and Hannah Cary, Dec. 13, 1781. C. R. 2.

James, of Randolph, and Hannah McIntire, Jan. 1, 1827.*

Joanna, and Sam[ue]ll Winchester, Nov. 19, 1747.

Sarah, and James Cornish, Apr. 20, 1765.

William C., of Chilmark, a. 27 y., mariner, s. George and Prudence, and Abby A. Luce of Tisbury, a. 21 y., d. Richard and Hepsabeth, June 13, 1849.

WESTACOTT, Robert G., cabinet maker, and Mary A. Donnelly, spinster, Dec. 6, 1845.*

WESTON, Mary D., and Thomas Danforth, Nov. 10, 1842.*

Thomas Q., of Middleboro, and Maria L. Tillson, int. Nov. 28, 1848.

WETERAU, Anna M., and Hammond H. Ortman, int. Nov. 23, 1848.

WETHERBEE (see also Weatherbee, Weatherby, Wetherby, Witherbee), Adeline, a. 28 y., d. John and Sarah, and James M. Keith, a. 30 y., attorney at law, s. Bethuel and Mary, Aug. 20, 1849.*

John, and Rebecca Tolman, Feb. 12, 1797. C. R. 2.

Sarah E., and Albert T. Elliot of Providence, int. Nov. 21, 1841.

Thomas, and Bathsheba Clewley, Nov. 4, 1751.

William, a. 24 y., broker, s. John and Sarah, and Cordelia B. Simmons, a. 23 y., d. David A. and Martha, June 10, 1847.*

WETHERBY (see also Wetherbee), Joseph, and Rhoda Packard, int. July 30, 1797.

* Intention also recorded.

**WETHERS,** Mary Ann, and Joseph Warren Cobb, int. Apr. 3, 1847.

**WHALEN,** Margarett, and Martin Maddan, int. July 26, 1849.

**WHARF** (see also Wharff, Whorf), James, and Mary W. Patrick, Oct. 1, 1820.*
Mary W. Mrs., and Charles Barry, int. Sept. 6, 1829.

**WHARFF** (see also Wharf), Sarah [of Gloucester. int.], and Nathaniel Jennings, Dec. 9, 1816. c. r. 2.*

**WHEALAN** (see also Whealen, Whelen), Phillip, and Catherine Gray, int. May 15, 1847.

**WHEALEN** (see also Whealan), Thomas, and Maria Cox, int. Aug. 3, 1845.

**WHEALER** (see also Wheeler), Henry [Wheeler. c. r. 2.], and Elizabeth Kelton, Dec. 28, 1773.

**WHEAT,** Hannah, and Thomas Small of Dedham, int. Nov. 20, 1842.
Sally, and Benjamin Bruce, int. Apr. 2, 1818.

**WHEATON** (see also Wheeton), James, and Sarah Child, Jan. 20, 1771.
Polly, and Samuel Davis, Dec. 4, 1794.*

**WHEELER** (see also Whealer), Abigail, and James Watson, Dec. 1, 1811.
Abraham, of Dorchester, and Dolly Woods, May 17, 1801.*
Betsey, of Ashby, and Daniel Tarbell, int. July 29, 1804.
Eben, and Hanna Cain, Jan. 1, 1804. c. r. 2.
Edmund, and Hannah Cain, int. Nov. 27, 1803.
Elizabeth, and Andrew Newman, May 19, 1826.*
Emily, and Philander Jones, July 4, 1841.
Hannah, of Concord, and Moses French, int. Nov. 24, 1811.
Jerahmeel, and Deborah Winchester of Brookline, Feb. 2, 1747-8.
Joseph N., and Mary Ann Willis, May 29, 1825.
Laura Ann, a. 22 y., d. Silas and Laura Ann, and Francis P. Beverstock, a. 21 y., morocco dresser, s. Edward and Hannah, Mar. 19, 1848.*
Margaret, and Nathaniel Brewer, at Boston, Dec. 6, 1763.
Mary, of Dorchester, and Willard Onion, int. May 19, 1833.

* Intention also recorded.

WHEELER, Mary Ann, and George Morse, int. Aug. 28, 1831.
Mary L., and Samuel Raymond of Charlestown, Dec. 7, 1809.*
Richard, and Prudence Pason [Payson. dup.], Dec. 2, 1702.
Ward, and Sarah A. Huckings, Aug. 6, 1843.*
William D., and Delia H. Gillen, Oct. 4, 1847.

WHEELOCK, Rebecca [Whelock. CT. R.], and John Craftes
[Crafts. CT. R.], June 7, 1654.
Sarah, of Medfield, and Henry Garnsoy, at Dedham, Nov. 7,
1700.

WHEELWRIGHT, Hannah, and Mason Basto, int. Apr. 29,
1827.

WHEETON (see also Wheaton), Nathan[ie]l, and Molly
Richards, Oct. 7, 1759.

WHELEN (see also Whealan), Bridget, and Cornelius Doherty, int. May 9, 1841.

WHIPPY, Mary, and Titus James, Jan. 1, 1718.

WHISTON, Sarah, and Ebenezer Swan, Oct. 25, 1770.

WHITAKER, Anne [Anna. int.], a. 23 y., d. Samuel and
Sarah, and Abraham Gladhill, a. 22 y., carpet weaver, s.
John and Betsey, Aug. 18, 1849.*
Susan, and Lewis Morse, July 16, 1820.*

WHITE (see also Wight), Abagail, of Brookline, and Samuel
Gore, int. June 22, 1800.
Abby, and Gardner Ewell of Dorchester, int. Oct. 4, 1840.
Bartholomew, and Hannah Davis, Nov. 29, 1798. C. R. 2.*
Benjamin, and Margaret Weld, July 16, 1701.
Benjamin, Capt., and Mrs. Elizabeth Aspinwall, both of
Brooklyn, Feb. 19, 1756.
Bridget, and Thomas Gibbins, int. Jan. 7, 1838.
Caroline M., and Jonathan [John. int.] H. Davis, Jan. 15,
1804.*
Charles, S., and Betsey Broad of Natick, int. Jan. 1, 1826.
Charlotte, and John Baker, jr., at Sharon, Feb. 4, 1798.*
David, and Margaret Sloper, Nov. 16, 1775.
David F., of Watertown, and Mary A. Bates, June 29, 1841.*
Ebenezer, Rev. [of Norton. C. R. 2.], and Mrs. Hannah
Richards, July 6, 1749.

* Intention also recorded.

WHITE, Ebenezer, of Brookline, and Hannah Davis, Apr. 21, 1766.

Eleanor, and John Williams, Sept. 29, 1803.*

Elisabeth, and Benjamin ——, Mar. 21 [22, 1749-50. c. r. 2.], 1750.

Eliza, of Deering, N. H., and William Brown, int. Sept. 27, 1835.

Elizabeth, and Edmund Weld, Nov. 10, 1687.

Elizabeth, Mrs., of Brookline, and William Goddard, at Brookline, Dec. 23, 1761.

Elizabeth, and Isaac Davis, Mar. 23, 1795.*

Elizabeth, and Squire Leonard of Dorchester, Nov. 24, 1799.*

Elizabeth, and Ebenezer Brewer, Apr. 8, 1807.*

Elizabeth, and Orray A. Taft, int. Apr. 19, 1840.

Ellen W[atson. int.], and Edward Baldwin, Aug. 8, 1838.*

Esther [Sarah. c. r. 2.], and Simeon Pond, Nov. 30 [Dec. 1. c. r. 2.], 1763.

George, and Frances Gibson, int. Oct. 31, 1846.

Hannah, and Ebenezer Davis, Apr. 18, 1700.

Harriet J., a. 18 y., d. William and Nancy, and John V. Woodhouse, a. 22 y., machinist, s. Thomas D. and Mary, Sept. 8, 1847.*

Harriet [H. int.], and John Reed, jr., Mar. 1, 1846.*

Isaac D., and Elizabeth H. Grosvenor of Paxton, int. Apr. 18, 1841.

Isaac H., and Mary W. Preston of Dorchester, int. Jan. 11, 1835.

Isaac H., widr., a. 48 y., carpenter, s. Micah and Jane, and Mary Ann Swazey, a. 19 y., d. Emanuel and Dorcas, Sept. 4, 1846.*

Isabella B., and Gideon Walker, int. June 2, 1848.

James, and Harriet E. Howe, int. May 20, 1838.

James A., and Charlotte Holmes, Oct. 13, 1833.

James T., a. 32 y., carpenter, s. James and Abba, and Julia T. Drake [of Newton. int.], a. 24 y., Jan. 9, 1848.

Joanna ,of Brookline, and Joseph Ruggles, Oct. 20, 1720.

John, and Esther Whitney, Mar. 8, 1745.

John, and Jemima Griggs, at Needham, Sept. 12, 1775.

John, and Polly Elisha, July 22, 1801.*

John, of Charlestown, and Rebecca Davis, Oct. 6, [July 2, c. r. 3.], 1805.*

* Intention also recorded.

White, John, jr., and Betsey Sanderson of Charlestown, int. Feb. 13, 1814.

John C., and Lydia B. Stanton of Lebanon, Me., int. Feb. 15, 1846.

John S., and Mary A. Barns, Aug. 17, 1844.

Joseph, of Brooklyn, and Mrs. Sarah Craft, May 26, 1730.

Katharine, and Ezekiel Hovey, Nov. 12, 1747.

Lerenzo [Lorenzo. int.], a. 24 y., cabinet maker, s. Joseph and Ruth, of Portsmouth, N. H., and Nancy Bell, a. 23 y., d. Benj[amin] and Sarah, Sept. 2, 1846.*

Lucy, and Stephen Brigham, Feb. 22, 1804.*

Luther, and Rebeccah Jackson, Dec. 18, 1798. c. r. 2.*

Martha, Mrs., and Jeremiah Parker, Nov. 15, 1750.

Mary, and John Davis, Sept. 30, 1742.

Mary, and Abiall Withington, Oct. 4, 1750.

Mary, and Ebenezer Bugbee, July 31, 1777.

Mary, and Daniel Craige, int. May 10, 1827.

Mary, and Christopher P. Shattuck, int. Apr. 12, 1835.

Mary, and John Dempsey, int. Oct. 30, 1848.

Mary C., and John James, Apr. [5. c. r. 3.], 1808.*

Mary E., of Dedham, and Sam[ue]l Leach, int. Apr. 6, 1828.

Matilda, and Royal Ellis [of Boston. c. r. 3.], Feb. 23, 1817.*

Moody, and Dorothy J. Rees, Aug. 13, 1843.

Moses, and Susanna Davis, Jan. 18, 1776.

Phebe Anne, and Gideon Eldridge, Aug. 11, 1834.*

Philip, of Newton, and Ann Pepper, at Boston, Dec. 2, 1730.

Polly W., and James H. Morgan, int. Nov. 3, 1837.

Rebecca, and Thomas Thayer Dec. 22, 1793.*

Rebecca, and Josiah Seavern, Sept. 2, 1801.*

Richard, and Hannah Gilford, int. May 25, 1823.

Ruth, and Otis Gould, Oct. 13, 1793.*

Sally [Sarah int.], of Newton, and Lemuel Pierce, at Newton, July 3, 1795.*

Sally, of Ossipee, N. H., and Bani Teague, int. Feb. 16, 1834.

Salome, and Isaac Davis, Dec. 9, 1813.*

Samuel, and Esther Lyon, Dec. 13, 1739.

Samuel, jr., and Hannah Bridge, May 21, 1763.

Samuel, jr., and Sarah Metcalf of Medway, at Medway, Apr. 29, 1766.

Samuel, and Sally Stoddard, int. Jan. 13, 1822.

* Intention also recorded.

WHITE, Samuel L., a. 22 y., s. Joseph and Elizabeth, and Orinda J. Keller of Lowell, a. 19 y., d. Matthew and' Hannah, Oct. 17, 1847.

Sam[ue]ll, and Mrs. Elizabeth Grenewood, Nov. 8, 1721.

Sarah, and Nath[anie]ll Pond, May —, 1756. C. R. 2.

Sarah, and Thomas Wyman, jr., Nov. 30, 1788.*

Sarah, of Dedham, and Isaac Chamberlain, at Dedham, [bet. 1796, and 1800 ?] [Nov. 6, 1796. int.]*

Sarah, and Elisha James, Dec. 23, 1817.*

Sarepta, and Ebenezer W. Scott, July 21, 1842.

Susan, and Magnus Lefstrom, Sept. 21, 1845.*

Susanna, and Jonathan Davenport of Dorchester, at Dorchester, Sept. 14, 1758.

Susanna [Whiting. int.], and Phinehas Child, Sept. 20, 1801.*

Thomas, and Catherine Green, int. Jan. 16, 1847.

Thomas, a. 21 y., ropemaker, s. William and Mary, and Susanna Ham, a. 20 y., d. John and Jerusha, Sept. 9, 1847.*

William, and Deborah Bosson, Dec. 22, 1767.

W[illia]m, and Nancy Avery of Holden, int. Dec. 7, 1806.

William, and Nancy Toby, Sept. 1, 1825.*

William, and Hannah Tuttle, June 26, 1827.

William, and Louisa L. Marsh, int. Jan. 20, 1833.

William, and Mary Ann Gould of Andover, int. July 16, 1839.

William A., of Watertown, and Harriet T. Sturgis, int. Mar. 29, 1845.

William H., a. 23 y., carpenter, s. James and Abigail, and Frances H. McDermot of Thomaston, Me., a. 19 y., d. John and Mary, June 1, 1845.*

Zenas, and Mary Draper, May 16, 1822. C. R. 2.*

WHITEHOUSE, Charles, and Sally Brown, Feb. 2 [9. C. R. 3.], 1817.*

WHITEING (see also Whiting), Rachel, and Ebenezer Healy [of Newton. C. R. 2.], Apr. 20, 1715.

WHITEMORE (see also Whittemore), Asa, and Sarah Jennison, Mar. 21, 1811.*

Elizabeth, and Edward P. W. Esty, May 20, 1827. C. R. 2.

Mary, and Amos Adams Mears, Nov. 7, 1805.*

Mary Ann, and Albert F. Mitchell of Brookline, int. Nov. 28, 1833.

William, and Elizabeth Clap, Apr. 9, 1812. C. R. 3.

* Intention also recorded.

**WHITFORD,** John, a. 21 y., miner, s. W[illia]m and Jane, and Ann Eleanor Morrow, a. 19 y., d. Thomas and Ellen, June 7, 1848.*

**WHITIMORE** (see also Whittemore), Ruthy, and Simeon Keys, Apr. 17, 1803.*

**WHITING** (see also Whiteing, Whitinge, Witing), Abigail, and James Draper, Feb. 18, 1680.

Abigail, and William Mackintash, Aug. 15, 1745.

Bathsheba, and Joseph Hay, Apr. 4, 1815. c. r. 2.*

Calvin [of Boston. c. r. 3.], and Adeline B. Gore, Oct. 29, 1829.*

Charlotte E., and Ozias Field, Feb. 16, 1837.*

Charlotte E., and William Leverett, Nov. 7, 1793.*

Deborah, and Edmund [Daniel. c. r. 2.] Gookin, Jan. 3, 1760.

Ebenezer, and Rhoda Colbourn, July 11, 1728.

Ebenezer, and Hulda Lyon, Oct. 30, 1748.

Ebenez[e]r, jr., and Rachel Tucker [May 10. c. r. 2.], 1753.

Ebenezer, 2d, and Ruth T. Walker, Nov. 7, 1816.*

Elizabeth [Mrs. c. r. 2.], and Ebenezer Swan, Oct. 31, 1780.

Hannah, and Seth Tucker of Milton, at Milton, Oct. 26, 1732.

Hannah, Mrs., and Thomas Dudley, Apr. 26, 1753.

Han[na]h, and Lemuel Billings, May 24, 1781. c. r. 2.

Henry, and Mary Davis, int. Apr. 4, 1784.

Isaiah, and Prudence Bridge, June —, 1754. c. r. 2.

Isaiah, and Abigail Harris of Brookline, Feb. —, 1759.

Isaiah, and Mehetable Shepherd of Dedham, at Dedham, May 10, 1779.

Joel, and Abigail Sumner Williams, Nov. 26, 1797.*

John, and Beulah Lewis of Dedham, at Dedham, Dec. 1, 1789.

Jonathan, and Anna Bullard of Dedham, at Dedham, Jan. 27, 1725-6.

Keziah, and William Draper, Sept. 24, 1767.

Leonard, and Susan Alden, int. Apr. 6, 1810.

Lucy, of Dedham, and James Morse, int. Mar. 24, 1805.

Lucy, and Joseph Hay, int. Oct. 10, 1841.

Mary, and Nathan[ie]ll Richards, Jan. 19, 1748-9.

Mary D., and Nathan Rand of Taunton, int. Oct. 28, 1832.

Mary F. P., a. 22 y., b. Southborough, d. Moses and Pesis R., and William Field of Dedham, a. 24 y., trader, b. North Bridgewater, s. Jabez and Mary, Sept. 19, 1849.*

Moses, and Jemima Tucker, May 26, 1764.

* Intention also recorded.

WHITING, Moses, of Dedham, and Mrs. Abigail Gay, Mar. 27, 1809.*

Moses, of Dedham, and Mrs. Isabel Dudley, Nov. 24, 1816.*

Nathaniel, and Hannah Lyon, May 1, 1729.

Nathaniel, jr., and Sarah Draper, at Boston, Sept. 23, 1767.

Priscilla, and Aaron Cass, Apr. 24, 1825. C. R. 2.*

Rachel, and Jacob Whitney, Nov. 15 [16. C. R. 2.], 1759.

Rhoda, and Thomas Lyon, Jan. 12, 1758.

Samuel K., and Mary I. G. Wilson, int. Sept. 12, 1841.

Sarah, Mrs., and James Prentice of Sutton, at Sutton, Dec. 24, 1770.

Seth Tucker, and Mrs. Lucy Dudley, Sept. 11, 1783.*

Solomon, and Lucy Mayo, Nov. 22, 1781. C. R. 2.

William, and Nancy Fellowes Davis, July 17, 1823.*

Zacharia, of Dedham, and Elizabeth Phillips, at Dedham, June 26, 1729.

WHITINGE (see also Whiting), Dorothy, and Thomas Weld, June 4, 1650.

WHITMORE (see also Whittemore), Sarah, and Charles Capron, both of Brookline, Aug. 20, 1792.

Stephen, jr., of Salem, and Esther S. Noyes, Sept. 17, 1832.*

WHITNEY, Abig[ai]l, and Joseph Haradon, May 30, 1781. C. R. 2.

Abigail, Mrs. [wid. int.], and Timothy Lewis, Aug. 7, 1785.*

Abigail, and Joseph Seaver, Nov. 17, 1799.*

Aibgail, and Abraham Spear, int. July 4, 1824.

Abigail H., and Lemuel Gay, Feb. 28, 1832.*

Abner, and Esther Jackson of Newton, at Newton, Mar. 21, 1768.

Amaziah, of Brookline, and Sarah Trull, Apr. 19, 1795.*

Ardelia L., and Thomas Crossley, Oct. 29, 1848.*

Caira R. [of Boston. C. R. 3.], a. 23 y., d. Eli and Sally, and Calvin Barrows[Burrows. C. R. 3.] of Lexington, a. 29 y., s. Samuel S. and Belinda, Oct. 14, 1849.*

Caroline L., of Quincy, and Charles Hill, int. July 21, 1833.

[Daniel, and Susannah Curtiss T. C.], ———, 1704.

Daniel ,and Sarah Gay, Mar. 7, 1769.

Daniel, and Elizabeth Champney, Nov. 14, 1802.*

Desire, and Edward Ward, Mar. 9, 1769.

Desire, and James Farrington, Apr. 3, 1828. C. R. 2.

* Intention also recorded.

WHITNEY, Dudley, and Mary S. Shove, int. Sept. 13, 1829.

Eli M., widr., a. 36 y., merchant, and Catherine Richards, wid. a. 32 y., d. Eliakin, Feb. 9, 1845.*

Elisha, jr., and Sally Heath, Feb. 26, 1804. c. r. 2.*

Elizabeth K., and Jesse Bills, int. Dec. 15, 1833.

Elnathan, and Sarah Perry, Sept. 24, 1729.

Esther, and John White, Mar. 8, 1745.

Ezekiel, of Watertown, and Katherine Draper, at Watertown, Dec. 6, 1763.

George, and Mary W. Mallard, Nov. 8, 1827.*

George, of Quincy, and Ann Greenough Gray, Dec. 15, 1829.*

Hannah, and Jesse [Jessee. int.] Herring, May 13, 1798. c. r. 2.*

Harriot W., and Joseph Strong of South Hadley, Feb. 11, 1813.*

Isaac, and Abigail Pond, Oct. 19, 1758.

Jacob, and Rachel Whiting, Nov. 15 [16. c. r. 2.], 1759.

Jane, of Marlborough, and William H. Brown, int. Nov. 16, 1828.

John, and Mary Payson, Apr. 22, 1773.

John H., and Sarah Skinner, Jan. 30, 1834.*

Jonas, and Sarah Perry, May 8, 1735.

Kimball, and Anna Leonard, int. Oct. 3, 1802.

Mary, of Watertown, and Abraham Chamberlin, at Watertown, Oct. 26, 1716.

Mary, and Joseph Libbey, Dec. 14, 1843.

Mary W., a. 42 y., and Luther C. Bailey, a. 24 y., s. Phineas and Dorcas, Dec. 31, 1848.*

Nancy, resident, and Benjamin Puffer of Stoughtonham, at Sharon, Oct. 20, 1778.

Pedy, and Joseph Dudley, June 14, 1801.*

Prudence [Whiting. c. r. 2.], and Lewis Jones, Dec. 29, 1790.*

Reuben, and Mary Brewer, Dec. 12, 1763. c. r. 2.

Ruth, and Joseph Adams, Apr. 22, 1701.

Sarah, and John Trull Mar. [17. int.; Apr. —, c. r. 3.], 1799.*

Stephen, and Ruth Whittemore, May 15, 1803. c. r. 2.*

Timothy, and Margaret Bacon, June 12, 1706.

W[illia]m, and Mary E. Jones [Glines. int.], June 4, 1840.*

———, Mr., of Boston, and ——— Richards, Feb. 9, 1845. c. r. 3.

WHITTEMORE (see also Whitemore, Whitimore, Whitmore), Abigail, and Ebenezer Smith, Nov. 15, 1774.

* Intention also recorded.

WHITTEMORE, Amos, and Mary Owen [Owens. c. r. 3.], Oct. 7, 1821.*

Andrew, and Mrs. Susan Newell, Aug. 3, 1841.*

Augusta A., and John L. Chenery, int. Mar. 5, 1843.

Betsey, and Elisha Toby of Dorchester, Dec. 5, 1802.*

Betsey T., and James M. Davis, int. June 12, 1836.

Ebbin W., and Sally A. Harvy, int. Mar. 18, 1838.

Eleanor, and Noah Parker, Dec. 10, 1772.

Elizabeth, and David Sloan, May 3, 1779.

Fanny T., and Clement Bartlett of Dedham, Sept. 26, 1824.*

Harriet, and William S. Keith, May 30, 1830.*

Henry S., a. 27 y., stone layer, s. Michael, jr. and Betsey, and Harriet M. Henry, a. 19 y., d. Jon[atha]n and Mary, Dec. 8, 1848.*

Jacob, and Mrs. Elizabeth Champney of Dorchester, at Dorchester, Oct. 7, 1777.

James, and Caroline Norcross of Newton, int. Mar. 10, 1839.

John, and Mary Ware, June 27, 1822.*

John, and Louisa Gale, int. Feb. 14, 1830.

John T., and Harriet [Hanah. int.] Lyon, Apr. [28.c. r. 3.], 1822.*

John T., and Sarah Henshaw, int. Aug. 18, 1844.

Judith Ann, and William Lewis of Walpole, int. Sept. 1, 1833.

Lois, of Dorchester, and John Mecuen, int. Apr. 26, 1812.

Lydia, of Malden, and Moses Collins, at Malden, May 20, 1746.

Mary, and Ralph Smith, Dec. 12, 1771.

Mary, and Sirus Knowlton, int. May 22, 1808. (banns forbidden by Mary Whittemore.)

Mary, and Sabin Holbrook, Jan. 10, 1813. c. r. 2.*

Mary A., and Jonas Pierce, jr., int. June 5, 1842.

Michael [jr. int.], and Elizabeth Titterton, June 10, 1804. c. r. 2.*

Oliver H., of Sharon. and Frances M. Bullard, Nov. 9, 1842.*

Rebecca, and Ephraim Chenery, Apr. 27, 1800. c. r. 2.*

Rebecca, Mrs., and John Hicks, int. Oct. 6, 1822.

Rebecca, of Boston, and John P. Beckwith, Nov. 19, 1843. c. r. 7.

Ruth, and Stephen Whitney, May 15, 1803. c. r. 2.*

Sam[ue]l, and Anne Dorby, Nov. 13, 1771.

Samuel, and Judith Caine, Mar. 31, 1811. c. r. 2.*

Samuel, and Olive Marden, Mar. 11, 1834.*

* Intention also recorded.

WHITTEMORE, Samuel, and Mary Follen, int. Nov. 24, 1848.
Sarah, and George W. Beckwith of Boston, Nov. 26, 1848.
Thomas R., and Augusta B. Richards, int. Nov. 19, 1843.
William, and Elizabeth Clap, Apr. 9, 1812.*
William, 2d, and Peggy Weatherbee, int. Feb. 18, 1816.

WHITTEN, Hannah, and Oliver Hide, at Dorchester, Oct. 14, 1800.

WHITTIER, Leonard D., and Tryphena Whittier, May 1, 1837.*
Reuben, and Lucy Chaplin, Feb. 25, 1808.*
Tryphena, and Leonard D. Whittier, May 1, 1837.*

WHITTLESY, Sarah E., of Litchfield, Conn., and Silas Stockman, int. Nov. 12, 1847.

WHORF (see also Wharf), Sylvanus H.[Sylvester H. of Boston. int.], a. 24 y., merchant, s. Samuel and Joanna R., and Henrietta Faxon, a. 18 y., b. Abington, d. Elisha and Hannah M., Sept. 2, 1849.*

WIGGEN (see also Wiggin), Margaret S., and Phinehas B. Smith, int. Mar. 26, 1837.

WIGGIN (see also Wiggen, Wiggins), Joseph, and Frances E. Hilton of Brentwood, N. H., int. Dec. 4, 1842.
Sarah, and Thomas J. Cate, int. Oct. 21, 1838.

WIGGINS (see also Wiggin), Abigail, and Silas R. Brown, int. Nov. 27, 1836.

WIGHT (see also White), Abigail, of Dedham, and Stephen H. Locke, int. Mar. 6, 1831.
Ann, of Needham, and Phillip Mills, at Needham, Dec. 22, 1774.
Charlotte, and Cornelius Sullivan, int. Apr. 1, 1847.
Nathaniel [resident. int.], and Sally Harding, Nov. 1, 1801. C. R. 2.*

WILBAR, Jane P. [Wilbur. dup.], and Edward F. Mecuen, May 1, 1842.*
Louisa, and Ansel Howard of Taunton, Oct. 22, 1826.*

WILBY Eliza Ann, and Hubbard G. Murray, Mar. 1, 1843.*

* Intention also recorded.

**WILCOX,** John D. F., and Paulina Hopkins of Orleans, int. June 23, 1848.

**WILD** (see also Weld), Edmund, and Mary Merry of Lynn, at Lynn, Nov. 25, 1779.
John [Weld. int.], of Cambridge, and Abigail B. Curtis, May 12, 1807.*
John, and Ann Kenney, int. Aug. 26, 1848.
Polly [Weld. int.], and Aaron Draper, Oct. 16, 1800. c. r. 2.*
Sarah, of Randolph, and Daniel Curtis, int. Nov. 13, 1848.

**WILDER,** Aretmas W., 2d m, of Montpelier, N. H. [Vt. int.], a. 30 y., merchant, b. Montpelier, s. Artemas and Sarah A. Stevens, a. 24 y., d. Amos and Susan T., Sept. 26, 1849.*

**WILDES** (see also Weld), Solomon, and Lucretia E. Peirce, of Boston, int. Oct. 17, 1849.

**WILDS** (see also Weld), Mary Ann, and Charles Samborn, June 16, 1825.

**WILEY** (see also Willey), James, of Charlestown, and Bethia Giles, int. Sept. 5, 1841.

**WILKERSON** (see also Wilkinson), Levi, and Bathsheba Tucker, Apr. 23, 1776.

**WILKINSON** (see also Wilkerson), John G., and Ellen Brown, Oct. 6, 1844.*

**WILLARD,** Aaron, and Mrs. Catharine Gates [both residents. int.], Mar. 6, 1783.*
Eliza Ann, and Jeremiah Lyon, Aug. 13, 1820.*
Hannah, and John Pond of Portsmouth, N. H., Dec. 31, 1809.*
Henry, and Frances A. Williams, ——, 1832.
Julia, and Isaac Cary, int. Dec. 26, 1830.
Mary, and Caleb Hobart, Esq., of Milton, Mar. 31, 1830.*
Moses, Dr., and Arabella Penny [both residents. int.], Oct. 4, 1785.*
Samuel S. [L. int.], and Mary J. Rowe, May 4, 1845.*
Sarah B., and Edward Bird of Dorchester, int. May 10, 1829.
Simon, and Mrs. Mary Leeds, Jan. 23, 1788.*
Simon, Jr., and Eliza Adams, Dec. 6, 1821.*

**WILLET** Abner, and Catherine Rhoads of Sharon, Feb. 17, 1814.*

* Intention also recorded.

**WILLEY** (see also Wiley), Caroline F., and Charles Foss, int. Sept. 18, 1831.

James, and Elizab[eth] Gallaghan, Aug. 23, 1843.*

**WILLIAMS,** Aaron D., and Nancy Bugbee, Dec. 8, 1814.*

Abiell, and Timothy Foster of Dorchester, Mar. 3, 1742-3.

Abigail, Mrs., and Edward Ruggles, Jan. 11, 1732-3.

Abigail, and Samuel May, Oct. 4, 1753.

Abigail, and Jonathan Balch, Dec. 5, 1771.

Abigail, and Ebenezer Smith, June 6, 1776.

Abigail, and Dr. John Bartlett, Feb. 17, 1789.*

Abigail, and Alpheus Williams of Charlton, Oct. 14, 1790.*

Abigail Sumner, and Joel Whiting, Nov. 26, 1797.*

Abigail, and William Ware of Needham, Jan. 1, 1812.*

Adaline, and Samuel McIntire, int. Sept. 9, 1827.

Adaline, and Jacob Stevens, int. July 27, 1828.

Alfred [of Boston. c. r. 3.], and Emily R. Pierce, Nov. 13, 1842.*

Alpheus, of Charlton, and Abigail Williams, Oct. 14, 1790.*

Amy, and David Baker, Mar. 22, 1809.*

Ann, and William Parry, both residents, Oct. 16, 1731.

Anna, and Joseph Houghton, Dec. 17, 1772.

Anna, and Samuel [Sam[u]ell. int.], Goff, Sept. 16, 1784.*

Benjamin, and Elisabeth Boylston, Mar. 9, 1756.

Benjamin, and Anna Fuller of Newton, at Newton, Apr. 29, 1766.

Benjamin Payson [Capt. int.], and Margaret Child, Feb. 3, 1814.*

Betsy, and Aaron D. Weld, Dec. 25, 1804.*

  ardson of Turner, Me., a. 24 y., s. Cornelius T. and Sarah R., Jan. 23, 1848.*

Caleb, and Eunice Clap, both of Dorchester, May 2, 1793.

Caroline, a. 27 y., d. Sam[ue]l S. and Lucy, and Abijah Rich-

Caroline M., and Alexander H. Twombly, int. Oct. 14, 1846.

Caroline R., and Benjamin Armstrong, Aug. 7, 1842.

Catherine, and Lt. Thomas Mayo, Apr. 27, 1773.

Charles, a. 22 y., clerk, s. Sam[ue]l S. and Lucy, and Hannah M. Rust, a. 21 y., d. Abednego and Hannah, June 8, 1848.*

Charlotte, and William Austin of Charleston, June 19 [17. c. r. 3.], 1806.*

Charlotte, and Samuel Seaverns, Aug. 31, 1806.*

Daniel, and Hanah Holbrook, June 25, 1724.

* Intention also recorded.

WILLIAMS, David, and Martha Cumings, Dec. 17, 1797.*

Deborah, and Isaac Parker, June 27, 1776.

Dorothy, and Ralph Holbrook, Jan. 9, 1739-40.

Dorothy, Mrs., and Capt. Thomas Wiswell, Apr. 20, 1749.

Dudley, and Mary Williams, Jan. 18, 1798. C. R. 3.

Dudley, and Isabella Everett, int. Aug. 26, 1832.

Edward, and Mrs. Sarah Trott, 3d, of Dorchester, at Dorchester, Feb. 19, 1740.

Edward Payson, and Mrs. Sarah Craft, May 21, 1772.

Elisabeth, and Samuel Holbrook, Sept. 1, 1755.

Elisha, of Hartford, and Abigail Livermore, Aug. 30, 1780.

Eliza, and Oren Peck, Dec. 6, 1821.*

Eliz[abe]th, Mrs., and Rev. Sam[ue]ll Ruggles of Billerica, Apr. 18, 1728.

Elizabeth, and John Williams, June 2, 1737.

Elizabeth, and Dea. Sam[ue]l Sumner, July 19, 1781.

Elizabeth, and Samuel Weld, Mar. 27, 1787.*

Elizabeth, and Stedman Williams, Jan. 31, 1796.*

Elizabeth, of Cambridge, and John Larrobee, int. Nov. 22, 1829.

Elizabeth S., a. 18 y., d. Thomas and Mary, and Charles B. Bryant, a. 24 y., currier, s. Edward and Mary, May 14, 1846.*

Elizabeth W., and Edward W. Bradley, May 25, 1825.*

Ellen M., and John S. Williams, int. Apr. 12, 1840.

Ezekiel, and Sarah Dana, Nov. 20, 1777.

Frances A., and Henry Willard, ——, 1832.

Franklin, a. 23 y., gilder, s. Sam[ue]l S. and Lucy, and Mary Elizabeth Seaver, a. 22 y., d. John C. and Mary, Dec. 24. 1846.*

George, and Sarah Forbes, int. June 19, 1842.

George Henry, and Hannah Ellis Coney, Sept. 27, 1838.*

Grace, and John Medcalf, Oct. 29, 1718.

Hannah, and Syranus Collins of Connecticut, May 22, 1777.

Hannah, and Thomas Dana, jr., Nov. 20, 1777.

Hannah, and Ebenezer Heath of Brookline, Jan. 11, 1791.*

Hannah, and Daniel Weld, May 29, 1800.*

Hannah, Mrs., and Calvin Granger, int. Aug. 26, 1810.

Hannah D., and Allen Putman of Hamilton, June 8, 1843.*

Harriet, and Thomas Child, int. Nov. 8, 1835.

Harriot A., and Lincoln Fearing, int. Dec. 25, 1831.

Henry, and Mary Payson, May 13, 1736.

* Intention also recorded.

WILLIAMS, Henry H., and Sally Williams, Sept. 25, 1800.*

Henry H., Capt., and Mary Dudley, int. Mar. 24, 1833.

Henry Howell, Lt., and Mrs. Elizabeth Bell, Jan. 28, 1762.

Henry J., and Sarah W. Robbins, Oct. 25, 1838.*

Howard S., and Sarah S. Waterman of Sandwich, int. June 2, 1849.

Isaac, and Elisabeth Davis, Nov. 12, 1767.

Isaac, and Nancy L. Brown of Mason, N. H., int. Feb. 9, 1848.

James, and Mary Ann Shaw Trefethen, int. Dec. 24, 1843.

Jane, Mrs., and Elisha Brewster, Feb. 1, 1779.

Jane, a. 21 y., d. Thomas and Mary, and Henry Maud, a. 25 y., carpet weaver, s. David, Aug. 31, 1849.*

Jeremiah, and Katherine Payson, Sept. 15, 1743.

Joanna, and Joseph Ruggles, Dec. 3, 1778.

John, and Sarah Weld, June 1, 1709.

John, and Mary Goad, Jan. 15, 1712.

John, and Dorothy Brewer, Mar. 15, 1715-16.

John, and Elizabeth Williams, June 2, 1737.

John, jr., and Ann Bird of Dorchester, at Dorchester, May 25, 1749.

John, Lt., and Mrs. Bethiah Steadman, Sept. 12, 1749.

John, and Mary Sumner, May 5, 1768.

John, and Mrs. Mary Champney of Dorchester, at Dorchester, May 15, 1770.

John, and Rebecca Winslow, Jan. 3, 1771.

John, and Eleanor White, Sept. 29, 1803.*

John, and Sarah Robbins of Cambridge, int. May 22, 1804.

John, and Mary Ann Davis, July 17, 1823.*

John Davis, and Hannah Davis, Dec. 15, 1768.

John Davis [jr. int.], and Hannah Weld, May 16, 1798. C. R. 2.*

John Evans [Evens. C. R. 3.], and Irene Coney, Mar. 21, 1833.*

John S., and Mrs. Nancy Hunt, May 6, 1807.*

John S., and Ellen M. Williams, int. Apr. 12, 1840.

Joseph, and Abigail Davis, May 22, 1706.

Joseph, and Mary Bass of Dorchester, at Dorchester, Jan. 1, 1750.

Joseph, and Mary Holmes, May 10, 1753.

Joseph, and Susanna May, Dec. 15, 1763.

Joseph, Esq., and Hannah Dudley, Apr. 5, 1770.

* Intention also recorded.

WILLIAMS, Jos[ep]h, Capt., and Mercy Davis of Brookline, int. Oct. 17, 1784.

Joseph D., and Emily Mirick, Aug. 16, 1826.*

Joseph S., of New Orleans, and Mrs. Susan King Williams, Sept. 14, 1825.*

Julia M. I., and Daniel Spalding of Nashville, N. H., Oct. 1, 1842.*

Katherine, Mrs., and John Ruggles, Jan. 20, 1741-2.

Lois, and Thomas Clark, July 24, 1777.

Louisa A[ugusta. int.], and James H. Lunt, Apr. 29, 1833.*

Lucretia, and William Campbell, Jan. 28, 1779.

Lucy, and Jacob Esty [Estey. resident. int.], July 16, 1782. C. R. 2.*

Lucy, and George Standdash of Dorchester, June 24, 1790.*

Lucy, and Charles Howe of Dorchester, Dec. 7, 1820.*

Margaret, and Thomas Griggs, Sept. 1, 1743.

Maria, a. 24 y., d. Sam[ue]l S. and Lucy, and James Porter, a. 26 y., carpenter, s. Alexander and Margarett, June 1, 1848.*

Martha, and Jacob Pason, Nov. 14, 1716.

Martha, and Thomas Cotton of Brookline, Apr. 14, 1725.

Martha, and Thomas Dana, Nov. 1, 1750.

Martha, and William Williams, Mar. 28, 1754.

Martha, and Nath[anie]l Ruggles, Dec. 8, 1767.

Martha, and Aaron D. Weld, May 27, 1819.*

Mary, and Samuel Chote, at Ipswich, 23 : 9 br. : 1688.

Mary, and Benjamin Pason, Nov. 25, 1713.

Mary, and Joseph Shed, Jan. 3, 1722-3.

Mary, and Samuel Gore, Feb. 23, 1727.

Mary, and Benjamin May, May 4, 1738.

Mary, and Jeremiah Parker, June 16, 1743.

Mary, and Timothy Parker, June. 10, 1764.

Mary, of Dorchester, and Job Walker, at Dorchester, Aug. 22, 1765.

Mary, and Nathan[ie]l Felton, jr., Dec. 21, 1769.

Mary, and John Smith, Dec. 9, 1779.

Mary, and Jonathan Brintnall, July 12, 1781.

Mary, Mrs., and Silvanus Burril [Burrill. int.], Jan. 16, 1783.*

Mary, and Dudley Williams, Jan. 18. 1798. C. R. 3.

Mary, and James Adams. Feb. 9, 1812.*

Mary, of New Market, N. H., and Thomas Garland, int. Feb. 15, 1843.

* Intention also recorded.

WILLIAMS, Mary L., and Henry Cunningham, May 22, 1822.*

Mary A., of Brooklyn, and Peter Smith, Nov. 2, 1837.*

Mehitabel, and John Shirley, Nov. 13, 1760.

Moses B., and Mary Jane Penniman, of Brookline, int. Feb. 26, 1843.

Nabby L., and Charles Durant, Apr. 6, 1806.*

Nancy, and Perez Ewell, Aug. 26, 1804.*

Nancy, of Dorchester, and John Houghton, int. Aug. 18, 1805.

Nathaniel W., and Mary Pratt, Mar. 1, 1796.*

Nath[anie]l W., and Mrs. Hannah Wells, int. Nov. 27, 1808.

Nehemiah D. Capt., and Sarah Heath, Dec. 14, 1815.*

Payson, and Rachel Child, June 13, 1776.

Payson, of Watertown, and Maria Durant, int. May 12, 1811.

Polly, and Robert Hooper of Marblehead, Dec. 21, 1809.*

Prudence, and William Heath, Oct. 20, 1748.

Rachel, Mrs., and Abraham Perrin, Apr. 29, 1779.

Rebecca, and Stephen Child, Dec. 22, 1803.*

Robert, and —— Fearing, wid., at Hingham, Nov. 3, 1675.

Robert, and Ann Boylstone, Mar. 29, 1750. C. R. 2.

Robert, and Elizabeth Bugbee, Apr. 28, 1774.

Salley, and Elijah Eastey, Oct. 22, 1791.*

Sally, and William Patten, Apr. 29, 1799.*

Sally, and Henry H. Williams, Sept. 25, 1800.*

Samuel, and Theoda Parkes, Mar. 2, 1653.

Samuel, and Mrs. Mary Capen, at Dorchester, Feb. 3, 1713-14.

Samuel, and Mrs. Dorothy Denison, Apr. 28, 1720.

Samuel, and Mrs. Hannah Chandler, May 17, 1750.

Samuel, and Mrs. Lucy Huntington of Norwich, d. Col. Hezekiah, Esq., and Hannah, May 31, 1762.

Sam[ue]l, and Mrs. Hannah Pierpont, Feb. 22, 1770.

Samuel C. Dr., of Shrewsbury, and Rebecca Sumner, May 5, 1818.*

Samuel S., and Lucy French of Dedham, int. June 5, 1814.

Samuell, s. Sam[uel], and Sarah May, Feb. 24, 1679.

Sam[ue]ll, jr., and [Mrs. C. R. 2.] Abigail May, Feb. 10, 1746-7.

Sarah, and John Polley, Jan. 1, 1704-5.

Sarah, and Samuell Barnard, May 22, 1718.

Sarah, Mrs., and Edward Brick of Dorchester, May 22, 1735.

Sarah, and Obadiah Davis, Sept. 13, 1744. C. R. 2.

Sarah, Mrs., and Rev. [Sylvanus. C. R. 2.] Conant [of Middleborough, C. R. 2.], May 16, 1751.

* Intention also recorded.

WILLIAMS, Sarah, and Cornelius Fellows, Dec. 20, 1763.

Sarah, and Gyles Alexander, May 4, 1773.

Sarah, and William Dudley, Feb. 22, 1774.

Sarah, and Jon[atha]n Davis, Oct. 31, 1781. C. R. 2.

Sarah, and Dr. Jonathan Davis, May 1, 1797.

Sarah, and Frederick G. Nicholls of Kingston, Jan. 29, 1823.*

Sarah C[hild. C. R. 3.], and Arthur W. Austin of Charlestown, May 29, 1834.*

Sarah Davies, and John Griggs, Nov. 23, 1820. P. R. 3.

Stedman, and Elizabeth Williams, Jan. 31, 1796.*

Stephen, jr., and Sarah Pason, Apr. 8, 1725.

Stephen, Capt., and Mrs. Elizabeth Lowder of Dorchester, at Dorchester, Dec. 14, 1738.

Stephen, and Theoda Perrin, Dec. 4, 1763.

Stephen, and Mary Langdon, Dec. 12, 1771.

Stephen, 3d, and Abigail Smith, Dec. 23, 1779.

Stephen [jr. C. R. 3.], and Mrs. Lois Cunningham, July 2, 1805.*

Stephen, 4th, and Louisa Palmer of Somersett, Jan. 25, 1807.*

Steven, and Mary Capen of Dorchester, at Dorchester, June 18 1700.

Susan, and Samuel Stodder, Jan. 28, 1816.*

Susan King, Mrs., and Joseph S. Williams of New Orleans, Sept. 14, 1825.*

Susanna, Mrs., and John Robinson of Dorchester, May 11, 1727.

Susanna A., and Benedict Berrien, int. Aug. 28, 1848.

Theoda, and Samuel Scarborough, Feb. 5, 1706.

Theoda, and Aaron Davis [jr. int.], Jan. 24, 1793.*

Thomas, jr., and Susannah Dana, Nov. 20, 1777.

Thomas, jr., and Elizabeth McCarthy, int. Sept. 18, 1791.

Thomas L., and Ann M. Gould, July 17, 1844.

Thomas L., and Nancy Rands, int. Apr. 13, 1845.

Thomas P., and Sarah Moore, Oct. 29, 1845.*

Tilson, and Mary Forbes, int. Mar. 26, 1826.

William, of Pomfret, and Sarah Stevens, Oct. 20, 1720.

William, and Sarah Payson of Dorchester, at Dorchester, May 28, 1752.

William, and Martha Williams, Mar. 28, 1754.

William, and Sarah May, Sept. 4, 1755. C. R. 2.

William, and Anne Maxwell, Dec. 2, 1762.

William [jr. int.], and Mrs. Sarah Crosby of Dorchester, at Dorchester, Dec. 25, 1782.*

WILLIAMS, William, jr., and Jane Howe, int. Nov. 4, 1821.
William, and Elizabeth Weld, Aug. 25, 1822.*
William, and Harriet H. Crane, int. Nov. 9, 1845.

**WILLIS,** Allen, and Polly Crawly [Crawley. int.], June 26, 1800. C. R. 2.*
Ephraim, and Charlotte Broad, int. May 4, 1828.
Experience [Mills. C. R. 2.], and Joseph Davis, May 11, 1726.
Hamilton, and Louisa M. Windship, Aug. 23, 1842.*
Martha, and Adam Kinsley, Esq., both of Canton, Dec. 31, 1823.
Mary, and William Peacock, Apr. 12, 1653.
Mary Ann, and Joseph N. Wheeler, May 29, 1825.
Milton, and Fanny Adams, Mar. 3, 1822.*
Relief D., and John H. Darling of Oxford, N. H., May 2, 1837.
Samuel, and Experience Newel, May 23, 1700.
Susanna, and Rev. Samuel Walter, at Boston, Aug. 7, 1735.

**WILLS,** Elizabeth R., and Francis A. Fuller, June 4, 1844. C. R. 5.

**WILLSON** (see also Wilson), Benjamin, and Esther Lyon, July 2, 1706.
John, and Sarah Goad, Dec. 13, 1711.
John, and Elizabeth Davenport, Jan. 25, 1720-21.
John, jr., and Abigail Mayo, Dec. 22, 1737.
John, and Mrs. Jane Scott, July 9, 1740.
Mary, and William Salter, May 15, 1746.
Mary, and Richard Lathbridge, Dec. 22, 1772.

**WILLUR,** Elizabeth Herrick, and Thomas Mickell Burnham, int. Oct. 6, 1844.

**WILSON** (see also Willson), Aaron, and Mrs. Judith Baker of Dorchester, at Dorchester, Nov. 19, 1778.
Benjamin, and Sally Payson of Sudbury, Dec. 5, 1802.*
Eliza, and William Waters, jr., July 11, 1815.*
Eliz[abe]th, and John Perigoe, Jan. 4, 1727-8.
Fanny T., and Nathan C. Carey, May 30, 1845.
Granville W., and Emily W. Hallowell, May 18, 1838.*
Hannah, and Subal Seaver, Feb. 7, 1668.
Harriet W., and Isaac Cook, jr., of Brookline, int. May 13, 1827.

* Intention also recorded.

WILSON, Henry, and Mary S. Champney, int. May 24, 1835.

John, and Mary H. Smith, int. Jan. 29, 1837.

John D., a. 21 y., merchant, s. Joseph and Jane J., and Mary Barker, a. 22 y., d. George and Susan, June 23, 1849.*

John L., of Philadelphia, and Francies M. P. Lewis, Oct. 26, 1837.*

Leonard J., of Milford, N. H., and Mary A. G. Sayer, Nov. 26, 1849.*

Lydia, and Nathaniel Seaver, Nov. 1, 1798.*

Maria J., and John A. Brown, int. Feb. 16, 1834.

Mary, and Joseph Gardner, May 11, 1732.

Mary, Mrs., and Samuell Danforth, Nov. 5, 1651.

Mary C., and Noah R. Garish, int. May 1, 1842.

Mary, I. G., and Samuel K. Whiting, int. Sept. 12, 1841.

Nathanael, and Hanna Crafts, Apr. 2, 1645.

Rebecca A., and Samuel S. Lyon of Bethel, Nov. 23, 1848.

Sally [Salley. int.], of Newton, and Nathaniel Richards, at Newton, Sept. 5, 1790.*

Sarah, and Daniel Machees, Mar. 18, 1662.

Sarah, of Newton, and Nathan Talbot, at Newton, June 12, 1770.

Sarah J., and Daniel T. Jewett, both of Bangor, Dec. 1, 1848.

Sukey, Mrs., and Ebenezer Leland, Aug. 4, 1793.*

Susannah, and Pharez Adams, Feb. 20, 1814.*

Thomas, of Cambridge, and Mrs. Mary Patricks, May 6, 1784.*

Thomas, and Deborah Crane, June 25, 1811.*

Thomas C., of Salem, and R. R. S. [Rhoda Rebecca Spencer. int.], Eldridge, Oct. 12, 1837.*

Ursilla, and Thomas Graves, Feb. 5, 1707.

WILTON, Susanna [Susana. dup.], of Cambridge, and Nath[anie]l Cunningham [resident. dup.], at Cambridge, Feb. 9 [Jan. 1. dup.], 1786.

WINCH, Jason, and Abig[ai]l How, Dec 13, 1777.

Jesse, and Lephy Sampson, int. Mar. 23, 1806.

WINCHESTER, Abigail, and Peter Stone, Dec. 5, 1749.

Benjamin, and Prudence May, Dec. 31, 1719.

Deborah, of Brookline, and Jerahmeel Wheeler, Feb. 2, 1747-8.

Elizabeth, of Brookline, and Daniel Rice, int. Apr. 8, 1787.

* Intention also recorded.

WINCHESTER, Henry, jr. [of Brookline.c. R. 2.], and Dorothy Brewer, Mar. 3, 1748. [1747-8. c. R. 2.]

Joanna, and Joseph Stevens, June 5, 1698.

Jonathan, and Sarah Craft [both of Brookline. c. R. 2.], May 5, 1748.

Joseph [of Brookline. c. R. 2.], and Margarett Brewer, Nov. 27, 1740.

Joseph, and Priscilla Gore, Mar. 1, 1758.

Josiah, and Sarah Sever, Mar. 25, 1707.

Lucretia, and Jabez Lewis, Feb. 8, 1807.*

Mehitabel, and Joseph Pason, Mar. 4, 1713.

Moses, and Mary Ames, Oct. 25, 1757.

Nathaniel, and Hannah Wyman, Nov. 9, 1815.*

Ruth, and Jonathan Corey [resident in Cambridge. c. R. 2.], ——, 1753. [May 10. c. R. 2.]

Samuel, and Hannah Bates, Dec. 10, 1808.*

Sam[ue]ll, and Joanna West, Nov. 19, 1747.

Sarah, and Robert Campbill, Jan. 2, 1763.

Susanna, and Abraham Dor, Nov. 5, 1747.

William Capt., and Anna Fuller of Newton, int. Sept. 28, 1800.

William, jr., and Mary P. Seaverns, Nov. 30, 1826.*

W[illia]m, jr., and Ann A. Seaverns, Oct. 18, 1842.*

**WINDSHIP** (see also Winship), Charles May, Dr., and Susan Barker, int. Feb. 27, 1831.

Charles W., Dr., and Patty R. Ziegler, Nov. 1, 1818.*

John [of Boston. c. R. c.], and Rhoda P[arker. c. R. 3.] Munroe, Apr. 21, 1805.*

Louisa M., and Hamilton Willis, Aug. 23, 1842.*

**WING,** John [Stephen. int.] B., b. Ireland, and Ann Hennessy [Hennessey. int.], b. Ireland, Oct. 11, 1849.*

**WINN,** Sarah, and John Murray, int. Mar. 7, 1849.

**WINSHIP** (see also Windship), Abiel, and Alice Shepard of Dorchester, Oct. 16, 1793.

Charles, Dr., and Catherine May, int. Feb. 28, 1808.

Charles, and Charlotte Munroe, July 10, 1808.*

Charles, and Sarah K. Bacon, of Dedham, Mar. 15, 1829.

Charlotte May, and Joseph Cowdin of Fitchburg, Dec. 1, 1813.*

Hephzibah, ad Thomas Shed, Dec. 26, 1771.

* Intention also recorded.

WINSHIP, Joshua, and Mary Cunningham, June 2, 1772.
Nathaniel, and Mary [Polly. int.] Freeman, at Boston, July 16, 1786.

**WINSLOW,** Isaac, and Jemima Debuke, at Boston, Nov. 25, 1770.
Lucy, and George Erving, Esq., Oct. 25, 1768.
Rebecca, and John Williams, Jan. 3, 1771.
Reuben, and Harriet Wyeth of Cambridge, int. May 16, 1824.
Sarah Louisa, a. 18 y., d. Reuben and Harriet, and George K. Goodwin, a. 22 y., carriage painter, s. Jeremiah and Caroline, Nov. 18, 1847.*

**WINSOR,** Joseph, widr., a. 57 y., merchant, s. Joshua and Olive, of Duxbury, and Temperance A. Downing, a. 52 y., Feb. 28, 1847.*
Sarah A., and Antepas Newton, jr., Nov. 8, 1840.*

**WINTER.** James, and Mrs. Susannah Bennit [Bennèt. dup.], d. John, Oct. 9, 1762.

**WINTHROP,** John, and Mrs. Anne Dudley, Dec. 16, 1707.

**WISE,** Joseph, and Mary Tompsonn, Dec. 3, 1641.
Marie, and Caleb Lamb, June 30, 1669.
Sarah, and Patrick Farrell, both b. Ireland, Nov. 16, 1849.*

**WISWALL** (see also Wiswel, Wiswell), Amasa C., and Clarissa Atwood, Jan. 7, 1830.*
Jeremiah, Dea., of Newton, and Mrs. Polly Harrington, int. Dec. 17, 1809.
Mary, and Timothy [W. int.] Bennet, Nov. 5, 1826.*
Payne, and Mary Ann Crane Mehoney, Sept. 5, 1824.*
Samuel, and Mary Ann Newton, Apr. 14, 1836.*
Sarah A. A., and James Davenport, Sept. 11, 1845.
Sarah C., and William H. Palmer, Nov. 28, 1839.*

**WISWEL** (see also Wiswall), Hannah, and Caleb Stedman, ——, 1697.

**WISWELL** (see also Wiswall), Hannah, Mrs., of Dorchester, and Ebenezer Pierpont, at Dorchester, Sept. 10, 1746.
Thomas, Capt., and Mrs. Dorothy Williams, Apr. 20, 1749.

**WITHERBEE** (see also Wetherbee), John B., and Sarah Goddard, int. May 16, 1841.

* Intention also recorded.

**WITHERO,** Simon, and Anna Maria Ortmans, int. Mar. 4, 1847.

**WITHERS,** John, and Martha Munsay of Wiscasset, Me., Nov. 12, 1845.

Mary Ann, a. 19 y., d. James and Margarett, and Joseph Warren Cobb, a. 23 y., morocco dresser, s. William and Sarah, Apr. 18, 1847.

**WITHINGTON,** Abel [Abial. c. R. 2.], and [Mrs. c. R. 2.] Hannah Weld, Dec. 14, 1774.

Abiall, and Mary White, Oct. 4, 1750.

Caroline P., and W[illia]m Cheever, Dec. 5, 1839.*

Eliza Ann, of Dedham, and Nelson Worthen, int. June 21, 1835.

Elizabeth, and David Beman, Nov. 2, 1806.*

Frances M., and George Homes of Dorchester, int. June 13, 1841.

Hannah, and Warren Marsh, Apr. 13, 1806.*

Isaac, jr., and Abigail Barnard, Oct. 14, 1841.*

Lewis, and Sarah Breck [Brick. int.] Robinson of Dorchester, at Dorchester, Nov. 12, 1795.

Lewis, and Lucy Goddard of Brookline, int. Apr. 30, 1820.

Lucy, and Stephen Goodnough, Sept. 15, 1796.*

Mary, and Capt. James Robinson, both of Dorchester, Dec. 5, 1793.

Mary, and Jacob Fisher, Jan. 13, 1799.*

Mirian, of Stoughton, and Joseph Colson, at Stoughton, Sept. 19, 1771.

Moses, and Jane Clap, Oct. 8, 1839.*

Nathaniel, and Sarah Crawley [Crowley. int.], Nov. 26, 1807. c. R. 2.*

Otis, of Brookline, and Sarah Ann Clap, Nov. 27, 1828.*

Samuel, and Sally Bruce, Nov. 13, 1804.*

Susan M., and Williard [Willard. int.] Hawes, Jan. 24, 1844.*

**WITING** (see also Whiting), Hannah, Mrs., and Oliver Hide, both residents, int. Sept. 21, 1800.

**WODDIS,** Hannah, and Thomas Cheiny, Sept. 24, 1684.

**WOESSNER** (see also Woessnor), Johannah, and John Hassold, int. May 5, 1844.

* Intention also recorded.

**WOESSNOR** (see also Woessner), Louisa, and Lewis Lion, int. Nov. 14, 1841.

**WOLCOT,** Joseph, of Needham, and Elisabeth Mosman, July 14, 1725.

**WOOD** (see also Woods), Caroline M., of Plymouth, and Lewis Brown, int. Aug. 14, 1836.
Cyrus, and Sally Alding, int. May 8, 1803.
Francis, and Katharine Pike, Dec. 28, 1780.
Harriet, and Allen Newell of Brookline, June 28, 1827.*
John, b. Ireland, and Bridget McLaughlin, b. Ireland, Dec. 14, 1849.
Lemuel, and Mary Salter, Mar. 31 [13. c. r. 2.], 1768.
Rebecca, and Ebenezer Webb, Feb. 8, 1773.
Susannah, and Joseph Allen, Oct. 3, 1745.

**WOODARD** (see also Woodward), Nancy [Woodward. int.], and Titus Pomroy [residents. int.], Feb. 26, 1804. c. r. 2.*

**WOODBRIDGE,** Rebecca A., a. 23 y., d. Thomas and Sophia, and William B. Howe, widr., a. 29 y., machinist, s. Levi and Abigail, June 8, 1847.*
Martha, and Samuell Ruggles, jr., July 8, 1680.

**WOODBURY,** Charles W., and Martha E. Gardner, int. June 2, 1846.
Nancy, and Caleb Joy, int. Jan. 1, 1815.

**WOODDY** (see also Woody), Mary, and Edmund Sheffield, Apr. 17, 1644.

**WOODFORTH,** Eunice H., a. 30 y., d. James, and John J. McKay, a. 39 y., clerk, s.Angus and Barbara, Mar. 15, 1849.*

**WOODHOUSE,** John V., a. 22 y., machinist, s. Thomas D. and Mary, and Harriet J. White, a. 18 y., d. William and Nancy, Sept. 8, 1847.*

**WOODMAN,** Truman [Freeman. int.], and Betsey Cummings. Sept. 7, 1834.*

**WOODS** (see also Wood), Abigail, and Samuel Sims, of Dorchester, Sept. 8, 1824.*
Benjamin, and Ann Turner of Scituate, Mar. 28, 1723.

* Intention also recorded.

WOODS, Dolly, and Abraham Wheeler of Dorchester, May 17, 1801.*

Elizabeth, Mrs., and William Gridley, Jan. 4, 1785.*

Elizabeth, and Enoch [A. int.] Smith of Newton, June 16, 1793.*

Eiizabeth Ann, and John M. Moulton, int. July 3, 1825.

George, and Dolly Brewer, Oct. 15, 1766.

Hannah, and John Levins, June 7, 1665.

Hannah, and Thomas Goold, Dec. 16, 1736.

Hervey, and Rebecca Metcalf of Royalston, int. Oct. 11, 1807.

Hervey, and Sally Pierce of Warwick, int. Mar. 21, 1819.

Jemima, and William Davis of Brooklyn, Dec. 29, 1743.

John, and Jemima Sever, Dec. 3, 1713.

John, jr., and Elizabeth Barber, Oct. 31, 1742.

John, and Sarah Barnard, at Boston, Aug. 20, 1747.

Maria, and Patrick Coffy, int. Sept. 10, 1849.

Miranda, and Horace Bacon, int. Jan. 7, 1838.

Prudence, of Dedham, and Augustus B. Keen, int. Aug. 17, 1834.

Sarah, and John Tileston of Dorchester, Dec. 16, 1725.

Sarah, and —— Seaver [of Wells. c. r. 2.], Nov. —, 1752.

Sarah, and John [E. c. r. 3.] Beck, June 22, 1807.*

William G., and Mary Shealds of Milton, int. Aug. 22, 1841.

**WOODSIDE,** Elbridge G., and Louisa Shepard of Canton, int. Oct. 4, 1835.

**WOODWARD** (see also Woodard), Abiel, and Daniel Seaver, Oct. 15, 1747.

Abraham, of Brookline, and Sarah Pierpont, June 4, 1728.

Abraham, jr., and Sarah Lethbridge, June 23, 1743.

Anne, and Kendal Johnson, Oct. 23, 1770.

Caleb [of Brookline. c. r. 2.], and Hannah Chever, Nov. 21, 1751.

Chauncey, of Brookline, farmer, and Augusta Draper, Nov. 25, 1847.*

Elizabeth F., of Brookline, and George W. Minns, int. Aug. 29, 1849.

Ester, and Isaac Morse, Oct. —, 1807.*

Ichabod, of Brookline, and Abigail Holbrook, at Brookline, July 1, 1725.

John, and Nancy Toleman of Brookline, int. May 7, 1786.

* Intention also recorded.

WOODWARD, Julia A., of Newton, and Warren Guild of Dedham, Mar. 1, 1843. C. R. 7.
Mary, and James Goddard, Nov. 27, 1713.
Mary E., and John Marshall of North Yarmouth, Me., Nov. 6, 1833.*
Nathanael, and Dorcas Gardiner [of Brookline. C. R. 2.], June 23, 1715.
Samuel, and Louis Hooper of Charlestown, int. Jan. 29, 1786.
Sarah Ann, and Phillip Sowden, jr., Mar. 27, 1838. C. R. 3.

WOODY (see also Wooddy), Richard, and Francis Dexter, Dec. 29, 1646.

WOOLRUCH, Christeanna, and Joseph Bownister, int. Jan. 4, 1846.

WORSLEY, Joseph, and Sarah Prince, Apr. 26, 1758.

WORTH, Elizabeth, and Samuel Pitcher of Milton, Jan. 6, 1703-4.

WORTHEN, Clarissa, and Joseph Calfe, int. Apr. 26, 1835.
Mary, and David P. Rowe, July 26, 1837.*
Nelson, and Hannah Young, June 2, 1844.*
Nelson, and Eliza Ann Withington of Dedham, int. June 21, 1835.

WREN, Susan, and John Hurly, int. May 4, 1849.

WRIGHT (see also Dwight), Benjamin F., and Lucinda Rundlet, Oct. 22, 1833.*
Caroline, of Cambridge, and Alfred Tufts, int. Dec. 25, 1842.
Elizabeth, and Solomon Sanborn, May 4, 1845.*
Frederick E., of Cambridge, and Anna C. Bell, d. Amory and Ann, Nov. 28, 1847.*
Jabash, and Susan Churchill of Plympton, int. May 6, 1821.
Jabesh, and Charlotte Cushing Clap, Jan. 1, 1811.*
Obadiah, and Nancy Ruggles, Aug. 13, 1797.*
Patrick, and Caroline Hill, [Jan. 20. int.], 18333.*
Rachell, and John Levnes, July 5, 1639.
Samuel, and Rebecca Craft, May 11, 1686.

WYAT, Samuel, and Mary H. Brown of Wenham, int. Jan. 5, 1823.

* Intention also recorded.

**WYETH,** Harriet, of Cambridge, and Reuben Winslow, int. May 16, 1824.

John, of Cambridge, and Mary Ann Newman, Nov. 12, 1839.*

**WYMAN,** Asa, jr., a. 24 y., wood dealer, s. Asa and Esther, and Louisa A. Ryerson, a. 18 y., d. Eben[eze]r and Mary, Aug. 2, 1847.*

Betsy, and John Pratt of Portland, Jan. 30, 1810.*

Catharine, and John Downer, Nov. 9, 1800.*

Edith, and Gershom Brown, Mar. 3, 1802.*

Edward, a. 27 y., merchant, s. Rufus and Ann. and Margarett [Margaret. int.], C. Boyde, a. 19 y., d. James and Margarett, Sept. 23, 1845.*

Elizabeth, and William Bacon, Jan. 15, 1815.*

Hannah, and Nathaniel Winchester, Nov. 9, 1815.*

Harriet, and Thomas Taber of New York, Apr. 15, 1824.*

Isaac, and Catharine Taber, Dec. 8, 1822.*

John, and Ann Payson of East Sudbury, at East Sudbury, Oct. 18, 1795.*

Joshua, of Woburn, and Mrs. Thankful Griggs, Sept. 11, 1798.*

Julia A., and Robert Ferguson, Sept. 8, 1844.*

Laura, and John Head of Haverhill, int. Mar. 8, 1835.

Mary, and William Pratt, Feb. 7, 1799.*

Rebecca, of Woburn, and Benjamin Thompson, at Woburn, Aug. 18, 1730.

Rebecca, and Lt. Isaac Sturtevent, Apr. 18, 1782.

Samuel, and Hannah Clark, Nov. 23, 1756.

Samuel, of Baltimore, and Hannah Davis Mayo, Oct. 19, 1820.*

Sarah, and Sewall Kendall, Feb. 22, 1820.*

Thomas, and Sarah Doubt, Apr. 19, 1757.

Thomas, jr., and Sarah White, Nov. 30, 1788.*

William [jr. int.], Capt., and Ruthy Davis, Sept. 4, 1806. c. R. 2.*

**YATES,** Nancy, and Ebenezer Hubbard, Dec. 28, 1848.*

**YENDLEY,** Joseph, and Elizabeth Dunmedy, int. Oct. 16, 1842.

**YOATON,** Betsey, and Joseph H. Burke, int. Dec. 11, 1842.

**YORK,** Stephen, and Keziah Griggs, Aug. 31, 1834.*

William, and Joanna Hale, Dec. 8, 1828.

* Intention also recorded.

**YOUNG,** Ann, and James Managhan, int. Apr. 11, 1841.
Calvin, and Submit Short, at Swansea, Sept. 18, 1842. p. r. 5.
Ezra, and Louisa Meserve, int. 12, 1846.
Frederick, and Aif Porstare, int. Mar. 8, 1846.
George, and Elisabeth [Elizabeth. int.] C. Rumril [Rumrill. int.], Oct. 17, 1844.*
Hannah, and Nelson Worthen, June 2, 1844.*
James G., and Julia A. Adams, Apr. 26, 1846.*
James S., and Mary B. Hopkins, int. Mar. 24, 1839.
John, and Anna Rockfort, Oct. 12, 1848.*
John D., and Elizabeth Pettee, June 6, 1832.*
Lot [Lott. p. r. 5.], and Keziah Pierce, Apr. 23, 1807.*
Mary, and Michael Kelley, int. Feb. 14, 1849.
Nancy, and William Rumrill, June 13, 1841.*
Nancy B., and Anthony Hankey, int. Nov. 17, 1846.
Olive, and Benjamin Gale, int. June 1, 1828.
Patrick, and Mary Collins, int. Mar. 18, 1847.
Rebecca, and John Parker, June 18, 1843.*
William, b. Ireland, and Margarett [Margerie. int.] Doherty, b. Ireland, July 19, 1849.*

**YOUNGMAN,** Anna, and Joseph Pepper, Dec. 15, 1720.
Eleanor, and Joseph Skellins of Richmond, Aug. 19, 1731.
Elizabeth, and John Craft, Feb. 5, 1722-3.
Francis, and Anna Heath, Dec. 2, 1685.
Sarah, and William Amos, Apr. 30, 1733.

**ZEIGLER,** George [Zegler. int.], and Mrs. Mary Blaney, Sept. 9, 1784.*
Patty R., and Dr. Charles W. Windship, Nov. 1, 1818.*

## SURNAMES MISSING

——, Benjamin, and Elisabeth White, Mar. 21, 1750. [Mar. 22, 1749-50. c. r. 2.]
——, Elizabeth, and Benjamin Sab[in. T. C.], ——, 1700.
——, Elizabeth, and Ebenezer Richards, Oct. —, 1769.
——Freeman, of Connecticut, and Mary Cheney, Jan. 5, 1776.
——, ——, and Elizabeth Newel, Apr. 9, 1690.
——, ——, and Robert Boilston, Mar. 29, 1750.

* Intention also recorded.

## NEGROES

**ANAN,** John, and Isabella Smith, Dec. 8, 1816. C. R. 2.

**ATKINSON,** Elizabeth, and William Dunkins, int. May 1, 1848.

**BANCROFT,** John, and Hannah Harrison, June 18, 1837. C. R. 3.

**BOSTON,** and Phebe, both free, July 28, 1776.
Zilpha, and Cuff Sumner, Nov. 4, 1801.*

**BRIDGHAM,** Simon, and Mrs. Hannah Roe, Apr. 5, 1804. C. R. 2.

**BURR,** Esther H., of Boston, and Thomas W. Steamburg, int. Nov. 11, 1846.

**CALE** [Catherine. dup.], and London [servant ?] of John Walley, Dec. 2, 1723.

**CATO,** and Ziporah, ——, 1770. C. R. 2.

**CATO,** and Jane, servants of Isaac Sears, Esq., Oct. 21, 1779.

**CLOSE,** Anna, resident, and Prince Robinson, int. Mar. 29, 1789.

**CRAIG,** James, and Nancy Otis, Oct. 14, 1798.*

**CRUMMELL,** Betty, and Peter, servant of Col. Dudley, June 27, 1741. C. R. 2.

**CUFFE,** and Grace servants to Rev. Nath[aniel] Walter, Oct. 10, 1745.

**DELEN,** Violet, and James D. Simpson, June 2, 1822.*

**DIXON,** Mary, and John Rowland, [Africans], [residents. int.], Dec. 4, 1800.*

**DUNKINS,** William, and Elizabeth Atkinson, int. May 1, 1848.

**FLOYD,** James M., and Mary Stevens, int. May 27, 1849.

**FREEMAN,** Mary Ann, and W[illia]m E. Johnston, Sept. 22, 1837. C. R. 3.

* Intention also recorded.

**GILES,** Simeon, and Hannah Robbins of Needham, int. Mar. 11, 1821.

**GINNEY,** servant to Madame Lucy Dudley, and James, servant to Joseph Williams, Feb. 26, 1756.

**GRACE,** and Cuffe, servants to Rev. Nath[aniel] Walter, Oct. 10, 1745.

**HARRISON,** Hannah, and John Bancroft, June 18, 1837. C. R. 3.

**JACK,** and Phillis, servant to Rev. Mr. Walters, Aug. 22, 1764. C. R. 2.

**JAMES,** servant to Joseph Williams, and Ginney, servant to Madam Lucy Dudley, Feb. 26, 1756.

**JANE,** servant to Mrs. Chick, and Jo, servant to Edw[ar]d Brinley, at Boston, Feb. 7, 1768.

**JANE,** and Cato, servants of Isaac Sears, Esq., Oct. 21, 1779.

**JO,** servant to Edw[ar]d Brinley, and Jane, servant to Mrs. Chick, at Boston, Feb. 7, 1768.

**JOHNSTON,** W[illia]m E., and Mary Ann Freeman, Sept. 22, 1837. C. R. 3.

**LONDON,** and Cale [Catherine. dup.] (servant. ?], of John Walley, Dec. 2, 1723.

**LUCY,** formerly belonging to Mr. Joshua Tilden of Marshfield, and Minervi, formerly belonging to the Rev. Mr. Robins of Milton, int. Feb. 20, 1780.

**MINERVI,** formerly belonging to the Rev. Mr. Robins of Milton, and Lucy, formerly belonging to Mr. Joshua Tilden of Marshfield, int. Feb. 20, 1780.

**OLIVER,** Judy, free, and Scipio, servant to Edward Brinley, at Boston, Feb. 16, 1769.

**OTIS,** Nancy, and James Craig, Oct. 14, 1798.*

**PETER,** servant of Col. Dudley, and Betty Crummell, June 27, 1741. C. R. 2.

* Intention also recorded.

**PHEBE,** and Boston, both free, July 28, 1776.

**PHEBE,** a Mulatto girl residing at Ens. Samuel Scarborough's, and Peter Spear, int. Dec. 9, 1787.

**PHILLIS,** servant to Rev. Mr. Walters, and Jack, Aug. 22, 1764. C. R. 2.

**ROBBINS,** Hannah, of Needham, and Simeon Giles, int. Mar. 11, 1821.

**ROBINSON,** Prince, and Anna Close, resident, int. Mar. 29, 1789.

**ROE,** Hannah, Mrs., and Simon Bridgham, Apr. 5, 1804. C. R. 2.

**ROWLAND,** John, and Mary Dixon, (Africans), [residents. int.], Dec. 4, 1800.*

**SCIPIO,** servant to Edward Brinley, and Judy Oliver, free, at Boston, Feb. 16, 1769.

**SIMPSON,** James D., and Violet Delen, June 2, 1822.*

**SMITH,** Isabella, and John Anan, Dec. 8, 1816. C. R. 2.

**SPEAR,** Peter, and Phebe, a mulatto girl residing at Ens. Samuel Scarborough's, int. Dec. 9, 1787.

**STEAMBURG,** Thomas W., and Esther H. Burr of Boston, int. Nov. 11, 1846.

**STEVENS,** Mary, and James M. Floyd, int. May 27, 1849.

**SUMNER,** Cuff, and Zilpha Boston, Nov. 4, 1801.*

**ZIPORAH,** and Cato, ———, 1770 C. R. 2.

* Intention also recorded.

# ROXBURY DEATHS

---

**ABBOT** (see also Abbott), William, Oct. 28, 1713.
William, s. William and Rebekah, Dec. 14, 1723, a. abt. 13 y.
  G. R. 1.
—all, Nov. 5, 1701, a. 40 y. G. R. 1.

**ABBOTT** (see also Abbot), Harriet Elizabeth, d. Rev. Jacob,
  Dec. 9, 1834, a. 6 m.
Harriet V., Sept. 12, 1843. C. R. 6.
John B., s. Rev. John S. C., May 24, 1839, a. 7 y.
Mary, d. William and Rebecca, May 16, 1714.
Nehimiah, June 21, 1807, a. 60 y.
Sarah Ann, wid., b. Newburyport, d. James and Aphia Bracket,
  consumption, Dec. 9, 1849, a. 28 y.

**ACREES,** Elizabeth, d. John, 24 : 5m : 1666. C. R. 1.

**ADAMS** (see also Addams), Amos (ordained Sept. 12, 1753),
  Oct. 5, 1775, a. 54 y. G. R. 1.
Edward W., Jan. 23, 1842, a. 27 y.
Elisha, youngest s., Dea. Ebenezer of Quincy, dec., issue
  of Dec. 22, 1798. N. R. 4.
Elizabeth, w. Rev. Amos, d. Dea. Henry Prentice of Cam-
  bridge, Aug. 11, 1769, in her 43d y. N. R. 2.
Hannah, d. Roger and Mary, ———, 1688.
Hannah, w. C. J., Oct. 21, 1838, a. 43 y.
Henry F., July —, 1830, a. 24 y.
Hiram [K. G. R. 5.], May 7, 1842, a. 25 y.
James, Apr. 25, 1843, a. 62 y.
John R., s. John Q. and Sarah C., bowel complaint, Sept. 4,
  1848, a. 5m. 7d.
Joseph, widr., gentleman, b. Stratham, N. H., s. Joseph and
  Mary, old age, Nov. 22, 1849, a. 99 y. 6 m.
Maria T., d. John, Sept. —, 1838, a. 3 y.
Mary, w. Roger, June 28, 1710.
Mary, d. Joseph, Jan. 30, 1828.

453

ADAMS, Phinehas [of Boston. G. R. 5.], Dec. 22 [20. G. R. 5.],
1831, a. 57 y. [a. 60 y. G. R. 5.]

Robert, s. Joseph and Elizabeth, lung complaint, Jan. 3, 1848.
a. 17 d.

Roger, s. Roger and Mary, May 26, 1710.

Roger, Mar. 2, 1714.

Thomas, s. Roger, Dec. 26, 1675.

Thomas, m., merchant, b. Pembroke, N. H., paralysis, Dec. 31,
1847, a. 64 y.

William Alleyne, s. W[illia]m J., July 23, 1841, a. 7 y.

W[illia]m H., unm., mariner, s. James and Mary, consumption,
May 29, 1846, a. 24 y.

Zabdiel, Mar. 24, 1820, a. 52 y.

————, ch. Zabdiel, Apr. 24, 1802, a. 2 y.

————, fracture of the brain caused by a fall, June 29, 1808,
a. 2 y. 9 m. C. R. 3.

————, ch. still born, Francis and Sarah L., Oct. 22, 1846.

ADDAMS (see also Adams), Amos [Adams. N. R. 2.], s. Rev.
Amos and Elizabeth, [scalded. N. R. 2.], June 2, 1761.
[in his 6th y. N. R. 2.]

ADDINGTON, Elizabeth, wid., Nov. 22, 1742, in her 88th y.
N. R. 1.

AINSWORTH, Allis, wid. Daniel, Jan. 9, 1684-5.

Daniel, Nov. 13, 1680.

Joanna, d. Edward and Joanna, ————, 30, 1699.

Joshua, s. Edward and Joanna, Jan. 25, 1688-9.

————, wid., bur. 10: 11m: 1684-5. C. R. 1.

AITIKISON, Andrew, Sept. 30, 1819, a. 40 y.

ALCOCK (see also Alcocke), George, Dea., bur. Dec. 30,
1640.

Joanna, d. John, Aug. 5, 1649.

John, Dr., at Boston, 27: 1m: 1667, a. 40 y. C. R. 1.

————, a young ch., 7: 7m: 1649. C. R. 1.

ALCOCKE (see also Alcock), John, May 5, 1690, in his 35th
y. G. R. 1.

Palsgrave [Allcock. G. R. 1.], Nov. 24, 1710. [a. 49 y. G. R. 1.]

Sarah, w. John, bur. 29: 9m: 1665, a. 44 y. C. R. 1.

**ALDIS** (see also Alldis, Auldice, Auldis), Eunice, w. Nathan, June 13, 1714.

Mary, d. Nathan and Mary, Dec. 28, 1716.

Nathan, s. Nathan and Eunice, Aug. 14, 1715.

Nathan, Feb. 10, 1749-50.

Rachel, Nov. 16, 1807.

**ALEXANDER,** Sarah, w. Giles [jr. N. R. 4.], Nov. 7, 1797, a. 50 y. [a. 49 y. N. R. 4.]

**ALLARD,** Cyrus D., s. Isaac T., Nov. 25, 1840. a. 3 y. 6m.

———, Frenchwoman, Aug. 11, 1717.

**ALLDIS** (see also Aldis), Ruth, d. John and Mary, Aug. 12, 1707.

**ALLEN**(see also Allin, Alling), Anna, June 8, 1718.

Calvin, s. Calvin and Abigil, Jan. 9 [11.C. R. 2.], 1809. [a. 16 w. C. R. 2.]

Hannah, wid. Robert, Esq., of Boston, June 24, 1841, a. 65 y.

James, Oct. —, 1822.

Joanna M., d. Asahel G. and Chestina, dysentery, Aug. 30, 1847, a. 1 y. 3 m. 15 d.

John W., July 18, 1844, a. 48 y. G. R. 5.

Joseph, Aug. —, 1817. [a. 43 y. C. R. 2.]

Mary Ann (Jennis), Aug. —, 1848. C. R. 4.

Peter, Sept. 7, 1728, a. abt. 60 y. G. R. 1.

Ralph Sanger, s. Calvin and Abigail, Aug. 20, 1812.

———,ch. Calvin and Abigail, Aug. 3, 1812, a. 2m. C. R. 2.

**ALLIN** (see also Allen), Elizabeth, d. Peter and Mary, June 5, 1709.

Sarah, d. Peter and Mary, May 31, 1709.

**ALLING** (see also Allen), Francis, bur. Dec. 1, 1692.

**ALLOTT,** Allice, b. England, consumption, Oct. 3, 1848, a. 12 y.

**AMES,** Louisa, Oct. —, 1841. C. R. 4.

Marietta, d. Asa and Mary, burnt, Dec. 18, 1846, a. 2 y. 6m.

**AMORY,** Caroline S., Aug. —, 1827, a. 35 y.

Catharine, w. John [decay of nature. C. R. 3.], July 20, 1831.

Charlotte Moryat, d. Rufus, July 17, 1813, a. 14 y.

John H., s. Thomas, Esq., dec., Sept. 16, 1839, a. 37 y.

AMORY, Mary Elizabeth, d. Tho[ma]s, Esq., dec. Jan 10, 1834. [a. 3̶3 y. C. R. 5.]

Philip [Phillip. C. R. 5.] D., s. Jonathan and Letitia, scarlet fever, May 11, 1849, a. 9 m.

Thomas, typhus fever, Oct. 31, 1822, a. 8 y. C. R. 3.

Thomas, [dropsy. C. R. 3.], Oct. 25 [27. C. R. 3.], 1823, a. 61 y.

**ANDERSON,** Eliza H., d. Rev. Rufus and Eliza H., consumption, Dec. 12, 1849, a. 18 y.

James, Apr. 8, 1813.

W[illia]m, m., b. Ireland, typhus fever, June 3, 1847, a. 40 y.

**ANDREWS,** Eliza P., d. Alfred A. and Harriet M., croup, Mar. 18, 1848, a. 1 y. 10 m.

John, Esq. [decay of nature. C. R. 3.], Oct. 17, 1822, a. 80 y.

Lucy H., d. Alfred A. and Harriet M., croup, Mar. 19, 1848, a. 5 y.

Ruth, Mrs. [old age. Mar. 26. C. R. 3.], 1831, a. 82 y.

Susan T., d. Lyman, consumption, Feb. 25, 1847, a. 4 y. 5 m.

**ANDUM,** George W., s. William and Mary B., lung fever, at Dorchester, (bur. at Roxbury), Mar. 1, 1849, a. 2 y. 7 m. 14 d.

**ANGUS,** Elizabeth N., Jan. 6, 1847, a. 53 y. G. R. 4.

**ANJAMANE,** Johannas, m., painter, b. Holland, consumption, Mar. 26, 1847, a. 33 y.

**ANNIS,** Susan, dropsy, at the alms house, Mar. 25, 1849, a. 67 y.

**APOLONIO,** Sarah, m., b. New York, Oct. 3, 1847, a. 28 y.

**APPEL,** Caroline J., d. Henry and Caroline J., croup, Dec. 13, 1846, a. 1 y. 4 m.

Henry, s. Henry and Caroline, bowel complaint, Oct. 26, 1849, a. 11 m.

———, s. still born, Henry, Jan. 14, 1848.

**APPLEGATE,** see Appleton.

**APPLETON,** W[illia]m S. [Applegate. dup.], July 5, 1837, a. 28 y.

**ARGAN,** Betsey, m., b. Ireland, lung fever, Feb. 11, 1848, a. 29 y.

**ARMSTRONG,** Caroline, d. Benj[ami]n and Caroline, fits, Jan. 1, 1848, a. 10 d.
Martha, Dec. 15, 1709.
Mercy, d. Jonathan, Oct. 2, 1694.

**ARNOLD,** Joseph, m., yeoman, apoplectic fit, Dec. 27, 1848, a. 72 y.
Lauretta, d. J. and E., Jan. 25, 1827, a. 8 y. c. r. 2.

**ASH,** James, s. J. M., Sept. 18, 1832, a. 6 m.

**ASHTON,** Mary, w. John [consumption. c. r. 3.], Dec. 15, 1840, a. 44 y. [a. 43 y. 6 m. c. r. 3.]

**ASPINWALL,** Peter, Dec. 1, 1687, a. abt. 75 y. g. r. 1.
Sarah, w. Samuel, Apr. 1, 1710, a. 42 y. g. r. 1.

**ASTWOOD** (see also Atwood), John, s. James, bur. Mar. 15, 1640.
John, s. John and Sarah, the end of 12m: 1640. c. r. 1.

**ATKIN** (see also Atkins), James, s. James, Feb. 21, 1683.

**ATKINS** (see also Atkin), Eliza, b. Ireland, d. H. and Allice, scarlet fever, at the alms house, Jan. 14, 1849, a. 3 m.
Mary, b. Ireland, scarlet fever, at the alms house, Oct. 13, 1848, a. 1 y.
Susan T., d. Fanny and Abraham [N. c. r. 5.], dysentery, Aug. 23, 1847, a. 3 y. 23 d.

**ATTEN,** Abagail, Sept. 25, 1805, a. 30 y.

**ATWOOD** (see also Astwood), Adeline, Mrs., Dec. 17, 1838, a. 30 y. [a. 20 y. c. r. 5.]
Benj[ami]n F. [T. c. r. 3.], s. Capt. Isaac [consumption. c. r. 3.], Jan. 25 [27. c. r. 3.], 1837, a. 21 y.
Charles H., s. Henry and Jane, scarlet fever, May 31, 1847, a. 3 y. 10 m. 6 d.

**AUGUSTA,** William, b. Ireland, consumption, Jan. 24, 1848, a. 17 y.

**AULDICE** (see also Aldis), John, Mar. 18, 1736-7, in his 83d. y.

**AULDIS** (see also Aldis), Mary, w. John, sr., Dec. 13, 1730, a. 77 y.

Nathanael, s. Nathan, June 10, 1736.

**AUSTIN,** Anna Jane, d. Dr. Benjamin [teething. c. r. 3.], Oct. 6, 1825, a. 22 m.

Charlotte Williams, dysentery, Sept. 21, 1821, a. 1 y. c. r. 3.

John [h. Mary. c. r. 5.], b. Ireland, typhus fever, Sept. 29, 1847, a. 25 y.

William Cleland, s. Dr. Benjamin [lung fever. c. r. 3.], June 25, 1823, a. 10 m. [a. 11 m. c. r. 3.]

**AVERBECK,** Catharine [Averbick. dup.], Sept. 9, 1838, a. 19 y.

**AVERY,** Adeline, at the alms house, Feb. 19, 1843, a. 40 y.

Eunice L. Mrs., Dec. 27, 1842, a. 31 y.

**AYERS** (see also Ayre, Eayers, Eayres), Almira, w. Benj[ami]n F., Apr. 23 1841, a. 24 y.

Dolly, Mrs., Dec. —, 1833, a. 50 y.

Dorithy, a pauper, Nov. 25, 1833, a. 68 y.

George C., unm., machinist, b. Wheelock, N. H., s. Samuel and Orpha, lung fever, Apr. 2, 1847, a. 30 y.

Jane F., w. Benj[ami]n F., Nov. 6, 1836, a. 25 y.

Nathaniel. of Boston, Aug. 10, 1800, a. 46 y. g. r. 3.

Nath[anie]l, Aug. 9, 1805, a. 44 y. [a. 46 y. c. r. 2.]

Nathaniel, s. Jonathan, Mar. 28, 1819, a. 5 w. c. r. 3.

Olive [Mrs. c. r. 2.], w. Eleazer [pleurisy, Feb. 20. c. r. 2.], 1834, a. 63 y. [a. 62 y. c. r. 2.]

William, a pauper, Aug. 6, 1834, a. 34 y.

————, Miss, Nov. 10, 1802, a. 30 y. c. r. 2.

————, ch. Jonathan, Sept. 24, 1805, a. 12 m. c. r. 2.

**AYRE** (see also Ayers), Lebbeus, suddenly at E. Whiting's, Feb. 3, 1776, a. 28 y. c. r. 2.

**BABBIT,** Abigail, Mrs., Jan. 28, 1821, a. 67 y.

**BABCOCK,** Euphemia F., bur. Nov. 13, 1844, a. 1 y. c. r. 5.

Sally, w. Robert G., Sept. 25, 1817, a. 19 y.

**BACHELDER** (see also Batchelder), Hannah L., b. Brunswick, Me., w. Albert, consumption, Mar. 25, 1849, a. 26 y.

**BACON** (see also Bacons, Beacon), Abigail Perry, d. William and Elizabeth, July 6, 1826.

BACON, Benjamin, s. John and Mary, June 28, 1709.

Caroline Susan, m., b. Dedham, d. William Herring, consumption, Sept. 4, 1849, a. 35 y.

Eleanor G., w. William B., child birth, Mar. 11, 1849, a. 24 y.

Elizabeth, w. Jacob, Feb. 27, 1713, a. 57 y. G. R. 2.

Elizabeth W., only d. William, May 13, 1840, a. 20 y.

George, s. Thomas, bur. 19 : 5m : 1672, a. 3 y. C. R. 1.

George [Beacon. C. R. 1.], "being at a Raising had a piece of timber fall upom him, and he dyed before the next morning," Sept. 19, 1715. [in his 41st y. G. R. 1.]

Harriet W., d. William and Eliza, July 26, 1824, a. 7 y.

James, Nov. 25, 1721.

Joseph, s. Philip and Patience, Oct. 23, 1727.

Joseph, a pauper [at the alms house. dup.], July 3, 1829, a. 65 y.

Margret, d. Tho[mas], bur. 18 : 8m : 1682. C. R. 1.

Sally, Sept. 11, 1800.

Sally, d. Jos[ep]h and Betsey, Sept. 11, 1801.

Thomas, Oct. 25, 1702.

William, Apr. 29, 1825, a. 23 y.

————, ch. still born, Tho[ma]s, 4 : 8m : 1673. C. R. 1.

————, ch. E. fever, Oct. 15, 1801, a. 18 m. C. R. 3.

————, ch. Joseph, Sept. 25, 1803, a. 14 m.

————, ch. David, dysentery, Sept. 26, 1822, a. 10 d. C. R. 3.

BACONS (see also Bacon), ————, ch. Jos[eph], Oct. 26, 1805, a. 18 m.

BAILEY (see also Bayley), Harriot E., d. Joseph and M. W., throat distemper, June 29, 1848, a. 3 m.

BAKER, Abigail, d. Thomas, jr. and Abigail, Jan. 1, 1741-2.

Abigail, w. John, Oct. 25, 1746, in her 34th y. G. R. 3.

Catharine, a pauper, Apr. 1, 1834, a. 70 y.

Charlotte H., d. Abel and Sarah, consumption, Oct. 29, 1848, a. 28 y.

David, Feb. 4 [9. C. R. 2.], 1803. [a. 47 y. C. R. 2.]

Elizabeth, d. Robert, Sept. 17, 1693.

Hannah, w. Thomas, jr., July 27, 1739. [in her 27th y. G. R. 1.]

Hannah, wid. Thomas, Mar. 6, 1776, in her 95th y. G. R. 3. [a. 95 y. C. R. 2.]

BAKER, James, clerk, unm., b. Topsham, s. Jonathan and Betsey
N., consumption, at New Orleans, bur. at Roxbury, Aug.
5, 1848, a. 22 y.

Jarvis, at the alms house, Sept. 19, 1842, a. 30 y.

Jonathan, s. Robert, Sept. 24, 1693.

John, s. Thomas and Sarah, Mar. 29, 1705.

John, Nov. 7, 1732, in his 88th y. G. R. 3.

John, Capt. Aug. 10, 1781, a. 75 y. G. R. 3.

John, Capt., Nov. 17, 1816, a. 81 y. C. R. 2.

John, Dec. 10, 1819, a. 36 y. C. R. 2.

John H., s. John and Elizabeth, dysentery, Aug. 18, 1847, a.
1 y. 10 m. 25 d.

Lucy, wid., Mar. 3, 1820, a. 74 y. C. R. 2.

Luke, apoplexy, July 19, 1833, a. 82 1-2 y. C. R. 2.

Martha W., Nov. —, 1838, a. 17 y.

Mary, d. Thomas, bur. July —, 1652.

Matthew, s. Robert, June 20, 1695.

Nabby, May 1, 1805, a. 37 y. C. R. 2.

Robert, s. Robert, Oct. 1, 1684.

Robert, Oct. 25, 1720.

Sarah, w. John, Nov. 29, 1715.

Thomas, sr., Jan. 28, 1683. [1683-4, a. 76 y. G. R. 1.]

Thomas, jr., under the command of Capt. Sam[ue]ll Wadsworth, slain by the Indians at Sudbury, Apr. 21, 1676.

Thomas, s. Thomas and Hannah, Oct. —, 1735.

Thomas, May 10, 1761, a. 83 y. G. R. 3.

———, ch, still born, John, bur. 27 : 3m : 1680. C. R. 1.

———, "old Blind Father" bur. 30 : 11 m : 1683-4. C. R. 1.

———, "old widow," bur. 6 : 6m : 1685. C. R. 1.

———, s. Capt., drowned in a tub of water, June 18, 1761, a.
abt. 3 y. N. R. 2.

———, d. John, jr., Feb. 21, 1776, a. 7 m. C. R. 2.

———, d. John, jr., Feb. 28, 1778, a. 8 y. C. R. 2.

———, w. Lemuel, Oct .8, 1784, a. 28 y. C. R. 2.

———, s. John, Apr. 1, 1785, a. 6 y. C. R. 2.

———, s. John, Aug. 18, 1792, a. 6 y. C. R. 2.

———, ch. John and Charlotte, Oct. 13, 1798, a. 3 m. C. R. 2.

BALCH, Frances, dysentery, Sept. 11, 1836, a. 10 w. C. R. 3.

Mary N., d. Joseph, Apr. 18, 1833, a. 2 m.

BALDNER (see also Baldnor), Elizabeth, d. Jacob and Mary,
dysentery, Aug. 26, 1848, a. 3 y.

Jacob, s. Jacob and Mary, June 12, 1839, a. 17 m. G. R. 5.

BALDNER, Jacob, m., b. Germany, liver complaint, Sept. 3, 1847, a. 45 y. 5 m.

BALDNOR (see also Baldner), Harriet, d. Jacob and Harriet, dysentery, Aug. 30, 1848, a. 1 y. 8 m.

BALDWIN, John H., s. Luke, Sept. 29, 1839, a. 1 y.
Mary, Mrs., Jan. 31, 1837, a. 67 y.
Thankful, w. Reuben, July 13, 1842, a. 42 y. G. R. 5.

BALIS, ———, w. Jonathan, Sept. 8, 1776, a. 31 y. C. R. 2.
———, ch. ———, Dec. 9, 1776, a. 5 m. C. R. 2.

BALLOW, Clarissa Hatch, d. Rev. Hosea, 2d, Jan. 30, 1829, a. 5 y.

BAMPTON, Elizabeth H., b. England, dysentery, Sept. 12, 1847, a. 45 y.

BANCE, Adrain, at the work house, May 30, 1801.

BANCROFT, Louisa Clouston Hales, d. William and Eliza, Mar. —, 1826, a. 5 m.

BANDLE, Mary, d. John F. and Mary S., dysentery, Oct. 12, 1848, a. 10 d.

BARDEN, Sarah, d. Hiram and Zilpah, dropsy in the head, Nov. 5, 1846, a. 3 m. 18 d.

BARKMAN, Mary, d. Frederick and Sarah, bowel complaint, Aug. 17, 1848, a. 7 m. 14 d.

BARLET (see also Bartlett), ———, ch. Dr. John, Sept. 3, 1802, a. 3 y.

BARLOW, Alessandross, s. Royal J. and Sarah E., Apr. 5, 1843, a. 1 y. 8 m. G. R. 5.
George R., s. Royal M. and Lucy P., Feb. 6, 1843, in his 4th y. G. R. 5.
Royal S. [M. Mar. 11, 1843, in his 28th y. G. R. 5.]

BARNABY, Richard, s. Timothy, croup, Mar. 6, 1849, a. 2 m.
———, d. Timothy and Eliza, teething, Mar. 23, 1847, a. 10 m.

BARNARD, Alexandine [Alexandrina. C. R. 3.] Fanning, d. Edward [cholera infantum. C. R. 3.], Sept. 10, 1825, a. 2 y. 1 m.

BARNARD, Betsy [Betsey. Mrs. C. R. 5.], influenza, July 10, 1843, a. 69 y. C. R. 3.

——, s. Lucy, Nov. 6, 1791, a. 2 y. C. R. 2.

**BARNES** (see also Barns), William, s. William and Jane, Nov. 19, 1815, a. 22 y.

**BARNS** (see also Barnes), Peggy, Dec. 31, 1804.

**BARON,** Mary Procter, d. William, Oct. 20, 1834, a. 5 y.

**BARRETT,** Michael, b. Ireland, ship fever, at the alms house, June 18, 1847, a. 19 y.

——, ch. ——, Sept. 12, 1805, a. 10 m.

**BARRY,** Margarett, b. Ireland, consumption, at the alms house, Apr. 4, 1849, a. 61 y.

**BARSTOW** (see also Basto, Brastow), ——, Mrs., b. Jamaica Plain, colic, May 29, 1844, a. 40 y.

**BARTLET** (see also Bartlett), ——, s. Dr. John, Sept. 19, 1802, a. 10 y.

**BARTLETT** (see also Barlet, Bartlet), Abby Kane, w. Enoch, June 5, 1842, a. 40 y.

Abigail, w. Dr. John, May 21, 1839, a. 68 y.

Abigail, m., d. Thomas and Francis Tilden, dysentery, Sept. 13, 1849, a. 48 y.

Ann Matilda, Jan. 31, 1821, a. 25 y.

Clarissa H., d. Hosea, Nov. —, 1842, a. 1 m.

George, s. Dr. John and Abigail, Jan. 18, 1825, a. 19 y.

George, widr., gentleman, b. Charlestown, old age, Dec. 25, 1848, a. 82 y.

Jane, d. Enoch and Abby, dysentery, Nov. 22, 1847, a. 26 y.

John, Jan. 24, 1823, a. 86 y.

Mary Williams, d. John and Abigail, Nov. 18, 1797.

Susan A., d. Enoch, Sept. 14, 1839, a. 8 m.

**BARTON,** Maria A., d. William and Harriet, dysentery, Aug. 11, 1847, a. 1 y. 5 m.

**BASFORD,** Nathan K., s. Henry and Mary J., dysentery, Aug. 30, 1847, a. 3 y. 1 m. 11d.

**BASTO** (see also Barstow., Mary E., enlargement of heart, June 11, 1849, a. 13 y. 10 m. 17 d.

**BASWELL,** Sybilla, b. Germany, w. George, consumption, Dec. 8, 1848, a. 38 y.

**BATCHELDER** (see also Bachelder), Elizabeth H., d. Joshua and Martha A., Nov. 10, 1833. G. R. 5.

John [P. T. G. R. 5.], s. Joshua [and Martha A., Feb. 10, 1834, a. 5 y. G. R. 5.]

Martha A. [Bacheller. C. R. 4.], wid., d. Alden and Elizabeth Jones, dropsy, Feb. 11, 1847, a. 40 y.

Mary E., d. Joshua and Martha A., Sept. 4, 1833, a. 10 m. G. R. 5.

Ruth, wid. Maj. Brade, at Keene, N. H., July —, 1840, a. 95 y.

**BATES,** Abby F., d. John H. and Hannah, dysentery, Sept. 5, 1847, a. 9 m.

Abigail, Mrs., May 26, 1839, a. 33 y.

Calvin Whiting, s. Gibson, Feb. 14, 1832.

Elizabeth Ann, d. Gibson, Feb. 17, 1832.

Gibson, June 29, 1842, a. 44 y.

Thomas, m., innholder, b. England, s. Thomas and Mary, disease of the heart, Nov. 13, 1849, a. 48 y. [a. 47 y. C. R. 5.]

**BAWN,** Josiah, s. Josiah and Martha, Jan. 21, 1837, a. 5 m.

**BAXTER** John, b. Ireland, s. Joseph and Sarah, consumption, Dec. 13, 1848, a. 2 y.

**BAYLEY** (see also Bailey), Hulda, d. James and Elizabeth, July 3, 1711.

James, Esq. [physician. N. R. 1.], Jan. 17, 1706-7. [a. 56 y. 4. m. N. R. 1.]

James, Lt., Oct. 24, 1715.

Mary, d. James and Elizabeth, Dec. 14, 1700.

Mary, d. James and Elizabeth, June 1, 1707.

Mary [Baley. G. R. 1.], wid. James, Esq. [w. Dr. James. G. R. 1.], Oct. 23, 1717. [a. 71 y. G. R. 1.]

**BEACON** (see also Bacon), Ephraim, in a storm on Boston Neck, Jan. 29, 1713.

John, s. John and Abiel, Feb. 1, 1710-11.

John, Oct. 28, 1713.

**BEAHN** (see also Bean), John M., laborer, b. Ireland, typhus fever, May 18, 1847, a. 26 y.

Mary, unm., b. Ireland, typhus fever, May 22, 1847, a. 21 y.

Patrick, laborer, b. Ireland, consumption, May 2, 1847, a. 17 y.

**BEALS,** Elizabeth, wid. Joshua, of Boston, May 7, 1839, a. 84 y.
Thomas, Sept. 2, 1814, a. 33 y.

**BEAN** (see also Beahn), John [old age. Jan. 25. c. R. 3.], 1836, a. 91 y.

**BEATS** (see also Beaty), Edward, s. James and Catherine, fever, Aug. 28, 1849, a. 6 y.

**BEATY** (see also Beats), Mary, d. James and Ann, measles, July 17, 1849, a. 10 m.

**BEAUMONT,** Laurana R., scrofula, June 13, 1843. c. R. 3.

**BECKS** [Nancy Beck, from Boston. c. R. 3.], w. W[illia]m [consumption. c. R. 3.], Jan. 23, 1807, a. 48 y.

**BEDUNAH** (see also Beduner), Benj[ami]n, Aug. 23, 1771, a. 67 y. G. R. 1.
Mary, a pauper, Aug. 2, 1830, a. 80 y.

**BEDUNER** (see also Bedunah), Elizabeth, July 19, 1799, a. 40 y.

**BEECHER,** ——, ——, 1845, a. 42 d.

**BEERE,** ——, inf. ch. Anthony, Sept. 16, 1657.

**BELKNAP,** Charles, July 13, 1830, a. 88 y.
Mary, May —, 1832, a. 80 y.
Polly, 2d, Feb. 11, 1832, a. 48 y.
Rebecca, consumption, Aug. 29, 1821, a. 46 y. c. R. 3.

**BELL,** Edward, s. William and Hannah (Crafts), Oct. 18, 1809. P. R. 2.
Franklin Heath, s. twin, Amory and Ann C., Jan. 18, 1836, a. 17 m.
Hannah, Sept. 8, 1829, a. 59 y. P. R. 2.
James, Feb. 19, 1824, a. 28 y.
James, bur. Apr. 18, 1840, a. 26 y. c. R. 5.
John, s. Thomas, bur. July 2, 1643.
Thomas, Oct. 28, 1808, a. 82 y. P. R. 2.
William, s. William and Hannah (Crafts), Nov. 21, 1804. P. R. 2.
William, widr., laborer, b. Gilling, old age, June 11, 1847, a. 82 y.

BELL, ——, d. ——, whooping cough, Sept. 29, 1846.

BEMIS, Jonathan, school master, Oct. 31, 1822, a. 27 y.

BENJAMIN, ——, ch. John, Sept. 4, 1787, a. 15 m. c. r. 2.
——, ch. John, Dec. 19, 1789, a. 22 m. c. r. 2.

BERGWYN, Anne, May 15, 1849, a. 4 y. 8 m. 23 d.

BERRY, ——, ch. Aug. 4, 1846.
——, inf. ch. John and Catherine, scarlet fever, May 6, 1847,
a. 1-2 d.

BERTLING, Ann, b. Germany, w. Anthony, child bed, Apr.
2, 1849, a. 36 y.

BEVERAGE (see also Beveridge), Jennett, b. Scotland, cholera, at the alms house, Sept. 21, 1849, a. 45 y.
John, b. Scotland, cholera, at the alms house, Sept. 16, 1849, a.
45 y.

BEVERIDGE (see also Beverage), Mary, b. Scotland, d. John
and Jenette, cholera, Sept. 19, 1849, a. 19 y.
——, ch. still born, John and Jenet, Sept. 9, 1849.

BEWDAIN (see also Bodwoin), Francis, s. Alexander and
Margaret, decline, Nov. 4, 1848, a. 5 m.

BICKNELL, Catharine Patridge, w. Charles, July 6, 1826, a.
21 y.
Charles, m., mason, s. Humphrey and Jemima, insanity, Aug.
7, 1848, a. 52 y.
Humphrey, widr., mason, b. Abington, old age, Dec. 31, 1848,
a. 86 v.
Jemima, b. Newton, w. Humphrey, paralytic, Oct. 15, 1848,
a. 82 y.
Lucy, d. Humphrey, Aug. —, 1842.

BILL (see also Bills), ——, Mrs., Sept. 3, 1789, c. r. 2.
——, ch. Jesse, whooping cough, June 25, 1833, a. 3 m. c. r. 2.

BILLINGS, Benjamin, s. Benjamin and Susannah, Sept. 12,
1793, a. 2 y. c. r. 2.
Benjamin, Aug. [20. c. r. 2.], 1829, a. 64 y.
George A., s. George and Lucy, bowel complaint, Aug. 31,
1848, a. 1 y. 3 m.
Hannah W., d. Benjamin, Sept. 17 [7. c. r. 2.], 1828, a. 23 y.

BILLINGS, Lemuel, Apr. 11, 1842, a. 85 y.
Rachel, Sept. 6, 1805, a. 21 y.

BILLS (see also Bill), Gustavus W., s. Gustavus and Ann A.,
    scarlet fever, July 15, 1849, a. 5 y. 7 m.
Sarah Ann C., w. Jesse, Mar. 31, 1833.
——, ch. Jesse, Feb. 1, 1830, a. 2 d.
——, ch. Shubael, June 16, 1834, a. 7 m.

BINGHAM, Eveline, d. Benj[a]m[in], Aug. 17, 1826, a. 3 y.
    C. R. 2.
Henry, apoplexy, bur. 8m: 10m: 1645. C. R. 1.
Mary Wellington, d. Benj[ami]n, Oct. —, 1834, a. 8 y.

BIRCHARD, ——, goodwife, 24: 1m: 1654-5. C. R. 1.

BIRD, Elizebeth, Jan. 16, 1806, a. 88 y.
James, at the work house, Jan. 17, 1809, a. 66 y.
James, Feb. 18, 1824, a. 58 y.
Louisa, d. James, jr. and Hannah, Aug. 26, 1800.

BIRK (see also Burk), Patrick, unm., laborer, b. Ireland, by
    falling into a well, Oct. 29, 1848, a. 28 y.

BISHOP, Anne, w. Thomas, Sept. 16, 1691.
Elizabeth, w. Tho[mas], bur. 4 : 10 m : 1681. C. R. 1.
Lydia, Mrs., Jan. 5, 1736-7.
Prudence, w. Thomas, Oct. 11, 1680.
Thomas, June 30, 1727. [in his 82d y. G. R. 3.]
——, "Sister," bur. 8 : 8 m : 1680. C. R. 1.

BLACK, Robert, m., b. Ireland, dropsy, Dec. 9, 1849, a. 40 y.

BLACKMAN, Moses, suddenly, of a bilious disorder, issue of
    Aug. 28, 1798, a. 44 y. N. R. 4.
Sarah, Mrs. [old age and lung fever, Mar. 24. C. R. 3.], 1840,
    a. 85 y.

BLACKSLEY, Edward, widr., bur. Nov. 3, 1637.
Sarah, d. Edward, bur. May —, 1638.

BLACKWELL, Margarett, b. Ireland, d. Thomas and Cath-
    erine, consumption, Apr. 5, 1848, a. 3 y. 6 m.

BLAGG, Sarah, Mrs., of New London, Conn., bur. Nov. 6,
    1839, a. 76 y. C. R. 5.

**BLAISDELL,** ——, Mrs., ——, 1839. C. R. 4.

**BLAKE,** Albanus M., s. Jesse and Nancy, inflammation of brain, July 22, 1849, a. 9 m.
Hannah, d. Samuel and Hannah, Feb. 3, 1714.
Martha, d. Joseph and Eliza, Sept. 19, 1823, a. 19 m. G. R. 5.
Nancy w. Jesse, liver complaint, Feb. 6, 1849, a. 74 y. 10 m.
Samuel, Dec. 1, 1747, in his 34th y. G. R. 1.
Sanborn, Apr. 26, 1824, a. 21 y.
——, ch. ——, croup, Aug. 12, 1846, a. 1 y.

**BLANCHARD,** Betsey H., Dec. 8, 1839, a. 30 y.
Francis, Apr. 1, 1827, a. 72 y.
Nehemiah, Aug. 15, 1835.
Susan L., d. Capt. W[illia]m, June 29, 1838, a. 18 y.

**BLANEY,** Anna, wid. Samuel, dropsy, Feb. 23, 1848, a. 83 y. 8 m.
Samuel, May 2, 1826, a. 66 y.
William, Apr. 17, 1780, a. 49 y. G. R. 1.
William, Jan. 5, 1824, a. 66 y.

**BLENDELL,** George B., June 27, 1832, a. 3 y. 4 m.

**BLENUS,** Julia A., b. Nova Scotia, d. Isaac W. and Olive, dysentery, Aug. 3, 1848, a. 5 y. 6 m.

**BLIN,** William, Capt., of Boston, shop keeper, Aug. 8, 1738. N. R. 1.

**BLOOD,** Sarah, July 28, 1690.

**BOACK,** Ellen, d. Leavit and Ellen, scarlet fever, Nov. 23, 1848, a. 3 y. 6 m.

**BOARDMAN** (see also Bordman), James [s. William, of Cambridge. G. R. 1.], Nov. 12, 1805, a. 20 y.
Pamelia H., Jan. 20, 1845. C. R. 6.

**BODGE,** Charles, Feb. 9, 1834, a. 26 y.
John, Apr. 22, 1837.
Joseph W., s. John, Jan. —, 1834, a. 8 y.
Mary, w. John, June —, 1831.
Samuel W., s. John, dec., Oct. 11, 1838, a. 33 y.
——, ch. ——, June 2, 1803, a. 18 m.
——, wid., Oct. 1, 1803, a. 59 y.
——, ch. John, Mar. 4, 1808, a. 5 y.

**BODIN** (see also Bowdoin), Caroline S., consumption, May 25, 1846, a. 12 y.

**BODOWIN** (see also Bowdoin), John [Boudoin. G. R. 1.], Sept. 12, 1706. [a. 45 y. G. R. 1.]

**BOGLE,** Alexander, Mar. 27, 1706.
——, goodwife, Sept. 2, 1712.

**BOHAWN,** John, m., laborer, b. Ireland, accidental, Apr. 17, 1848, a. 35 y.

**BOILER,** James, s. James and Mary, Sept. 29, 1849, a. 6 m.

**BOIT,** Ellen d. John, at Charleston, S. C., "beginning of" Aug. 1821, a. 18 y. C. R. 3.

**BOLFORD,** Mary, wid., b. Ireland, dysentery, Nov. 16, 1848, a. 75 y.

**BOLLMAN,** John, s. Christopher L. and Dorothy, Nov. 18, 1847, a. 12 d.

**BOMAN** (see also Bowman), Mary J [Bowman. C. R. 6.], w. A. H., June 19, 1837, a. 32 y.

**BOOHAN,** Ellen, d. Patrick and Hannah, scarlet fever, Mar. 4, 1849, a. 3 y.

**BORDMAN** (see also Boardman), Lydia, Mrs., Feb. —, 1821.

**BORDEN,** Alice H., b. New Bedford, d. Jeremiah and Alice, consumption, Oct. 9, 1848, a. 19 y.

**BOSSON,** Abigail, w. William, July 28, 1766, in her 39th y. G. R. 1.
Charles, s. William and Ruth, Apr. 12, 1768, a. 5 w. G. R. 1.
Hannah, Dec. 27, 1805.
Ruth, w. William, May 13, 1769, in her 34th y. G. R. 1.
Ruth, d. William and Ruth, May 20, 1769, a. 15 d. G. R. 1.
Thaddeus, s. Will[ia]m and Abigail, Aug. 29, 1747, a. 15 m. G. R. 1.
——, ch. William, Jan. 21, 1803, a. 4 y.

**BOSSUET,** Catharine Rumport DeVous Doncour, Mrs., June 20, 1830, a. 52 y.

**BOUNDS,** Patience, d. Daniel T., and Alvira, scarlet fever, June 27, 1848, a. 1 y.

**BOURN,** Johanna, wid. Rev. Shearjashub, Apr. 16, 1776, in her 71st y. G. R. 1.

Shearjashub, Rev., late minister of the First Parish in Scituate, s. Hon. Melatiah, Esq., of Sandwich, dec., Aug. 14, 1768, a. 69 y. G. R. 1.

**BOWDITCH,** Jonathan, m., yeoman, b. Braintree, old age, Sept. 16, 1847, a. 83 y.

Martha W., Mrs., Feb. 22, 1834.

Martha W., d. Galen and Susan, Sept. 20, 1836, a. 6 w.

**BOWDLEAR,** Joseph, s. John and Mary Ann, teething, Oct. 14, 1849, a. 7 m. 14 d.

Samuel, Jan. 26, 1845, a. 1 y. 4 m.

**BOWDOIN** (see also Bewdain, Bodin, Bodowin), William, Esq., Feb. 25, 1773, in his 61st y. N. R. 2.

**BOWEN** (see also Bowin), Elizabeth, wid. Henry, Apr. 30, 1702. [in her 63d y. C. R. 1.]

Hannah, w. Isaac, Jan. 22, 1717.

Hester, "a younge maide," Mar. 28, 1654.

John, b. Ireland, lung complaint, at the alms house, Nov. 19, 1849, a. 24 y.

Samuel, Dec. 14, 1802, a. 56 y.

Sarah, d. John and Hannah, Jan. 29, 1704-5.

Sarah, d. Isaac and Hannah, Aug. 20, 1716.

**BOWERS,** Lewis, m., b. Germany, cold water, Aug. 18, 1849, a. 37 y.

Wilder, Oct. 2, 1800, a. 28 y.

**BOWHANNUS,** Johannus, s. Cornelius and Catherine, dysentery, Sept. 25, 1848, a. 14 d.

**BOWIN** (see also Bowen), Benjamin, s. Isaack and Elizabeth, Dec. 1, 1721.

Margaret, d. Henry, bur. — : 7 m : 1665. C. R. 1.

——, inf. ch. Henry, bur. 4 : 5 m : 1664. C. R. 1.

**BOWLES** (see also Bowls), Dorothy, w. John, bur. Nov. 3, 1649.

BOWLES, Elizabeth [Elizabeth, d. Elder Heath. C. R. 1.], w.
John, July 6, 1655.
Francis Burrows, s. William, Dec. —, 1831, a. 9 m.
Hannah, wid., b. Taunton, old age, July 10, 1847, a. 82 y.
Isaack [Isaac. C. R. 1.], s. John, bur. Nov. 3, 1652.
John, Mar. 30, 1691.
John, frozen to death, Dec. 14, 1747. N. R. 1.
Lidya, w. Maj., Nov. 16, 1722.
Lucius Q. C., June 27, 1842, a. 54 y.
Sarah, inf. d. John, bur. 23 : 3 m : 1687. C. R. 1.
Stephen J., Mar. 26, 1846. C. R. 6.
——, "Sister," smallpox, 3 : 9 m : 1649. C. R. 1.
——, Elder, bur. 24 : 7 m : 1680. C. R. 1.
——, wid., aged, bur. 4 : 7 m : 1686. C. R. 1.

BOWLS (see also Bowles), John, s. John, Jan. 17, 1683.
Sarah [Bowles. C. R. 1.], w. John, May 23, 1687.
——, Mrs., wid. John, Sept. 2, 1686.

BOWMAN (see also Boman), Brooks, m., gentleman, b. Mere-
dith, N. H., s. Zadoc and Sarah, Sept. 18, 1849, a. 54 y.
Jonathan, July 23, 1798, a. 21 y.
Lucy, Mrs., Mar. 12, 1813, a. 65 y.
Lucy Ann, d. Brooks and Lucy, consumption, Mar. 22, 1847,
a. 25 y.
Sylvanus, jr., s. Sylvester, bowel complaint, Sept. 2, 1846, a.
2 y.

BOYDEN, Joseph Ezra, s. Obed[iah] Ambrose, bur. Oct. 1,
1831, a. 2 y. C. R. 2.

BOYLE (see also Boyllan), James, m., laborer, b. Ireland,
stoppage in the throat, Nov. 21, 1848, a. 30 y.
Neal O., b. Ireland, ship fever, at alms house, May 28, 1847,
a 36 y.
Patrick, m., laborer, b. Ireland, consumption, Oct. 2, 1847, a.
48 y.
Patrick Henry, s. Patrick and Rosanna, dysentery, Sept. 2,
1848, a. 2 m. 22 d.

BOYLLAN (see also Boyle), Mary, b. Ireland, wid. James,
child bed, Apr. 9, 1849, a. 22 v.

BOYLSTON, Luke, May 24, 1800.
Thomas, suicide, Feb. 15, 1812, a. 29 y. C. R. 3.

BOYLSTON, Ward N[icholas. c. R. 3.], Esq. [dropsy in the chest. c. R. 3.], Jan. 7, 1828, a. 78 y.

**BRABROOKE,** Ann, "an old woman," May 20, 1648.

**BRADFORD,** Ann, wid. [Col. c. R. 3.] Samuel, Esq. [of Boston, consumption, Oct. 14, c. R. 3.], 1824, a. 64 y.
Benjamin, Jan. 10, 1730, a. abt. 30 y. G. R. 1.
John, Rev., Jan. 27, 1825, a. 69 y. [a. 68 y. c. R. 2.]
Margaret [Margarett. c. R. 2.], d. Rev. John, Sept. 8, 1822. [a. 42 y. c. R. 2.]
Mary, w. Rev. J., May 5, 1828, a. 74 y. c. R. 2.
Stewart L., s. S. D. and Julia Emma, inflammation of the lungs, July 2, 1846, a. 11 m. 29 d.
——, Mr., from Plymouth, gravel, Jan. —, 1794. c. R. 3.

**BRADHURST** (see also Brodhurst), Martha, w. Ralph, Aug. 6, 1693.

**BRADLEE** (see also Bradley), Sarah, w. Lemuel, Sept. 17, 1822, a. 35 y.
Susan, w. Lemuel, Oct. 13, 1835, a. 41 y.

**BRADLEY** (see also Bradlee), Elizabeth Weld, w. Edward W., d. Stedman Williams, Oct. 23, 1825, a. 17 y.
Joanna, Jan. 6, 1808, a. 56 y.
——, ch. L., Mar. 28, 1803, a. 3 y.

**BRADY,** Michael, laborer, b. Ireland, drowned, May 25, 1848, a. 25 y.

**BRAGG,** Horatio N., bowel complaint, Aug. 1, 1847, a. 4 m. 4 d.
Samuel, inf. s. Horatio Nelson and Mary, Mar. 5, 1835. c. R. 5.

**BRAID,** John [s. John B. and Maria. dup.], Oct. 2, 1799.

**BRAILSFORD,** Norton, Oct. 10, 1805, a. 60 y.
——, w. Norton, Sept. 17, 1805, a. 56 y.

**BRAISLER,** Bridget M., b. Ireland, w. W[illia]m, fever, Jan. 29, 1849, a. 30 y.

**BRAMAN,** Mary, d. Michael and Ann, fever, May 17, 1849, a. 9 y.

**BRAND,** Martha, wid. ["old widow." c. R. 1.] George, Aug. 1, 1686.

**BRANNEL** (see also Brannell), Thomas, m., laborer, b. Ireland, fever, July 7, 1847, a. 35 y.

**BRANNELL** (see also Brannel), Lawrence, unm., laborer, b. Ireland, inflammation of bowels, Mar. 18, 1849, a. 27 y.

**BRANNIN,** John, s. John and Catherine, teething, Oct. 12, 1848, a. 1 y. 10 m.

**BRASTOW** (see also Barstow), Mason [Basto. C. R. 2.], s. Mason [lung fever. C. R. 2.], Mar. —, 1834, a. 6 w. [Feb. 27, a. 10 w. C. R. 2.]

**BRAWDRIC,** Edward, laborer, b. Ireland, ship fever, Aug. 5, 1847, a. 24 y.

**BREMMER,** Martin [Brimmer, Esq., mortification of the bowels. C. R. 3.], Sept. 26, 1804.

**BRERETON,** Amelia, wid., b. Maryland, dysentery, Sept. 18, 1847, a. 54 y.

**BRERN,** Christiana, m., b. Germany, consumption, July 3, 1848, a. 31 y.

**BRETT,** Michael, unm., laborer, b. Ireland, ship fever, June 18, 1847, a. 19 y.

**BREWER** (see also Bruer), Abigail, w. Joseph, jaundice and mortification, Nov. 15, 1818. C. R. 3.
Abigail, wid., old age, Apr. 23, 1849, a. 78 y.
Daniel, Jan. 9, 1708, a. 84 y.
Ebenezer, June 23, 1814, a. 49 y.
Ebenezer, Jan. 25, 1828, a. 29 y.
Elizabeth, w. Nathaniell, bur. June 25, 1661. CT. R.
Elizabeth, w. Nathaniel, Mar. 24, 1763, a. 68 y. G. R. 1.
Elizabeth, Mrs., Sept. 12, 1827, a. 67 y.
Hannah, wid. Daniel, Oct. 6, 1717, a. 81 y.
Joanna, Feb. 7, 1688-9, a. 87 y.
John, s. Nathanael and Elizabeth, Sept. 1, 1733. [a. 18 m. 8 d. G. R. 1.]
Joseph, small pox, June 26, 1777, a. 54 y. G. R. 1.
Joseph [decay of nature. C. R. 3.], May 16, 1823, a. 72 y.
Julia A., Oct. 23, 1839, a. 25 y.
Margaret, d. Nathanael and Margaret [Margarett. dup.], May 4, 1693. [a. 5 w. G. R. 1.]
Margarett, w. Nathaniel, July 25, 1704.

Brewer, Mary, scrofula, July 4, 1838, a. 76 y. c. r. 3.
Nathanael, sr., Feb. 26, 1692-3. [a. 57 y. g. r. 1.]
Nathanael, Dea., Apr. 22, 1733.
Natha[nie]l, June 14, 1747, a. 52 y. 9 m. g. r. 1.
Nath[aniel], consumption, May 10, 1793, a. 66 y. c. r. 3.
Nathaniel, Nov. 7, 1829, a. 44 y.
Rebecca, w. W[illia]m, Apr. 3, 1802.
Sarah [old age. Apr. 7. c. r. 3.], 1836, a. 82 y. [a. 83 y. c.
    r. 3.]
Susannah, wid., bur. Feb. 20, 1794, a. 72 y. n. r. 4.
William, Esq., July 30, 1817, a. 59 y.
——, "bro." ulcer on the lungs, bur. 28 : 1 m : 1646. c. r. 1.
——, ch. stillborn, Daniel, bur. 11 : 1 m : 1660-61. c. r. 1.
——, d. Nath[aniel], Nov. 20, 1794, a. 4 y. c. r. 3.
——, w. Eben[eze]r, June 14, 1805, a. 31 y.

BRICKETT Frederick Park, s. [only ch. g. r. 5.] Nath[anie]l
    [jr., and Catharine G. g. r. 5.], Aug. 24, 1842, a. 7 m.
Nathaniel, sr., Mar. —, 1845 [Mar. 13, 1846. g. r. 5.], a.
    51 y.

BRIDG (see also Bridge), Margaret, 19 : 1 m : 1671, a. 4 y.
    g. r. 1.

BRIDGE (see also Bridg), Anna, w. Edward, jr., June 21,
    1729. [1722, in her 30th y. g. r. 3.]
Edward [Bridg. c. r. 1.], Dec. 20, 1683, a. abt. 82 y.
Edward, jr., Sept. 23, 1733.
Hannah, d. Lt. John and Hannah, Dec. 15, 1742.
John, colic, 20 : 6 m : 1674. c. r 1.
John, s. Edward and Mary, July — [June 27. g. r. 1.], 1691,
    [a. 2 m. g. r. 1.]
John, s. John and Elizabeth, Sept. 22, 1741.
John, Lt., Nov. 23, 1748.
Margaret, d. John, bur. 22 : 1m : 1670-71. c. r. 1.
Mary, w. Capt. Edward, July 18, 1724, a. 56 y. 3 m.

BRIGGS, Charles W., s. Rev. Charles, Feb. 2, 1840, a. 14 y.
Cornelius, m., cabinet maker, b. Weymouth, s. Joshua and Car-
    oline, heart complaint, Feb. 2, 1848, a. 60 y.
Franklin, s. Benj[amin] and Mary Ann, consumption, Mar.
    15, 1849, a. 5 m. 14 d.

BRIGHAM, Caroline, Feb. —, 1832, a. 19 y.
Lucy, Mrs., Nov. 4, 1820, a. 44 y.

BRIGHAM, Lucy, w. Capt. Samuel, Sept. 9, 1824, a. 50 y.

Mary, w. Peter, Nov. —, 1836, a. 46 y.

Nancy, complication of disorders, Nov. 28, 1813. a. 18 m, C. R. 3.

Stephen, Mar. 9, 1820, a. 41 y. G. R. 1.

William White, s. Stephen and Lucy, Sept. 21 [20. dup.], 1806, [a. 2 y. dup.; a. 23 m. G. R. 1.]

**BRIMMER,** see Bremmer.

**BRINLEY,** Francis, Col., Nov. 26, 1765. N. R. 5.

Francis, Mar. 1, 1838, a. 66 y.

Jerusha, w. Francis, Oct. 19, 1827, a. 39 y.

**BRITTON,** Alonzo, s. John L. and Mary C., Aug. 23, 1843, a. 4 m. G. R. 5.

John W., s. John L. and Mary C., Sept. 19, 1845, a. 3 m. G. R. 5.

Mary A., d. John L. and Mary C., Sept. 13, 1838, a. 7 m. G. R. 5.

Mary C., b. Medway, [w. John L. G. R. 5.], d. Faxon and Mary Dean, consumption, Nov. 10 [Oct. 10. G. R. 5.], 1847, a. 28 y.

William H[enry, eldest. G. R. 5.], s. John L. and Mary [C. G. R. 5.], consumption, Jan. 28, 1847, a. 7 y. 4 m.

**BROAD,** John, s. John and Mary [Molly. C. R. 2.], Feb. 21, 1812. [a. 17 m. C. R. 2.]

Lucy, d. John and Mary, Oct. 15, 1813. [a. 8 m. C. R. 2.]

**BRODHURST** (see also Bradhurst), Hannah [Bradhurst. C. R. 1.], w. Ralph, July 10, 1686, a. 42 y.

Hannah, w. Ralph, Apr. 18, 1710. [1719, a. 55 y. G. R. 1.]

**BROMFIELD,** Thomas, Dec. 26, 1776, a. 65 y. N. R. 2.

**BROOK** (see also Brooks), Adelaide W., d. John and Sarah, dropsy, May 13, 1847, a. 5 y. 10 m.

**BROOKS** (see also Brook), Adelaide E., d. John and Louisa, dysentery, Sept. 25, 1847, a. 1 y. 11 m.

Avis, w. John, June 14, 1834, a. 31 y.

Charlotte E., d. John and Sarah M., dysentery, Sept. 15, 1847, a. 1 y. 9 m.

Eunice, w. Kendall, Nov. 11, 1817, a. 21 y.

Louisa, d. Benjamin, Aug. 16, 1825, a. 14 m.

BROOKS, Louisa T., [w. J. C. R. 4.], b. Windham, Conn., dysentery, Oct. 12, 1847, a. 29 y.

William H., s. John and Sarah Ann, croup, Oct. 11, 1848, a. 4 y. 6 m.

———, ch. Kendall, fits, June 20, 1846, a. 3 y.

**BROWING,** William D[ennis Browning, nervous fever. C. R. 3.], Oct. — [Sept. 28. C. R. 3.], 1831, a. 20 y.

**BROWN** (see also Browne, Browns), Adam, m., weaver, b. Scotland, dysentery, Sept. 26, 1847, a. 42 y.

Ann Maria, dropsy of the brain, Nov. —, 1836, a. 4 y. C. R. 3.

Bartha V., w. Dr. John G., Oct. 4, 1839, a. 38 y.

Calvin, s. Haman and Mardia, Oct. 8, 1813. [a. 10 m. G. R. 1.]

Clara P., d. W[illia]m B. and Maria D., brain fever, Jan. 6, 1848, a. 1 y. 5 m.

George Warren, s. Joseph and Sarah H., May 9, 1830.

Eliza P., w. Samuel R., inflammation of bowels, May 25, 1849, a. 24 y.

Eliza P., d. Sam[ue]l R. and Eliza P., May 27, 1849, a. 7 d.

Elizabeth, d. John and Sarah, Apr. 2, 1710.

Ellen A., d. W[illia]m H. and Jane, dysentery, Sept. 1, 1847, a. 1 y. 3 m.

Francis B., m., custom house, b. Ipswich, s. Nathan and Abigail, lung and pleurisy fever, Feb. 3, 1848, a. 48 y.

Haman, Capt., Aug. 31, 1824, a. 42 y.

Henry H., s. Henry and Adeline, dropsy on brain, July 31, 1847, a. 1 y. 6 m.

James, unm., b. Ireland, consumption, Sept. 11, 1847, a. 38 y.

James, b. Scotland, s. Adam and Jane, dysentery, Sept. 13, 1847, a. 10 y.

James Edwin, scarletina, Feb. 24, 1839, a. 4 y. C. R. 3.

James Russell, s. Capt. Elisha, hydrocephalus, July 11, 1845, a. 2 y. 8 m. C. R. 3.

Jane, m., b. Grafton, Vt., d. Lemuel and Dorcas, heart complaint, Nov. 18, 1849, a. 46 y. 6 m.

Jane Augusta, d. William H. and Jane, consumption, May 30, 1847, a. 17 y. 7 m.

Jeremiah, debility, Aug. 9, 1818, a. 55 y. C. R. 3.

Jesse, m., baker, b. Sudbury, s. William and Susan, rheumatism and gout, July 10, 1848, a. 57 y.

John, m., machinist [a native of Aberdeen, Scotland. G. R. 5.], consumption, July 31, 1846, a. 35 y. [a. 34 y. G. R. 5.]

BROWN, John, widr., farmer, b. England, lung fever, Jan. 13, 1847, a. 79 y.

John William, s. Chester and Anna G., lung fever, Dec. 7, 1846, a. 5 m. 6 d.

Mardia, w. Haman, Aug. 17, 1813. [a. 22 y. G. R. 1.]

Margarett, m., b. Ireland, colic, Jan. 28, 1848, a. 65 y.

Mary, b. Brighton, wid. Charles, dysentery, Sept. 2, 1848, a. 52 y.

Serena, m., b. Scituate, d. Galen and Serena, consumption, July 7, 1847, a. 22 y.

Sophronia A., d. Luke, July 2, 1838, a. 14 m.

Timothy D., Apr. —, 1820.

———, ch. still born, John and Margarett, Apr. 17, 1849.

**BROWNE** (see also Brown), ———, inf. ch. John, bur. 17 : 8m : 1681. C. R. 1.

**BROWNELL** Mary Louisa, d. Uriah T. and Nancy C., dropsy on brain, Mar. 28, 1848, a. 4 y. 11 m.

Sarah, wid., Aug. 1, 1806, a. 72 y.

**BROWNING,** see Browing.

**BROWNS** (see also Brown), ———, ch. Joseph [Brown. dup.], Nov. 2, 1800, a. 1 y. 9 m. [a. 21 m. dup.]

**BROWSE,** Catherine, m., b. Ireland, consumption, July 7, 1847, a. 33 y.

**BRUER** (see also Brewer), Ann [Anne Brewer. C. R. 1.], wid., Mar. 13, 1658. [1658-9. C. R. 1.]

Elizabeth [Brewer. CT. R.], w. Nathaniel [Nathaniell. CT. R.], June 25, 1661.

**BRYANT,** Benaiah, bur. Oct. 2, 1845, a. 73 y. C. R. 5.

Francis C., drowned in Jamaica Pond, July 28, 1832.

Mary A., w. James, Apr. —, 1835, a. 23 y.

Mary Ann, w. Geo[rge] W. of Medford, consumption, at Dorchester, Sept. 29, 1846, a. 22 y.

**BUCKMASTER** (see also Buckminster), Joseph, bur. 20 : 9m : 1668. C. R. 1.

**BUCKMINSTER** (see also Buckmaster), Jabez [Buckmaster. C. R. 1.], of Muddy River, Sept. [22. C. R. 1.], 1686.

Sarah, wid. Zachariah, June 27, 1704.

**BUFFORD,** Anna Milora, inf. d. John H., bur. Jan. 1, 1844.
C. R. 5.

**BUGBE** (see also Bugbee), Sarah, w. Thomas, small pox, Dec. 19, 1721.
Thomas, s. Thomas and Sarah, small pox, Dec. 24, 1721.

**BUGBEE** (see also Bugbe, Bugbey, Bugbie, Bugby, Bugbyes).
Aaron W., m., carpenter, b. St. Stephens, N. B., s. Ebenezer and Nancy, cancer tumor, Nov. 17, 1848, a. 29 y.
Abigail, wid. Edward, Oct. 22, 1729, in her 56th y. G. R. 1.
Abigail, wid., issue of Aug. 25, 1792, a. 79 y. N. R. 4.
Asa, Dec. 15, 1831, a. 41 y.
Ebenezer, s. Thomas and Sarah, May 29, 1703.
Ebenezer, Jan. —, 1834, a. 84 y.
Edward, Jan. 29, 1702-3.
Ephraim, s. Thomas and Sarah, Mar. 30, 1709.
Joanna, w. John, July 11, 1690.
John, Jan. 16, 1703-4.
Mary, w. Daniel, jr., June 1, 1763, a. 25 y. 9 d. G. R. 1.
Mary, w. Ebeneser, May 1, 1810.
Martha Louisa, d. Asa, Nov. 9, 1831, a. 3 y.
Polly, d. Eben[eze]r and Mary, Feb. 17 [18. dup.], 1802, a. 24 y.
———, ch. Edward, July 9, 1800.
———, ch. Edw[ard], July 9, 1800, a. 4 y.

**BUGBEY** (see also Bugbee), Edward, bur. 27:11m:1668-9.
a. abt. 80 y. C. R. 1.

**BUGBIE** (see also Bugbee), ———, inf. ch. Edward, bur. —:
9m:1642. CT. R.

**BUGBY** (see also Bugbee), ———, inf. ch. Joseph, bur. 10:
11m:1686-7. C. R. 1.

**BUGBYES** (see also Bugbee), ———, inf. ch. Edward, bur.
Aug. 31, 1642.

**BULLOCK,** ———, s. Luther, bowel complaint, Sept. 22, 1846, a. 1 y. 8 m.

**BUNNELL,** Mary W., d. E. F., Mar. —, 1841, a. 7 y.

**BUNTIN,** Ellen, at the alms house, Sept. 5, 1839, a. 12 y.

**BURBANK,** ———, ch. still born, Otis and Hannah, June 4, 1848.

**BURDEN,** Mary, Dec. 2, 1707.

**BURDETTS** (see also Burditt), ———, ch. wid., Sept. 9, 1802, a. 3 y.

**BURDITT** (see also Burdetts), Nathan, Sept. 9, 1800. [a. 31 y. dup]
Nathan, s. Nathan, Aug. —, 1830, a. 3 y. 4 m.
Polly, d. Nathan and Elizabeth, [1799?]

**BURGE** (see also Burgess), Margaret, formerly w. W[illia]m Cheiny, sr., July 2, 1686.

**BURGES** (see also Burgess), Esther, Jan. —, 1709, a. 28 y. G. R. 1.

**BURGESS** (see also Burge, Burges), Edwin H., s. John, Jan. 27, 1843, a. 6 m.
John W., m., laborer, consumption, Sept. 23, 1846, a. 40 y.

**BURGUIN,** John F., s. John R. and Ann, teething, July 13, 1846, a. 1 y.

**BURK** (see also Birk), Edward, m., laborer, b. Ireland, palsy, Mar. 31, 1847, a. 40 y.
John, s. Michael and Catherine, croup, Mar. 17, 1848, a. 1 y. 1 m.
Margaret, ship fever, at the alms house, Sept. 1, 1847, a. 7 d.
Margarett [wid. dup.], b. Ireland, fever [consumption, at the alms house. dup.], May 23, 1849, a. 60 y. [a. 61 y. dup.]
Mary, ship fever, at the alms house, Sept. 1, 1847, a. 7 d.
Peter, b. Ireland, ship fever, at the alms house, June 18, 1847, a. 24 y.
William, unm., laborer, b. Ireland, drowned, Aug. 27, 1848, a. 25 y.

**BURNETS,** ———, inf. ch. Robart, bur. Nov. 18, 1642.

**BURNHAM,** Clara, d. Geo[rge] P. and Achsa B., worms, May 17, 1849, a. 5 y.
Hannah Maria, w. Ira, Mar. 25, 1841, a. 30 y. [a. 31 y. G. R. 5.]
Jane, Mrs., June 19, 1811, a. 70 y. G. R. 1.
Sarah M., d. Ira [and Hannah M. G. R. 5.], Oct. 21, 1840. [a. 6 m. G. R. 5.]

BURNHAM, Susan B., wid., dysentery, Sept. 23, 1849, a. 64 y. 6 m.

**BURNOP,** ———, inf. ch. Robert, bur. —: 9m: 1642. CT. R.

**BURNS** (see also Byrnes), Ann, m., b. Ireland, consumption, Feb. 7, 1848, a. 68 y.
Patrick, b. Ireland, ship fever, at the alms house, Mar. 18, 1849, a. 35 y.

**BURRELL** (see also Burrells, Burril, Burrill), George, unm., s. Lemuel and Jerusha, fits, July 24, 1848, a. 52 y.
———, ch. James, Sept. 16, 1797, a. 9 y.

**BURRELLS** (see also Burrell), ———, ch. Sylvanus [Burrell. dup.], Oct. 3, 1797, a. 2 y.

**BURRIL** (see also Burrell), Josiah, June 18, 1809, a. 28 y. C. R. 2.

**BURRILL** (see also Burrell), Alathea, at Wrentham, May —, 1840. C. R. 4.
Marcy, July 30, 1817.
Rebecca, Oct. 14, 1826, a. 32 y.

**BURROUGHS** (see also Burrows), William, Jan. 2, 1778, a. 94 y. N. R. 2.

**BURROWS** (see also Burroughs), Francis, affection of the brain, Dec. 24, 1831, a. 6 m. C. R. 3.
William, Capt. [affection of brain and lungs. C. R. 3.], Oct. 21, 1837, a. 65 y.

**BURTON,** Mary Thomas, d. John and Louisa P., Apr. 17, 1814.

**BUSH,** Hanna [Hannah. CT. R.], maid servant of Joseph Wise, June 2, 1655. [1654. CT. R.]

**BUSSEY,** Benjamin, old age, Jan. 13, 1842, a. 85 y. C. R. 3.
Judith, b. Dedham, wid. Benjamin, paralysis, May 1, 1849, a. 86 y. 8 m.

**BUTCHER,** John, Nov. 10, 1699.

**BUTLER,** Charlotte, May 16, 1803, a. 18 y.
Maria, b. Ireland, w. Barnard, child bed, Jan. 27, 1849, a. 29 y.

BUTLER, Rebecca, wid., June 1, 1803, a. 55 y.

BUTTERFIELD, Unice, imperfect, born without a back bone, Sept. 22, 1815, a. 6 m. c. R. 3.

BUTTERS, Levi Bartlett, s. W[illia]m, Esq., Feb. —, 1833, a. 13 m.

BYRNES (see also Burns), Hannah, d. John and Hannah, bowel complaint, Aug. 3, 1848, a. 1 y. 10 m.
Thomas, m., starch manufacturer, b. Ireland, cholera, Sept. 18, 1849, a. 40 y.

BYRON, Ellen, d. James and Ann, dropsy on the brain, June 29, 1848, a. 1 y. 3 m.
Joseph Edward, s. Joseph [and Rebecca. c. R. 5.], Sept. 4, 1838. [a. 8 y. c. R. 5.]
Mary, b. Ireland, ship fever, at the alms house, June 20, 1849, a. 20 y.
Sophia, b. Bucksport, wid. Thomas, consumption, Mar. 10, 1849, a. 48 y.

CABOT, Lucy, unm., b. Beverly, dysentery, Aug. 18, 1848, a. 63 y.

CADY, James, Sept. 16, 1832, a. 42 y.
W[illia]m, b. Ireland, ship fever, at the alms house, May 16, 1847, a. 25 y.

CAFFY, John, b. Ireland, s. Bernard and Catherine, convulsions, Apr. 10, 1848, a. 59 y.

CAIN, Sarah, m., b. Ireland, poison, Apr. 7, 1848, a. 41 y.

CALDER, ———, s. Nath[anie]l, diarrhoea, July 28, 1846, a. 10 m.

CALEF (see also Calfe), Mary, w. Robert, Nov. 12, 1719.
Robert, Apr. 13, 1719. [a. 71 y. G. R. 1.]

CALEHAN (see also Callehand), Mary, a pauper, Oct. 17, 1734, a. 12 d.

CALFE (see also Calef), Daniel [Calef. G. R. 1.], Aug. 13, 1712. [in his 21st y. G. R. 1.]

CALLAHAND (see also Calehan), Peter, b. Ireland, ship fever, at the alms house, July 26, 1847, a. 36 y.

**CALLANANE,** James, consumption, Dec. 24, 1848, a. 6 y. 9 m.

**CALLENDER,** Sarah E. H. Ashton, w. Benjamin, Feb. 3, 1848, a. 31 y. G. R. 4.
———, s. Joseph, Aug. 19, 1832, a. 3 m.

**CALLER,** ———, ch. still born, James and Catherine, Aug. 29, 1848.

**CALPIN,** James, unm., laborer, b. Ireland, cholera, Sept. 5, 1849, a. 38 y.

**CAMNAR,** ———, ch. still born, John and Margarett, July 27, 1848.

**CAMPBELL,** Adam, b. Liverpool, s. James and J. McGill, inflammation of lungs, Apr. 15, 1847, a. 8 y.
George, s. James and Jennett McGill, bowel complaint, Dec. 25, 1846, a. 1 m. 14 d.
Henry Clay, s. Benj[ami]n F., Dec. —, 1840, a. 8 m.
William Cheney, s. Robert C., Aug. 11, 1842, a. 3 y. 10 m.

**CANAAN,** Mary [Canan. c. r. 3.], Mrs., [consumption. c. r. 3.], June 25, 1832. [a. 40 y. c. r. 3.]

**CAR** (see also Carr), ———, w. Dominick, Mar. 12, 1807.

**CARD,** ———, ch. ———, Sept. —, 1840.

**CARDIS,** Ebenezer, inf. s. Isack, bur. 9 : 10m : 1674. c. r. 1.

**CAREY** (see also Cary), William, Oct. —, 1827, a. 73 y.

**CARLETON** (see also Carlton), Guy, Jan. 31, 1840, a. 51 y.
Harriet, d. Guy, Apr. 21, 1836, a. 20 y.
Isaac, s. Guy, Jan. 31, 1837, a. 15 y.
Maria, d. Guy, dec., July 29, 1840, a. 15 y.

**CARLTON** (see also Carleton), Sarah, w. W[illia]m, Dec. 23, 1811, a. 63 y.

**CARNEY,** John, m., b. Ireland, palsy, Aug. 11, 1848, a. 58 y.
Mary, d. Mary, fits, at the alms house, Dec. 13, 1848, a. 2 y.
William, s. Daniel and Margaret, fever, July 23, 1848, a. 5 y.

**CARR** (see also Car), Jacob S., s. Charles, May 23, 1842, a. 2 1-2 y.

CARR, John F., s. John B., Aug. 3, 1835, a. 6 y. 7 m.

Patrick, unm., laborer, b. Ireland, ship fever [at the alms house. dup.], June 14, 1847, a. 35 y.

**CARROL** (see also Carroll), Bridgett, b. Ireland, w. W[illia]m disease of lungs, Sept. 4, 1848, a. 30 y.

**CARROLINE,** Mary, at the alms house, Sept. 19, 1849, a. 8 m.

**CARROLL** (see also Carrol, Caryl), James, widr., laborer, b. Ireland, dysentery, July 21, 1848, a. 65 y.

Joseph, s. Joseph and Catherine, dysentery, July 12, 1848, a. 1 y. and 4 m.

**CARTER,** Maria, d. George and Bridget, dysentery, Aug. 9, 1849, a. 9 m.

Samuel, s. John, of Fitchburg, and Lydia, Sept. 28, 1800, a. 19 y. G. R. 1.

Thomas, Oct. 8, 1805, a. 25 y.

Williams, unm., laborer, b. Portland, Me., s. James and Rosanna, consumption, Mar. 8, 1849, a. 24 y.

**CARTILLO,** Edward, s. Michael and Mary, croup, Jan. 2, 1849, a. 1 y. 6 m.

**CARTRET** (see also Cartwright), Louisa, d. Phillip and Louisa, July 19, 1844, a. 5 w. G. R. 5.

**CARTRIT** (see also Cartwright), Lucy, d. Francis, July —, 1832.

Lydia M., d. Francis, July —, 1832, a. 5 y.

**CARTWRIGHT** (see also Cartret, Cartrit), Elizabeth, sister of Edw[ar]d Morrice, bur. 6 : 8m : 1673. C. R. 1.

Elizabeth, Aug. —, 1836.

**CARVER,** Mary, Dec. 9, 1752.

**CARY** (see also Carey), William George, s. Isaac H. and Phebe P., Aug. —, 1837, a. 1 y.

**CARYL** (see also Carroll), Elizabeth, Dec. 1, 1780, a. 29 y. C. R. 2.

**CASEY,** John, inflammation of brain, at the alms house, June 8, 1849, a. 1 y.

**CASS,** Priscilla, Mrs., Dec. —, 1832, a. 37 y.
Sarah, Oct. —, 1833, a. 36 y.

**CASSADY,** James, b. New York, at the alms house, July 23, 1849, a. 6 m.
Margarett, b. Ireland, w. John, consumption, Mar. 22, 1849, a. 45 y.

**CASWELL,** James S., b. West Cambridge, s. James and Betsey, scarlet fever, Mar. 10, 1849, a. 13 y. 5 m.
Sarah E., d. James and Betsey, scarlet fever, Mar. 3, 1849, a. 3 y.
William, at Matanzas, ———, 1820, a. 40 y.

**CATEN,** John, b. Ireland, ship fever, at the alms house, Mar. 15, 1848, a. 54 y.

**CAUGHLIN** (see also Coughlin), W[illia]m, b. Ireland, ship fever, at the alms house, June 11, 1847, a. 39 y.

**CAWTE,** ———, ch. James, Apr. 17, 1808, a. 2 y.

**CAYLA,** Ellen, m., b. Ireland, fever, Feb. 28, 1847, a. 35 y.

**CAZNEAU,** Andrew, Hon., Chief Justice of the Vice Admiralty Court in Bermuda, bur. May 2, 1792. N. R. 4.
Samuel J., May 13, 1814, a. 72 y.

**CELLEY** (see also Celly), Nancy, w. Benj[ami]n, Nov. 2, 1834, a. 28 y.
Nancy Maria, d. Benj[ami]n, Jan. 22, 1836, a. 4 y.

**CELLY** (see also Celley), James, b. England, cholera, at the alms house, Aug. 16, 1849, a. 42 y.

**CENTER** (see also Senter), Hiram B., s. George and Betsey, fits, Nov. 28, 1847, a. 4 m.

**CESLER,** Christiana, d. John and Christiana, July 29, 1848, a. 6 m.
Louisa, d. Jacob and Christiana, Feb. 28, 1849, a. 11 m.

**CHADWICK,** Betsey [Betsy. G. R. 5.], Mrs., Apr. 20, 1842, a. 37 y.
Helen Frances, d. Betsy, Aug. 8, 1843, a. 15 m. G. R. 5.
———, ch. W[illia]m T. and Mehitable, Mar. 14, 1849, a. 2 d.

**CHAFFEE,** Sarah Jane, d. Edwin M. and Sarah A., Sept. 11, 1837, a. 2 1-2 y.

**CHAMBERLAIN** (see also Chamberlaine, Chamberlin), Aaron, Nov. 27, 1817, a. 33 y.

Caroline Tilden, d. Henry P., Apr. —, 1832, a. 2 y.

Hannah, Sept. 3, 1811, a. 43 y. C. R. 2.

Hannah, June 29, 1814, a. 21 y. C. R. 2.

Jacob [Chamberlaine. G. R. 1.], small pox, Nov. 7, 1721. [a. 63 y. G. R. 1.]

John, s. Jacob and Sarah, July 1, 1729, a. 1 m. G. R. 3.

John, Apr. 8, 1776, a. 92 y. C. R. 2.

John, Aug. 29, 1790, a. 20 y. C. R. 2.

John, Feb. 8, 1794. C. R. 2.

John Payson, s. Steph[e]n and Sarah [canker fever, Sept. 17, 1797, a. 7 m. C. R. 3.]

Lucy, wid., Dec. 27, 1830, a. 41 y. C. R. 2.

Margarett, m., b. Cambridge, w. Isaac, heart complaint and dropsy, Apr. 8, 1847, a. 40 y. 7 m. 22 d.

Mary, w. Edmund, of Chelmsford, at Samuel Ruggles' house, bur. 7 : 10m : 1669. C. R. 1.

Mary, w. Jacob, Oct. 12, 1718.

Mary A., d. Daniel and Mary, cholera infantum, July 26, 1846, a. 1 y. 6 m.

Moses, Sept. 5, 1825, a. 49 y. C. R. 2.

Nehemiah, Feb. 14, 1817, a. 59 y.

Patience, d. Jacob and Sarah, Dec. 14, 1727, a. 1 m. G. R. 3.

Payson, s. Stephen, Nov. 11, 1796, a. 16 y. C. R. 2.

Sarah, w. Jacob, Oct. 14, 1745, a. 84 y. G. R. 3.

Sarah, wid., Jan. 23, 1819, a. 55 y. C. R. 2.

Sarah, wid., Jan. 13, 1820, a. 81 y. C. R. 2.

Sarah, wid., Mar. 15, 1823, a. 84 y.

Stephen, s. Jacob and Sarah, July 20, 1731, a. 3 m. G. R. 3.

Stephen, Jan. 12, 1803, a. 70 y. C. R. 2.

Thomas, Sept. 14, 1714.

William Frederick, July 28, 1827, a. 17 m. C. R. 2.

——— w. Stephen, May 15, 1778, a. 42 y. C. R. 2.

———, ch. John, Oct. 14, 1778, a. 5 y. C. R. 2.

———, ch. Nehemiah and Sarah, Nov. 13, 1787, a. 9 m. C. R. 2.

———, ch. Moses and Lucy, Sept. 29, 1818, a. 14 m. C. R. 2.

———, ch. ———, Oct. 13, 1837, a. 7 m. C. R. 2.

CHAMBERLAIN, ——, Mrs., bur. Dec. 9, 1844, a. 76 y. c. R. 5.

——, d. Ebenezer, brain complaint, July 20, 1846, a. 3 y.

**CHAMBERLAINE** (see also Chamberlain), Hannah, w. John, Oct. 31, 1735.

**CHAMBERLIN** (see also Chamberlain), Austin, s. Daniel M., heart complaint, Oct. 28, 1849, a. 7 y. 3 m.

**CHAMPNEY,** Elizabeth, Mrs., Jan. 30, 1829, a. 83 y.

Henrietta, d. John, Oct. 14, 1831, a. 10 y.

Henry, m., clerk, s. John and Lydia, typhus fever, Dec. 19, 1846, a. 28 y.

John, m., gentleman, s. Jonathan and Elizabeth, jaundice and palsy, Mar. 23, 1847, a. 68 y.

Jonathan, May 14, 1809, a. 71 y.

Joseph, Dec. 11, 1799, a. 47 y.

Maria S., w. John, d. Hon. Charles Wells, Sept. 15, 1839, a. 21 y.

Mary, w. Jonathan, Jan. 16, 1771, in her 33d y. G. R. 1.

Sarah, only d. Jonathan and Eliz[abe]th, Apr. 24, 1792, a. 11 y. G. R. 1.

**CHANDLAR** (see also Chandler), Joseph [Chandler, s. John. C. R. 1.], 29 : 7m : 1668, a. 18 m. G. R. 1.

**CHANDLER** (see also Chandlar), Frederick, s. Frederick [and Elizabeth. G. R. 4.], drowned, Dec. [14. G. R. 4.], 1830, a. 13 y.

Frederick, June 9, 1832. [a. 40 y. G. R. 4.]

Gardiner L., Esq., Dec. 18, 1840, a. 72 y.

Hervey, Jan. 17, 1830, a. 40 y.

John [Chandlar. G. R. 1.], s. John, bur. Dec. 15, 1660. [a. 9 m. G. R. 1.]

Margaret, d. Zachariah and Margar[e]t, Jan. 9, 1725, a. 7 y.

Sarah, d. Zachariah and Margaret, Jan. 7, 1725, a. 5 y.

Willia[m], consumption, 26 : 11m : 1640-41. C. R. 1.

William, householder, [housekeeper. CT. R.], bur. June 19, [19 : 11m. CT. R.], 1641.

Zecheriah, s. Zecheriah and Margarett, Jan. 19, 1728-9.

**CHAPIN,** Maria L., d. Judson, heart complaint, May 12, 1849, a. 21 y.

Roxana [Roxania. C. R. 2.], w. Judson, Nov. 24, 1830. [a. 27 y. C. R. 2.]

**CHEANEY** (see also Cheney), Tho[ma]s, Feb. 22, 1808, a. 57 y.

**CHEANIE** (see also Cheney), John [Cheny. G. R. 1.], drowned, bur. 12 : 10m : 1671. C. R. 1. [a. 31 y. G. R. 1.]

**CHEANY** (see also Cheney), ——, inf. ch. Will[iam], jr., bur. —: 8m : 1661. C. R. 1.

**CHEEVER** (see also Chever), Hannah, w. John, Feb. 14, 1734.

**CHEINY** (see also Cheney), Henry [Cheny, inf. ch. C. R. 1.], s. Thomas and Hanna, Sept. 25, 1687.
Thomas [Cheney, twin. C. R. 1.], s. Thomas and Hanna, Sept. 18, 1687.

**CHENERY** (see also Cheney), Ephraim, July 15, 1825, a .49 y. C. R. 2.
——, ch. Ephraim and Rebecca, July 13, 1812, a. 2 y. C. R. 2.

**CHENEY** (see also Cheaney, Cheanie, Cheany, Cheiny, Chenery, Cheny), Benja[min], s. Henry and Mary, Dec. 23, 1739, a. 6 y. G. R. 1.
Deborah, Nov. 7, 1812, a. 85 y.
Ebenezer, s. Eben[eze]r and Elizabeth, Aug. 22, 1742, a. 21 m. 12 d. G. R. 1.
Ebenezer, Lt., Mar. 24, 1780. [in his 82d y. G. R. 1.]
Eben[eze]r, Feb. 15, 1845, a. 22 y.
Elizabeth, d. Eben[eze]r and Elizabeth, Aug. 17, 1742, a. 11 y. 10 m. 16 d. G. R. 1.
Elizabeth, w. Lt. Ebenezer, Apr. 17, 1769. [in her 65 th y. G. R. 1.]
Hannah, wid. Thomas, June 5, 1720, in her 63d y. G. R. 1.
Hannah, d. Eben[eze]r and Elizabeth, Aug. 11, 1742, a. 6 y. 4 d. G. R. 1.
Henry, Dec. 22, 1737, in his 41st y. G. R. 1.
Jane, Mrs., July 26, 1845, a. 91 y. G. R. 5.
Jane (Ayers), Nov. —, 1836. C. R. 4.
Joseph, jr., m., harness maker, s. Joseph, consumption, Mar. 21, 1848, a. 26 y.
Mary, d. Henry and Mary, Aug. 28, 1731.
Mary, d. Henry and Mary, Nov. 18, 1735.
Mary, wid. Henry, Feb. 16, 1739, in her —3t[h] y. G. R. 1.

CHENEY, Sarah, d. Ebenezer and Elizabeth, Feb. 11, 1739, a. 15 m. 1 d. G. R. 1.

Thomas, s. Ebenezer and Elizabeth, Aug. 1, 1742, a. 9 y. 3 m. 5 d. G. R. 1.

Thomas, Dec. 16, 1822, a. 38 y.

William [Cheany, sr. C. R. 1.], June 30, 1667, a. 63 y.

William, Jan. 5, 1830.

——, [female], dropsy [bet. Feb. 5 and Dec. 21.], 1807. C. R. 3.

CHENY (see also Cheney), Rebecca, d. William and Rebecca, June 17, 1706.

Samuel, s. Thomas and Hannah, Nov. 29, 1704.

Thomas, s. William, Apr. 20, 1714.

Thomas, sr., Mar. 7, 1717.

William, Mar. 25, 1695.

——, "Sister," aged, bur. 3 : 5m : 1686. C. R. 1.

CHESBROUGH, Elizabeth Reese, b. Baltimore, d. Isaac M. and Phrania J., disease of the brain, Oct. 9, 1848, a. 32 y. 5 d.

CHESMAN, Anna S., Apr. 10, 1829, a. 15 m.

CHESWORTH, Elizabeth, Mrs., Dec. —, 1836, a. 49 y.

CHEVER (see also Cheever), Edward, s. John and Hannah, Oct. 8, 1743.

John, Oct. 13, 1751.

Margarett, w. John, Mar. 14, 1741-2.

CHICK, Richard [Chik. C. R. 1.], Oct. 13, 1686, a. 48 y.

——, wid. Mar. 19, 1698-9.

CHICKERING, Deborah F., Mrs., bur. Aug. 1, 1843, a. 54 y. C. R. 5.

CHIELD (see also Child), Elizabeth, w. Joshua, Mar. 6, 1752, a. 87 y. G. R. 3.

Isaac, Sept. [1]2, 1765, in his 77th y. G. R. 3.

CHILD (see also Chield, Childe, Childs), Aaron, jr., Aug. 31, 1839, a. 43 y.

Abigail, d. Phineas and Elizabeth, May 10, 1795, a. 6 y. G. R. 4.

Anna, d. Joshua and Deborah, May 10, 1729, in her 1st y. G. R. 3.

CHILD, Benjamin, Jan. 26 [24. C. R. 3.], 1723, [1723-4, in his 66th y. G. R. 3.]

Caroline, Sept. 27, 1805.

Charlotte, m., b. Falmouth, Me., w. Thomas, consumption, Aug. 12, 1848, a. 63 y.

David, s. Isaac and Elizabeth, Oct. 16, 1766, in his 19th y. G. R. 3.

David, Oct. —, 1798, a. 7 m. C. R. 3.

David Weld, s. Stephen and Sarah, Sept. 20, 1799.

Deborah, w. Joshua, Apr. 21, 1732, in her 40th y. G. R. 3.

Elizabeth, w. Isaac, Apr. —, 1754, in her 62d y. G. R. 3.

Elizabeth, w. Phineas [dropsy. C. R. 3.], Sept. 28, 1800, a. 49 y. G. R. 4.

Esther Maria, d. Stephen and Sarah, whooping cough [bet. Aug. 20 and Nov. 21], 1805, a. 4 y. C. R. 3.

George H., Aug. 21, 1841, a. 26 y.

Grace, w. Benjamin, Dec. 10, 1723. [in her 63d y. G. R. 3.]

Hannah, d. Daniel and Rebecca, Jan. 30, 1809, a. 14 y. C. R. 2.

Hannah R., d. Daniel, drowned in a well, Apr. 6, 1831, a. 22 y. C. R. 2.

Joshua, s. Joshua and Deborah, Aug. 4, 1728, in his 3d y. G. R. 3.

Joshua, Jan. 18, 1729-30, in his 73d y. G. R. 3.

Joshua, July 20, 1756, in his 70th y. G. R. 3.

Margaret, w. Edward, Dec. 1, 1754, in her 66th y. G. R. 3.

Margaret, d. Benjamin F., of Calhoun Co., Ill. [dysentery, Aug. 18. C. R. 3.], 1839, a. 19 m.

Mary, wid., Oct. 31, 1707.

Mary, wid., b. Newton, dysentery, July 26, 1847, a. 76 y.

Mehitabel, May 1, 1822, a. 20 y. C. R. 2.

Phineas, Mar. 17, 1813, a. 64 y. G. R. 4.

Priscilla, d. John and Esther, Apr. 14, 1750, in her 2d y. G. R. 3.

Richard, May 18, 1759, a. 57 y. G. R. 3.

Robert [Robart P. C. R. 2.], Jan. 3, 1830, a. 44 y. [a. 43 y. C. R. 2.]

Samuel, s. Joshua and Elizabeth, Feb. 7, 1705-6.

Sarah, w. Stephen [gradual decay of constitution. C. R. 3.], Nov. 9, 1826, a. 63 y.

Sarah Richards, d. Abner and Betsy, whooping cough, Aug. 20, 1805, a. 18 m. C. R. 3.

Sarah W., typhus fever, Mar. 22, 1811, in her 16th y. C. R. 3.

Stephen, old age, consumption, Sept. 15, 1833, a. 75 y. C. R. 3.

CHILD, William, s. William and Deborah, June 18, 1724.
——, ch. Daniel and Rebecca, Apr. 7, 1791, a. 2 w. C. R. 2.
——, ch. Daniel and Rebecca, Sept. 28, 1800, a. 14 m. C. R. 2.
——, w. Daniel, May 10, 1826. C. R. 2.

CHILDE (see also Child), Joseph, s. Benjamin, bur. 10 : 12
m : 1673-4. C. R. 1.
——, inf. ch. Benjamin, bur. —: 10m: 1662. C. R. 1.

CHILDS (see also Child), Aaron, suddenly, issue of Aug. 28,
1795, a. 58 y. N. R. 4.
Aaron, m., carpenter, s. Aaron and Susanna, inflammation of
bowels, May 11, 1847, a. 77 y.
Elizabeth, d. Stephen and Sarah, consumption, ——, 1805, a.
19 d. C. R. 3.
Ellen, b. Watertown, d. James and Julia, canker, Sept. 28,
1847, a. 8 m.
——, inf. s. Francis L. and Sarah A., inflammation of bowels,
Oct. 15, 1846, a. 2 m. 14 d.

CHOATE, William, Dec. 1, 1727, in his 25th y. G. R. 1.

CHORLEY, Catharine E., d. John, Apr. 13, 1838, a. 4 y. 7 m.

CHRISTY, Robert, Nov. —, 1805, a. 54 y.

CHURCHILL, George G., s. W[illia]m F. and Caroline,
dysentery, Aug. 21, 1847, a. 2 y.

CIRTY, Catherine, unm., b. Ireland, lung fever, Mar. 23, 1847,
a. 26 y.

CLAFLEN (see also Claflin, Claflon), Cynthia, w. Ebenezer,
June 28, 1824, a. 67 y. G. R. 1.
Ebenezer, soldier during Revolutionary War, Mar. 28, 1831,
in his 79th y. G. R. 1.

CLAFLIN (see also Claflen), Royal, dysentery, Oct. 29, 1802,
a. 18 y. C. R. 3.

CLAFLON (see also Claflen), Elizabeth, Dec. 30, 1814, a. 20
y. G. R. 1.

CLAP (see also Clapp), Daniel, m., carpenter, b. Marl-
borough, N. H., by a fall, July 30, 1846, a. 42 y.
Edward, s. John, drowned, July 28, 1826, a. 19 y.
George, Dec. 30, 1829.

CLAP, John, s. John, drowned, July 28, 1826, a. 17 y.

John, Dea., Sept. 23, 1840, a. 76 y.

Priscilla, w. John, Jan. 24, 1822, a. 45 y.

Sarah, wid., Apr. 21, 1843, a. 78 y.

Susannah [Clapps. dup.], w. John, May 9, [6. dup.], 1802, a. 31 y.

—— [Claps. dup], w. John, July 1, 1800.

—— [Clapps. dup.], ch. Caleb and Ann, Mar. 1, 1801, a. 1 w.

**CLAPP** (see also Clap), Caroline A., w. Joseph H., d. Jacob Allen, Dec. 15, 1839, a. 27 y.

Elizabeth, July —, 1825. c. r. 4.    ,

——, inf. ch. John and Susannah, May 6, 1802, a. 7 hrs.

**CLARK** (see also Clarke), Abigail, M., wid., b. Sanbornton, N. H., d. Elisha and Abigail, consumption, d. at Haverhill, bur. Roxbury, June 29, 1848, a. 37 y.

Elizabeth, d. John and Mary, heart complaint, Aug. 28, 1847, a. 27 y.

George, Jan. 8, 1849, a. 59 y. c. r. 6.

Hanna, d. James, bur. 25 : 7 m : 1669. c. r. 1.

Hannah, w. James, May 30, 1683.

James, bleeding of the lungs, 18 : 10 m : 1674. c. r. 1.

John, m., victualler, b. Ireland, insane, May 23, 1847, a. 56 y.

Seth, s. Chenery, Mar. 14, 1820, a. 9 y.

Susan F., d. W[illia]m D. and Eliza S., dysentery, Aug. 19, 1847, a. 4 y.

Susanna, Mar. 9, 1802.

——, inf. ch. Uriah, bur. 22 : 12 m : 1687-8. c. r. 1.

**CLARKE** (see also Clark), George, Sept. 3, 1696.

Hannah, w. Uriah, Feb. 28, 1681, a. 25 y. g. r. 1.

Hugh, July 20, 1693.

John, July 10, 1762, a. 70 y. g. r. 1.

Nabby, d. Thomas, Esq. and Mrs. Louis, Mar. 10, 1787, [a. 10 m. g. r. 1.]

Sarah, wid. John, July 5, 1764, a. 67 y. g. r. 1.

Susy [Susa. dup.], at the work house, May 31, 1802.

——, w. Hugh, Dec. 11, 1692.

**CLEAVES** W[illia]m, under the command of Capt. Sam[u]ell Wadsworth, slain by the Indians at Sudbury, Apr. 21, 1676.

**CLENDENIN,** Charlotte L., d. John L. and Charlotte A., Sept. 22, 1836, a. 19 m.

**CLEREY,** Betsey, b. Ireland, consumption, Mar. 3, 1848, a. 21 y.

**CLIFFORD,** Ellen, d. Thomas and Mary, brain fever, at Dedham, (bur. at Roxbury), Jan. 30, 1849, a. 18 y.
Ira S., s. Ira and Elizabeth, lung complaint, May 3, 1847, a. 1 y. 5 m.

**CLOUGH,** ——, ch. still born, Ellick and Catherine M., Oct. 5, 1846.

**CLOUSTON,** Esther, m., b. Newburyport, dysentery, Sept. 17, 1849, a. 68 y.

**CLOUTMAN,** Deborah K., Mrs., Jan. 14, 1840, a. 27 y.

**COBB,** George W., s. Joseph L. and Elizabeth M. S., Oct. 22, 1836, a. 7 y.
Sarah,, m., b. Kingston, d. Nathaniel and Rebecca, consumption, Aug. 22, 1847, a. 54 y. 1 m. 21 d.
——, ch. Capt. William, Sept. —, 1831, a. 13 m.

**COBINE,** Mary, wid., b. Ireland, ship fever, July 29, 1847, a. 32 y.

**COBLEIGH,** William H[enry, Aug. 21. G. R. 4.], 1836, a. 18 y. [a. 17 y. G. R. 4.]

**COCHE,** David, unm., laborer, b. Ireland, ship fever, June 13, 1847, a. 20 y.

**COCHRAN** (see also Cochrane), Eliza J[ane. C. R. 5.], d. Thomas and Catherine, teething, Aug. 2, 1848, a. 1 y. [a. 1 y. 1 m. C. R. 5.]
Mary, at Reading, (bur. at Roxbury), Aug. 31, 1848, a. 61 y.

**CODINGTON,** Hannah [Cuddington. CT. R.; an aged woman. C. R. 1.], w. Stockdale, [apoplexy. C. R. 1.], bur. July 20, 1644.

**COGGSWELL,** Abigail, b. Nova Scotia, d. Daniel and Abigail, fever, Sept. 14, 1848, a. 8 y.
Sophia, b. Nova Scotia, d. Daniel and Sophia, measles, June 5, 1848, a. 5 y.

**COHALER,** Johanna, m., b. Ireland, fever, June 27, 1847, a. 67 y.

**COILE,** David, b. Ireland, old age, at the alms house, Dec. 16, 1849, a. 72 y.

**COLBART** (see also Colbert), Mary, at the work house, Jan. 16, 1809, a. 77 y.

**COLBERT** (see also Colbart), John, s. Michael and Mary, convulsions, Dec. 19, 1848, a. 3 y. 1 m.

Lawrence, m., b. Ireland, fever, Mar. 5, 1848, a. 34 y.

Thomas, from [at. dup.], work house, Dec. 26, [25. dup.], 1801, [1802. dup], a. 80 y.

**COLBURN** (see also Colburne), Ann Eliza[beth. c. r. 3.], d. Nath[anie]l, dec., Nov. 1, 1835, a. 16 m.

Eliza Armsby, cholera infantum, Aug. 22, 1830, a. 6 m. c. r. 3.

Eliza K[ingsbury. c. r. 3.], w. Capt. Nath[anie]l [confinement. c. r. 3.], Mar. 8, 1830, a. 33 y.

Elizabeth, b. Surrey, N. H., w. William, paralysis, Aug. 3, 1849, a. 48 y.

John, s. John and Rhoda, Dec. 6, 1716.

John, June 7, 1732, in his 57th y. g. r. 2.

John Armsby, s. Nathaniel and Eliza [lung fever. c. r. 3.], Apr. 12, 1825, a. 2 y.

Nath[anie]l [suicide, July 6. c. r. 3.], 1834, a. 39 y.

Sarah D., Mrs., May 17, 1836, a. 45 y.

Thomas, a foreigner, Feb. 25, 1801.

**COLBURNE** (see also Colburn), John, nervous fever, Mar. 21, 1802, a. 48 y. c. r. 3.

**COLBY,** William Henry, dropsy of the brain, Aug. 21, 1836, a. 18 y. c. r. 3.

**COLEN,** Mary, b. Ireland, delirium tremens, at the alms house, Mar. 19, 1848, a. 40 y.

**COLLEGAN** (see also Colligen), Nancy, d. Thomas and Margarett, dysentery, Sept. 26, 1848, a. 10 y. 5 m.

**COLLIGEN** (see also Collegan), Deborah, Mrs., Mar. —, 1829, a. 52 y.

**COLLINS,** Martin, at the alms house, Dec. 23, 1843, a. 18 y.
Oliver, bur. June 27, 1845, a. 13 m. C. R. 5.
Patrick, a pauper, Feb. 1, 1829, a. 75 y.
Siranus [Seranus. dup.], Jan. 4, 1798, a. 44 y.
——, Mrs., b. Jamaica Plain, Nov. —, 1844, a. 40 y.

**COLTMAN,** John W., Nov. —, 1832, a. 20 y.

**COMEGYS,** John, s. Jacob, Mar. 16, 1832, a. 6 y.

**CONANT,** Alfred M., s. Henry, Aug. 3, 1839, a. 9 w. G. R. 5.
Charles E., s. Henry, Jan. 18, 1841, a. 9 m. G. R. 5.
Cynthia [A. G. R. 5.], d. Maj. Henry, Dec. — [Oct. 9. G. R.
    5.], 1830, a. 16 m.
Eliza [C. G. R. 5.], d. Maj. Henry, Nov. [13. G. R. 5.], 1830, a.
    6 y. [a. 7 y. G. R. 5.]
Helen M., d. Henry, Sept. 8, 1839, a. 4 y. G. R. 5.
Henry [jr. G. R. 5.], s. Maj. Henry, Nov. [8. G. R. 5.], 1830,
    a. 4 y. [a. 5 y. G. R. 5.]
Henry, laborer, consumption, Aug. 23, 1846, a. 49 y. [a. 48 y.
    G. R. 5.]

**CONDEN,** Rebecca, Mrs., Dec. 30, 1820, a. 71 y.

**CONDER,** David, s. James and Mary, dysentery, Oct. 21,
    1848, a. 2 y. 2 m.

**CONETY,** John, s. John and Jane, measles, July 9, 1849, a.
    2 m.

**CONEY,** Jabez [fever. C. R. 2.], May 24, 1841, a. 67 y.
Susannah, d. John and Susannah, Sept. 23, 1800.

**CONKEY,** John A., Jan. 12, 1843, a. 32 y.

**CONNELL,** Joseph, July 16, 1833, a. 32 y.

**CONNER** (see also O'Connor), Honora, m., b. Ireland, child
    bed, Oct. 11, 1847, a. 28 y.

**CONNOLLY,** Betsy, Nov. 21, 1798, a. 20 y. C. R. 2.

**CONNOR** (see also O'Connor), William, s. William and Cath-
    erine, scarlet fever, Oct. 28, 1849, a. 1 y. 3 m.

**CONSAELINE,** Ann, b. Ireland, ship fever, at the alms house,
    Oct. 10, 1847, a. 2 m.

**CONVERSE,** ——, ch. ——, July 5, 1816, a. 9 m. c. r. 2.

**CONWAY,** James, at the alms house, Dec. 18, 1848, a. 6 m.

**COOK,** Caroline Georgianna, d. James M. and Mary W., Dec. 25, 18—, a. 1 y.

George F. [Cooks. dup.], s. Jona[than] F. and Mary, Mar. 14 [12. dup.], 1807. [a. 12 m. dup.]

Henrietta Josephine, d. James M. and Mary W., Aug. 7, 1837, a. 3 y. 3 m. g. r. 5.

Jane Alice, d. James M. and Mary W., Apr. 26, 1846, a. 6 m. g. r. 5.

Jonathan, Sept. 12, 1805, a. 35 y.

Josephus Waterman, s. James M. and Mary W., Feb. 21, 1839, a. 15 m. g. r. 5.

Mayo [consumption. c. r. 2.], Dec. [11. c. r. 2.], 1832, a. 34 y. [a. 33 y. c. r. 2.]

——, s. James and Rosannah, dropsy, Dec. 18, 1846, a. 2 m.

**COOKSON,** Samuel, Mar. 7, 1806, a. 63 y.

——, ch. Sam[ue]l and Susanna, Dec. 17, 1795, a. 4 d. c. r. 2.

**COOPER,** James Robert, s. John and Ann, bur. Mar. 25, 1837, a. 7 w. c. r. 5.

**COPELAND,** Charles, s. Charles and Susan R., Aug. 18, 1835.

**CORBAN** (see also Corbin), Margret, bur. 24 : 7 m : 1675. c. r. 1.

**CORBETT,** Mary B., b. Swanzey, w. David, consumption, Nov. 12, 1848, a. 48 y.

Robert A., s. Robert L. and Frances P., cholera infantum, Aug. 25, 1848, a. 8 m. 5 d.

**CORBIN** (see also Corban), Hannah, bur. 6 : 8 m : 1686. c. r. 1.

**CORDWELL,** Elizabeth, old age, Sept. 22, 1846, a. 87 y.

**COREY,** Benjamin, Mar. 19, 1820, a. 62 y.

David, Dea., Jan. 9, 1823, a. 62 y.

Ebenezer, Jan. 22, 1782, a. 63 y. c. r. 2.

Ebenezer, Nov. 22, 1793, a. 38 y. c. r. 2.

Hannah, Mar. 7, 1779, a. 88 y. c. r. 2.

Hannah, wid., Nov. 16, 1810, a. 84 y. c. r. 2.

Hannah, Aug. 1, 1811, a. 26 y. c. r. 2.

COREY, Mary, d. Ebenezer and Hannah, Nov. 25, 1755.
Rebecca, d. Eben[eze]r, Apr. 9, 1778, a. 27 y. C. R. 2.
Sarah, wid. of Dea. David, Apr. 10, 1830, a. 61 y.

COROHAN, Bridget, m., b. Ireland, Mar. 3, 1847, a. 30 y.

COSTELLY, Mary Ann, d. Patrick and Bridget, worm fever,
Apr. 1, 1849, a. 1 y. 11 m.

COTTREL, Samuel, May 15, 1807.

COUGHLIN (see also Caughlin), Johanna, unm., b. Ireland,
cholera, Sept. 9, 1849, a. 24 y.

COVERLEY (see also Coverly), Elizabeth, wid. Nath[anie]l,
dysentery, Aug. 11, 1848, a. 79 y.
Polly F., b. Meredith, N. H., w. Eben, dysentery, Aug. 18,
1848, a. 56 y.

COVERLY (see also Coverley), Mary Ann, d. Charles, Apr.
21, 1843, a. 8 y.
Thomas D., b. N. H., s. Eben[eze]r C. and Mary H., Mar. 21,
1848, a. 29 y.

COWING, Ann Gordon, housewife, w. Cornelius, d. James and
Eliza Gordon, dysentery, Sept. 30, 1847, a. 51 y. 6 m.
15 d.

COYLE, Mary, d. John and Catherine, bowel complaint, Aug.
9, 1848, a. 1 y. 2 m.
Mary, wid., b. Ireland, consumption, Apr. 26, 1849, a. 50 y.
Michael, b. Ireland, ship fever, at the alms house, Aug. 21,
1847, a. 1 y.

CRACKLIN, Caroline O. [Caroline R. Cracknell. C. R. 5.], d.
William and Francis, complaint of head, May 31, 1848,
a. 17 y.
Eliza R., w. Lemuel, consumption, May 4, 1849, a. 51 y.
William, May 24, 1840, a. 54 y.

CRACKNELL, see Cracklin.

CRAFT (see also Crafts), Aaron, s. Samuel and Elizabeth,
Dec. 30, 1711.
Aaron, s. Benjamin and Abigail, Oct. 15, 1714.
Alice, bur. 26 : 1 m : 1673, a. 73 y. C. R. 1.
Daniel, May 5, 1728, in his 21st y. G. R. 1.

CRAFT, Dorcas, wid. Griffin, Dec. 30, 1697.

Ebenezer, Ens., Aug. 13, 1722, a. 43 y. G. R. 1.

Elizabeth, d. Ebenezer and Elizabeth, July 1, 1714.

Elizabeth, wid. [Lt. Samuel. G. R. 1.], Dec. 9, 1731. [in her 88th y. G. R. 1.]

John, Oct. 3, 1685, a. 55 y.

Jonathan, bur. Mar. 5, 1795, a. 88 y. N. R. 4.

Mary, d. Ephraim and Hannah, [1712 ?]

Mary, wid., Jan. 3, 1724.

Moses, s. Moses and Rebeckah, May 3, 1672.

Nathaniel, s. Nath[anie]l and Patience, Jan. 13, 1727-8, in his 24th y. G. R. 1.

Nathaniel, Sept. 8, 1746, in his 70th y. G. R. 1.

Patience, d. Nathan[ie]ll, Mar. 10, 1720. [1720-21, a. 43 y. G. R. 1.]

Rebecca, w. John, childbirth, bur. 28 : 9 m : 1667. C. R. 1.

Rebecca, d. Moses, bur. 20 : 7 m : 1669. C. R. 1.

Samuel, Dec. 9, 1709.

Sukey [Susannah Crafts. G. R. 1.], Sept. 22, 1800. [a. 22 y. dup ; a. 21 y. G. R. 1.]

Susannah, Feb. 10, 1803, a. 92 y.

——, w. Jos[eph], Mar. 9, 1808, a. 28 y.

**CRAFTS** (see also Craft), Abigail, wid., Jan. 28, 1823, a. 78 y.

Abigail Frances, d. Ebenezer and Sarah H., Dec. 18, 1824, a. 2 y.

Jacob, m., laborer, b. France, old age, Dec. 3, 1848, a. 77 y.

John [jr. C. R. 1.], s. John, drowned [off the oyster banks. C. R. 1.], May 5, 1684.

John, bur. 3 : 7 m : 1685. C. R. 1.

Joseph, s. John, bur. July 20, 1666.

Martha, Feb. 9, 1825, a. 50 y.

Mary Elizabeth, d. Ebenezer, Sept. 11, 1823, a. 15 y.

Rebecah, w. John, bur. Nov. 24, 1667.

Rebeccah, d. Moses, Sept. 20, 1669.

Samuell, s. Samuel, bur. June 5, 1663.

Sarah Ann, d. Ebenezer, Sept. 23, 1823, a. 6 y.

Tho[ma]s, Esq., Jan. 14, 1799. P. R. 2.

William, Dec. 14, 1800, a. 63 y. P. R. 2.

——, "Father," Nov. 17, 1789. P. R. 2.

——, "Mother," Jan. 31, 1796. P. R. 2.

CRAIGE, George [Craig. c. r. 5.], unm., laborer, b. Ireland, [ship. c. r. 5.] fever, Apr. 10, 1847, a. 16 y. [a. 17 y. c. r. 5.]

Thomas [Craig. c. r. 5.], m., laborer, b. Ireland, accidental, Feb. 27, 1849, a. 30 y. [a. 28 y. c. r. 5.]

CRAMPTON, John G., m., b. Scotland, consumption, Sept. 18, 1847, a. 29 y.

CRANCH, Joseph, from Milton, consumption, Nov. 21 [17. g. r. 4.], 1806, a. 60 y. c. r. 3.

Maria Vietch, May 29, 1810, a. 22 y. g. r. 4.

CRANE, Abigail, b. Mt. Desert, Me., d. Elisha, dysentery, Sept. 9, 1847, a. 12 y.

Charles, of Canton, June 11, 1843, a. 36 y. g. r. 5.

Theodore E., s. Charles and Harriet, Feb. 13, 1845, a. 1 y. 6 m. g. r. 5.

CRAWLEY (see also Crowley), Florance, d. Daniel and Ellen, bowel complaint, Aug. 13, 1848, a. 1 y. 9 m.

Margaret, Oct. 12. 1802, a. 45 y. c. r. 2.

——, inf. ch. Abraham, Sept. 30, 1799. c. r. 2.

CREASE (see also Crees, Creese, Crese), Richard, drowned, May 13, 1737.

CREES (see also Crease), Elizabeth, wid. Richard, Dec. 15, 1749, in her 49th y. g. r. 1.

CREESE (see also Crease), William, s. Richard and Elizabeth, May 29, 1736.

CREHORE, Joseph, Jan. 23, 1813.

Julia, d. wid. Catharine, small pox, Jan. 7, 1828, a. 20 y.

CRESE (see also Crease), Richard, Apr. 13, 1792, a. 60 y. g. r. 1.

CRISP, John, a soldier, Apr. 11, 1710.

CROCKS, ——, ch. stillborn, Samuel, Aug. 13, 1846.

CROMBEA (see also Crumbee), ——, Mrs., w. W[illia]m, fever, Sept. 18, 1846.

CROOKER, Horace Tower, s. Ralph, Nov. 3, 1833, a. 14 m.

——, ch. ——, bur. Oct. 22, 1841. c. r. 5.

**CROOME,** Emma, d. William [and Sarah H. c. r. 5.], Aug. 24, 1838, a. 8 m. [21 d. c. r. 5.]
Sarah H., Mrs., bur. Oct. 11, 1838, a. 26 y. c. r. 5.

**CROSBY,** Lydia, w. Josiah, June —, 1841, a. 25 y.
——, Mrs., Apr. —, 1830. c. r. 4.

**CROSHER,** Mezilla, b. Scotland, d. Samuel and Sarah, canker, Dec. 5, 1848, a. 2 y. 5 m.

**CROTHERS,** Ann, Mrs., Sept. —, 1820.

**CROUCH,** Edward, bur. Oct. 14, 1845, a. 4 y. 6 m. c. r. 5.
Jane, m., b. Nova Scotia, small pox, Sept. 15, 1847, a. 34 y.
Julia, d. Thomas and Jane, disease on brain, Aug. 8, 1847, a. 11 m.
Mary Ellen, bur. Aug. 1, 1845, a. 6 y. c. r. 5.
Nancy, bur. July 8, 1845, a. 7 m. c. r. 5.
William, b. Nova Scotia, s. Thomas and Jane, typhus fever, Nov. 30, 1846, a. 15 y.

**CROWLEY** (see also Crawley), John, b. Ireland, ship fever, at the alms house, June 1, 1848, a. 25 y. [a. 27 y. dup.]

**CROXFORD,** Lydia, a pauper, Nov. 4, 1832, a. 83 y.

**CRUDY,** Anthony, b. Ireland, ship fever, June 27, 1847, a. 20 y.

**CRUFFY,** ——, ch. stillborn, Mark and Mary, Apr. 10, 1849.

**CRUMBEE** (see also Crombea), Mary, m., b. Scotland, child birth, Sept. 20, 1847, a. 32 y.

**CRUSTY,** Charles, s. Michael and Harriet, croup, Sept. 6, 1849, a. 1 y 9 m.

**CUDDY** (see also Cudehy), Andrew, unm., laborer, b. Ireland, ship fever, June 27, 1847, a. 22 y.

**CUDEHY** (see also Cuddy), Edward, unm., b. Ireland, accidental, Jan. 24, 1849, a. 33 y.

**CULVER,** ——, inf. d. ——, 21 : 11 m : 1650-51. c. r. 1.

**CUMMENS** (see also Cummings), Mary, w. William, Apr. 29, 1832, a. 69 y.

Sally, Mrs., issue of Aug. 11, 1792, a. 22 y. N. R. 4.

——, Mrs. [Cummins. dup], May 15, 1799.

**CUMMINGS** (see also Cummens, Cummins), Lucius, m., machinist, b. New Hampton, s. Manton and Mary, accidental, at Canton, (bur. at Roxbury), Feb. 1, 1849, a. 34 y.

Otis, Apr. —, 1833, a. 33 y.

**CUMMINS** (see also Cummings), Jacob [Cummens. dup.], Jan. 6, 1802, a. 59 .

Polley, Nov. 1, 1803, a. 20 y.

William, Apr. 20, 1834, a. 66 y.

**CUNNIGHAM** (see also Cunningham), Andrew, Esq., ——, 1829, a. 69 y.

**CUNNINGHAM** (see also Cunnigham), Elizabeth, at the alms house, Sept. 14, 1839, a. 1 y.

James, s. Josiah and Louis, July 30, 1787, a. 2 y. 6 m. G. R. 1.

John, Jan. [16. G. R. 1.], 1829, a. 65 y. [a. 60 y. G. R. 1.]

Josiah, Nov. 19, 1798, a. 41 y.

Phebe, Mrs., bur. Dec. 3, 1845, a. 72 y. C. R. 5.

Sarah A., Mrs., bur. July 15, 1844, a. 63 y. C. R. 5.

William, Oct. 6, 1805, a. 84 y.

**CURLEY** (see also Curly), Mary, d. John and Bridget, water on brain, Nov. 11, 1849.

Matthew, m., laborer, b. Ireland, fever, July 15, 1847, a. 30 y.

Matthew, b. Ireland, dropsy, at the alms house, Sept. 6, 1847, a. 45 y.

Thomas, m., laborer, b. Ireland, fever, July 9, 1847, a. 35 y.

Thomas, s. Peter and Seria, brain fever, May 2, 1849, a. 1 y. 4 m.

**CURLY** (see also Curley), Mary, m., child bed, Mar. 8, 1849, a. 32 y.

Matthew, s .Matthew and Catherine, bowel complaint, Sept. 24, 1848, a. 11 m.

**CURNISKEY,** Mary, w. James, Feb. 10, 1835, a. 54 y.

**CURRIER,** Nath[anie]l, Feb. —, 1821.

**CURRY**, Agnes, unm., laborer, b. Scotland, consumption, July 2, 1847, a. 28 y.

**CURTIS** (see also Curtise, Curtiss), Abigail, d. Philip, bur. June 20, 1663.

Abigail, Mrs., July 16, 1773.

Ann, Oct. 22, 1823, a. 78 y.

Benjamin [Curtiss, hatter. N. R. 2.], Feb. 6, 1773.

Benjamin, Dr., Nov. 26, 1784.

Christopher, m., farmer, b. England, cholera morbus, Sept. 20, 1846, a. 71 y.

Elizabeth, d. Sam[ue]ll and Hannah, Nov. 13, 1734. [in her 7th y. G. R. 1.]

Hannah, wid. Isaac, Feb. 6, 1719-20, in her 68th y. G. R. 1.

Hannah, d. Isaac [Samuel. G. R. 1.] and Hannah, Oct. 20, 1733. [in her 20th y. G. R. 1.]

Hannah, Mrs., Feb. 17, 1824, a. 67 y.

Isaac, s. Isaac and Mehittabel, July 20, 1728.

Isaac, s. Isaac and Mehitabel, Oct. 10, 1730.

Isaac, May 23, 1748, in his 63d y. G. R. 1.

Isaac, Mrs., Nov. 27, 1805, a. 27 y.

Isaak, s. Isaak, a flux, bur. 13 : 8m : 1682. C. R. 1.

John, July 26, 1793. [a. 40 y. N. R. 4.]

John, m., yeoman, s. Isaac and Ann, paralysis, Nov. 12, 1849, a. 78 y.

Joseph, issue of Feb. 1, 1792, a. 70 y. N. R. 4.

Joseph, Capt., jr., Apr. —, 1830, a. 27 y.

Katherine [Catherine, Mrs., bilious fever. C. R. 3.], June 15, 1802, a. 67 y.

Lydia M., b. Abington, d. Nahum and Betsey, fits, Oct. 17, 1849, a. 2 y. 6 m.

Mary, inf. d. Isaak, bur. 1 : 12m : 1682-3. C. R. 1.

Mehitable, unm., old age, Aug. 4, 1846, a. 84 y.

Mehitable, d. Isaac and Peggy, consumption, Sept. 4, 1847, a. 36 y.

Philip, s. Philip, bur. 5 : 10m : 1659. C. R. 1.

Philip, s. Samuel and Hannah, Nov. 14, 1716.

Rebecca, w. John, humors, 16 : 3m : 1675. C. R. 1.

Rosana, w. Nath[anie]l, Esq. [affection of the heart. C. R. 3.], Jan. 2 [Feb. 3. C. R. 3.], 1841, a. 64 y. [a. 65 y. C. R. 3.]

Sally, w. Isaac, Nov. 28, 1805.

Samuel, s. Isack, scalded, 18 : 2m : 1679. C. R. 1.

Curtis, Samuell, s. .Sam[ue]ll and Hanah [June. G. R. 1.] 25, 1733. [in his 22d y. G. R. 1.]

Sarah, d. Philip, Dec. 8, 1659.

Thomas, s. William [consumption. C. R. 1.], bur. June 26, 1650.

William, Dec. 8, 1672, a. 80 y.

William, s. Samuel and Hanah, May 10, 1728. [a. 19 m. G. R. 1.]

————, Mrs., Mary "alias" June 11, 1799, a. 65 y.

————, d. John and Sarah, July 25, 1846, a. 35 d.

**CURTISE** (see also Curtis), Sarah [Curtis. G. R. 1.], Mar. 26, 1673, a. 73 y.

**CURTISS** (see also Curtis), Isaac [Curtis. G. R. 1.], May 31, 1695. [in his 55th y. G. R. 1.]

Joseph, s. Philip, Nov. 27, 1690.

Philip, Lt., slain by the Indians at Hassanameset, Nov. 9, 1675.

**CUSHING,** Catharine B. O. [grand d. Madam Orne. C. R. 5.], Nov. 10, 1836, a. 30 y.

Hannah B., Mrs., bur. Oct. 18, 1841. C. R. 5.

————, inf. ch. James, May 31, 1846, a. 1 m. 14 d.

**CUSHMAN,** Eliza Ann, Mar. 15, 1845. C. R. 6.

**CUSICK,** Elizabeth, m., b. Ireland, w. Michael, child bed, June 8, 1848, a. 38 y.

**CUTHBERTON,** Hugh, s. Thomas and Mary, consumption, Aug. 4, 1848, a. 1 y. 4 m.

**CUTLER,** Benjamin C., Esq., suicide, Apr. 3, 1810, a. 54 y. C. R. 3.

**DALTON,** Daniel H., widr., ropemaker, b. Wiscasset, disease of the brain, Oct. 5, 1846, a. 30 y.

Louisa A., d. Daniel H., bowel complaint, Oct. 2, 1846, a. 1 y. 4 m.

**DALY,** Carrol, m., laborer, b. Ireland, accidental, May 22, 1848, a. 50 y.

**DAME,** George R., s. William and S., dysentery, Oct. 5, 1848, a. 3 y.

**DAMON,** Adaline [Adeline, consumption. C. R. 3.], Aug. 28, 1831, a. 21 y.

Serena, w. E. L., July 8, 1847, a. 22 y. G. R. 5.

**DANA,** Daniel, Nov. 15, 1787, a. 70 y. G. R. 3.

Esther D., May —, 1842, a. 23 y.

Martha Ann, d. Francis, Apr. 18, 1842, a. 10 y. 6 m.

William, Sept. 1, 1805, a. 19 y.

**DANE,** John, Sept. 14, 1658.

John, s. John, Dec. —, 1839, a. 3 w.

**DANFORTH,** Elizabeth, d. Samuel, Dec. 15, 1659. [1660. CT. R.; a. 1 y. 5 m. G. R. 1.]

Elizabeth, d. Samuel [putrid fever. C. R. 1.], Oct. 26, 1672.

Elizabeth, d. Samuel, Oct. 30, 1673. [a. 2 w. G. R. 1.]

Mary, d. Samuel, Dec. 7, 1659. [1660. CT. R.; a. 5 y. 7 m. G. R. 1.]

Rhoda, Oct. —, 1841. C. R. 4.

Samuel, Rev. [putrid fever. C. R. 1.], Nov. 20 [19. different ink.], 1674. [a. abt. 48 y. C. R. 1.]

Samuell, s. Rev., bur. July 22, 1653. [a. 6 m. G. R. 1.]

Sarah, d. Samuel, Dec. 5, 1659. [1660. CT. R.; a. 1 y. G. R. 1.]

Thomas, s. Samuel, Apr. 13, 1672. [a. 10 d. G. R. 1.]

**DANIEL** (see also Daniels), Anna B., d. Josiah N. and Sarah H., scarlet fever, Feb. 16, 1849, a. 4 y. 2 m.

**DANIELS** (see also Daniel), Elizabeth, Nov. 4, 1819. a. 26 y. C. R. 2.

Ephraim W.. m., s. Margaret, b. Charlestown, fit, Nov. 23, 1847, a. 40 y.

Martha, Mrs., Nov. —, 1829.

Oliver, s. John and Henrietta, inflammation of bowels, Sept. 29, 1849, a. 2 y. 1 m.

Richards, Feb. 16, 1829, a. 68 y. C. R. 2.

Rufus, m., b. N. H., consumption, d. at Brookline, bur. Roxbury, July 14, 1848, a. 52 y.

William, at the alms house, Apr. 8, 1841, a. 30 y.

**DARLING,** Susan C., w. Thomas H., June 3, 1840, a. 36 y.

**DART,** Theodore, s. Thomas and Betsey, Sept. 23, 1836, a. 20 m.

**DASCOMB,** Mary [Dascom. c. r. 2.], d. John and Hannah, Oct. 12, 1800. [a. 15 m. c. r. 2.]

**DAUNT,** Daniel, b. Ireland, ship fever, at the alms house, Dec. 27, 1849, a. 20 y.

**DAVENPORT** (see also Devenport), Addington, Jan. 16, 1836, a. 69 y.
Emeline, d. Enoch, Aug. 2, 1818, a. 4 y.
Enoch, Oct. 8, 1823, a. 37 y.
George, only s. Enoch, Aug. 9, 1818.
Joseph, Nov. 30, 1827, a. 74 y.
Susannah, Mrs., May 29, 1841, a. 79 y.
————, d. Enoch, Aug. 16, 1818.

**DAVIS** (see also Daviss), Aaron, Capt., merchant, Oct. 12, 1773. n. r. 2.
Aaron Col., small pox, June 11, 1777. c. r. 2.
Aaron, May 29, 1812, a. 71 y.
Aaron, Mar. 26, 1813, a. 23 y. c. r. 2.
Abigail L., w. Barnabas, Aug. 13, 1840, a. 33 y.
Abijah W., s. John and Locata, consumption, Feb. 28, 1848, a. 51 y.
Alice, w. William, childbirth, bur. 24 : 12m : 1667-8. c. r. 1.
Amasa, Mar. 30, 1800, a. 39 y. c. r. 2.
Augusta Ann, d. Charles and Harriet, May 6, 1804.
Benjamin, s. William, Nov. 20, 1695.
Benjamin, s. Joseph and Sarah, June 19, 1707.
Benj[ami]n, July 4, 1836, a. 65 y.
Bethia, d. Ichabod and Bethia, June 7, 1706.
Bethiah, w. Ichabod, Apr. 23, 1768, in her 92d y. g. r. 3.
Bethia[h], consumption, Jan. 23, 1810, a. 59 y. c. r. 3.
Caleb, consumption, Dec. 23, 1799, a. 27 y. c. r. 3. [a. 26 y. n. r. 4.]
Charles, s. Charles, Esq., Oct. 24, 1825, a. 25 y.
Charles, Esq., Feb. 11, 1842, a. 70 y.
Charles H., s. Joseph N. and Caroline, bowel complaint, Sept. 6, 1848, a. 8 m.
Dorothy, Mrs., Mar. 18, 1820, a. 76 y.
Ebenezer, May 14, 1712.
Edward Horatio, s. John H. and Caroline M. [fever on the lungs. c. r. 3.], Sept. 3, 1816. [a. 14 m. c. r. 3.]
Edward Reed, s. George B. and Nancy B., Nov. 15, 1839, a. 2 y. 7 m. 5 d.

DAVIS, Elisabeth, bur. Dec. 19, 1845. C. R. 5.

Elizabeth, w. W[illia]m, bur. May 4, 1658.

Elizabeth, wid., Jan. 28, 1812, a. 68 y. C. R. 2.

Elizabeth Dorothy, d. Stephen and Martha, Feb. 14, 1818, a. 9 y.

Ezra, Dea., Mar. 4, 1784, a. 74 y. G. R. 3.

Ezra, Feb. 6, 1831, a. 50 y.

Ezra, Dea., Jan. 7 [old age. C. R. 3.], 1832. a. 87 y.

Ezra, consumption, bur. Feb. 10, 1832, a. 50 y. C. R. 2.

Ezra, bur. June 11, 1842, a. 67 y. C. R. 5.

George Hutchins, s. William, jr., July 1, 1840, a. 31-2 y.

Gideon, s. Aaron, Sept. 7, 1775, a. 8 y. C. R. 2.

Hannah, d. Aaron, Sept. 7, 1775, a. 10 y. C. R. 2.

Hannah, w. Moses, eldest d. Ebenezer Pierpont, dec., Aug. 5, 1787, a. 37 y. G. R. 1.

Hannah, s. [d. sic.], Amasa and Martha, Mar. 10, 1798. [a. 1 w. C. R. 2.]

Hannah, Sept. 26, 1800, a. 30 y.

Hannah Mrs., [lung attack. bur. Nov. 4. C. R. 2.], 1831, a. 86 y.

Harriet, wid., d. Corneluis and Sarah, consumption, June 25, 1847, a. 65 y.

Harriet F., d. Charles and Harriet, Sept. 17, 1805.

Henry P., bur. Nov. 1, 1844, a. 28 y. C. R. 5.

Ichabod, Dea., Mar. 16, 1754, in his 78th y. G. R. 3.

Ichabod T., s. Lt., B., dec., May 27, 1839, a. 35 y.

Isaac, s. Dea. Ezra, dec., Mar. —, 1832, a. 61 y.

Isaak [Issac. G. R. 1.], a. flux, bur. 30 : 8m : 1682. C. R. 1. [a. 27 y. G. R. 1.]

Jacob, s. Jacob and Jemima, Sept. 20, 1734.

Jacob, July 4, 1809, a. 67 y. G. R. 1.

Jane, wid., at Watertown, May 12, 1714.

John, sr., Mar. 16, 1704-5. [a. abt. 62 y. G. R. 1.]

John, Ensign, Mar. 11, 1717. [1716-17, a. 66 y. G. R. 1.]

John, s. Sam[ue]ll and Mary, Mar. 21, 1724.

John, Dea., July 22 [June 21. C. R. 2.], 1776. [a. 74 y. C. R. 2.]

John, July —, 1783, a. 45 y. C. R. 2.

John, jr., Nov. 20, 1801, a. 42 y.

John, Aug. 1, 1802, a. 62 y. [a. 63 y. C. R. 2.]

John, jr., Nov. 20, 1802.

John, July 15, 1819, a. 38 y.

John, Jan. 12, 1819, a. 50 y.

Davis, John Heath, m., constable, s. Ezra, gravel, Mar. 16, 1849, a. 69 y. 8 m.

John T., s. Aaron and Mary Ann, dysentery, Sept. 16, 1848, a. 2 y. 9 m.

Jonas, Capt., Jan. —, 1831, a. 46 y.

Jonathan, Dr., Feb. 12 [10. dup.], 1801, a. 85 y.

Joseph, sr. [jr. dup.], Dec. 25 [23. dup.], 1717.

Joseph, May 8, 1814, a. 35 y.

Joseph P[epper. c. r. 3.], s. John H. and Caroline M., drowned in Jamaica Pond, Dec. 28, 1822. [a. 10 y. c. r. 3.]

Lemuel Baker, Feb. 15, 1826, a. 28 y.

Lucy, d. Noah and Elizabeth, Mar. 14, 1804, a. 21 y. c. r. 2.

Lydia, wid., July 25, 1811, a. 85 y. c. r. 2.

Martha, wid. Stephen [w. Stephen. g. r. 1.], Nov. 14, 1825, a. 57 y.

Mary, w. John, Jan. 12, 1683. [a. 35 y. g. r. 1.]

Mary, d. John and Mary, Oct. 6, 1694.

Mary, wid. Ens. John, Nov. 11, 1719, in her 66th y. g. r. 1.

Mary, wid., July 1, 1785, a. 71 y. c. r. 2.

Mary, Apr. —, 1808.

Mary, wid., Feb. 11, 1813, a. 77 y. c. r. 2.

Mary, d. wid. Relief, Jan. 22, 1818, a. 17 y.

Mary, Mrs. [a pauper. dup.], Apr. 10, 1834, a. 70 y.

Mary, ———, 1840. c. r. 5.

Moses, s. William and Sally, Aug. 20, 1805.

Moses, June 2, 1823, a. 79 y.

Nathaniel A. M., Mar. 5, 1731, in his 26th y. g. r. 3.

Nathaniel, Feb. 7, 1775, in his 59th y. c. r. 2.

Nath[anie]l Weld, s. Noah and Elizabeth, Dec. 7, 1778.

Nath[anie]l, May 20, 1804, a. 63 y. [a. 62 y. c. r. 2.]

Nathaniel, Feb. 16, 1809, a. 46 y. c. r. 2.

Noah, Dea., Jan. 30, 1809, a. 67 y. c. r. 2.

Noah [lung fever. c. r. 2.], Mar. 10 [Apr.13. c. r. 2.], 1832, a. 66 y.

Obadiah, Dec. 31, 1775, a. 62 y. c. r. 2.

Polly, w. William, Aug. 4, 1798, a. 25 y.

Sally Ruggles, d. Dea. William, Aug. 16, 1825, a. 23 y.

Samuel, s. Tobias, bur. 8 : 12m : 1660-61. c. r. 1. [a. 2 y. g. r. 1.]

Samuel, s. Toby, small pox, bur. 10 : 2m : 1679. c. r. 1.

Samuel, Aug. 1, 1811, a. 42 y. c. r. 2.

Sarah, w. Tobias, bur. Feb. 15, 1648.

Sarah, d. bro. Morel, cold, bur. 23 : 11m : 1648. c. r. 1.

DAVIS, Sarah, d. Ebenezer and Hannah, Sept. 5, 1723.

Sarah, d. Dea. John and Sarah, Oct. 21, 1767.

Sarah, wid. Dea. Ezra, Feb. 14, 1789, a. 75 y. G. R. 3.

Sarah, wid. Dea. John, Mar. 27, 1792. [a. 78 y. C. R. 3.]

Sarah [wid. C. R. 2.], Mar. 8, 1806, a. 98 y. [a. 94 y. C. R. 2.]

Sarah, wid., Oct. 19, 1822, a. 83 y.

Sarah, May 25, 1828, a. 83 y. C. R. 2.

Sarah, w. Dea. Ezra, [cholera morbus, Jan. 11. C. R. 3.], 1831, a. 79 y.

Sarah, d. Aaron and Susannah, lung fever, Mar. 26, 1847, a. 81 y.

Stephen, Mar. [22. G. R. 1.], 1821, a. 57 y. [a. 56 y. G. R. 1.]

Susannah, [Susanna. dup.], Aug. 14, 1801, a. 65 y.

Thankful E. W., d. John and Thankful, Dec. 19, 1818, a. 5 y.

Thomas, s. Samuel and Mary, Feb. 19, 1713.

Thomas, s. Aaron and Hannah, June 17, 1795, a. 16 y. C. R. 2.

Thomas, Capt. [dropsy of the chest. G. R. 3.], Mar. 9, 1827, a. 39 y.

Tobias, Apr. 25, 1690.

Victoria, d. Charles, Apr. 17, 1842, a. 4 y. 5 m.

Willia[m], small pox, at Boston, bur. 18 : 10m : 1678. C. R. 1.

William, Dec. 9, 1683, a. 66 y.

William, Jan. 23, 1705-6.

William, s. Dea. John and Sarah, Oct. 6, 1760.

————, inf. ch. twin, Joseph, bur. 19 : 1m : 1679-80. C. R. 1.

————, inf. ch. Joh[n], sr., bur. 7 : 11m : 1683-4. C. R. 1.

————, s. Aaron, Sept. 11, 1775, a. 1 y. 4 m. C. R. 2.

————, s. Noah, Dec. 6, 1778, a. 11 m. C. R. 2.

————, w. Nehemiah, of Partridgefield, at Seth T. Whiting's, Oct. 6, 1795. C. R. 2.

————, wid. Amasa, Oct. 3, 1802. C. R. 2.

————, d. Dea. Noah, Mar. 12, 1804, a. 18 y.

————, ch. L. B., July 8, 1805, a. 2 y. 7 m.

————, ch. W[illia]m, July 20, 1805, a. 18 m.

————, ch. Samuel and Mary, Sept. 10, 1805, a. 2 y. 7 m. C. R. 2.

————, ch. C., Sept. 16, 1805, a. 2 y.

————, ch. Samuel and Mary, Sept. 25, 1805, a. 16 m. C. R. 2.

————, ch. Steph[e]n, Sept. 15, 1806, a. 4 m.

————, ch. Charles, May 6, 1807, a. 2 y.

————, inf. ch. ————, Aug. 14, 1846.

**DAVISS** (see also Davis), Mary, w. Ens. John, Nov. 11, 1719.

**DAWLIN,** Thomas, s. James and Ellen, decline, July 28, 1849, a. 10 m.

**DAWSON,** ———, a stranger, at Maj. Whiting's, July 30, 1797. c. r. 2.

**DAY,** Alfred E., s. Erastmus and Sarah, teething, Sept. 4, 1849, a. 9 m. 6 d.

Charles, s. Richard and Julia, teething, Feb. 13, 1849, a. 1 y. 1 m.

Chester A., s. Moses, Dec. —, 1835, a. 2 y.

Jabez, widr., yeoman, b. Dudley, typhus fever, Nov. 3, 1846, a. 74 y.

Sarah N. Mrs., Jan. 1, 1831, a. 36 y.

Sarah N., m., d. Antipas and Elizabeth Newton, consumption, Sept. 18, 1849, a. 35 y.

——, d. —— —, of Dedham, a servant to Sam[ue]l Ruggles, bur. 24 : 8 m : 1669. c. r. 1.

**DAYERS,** Gerald, M. D., surgeon in the U. S. Navy, May 21, 1835.

**DEALY,** Mary E., d. Thomas and Mary, decline, Apr. 20, 1849, a. 7 m.

**DEAN,** Alfred E., m., b. Gibralter, s. W[illia]m S. and Sarah, consumption, Oct. 23, 1848, a. 33 y.

William H., Sept. 30, 1835, a. 30 y.

**DE ARANGUREN,** Don Miguel, of Havana, drowned in Jamaica Pond, July 7, 1845, a. 17 y. c. r. 3.

**DEARBORN,** Henry, Gen., June 6, 1829, a. 78 y. 3 m.

Henry, s. Henry G. R., Sept. 4, 1842, a. 10 m.

**DECOEN,** Patrick, b. Ireland, fever, Mar. 3, 1848, a. 28 y.

**DEGAN,** Paitrick, s. Michael and Catherine, croup, Dec. 20, 1848, a. 2 y. 2 m.

**DELESTDERNIES,** Mary, b. Eastport, d. Gustavus and Hannah, whooping cough, Aug. 11, 1848, a. 5 y.

**DELLON,** Mary, b. Ireland, w. James, hemorrhage, June 6, 1849, a. 40 y.

**DENISON** (see also Dennison), Bridget, w. George [fever and consumption. c. r. 1.], bur. Aug. —, 1643.

DENISON, Deborah, d. Edw[ar]d, bur. 18 ; 4m : 1663. c. r. 1.

Deborah, d. Edw[ar]d, bur. 27 : 2 m : 1667. c. r. 1.

Edward, s. Edward, bur. Jan. —, 1645.

Edward, Apr. 26, 1668.

Elizabeth, wid. Edward, Feb. 5, 1716, a. 91 y. [1716-17. g. r. 1.]

Jeremiah [Dennison. c. r. 1.], s. Edward, bur. May —, 1649.

Joseph, s. Edward, bur. May —, 1649.

Margret [Dennison, "old mother." c. r. 1.], w. William, bur. Feb. 3, 1645. [1645-6. c. r. 1.]

William [A. M. g. r. 1.], Mar. 22, 1717-18. [a. 54 y. g. r. 1.]

——, s. Edward, convulsions, bur. 6 : 8 m : 1646. c. r. 1.

——, ch. still born, Edward, bur. 2 : 4 m : 1663. c. r. 1.

**DENNISON** (see also Denison), John, s. Edward, 7 : 7 m : 1644. c. r. 1.

William [Denyson. c. r. 1.], "old," bur. Jan. 25, 1653.

——, d. I. N., Sept. 4, 1840, a. 9 1-2 m.

**DEPOLT,** Mary Ann, unm., b. France, consumption, Oct. 31, 1848, a. 23 y.

**DERBY,** Daniel, b. Ireland, ship fever, at the alms house, July 9, 1847, a. 40 y.

Ferdinand, Jan. 9, 1845, a. 45 y.

**DESILVY,** George, at the work house, Mar. 22, 1810, a. abt. 50 y.

**DEVENPORT** (see also Davenport), Abby Ann, d. Elijah L., Mar. 7, 1838, a. 5 y.

**DEVINE,** Martin, b. Ireland, ship fever, at the alms house, July 8, 1847, a. 25 y.

Pat[rick], b. Ireland, at the alms house, Feb. 25, 1848, a. 45 y.

**DEVOTION,** Deborah, bur. 20 : 8 m : 1682. c. r. 1.

Edward ["Father." c. r. 1.], Sept. 21, 1685, a. abt. 64 y. g. r. 1.

Mary, wid. Dec. 29, 1713.

——, inf. ch. Edw[ar]d, bur. 12 : 4 m : 1664. c. r. 1.

**DEWGARE,** John, s. Adam and Margarett, bowel complaint, Aug. 3, 1848, a. 5 m.

**DEXTER,** Samuel, m., gentleman, b. Gloucester, consumption, Jan. 30, 1849, a. 53 y. 4 m. 12 d.

**DICKENSON** (see also Dickinson), Dexter O., m., b. Ludlow, s. Erastmus and Olive, consumption, May 16, 1849, a. 40 y.
Louisa, m., d. Abel Baker , inflammation of the bowels, Oct. 21, 1847, a. 28 y.

**DICKERMAN,** Lemuel [Dickeman. Nov. 1. c. r. 3.], 1817, a. 66 y.

**DICKINSON** (see also Dickenson), Harriet L., Oct. 21, 1847. c. r. 6.
Samuel N., m., printer and Editor of Boston Almanac, consumption, Dec. 16, 1848, a. 47 y.

**DICKSON** (see also Dixon), Catharine Bates, d. Capt. Joshua G. and Sarah [cholera infantum. c. r. 3.], July 30, 1828, a. 1 y.

**DILLAWAY** (see also Dilleway), Caroline Porter, d. Charles K., Apr. 8, 1839, a. 2 y. 11 m.
Francis Henry, s. Charles K. and Martha R., ——, 1844, a. 1 y.

**DILLEWAY** (see also Dillaway.), ——, ch. Sam[ue]l, July 14, 1805, a. 7 y.

**DIMSEY,** John, m., laborer, b. Ireland, dysentery [ship fever, at the alms house. dup.], Oct. 8, 1848, a. 60 y.

**DINSDELL,** Charles, s. Charles and Elsee, Dec. 8, 1796.
Charles, Dec. 18, 1827, a. 30 y.
Lucy, Mrs., July 8, 1798, a. 67 y.

**DIXON** (see also Dickson), [William Thompson. c. r. 5.], s. John and Jane, dropsy, Dec. 8, 1846, a. 5 m. 15 d. [a. 6 m. c. r. 5.]
——, Mrs., cholera, at the alms house, Sept. 2, 1849, a. 28 y.

**DOANE,** John, consumption, Apr. 9, 1795, a. 22 y. c. r. 3.

**DODD,** George Henry, s. George W., and Catharine H., Dec. 14, 1843, a. 4 y. 3 m.

**DODGE**, Ann, m., b. Tunbridge, Vt., consumption, Apr. 20, 1847, a. 29 y.

Frances J., cholera infantum, July 27, 1847, a. 9 m.

——, ch. Solomon, Aug. 7, 1846, a. 3 y.

**DOGGET** (see also Doggett), Lois, w. Sam[ue]l, Nov. 23, 1839, a. 44 y.

**DOGGETT** (see also Dogget), Abigail W., d. wid. Elizabeth, Oct. 5, 1822, a. 18 y.

Francis Miller, s. John and Sophia, Oct. 8, 1813.

Increase Sumner, Nov. 8, 1820, a. 20 y.

Jesse, Capt., Aug. 10, 1813, a. 52 y.

——, ch. Jesse, Apr. 24, 1802, a. 7 y.

——, ch. Jesse, July 3, 1805, a. 3 m.

**DOLAN** (see also Doland, Dollan, Doolan), Bartholomew, m., laborer, b. Ireland, lung complaint, Oct. 19, 1847, a. 52 y.

Catherine, b. Ireland, fever, Jan. 28, 1848, a. 15 y.

Catherine, m., b. Ireland, dysentery, Oct. 1, 1848, a. 55 y.

James, s. Patrick and Ellen, dysentery, Aug. 20, 1848, a. 9 m.

John, jr., b. Ireland, s. John, brain fever, Jan. 9, 1848, a. 13 y.

Thomas, s. Thomas and Margarett, whooping cough, Mar. 21, 1848, a. 2 y.

William, s. Timothy and Mary, decline, Sept. 10, 1849, a. 15 d.

**DOLAND** (see also Dolan), Edward, s. Thomas and Bridget, dysentery, Aug. 9, 1848, a. 1 y. 3 m.

Julia [wid. dup.], b. Ireland, bowel complaint [fever. dup.], at the alms house, Oct. 27, 1847, a. 50 y. [a. 52 y. dup.]

Martin, at the alms house, May 14, 1839, a. 38 y.

**DOLLAN** (see also Dolan), Mary E., d. Thomas and Hannah, decline, Sept. 28, 1848, a. 7 d.

**DONALD** (see also McDonald), John, m., laborer, b. Ireland, fever, June 23, 1847, a. 36 y.

John, m., laborer, b. Ireland, cold water, June 22, 1849, a. 60 y.

Thomas, m., laborer, consumption, Aug. 10, 1847, a. 30 y.

**DONALLY** (see also Donnelly), ——, Mrs., b. Jamaica Plain, child birth, Nov. —, 1844, a. 38 y.

——, inf. ch. ——, b. Jamaica Plain, Nov. —, 1844.

**DONELLY** (see also Donnelly), Patrick [Donala. dup.], b.
Ireland, ship fever, at the alms house, May 16 [18. dup.],
1848, a. 26 y.

**DONEVAN**, Cornelius, s. Michael and Bridget, decline, Nov.
14, 1848, a. 1 m. 7 d.

**DONNELL** (see also Donnelly), Mary J., d. Martin and Mary,
whooping cough, Mar. 11, 1849, a. 1 y. 9 m.

**DONNELLY** (see also Donally, Donelly, Donnell), John, s.
Owen and Bridget, decline, Nov. 8, 1849, a. 7 m.
Mary, unm., b. Ireland, fever, at the almshouse, Mar. 9, 1847,
a. 17 y.
Owen, m., laborer, b. Ireland, brain fever, Apr. 16, 1849, a.
50 y.
Patrick, m., laborer, b. Ireland, consumption, Feb. 22, 1847, a.
56 y.

**DOOLAN** (see also Dolan), Ann, d. Patrick and Seria, croup,
Sept. 25, 1849, a. 1 y. 2 m.

**DOR** (see also Dorr), Edward [inf. c. r. 1.], s. Edward, Nov.
28, 1683.
Elizabeth, w. Edward, Jan. 30, 1732-3, in her 64th y. G. R. 1.
——, inf. ch. Edward, bur. 10 : 11 m : 1684-5. c. r. 1.

**DORAND**, Eliza Ann, b. Calais, Me., d. William and Mary.
dysentery, Nov. 7, 1846, a. 3 y. 9 m.

**DORETY** (see also Dorherty), Ann, unm., consumption, at
Lynn, (bur. at Roxbury), Mar. 10, 1849, a. 26 y.

**DORHERTY** (see also Dorety), Mary A., at the alms house,
Feb. 20, 1848, a. 5 m.

**DORN**, Ebenezer, Aug. 8, 1782, in his 70th y. N. R. 2.

**DORNBACK**, Elizabeth, d. Christian and Elizabeth, dropsy,
Jan. 23, 1849, a. 5 y. 10 m.

**DORR** (see also Dor), Aaron, s. Ebenezer and Mary, June 25,
1716. [a. 10 w. G. R. 1.]
Abigail, w. Edward, Apr. 6, 1743, in her 31st y. G. R. 1.
Abigail, w. Edward, June 5, 1745, a. 19 y. G. R. 1.
Ama [Ame. wid. N. R. 2.], w. Ebenezer, Nov. 21, 1782, in her
68th y. G. R. 1. [a. 68 y. N. R. 2.]

DORR, Amanda M., w. Horatio, Sept. 14, 1833, a. 20 y.

Ann, d. [inf. ch. C. R. 1.] Edward, Oct. 5, 1683.

Ebenezer, Capt., Feb. 25, 1760, a. 72 y. G. R. 1.

Ebenezer, sr., Aug. 8, 1782, in his 70th y. G. R. 1.

Ebenezer, bur. Jan. 16, 1847, a. 86 y. C. R. 5.

Edward, Feb. 9, 1733-4, in his 86th y. G. R. 1.

Edward, s. Edward and Abigail, Dec. 7, 1753, a. 3 y. G. R. 1.

Eliza, wid. Jonathan, Esq., Sept. 30, 1842, a. 59 y.

Elizabeth, w. Edward, Dec. 7, 1719, a. 63 y. G. R. 1.

Elizabeth, Mrs., June —, 1831, a. 80 y.

Hannah, 2d, w. Capt. Ebenezer, Mar. 17, 1747-8. G. R. 1.

Jane, w. Ebenezer, May 13, 1814, a. 42 y.

Julia Ann, typhus fever, Nov. 20, 1835, a. 22 y. C. R. 2.

Margaret, drowned, Sept. —, 1827. C. R. 4.

Mary, w. Ebenezer, June 12, 1728, in her 40th y. G. R. 1.

Moses, s. Ebenezer and Mary, Oct. 3, 1736, a. 15 y. G. R. 1.

Nancy Williams, w. Ralph Smith, Oct. 18, 1843, a. 29 y.

Nathaniel, jr., m., yeoman, s. Nath[anie]l and Susan, tumor, Oct. 25, 1846, a. 36 y.

Susan, w. Nath[anie]l, Dec. 28, 1834, a. 45 y.

Susannah, wid. Capt. Ebenezer, Nov. 21, 1769, a. 86 y. G. R. 1.

William, Aug. 13, 1840, a. 84 y.

**DORSEY,** Lydia, d. Nath[anie]l and Louis, lung fever, Mar. 8, 1847, a. 8 m.

**DOUGHTY,** Elizabeth, d. John and Catherine, lung fever, Apr. 13, 1847, a. 1 y. 4 m.

**DOVE,** Amos, s. John and Mary, teething, Aug. 4, 1848, a. 10 m.

Elizabeth, d. Will[ia]m and Mary, Au. 6, 1813, a. 2 y. 4 m. G. R. 1.

Mary Ann, d. William, Sept. 10, 1823, a. 8 y.

Mary Elisabeth, d. William and Mary, Aug. 10, 1813.

Sally, Dec. 23, 1802, a. 44 y.

Susanna Maria, d. William and Mary, Apr. 24, 1813. [a. 4 m. G. R. 1.]

**DOW,** George E., b. Tamworth, N. H., s. Eben and Harriet N., dysentery, July 31, 1848, a. 4 y. 5 m.

Mary, Aug. 12, 1810, a. 32 y.

——, inf. ch. Charles H., Aug. 17, 1847.

**DOWNER,** Eliphelit, Dr., Apr. 3, 1806, a. 62 y.

**DOWNES** (see also Downs), Lawrence, ship fever, at the alms house, June 30, 1847, a. 71 y.
Mary F., bowel complaint, Aug. 12, 1849, a. 1 y. 3 m.

**DOWNEY** (see also Downing), Ellen, b. Ireland, ship fever, at the alms house, July 30, 1847, a. 36 y.
——, ch. Ellen, at the alms house, July 25, 1847, a. 2 d.

**DOWNING** (see also Downey, Downy), George, s. George and Ellen, scarlet fever, Feb. 2, 1847, a. 6 y. 7 m.
Nancy, d. George and Ellen, scarlet fever, Jan. 28, 1847, a. 7 y. 9 m.

**DOWNS** (see also Downes), ——, ch. L. P., Sept. 25, 1804, a. 7 m.
——, ch. Laurence P., Apr. 18, 1807.

**DOWNY** (see also Downing), Thomas, m.. laborer, b. Ireland, consumption, July 5, 1847, a. 35 y.

**DOWS** (see also Dowse), Mary, w. Benjamin, Nov. 3, 1708.

**DOWSE** (see also Dows), John, Apr. 29, 1790, in his 73d y. G. R. 1.
John, Apr. 26, 1814.

**DOYLE,** James. b. Ireland, ship fever, at the alms house, June 3, 1847, a. 19 y.

**DRAKE,** Andrew Jackson, June 13, 1837, a. 3 y. 8 m.

**DRAPER,** Aaron, Jan. 15, 1802, a. 24 y. C. R. 2.
Abigail, w. James, Oct. 25, 1721, in her 59th y. G. R. 2.
Abijah, Dr., Mar. 25, 1836, a. 62 y. [a. 60 y. C. R. 2.]
Ann, d. Richard, Dec. 21, 1702. [Feb. 5, 1702-3. dup.]
Benjamin, s. Nathanael and Abigail, Sept. 15, 1711.
Charles W., s. Charles R. and Mary, lung fever, May 30, 1847, a. 1 y. 2 m. 3 d.
Elisabeth, d. Moses and Hannah, Nov. 17, 1688.
Elizabeth, w. William, Oct. 28, 1761, in her 26th y. G. R. 2.
Esther [d. [Rich]ard and Sarah?] Feb. 7, 1702, a. 8 y G. R. 1.
Hanah, w. Moses, June 9, 1692. [a. 22 y. 8 m. 21 d. G. R. 1.]
James, July —, 1691, a. abt. 73 y. G. R. 2.
James, sr., July 13, 1697.

DRAPER, James, Sergt., Apr. 30, 1698. [in his 44th y. G. R. 2.]
John, s. James and Rachel, Mar. 10, 1716.
John, July 28, 1806, a. 28 y.
Jonathan, Capt. Feb. 28, 1746-7. [1747, in his 77th y. G. R. 2.]
Lydia Frances, w. Abijah W., Apr. 29, 1846.
Marriam, w. James, Jan. —, 1691, a. abt. 77 y. G. R. 2.
Mary, d. Nathan and Hannah, Dec. 9, 1800. [a. 2 w. C. R. 2.]
Mehitabel, w. Nathan[ie]l, Mar. 18, 1757, in her 42d y.
Moses, s. Moses and Sally, May 19, 1796.
Moses, Jan. 21, 1775, in his 56th year. C. R. 2.
Moses, Col., Feb. 11, 1798, a. 54 y. C. R. 2.
Moses, May 19, 1798.
Nancy M., Mrs., June 3, 1839. C. R. 7.
Nathaniel, Dec. 30, 1721, a. 38 y. G. R. 2.
Nathaniel, Mar. 28, 1767, in his 61st y. G. R. 2.
Paul, Feb. 1, 1788, a. 44 y. C. R. 2.
Rebeckah, w. W[illia]m D., consumption, Nov. 19, 1833, a.
    70 y. C. R. 2.
Rosamund, w. Lorenzo, May 31, 1825, a. 27 y.
Sally, d. Moses and Sally, Feb. 13, 1814. [a. 15 y. C. R. 2.]
Sally, w. Moses, Nov. —, 1822, a. 50 y.
Samuel, June 12, 1744, in his 31st y. G. R. 2.
William, paralytic, Oct. 19, 1834, a. 75 y. C. R. 2.
William E., s. William and E., dysentery, Oct. 4, 1848, a. 2 m.
    7 d.
——mas, Feb. 3, 1702, a. 2 y. G. R. 1.
——, ch. Richard, Feb. 6, 1702-3.
——, ch. Moses, May 27, 1775, a. 8 m. C. R. 2.
——, ch. Paul, Sept. 20, 1777, a. 14 m. C. R. 2.
——, s. Paul, Sept. 28, 1778, a. 5 y. C. R. 2.
——, ch. Moses and Sarah, May 22, 1797, a. 11 w. C. R. 2.
——, ch. Paul and Sarah, June —, 1787, a. 17 m. C. R. 2.
——, d. Paul, Sept. 30, 1782, a. 1 y. 9 m. C. R. 2.
——, ch. Moses and Sarah, July 28, 1816, a. 3 y. C. R. 2.

DREW (see also Drue), Albert W., s. Lorain J. and Louisa
    E., inflammation on brain, Dec. 31, 1849, a. 4 y. 6 m.
Enoch, Apr. 16, 1830, a. 27 y.
James W., s. George E. and Rhoda, fits, Mar. 25, 1847, a. 1 y.
    1 m. 13 d.
Lucy Ann, b. Salem, d. Samuel and Lucretia, dropsy, Mar. 3,
    1849, a. 40 y.

DREW, Nath[anie]l, Sept. 16, 1832.
Richard, widr., carpenter, b. Dover, N. H., consumption, Aug. 24, 1848, a. 44 y.

**DRISCOLL,** Daniel, s. Cornelius and Julia, dysentery, Aug. 13, 1848, a. 7 m. 15 d.
Mary, d. Cornelia and Julia, May 14, 1848, a. 2 y. 11 m.

**DRUE** (see also Drew), James, m., b. Ireland, consumption, Feb. 25, 1849, a. 28 y.

**DRUSE,** John, in the wars, bur. 24 : 5 m : 1675. C. R. 1.
Sarah [Druth. N. R. 4.], Dec. 23, 1792, a. 42 y. G. R. 4.

**DUDLEY** (see also Dudly, Dudlye), Abigail, wid., Oct. 30, 1807. C. R. 2.
Benjamin, Mar. 16, 1814, a. 21 y. G. R. 1.
Betsey, Jan. 29, 1837, a. 22 y. C. R. 2.
[Caroline. G. R. 1.], ch. Elijah [and Isabel. G. R. 1.], Nov. 1, 1802, a. 9 m. [a. 9 m. 6 d. G. R. 1.]
Charles D., s. David, July 15, 1840, a. 18 y.
Charles E., s. W[illia]m D., scarlet fever, May 25, 1849, a. 5 y. 11 m.
David, Esq., Apr. 21, 1841, a. 52 y.
Eben[eze]r [consumption. C. R. 2.], Aug. 2, 1833. [a. 62 y. C. R. 2.]
Edward [Dudly. 2d. C. R. 1.], s. Joseph, Esq., and Rebeca, Feb. 1, 1683, a. 12 y. [1682-3. C. R. 1.]
Elijah, Sept. 6, 1805, a. 42 y. [a. 41 y. G. R. 1.]
Joseph, late Governor of New England, Apr. 2, 1720, a. 73 y.
Joseph, Col., Feb. 28, 1827, a. 46 y.
Katherin [Dudly. C. R. 1.], d. Joseph, Esq., Jan. 7, 1682-3, a. abt. 3 h.
Paul, Hon., Jan. 25, 1751, in his 76th y. N. R. 1.
Rebecca, w., Gov., dec., Sept. 21, 1722, a. 71 y.
Thomas, Feb. 28, 1826, a. 43 y.
Thomas, May —, 1832.
William, Hon., Col. of the First Regiment, suddenly, Aug. 5, 1743. N. R. 1 .
William, Oct. 4, 1786, a. 33 y.
William, s. Joseph and Pedy, Dec. 29, 1801, a. 2 m. 24 d.
William, Nov. 12, 1833, a. 25 y.
W[illia]m Davis, lung fever, at the alms house, Apr. 31, 1849, a. 43 y.

DUDLEY, W[illia]m Davis, s. wid., measles, May 14, 1849, a.
3 y. 6 m.

——, d. still born, Thomas, Aug. 30, 1779. C. R. 2.

——, ch. Eben[eze]r, burnt to death, Dec. 1, 1833. C. R. 2.

**DUDLY** (see also Dudley), John, inf. s. ——, bur. 18 : 6 m :
1680. C. R. 1.

Thomas [Dudley, Esq. C. R. 1.], bur. July 31, 1653.

**DUDLYE** (see also Dudley), Dorothy [Dudley. CT. R; Dudly.
C. R. 1.], w. Thomas [Esq., colic. C. R. 1.], bur. Dec. 27,
1643. [27 : 7 m : CT. R.]

**DUFF** (see also Duffa, Duffee, Duffy, Maduff), James, May 5,
1776, a. 45 y. C. R. 2.

Nabby, a pauper, Nov. 8, 1833, a. 70 y.

William, ship fever, at the alms house, Aug. 23, 1847, a. 103 y.

——, w. James, Apr. 6, 1774, a. 38 y. C. R. 2.

——, ch. James, Nov. 6, 1774, a. 7 m. C. R. 2.

**DUFFA** (see also Duff), James, b. Ireland, scarlet fever, at
the alms house, Feb. 15, 1849, a. 6 m.

**DUFFEE** (see also Duff), Mary A., b. Ireland, ship fever,
at the alms house, Aug. 7, 1847, a. 32 y.

**DUFFY** (see also Duff), James, s. Patrick and Mary, burnt
to death, Mar. 1, 1849, a. 4 y.

Mary J., d. W[illia]m and Mary Ann, water on the brain,
July 13, 1848, a. 10 m.

Seria, d. Edward and Mary, bowel complaint, Aug. 12, 1848,
a. 1 y. 6 m.

**DUGAN,** Margarett, d. Charles and Bridget, bowel complaint,
Aug. 23, 1848, a. 5 m.

**DUHAMEL,** Jacques Louis, Monsieur, late of Martinque, merchant, at Jamaica Plain, issue of Aug. 22, 1792. N. R. 4.

**DUICK,** Esther, w. Benjamin, bur. Jan. 3, 1794. N. R. 4.

[Hannah. N. R. 4 ; Hannah Duicks. dup.], w. Benjamin, Mar.
5, 1799, a. 41 y.

**DUMARESQ,** Margaretta, d. Philip and Margaretta, scarlet
fever, June 17, 1849, a. 12 y.

**DUNBAR** (see also Dunbark), Anne Maria, bur. Oct. 13, 1844, a. 7 y. C. R. 5.

Charles H., s. Calvin and Adeline, dropsy on head, July 3, 1847, a. 2 y. 4 m.

Sophia, d. Christian and Elizabeth, dysentery, Sept. 5, 1848, a. 2 m. 9 d.

William, bur. Oct. 14, 1844, a. 4 y. C. R. 5.

——, ch. Elias, Dec. 1, 1805, a. 22 y.

**DUNBARK** (see also Dunbar), Margarett, d. Christian and Elizabeth, fits, Sept. 18, 1849, a. 14 d.

**DUNCAN,** see Dunecan.

**DUNECAN** (see also Dunkin), Mary, d. Brine and Bridget, scarlet fever, Dec. 19, 1849, a. 6 y.

**DUNHAM,** Silvanus, Aug. 27, 1805.

**DUNKAN** (see also Dunkin), Sarah, ch. Sam[uel], bur. 26 : 5 m : 1675. C. R. 1.

**DUNKIN** (see also Dunecan, Dunkan, Dunklin), Samuel, s. Samuel and Deliverance, Oct. 5, 1689.

Samuel, Nov. 19, 1693.

**DUNKLIN** (see also Dunkin), Samuel, 28 : 10 m : 1672, a. 6 w. G. R. 1.

**DUNLAP,** William, m., cabinet maker, s. Moses, consumption, Aug. 30, 1847, a. 29 y.

**DUNN,** Michael, s. John and Hannah, bowel complaint, Sept. 5, 1848, a. 10 m.

William Gustavus, s. Theodore and Caroline M., bronchitis, Jan. 1, 1847, a. 3 m. 16 d.

**DUNSTER,** Isaiah, Capt., Aug. [26. C. R. 2.], 1817. [a. 56 y. C. R. 2.]

**DUNTON,** Rebecca, d. Ebenezer and Sarah, Aug. 14, 1717.

Rebekah, d. Samu[e]ll and Anna, Apr. 10, 1718.

**DURAND** (see also Durant), Ellen Louisa, d. Milton, Mar. 6, 1838, a. 4 m.

——, ch. W[illia]m and Mary, typhus fever, Aug. 20, 1846, a. 15 m.

**DURANT** (see also Durand), Abby L., d. Charles, dec., June 6, 1839, a. 26 y.
Charles, Oct. 23, 1832, a. 55 y.
Charles M., Aug. 4, 1829, a. 21 y.
Henrietta, July 21, 1829, a. 13 y. 7 m.
Nabby Williams, d. Charles and Nabby, Mar. 12, 1811.
——, ch. Charles, Jan. 28, 1830, a. 1 d.

**DURGE,** Charles, b. Italy, insane, at the alms house, Feb. 12, 1849, a. 50 y.

**DURSEY** (see also Dusey), ——, an aged man, drowned, Dec. 21, 1752. N. R. 1.

**DUSEY** (see also Dursey), Mary, June 25, 1718.

**DUTTON,** Emma L., d. W[illia]m P. and Susan M., scarlet fever, May 7, 1849, a. 4 y. 6 m.

**DWYER** (see also Dyer), Rosa, m., b. Ireland, child bed, Dec. 9, 1849, a. 26 y.

**DYER** (see also Dwyer), Benjamin, jr. [from Providence, dropsy of the brain, Aug. 2. C. R. 3.], 1834, a. 10 y. [a. 9 y. C. R. 3.]
William, m., b. Ireland, accidental, June 7, 1847, a. 25 y.

**EAGAN** (see also Egan), James, s. John and Rose, croup, Jan. 21, 1849, a. 2 y. 8 m.
Maria, d. Timothy and Catherine, diarrhoea, Aug. 31, 1849, a. 1 y. 3 m.

**EAGLES,** Jacob, Sept. —, 1834.

**EARLY,** Elizabeth J., d. John and Margarett, bowel complaint, July 9, 1848, a. 1 y.
Francis, laborer, b. Ireland, Apr. 2, 1848, a. 21 y.

**EASTMAN,** Francis S., m., teacher, b. Randolph, Vt., insanity, Apr. 18, 1847, a. 43 y.

**EASTY,** Abigail Smith, Sept. 24, 1800, a. 15 m. C. R. 3.
Abigail Williams, Oct. 14, 1794, a. 6 m. C. R. 3.
Jacob, internal wound, Apr. 21, 1799, a. 42 y. C. R. 3.

**EATON,** Abby Eliza, d. Richard and Lydia A., fits, Sept. 17, 1847, a. 1 y. 2 m.

EATON, Adaline, w. John A., Sept. 10, 1832, a. 36 y.
Benjamin, small pox, Jan. 2, 1721-2.
Charles A., s. Jonathan and Ann, Oct. 22, 1848, a. 2 y. 8 m.
Katherine, d. Benjamin and Mercy, June 25, 1719.
Lucy Ann, b. Lynnfield, w. James L., consumption, Nov. 2, 1848, a. 23 y. 8 m. 12 d.
P., Dec. 23, 1835, a. 38 y.
Robert, s. Benjamin and Mercy, Sept. 1, 1713.
Sarah, ——, 1740, a. 11 [y] 2 d. G. R. 1.
William Henry, s. W[illia]m G. and Elizabeth W., bronchitis, Feb. 9, 1848, a. 8 m.

EAYERS (see also Ayers), Elizabeth [Eayes. N. R. 4.], wid. Solomon, Aug. 27, 1793, a. 64 y. G. R. 1.

EAYRES (see alsó Ayers), John, s. Solomon and Elizabeth, Dec. 12, 1753, in his 2d y. G. R. 1.

EBERT, George E., s. George M., dysentery, Sept. 3, 1848, a. 12 y. 3 m.

ECHEVERIRE, Martina A. M., July 19, 1844. C. R. 6.

EDDY, ——, d. Levi and Susan, lung fever, Apr. 18, 1847, a. 4 m.

EDES, Josiah, Capt., consumption, Aug. 30, 1795. C. R. 3.
Susan, Oct. 4, 1826, a. 42 y.

EDMUNDS, Thankfull, Sept. 3, 1797, a. 31 y.

EDWARDS, Sarah, Mrs. [old age. C. R. 3.], Jan. 12, 1823, a. 87 y.

EGAN (see also Eagan), Rose, d. John and Rose, measles, Jan. 31, 1849, a. 11 y.

ELIOT (see also Elliot), Anne, w. John, Mar. 22, 1686-7.
Benjamin, Oct. 15, 1687.
John [Rev., "The Apostle to the Indians" (ordained over First Church, Nov. 5, 1832). G. R. 1.], May 20, 1690, a. 86 y.
Samuel, bur. 1 : 9 m : 1664. C. R. 1.

ELKINS, Charles, s. James L. and Mary, bowel complaint, Aug. 4, 1848, a. 8 y.

**ELKS,** Christiana, d. Andrew and Christiana, bowel complaint, July 11, 1849, a. 6 m.

**ELLERY,** John S., apoplexy, at New York, Nov. 18, 1846, a. 73 y. c. R. 3.

**ELLIOT** (see also Eliot), Amanda M., w. Charles A., b. Providence, R. I., consumption, Sept. 19, 1846, a. 17 y.
Aron [Aaron Eliot. c. R. 1.], s. John, Nov. 18, 1655.
Lucius Addison, s. Rev. Joseph, July 10, 1822, a. 12 y.
Phillip [Elliott. cr. R; Philip Eliot. c. R. 1.], Dea., Oct. 24, 1657.

**ELLIS,** John N[athaniel, s. Charles S. c. R. 5.], Mar. 25, 1840, a. 15 m.
Martha, w. Amasa [colic. c. R. 3.], Nov. 26, 1812.
Mary Jane, d. Charles S. [and H. c. R. 5.], Mar. 5, 1838, a. 4 y. 4 m.
Nathaniel, Feb. 17, 1843, a. 63 y.
Sarah, wid., d. Jonathan Robbins, dysentery, d. at Worcester, bur. at Roxbury, Sept. 10, 1849, a. 80 y.
——, ch. M., Nov. 4, 1806, a. 19 m.

**ELWELL,** Mary W., Feb. 8, 1843, a. 29 y.

**EMERSON,** Mary, Dec. —, 1830. c. R. 4.
Timothy, Sept. —, 1823, a. 34 y.

**EMERY,** Sophronia, w. Francis W. R., Dec. 21, 1837, a. 37 y.
Sophronia Faulkner, d. F. W. R., Dec. 21, 1833, a. 2 y.

**ENESER,** George, m., laborer, b. France, lung complaint, Sept. 5, 1847, a. 26 y.

**ENTHIS,** Louis Philip s. Philip and Elizabeth, fits, Aug. 10, 1848, a. 1 m. 4 d.

**ERVING,** William, Esq., issue of June 1, 1791. N. R. 4.

**ESTABROOK** (see also Estabrooks), Mary, w. Samuel, d. Richard Creas, Mar. 9, 1799, a. 42 y. G. R. 1.
Mary, d. Samuel and Mary, Oct. 4, 1800, a. 7 m. G. R. 1.

**ESTABROOKS** (see also Estabrook), John C., Dec. 4, 1830, a. 37 y.

**EUSTIS,** Rebecca, w. Col. Abraham, inflammation of liver, June 10, 1820, a. 33 y. C. R. 3.
William, Gov., b. Cambridge, Feb. 6, 1825.

**EVANS,** Eugene F., s. W[illia]m and H., water on the brain, Mar. 3, 1848, a. 4 y. 11 m. 26 d.
John, bur. Jan. 15, 1843, a. 43 y. C. R. 5.
Richard Elbert, inf. s. Richard, bur. Mar. 20, 1842. C. R. 5.
Susan E., m., b. Dedham, d. Joshua and Clara Fairbanks, dysentery, Sept. 15, 1849, a. 28 y. 8 m.
——, inf. ch. Abraham and Ann, Mar. 5, 1848, a. 7 d.

**EVELETH** ——, ch. Zimri, Sept. 19, 1801.

**EVERETT,** Eliphalet, Apr. 11, 1835, a. 52 y.
Lucy, w. Peter, Sept. 20, 1788, a. 38 y. C. R. 2.
Moses, consumption, Jan. 14, 1798, a. 17 y. C. R. 2.
Nathaniel, Aug. 17, 1807. C. R. 2.
Peter, Nov. 25, 1804, a. 58 y. C. R. 2.
——, ch. Peter, Sept. 20, 1790, a. 2 y. C. R. 2.
——, ch. Nathaniel and Sally, Dec. —, 1804. C. R. 2.

**EWER,** Francis G., s. Warren B. and Hosopher, dysentery, Jan. 11, 1849, a. 6 y. 6 m.
Samuel B., s. Warren B. and Hosopher, dysentery, Dec. 25, 1848, a. 1 y. 2 m.

**FAGAN,** John, at the alms house, May 24, 1841, a. 39 y.

**FAIRBANKS,** Samuel S., Feb. 25, 1838, a. 24 y.

**FALLIN** (see also Follen), John, s. Michael and Ellen, bowel complaint, Aug. 25, 1848, a. 2 y.

**FALLON** (see also Follen), Michael, laborer, b. Ireland, ship fever, May 20, 1848, a. 20 y.

**FAREWELL** (see also Farwell), ——, ch. Addison and Malinda, Mar. 14, 1849, a. 5 d.

**FARLEY** (see also Farly), Caleb, Mar. 16, 1711-12.
Lydea, wid. Caleb, Nov. 19, 1715.
Lydea, d. Benjamin and Anna, Nov. 24, 1716.

**FARLON** (see also Follen), Catherine, m., b. Ireland, fits, Nov. 16, 1848, a. 32 y.

**FARLY** (see also Farley), Benjamin, Mar. 12, 1717-18.

**FARNAM** (see also Farnham), Nancy, w. Henry, Esq., May 8, 1840, a. 59 y.

**FARNHAM** (see also Farnam), Benj[amin] [Farnum. dup.], Oct. 12, 1797, a. 22 y.

**FARNSWORTH** (see also Farnworth), Catharine, w. William, Feb. 1, 1843, a. 56 y.
Harriet C. [E. c. r. 4.], d. William and Catherine, consumption, Nov. 5, 1847, a. 27 y.
William Lawrence, June 17, 1845, a. 28 y. G. R. 5.

**FARNWORTH** (see also Farnsworth), Jonas, s. Lt. Jonas, of Groton, and Jane, Sept. 21, 1800, a. 18 y. G. R. 1.

**FARQUHARSON,** John W., s. Alexander and Elisabeth, bur. July 6, 1839, a. 4 y.
———, ch. Alexander and Elisabeth, bur. May 2, 1841, a. 11 y. c. r. 5.

**FARRELL** (see also Farrill), Ambrose, Feb. —, 1839, a. 55 y.
Martin, s. Patrick and Hannah, Nov. 7, 1849, a. 19 d.

**FARRIER,** Betsey, Mrs., Aug. 3, 1831, a. 24 y.

**FARRILL** (see also Farrell), James, s. John and Bridgett, decline, Sept. 28, 1848, a. 11 d.
Mary Ann, d. Patrick and Julia, bowel complaint, Aug. 27, 1848, a. 1 y. 2 m.

**FARRINGTON,** Betsey, w. Capt. Benj[amin], May 26, 1818, a. 36 y. c. r. 2.
George Lyon, Nov. 30, 1823, a 59 y.
Rhoda T., at the alms house, Aug. 18, 1837, a. 26 y.
———, ch. G. L., Oct. 25, 1803.
———, w. Geo[rge] L., Mar. 4, 1805.

**FARROW,** wid., May 10, 1804.

**FARWELL** (see also Farewell), ———, s. Thomas, June —, 1829.

**FAUNCE,** Edwin J., s. Calvin B., Feb. 6, 1843, a. 9 m. 16 d.
James B., Jan. 14, 1840, a. 23 y.

FAUNCE, John E., b. Baltimore, s. John and Virginia, disease of lungs, Sept. 5, 1847, a. 6 m. 12 d.

FAXON (see also Faxons, Foxon), Eleb, Oct. 6, 1820, a. 64 y.
Frances, d. Eleb and Charlotte C., dysentery, at Truro, bur. at Roxbury, Aug. 27, 1848, a. 1 y. 3 m.
Mary, d. Nathaniel and Mary, Apr. 28, 1789.
Mary, wid. Nath[anie]l, Dec. 11, 1818.
Nathaniel, s. Nathaniel and Mary, July 24, 1782.
Ruth, wid. Eleb, Apr. 15, 1824.
Thomas, Apr. 29, 1834, a. 36 y.
William, s. Nathaniel and Mary, Sept. 7, 1785.

FAXONS (see also Faxon), ——, ch. Elib, Sept. 21, 1802, a. 3 y.

FAY (see also Feay), Anna G., d. Cyrus H. and Anna, complaint on the brain, Feb. 13, 1847, a. 4 y. 11 m.
Joseph P., jr., unm., druggist, b. Lebanon, N. H., s. Joseph P. and Charlotte, inflammation of the bowels, Mar. 13, 1847, a. 22 y.

FEAGAGE, James, s. John and Mary, July 23, 1848, a. 1 d.

FEARING, Noah, Dr., formerly of South Bridgewater, June 20, 1824.

FEATHERGILL, Mary, d. Robert, Sept. 19, 1714.

FEAY (see also Fay), Barbary, d. John and Roase, decline, Apr. 7, 1849, a. 1 m. 7 d.

FEHELY, John, s. Michael and Mary, diarrhea, Aug. 29, 1849, a. 2 y. 8 m.
Margarett, d. Thomas and Margarett, whooping cough, Jan. 16, 1849, a. 2 y. 9 m.
Michael, s. Patrick and Margarett, bowel complaint, Sept. 8, 1848, a. 15 d.

FELLOWES, George, Mar. —, 1838, a. 41 y.
George Frederick, s. John W. and Sally, Sept. 7, 1796.
John, s. Thomis and Sally [Rumrill. in pencil], Apr. 1, 1813.
Joseph, s. Nathaniel and Sally, Sept. 25, 1800.
Lucy, w. Nath[anie]l, Esq., of the Island of Cuba, d. the late William Lambert, Esq., ——, 1829, a. 35 y.

**FELTON** (see also Filton), Hannah, June 18, 1807, a. 58 y.
Joshua, a pauper, May 26, 1835, a. 49 y.
Lois, wid. Dea. Joshua, Aug. 15, 1824, a. 74 y.

**FENAUGHTY** (see also Finerty), Ann, d. Patrick and Mary,
bowel complaint, July 30, 1848, a. 1 y. 9 m.

**FENERAN,** Thomas, at the alms house, Apr. 5, 1843, a. 63 y.

**FENLEE,** Mary, wid. Austin, of Boston, Sept. 7, 1840, a. 59 y.

**FENNO,** Joseph, Oct. 7, 1787, a. 18 y. C. R. 2.

**FERNALD,** Guy Frederick, s. Guy C., Sept. 27, 1834, a. 8 m.

**FESSENDEN,** John, Esq. [old age. C. R. 3.], Nov. 16, 1845,
a. 75 y. G. R. 4. [a. 71 y. C. R. 3.]
William D., unm., s. W[illia]m and Olive, ship fever, Apr.
3, 1849, a. 57 y.

**FIELD** (see also Fields), Elizabeth [Fields, w. Robert, Esq.
G. R. 1.], wid., b. England [at Bath, Me. G. R. 1.], debility,
Apr. 11 [Jan. 13. G. R. 1.], 1848, a. 76 y.
Susannah, Mrs., Sept. —, 1831, a. 23 y.
William O., s. Ozias, Jan. 4, 1841, a. 3 y.

**FIELDS** (see also Field), Robert, Esq., a native of England,
Jan. 24, 1812, a. 57 y. G. R. 1.

**FILBER,** Johannis, d. Johannas and Jane, typhus fever, Dec.
7, 1848, a. 5 y. 9 m.

**FILTON** (see also Felton), Nath[anie]l [Felton. G. R. 1.],
Feb. 24, 1807, a. 93 y.

**FINCH,** Samuel, bur. 27 : 11m : 1673-4. C. R. 1.
————, "old Sister," bur. 10 : 8m : 1683. C. R. 1.

**FINEREN,** Mary, m., b. Ireland, heart complaint, Aug. 9,
1847, a. 33 y.

**FINERTY** (see also Fenaughty), Peter, m., laborer, b. Ireland,
consumption, July 11, 1849, a. 43 y.

**FINN,** John, s. John and Hannah, decline, Sept. 15, 1848, a.
21 d.
Michael, b. Ireland, ship fever, at the alms house, June 19,
1849, a. 10 y.

**FINNERSON,** Thomas, Nov. 19, 1830, a. 23 y.

**FISH,** Deborah, a stranger from Milton, N. H., fever, Nov. 8, 1821, a. 23 y. C. R. 3.

**FISHER,** Eliza, w. Amos, Mar. 26, 1811, a. 24 y. G. R. 1.
George Lewis, s. Lewis and Lydia, Jan. 29, 1828, a. 26 m.
Jerusia, consumption, Dec. 26, 1813, a. 23 y. C. R. 3.
Lewis, Aug. 25, 1824, a. 51 y.
————, d. Frederick, Apr. 26, 1847, a. 2 y.

**FISK,** Adelia L., w. Samuel, Apr. —, 1833, a. 38 y.
Ann, Feb. 20, 1776, a. 40 y. C. R. 2.
Thomas, Dec. 17, 1803, a. 59 y.

**FITCH,** ————, ch. still born, Mary Ann, Apr. 3, 1849.

**FLAGG,** John, Rev., Mar. 14, 1831, a. 41 y.

**FLANAGAN,** Edward [Flannegan. dup.], m., laborer, b. Ireland, consumption, [ship fever, at the alms house. dup.], June 20, 1848, a. 45 y.

**FLATURLY,** Mary, d. Patrick and Bridget, Jan. 28, 1849, a. 2 d.

**FLETCHER,** Lyman, Feb. —, 1834.

**FLIENOTT,** ————, ch. Andrew, consumption, Aug. 28, 1846, a. 2 y.

**FLINN** (see also Flynn), Lawrence, s. John and Bridget, dropsy, Mar. 30, 1849, a. 8 m.
Margarett, d. Patrick and Margarett, decline, Aug. 7, 1848, a. 1 m. 5 d.

**FLYNN** (see also Flinn), Margarett, b. Ireland, ship fever, at the alms house, Aug. 13, 1847, a. 19 y.

**FOLLA,** Julia, unm., b. Ireland, dysentery, Aug. 25, 1848, a. 22 y.

**FOLLEN** (see also Fallon, Fallin, Farlon), Edward, [Farlin, unm. dup.], b. Ireland, ship fever, at the alms house, Apr. 20, 1849, a. 20 y. [a. 19 y. dup.]
Mary, m., b. Ireland, fever, Mar. 28, 1848, a. 56 y.
Mary, d. Margrett, fever, at the alms house, Sept. 1, 1849, a. 28 d.

FOLLEN, Patrick, b. Ireland, ship fever, at the alms house, May 20, 1848, a. 23 y.

**FOLSOM,** Harriet, teething, Oct. 21, 1849, a. 10 m.

Robinson, Feb. —, 1836, a. 23 y.

———, inf. still born, Levi G. and Leah, Nov. 5, 1847.

**FORBES,** Elisha, Jan. 29, 1821, a. 47 y.

William Brown, dropsy of brain, Jan. 16, 1817, a. 7 m. c. r. 3.

**FORD,** John P., jr., s. John P., Nov. —, 1836, a. 1 y.

**FOSS,** Albert W., s. Charles and Caroline F., croup, Nov. 10, 1848, a. 2 y. 6 m.

———, Mrs., w. Sam[ue]l A., mortification of bowels, bur. at Dorchester, May 8, 1846, a. 31 y.

**FOSTER,** Almira, w. Isaac, jr., Apr. 30, 1834, a. 27 y.

John, a stranger, Oct. 26, 1806.

John M., carpenter, b. Poland, Me., s. Joseph and Susan, consumption, Nov. 26, 1848, a. 24 y.

Lois, w. Andrew B., Aug. 4, 1817, a. 25 y. g. r. 1.

Mary, erysipelas, Oct. 11, 1822, a. 11 w. c. r. 3.

Mary Conant, cholera morbus, Aug. 14, 1825, a. 13 m. c. r. 3.

Mary Francis, d. Lemuel, Aug. 22, 1826, a. 1 y.

Samuel, May —, 1820, a. 33 y.

Thomas, s. Thomas, bur. Aug. 14, 1663.

———, ch. still born, Tho[mas], bur. 17 : 12m : 1667-8. c. r. 1.

**FOWLE** (see also Fowls), Charlotte, d. Joshua B., June 20, 1832, a. 4 y.

Nancy, w. Isaac, cholera, Aug. 12, 1849, a. 63 y. 7 m. 18 d.

Sarah Ann, d. Joshua B., June 20, 1832, a. 8 y.

Susan, Nov. 1, 1828, a. 45 y. c. r. 2.

William W[hitney. c. r. 3.], s. John and Prudence [cholera infantum. c. r. 3.], Oct. 15, 1826, a. 13 m.

William Whitney, s. John [canker. c. r. 3.], Nov. 27, 1829, a. 15 d. [a. 3 w. c. r. 3.]

**FOWLS** (see also Fowle), [Sarah Fowle. n. r. 4.], w. Jonathan, Dec. 14, 1799, a. 42 y. [a. 40 y. n. r. 4.]

**FOX,** Abraham S., Feb. 26, 1810, a. 24 y.

Anna, b. Dorchester, wid Ebenezer, old age, at Dorchester, bur. at Roxbury, Feb. 25, 1849, a. 88 y.

Ebenezer, Dec. 14, 1842, a. 80 y.

Fox, Elizabeth, wid. Richards, Nov. 4, 1792, a. 58 y. G. R. 1.

Joseph Ferdinand, s. Joseph, cholera infantum, Oct. 12, 1827, a. 10 m. C. R. 3.

Louisa, d. Dr. Charles, May 20, 1824, a. 9 m.

Mary Anna, d. Charles, Aug. 17, 1840, a. 24 y.

Richard, s. Charles and Mary Louisa, Nov. —, 1825, a. 10 w.

**FOXON** (see also Faxon), Seymour, Feb. —, 1829, a. 37 y.

**FOY,** Elizabeth, d. John and Sarah A., lung fever, Feb. 17, 1849, a. 8 m. 17 d.

**FRANCIS,** Charles, Jan. 14, 1841, a. 21 y.

George W., s. Geo[rge] W. and Matilda, bowel complaint, Aug. 18, 1849, a. 1 y. 5 m.

Nathaniel, jr., unm., secretary, s. Nathaniel and Eliza, typhoid fever, Aug. 4, 1848, a. 29 y.

Samantha, May —, 1829, a. 34 y.

William, Feb. 6, 1835, a. 47 y.

**FRANK,** Dominick Carlo, Aug. 22, 1812, a. abt. 60 y.

**FRANKLIN,** Benjamin H., s. Benj[ami]n, Feb. 21, 1841, a. 10 m. 6 d.

**FREEMAN** (see also Freemans), Caroline, d. Leonard, July —, 1832, a. 2 y.

Charlotte Rebecca, d. ———, of Boston, dysentery, Oct. 31, 1821, a. 2 y. C. R. 3.

Lendell E. W., unm., engineer, b. New Portland, Me., typhoid fever, Aug. 18, 1849, a. 20 y.

Sarah, d. Leonard, Apr. —, 1832, a. 6 y.

Sarah, Nov. 19, 1833, a. 4 y.

Synthia, June —, 1831, a. 17 y.

———, ch. Samuel, Oct. 5, 1800, a. 9 m.

**FREEMANS** (see also Freeman), ——— [Freeman. dup.], ch. Samuel, Feb. 8, 1798, a. 1 d.

———, ch. Sam[ue]l, Oct. 14, 1802, a. 15 m.

**FRENCH,** Bela, Sept. 5, 1826, a. 35 y.

Charles, Nov. 18, 1822, a. 36 y.

Charles, s. Daniel, Apr. 10, 1827.

Daniel, Aug. 3, 1828, a. 52 y.

Moses, Oct. 6, 1813. [a. 30 y. G. R. 1.]

**FRIDAY,** Ellen, b. Ireland, w. Thomas, consumption, Apr. 19, 1849, a. 24 y.

**FRISSEL,** Benjamin [Frizal, "a youth." c. r. 1.], Nov. 9, 1683.
James, Feb. 6, 1716, a. abt. 90 y.
Sarah, w. James, sr., Feb. 11, 1712.

**FROST,** Benjamin H., s. W[illia]m O. and Caroline, dysentery, July 15, 1849, a. 9 m.
Elizabeth, Mrs., Dec. —, 1835, a. 63 y.
———, of Portsmouth, N. H., killed by falling from the top of a house, Mar. 20, 1819, a. 40 y. c. r. 3.

**FROTHINGHAM,** Charles, Nov. —, 1832, a. 4 y.

**FULLER,** George, unm., laborer, b. Ireland, cold water, June 22, 1849, a. 19 y.
John, s. John and Bethya, Nov. 3, 1711.
John, at New York, Jan. 4, 1840, a. 43 y.
Josiah, Mar. 22, 1843, a. 53 y.
Sarah Elizabeth [d. Asa and Sarah. c. r. 2.], cholera morbus, Aug. 21 [20. c. r. 2.], 1825, a. 9 m. c. r. 3.
———, ch. Ebenezer, Sept. 17, 1797. [a. 1 y. 3 m. dup.]
———, ch. Eben[eze]r, July 25, 1803, a. 28 m.
———, ch. Asa, canker, Sept. 7, 1834, a. 11 m. c. r. 2.

**FULMER,** Martin, s. Andrew and Mary, measles, Aug. 1, 1849, a. 3 y. 8 m.

**GAFFERY,** John, laborer, b. Ireland, dysentery, Oct. 18, 1847, a. 19 y.

**GALAGHER** (see also Gallager, Gallagher), Michael, s. James and Mary, Mar. 1, 1848, a. 1 d.
Patrick, laborer, b. Ireland, s. John, accidental drowning, June 17, 1849, a. 28 y.

**GALASPY** (see also Gilspia), David, ship fever, at the alms house, July 19, 1847, a. 24 y.

**GALE,** Anna, w. Capt. Isaac, Feb. 14, 1813.
Benjamin, Mar. —, 1838, a. 36 y.
Calvin, Dec. 6, 1805, a. 39 y.
Fanny Winchester, d. Capt. Isaac, Jan. 2, 1813.
Hannah, Mrs., June —, 1831, a. 65 y.

GALE, Luther, Mar. 23, 1821, a. 28 y.
Sally, d. Hannah, Jan. 4, 1819, a. 13 y.
William, Feb. 4, 1834, a. 36 y.
———, ch. William, Sept. —, 1830.
———, ch. Maj. Isaac, May —, 1832.

GALLAGER (see also Galagher), Bridget, b. Ireland, ship fever, at the alms house, July 26, 1847, a. 32 y.

GALLAGHER (see also Galagher), Eliza, d. Thomas and Margaret, consumption, Nov. 30, 1848, a. 1 y.

GALLOOP (see also Galloope), ———, ch. Rich[ar]d, Sept. 25, 1805, a. 2 y.

GALLOOPE (see also Galloop, Gallup), Mary, d. Richard and Mary, Sept. 19, 1798. [a. 1 y. G. R. 1.]

GALLUP (see also Galloope), J. H. E., m., b. Demerrara, disease of heart, May 28, 1848, a. 33 y.

GALVER, Julia, d. Philip and Joannah, canker, Nov. 23, 1848, a. 1 y. 2 m.

GALVIN, Frances T., Mrs., bur. Oct. 17, 1841. C. R. 5.
Mary, b. Ireland, w. James, d. at Cambridge, bur. at Roxbury, child bed, Nov. 3, 1848, a. 33 y.

GAMAGE, Sarah E., Aug. 25, 1845. C. R. 6.

GAMBLIN (see also Gamlin), Benjamin, Sept. 21, 1718, in his 80th y. G. R. 1.
Joseph, s. Robert, bur. Nov. 30, 1653.
Obedience, d. Benjamin and Obedience, Aug. 10, 1687.
Robert [Gamlin. C. R. 1.], s. Benjamin, Dec. 27, 1684.

GAMLIN (see also Gamblin), Robert, bur. 7 : 9m : 1663. C. R. 1.
———, inf. ch. Benjamin, bur. 8 : 8m : 1680. C. R. 1.
———, "aged Sister," bur. 2 : 11 m : 1681-2. C. R. 1.
———, inf. ch. Ben[ja]min, bur. 5 : 6m : 1687. C. R. 1.

GANNON, Ellen, d. Thomas and Ellen, bowel complaint, Aug. 20, 1848, a. 1 y. 2 m.
Ellen, d. Patrick and Catherine, inflammation of lungs, Sept. 12, 1848, a. 7 m.
Patrick, m., laborer, b. Ireland, typhus fever, June 9, 1848, a. 30 y.

**GARDINER** (see also Gardner), Peter, s. Peter, consumption, bur. 31 : 8 m : 1674. C. R. 1.

Sarah, d. Peter, bur. 20 : 12 m : 1660-61. C. R. 1.

——, "aged Sister," bur. 7 :8 : m 1658. C. R. 1.

**GARDNER** (see also Gardiner, Garner), Abigail, inf. d. Andrew, bur. 30 : 11 m 1681-2. C. R. 1.

Andrew, s. Andrew and Mary, May 7, 1704.

Benj[ami]n, Sept. —, 1834, a. 32 y.

Caleb, s. Thomas, Dec. 13, 1681.

Ebenezer, s. Peter, May 13, 1683.

Elizabeth, d. Isaac S. dec., [consumption. C. R. 3.], Jan. 10, 1835, a. 35 y.

Francis, Hon., June —, 1835, a. 63 y.

Gideon, jr., s. Gideon and Tabetha, of Boston, Jan. 29, 1766, a. 4 y. 2 m. G. R. 1.

Henry Jackson, s. Sam[ue]l J., Esq., July 2, 1831, a. 2 y.

Joseph Henry, s. Joseph H., Sept. 16, 1837, a. 15 m.

Joshuah [Gadner. C. R. 1.], s. Joshuah [inf. ch. Joshuah. C. R. 1.], Oct. 22, 1682.

Lucy ["old Sister." C. R. 1.], w. Thomas, Nov. 4, 1687.

Mary, w. Samuel, bur. Mar. 2, 1793, a. 40 y. N. R. 4.

Peter, s. Thomas, bur. Aug. 24, 1653.

Peter, s. Peter, Oct. 30, 1673.

Peter, Nov. 5, 1698.

Rebecka, w. Peter, June 10, 1675, in her 45th y.

Richard Ward, s. Joseph H., Aug. —, 1837, a. 15 m.

Ruth (Babcock), May —, 1848. C. R. 4.

Samuell [Lt. dup.], s. Peter [under the command of Capt. Sam[ue]ll Wadsworth. dup.], slain by the Indians [at Sudbury. dup.], Apr. 21, 1676.

Sarah, d. Sam[ue]l J., Esq., May 15, 1832, a. 10 m.

Sarah, Mrs., Sept. 16, 1832, a. 68 y.

Thomas [Gardiner. CT. R.], householder [housekeeper. T. C.], bur. Nov. —, 1638.

Thomas, s. Peter, bur. Aug. 10, 1653.

Thomas, sr., July 15, 1689.

——, ch still born, Joshua, bur. 8 : 6 m : 1686. C. R. 1.

——, inf. ch. Andrew, bur. 3 : 12 m : 1686-7. C. R. 1.

**GAREE** (see also Gary), Francis [Fransis Gary. G. R. 1.], wid. Arthur, bur. 1 : 8 m : 1672. C. R. 1. [a. 71 y. G. R. 1.]

**GARETTY** (see also Garety) Eliza, inflammation on brain, at the alms house, July 10, 1849, a. 1 y.

**GARETY** (see also Garetty, Geraughty), John, m., laborer, b. Ireland, dysentery, Sept. 5, 1847, a. 61 y.
Patrick, m., b. Ireland, fits, May 24, 1849, a. 3̷5 y.

**GARLAND,** John B. Jones, Oct. 7, 1832, a. 13 m.
Mary A. Jones, d. W[illia]m, July —, 1834, a. 7 m.

**GARNER** (see also Gardner), Abigaile [Abigal Gardner. c. R. 1.], d. Thomas [fever. c. R. 1.], Aug. 28, 1649.

**GARRIN,** Bridget, d. John and Bridget, June 22, 1849, a. 1 m. 14 d.

**GARRISON,** ——, s. Robert D. and Mary, Sept. 15, 1846, a. 42 d.

**GARVIN,** John, b. Ireland, ship fever, Sept. 15, 1847, a. 24 y.

**GARY** (see also Garee, Gery), Dorcas, inf. d. ——, wid. Nath[aniel], small pox, bur. 21 : 12 m : 1678-9. c. R. 1.
Hannah [Hanna Garee. c. R. 1.], d. Nathaniell, Jan. 28, 1670, a. 11 y. [1670-71. c. R. 1.]
Samuel, Oct. 12, 1715.
William, Dea., Sept. 4, 1712, a. abt. 83 y.

**GATELY,** Honour, w. John, Dec. 7, 1823, a. 37 y.
Malichi, Oct. 18, 1827, a. 47 y.
Thomas, s. Thomas and Ellen, fits, July 23, 1848, a. 3 m.
Timothy, m., laborer, b. Ireland, accidental, Sept. 17, 1848, a. 28 y.

**GAVET,** Charles S., May —, 1826.

**GAY,** Aaron, at the almshouse, June 7, 1837, a. 59 y.
Amos M., currier, s. Timothy and Susan, dysentery, Aug. 7, 1849, a. 27 y.
Ann C., d. Aaron, July —, 1836, a. 23 y.
Joel, Dec 19 [21. dup.], 1800, a. 35 y.
Joseph Anthony, s. Joel and Abigail, Nov. 2 [1. dup; Oct. 30. G. R. 1.], 1800. [a. 9 y. dup.]
Leonard, June —, 1836, a. 20 y.
Louisa, w. Aaron, Feb. 13, 1828, a. 47 y.
Otis, s. Amasa and Rebecca, May 16, 1802, a. 10 y. c. R. 2.
Rebecca, Mrs., lung fever, May 18, 1834, a. 64 y. c. R. 2.

GAY, Samuel, of Dedham, Sept. 9, 1820, a. 78 y. C. R. 2.
Susanna, w. Timothy, Feb. 8, 1833, a. 49 y.
Timothy, Mar. —, 1840.
Willard, July 7, 1833.
——, w. Samuel, Aug. 20, 1797. C. R. 2.

GEANER, John, s. Bernard and Bridget, Nov. 23, 1849, a.
9 m.

GEE, —, ch. still born, Mary, June 27, 1849.

GEISON, Eliza, b. Marlborough, w. Benj[amin], erysipelas,
June 20, 1849, a. 58 y.

GEORGE, Abigail M., m., b. Newburyport, d. Horace and
Nancy Norton, consumption, June 28, 1847, a. 50 y.
Henry Phillips, s. Jacob Phillips and Caroline, fits, Dec. 26,
1846, a. 3 m.
James [A. drowned. C. R. 5.], Oct. 2, 1836, a. 18 y.

GERAUGHTY (see also Garety), John H., s. Patrick and
Bridget, dysentery, July 31, 1848, a. 5 m. 18 d.

GERY (see also Gary), Arther [Garee. C. R. 1.], Dec. 17,
1666, a. 67 y.
Deborah [Gary, d. wid., small pox. C. R. 1.], Mar. 8, 1678
[1678-9. C. R. 1.]
Elisebeth, w. Samuell, Nov. 20, 1676.
Nathaniel [Gary, small pox. C. R. 1.], Jan. 28, 1678. [1678-9.
C. R. 1.]
Rebecah, Feb. 19, 1678.
Rebeccah, d. Nathaniel, bur. Feb. 3, 1676.

GHADBURN, Paul, Sept. —, 1830.

GIBBS, Matilda Bartlett, d. Alexander H. and Ellen Mary,
Aug. —, 1821.

GIBSON, ——, w. ——, of Cambridge, bur. 1 : 10 m : 1661.
C. R. 1.

GILBERT, Mary, wid. Capt. John, of Newton, Apr. 6, 1840, a.
79 y.
Polly, May —, 1840. C. R. 4.

GILMAN, Rhoda, w. William, Sept. 8, 1801. C. R. 2.

**GILMORE,** Thomas, s. Patrick and Mary, croup, Apr. 10, 1848, a. 1 y. 2 m.

**GILSON,** Eusebia, b. Redding, Vt., w. Calvin, liver complaint, Jan. 9, 1847, a. 41 y.

**GILSPIA** (see also Galaspy), Daniel, unm., laborer, b. Ireland, sun struck, July 18, 1847, a. 23 y.

**GIRE,** George, s. Jacob and Catherine, scarlet fever, Jan. 8, 1849, a. 6 y.

**GLARY,** Daniel, s. John and Mary, croup, Feb. 19, 1849, a. 5 m.

**GLAVEIN,** Mary, d. Daniel and Mary, scarlet fever, Feb. 28, 1848, a. 3 y. 8 m.

**GLEANAN** (see also Gleanon), Mary, d. Patrick and Ellen, decline, July 17, 1849, a. 11 m.

**GLEANON** (see also Gleanan), Mary, d. James and Honora, convulsions, June 3, 1849, a. 1 y. 1 m.
John, s. John and Hannah, consumption, Feb. 25, 1848, a. 8 d.

**GLIDDEN,** Harriet E., d. Daniel W., Sept. 17, 1836, a. 1 y. 12 d.

**GLOVER,** Eunice, fits, Mar. 15, 1848, a. 63 y.
Hanna, d. Hab., 22 : 7 m : 1654. c. r. 1.
Mary, w. Thomas [rapid consumption. c. r. 3.], Sept. [17. c. r. 3.], 1838, a. 38 y.
Rebecca P., wid. Stephen, tumor, Dec. 13, 1846, a. 56 y.

**GLYNN,** Michael, suicide, Jan. 7, 1831.

**GOARD** (see also Gorde), Benjamine, s. Richard, 31 : 8 m : 1654. ct. r.
John [a young man], small pox, bur. 18 : 12m : 1678-9. c. r. 1.
Joseph, s. Richard [convulsions. c. r. 1.], bur. May 30, 1648.
Phebe, w. Richard, small pox, bur. 28 : 12 m : 1678-9. c. r. 1.
———, "Blind Father," bur. 29 : 7m : 1683. c. r. 1.

**GOARE** (see also Gore), Abigaile [Abigail Gore. c. r. 1.], d. John, Apr. 13, 1642.
Obadia [Obadiah Gore. c. r. 1.], s. John [consumption. c. r. 1.], May 12, 1646. [a. 10 y. c. r. 1.]

GOARE, Obadia [Obediah Gore. C. R. 1.], s. John, bur. Sept. 3, 1653.

**GOARES** (see also Gore), ——, twin ch. John, Jan. 11, 1651.

**GODDARD,** Ann, Aug. 26, 1831, a. 31 y.
Deborah, w. Joseph, June 8, 1714, a. 57 y. G. R. 1.
Ebenezer, Apr. 8 [May 8. G. R. 5.], 1827, a. 75 y.
Ebenezer, Capt., Dec. 15, 1838, a. 59 y.
Elizabeth, June 19, 1824, a. 77 y.
Leah, wid. William, Sept. 10, 1720, in her 64th y. G. R. 1.
Lucy, w. Thacher, Esq., Aug. 30, 1827, a. 62 y.
Rebecca, d. Samuel and Joanna [consumption. June ——. C. R. 3.]
Mar. 26, 1798, in her 12th y. G. R. 4.
Sarah, w. Lt. John, May 22, 1732, in her 56th y. G. R. 1.
[Sarah. N. R. 4.], w. Ebenezer, Nov. 1, 1799, a. 44 y.
Susannah, Nov. 26, 1803, a. 18 y.
Susannah, wid., d. Lewis and Susannah Charmil, consumption, Dec. 11, 1849, a. 78 y.
Thacher, Esq., June 29, 1829, a. 68 y.
Vashti, wid. Ebenezer [w. Ebenezer. G. R. 5.], Apr. 1, 1834, a. 67 y. [a. 68 y. G. R. 5.]
——, ch. Eben[eze]r, jr., Dec. 3, 1803, a. 2 y.

**GODFREY,** Nathaniel G., s. Nathaniel and Emeline, lung fever, Oct. 26, 1846, a. 1 y 4 m.

**GOFF,** Amasa Davis, s. William, Aug. 15, 1832, a. 2 m.
Ann, old age, May 26, 1844, a. 86 y. C. R. 3.
John Farrie, June 25, 1832, a. 4 y.
Sarah, wid., b. Marblehead, jaundice, Nov. 18, 1847, a. 73 y.
Sarah Jane Farrier d. W[illia]m, Nov. 21, 1831, a. 6 y.

**GOHALAR,** Richard, m., b. Ireland, cramp in bowels, July 25, 1847, a. 35 y.

**GOLDSMITH,** George, s. Solomon, Dec. 6, 1835, a. 1 y.
——, b. Jamaica Plain, nutshell in throat, Dec. ——, 1844, a. 10 m.

**GOODENOW,** Lucy [Goodenough. C. R. 2.], d. Ephraim and Elizabeth, Oct. 19 [14. dup.], 1799.

**GOODHUE,** John, m., carpenter, heart complaint, Jan. 3, 1849, a. 43 y.

**GOODWIN,** Ann, Mrs., Nov. 26, 1827, a. 42 y. C. R. 2.
Rebecca, Sept. 27, 1806, a. 19 y.

**GOODYEAR,** ——, inf. ch. ——, bur. Dec. 3, 1844. C. R. 5.

**GOOKIN** (see also Gookins), Edmund, July 10, 1810, a. 73 y.
C. R. 2.
Hannah, w. Edmond, Dec. 6, 1748, a. 23 y. G. R. 2.

**GOOKINS** (see also Gookin), Hannah, inf. d. Daniel, bur.
2 : 6 m : 1647. C. R. 1.

**GORDE** (see also Goard), Joseph, Aug. 12, 1691.
Richard, Sept. 29, 1683.
Sarah [Goad. dup.], d. Joseph [and Anna. dup.], Dec. 29,
1684.

**GORDON** (see also Gorton), Elisabeth, d. Robert and Mary,
bur. Jan. 13, 1837, a. 19 m. C. R. 5.
John, s. Patrick and Margarett, bowel complaint, July 30, 1848,
a. 1 y. 1 m.
William, a stranger, sailed from Liverpool for the West In-
dies with Capt. Robinson, Oct. 11, 1773, a. 52 y. N. R. 2.

**GORE** (see also Goare, Goares, Gores), Aaron Willard, s.
Watson, Oct. —, 1830, a. 17 m.
Abigail, d. John, sr., Oct. 21, 1671.
Abigail, d. Samuel, bur. 5 : 1 m : 1673-4. C. R. 1.
Abigail, d. John and Sarah, Aug. 11, 1691-2.
Abigail, d. John and Sarah, Aug. 11, 1693.
Charles W., s. Charles F., Jan. 27, 1842, a. 3 y.
Charlotte, d. Josh[u]a and Julia, Nov. 3, 1801.
Charlotte Louisa, w. Watson, jr., June 21, 1842, a. 18 y. 7 m.
Ebenezer, Capt., Nov. 13, 1763, a. 74 y. G. R. 1.
Ebenezer, Capt., Aug. 16, 1791, in his 44th y. G. R. 1.
Frederick Augustus, s. Joshua and Polly, small pox, Oct. 4,
1792, in his 2d y. G. R. 1.
John, June 4, 1657.
John, inf. s. Sam[uel], bur. 10 : 1 m : 1678-9. C. R. 1.
John, June 26, 1705.
Jos[eph], Oct. 12, 1803, a. 54 y.
Joseph, Feb. 3, 1824, a. 71 y.
Joseph, premature age, May 10, 1836, a. 67 y. C. R. 3.
Julia, w. Joshua, Apr. 19, 1801, a. 27 y.
Mary, d. John and Mary, Mar. 11, 1715. [1714-15. a. 5 y. 8
m. G. R. 1.]
Mary, w. Jeremiah, Feb. 11, 1766, in her 24th y. G. R. 1.

GORE, Mary, Apr. 27, 1818, a. 73 y.

Mary, w. John C., Feb. 25, 1843, a. 27 y.

Polly, w. Joshua, Mar. 14, 1794, in her 27th y. G. R. 1.

Rebecca, d. John and Mary, Sept. 2, 1730, a. 16 y. 3 m. 21 d.
   G. R. 1.

Samuel, s. John and Sarah, Feb. 15, 1695.

Samuel (2d), s. John and Sarah, June 9, 1697.

Samuel, s. Samuel and Hannah, May 22, 1706.

Samuel, s. Samuel and Mary, Jan. 13, 1730, in his 3d y. G. R. 1.

Samuel, Nov. 29, 1757, a. 58 y. 2 m. 17 d. G. R. 1.

Samuel, Nov. 3, 1814, a. 84 y.

Samuel, Dec. 11, 1824, a. 50 y.

Sarah [Goare. G. R. 1.], d. John and Mary, Apr. 2, 1711. [a.
   1 m. 2 d. G. R. 1.]

Stephen, s. Joshua and Polly, small pox, Oct. 4, 1792, in his
   5th y. G. R. 1.

Susannah, d. Ebenezer and Susannah, July 18, 1769, a. 20 y. G.
   R. 1.

Susannah, wid. Capt. Ebenezer, Nov. 21, 1769, a. 86 y. G. R. 1.

Thomas, s. Samuel and Elisabeth, Oct. 17, 1689.

——, inf. ch. Samuel, bur. 24 : 5 m : 1675. C. R. 1.

——, inf. ch. Sam[uel], bur. 24 : 7 m : 1680. C. R. 1.

——, d. Joseph, Nov. 3, 1801, a. 18 y.

——, ch. Sam[ue]l, jr., Oct. 17, 1802, a. 14 m.

——, wid., Aug. 6, 1803, a. 95 y.

**GORES** (see also Gore), ——, w. Joshua, Apr. 19, 1801, a.
   27 y.

**GORHAM,** Leander V., see Lyon, Leander V. Gorham.

Leander V., s. Henry, Apr. 10, 1840, a. 3 y. 3 m.

**GORMLY,** Ann, d. John and Catherine, bowel complaint, Aug.
   11, 1848, a. 5 m. 15 d.

Ellen, d. Michael and Catherine, decline, Sept. 14, 1848, a.
   1 m. 7 d.

——, ch. still born, Mark and Mariah, Nov. 20, 1848.

**GORTON** (see also Gordon), Elizabeth, d. John, Aug. 6, 1654.

Hanna, d. John, bur. 9 : 1 m : 1669-70. C. R. 1.

Mary, d. John, Aug. —, 1636.

——, d. John, — : 9 m : 1646. C. R. 1.

**GORVEN,** John, b. Ireland, fever, Sept. 16, 1847, a. 25 y.

**GOSS,** Hannah, inf. d. Philip, bur. 20 : 1 m : 1678-9. C. R. 1.
Sally, w. William, town poor of Newton, consumption, Apr.
24, 1832, a. 32 y. C. R. 2.

**GOULD,** Clarissa, d. Otis and Ruth, Oct. 19, 1799, a. 5 d.
G. R. 1.
[Eliza. G. R. 1.], ch. Otis [d. Otis and Ruth. G. R. 1], Aug.
4, 1803, a. 10 y. [a. 9 y. 4 m. G. R. 1.]
[Eliza. G. R. 1.], ch. Otis [d. Otis and Ruth. G. R. 1.], Sept.
18, 1807, a. 13 m.
Elizabeth S., wid., consumption, bur. at Jamaica Plain, Dec.
6, 1849, a. 73 y. 9 m. 26 d.
Jacob, Sept. 25, 1811, a. 47 y. G. R. 1.
James Ward, s. Joseph D., Sept. 28, 1837, a. 7 w.
John, Capt. [fever. C. R. 3.], Jan. 10 [5. C. R. 3.], 1814, a. 41
y. G R. 4.
Otis, Sept. —, 1835, a. 18 y.
Richard, measles, Mar. 28, 1802, a. 26 y. C. R. 3.
Royall, drowned in Jamaica pond, July 13, 1822, a. 35 y. C.
R. 3.
Ruth, w. Otis, Mar. 4, 1812, a. 39 y.
Sally R., d. Jacob and Lucy, Mar. 6, 1813, a. 13 y. G. R. 1.
Samuel, Dr., Nov. 13, 1845. C. R. 7.
——, ch. Otis, Oct. 19, 1800.
——, d. wid., of Dedham, Dec. 19, 1825, a. 3 d. C. R. 3.

**GOVENER,** Mary, unm., foreigner, fits, July 10, 1846, a. 21 y.

**GRACE,** Nicholas, servant to John Newell, Jan. 8, 1682-3.

**GRAHAM,** Elisabeth S., June 7, 1848. C. R. 6.

**GRANT,** Abby B., b. Acton, Me., d. Arvis and Charlotte,
dysentery, Sept. 5, 1848. 1 y. 8 m.

**GRAVE** (see also Graves), John, ulcer on the lungs, bur. 5 :
10 m : 1645. C. R. 1.

**GRAVES** (see also Grave), George F., s. George and Sarah
L., dysentery, Aug. 17, 1848, a. 1 y. 2 m.
John [Grave. C. R. 1.], householder, bur. Nov. 15, 1644.
Mary, d. Thomas and Ursilla, Aug. 17, 1715.
Thomas, s. Thomas and Ursilla, Sept. 11, 1709.
——, "Old Mother." bur. Feb. 24, 1644, a. 80 y.
——, wid., Oct. 11, 1805, a. 65 y.

**GRAVNER** (see also Grosvenor), ———, ch. still born, John, bur. 21 : 7m : 1683. c. r. 1.

**GRAY,** Abby T., d. Thomas and Sarah A., bur. Oct. 2, 1837, a. 16 m. c. r. 5.

Deborah, w. Rev. Thomas, D. D., youngest d. Sam[ue]l Stillman, D. D. [dyspepsia. c. r. 3.], Sept. 9, 1829, a. 59 y.

Elizabeth, mother of Rev. Thomas [old age. c. r. 3.], Dec. 24, 1825, a. 89 y.

Frances Ellen, d. Harrison, Mar. 11, 1835, a. 13 y.

Francis, s. Henry, Esq., Nov. 16, 1828.

Francis, w. Henry, Esq., Mar. 22, 1830, a. 36 y.

Hannah Stillman, d. Tho[ma]s and Deb[ora]h [consumption. c. r. 3.], Mar. 2, 1798. [a. 18 m. c. r. 3.]

Henry, architect, Oct. —, 1833, a. 41 y.

Jane Richards [Jane P. dup.], d. Alfred T. and Mary W., Jan. 17, 1840. [a. 6 m. dup.]

Michael, Sept. 14, 1848.

Nancy, by a fall, Oct. 27, 1795, a. 4 y. c. r. 3.

Thomas, Rev. D. D., widr, s. William and Elizabeth, paralysis, June 1, 1847, a. 75 y.

**GREANWOOD,** James, May 26, 1720.

**GREATON,** Katharine, w. John, issue of Feb. 21, 1774. n. r. 2.

———, ch. Col., Sept. —, 1775, a. 10 m. c. r. 2.

**GREELY,** James, Jan. 1, 1813, a. 71 y.

**GREEN** (see also Greene, Greens), Mary Elizabeth, d. Abel and Elizabeth, Aug. 22, 1826, a. 11 m.

Patrick, m., laborer, b. Ireland, dysentery, Aug. 28, 1848, a. 30 y.

Samuel, laborer, consumption, Feb. 23, 1844, a. 48 y.

Simon, a pauper, Aug. 25, 1833, a. 23 y.

Sukey, May 31, 1799, a. 21 y.

———, inf. ch. Samuel and Phebe, May 25, 1848, a. 21 d.

**GREENE** (see also Green), John, Apr. 18, 1808, a. 55 y.

———, Mr., a foreigner, June 24, 1808. c. r. 2.

**GREENLEAF,** Samuel B., unm., laborer, b. Stafford, N. H., s. John and Rebecca, lung complaint, Mar. 21, 1847, a. 22 y.

**GREENOUGH,** Ada Mariah, d. James and Mary, Sept. 6, 1849, a. 1 y. 4 m.

Anna [Mrs. Anne. mortification. C. R. 3.], July 6, 1802, a. 57 y.

David S., Esq., at Cohasset [hernia. C. R. 3.], Aug. 24, 1826, a. 74 y.

David S., Esq. [ossification of the heart. C. R. 3.], Aug. 6, 1830, a. 43 y. [a. 43 y. 5 m. C. R. 3.]

George, s. D. S., dropsy of brain, Aug. 23, 1824, a. 6 w. C. R. 3.

Jane D. [at Newberne, N. C. C. R. 3.], d. David S. and Maria F., bur. Roxbury, consumption, Mar. 29, 1847, a. 16 y. 3 m. 3 d.

John, consumption, at Havana, Mar. 6, 1842, a. 26 1-2 y. C. R. 3.

Maria, dropsy of brain, Aug. 23, 1820, a. 7 m. C. R. 3.

Maria, d. David S., Esq. cholera infantum. C. R. 3.], Aug. 13, 1830, a. 2 y.

Newman, Aug. 2, 1824, a. 48 y.

Phebe, Mrs., June 18, 1828, a. 43 y.

**GREENS** (see also Green), ——, ch. John, Oct. 5, 1802, a. 2 y.

**GREGORY** (see also Grigory), Betsy [Betsey S. G. R. 4.], inflammation of bowels, Jan. 4, 1834, a. 17 y. C. R. 3.

**GRIDLEY,** Abigail, w. Samuel, May 2, 1743.

Abigail, wid. Dea. Samuel, Aug. 17, 1781, a. 70 y. G. R. 1.

Charlotte, unm., old age, June 24, 1849, a. 86 y.

Lucy, d. William and Lidia, Apr. 23, 1759.

Lydia [wid. William. N. R. 4.], Oct. 5, 1796, a. 63 y.

Lydia, ——, 1832, a. 68 y.

Mary, w. [Dea. G. R. 1.] Samuel, Oct. 28, 1746. [a. abt. 27 y. G. R. 1.]

Samuel, s. Sam[ue]ll, Feb. 4, 1746-7.

William, Dea., Dec. 10, 1786, in his 55th y. N. R. 3.

**GRIFFIN,** James, Nov. 20, 1802.

Joseph, Feb. 17, 1714.

Michael, m., laborer, b. Ireland, dysentery, Sept. 2, 1848, a. 56 y.

Rich[ar]d, bur. 28 : 12 m : 1666-7. C. R. 1.

Sarah, d. Joseph, bur. 11 : 12 m : 1687-8. C. R. 1.

**GRIGGS** (see also Grigs), Betsey, d. Moses and Peggy, Aug. 24, 1805.

GRIGGS, George, Dr., Jan. 10, 1724-5, a. 58 y. G. R. 1.

Hannah [Grigs. C. R. 1.], w. Joseph, Jan. 9, 1683. [1683-4.
C. R. 1.]

Henry Augustus, Aug. 29, 1834, a. 14 m. P. R. 3.

Ichabod, Feb. 20, 1717-18.

James, Nov. 24, 1798, a. 95 y. C. R. 2.

James, Dec. 27, 1816, a. 67 y. C. R. 2.

Joseph, s. John, June 15, 1703.

Joseph, Feb. 10, 1714, a. 90 y.

Lemuel, Sept. —, 1840, a. 77 y.

Mary, w. Thomas, bur. Nov. 29, 1639.

Mary, w. Joseph [d. —— Crafts. C. R. 1.], bur. June 30, 1653.

Moses, by a fall, Dec. 14, 1830, a. 75 y. C. R. 3.

Prudence, w. Thomas, May ——, 1832, a. 86 y.

Rebecca, a pauper, Feb. 7, 1830, a. 82 y.

Ruth, d. John, bur. 28 : 9 m : 1673. C. R. 1.

Ruth, b. Sudbury, wid. Lemuel, cancer, Sept. 3, 1848, a. 63 y.

Samuel, s. Joseph, — : 11 m : 1656-7. C. R. 1.

Samuel, Mar. 14, 1798, a. 95 y.

Sarah Davies, 1st, Sept. 1, 1821, a. 3 d. P. R. 3.

Sarah Davies, 2nd, Aug. 7, 1825, a. 8 m. P. R. 3.

Thomas, householder, May 23, 1646.

Thomas, a pauper, Dec. 25, 1833, a. 82 y. [a. 83 y. dup.]

William, July 5, 1811, a. 57 y. C. R. 2.

——, d. ——, cachexy, — : 1645. a. abt. 12 y. C. R. 1.

——, inf. ch. John, bur. 21 : 5 m : 1663. C. R. 1.

——, grand ch. Mr., Jan. 4, 1774, a. 2 y. 8 m. C. R. 2.

——, w. James, Dec. 14, 1778, a. 60 y. C. R. 2.

——, ch. Sam[ue]l, Mar. 14, 1798.

——, ch. Lemuel and Ruthy, Feb. 17, 1807, a. 3 d. C. R. 2.

——, inf. ch. Charles and Hannah, Jan. 26, 1829. C. R. 2.

GRIGORY (see also Gregory), Hannah, w. Patrick, Nov. 18,
1754, a. 63 y. G. R. 1.

GRIGS (see also Griggs), John, sr., Jan. 23, 1691-2.

GROCER, Thomas, a stranger, bur. 2 : 12 m : 1664-5. C. R. 1.

GROSSVENOR (see also Grosvenor), John [Grosvenor. G. R.
1], Sept. 26, 1691. [in his 49th y. G. R. 1.]

GROSVENOR (see also Gravner, Grossvenor), Thomas, s.
John and Esther, June 30, 1687.

**GROVER,** Asaph C., s. Asaph and Hannah, June 19, 1813.

**GURNEY,** Michael, b. Ireland, s. Thomas and Bridget, dysentery, Sept. 13, 1848, a. 19 y.

**GRUSH,** Abigail, w. Job T., Sept. 2, 1842, a. 42 y.
George G., s. Job T., Dec. 20, 1838. [a. 3 y. dup; a. 2 y. 9 m. G. R. 5.]
Hellen Maria, d. Job T., Aug. 19, 1839. [a. 6 m. G. R. 5.]

**GUILD,** Samuel, jr., m., tanner, affection of the heart, Sept. 20, 1846, a. 37 y.

**GUNDER,** Thomas, Esq., merchant, July 12, 1760, in his 54th y. N. R. 2.

**GUNNING,** Patrick, s. Timothy and Margarett, whooping cough, Dec. 20, 1848, a. 1 y.

**GURNEY,** Daniel, July —, 1830.
Susan, w. James H., Nov. 7, 1811.

**GUTRIDGE,** Elizabeth, a pauper, Dec. 14, 1831, a. 80 y.

**GUYRN** (see also Gwinn), Daniel, at the almshouse, July 21, 1830, a. 4 m.

**GWINN** (see also Guyrn, Gwynne), Edward Horatio, inf. s. G. F., Mar. 24, 1833. c. R. 5.

**GWYNNE** (see also Gwinn), Margarett, b. Ireland, w. Samuel, child bed, June 27, 1849, a. 25 y.
——, ch. still born, Sam[ue]l and Margarett, June 23, 1849.

**GYLES,** John, Esq., May 29, 1755, a. abt. 77 y.

**G——,** Elizabeth, Dec. 31, 1681, a. 80 y. G. R. 1.

**HADLOCK,** ——, w. ——, bur. 23 : 5 m : 1675. c. R. 1.

**HAGAR** (see also Hager), ——, ch. Samuel and Cyrene, May 11, 1818, a. 6 m. c. R. 2.

**HAGBORNE,** Samuel [Hagbourne. c. R. 1.], housekeeper, [father of John and Hanna. cT. R; fever, "upon a deepe could and stopt up with flegme," c. R. 1.], Dec. 27, 1642. [1642-3. c. R. 1.]

**HAGER** (see also Hagar), Philip, b. Ireland, consumption, at the alms house, June 28, 1847, a. 2 y.

**HAINES** (see also Haynes), ——, ch. Peter and Sally, Dec. 27, 1809, a. 3 m. C. R. 2.

**HALAN,** John F., m., laborer, b. Ireland, consumption, Mar. 24, 1848, a. 32 y.

**HALE,** Abigail, w. Eliphalet, Sept. ——, 1829, a. 54 y.
Jonathan, Capt., of Glastonbury, Conn., Mar. 7, 1776, in his 56th y. G. R. 3.

**HALEY** (see also Halley), James, b. Ireland, croup, at the alms house, June 1, 1847, a. 1 y.

**HALL,** Benjamin, s. Ephraim and Thankfull, killed by over-turning of a cart, May 16, 1740.
Eleanor, w. Jonathan, July 3, 1764, a. 33 y. G. R. 1.
Elizabeth, w. Richard, Nov. 30, 1719, a. 74 y. 6 m. G. R. 1.
Hendrick, Jan. ——, 1838.
Hopestill, Sept. 25, 1822, a. 52 y.
John, jr. [cancer in the bowels. C. R. 3.], Aug. 16, 1837, a. 42 y.
John, b. Connecticut, s. Archibald and Mary, rupture, May 14, 1848, a. 5 y.
Lucretia Bates, d. Joseph, Aug. 25, 1828, a. 9 m.
Lucy, d. Hopestill and Lydia, Mar. 28, 1806.
Martha, d. Richard [and Elizabeth. G. R. 1.], Nov. 12, 1701. [a. 21 y. 2 m. G. R. 1.]
Mary, d. Richard and Elizabeth, Sept. 23, 1708.
Mary, w. David, July 25, 1843, a. 43 y.
Mercy, w. Jonathan, Mar. 30, 1761, in her 29th y. G. R. 1.
Rebecca B., d. Hiram and Rebecca, bowel complaint, Feb. 2, 1848, a. 1 y. 2 m.
Richard, s. Richard and Elizabeth, Dec. 23, 1712.
Richard, small pox, Nov. 28, 1721.
Richard, Apr. 9, 1727, in his 71st y. G. R. 1.
Sarah, d. Hopestill and Lydia, Mar. 6, 1803.
Susan, mortification of knee, Mar. 30, 1816, a. 2 w. C. R. 3.
——, ch. Hopestill, Mar. 6, 1803, a. 18 m.
——, ch. ——, consumption, Jan. 4, 1804, a. 8 m. C. R. 3.
——, ch. Hope, Mar. 28, 1806, a. 11 m.
——, inf. ch. C. G., bur. Aug. 1, 1843. C. R. 5.

**HALLET,** Geo[rge], internal cancer, Sept. 13, 1845, a. 61 y. 2 m. c. r. 3.

**HALLEY** (see also Haley), Dorothy, wid. Thomas, Jan. 28, 1697-8.

**HAMBLIN,** Mary C., w. Perez, Mar. 24, 1836, a. 22 y.

**HAMILTON,** Alexander, Scotchman, Jan. —, 1830.
Joanna b. Ireland [w. George. c. r. 5.], consumption, Aug. 6, 1847, a. 25 y.
Mary, d. George and Joanna, consumption, Aug. 11, 1847, a 4 m.

**HAMMATT,** Mary, Feb. 13, 1837, a. 58 y.

**HAMMOND,** Benjamin, Aug. 19, 1838, a. 79 y.
Eliza, Nov. 5, 1803, a. 13 y. .c. r. 2.
Frederick, b. Germany, ship fever, at the alms house, Sept. 16, 1847, a. 25 y.
Isaac, s. James and Rebecca, brain fever, Feb. 28, 1848, a. 1 y. 1 m.
John, b. Glasgow, Scotland, s. James and Martha Hamilton, dropsy, Oct. 30, 1846, a. 1 y. 6 m.
Sarah M., w. Stephen, Apr. 25, 1841, a. 32 y.
——, inf. ch. Alexander, bur. Mar. —, 1844. c. r. 5.

**HANCHET** (see also Hanset), John [Hanshet, "old." c. r. 1.], Feb. 21, 1683. [1683-4. c. r. 1.]
Thomas, May 6, 1719.

**HANCHETT** (see also Hanset), Elisabeth [Elizabeth Hanchet. c. r. 1.], d. John, June —, 1668. [bur. 9 : 4 m : 1668. c. r. 1.]

**HANCOCK,** Belcher, Capt., May 14, 1813.
——, ch. ——, Feb. 24, 1776, a. 3 y. c. r. 2.
——, ch. Belcher, Sept. 28, 1797, a. 2 y.

**HANLY,** Julia G., b. Ireland, w. John, child bed, Mar. 31, 1849, a. 30 y.

**HANSCOM** (see also Hanscomb), John [Hanscomb. c. r. 3.], at Jamaica Plain [consumption. c. r. 3.], July 11, 1840 a. 41 y.

**HANSCOMB** (see also Hanscom), Emaline Frances, d. John M. [d. J. H., whooping cough. c. R. 3.], July 15, 1831, a. 2 y. 7 m.

Henry M., s. John M. [typhus fever. c. R. 3.], July 3, 1839, a. 7 y.

**HANSET** (see also Hanchet, Hanchett), Hanna [Hanshet. c. R. 1.], d. John [convulsions. c. R. 1.], bur. May 27, 1648.

Hanna [Hanshet. c. R. 1.], d. John [cough. c. R. 1.], bur. Oct. 2, 1649.

John [Hanchet. c. R. 1.], s. John, bur. Apr. 2, 1654.

**HANSON**, Charlotte E., b. Saco, Me., w. John L., consumption, Sept. 23, 1848, a. 30 y.

Ellen Maria, Feb. 22, 1845, a. 4 m.

Moses, Oct. —, 1844. c. R. 4.

**HARADEN**, Thomas, Capt., Jan. 28, 1839, a. 67 y.

**HARDEN** (see also Harding), Daniel Sharp, s. Chester C., Aug. 28, 1828, a. 11 m.

Seth, a stranger from Cape Cod, Sept. 15, 1779, a. 23 y. c. R. 2.

William, July 3, 1798. c. R. 2.

**HARDING** (see also Harden), Chester C., Sept. —, 1834, a. 30 y.

Elizabeth, wid. [old age. c. R. 3.], Oct. 5, 1827, a. 85 y.

Harriet N., unm., b. Providence, R. I., bur. at Providence, cholera, Aug. 31, 1849, a. 30 y.

James, Jan. —, 1818, a. 40 y.

**HARDY**, Bridget, d. Edward and Winneford, at Dorchester, bur. at Roxbury, disease of the brain, Jan. 19, 1849, a. 11 y. 6 m.

**HARLOW**, Lavina, Mrs., May 3, 1833, a. 38 y.

Warren, s. Z. and Aveline, dropsy in the head, June 19, 1846, a. 8 m.

**HARNED**, George, unm., b. Nova Scotia, s. William and Sarah B. dropsy, Sept. 11, 1848, a. 19 y.

**HARNEY**, Catherine, d. Thomas and Mary, croup, May 9, 1848.

Hannah, d. Edward and Betsey, whooping cough, Dec. 20, 1848.

HARNEY, Mary, b. Ireland, w. Patrick, Aug. 15, 1849, a. 32 y.
Timothy, s. Patrick and Mary, bowel complaint, Feb. 6, 1849,
a. 7 m.
William, ship fever, at the alms house, Sept. 10, 1847, a. 3 y.

HARPER, Horatio Randall, inf. s. Joseph and Abigail, Oct.
23, 1834. C. R. 5.
Mary Anne, d. James, bur. Feb. 2, 1839, a. 9 y. C. R. 5.
Varnam, d. William and Medelaine, dysentery, Dec. —, 1849,
a. 11 m.
——, ch. Joseph, teething, Aug. 29, 1835, a. 11 m. C. R. 2.

HARRAHS, —— [Harrah. dup.], ch. Elisha, Dec. 5, 1796, a.
3 y.

HARRINGTON (see also Huntington) Caroline A., Jan. 22,
1822, a. 14 y. G. R. 1.
Catherine, wid., b. Ireland, consumption, July 22, 1848, a.
38 y.
Elizabeth, Mrs. [w. George W., suddenly. G. R. 2.], Nov. 8,
1831, a. 21 y.
Leonard H. [Huntington. G. R. 5.], s. David and Jane, dysentery, Oct. 1 [Dec. 1. G. R. 5.], 1847, a. 1 y. 3 m. [a. 11 m.
16 d. G. R. 5.]
Mary, d. Patrick and Bridget, brain fever, Feb. 4, 1849, a. 3 y.
——, w. Stephen, Jan. 15, 1805, a. 31 y.
——, ch. S., Feb. 24, 1805, a. 3 m.

HARRIS, John [old age. Dec. 6. C. R. 3.], 1831, a. 81 y.
Leafe, May —, 1833. C. R. 4.
Mary, d. John, bur. 4 : 12 m : 1673-4. C. R. 1.
Mary, w. John [of Brookline, typhus fever. C. R. 3.], May 7,
1814, in her 57th y. G. R. 4.
Robert, Apr. 11 [8. G. R. 4.], 1826, a. 40 y. C. R. 3.
Robert, scarletina, Oct. 19, 1835, a. 2 y. C. R. 3.
Thomas, servant to John Johnson, 2 : 7 m : 1640. CT. R.
——, laborer, killed by the falling of a large stone while at
work in a well, issue of Nov. 23, 1793. N. R. 4.

HARRISON, Charlotte, consumption of the blood, Mar. —,
1816, a 41 y. C. R. 3.
Mary, d. Patrick and Bridget, decline, Sept. 24, 1849, a. 3 y.
5 m.

**HART** (see also Hartt), Lydia T., w. Peter, Nov. 25, 1837 a. 35 y.

**HARTSHORN,** Francis T., suicide, June 9, 1834, a. 25 y. c. r. 3.
Hannah, w. Capt. Warren, May 24, 1814, a. 29 y.
Jason [nervous fever. c. r. 3.], Dec. 1, 1822, a. 53 y.
Margaret, consumption, Mar. 24, 1826, a. 20 y. c. r. 3.
Rebecca, teething, July 28, 1814, a. 11 m. c. r. 3.
Rebecca, w. Jason [consumption. c. r. 3.], Nov. 2, 1815, a. 35 y. [a. 36 y. c. r. 3.]

**HARTT** (see also Hart), Betsey E., wid. Joseph, ulcers in bowels, Apr. 9, 1849, a. 66 y.
——, ch. still born, Roger and Margarett, Apr. 6, 1849.

**HARTWELL,** George A. C., widr., laborer, b. Maine, s. George and Susan, Aug. 23, 1846, a. 42 y.

**HARVEY,** John, of Brookline, Apr. 21, 1820, a. 31 y. c. r. 2.
Mary, wid., Apr. 11, 1826, a. 78 y. c. r. 2.
Samuel, May 2, 1826, a. 41 y. c. r. 2.

**HASKINS** Elizabeth T., m., b. Brookfield, d. Francis and Sarah Doxcrift, influenza, Sept. 21, 1849, a. 68 y.
Helen Maria, d. Thomas W. and S., bur. Oct. 2, 1838, a. 2 w. c. r. 5.
Thomas W[ilson. c. r. 5.], s. Thomas W. [and Mary. c. r. 5.], Aug. 11, 1839, a. 11 m.

**HASSEN,** Chester, bilious fever [bet. Feb. 5 and Dec. 21], 1807, a. 27 y. c. r. 3.

**HASSETT,** Catherine, b. Ireland, cancer, at the alms house, Mar. 27, 1848, a. 54 y.

**HASTINGS,** Joseph, Maj., Dec. 20, 1826, a. 41 y.
Mary, w. Thomas, July 12, 1818, a. 26 y.
Mary B., w. John [I. dup.], Dec. 4 [15. dup.], 1836, a. 23 y.
——, inf. ch. John I., Dec. 15, 1836, a. 2 d.

**HATCH,** Crowel, liver complaint, Nov. 3, 1814, a. 77 y. c. r. 3.
Hannah, w. Crowel, lying in convulsion fits, Apr. 29, 1800, a. 35 y. g. r. 3.

**HATHAWAY,** Richard, cholera infantum, at the alms house, Aug. 3, 1848, a. 5 m.

**HAUKINS,** ——, "goodwife," of Boston, bur. 25 : 7 m : 1683. C. R. 1.

**HAVEN,** Samuel, m., gentleman, b. Dedham, s. Jason and Catherine, old age, Sept. 4, 1847, a. 76 y.

**HAWES,** Achsah, w. John H., Sept. 8, 1822.
Caroline S., d. Benj[amin], jr. and Caroline, dysentery, Sept. 16, 1847, a. 1 y. 1 m.
Joseph, s. Stephen and Mary, Mar. 7, 1789, a. 2 d. G. R. 1.
Rob[er]t, bur. 29 : 10 m : 1666, a. abt. 84 y. C. R. 1.
Stephen, ——, 1799, a. 44 y.
William E., Jan. 3, 1832, a. 5 y. 7 m.

**HAWLEY** (see also Hawly), Thomas, sr., under the command of Capt. Sam[ue]ll Wadsworth, slain by the Indians at Sudbury, Apr. 21, 1676.

**HAWLY** (see also Hawley), Emm, w. Thomas, bur. Nov. 29, 1651.
Joseph, s. Thomas, bur. Nov. 23, 1653.

**HAY** (see also Hoy), Elizabeth [Hoy. C. R. 5.], wid., b. Wales [emigrant. C. R. 5.], fatigue from Europe, at Deer Island, bur. at Roxbury, consumption, Feb. 8, 1849, a. 66 y. [a. 60 y. C. R. 5.]

**HAYARD** (see also Hayward), Charles [Hayward. C. R. 2.], suicide, Jan. [10. C. R. 2.], 1834. [a. 20 y. C. R. 2.]

**HAYCOCK,** Jesse, at Sacramento, Cal., Oct. —, 1850. C. R. 4.

**HAYDEN,** Abner, June 14, 1801, a. 34 y.
Deborah Wales, d. Abner and Debo[ra]h, Aug. 15, 1800.
Edwin Leonard, s. Joseph P., Dec. 6, 1840.
George W., machinist, b. Exeter, s. Michael, cholera, Sept. 5, 1849, a. 20 y. 9 m.
Hannah, Mrs., bur. July 24, 1844, a. 68 y. C. R. 5.
Sally Wales, d. Abner and Debo[ra]h, Aug. 17, 1800.

**HAYES,** Joanna, d. Owen and Mary, decline, Oct. 31, 1849, a. 1 m. 15 d.
Martha W., m., d. Lemuel and Beulah Richards, consumption, Sept. 23, 1849, a. 34 y. 2 m. 3 d.

**HAYNES** (see also Haines), Anna Payson [Hayny, d. Daniel and Tamson. dup.], Oct. 29, 1799.
Hannah W., d. Opher, dec., Nov. 7, 1830, a. 18 y.
Leonard, m., laborer, s. Opher and Harriet, suicide, Oct. 2, 1849, a. 38 y.
Margarett, m., b. Ireland, child bed, July 7, 1847, a. 30 y.
Mesach, Sept. 10, 1807, a. 30 y. c. r. 2.
Opher, July 25, 1826, a. 41 y.
——, w. Samuel, Dec. 2, 1806, a. 52 y.
——, ch. still born, Nathan, Feb. 24, 1847.

**HAYT** (see also Hoyt), ——, w. Luvis, Oct. 12, 1802, a. 40 y.

**HAYWARD** (see also Hayard, Heywood), John, July 29, 1695, a. 45 y. g. r. 1.
Louis, unm., s. Samuel and Sarah, consumption, Feb. 2, 1847, a. 56 y.
Samuel, Sept. 11, 1812, a. 53 y.
Samuel, m., printer, consumption, May 27, 1849, a. 51 y.

**HAZELTON**, Jeremiah, m., laborer, b. Vermont, dysentery, Oct. 16, 1849, a. 39 y.
Mary P., b. Hill, N. H., d. Jeremiah and Mariah, complaint of head, Nov. 5, 1847, a. 14 y.

**HAZLETT**, William, July 17, 1823, a. 53 y.
——, ch. W[illia]m, June 6, 1804, a. 7 m.
——, ch. W[illia]m, Nov. 18, 1805, a. 6 m.

**HAZLEWOOD**, F. J., dysentery, Sept. 30, 1848, a. 1 y. 6 m.
——, inf. ch. Mary Ann, Aug. 31, 1832. c. r. 2.

**HEAD**, Judith Bussy, quinsy, Jan. 30, 1831, a. 5 m. c. r. 3.

**HEALEY** (see also Healy), John, s. John and Hannah, Sept. 16, 1726.
Nancy, a pauper, Mar. 23, 1835, a. 45 y.
Nathaniell, s. Samuell and Margaret, small pox, Nov. 15, 1721.
Samuell, small pox, Nov. 25, 1721.

**HEALY** (see also Healey, Hearly, Heeley, Heely, Heli, Hely), Aaron, June 2, 1785, a. 50 y. c. r. 2.
Eliza, d. William and Mary, summer complaint, Oct. 9, 1848.
Hannah, w. John, Sept. 23, 1751, in her 50th y. g. r. 2.
Hannah, d. Morris and Hannah, Apr. 6, 1849, a. 2 hours.
John, May — [June 5. c. r. 2.], 1783, in his 85th y. g. r. 2.

HEALY, Margarett, b. Ireland, w. Daniel, at Dorchester, bur. at Roxbury, dysentery, Aug. 31, 1848, a. 22 y.

Nathaniel, June 2, 1734, in his 76th y. G. R. 2.

Rebeckah, wid. Nathaniel, Jan. 6, 1734-5, in her 74th v. G. R. 2.

Rebeckah, Oct. 24, 1798, a. 24 y. C. R. 2.

———, d. Aaron, Sept. —, 1783, a. 10 y. C. R. 2.

——, d. Aaron, Oct. 1, 1783, a. 15 y. C. R. 2.

———, ch. Mrs., May 9, 1790, a. 3 y. C. R. 2.

———, d. Mrs., Nov. 9, 1806, a. 18 y.

**HEARD** (see also Hurd), Sarah N., w. John J., consumption, Aug. 13, 1848, a. 39 y.

**HEARGERTY,** John, s. Martin and Grace, decline, June 15, 1849, a. 5 m.

**HEARLY** (see also Healy), Mary, b. Ireland, d. James, consumption, Aug. 27, 1848, a. 23 y.

**HEARSEY** (see also Hersey), ———, ch. Zerubabel, Nov. 20, 1801, a. 6 m.

———, ch. Zerubabel, Nov. 20, 1802.

**HEARSY** (see also Hersey), John, old age, Dec. 2, 1822, a. 80 y. C. R. 3.

**HEATH,** Abigail, d. William and Anna, Dec. 28, 1707.

Abigail, wid. Capt. William, July 7, 1791.

Adaline [Adeline Maria. C. R. 3.], w. Joseph, jr. [hectic, Mar. 19. C. R. 3.], 1832, a. 31 y.

Ann [G., Mrs., dropsy of chest. Nov. 29. C. R. 3.], 1831, a. 69 y.

Anna, d. Isaac, jr., Nov. 17, 1681.

Dorothy, d. wid., small pox, 3 : 11m : 1678-9. C. R. 1.

Elisabeth, wid. "Elder," bur. 14 : 11m : 1664-5. C. R. 1.

Elizabeth, w. Lt. Samuel, May 17, 1763.

Elizabeth, w. William, Esq., Oct. 2, 1820, a. 52 y.

Hannah, w. William, June 21, 1697.

Hannah, Mar. 27, 1803, a. 29 y.

Henry, s. Capt. William and Sarah, Mar. 15, 1773.

Isaac, "Elder," 21 : 11m : 1660. C. R. 1.

Isaac, jr., Dec. 22, 1684.

Isaac, sr., Dec. 29, 1694.

Joseph, s. Peleg, bur. Jan. 8, 1660. [1660-61. C. R. 1.]

HEATH, Joseph, s. ——, wid. Peleg, stoppage of the stomach, bur. 10 : 10m : 1674. C. R. 1.
Joseph, Esq., Justice of the Peace, fever, May 12, 1752. N. R. 1.
Joseph, old age, consumption, July 6, 1842, a. 76 y. C. R. 3.
Mary, d. Isaac, bur. 14 : 3m : 1668. C. R. 1.
Mary, w. Capt. Samuel, Sept. 23, 1794, a. 56 y. N. R. 4.
Naomi, w. Joseph, Esq., Sept. 21, 1810.
Peggy, wid. Peleg, Apr. 10, 1837, a. 60 y.
Peleg, wound in the knee, bur 18 : 9 m : 1671. C. R. 1.
Peleg, s. William and Hannah, Jan. 27, 1696-7.
Peleg, jr., Oct. 21, 1812, a. 41 y.
Peleg, July 17, 1813, a. 72 y.
Samuel, Lt., Sept. 13, 1763.
Samuel, jr., Dec. 26, 1804, a. 31 y.
Samuel, Capt., Sept. 7, 1817, a. 78 y.
Samuel, old age, Sept. 24, 1841, a. 82 y. C. R. 3.
Sarah, wid. Gen. William, Oct. 10, 1814, a. 78 y. 8 m. 7 d.
William, householder, bur. May 30, 1652.
William, Capt., Nov. 3, 1738.
William, Capt., issue of June 13, 1789, a. 34 y. N. R. 3.
William, Capt., June 6, 1798.
William, Gen., Jan. 24, 1814, a. 76 y. 10 m. 11 d.
William, jr., Sept. 3, 1817, a. 24 y.
William, Esq., Mar. 8, 1836, a. 74 y.
William Alfred, s. Joseph and Naomi, Nov. 25, 1805. [a. 17 m. dup.]
——, inf. ch. Isaack, jr., bur. June 2, 1651.
——, inf. ch. Isaac, jr., bur. 2 : 11m : 1651-2. C. R. 1.
——, "aged," wid. Will[iam], bur. 15 : 10m : 1659. C. R. 1.
——, inf. ch. Isaac, bur. 6 : 11m : 1667-8. C. R. 1.
——, ch. Jos[eph], Nov. 26, 1805, a. 17 m.
——, w. Peleg, Dec. 25, 1806, a. 67 y.

HECTOR, Charles, s. Thomas and Seria, decline, Apr. 8, 1849, a. 3 m.

HEELEY (see also Healy), Timothy, Oct. 9, 1790.

HEELY (see also Healy), Rebecca Mason, d. Benj[amin] and Sarah, Oct. 6, 1800.
Timothy, July 23, 1800, a. 37 y.

HELI (see also Healy), ——, childbirth, 8 : 9m : 1649. C. R. 1.

**HELY** (see also Healy), Samuel, Nov. 25, 1721, in his 33d y. G. R. 1.

Samuell, s. William, Jan. 15, 1646.

**HEMINGWAY** (see also Hemmenway, Hemmingway, Heminway, Hinningway), John, Oct. 4, 1723.

Marah, d. Raph, bur. Apr. 4, 1634.

Mary, w. Joshua, sr., May 5, 1703.

Ralph, June 1, 1699.

**HEMINWAY** (see also Hemingway), John, inf. s. John, bur. latter end of 12 m : 1687-8. C. R. 1.

**HEMMEN** (see also Hemmer), Amelia, b. Germany, d. Charles and Phillipine, scarlet fever, Aug. 9, 1849, a. 4 y.

**HEMMENWAY** (see also Hemingway), Elisebeth, wid. Ralph, sr., Jan. 2, 1684-5, a. 82 y.

Mary, Mrs., at W[illia]m May's, Apr. 10, 1819, a. 62 y.

Ruth, July 17, 1684.

Sarah, d. John, Feb. 26, 1687-8.

**HEMMER** (see also Hemmen), Maria, b. Germany, wid. Christopher, old age, Apr. 24, 1849, a. 77 y.

**HEMMINGWAY** (see also Hemingway), Marah, d. Raph, bur. 4 : 3m : 1635. CT. R.

Mary, d. Raph, bur. Dec. 21, 1653.

**HENDERSON,** Catherine Leland, at Portland, Oregon, Apr. 1, 1808, aged 89 y. 6 m. P. R. 4.

Joseph, laborer, consumption, Feb. 25, 1844, a. 62 y.

Nabby, w. Nathan, Aug. 9, 1801, a. 28 y.

William, s. James and Polly, Sept. 19, 1799, a. 13 m. G. R. 1.

**HENDEY,** Daniel W., at Mobile, ——, 1832, a. 26 y.

**HENDLEY,** Mary, w. William, Nov. 8, 1814, a. 63 y.

Mary, Mrs. [w. Jacob. G. R. 5.], Jan. 5 [Feb. 5. G. R. 1.], 1830, a. 52 y.

**HENDRESCH,** Christian, s. Martin, bowel complaint, Aug. 15, 1848, a. 4 y.

**HENERY,** Eliza, b. Ireland, w. James, cholera, July 26, 1849, a. 27 y.

Thomas, s. John and Catherine, scarlet fever, Nov. 11, 1849, a. 2 y. 6 m.

**HENNESY,** Joseph, s. W[illia]m and Julia, Mar. 4, 1849, a. 1 d.

**HENSHAW,** Elizabeth F., b. Dover, w. Charles, child bed, Mar. 9, 1849, a. 25 y. 6 m.
Herbert, s. Charles and Elizabeth, Feb. 26, 1849, a. 3 d.
John, Sept. 21, 1721 [1821?], a. 72 y. c. r. 2.
John, consumption, Feb. 16, 1833, a. 41 y. c. r. 3.
Sarah, wid., Feb. 22, 1825, a. 57 y. [a. 58 y. c. r. 2.]
———, ch. John and Sarah, Oct. 24, 1795, a. 3 d. c. r. 2.
———, ch. John and Sarah, May 18, 1802, a. 6 y. c. r. 2.
———, ch. John and Sarah, Nov. 5, 1808, a. 1 w. c. r. 2.

**HERING** (see also Herring), Ezra T., consumption, Sept. 14, 1848, a. 33 y.

**HERMANS,** Ellen A., d. Ferdinand and Mercy, disease of the brain, Oct. 5, 1848, a. 6 y.

**HERRING** (see also Hering), James, Mar. 18, 1731-2. [in his 76th y. g. r. 2.]
James, May 5, 1779, a. 76 y. c. r. 2.
James, Mar. 29, 1798. c. r. 2.
Jesse, Feb. 8, 1816, a. 48 y. c. r. 2.
Lemuel [Harring. g. r. 4.], consumption, June 22, 1815, a. 20 y. c. r. 3.
Sarah, w. James, Dec. 2, 1721.
Sarah, w. James, June 18, 1724, in her 51st y. g. r. 2.
Thankful, wid., May 25, 1826, a. 78 y. c. r. 2.
———, w. James, June 23, 1774. c. r. 2.

**HERSEY** (see also Hearsey, Hearsy), Ebenezer, Aug. 15, 1829, a. 48 y.
Elizabeth, w. Zerubbabel, Nov. 18, 1819, a. 38 y. g. r. 1.
Freeman, Feb. 11, 1826, a. 22 y. g. r. 5.
Harriet, b. Rutland, w. Sam[ue]l M., paralytic, Sept. 27, 1848, a. 41 y.
Mary, Mrs., Nov. —, 1832, a. 80 y.

**HEWES,** Ann Fry, d. Shubael, grand d. Richard Fry, Esq., formerly of London, Eng., Oct. 12, 1820.
Joshuah [Joshua. c. r. 1.], s. Joshuah [and —— Gould, convulsions. c. r. 1.], bur. Dec. 20, 1639.
Thomas F. C., s. John M., Nov. 11, 1840, a. 3 w.

**HEWINS,** Keziah, affection of kidneys, Jan. 29, 1844, a. 67 y. c. R. 3.

**HEYWOOD** (see also Hayward), Mary Elizabeth [Haywood. c. R. 3.], d. Sam[ue]l P. and Sarah H., [whooping cough, Sept. 6. c. R. 3.], 1828, a. 14 m.

**HIBBERD,** ——, ch. M., fits, July 15, 1846, a. 1 y. 6 m.

**HICKS,** John, Jan. —, 1827, a. 34 y.

**HICKSON,** Abigail Cooper, wid., Oct. 6, 1826, a. 70 y. c. R. 2.

**HIDES** (see also Hyde), Mary wid., b. Germany, consumption, June 18, 1848, a. 66 y.

**HILBERT,** Abbot A., s. Anthony and Henrietta, consumption, May 20, 1849, a. 7 y. 2 m.
Edward F., s. Anthony and Henrietta, bilious fever, Nov. 14, 1849, a. 2 y. 8 m.

**HILDRETH** (see also Hildrith), William N., s. William, July 20, 1838, a. 2 1-2 y.

**HILDRITH** (see also Hildreth), John W., s. W[illia]m, Aug. 4, 1839, a. 4 m.
William, Aug. 29, 1840, a. 33 y.

**HILL,** Ann Maria, w. George, Mar. 2, 1838, a. 27 y.
Charles, s. Sylvester and Mary, bowel complaint, Aug. 12, 1848, a. 4 m. 15 d.
Martha Louise, typhus fever, June 24, 1835, a. 3 y. c. R. 3.
Oliver, May 12, 1820, a. 72 y.
Richard, old age, Sept. 9, 1846, a. 84 y.
Susan Bosson, d. Jonathan, Jan. 13, 1827, a. 8 m.
Thomas M. B., s. Jonathan, Oct. 17, 1826, a. 17 y.

**HILLEY,** John, b. Ireland, heart complaint, Mar. 5, 1848, a. 20 y.

**HILLIARD,** Thomas, unm., b. South Carolina, fever, Aug. 27, 1847, a. 22 y.

**HILLMAN** (see also Hillsman), Frederick, b. Germany, s. Henry and Caroline, measles, June 6, 1848, a. 6 y.
Henry, b. Germany, dropsy, at the alms house, Nov. 10, 1849, a. 7 y.

HILLMAN, Mary, d. Henry and Charlotte, dysentery, Aug. 16, 1848, a. 9 m.

HILLSMAN (see also Hillman), Charlotte, m., b. Germany, dysentery, Oct. 27, 1849, a. 32 y.

HILTON, Lydia, Mrs., Oct. —, 1837, a. 87 y.

HINDRES, Ferdinand, s. Ferdinand and Amelia, decline, Oct. 22, 1848, a. 3 m.

HINERSON, Mary, b. England, d. Samuel, measles, June 28, 1848, a. 2 y.

HINGS, Phillip, s. Michael and Barbary, dysentery, Oct. 8, 1848, a. 10 m.

HINNINGWAY (see also Hemingway), Ruth, bur. 18:5m: 1684. C. R. 1.
———, "old Widdow," bur. 3:12m:1685-6. C. R. 1.

HOAS, ———, inf. ch. John and Winderlin, May 17, 1847, a. 7 d.

HOBART (see also Hobert), Betsey, w. Peter, Aug. 27, 1835, a. 52 y.
Mary, at New Ipswich, N. H., Sept. 17, 1842, C. R. 7.

HOBBS, Ellen, m., b. Ireland, child bed, Nov. 19, 1847, a. 33 y.
William F., s. Robert L. and Mary Ann, burnt, July 16, 1848, a. 5 y.

HOBERT (see also Hobart), Sarah F., w. Albert, Oct. 9, 1838, a. 35 y.

HODGDON, A. P., ch. Abraham and Emily, Apr. 3, 1836, a. 3 y. 9 m. G. R. 4.
Abram Parker, lung fever, Apr. 24, 1835, a. 4 y. C. R. 3.
Emily, w. Abraham [paralytic. C. R. 3.], July 1, 1843, a. 41 y. G. R. 4. [a. 40 y. C. R. 3.]
J. W., ch. Abraham and Emily, July 7, 1842, a. 2 y. G. R. 4.
Parker E., b. Lebanon, Me., apoplexy, June 13, 1849, a. 77 y. 9 m. 15 d.

HODGES, George C., m., clerk, b. Rutland, s. Jeremiah and Relief, rupture of blood vessel, Oct. 10, 1847, a. 42 y.

HODGES, Martha C., m., b. Lansingburg, N. Y., d. Samuel and Sally Ellis, bur. Providence, R. I., cholera, Aug. 29, a. 42 y.

HOFFMAN (see also Hofman), W[illia]m, s. Barbary, bowel complaint, Aug. 20, 1849, a. 6 m.

HOFMAN (see also Hoffman), Andrew, widr., laborer, b. Germany, gravel, July 17, 1847, a. 73 y.

HOGAN, Joanna, d. Philip and Joanna, decline, Nov. 22, 1848, a. 22 d.

John, s. Ellen, measles, July 20, 1849, a. 6 m.

HOLAHAN, Christopher, m., b. Ireland, consumption, Feb. 16, 1849, a. 42 y.

HOLAND (see also Holland), Josiah, Sept. 25, 1729, a. 83 y. G. R. 1.

HOLBROKE (see also Holbrook), John [Holbrook, small pox. C. R. 1.], Dec. 25, 1678.

HOLBROOK (see also Holbroke, Holbrooke, Holdbrook), Daniell, drowned, July 31, 1719.

Daniel, Oct. 7, 1827, a. 83 y.

Elizabeth, d. Ralph and Dorothy, Aug. 31, 1747, a. 1 y. 6 m. G. R. 1.

Elizabeth, d. Amos [inflammation of bowels. C. R. 3.], July 11, 1827, a. 17 y.

Harriot, erysipelas, Jan. 22, 1816, a. 5 w. C. R. 3.

Henry E., s. Theodore and Rachel B., convulsions May 13, 1849, a. 8 y. 9 m.

John, inf. s. John, bur. 27 : 6m : 1687. C. R. 1.

John, Sept. 26, 1735. [a. 71 y. G. R. 1.]

Mary, wid. John, Apr. 24, 1751, in her 87th y. G. R. 1.

Parker Craft, dysentery, Sept. 26, 1814, a. 23 m. C. R. 3.

Ralph, jr., s. Ralph and Dorothy, Aug. 23, 1747, a. 3 y. 6 m. G. R. 1.

Sally, w. Ezra, June 11, 1827, a. 45 y.

Sarah, complication of disorders occasioned by intemperance, [bet. Mar. and May], 1827, a. 45 y. C. R. 3.

Stephen [H., s. Amos. C. R. 3.], drowned [in wreck of the "Massasoit" from Calcutta off Point Allerton. C. R. 3.], Dec. 15, 1844, a. 24 y. [a. 23 y. C. R. 3. ; a. 22 y. C. R. 5.]

Willard, at the alms house, Aug. 3, 1840, a. 40 y.

**HOLBROOKE** (see also Holbrook), Abel, s. Daniel and Elizabeth, Apr. 27, 1706.

Abigail, w. Daniel, Nov. 5, 1702.

Daniel, s. Daniel and Elisabeth [Elizabeth. dup.], July 12, 1697.

Elizabeth, d. Daniel and Elizabeth, Nov. 7, 1702.

Elizabeth, d. John and Mary, Feb. 5, 1715-16.

Mary [Holbrook. G. R. 1.], d. John and Mary, Sept. 7, 1712. [a. 21 y. 11 m. 15 d. G. R. 1.]

Samuel, s. Daniel and Elizabeth, July 25, 1714.

Sarah, d. John and Mary, Oct. 13, 1704.

Sarah, d. Daniel and Elizabeth, Sept. 12, 1714.

**HOLDBROOK** (see also Holbrook), Daniel, injured by a knife in his pocket as he fell, going over a wall, bur. 23: [7m?] 1673. C. R. 1.

**HOLDEN,** Mary Ann J., Nov. 17, 1831, a. 25 y.

**HOLDRIDGE,** Sarah, Aug. 3, 1707.

**HOLLAND** (see also Holand), John, b. Ireland, ship fever, at the alms house, May 2, 1849, a. 31 y.

Thomas, m., b. Ireland, fever, May 1, 1849, a. 32 y.

**HOLLOWAY,** Jarrott, [Jarritt, a native of England, Sept. 29. G. R. 5.], 1842, a. over 80 y. [a. 84 1-2 y. G. R. 5.; a. 85 y. C. R. 5.]

[Sarah, a native of England. G. R. 5.], w. Jarett, Dec. 19, 1831. [a. 64 y. G. R. 5.]

**HOLMES** (see also Holms, Homes), Benjamin D., Jan. —, 1840. C. R. 4.

Debora, d. George, Mar. —, 1646.

Deborah [Holms. CT. R.], d. George, bur. Feb. 5, 1641.

Deborah, inf. d. ————, bur. 29: 7m: 1646. C. R. 1.

Elizabeth, w. W[illia]m [consumption. C. R. 3.], Jan. 20, 1835, a. 45 y. [a. 50 y. G. R. 4.]

George, householder [fever. C. R. 1.], bur. Dec. 18, 1645. [1645-6. C. R. 1.]

Mary, Mrs., apoplexy, at Dorchester, Mar. 16, 1834, a. 74 y. C. R. 2.

Nathanael, Feb. 12, 1712.

Nathaniel, jr., June 12, 1699.

————, inf. ch. George, 3: 1m: 1641-2. C. R. 1.

HOLMES, ——, inf. ch. George, bur. Oct. 28, 1642.
——, inf. ch. George, bur. Oct. 30, 1642.
——, w. Nathaniel, Mar. 11, 1695-6.
——, ch. Norman, Oct. 6, 1803, a. 10 m.

**HOLMS** (see also Holmes), ——, ch. Nor[ma]n, Dec. 19, 1807, a. 5 m.

**HOLT,** Ruth K., Jan. —, 1839, a. 29 y.

**HOMAN** (see also Homans), Mary, m., b. Germany, lung complaint, Nov. 11, 1847, a. 36 y.

**HOMANS** (see also Homan), Henry, b. Germany, s. Frederick and Mary, consumption, July 20, 1849, a. 4 y.
Mary, bur. Mar. 7, 1849, a. 75 y. C. R. 5.

**HOMER,** Josephine, d. George and Francis, lung fever, May 10, 1849, a. 1 y. 2 m.

**HOMES** (see also Holmes), ——, wid., bur. 6 : 11m : 1662-3.
C. R. 1.
——, inf. ch. Nath[aniel], cripple, bur. 18 : 9m : 1671. G. R. 1.

**HOMMIGERS,** ——, w. Thomas, July 26, 1807.

**HOPKINS,** Ebenezer, s. William, bur. 19 : 8m : 1674. C. R. 1.
Hannah, w. Willia[m], small pox, 5 : 11m : 1678-9. C. R. 1.
Mary, small pox, bur. 8 : 12m : 1678-9. C. R. 1.
Thomas under the command of Capt. Sam[ue]ll Wadsworth, slain by the Indians at Sudbury, Apr. 21, 1676.
William, sr., Nov. 8, 1688.

**HORN,** Abigail, w. Richard, Sept. 1, 1840, a. 23 y.
Richard, m., carpenter, b. Lebanon, Me., s. Richard and Sarah, paralytic, Apr. 26, 1847, a. 40 y.
——, inf. ch. Richard, Sept. —, 1837.

**HOUGHTON,** Abigail, Mrs., Dec. 15, 1838, a. 83 y.
Adeline, d. Jorn, dec., Jan. 11, 1836, a. 18 y.
Elijah, apoplexy, Apr. 7, 1822, a. 24 y. C. R. 3.
Eliza Ann, cholera infantum, Sept. —, 1819, a. 1 y. C. R. 3.
Elizabeth, w. Thomas, consumption, Aug. 6, 1820, a. 23 y.
C. R. 3.
Elizabeth, Aug. 13, 1838, a. 25 y.
Henry, cholera infantum, Aug. 25, 1825, a. 16 m. C. R. 3.

HOUGHTON, John, Sept. 27, 1828, a. 56 y.
Nancy, wid., b. Dorchester, Sept. 1, 1846, a. 66 y.
Zelia Adams, d. Isaac and Zebiah, June 8, 1835, a. 15 y.

**HOUSEMAN** (see also Housman), Elizabeth, d. Fred[eric]k and Catherine, fits, Jan. 23, 1849, a. 1 y. 11 m.

**HOUSMAN** (see also Houseman), Sophia, d. Godfrey and Catherine, scarlet fever, July 25, 1849, a. 1 y. 2 m.

**HOW** (see also Howe), Abraham, jr., Jan. 12, 1683. [1683-4. C. R. 1.]
Abraham, sr., Nov. 20, 1683.
Amory, s. Rev. Mark Anthony DeWolfe, Feb. —, 1840, a. 4 y.
————, w. Abraham, stopping of the lungs, bur. 7 : 10m : 1645. C. R. 1.

**HOWARD,** Charles, s. John, Sept. 22, 1834, a. 14 m.
Francis, b. Dorchester, s. John and Deborah, croup, Oct. 13, 1846, a. 2 y. 10 m.
George H., s. Phineas and Deborah, inflammation, May 24, 1848, a. 14 y.
Henry F., Dec. 27, 1840, a. 18 y.
John, inf. s. John, bur. 29 : 5m : 1680. C. R. 1.
John, July 29, 1695.
Joseph C., unm., architect, s. John and Clarissa C. consumption, Oct. 27, 1846, a. 26 y.
Mary, Mrs., confinement, Feb. 20, 1834. C. R. 2.
————, inf. ch. John, bur. 7 : 7m : 1681. C. R. 1.
————, inf. ch. ————, Aug. —, 1832.
————, ch. Geo[rge] B., croup, Sept. 30, 1834, a. 7 m. C. R. 2.

**HOWE** (see also How, Howes), Betsey, w. Alvan, Apr. 24, 1826, a. 26 y. C. R. 2.
Charlotte [Catherine C. R. 3.] [Hewes. in pencil.], [consumption. C. R. 3.], Mar. 2, 1837, a. 37 y.
David, old age, Dec. 19, 1825, a. 78 y. C. R. 3.
David, July —, 1830, a. 42 y.
Elizabeth, w. David, bilious fever, Dec. 2, 1803, a. 41 y. C. R. 3.
Freemaetta, d. Freeman F. and Caroline, bur. at Jamaica Plain, dropsy on brain, Sept. 6, 1849, a. 1 y. 4 m.
Georgiana, d. Albert, Feb. 29, 1840, a. 13 m.
Han[n]a[h], Mrs., Oct. 27, 1804, a. 25 y.

Howe, Hannah, Mrs. [wid. lung fever. c. r. 3.], Apr. 27, 1837, a. 76 y.

Helen Maria, d. Rev. Mark R. DeWolf and Julia B., Apr. 7, 1839. [a. 8 m. 9 d. c. r. 5.]

Henrietta, w. John, Oct. 26, 1804, a. 25 y. g. r. 1.

James, Jan. 12, 1798, a. 50 y. [a. 51 y. g. r. 1.]

James, s. James and Susanna, June 23, 1801, a. 24 y. [a. 25 y. g. r. 1.]

John [intemperance. Mar. 31. c. r. 3.], 1828, a. 49 y. [a. 39 y. c. r. 3.]

Julia B [owen, at St. Croix. c. r. 5.], w. Rev. Mark A. DeW., Feb. 5, 1841, [a. 35 y. c. r. 5.]

Julia Amory, d. Rev. M. A. DeW., bur. May 11, 1841, a. 1 y. c. r. 5.

Louisa Smith, bur. Mar. 20, 1845, a. 10 y. 5 m. c. r. 5.

Mary, w. Abraham F., Esq., Feb. —, 1842, a. 61 y.

Thomas Amory, s. M. A. DeW. and Julia B., bur. Feb. 8, 1840, a. 3 y. 10 m. c. r. 5.

——, s. Geo[rge], June 18, 1802, a. 10 y.

HOWELL, Sarah [at Capt. Jos[eph] Williams'. in pencil.], Dec. 14, 1804, a. 89 y.

HOWES (see also Howe), ——, ch. Geo[rge], Apr. 15, 1807, a. 11 m.

HOY (see also Hay), ——, ch. still born, James and Mary, Sept. 19, 1848.

HOYT (see also Hayt), Elna, Apr. 4, 1808, a. 47 y.

HUCKINS, Cordelia E., d. Jason and Caroline M., inflammation of head, Apr. 26, 1847, a. 2 y. 2 m.

HUDDLESTON, Ann Maria, a pauper [inf. d. James and Eliza. c. r. 5.], July 26, 1834, a. 1 y.

Nancy, b. Gardiner, Me., w. J. S. F., d. Michael and Deborah Burns, rheumatic complaint, Jan. 23, 1848, a. 31 y.

HUDSON, Solomon, son in law to Amasa Gay, Sept. —, 1822. c. r. 2.

HUGGINS, ——, Mrs., Jan. 26, 1837, a. 40 y. c. r. 2.

HUMPHREY (see also Humphries), Maria Matilda, Mrs., Mar. —, 1831, a. 20 y.

**HUMPHREYS** (see also Humphries), Elizabeth, w. William, May 15, 1824, a. 39 y.
George, s. Edward, Aug. —, 1828, a. 21 y.

**HUMPHRIES** (see also Humphrey, Humphreys, Humphris), Elizabeth, Mrs. [suddenly. c. r. 4.], July 4, 1829, a. 55 y.
Rebecca, w. Edward, Dec. 22, 1817, a. 38 y.

**HUMPHRIS** (see also Humphries), Emeline [Humphries. c. r. 4.] d. Edward and Emeline, obstruction in throat, Mar. 22, 1849, a. 47 y.

**HUNEWELL** (see also Hunnewell), Theoda, w. Hon. Jona-[than], May 21, 1834, a. 70 y.

**HUNNEMAN,** Abby Hewes, d. Dea. W[illia]m C., Dec. 18, 1836, a. 19 y.
Hannah, w. W[illia]m C., malignant hemorrhoids, Mar. 24, 1849, a. 72 y.
Sarah C., d. Dea. William C., Dec. 11, 1831, a. 21 y.

**HUNNEWELL** (see also Hunewell), Jonathan, Hon., Apr. 3, 1842, a. 83 y.

**HUNT,** Caroline, bur. Apr. 29, 1839, a. 21 y. c. r. 5.
Emely, d. James and Althea, cholera infantum, Aug. 5, 1849, a. 1 y. 3 m.
Moses, Oct. 12, 1814, a. 26 y.

**HUNTER,** Forester, s. Robert and Jane P., dysentery, Aug. 15, 1847, a. 8 m.

**HUNTING,** George, Dec. —, 1825, a. 40 y.
Samuel, s. Asa and Abigail, Mar. 17, 1798.
Sarah, d. Reuben, Sept. 3, 1824, a. 6 y.
——, consumption [after June 29], 1808. c. r. 3.

**HUNTINGTON** (see also Harrington), Leonard H., s. David and Jane, Dec. 1, 1847, a. 11 m. 16 d. g. r. 5.

**HUNTRESS,** Eleanor, unm., b. N. H., dysentery, Sept. 14, 1848, a. 46 y.

**HURD** (see also Heard), Benjamin, goldsmith, s. Capt. Jacob, June 2, 1781, in his 40th y. n. r. 2.

**HURLEY,** Deborah, Dec. 14, 1799, a. 54 y.
Mary, b. Ireland, w. James, cancer, Dec. 16, 1848, a. 44 y.

**HUTCHINS,** Lucinda, Oct. 24, 1819, a. 3 m. C. R. 3.

**HUTCHINSON,** Abigail, w. Dea. Israel, Dec. —, 1833, a. 69 y.

**HYDE** (see also Hides), Fanny A., Mrs., at Cambridgeport, bur. May 8, 1839, a. 22 y. C. R. 5.
Phillip, Nov. 15, 1798, a. 45 y.
Rebecca Smith, m., d. William and Sally, consumption, Nov. 5, 1849, a. 38 y.

**HYLAND,** Polly, Feb. —, 1829, a. 64 y.

**INNESON,** William J., b. England, s. Sam[ue]l and Elizabeth, consumption, Sept. 10, 1847, a. 10 y.

**IRVING,** see Erving.

**IVERS,** James A., s. George and Eunice, heart complaint, Mar. 27, 1849, a. 9 m. 5 d.
Jane, mother of James, bur. Mar. 30, 1789, a. 90 y. N. R. 3.

**JACSON** (see also Jackson), Sarah [Jackson, wid. Sebes. G. R. 2.], Apr. 20, 1725. [a. 75 y. G. R. 2.]

**JACKMAN,** Charles O., Jan. 9, 1845, a. 6 m.

**JACKSON** (see also Jacson), Andrew, jr., s. Andrew and Mary E., scarlet fever, Mar. 16, 1849, a. 1 y. 6 m.
Antipas, carpenter, b. Newton, old age, July 27, 1846, a. 73 y.
Charles Henry, s. Edmund and Mary Harriet, Sept. 12, 1828.
George Henry, s. Andrew and Mary E., May 1, 1843. G. R. 5.
Gershom, Jan. 10, 1799, a. 53 y. C. R. 2.
Hannah, d. Antipass and Hannah, Aug. 5, 1805. [a. 2 m. dup.]
Hannah, July —, 1821. C. R. 4.
Mary Elizabeth, d. Andrew and Mary E., dropsy in the brain, Nov. 6, 1846, a. 11 m.
N., Oct. 5, 1800, a. 18 y.
——, ch. Gershom, Dec. 19, 1773, a. 3 y. C. R. 2.
——, d. Gershom, Sept. —, 1783, a. 20 m. C. R. 2.
——, w. Gersham, Dec. 1, 1788. C. R. 2.
——, ch. Joel, Feb. 19, 1827, a. 4 w. C. R. 3.
——, inf. ch. Daniel and Laura, Aug. 1, 1846.

**JAMES,** Benj[ami]n F., jr., s. Benj[ami]n F. and Sarah, dropsy, June 6, 1849, a. 5 y.
Charles, s. Jos[eph] and Mary, Oct. 31, 1798.
Elisha, consumption, May 14, 1837, a. 58 y. C. R. 3.

JAMES, Eliza G[reenman. c. r. 3.], d. Elisha, dec. [typhus fever. c. r. 3.], Nov. 1, 1842, a. 20 y.

John, jr. [consumption. c. r. 3.], Aug. 6, 1833, a. 21 y.

John, carpenter [consumption. c. r. 3.], Aug. 27, 1844, a. 60 y.

Joseph, Oct. 11, 1801, a. 10 m.

Joseph, Nov. 18, 1838, a. 65 y.

Lewis, dropsy of chest, Apr. 25, 1830, a. 73 y. c. r. 3.

Martha Washington, d. Joseph [and Mary. Oct. 20. g. r. 5.], 1823, a. 18 y.

Mary, dysentery, Sept. 14, 1810, a. 16 m. c. r. 3.

Mary, d. Joseph [and Mary. g. r. 5.], Nov. 5, 1822, a. 20 y.

Sarah A., d. Benj[amin] F. and Sarah, dysentery, Sept. 1, 1847, a. 5 y. 3 m.

William, s. George and Dorothy, consumption, Oct. 12, 1846, a. 1 y. 7 m.

William Ellery, s. John [fever. Jan. 26. c. r. 3.], 1823, a. 2 y.

——, ch. Joseph, Oct. 4, 1802, a. 3 y.

——, ch. Charles, June 15, 1803, a. 14 m.

**JAMESON** (see also Jamison, Jemerson), Emely, Mrs., Apr 16, 1830, a. 28 y.

**JAMISON** (see also Jameson), William, jr., Sept. 28, 1834, a. 27 y.

**JEDKINS** (see also Judkins), Charles H., s. Sam[ue]l and Ellen F., canker, Nov. 10, 1848, a. 10 m.

**JEMERSON** (see also Jameson), Louisa, d. William, Oct. 15, 1844, a. 38 y. g. r. 4.

Mary [Jamerson. c. r. 3.], w. William [consumption. c. r. 3.], Aug. 31, 1839, a. 63 y.

**JENKINS**, Hannah, w. William F., consumption, Jan. 12, 1847, a. 26 y.

**JENNESS**, Charles, Feb. 25, 1845, a. 49 d.

Mary Ann, w. Josiah, canker, Aug. 1, 1848, a. 28 y.

Sarah, d. Josiah and Mary Ann, diarrhoea, July 31, 1848, a. 4 m.

**JERG**, Julia Howe, d. Jacob and Christina, Aug. 30, 1834. c. r. 5.

**JERVIS**, James, Capt., Nov. 18, 1750, in his 51st y. g. r. 1.

**JILICK,** Andrew, s. Andrew and Christiana, fits, Aug. 5, 1848, a. 1 y.

**JOCELIN** (see also Josselyn), Dorothy, maid servant of Mr. Dudly, apoplexy, bur. 2 : 10 m : 1645. c. r. 1.

**JOHNSON,** Abigail, d. Elisha and Abigail, Nov. 28, 1714.
Elisabeth ["old Sister." c. r. 1.], wid. Capt. Isaac, suddenly, Aug. 13, 1683.
Elizabeth, b. N. H., at the alms house, Sept. 13, 1849, a. 25 y.
Eunice, d. John and Mary, Apr. 6, 1709.
John, the elder ["Surveyor General of all ye armes." c. r. 1.], Sept. 29, 1659.
John, s. Capt., Dec. 18, 1661.
Joseph, s. Capt. Isaack, Dec. 12, 1645.
Margery, w. John, bur. 9 : 4m : 1655. c. r. 1.
Peter, m., ropemaker, b. N. Y., cholera, Sept. 19, 1849, a. 45 y.
Sarah, unm., b. Londonderry, N. S., dysentery, Aug. 31, 1841, a. 21 y
Sarah R., Aug. 31, 1848. c. r. 6.
Susan, wid., d. Charles and Harriet Davis, consumption, Aug. 1, 1849, a. 36 y. 6 m. 17 d.

**JONES,** Alden, m., carpenter, b. Bridgewater, dropsy, June 7, 1846, a. 58 y.
Ann, Mrs., a native of England, Dec. 15, 1825, a. 42 y.
Caroline W., s. John and Elizabeth, disease on the brain, Sept. 17, 1849, a. 7 y. 2 m.
Catharine Shirley, d. William H. and Catharine, July 20, 1836.
Daniel K., b. Dorchester, s. Sam[ue]l R. and Zoa, croup, Mar. 1, 1848, a. 1 y. 6 m.
Elizabeth, suddenly, in fits, Aug. 2, 1810 a. 14 y. c. r. 3.
Hannah, w. John, d. Stephen and Sarah Payson, Mar. 3, 1800.
Huldath V., widr., b. Barrington, N. S., consumption, July 10, 1847, a. 35 y.
James, Dec. 3, 1826, a. 31 y.
John Cluly, June 6, 1812, a. 66 y. c. r. 2.
Julia A., d. Thomas S., Dec. 8, 1839.
Lewis, Apr. 23, 1830, a. 73 y.
Lucy Ann A., d. Thomas and Lucy Ann, at Somerville, bur. at Roxbury, scarlet fever, Nov. 2, 1848, a. 10 y.
Mary B., d. William H., Feb. 24, 1840, a. 2 y. 3 m.

JONES, Mary, d. John and Elizabeth, consumption, Mar. 14, 1848, a. 19 y. 6 m.

Nabby B., d. Solomon and Nabby, Sept. 2, 1817, a. 4 y.

Nabby, wid. Solomon, at Prospect, Me., June 1, 1832.

Nath[anie]l D., s. W[illia]m and Nancy, canker, Sept. 23, 1849, a. 3 m.

Phebe, scald, 6 : 5 m : 1650. C. R. 1.

Prudence, consumption, Dec. 20, 1833, a. 73 y. C. R. 3.

Solomon, Mar. 13, 1820, a. 54 y.

Susanna Goddard, d. James and Susanna, Nov. —, 1824, a. 1 y. 10 m.

William B., s. William H., Dec. 3, 1836, a. 2 y. 5 m.

——, ch. John C., Dec. 31, 1775, a. 4 y. C. R. 2.

——, s. John Cluly, Aug. —, 1783, a. 16 y. C. R. 2.

——, ch. John Cluly and Rebecca, Mar. 23, 1788, a. 2 m. C. R. 2.

——, w. John, July 10, 1788. C. R. 2.

——, ch. Lewes, Aug. 9, 1805, a. 20 m.

——, ch. William, fits, Aug. 6, 1846, a. 2 m.

——, ch. Miss Mary, June 11, 1849, a. 6 d.

JORDAN, Henry A., Oct. —, 1833, a. 26 y.

John B., s. Chancey and Sarah J., dysentery, Sept. 13, 1847, a. 6 y.

Sarah D., Mrs., Mar. 5, 1831, a. 29 y.

JOSSELYN (see also Jocelin), Hannah, Mrs., May 4, 1837, a. 61 y.

JOULE, William Guy, June 3, 1811, a. abt. 50 y.

JOY, Charles, at the alms house, July 10, 1838, a. 68 y.

David, Mar. 13, 1826, a. 28 y.

Margery Ellen, scarlatina, Oct. 19, 1835, a. 5 y. C. R. 3.

JOYCE, Jane E., b. St. Johns, N. B., w. Sam[ue]l C., consumption, Jan. 11, 1849, a. 47 y.

Martha M., b. New Brunswick, d. Sam[ue]l C. and Jane E., consumption, June 25, 1848, a. 17 y.

JUDKINS (see also Jedkins), Ellen F., b. Gilmanton, N. H., w. Samuel, typhoid fever, Nov. 25, 1848, a. 34 y.

JUSOE, Mary, d. Peter and Mary, Jan. 28, 1719-20.

**KALLOCK** (see also Kellack), George, Rev., Nov. 16, 1831.
C. R. 4.

**KANGLY,** John. b. Ireland, ship fever, at the alms house, Mar.
30, 1848, a. 53 y.

**KEATING,** Ann E., d. Michael and Mary, croup, Mar. 13,
1849, a. 5 y. 8 m.
James, s. James and Bridget, brain fever, Aug. 18, 1848, a.
8 m.

**KEBEY,** John, s. Edward, bur. Dec. 20, 1652.
Rewben, s. Edward, bur. Feb. 8, 1652.

**KEEF,** Ellen, d. James and Margarett, July 8, 1848, a. 2 d.

**KEELIN,** Nathan Prince, s. Christian, June 23, 1842, a. 4 y.
8 m.

**KEENAUGH** (see also Kenaugh), Bridget, d. Brine and Rose,
diarrhoea, Aug. 14, 1849, a. 3 y. 6 m.
Martin, s. John and Eliza, whooping cough, Jan. 15, 1849, a.
3 m.

**KEENE** Catherine, d. Owen and Bridget, decline, Sept. 10,
1849, a. 5 m.

**KEIGLE,** Joseph, b. Germany, ship fever, at the alms house,
Mar. 12, 1848, a. 40 y.

**KEITH,** John [cancer on the leg. C. R. 2.], Apr. 8, 1833, a.
76 y. [a. 77 y. C. R. 2.]
Sarah C., w. William, Aug. 22, 1841, a. 50 y.

**KELLACK** (see also Kallock), Lemuel, of Wrentham, suddenly, by a fall from his house, July 14, 1795, a. 66 y.
N. R. 4.

**KELLEY** (see also Kelly), Catherine, unm., b. Ireland, consumption, Oct. 1, 1848, a. 22 y.
Daniel, Sept. 28, 1829, a. 40 y.
John, b. Ireland, ship fever, at the alms house, Apr. 21, 1849,
a. 51 y.
Joseph, cholera infantum, at the alms house, Aug. 8, 1848, a.
5 m.
Joseph, s. Bridget, disease of the brain, at the alms house, Feb.
20, 1849, a. 1 m.

KELLY, Patrick, m., b. Ireland, consumption, Nov. 16, 1848, a. 24 y.

Peggy, Mar. 16, 1803, a. 22 y.

**KELLOGG,** Warren, May —, 1839, a. 4 y. 8 m.

**KELLY** (see also Kelley), Abigail, Feb. 15, 1799, a. 50 y.

Abigail, Oct. 23 [25. dup.], 1800, a. 21 y.

Andrew, laborer, b. Ireland, consumption, Aug. 17, 1847, a. 50 y.

Ann, m., b. Ireland, consumption, Sept. 19, 1847, a. 26 y.

Barnard [Barney. dup.], s. Patrick and Catherine, decline [measles. dup.], June 28 [20. dup.], 1849, a. 3 y.

Bridget, wid., b. Ireland, dysentery, Oct. 30, 1847, a. 50 y.

Bridget, d. Thomas and Bridget, whooping cough, Feb. 26, 1848, a. 11 m.

Bridget, b. Ireland, fever, at the alms house, Oct. 8, 1849, a. 23 y.

Catherine, at the alms house, Sept. 27, 1847, a. 6 m.

Catherine, m., b. Ireland, consumption, Nov. 24, 1847, a. 30 y.

Elizabeth, unm., b. Ireland, dysentery, Sept. 9, 1848, a. 24 y.

Elnora, b. Ireland, w. Luke, consumption, Feb. 11, 1849, a. 50 y.

James, s. Denis and Ann, dysentery, Aug. 4, 1848, a. 1 y. 3 m. 3 d.

Jane Mary, b. Ireland, w. William, decline, Sept. 1, 1849, a. 16 y .

John, s. John and Mary, dysentery, Sept. 21, 1848, a. 1 y. 4 m.

John Hubert, s. Michael and Bridget, bowel complaint, Aug. 31, 1848, a. 1 y. 3 m.

Malary, d. John and Honora, whooping cough, Nov. 12, 1848, a. 11 m.

Margaret, d. Andrew and Abigail, Apr. 17, 1804, a. 23 y. c. R. 1.

Mary, b. Ireland, bowel complaint, Sept. 19, 1847, a. 29 y.

Mary, wid., b. Ireland, consumption, Sept. 19, 1848, a. 63 y.

Mary, b. Ireland, d. Barney and Mary, erysipelas, May 10, 1849, a. 24 m.

Patrick, m., laborer, b. Ireland, fever, Oct. 16, 1847, a. 32 y.

Thomas, b. Ireland, ship fever, at the alms house, June 8, 1848, a. 21 y.

——, ch. still born, Thomas and Ellen, Nov. 23, 1849.

**KENAUGH** (see also Keenaugh), Mary, d. Daniel and Eliza, decline, Dec. 18, 1848, a. 1 y. 11 m.

KENDALL, Abbott Lawrence, s. Abel, jr., Aug. —, 1837, a. 15 m.

KENDRICK (see also Kenrick), Nancy M., Sept. 1, 1846. c. r. 6.

KENNEDY (see also Kinneday), Flora, d. Donald and Ann, measles, May 29, 1849, a. 3 y. 5 m.

KENNEY (see also Kenny), Betsey, old age, July —, 1834, a. 72 y. c. r. 3.
John [Kenny, laborer. dup.], b. Ireland, ship fever, at the alms house, Feb. 6 [4. dup.], 1848, a. 32 y.
Mary, at the almshouse, July 5, 1839, a. 22 y.
Michael, s. Francis and Julia, bowel complaint, Sept. 25, 1848, a. 4 y. 6 m.

KENNY (see also Kenney), Daniel, s. John and Elizabeth, croup, Apr. 8, 1848, a. 1 y.
Hannah, b. Ireland, d. Andrew and Mary, June 18, 1849, a. 17 y.
Josiah, June 19, 1778, a. 23 y. c. r. 2.
Stephen, m., b. Ireland, brain fever, Apr. 13, 1849, a. 39 y.
——, d. Catherine, consumption, Jan. 28, 1847, a. 4 m. 14 d.
——, ch. still born, Thomas and Catherine, Oct. 2, 1846.

KENRICK (see also Kendrick), Judah, wid. John, Aug. 23, 1687.
Mary, w. Elijah, July 20, 1714, a. 36 y. g. r. 1.
William, consumption, June 1, 1833, a. 65 y. c. r. 2.

KENT, David, May 3, 1840, a. 37 y.
Stephen, jr., s. Stephen and Elizabeth, Apr. 16, 1760, a. 20 y. g. r. 3.
——, wid., Nov. 30, 1803, a. 86 y.

KETTELL (see also Kettle), Hannah, w. Samuel, Oct. 10, 1808, a. 36 y.
Joseph Pierce [Kettle. dup.], s. Samuel and Hannah, Oct. 2 [4. dup.], 1805. [a. 13 m. dup.]

KETTLE (see also Kettell), ——, ch. S., Sept. 6, 1805.

KEVER, Thomas, b. Ireland, bowel complaint, at the alms house, Sept. 12, 1847, a. 55 y.

**KEYES** (see also Keys), Elizabeth, w. John, consumption, Aug. 6, 1793, a. 46 y. c. r. 3.
Mary, w. John, Apr. 21, 1774.
Samuel, Oct. 26, 1785, a. 9 w. g. r. 4.
Simeon, June 19, 1814, a. 35 y.
Thomas, widr., laborer, b. Ireland, old age, Nov. 30, 1849, a. 90 y.

**KEYS** (see also Keyes), Ruth, Mrs., Mar. 3, 1824, a. 60 y.

**KIDD,** John Thomas, unm., blacksmith, b. England, bank of earth falling on him, Oct. 29, 1846, a. 50 y.

**KIDDER,** Joseph B., Aug. 5, 1824.

**KIGGY,** Ellen, b. Ireland, w. Martin, consumption, July 21, 1848, a. 35 y.
Hannah, b. Ireland, croup, at the alms house, June 1, 1849, a. 5 y.
Hannah, d. Martin and Ellen, croup, June 21, 1849, a. 7 y.

**KILDAY,** Ann, b. Ireland, w. Andrew, child bed, May 22, 1849, a. 35 y.

**KILDUFF,** John, m., laborer, b. Ireland, fever, July 23, 1849, a. 31 y.

**KILHAM,** Rebecca, w. George W., Dec. 7, 1823, a. 33 y.

**KILLIAN** (see also Killion), John, m., laborer, b. Ireland, consumption, June 8, 1848, a. 38 y.

**KILLION** (see also Killian), Ann, m., b. Ireland, child bed, July 24, 1848, a. 30 y.
Bridget, m., b. Ireland, typhus fever, June 7, 1847, a. 30 y.
Mary, d. Michael and Bridget A., summer complaint, Sept. 19, 1848.

**KILLROY,** Michael, m., laborer, b. Ireland, cholera, Aug. 30, 1849, a. 35 y.

**KINDER,** Mrs., Apr. —, 1803.

**KINE,** Thomas, m., laborer, b. Ireland, bowel complaint, Sept. 2, 1849, a. 38 y.

**KING,** Charles Horace, s. Horace and Catharine, Oct. 15, 1839, a. 15 m.

KING, Oren [Oran, a stranger, typhus fever. C. R. 3.], Nov. —,
1828, a. 20 y.
Samuel, s. George, Jan. —, 1841, a. 4 w.

KINGMAN, Thomas, Mar. —, 1829, a. 43 y.

KINGSBURY (see also Kinsbury), Aaron, Apr. 12, 1839, a.
63 y.
Charlotte S., d. Aaron, dysentery, Sept. 10, 1803, a. 4 y. 4 m.
C. R. 3.
Noah, June 4, 1826, a. 68 y.
Thomas N., m., merchant, b. Needham, consumption, June 18,
1848, a. 49 y.

KINNEDAY (see also Kennedy), James, Feb. 2, 1807.

KINSBURY (see also Kingsbury), Theodore, Mar. 6, 1807, a.
12 m.

KINSLEY, Martin, Hon. [in a fit. C. R. 4.], June 20, 1835,
a. 81 y.
Polly, at Walpole, N. H., Aug. 21, 1849, a. 85 y. C. R. 4.

KITTERIDGE (see also Kittredge), Royal, s. Leonard and
Almira, inflammation of bowels, Feb. 2, 1849, a. 18 d.

KITTREDGE (see also Kitteridge), Maria G., d. Dea. Alvah,
Sept. 4, 1838, a. 22 m.

KNAPP, William, m., b. England, typhus fever, May 21, 1849,
a. 41 y.

KNELAND, John, Aug. 11, 1691, a. 59 y. 9 d. G. R. 1.

KNIGHT, James, suicide, Feb. 13, 1831, a. 30 y.
Mehitabel, d. Samuel, Apr. 20, 1703.
Samuel, s. Samuel and Sarah, May 20, 1689.

KNOWER (see also Knowers), Benja[min], Nov. 9, 1806, a.
52 y.
Charles Henry, s. Samuel, Nov. —, 1828.
Elizabeth, w. Benja[min], Sept. 7, 1802, a. 49 y.
Samuel, July 16, 1806, a. 40 y.
Susan Maria, d. Samuel, June 19, 1833, a. 10 m.

KNOWERS (see also Knower), —— [Knower. dup.], ch.
Benjamin, Mar. 3, 1797, a. 5 y.

**KNOX,** Sarah D., incipient pregnancy, Aug. 5, 1818, a. 20 y. 8 m. C. R. 3.

**KOHLER,** ——, ch. still born, Martin and Caroline, May 29, 1849.

**KOOITS,** ——, s. C. J., fits, July 29, 1846, a. 3 y.

**KOVITS,** Sicily, b. New York, ch. Charles and Elizabeth, bowel complaint, Aug. 24, 1849, a. 13 y. 5 m.

**KRAMER,** Sebastine, s. Sebastine, Sept. —, 1833, a. 1 y.

**KRANIER,** Mary, at the alms house, July 19, 1847, a. 4 m.

**KUHN,** Elizabeth M., Mar. 22, 1845. C. R. 6.
——, ch. still born, John and Ellen, June 12, 1849.

**KURR,** Mary W., m., b. Newburyport, d. Nathaniel and Sarah Hawes, fits, Feb. 5, 1848, a. 39 y.

**KYTE,** John, m., laborer, b. England, accidental, July 22, 1847, a. 31 y.

**LADWIG,** Mary E., m., b. Germany, dropsy, Nov. 23, 1848, a. 50 y.

**LAGALLEE,** ——, ch. Thomas, May 17, 1721 [1821 ?], a. 6 W. C. R. 2.

**LAGGETT,** Emma, unm., b. Amherst, N. H., rupture of blood vessel on lungs, Oct. 20, 1848, a. 54 y.

**LAHA,** Mary, d. Thomas and Abigail, Mar. —, 1837.

**LAIFFLER,** William, b. Germany, at the alms house, Oct. 15, 1849, a. 32 y.

**LAKEMAN,** John, Feb. 21, 1841, a. 54 y.

**LALLY,** Bridget, b. Ireland, w. James, fever, Feb. 1, 1849, a. 62 y.
Dennis, m., b. Ireland, dysentery, Aug. 14, 1848, a. 58 y.
Ellen A., m., b. Ireland, fever, Sept. 21, 1847, a. 22 y.
John, b. Ireland, dysentery, Sept. 4, 1848, a. 34 y.

**LAMB** (see also Lambe), [Benjamin Lambe. C. R. 1.], inf. ch. Thomas, bur. 28 : 9m : 1639.CT. R. [a. a few h. C. R. 1.]
Elisabeth, d. Joshua, June 9, 1683.

LAMB, John, s. [inf. ch. C. R. 1.], Joshua, June 16, 1685.
Joseph, s. Caleb, bur. Dec. 26, 1692.
Joshua, Sept. 23, 1690.
Joshua, Col., July 20, 1754, in an advanced age. N. R. 1.
Mary, d. Caleb [small pox. C. R. 1.], July 4, 1679.
Mary, wid. Joshua, Oct. 9, 1700.
Mary A., at the alms house, Aug. 30, 1849, a. 8 m.

**LAMBE** (see also Lamb), Elizabeth [Elisabeth Lamb. CT. R.],
    w. Thomas [child birth. C. R. 1.], bur. Nov. 28, 1639.
Elizabeth, inf. d. Joshua, bur. 10 . 4 m . 1683. C. R. 1.
Joseph, inf. s. Caleb, bur. 11 : 4 m : 1683. C. R. 1.
Thomas, householder, Apr. 3, 1646.
——, "Bro.", calenture, bur. 28 : 1 m : 1646. C. R. 1.

**LAMBERT** (see also Lombard), Susanna, wid. William, Esq.,
    July 3, 1830, a. 71 y.
William, jr., at Rotterdam, Aug. —, 1807, a. 24 y.
William, June 17, 1823, a. 80 y.
——, ch. William, Oct. 7, 1779.
——, ch. William, Oct. 7, 1797, a. 6 y.

**LANDERS**, Mehitable, wid., consumption, Feb. 25, 1848, a.
    83 y.
William, a pauper, Jan. 23, 1829, a. 55 y. [a. 56 y. dup.]
—— [Lander. dup.], ch. William, Aug. 7, 1797, a. 2 m.
——, ch. William. May 5, 1801.

**LANE** (see also Laynes), Charles, Nov. —, 1833, a. 36 y.

**LANG**, Susan, d. Edward and Eliza, croup, Feb. 8, 1847, a.
    7 y.

**LANGLEY**, Samuel, May 12, 1800, a. 58 y.
Sarah, Feb. 17 [19. dup.], 1801, a. 85 y.

**LANNON** (see also Lennon), William E., s. Patrick and Mar-
    garet, dysentery, Oct. 31, 1848, a. 4 y. 7 m.

**LANRAGIN**, Patrick, b. Ireland, ship fever, at the alms house,
    May 30, 1848, a. 60 y.

**LANSFORD**, ——, ch. Henry, Sept. 13, 1805, a. 14 m.

**LARABEE**, Hannah [Larrabee, w. John. G. R. 5.], June 21,
    1827, a. 25 y.

LARABEE, Lydia, d. John, Mar. —, 1834, a. 14 m.
Thomas, Feb. —, 1834, a. 37 y.

LARKIN, Joseph, m., clock maker, consumption, Aug. 10, 1847, a. 41 y.

LARLY, Thomas, m., laborer, b. Ireland, dysentery, Sept. 7, 1849, a. 36 y.

LARVERY (see also Laverie, Lavers, Lavery), Robert, b. Scotland, disease of brain, at the alms house, July 17, 1847, a. 6 y.

LATHROP, Tisdale, Nov. 5, 1815, a. 25 y.

LAUCHLEN (see also Lochlin), Anna, wid., Dec. 4, 1773, a. 84 y. C. R. 2.

LAUCHLENS (see also Lochlin), ———, ch. ———, Jan. 23, 1774, a. 12 h. C. R. 2.

LAUGHHIFF, Michael, unm., laborer, b. Ireland, consumption, July 3, 1849, a. 23 y.

LAUGHLIN (see also McLaughlin), Mary E., d. Timothy and Mary, croup, Apr. 22, 1848, a. 2 y. 2 m.

LAVERIE (see also Larvery), William Garrick, s. Robert, (Scotch), cholera infantum, July 29, 1845, a. 5 m. C. R. 3.

LAVERS (see also Larvery), ———, ch. still born, W[illia]m G., Oct. 16, 1848.

LAVERY (see also Larvery), Robert, internal ulceration, Oct. 5, 1845, a. 28 y. C. R. 3.

LAW, Aurther S., s. Thomas T. and Elizabeth H., bowel complaint, Aug. 15, 1848, a. 2 m.

LAWRENCE, Elizabeth w. Rev. Byrem, d. Dr. Nath[anie]l S. Prentiss, at Charlestown, Indiana, Apr. 18, 1834, a. 34 y.
Hannah S., d. Reuben and Rosina [inflammation of the bowels. C. R. 3.], Mar. 7, 1841, a. 8 y. G. R. 4.
Rosina, w. Reuben, Dec. 3, 1842, a. 36 y. G. R. 4.
Roxana of Pepperell, Sept 18, 1826, a. 18 y.
W[illia]m M., m., tinplate worker, b. Hollis, N. H., s. Nathan and Elizabeth, consumption, Oct. 2, 1847, a. 28 y.

**LAWTON,** Samuel, laborer, pleurisy fever, Feb. 20, 1844, a. 33 y.

**LAYMAN,** ———, Mrs., Oct. 5, 1832.

**LAYN** (see also Laynes), Mary, d. Joseph and Mary, Jan. 1, 1711.

**LAYNES** (see also Lane, Layn), Bernard, s. Timothy and Mary, teething, Aug. 29, 1848, a. 8 m.
Leria, d. Bernard and Catherine, teething, Aug. 31, 1848, a. 11 m. 14 d.

**LEACH,** Thomas [Leech. c. r. 5.], widr., laborer, b. Ireland, fever, Apr. 10, 1847, a. 40 y. [a. 44 y. c. r. 5.]

**LEARNARDS** (see also Leonard), ———, d. Jonas, Sept. 13, 1805, a. 16 y.

**LEARNED** (see also Leonard), Henry, s. Grant and Martha, Sept. 6, 1800.

**LEARY,** Catherine, b. Maine, w. Timothy, consumption, Jan. 22, 1849, a. 28 y.
Richard, s. John and Catherine, bowel complaint, Aug. 14, 1848, a. 10 m.

**LEATHBRIDG** (see also Lethbridge), Adams, s. Richard and Hopstil, Oct. 24, 1766, a. 3 m. g. r. 1.
Hopstil, w. Richard, Aug. 8, 1766, in her 46th y. g. r. 1.

**LEATHBRIDGE** (see also Lethbridge), Richard, issue of Aug. 27, 1791, a. 70 y. n. r. 4.

**LEAVERETT** (see also Leveret), Daniel Sharp, s. Rev. William, Mar. —, 1837, a. 9 m.

**LEAVINS** (see also Levins), Sarah, w. John, bur. 25 : 8m : 1666. c. r. 1.

**LEAVY,** Jane, d. W[illia]m and Bridget, croup, July 20, 1849, a. 11 m. 17 d.

**LEE** (see also Leigh), Mary E., w. W[illia]m Raymond, June 23, 1839, a. 25 y.
Mary L., July 6, 1825, a. 80 y.

LEE, Sarah, wid. Hon. Samuel, of Province of New Brunswick, Nov. 5, 1831.

Susan T., w. George, Aug. —, 1837.

Tracy, s. W. Ramond [inf. s. William R. and Mary. c. r. 5.], Mar. 4, 1836.

LEEDS, James [Blake. c. r. 3.], s. James B. [inflammatory fever. c. r. 3.], July 1, 1831, a. 8 y.

James, intemperance, Dec. 28, 1834, a. 39 y. c. r. 3.

LeFAVOUR, Richard M., m., inn holder, b. Salem, typhus fever, Nov. 23, 1846, a. 31 y. 3 m. 22 d.

LEHNART, Jacob Henry, s. Henry and Elizabeth, June 23, 1847, a. 1 y. 15 d. g. r. 5.

LEIGH (see also Lee), Thomas [nephew Capt. Thomas Brattle of Boston. g. r. 1.], July 19, 1694. [a. 30 y. g. r. 1.]

LEIGHTON, Harriet A., d. Abel and Abigail, croup, Mar. 30, 1848, a. 7 y. 4 m.

Juliette, d. Abel and Abigail, croup, Apr. 5, 1848, a. 3 y.

LELAND, Anna B., d. Sherman and Betsey (Adams), May 19, 1844, a. 9 y. 6 m. p. r. 4.

Elizabeth A[dams, d. Sherman and Betsey (Adams). p. r. 4.], rupture of blood vessel, Oct. 28, 1847, a. 33 y. [a. 33 y. 2 m. 24 d. p. r. 4.]

George, s. Hon. Sherman, June 6, 1832, a. 3 y. [a. 3 y. 3 m. 12 d. p. r. 4.]

Julia, d. Hon. Sherman [and Betsey (Adams) in Oregon, Illinois. p. r. 4.], Nov. 27, 1840, a. 23 y. [a. 23 y. 11 m. p. r. 4.]

LEMIST, John, perished when the steamboat Lexington was burnt, on Long Island Sound, Jan. 13, 1840.

John Russell Langdon, s. John, Sept. 21, 1831, a. 7 y.

William Clarke, s. Edwin, July 14, 1840, a. 18 m.

LENDOL, William, s. Silvanus and Abigail, Dec. 29, 1825, a. 8 m. c. r. 2.

LENNON (see also Lannon), James, at the alms house, Dec. 14, 1841, a. 38 y.

LEONARD (see also Learnards, Learned), Bridget, 2d, ship fever, at the alms house, June 2, 1847, a. 1 d.

LEONARD, Bridget, b. Ireland, ship fever, at the alms house, June 7, 1847, a. 24 y.

Elizabeth, wid., d. James and Elizabeth, old age, May 3, 1848, a. 76 y.

Jacob H., s. Henry and Elizabeth, lung fever, June 21, 1847, a. 1 y. 15 d.

Mary, d. Michael and Ellen, small pox, Aug. 26, 1849, a. 11 m.

**LEPIERE,** Martha Crafts, Feb. 12, 1825, a. 51 y. C. R. 3.

**LEPRILETE,** Ludovici, Dr., Mass. Med. Soc., July 29, 1804, a. 54 y. G. R. 4.

Ludovicus [Lewis. N. R. 4.], only s. Dr. Ludovici, Oct. 30, 1792, a. 7 y. G. R. 4.

**LETHBRIDGE** (see also Leathbrigd, Leathbridge), George, s. Richard and Mary [dysentery, Sept. 21. G. R. 4.], Aug. 21, 1818. [a. 5 m. 14 d. G. R. 4.]

Mary, old age, Feb. 5, 1807, a. 84 y. C. R. 3.

Mary, w. Richard [consumption. C. R. 3.], Dec. 28, 1818, a. 32 y.

Richard, m., accidental drowning, Sept. 4, 1847, a. 61 y.

**LEVENS** (see also Levins), John, palsy, bur. 15:9m:1647. C. R. 1.

**LEVERET** (see also Leaverett), ———, wid. Hudson, Dec. 16, 1714.

**LEVINS** (see also Leavins, Levens), Elizabeth, w. John, bur. Oct. 10, 1638.

Hannah, Oct. 24, 1666, a. 28 y.

John, householder, Nov. 16, 1647.

Peter [Leavins, s. twin. C. R. 1.], John, bur. 15:11m:1644. CT. R. [1644-5. C. R. 1.]

**LEWIN,** John, m., shoe maker, b. England, asthma, Feb. 18, 1848, a. 53 y.

**LEWIS,** Abigail, Mrs., ———, 1829, a. 85 y.

Barichiah, Apr. 18, 1785, a. 75 y. C. R. 2.

Esther, Sept. 8, 1796, a. 31 y.

Hannah, wid. James, May 2, 1840, a. 83 y. G. R. 5.

Jabez [complaint of the heart. C. R. 3.], Feb. 21, 1827, a. 51 y.

James, Dec. 17, 1826, a. 84 y. G. R. 5.

John, yeoman, old age, Feb. 15, 1844, a. 80 y.

LEWIS, Joshua S., Capt., Dec. 13, 1837, a. 45 y. G. R. 5.
Mary, July 11, 1777, a. 41 y. C. R. 2.
———, ch. Samuel, Apr. 10, 1779, a. 2 y. C. R. 2.
———, w. Timothy, May 24, 1808. C. R. 2.

LIGHTNER, Margaret, w. John, Aug. 25, 1841, a. 34 y.

LILIKIN (see also Linikin), Delilah Ann, b. New Brunswick,
d. Abner T. and Lucretia, consumption, July 10, 1849, a.
19 y.

LILLY, ———, Mr., a stranger, Aug. —, 1821. C. R. 3.

LILLYMAN, W., bur. Mar. 8, 1846, a. 50 y. C. R. 5.

LINCOLN, John E[lliot, consumption. C. R. 3.], Jan. 13, 1840,
a. 31 y.
Oliver, m., gentleman, b. Norton, s. Abiel, tumor, July 30,
1848, a. 73 y.

LINDEMUTH, Christian, widr., laborer, b. Germany, Aug. 19,
1849, a. 84 y.

LINE (see also Lines), Patrick, m., laborer, b. Ireland, consumption, Mar. 28, 1848, a. 33 y.

LINES (see also Line), Patrick, unm., b. Ireland, lung fever,
Apr. 2, 1849, a. 20 y.

LINFIELD, Jonathan W., s. Jona[than] and Sally, Sept. 9,
1809, a. 1 y. 1 m. 11 d. G. R. 1.

LINIKIN (see also Lilikin), Mary E., b. Maine, d. Abner T.
and Lucretia, dropsy, May 3, 1847, a. 10 y. 4 m.

LION (see also Lyon), Johnathan [Jonathan Lyons. C. R. 1.],
s. Willyam [William. C. R. 1.], bur. June 5, 1668.
Mary, d. Joseph and Mary, Aug. 7, 1687, a. 9 m. 3 w. 2 d.
G. R. 1.
Mary, small pox, Sept. 19, 1792. C. R. 2.

LISCOM, ———, ch. still born, John and Eliza E., Oct. 5,
1848.

LITCHFIELD, Edward, b. Lewiston, Me., s. Vassal and
Nancy, dropsy on brain, Sept. 15, 1848, a. 1 y. 11 m. 15 d.

LITHGO, Arthur, Col., Aug. 14, 1835, a. 76 y.

**LITTLE,** Israel, Nov. 22, 1828, a. 27 y.

**LITTLEFIELD,** Clarissa W., m., d. Samuel and Clarisa Rumrill, heart complaint, Apr. 13, 1848, a. 37 y.

**LITTLETON,** Irene, m., b. Woodstock, Vt., d. Isaac and Clarissa Stanton, consumption, Sept. 15, 1849, a. 32 y.

**LIVERMORE,** Charles, s. William, dropsy, Sept. 4, 1849, a. 4 y.
John, Sept. 17, 1807, a. 47 y.

**LLOYD,** Benj[amin] Daniel, s. David and Sarah, croup, Nov. 16, 1847, a. 2 y. 6 m.
David Thomas, s. David and Sarah, Nov. 6, 1845, a. 3 y. 9 m. G. R. 5.
Mary Pamela, d. David and Sarah, Nov. 3, 1845, a. 1 y. 4 m. 5 d. G. R. 5.
————, ch. still born, David and Sarah, July 1, 1848.

**LOCHLIN** (see also Lauchlen, Lauchlens), George, Mar. 2, 1750, a. 62 y. G. R. 1.

**LOMBARD** (see also Lambert), Thomas, of the Island of Jamaica, Oct. 12, 1745, a. 53 y. G. R. 1.

**LONG,** Almira, Dec. 14, 1831, a. 22 y.
Caleb, Dec. —, 1825.

**LONGER,** Charles [Longen. dup.], Aug. 30 [24. dup.], 1802. [a. 12 y. dup.]
James, Jan. 16 [18. dup.], 1806, a. 58 y.
————, ch. Janet, Oct. 29, 1808, a. 1 y. C. R. 2.

**LOOP,** Julia, d. W[illia]m P. and Dorothy, teething, Sept. 6, 1849, a. 1 y. 5 m.

**LORD,** Charles H., s. John W. and Maria, dysentery, Aug. 27, 1847, a. 2 y. 20 d.

**LORING,** Ruth, Oct. —, 1830.

**LOUBET,** John G., Sept. —, 1830, a. 34 y.

**LOUD** (see also Lowd), Joanna, Mrs., Apr. 11, 1819, a. 82 y.

**LOUDER** (see also Lowder), William, a pauper, Mar. 31, 1835, a. 48 y.

**LOVE,** Rosanna, Mrs., bur. Nov. 11, 1841, a. 29 y. c. R. 5.

**LOVEJOY,** W. H., s. Joseph and Margarett, Aug. 17, 1846, a. 9 m.

**LOVERING,** Hannah, consumption, Apr. 12, 1803, a. 57 y. c. R. 3.
Joseph, mortification, Sept. 1, 1802, a. 67 y. c. R. 3.
William, s. Robert and Alice, June 21, 1713.

**LOWD** (see also Loud), Charles Henry, s. Henry and Lucy, fever, Jan. 9, 1848, a. 1 y. 6 m.
Edwin L., s. Henry and Lucy, fever, Jan. 12, 1848, a. 3 y. 6 m.

**LOWDER** (see also Louder), Betsey, ship fever, at the alms house, Aug. 24, 1847, a. 69 y.
Charles W., s. Phillip and Sarah Ann, dysentery, Sept. 14, 1847, a. 2 y. 7 m.
John, consumption, June —, 1799, a. 75 y. c. R. 3.
John, dropsy, ————, 1806, a. 59 y. c. R. 3.
John, m. victualler, s. John and Mary, affection of the heart, Feb. 7, 1847, a. 66 y. [a. 47 y. c. R. 3.]
Mary, dropsy, Dec. 31, 1818, a. 66 y. c. R. 3.
————, w. John, jr., consumption, Feb. 15, 1793. c. R. 3.

**LOWE,** Charlotte, Mar. 25, 1845, a. 2 y. 10 m.

**LOWELL,** John, Esq., May 9, 1802, a. 39 y.
John, Hon., Mar. 13, 1840, a. 70 y.
————, s. Charles, Sept. 26, 1846, a. 2 y. 18 m.

**LOWNDES,** Hannah, Mrs., June 12, 1832, a. 24 y.

**LOWNY,** W[illia]m A., s. W[illia]m and Sarah Jane, fits, Oct. 17, 1848, a. 1 y. 8 m.

**LUBY,** John, m., laborer, b. Ireland, at Cambridge, bur. at Roxbury, cramp, Dec. 4, 1848, a. 34 y.

**LYAN** (see also Lyon), Joseph, s. Joseph and Mary, Feb. 27, 1703.

**LYNCH,** Julia [Linch. dup.], b. Ireland, bowel complaint, at the alms house, June 4, 1848, a. 27 y. [a. 30 y. dup.]
Michael [Linch, s. Julia. dup.], b. Ireland, bowel complaint, at the alms house, June 4, 1848, a. 2 y.
Thomas, s. John, quinsy, June 23, 1811, a. 7 m. c. R. 3.

**LYNDEN** (see also Lyndon), Thomas, bur. Dec. 4, 1849, a. 65 y. c. r. 5.

**LYNDON** (see also Lynden), Edward, m., laborer, b. Ireland, consumption, Dec. 1, 1849, a. 64 y.

**LYON** (see also Lion, Lyan, Lyons), [Abigail. g. r. 2.], w. John, Jan. 15, 1702-3. [a. 48 y. g. r. 2.]

Abigail, w. Ephraim, Nov. 28, 1721.

Achin, s. Thomas, jr. and Anne, Oct. 16 [abt. Oct. 17. dup.], 1693.

Anna, d. Thomas, May 29, 1683.

Anna, d. Thomas and Abigail, Oct. 16, 1693.

Anna, d. Benjamin and Anna, Oct. 3, 1747.

Anna, wid., Sept. 17, 1775. c. r. 2.

Anne, w. Thomas, jr., Oct. 17, 1693.

Benjamin, inf. s. John, bur. 14 : 12m : 1679-80. c. r. 1.

Benjamin, s. William, jr., Apr. 2, 1683.

Benjamin, Feb. 20, 1752, in his 44th y. g. r. 2.

Benja[min], June 14, 1785, a. 53 y. c. r. 2.

Benjamin, June [3. c. r. 2.], 1821, a. 47 y.

Daniel, Sept. 13, 1776, a. 29 y. c. r. 2.

Deborah, wid. William, Mar. 12, 1717.

Elisha, s. Joseph and Mary, Feb. 10, 1705-6.

Elizabeth, d. Eliphalet, Apr. 3, 1747, in her 17th y. g. r. 2.

Elizabeth, w. Daniel, Apr. 14, 1774. [a. 25 y. c. r. 2.]

Elizabeth, May 27, 1780, a. 90 y. c. r. 2.

Hannah, w. Benjamin, May 11, 1738. [in her 31st y. g. r. 2.]

Hannah, Aug. 16, 1804.

Jonathan, s. Thomas, Oct. 25, 1675.

Jonathan, s. Thomas, Nov. 29, 1683.

John, Jan. 15, 1702-3. [a. 55 y. g. r. 2.]

Joseph, s. Joseph and Mary, Mar. 19, 1705.

Joseph, June 19, 1724.

Joseph, Dec. 19, 1724, in his 47th y. g. r. 2.

Leander V. Goreham (?), s. adopted, John and Eliza, Apr. 9, 1840, a. 3 y. 3 m. g. r. 5.

Lucy, Mrs., bur. July 27, 1844, a. 83 y. c. r. 5.

Maria, d. Samuel, Apr. 25, 1704.

Martha, wid. William, abt. Aug. 4, 1694.

Mary, d. Joseph, s. W[illia]m, Jan. 9, 1682-3, a. 3 hrs.

Mary Windship, d. Jason and Lucy, Oct. 4, 1801.

Mehittable, Nov. 28, 1724.

LYON, Olive, Feb. 7, 1817, a. 34 y. C. R. 2.
Rhoda, wid., June 26, 1816, a. 78 y. C. R. 2.
Samuel, s. Samuel and Elizabeth, Mar. —, 1712.
Samuel, sr., Apr. 7, 1713.
Sarah, w. William, Feb. 9, 1688-9.
Susanna, d. John and Abigail, Dec. 25, 1698.
Thomas, Nov. 30, 1810, a. 75 y. C. R. 2.
William, sr., bur. May 21, 1692.
William, sr., Aug. 10, 1714. [a. abt. 62 y. G. R. 2.]
————, ch. Benj[ami]n, Oct. 27, 1774, a. 3 y. 2 m. C. R. 2.
————, ch. Thomas, Feb. 21, 1775, a. 4 y. C. R. 2.
————, ch. Eliphalet, July 15, 1777, a. 2 y. C. R. 2.
————, d. Eliphelet, June 14, 1777, a. 5 y. C. R. 2.
———— ch. Tho[ma]s, May 31, 1780, a. 3 d. C. R. 2.
————, d. Benjamin and Elizabeth, Sept. 14, 1817, a. 4 y.
     C. R. 2.
————, ch. Charles, scalded, Jan. —, 1838, a. 4 w. C. R. 2.

**LYONS** (see also Lyon), Joseph, b. Ireland, small pox, at the
     alms house, Feb. 22, 1848, a. 3 y.
Mary, b. Ireland, small pox, at the alms house, Mar. 5, 1848, a.
     2 y.

**MABIN,** Caroline, Dec. —, 1842, a. over 40 y.

**MACARTY** (see also McCarty), Susannah, wid., Apr. 4, 1838,
     a. 78 y.

**McCAMEY,** Bridget, wid., b. Ireland, dysentery, Sept. 14,
     1847, a. 47 y.

**McCANDLISH,** John G., s. Thomas and Jennett, croup, May
     14, 1848, a. 1 y. 7 m.

**MacCARTHY** (see also McCarty), [Anna McCarthy, lung
     fever. C. R. 3.], wid., Mar. 21, 1803, a. 70 y.
Judeth, wid., issue of Mar. 2, 1791. N. R. 4.
Sally, July 6, 1805, a. 26 y.

**MACCARTI** (see also McCarty), Florence, June 13, 1712.

**McCARTNEY** (see also McCarty), Alexander, a pauper, Sept.
     9, 1834, a. 60 y.

**McCARTY** (see also Macarty, MacCarthy, McCarthy, Mac-
     carti, McCartney), Catherine, wid., b. Ireland, dropsy,
     Apr. 27, 1847, a. 47 y.

McCARTY, Charles, s. William and Susanna, Sept. 11, 1810.

Ellen, d. John and Bridget, croup, Apr. 2, 1849, a. 2 y. 4 m.

Henry F., Sept. 13, 1836, a. 28 y.

Jeremiah, jr., b. Ireland, d. at New Market, N. H., bur. Roxbury, brain fever, June 7, 1848, a. 16 y.

John, laborer, b. Ireland, lung complaint, Apr. 2, 1848, a. 19 y.

John, b. Ireland, Aug. 20, 1848.

Julia, d. Dan[ie]l and Catherine, decline, Feb. 3, 1849, a. 1 m. 7 d.

Margaret [Maccarty. N. R. 4.], d. Tho[ma]s and Sarah, July 17, 1799. [a. 23 y. N. R. 4.]

Maria, d. Daniel and Catherine, measles, July 12, 1848, a. 2 y. 2 m.

Martha, w. William, Nov. 12, 1803, a. 27 y.

Mary, d. John and Mary C., teething, July 13, 1848, a. 1 y. 3 m.

Mary, d. John and Julia, consumption, Mar. 23, 1849, a. 3 m.

Patrick, m., laborer, b. Ireland, fever, Aug. 13, 1847, a. 37 y.

Patrick, unm., laborer, b. Ireland, dysentery, Sept. 1, 1848, a. 19 y.

Richard, laborer, b. Ireland, diarrhoea, Apr. 2, 1848, a. 22 y.

Sarah, wid., Oct. 19, 1820, a. 68 y.

Thomas, Capt., May 20, 1783, a. 64 y. G. R. 1.

William, Dec. 3, 1830, a. 57 y.

McCEW, Richard, s. Timothy and Mary, fever, Apr. 8, 1849, a. 7 y.

McCLURE, Martha W., d. Mark and Mary, consumption, June 9, 1849, a. 14 y. 4m.

McCORMICK, Mary A., d. Patrick and Catherine, dysentery, Aug. 4, 1849, a. 9 m.

McCRACKER, Charles, s. Charles and Mariah, debility, Sept. 30, 1848, a. 1 m. 26 d.

McCUEN (see also Mecuen), Michael, b. Ireland, ship fever, at the alms house, Mar. 14, 1848, a. 9 y.

Rosea, at the alms house, Jan. 20, 1848, a. 35 y.

McDANIEL (see also McDaniell, McDaniels), Jacob, Capt., on the coast of Affica, ——, 1817.

McDANIELL (see also McDaniel), James G., s. Jacob and Eliza, Sept. —, 1810, a. 9 m. G. R. 1.

**McDANIELS** (see also McDaniel), Mary, m., b. England, consumption, Mar. 8, 1847, a. 23 y.

**McDONALD** (see also Donald), Emily, m., b. Brooks, Me., d. William and Fanny Cilley, fever, Apr. 3, 1847, a. 26 y.,

**McDONELL** (see also McDonnell), Edward, s. Michael and Margarett, bowel complaint, Aug. 4, 1849, a. 6 y. 4 m.
James, d. Michael and Mary, whooping cough, Mar. 8, 1849, a. 1 y. 8 m.

**McDONNELL** (see also McDonell), John, s. Patrick and Catherine, decline, Apr. 22, 1849, a. 21 d.
Margarett, b. Ireland, w. Francis, child bed, Mar. 19, 1849, a. 20 y.
Michael, s. Patrick and Alice, decline, Nov. 12, 1849.

**McELORY** (see also McElroy), Mary, d. John, Nov. 3, 1833, a. 7 m.

**McELROY** (see also McElory), Mary, Mrs., May 8, 1830, a. 35 y.
——, inf. s. John and Wealthy, cholera infantum, Oct. 20, 1847, a. 16 d.

**McEVANS**, Catherine, scarlet fever, Dec. 24, 1848, a. 5 y. 9 m.
John, s. James and Scaria, scarlet fever, Dec. 19, 1848, a. 7 y. 6 m.
Seria, d. James and Seria, summer complaint, Oct. 16, 1848, a. 3 y. 4 m.

**McFADDIN** (see also McFarden), ——, ch. John, Aug. 6, 1777, a. 16 m. c. r. 2.

**McFADDING** (see also McFarden), ——, s. John, Feb. 24, 1778, a. 2 w. c. r. 2.

**McFARDEN** (see also McFaddin, McFadding), Thomas [McFarlin, laborer. dup.], b. Ireland, ship fever, at the alms house, June 19, 1848, a. 45 y. [a. 50 y. dup.]

**McFARLIN**, see McFarden.

**McGANN** (see also McHann), James, s. Michael and Rosanna, decline, Sept. 19, 1848, a. 21 d.
Rosanna, m., b. Ireland, at Cambridge, bur. at Roxbury, child bed, Sept. 21, 1848, a. 26 y.

**McGAWLY,** Francis, s. Francis and Bridget, bowel complaint, Aug. 25, 1848, a. 1 y. 15 d.

**McGEE** (see also Magee), Henry F., at Woonsocket, ——, 1840. C. R. 4.

Margarett, b. Ireland, w. John, child bed, Aug. 4, 1849, a. 27 y.

Michael, s. Michael and Ann, jaundice, Dec. 9, 1849, a. 1 y. 1 m. 21 d.

——, ch. still born, John and Margarett, July 24, 1849.

**McGLAFLING** (see also McLaughlin), Lawrence, Mar. 15, 1822, a. 79 y. C. R. 2.

**McGLONE,** Stephen, m., laborer, b. Ireland, inflammation of bowels, July 3, 1847, a. 35 y.

**McGONN,** Frances, d. Thomas and Catherine, dysentery, Sept. 1, 1848, a. 11 m. 5 d.

**McGOWNAGE,** Hannah, b. Ireland, d. Michael and Margarett, bowel complaint, Sept. 8, 1848, a. 21 d.

**McGRAW** (see also Magrath), Bartley, b. Ireland, ship fever, at the alms house, Dec. 30, 1848, a. 30 y.

**McGREGOR,** James I., bur. Sept. 23, 1845, a. 1 y. 7 m. C. R. 5.

**McGUIRE** (see also McGuyre), Dennis, tailor, b. Ireland, cholera, Sept. 8, 1849, a. 42 y.

James, s. Michael and Margarett, dysentery, Aug. 9, 1848, a. 9 m. 9 d.

Winneford, m., b. Ireland, consumption, Oct. 16, 1849, a. 27 y.

**McGUYRE** (see also McGuire), Charles Henry Swett, s. twin, J., original defect of constitution, Aug. 13, 1818, a. 2 m. C. R. 3.

**McHANN** (see also McGann), Rosanna, b. Ireland, consumption, July 3, 1848, a. 28 y.

**McINTIRE** (see also McIntyre), Mary, Mrs., Feb. 1, 1824, a. 61 y.

**McINTOSH** (see also Mackingtosh), Warren, s. Michael and Mary, lung fever, Apr. 4, 1847, a. 2 y.

——, inf. ch. still born, Sam[ue]l and Susan, Sept. 29, 1847.

**McINTYRE** (see also McIntire), Daniel, s. Daniel and Mary, whooping cough, Jan. 4, 1849, a. 1 y.

**McJENNESS,** William, s. W[illia]m and Seria, scarlet fever, Apr. 7, 1849, a. 4 y. 2 m.

**MACK,** John, b. Ireland, ship fever, at the alms house, June 20, 1847, a. 3 y.

——, infantile, at the alms house, Feb. 23, 1849, a. 1 d.

**McKANAUGH** (see also McKenna), ——, ch. still born, John and Mary, Sept. 10, 1849.

**McKENNA** (see also McKanaugh), Mary, Mrs., Oct. 6, 1842, a. 74 y.

**MACKINGTOSH** (see also McIntosh), Sarah, domestic of John Amory, dropsy of the heart, Aug. 22, 1827, a. 17 y. C. R. 3.

**McLANE,** Archibald, m., laborer, b. Scotland, typhus fever, Dec. 10, 1847, a. 40 y.

John, at the alms house, Sept. 24, 1835, a. 2 y.

**McLAUGHLAN** (see also McLaughlin), Bridget, wid., b. Ireland, dysentery, Sept. 1, 1847, a. 60 y.

**McLAUGHLIN** (see also Laughlin, McLaughlan), Andrew, s. Richard and Hannah, teething, Sept. 9, 1848, a. 1 y. 3 m.

John, b. Ireland, consumption, Dec. 27, 1848, a. 16 y.

Timothy, m., s. farmer, b. Ireland, dysentery, Nov. 22, 1847, a. 30 y.

**McLOUD,** ——, s. still born, Alexander and Mary, Jan. 14, 1848.

**McMAHON,** Thomas, b. Ireland, diarrhoea, Aug. 16, 1848, a. 30 y.

**McMANNUS,** Ellen, b. Ireland, w. Patrick, at Dover, N. H., bur. at Roxbury, dysentery, Sept. 20, 1848, a. 40 y.

**McMULLEN,** Margarett, d. Ann, disease of the brain, at the alms house, Jan. 30, 1849, a. 7 m.

**McNABB,** James, at the almshouse, Oct. 2, 1836, a. 1 y.

**McNAMARA,** Bernard, s. Patrick and Bridget, scarlet fever, Nov. 28, 1848, a. 2 y. 2 m.

**McNAUGHT,** Emeline, b. Canton, d. Peter and A., whooping cough, May 28, 1849, a. 1 y. 7 m.

**McNEAL** (see also McNiel), Alice, m., b. Ireland, child bed fever, Feb. 8, 1848, a. 28 y.

**McNEE,** Mary [Mary Douglass Macnee, w. Robert, a native of Paisley, Scotland. G. R. 5.], heart complaint, Nov. 19, 1847, a. 28 y. [a. 23 y. G. R. 5.]

**McNIEL** (see also McNeal), ——, ch. W[illia]m, Aug. 26, 1806, a. 18 m.

**McNULTY,** George, b. Ireland, diarrhoea, July 20, 1848, a. 22 y.
Margarett, d. Peter and Bridget, dysentery, Aug. 5, 1848, a. 7 m.

**MACOCK,** Eben[eze]r, killed instantly by a wheel running over him, Mar. 27, 1776, a. 15 y. C. R. 2.

**MACOMBER,** Charlotte, Mrs., Dec. 5, 1823.

**McSWENEY,** Michael, m., b. Ireland, cold water, July 21, 1849, a. 32 y.

**McTEAMAN,** John, b. Ireland, ship fever, at the alms house, Mar. 24, 1848, a. 23 y.

**MADDISON,** ——, "dyed suddenly being melted as was thought and sitting down in the higheway by Daniel Brewers house dyed there," Aug. 10, 1683.

**MADUFF** (see also Duff), Charles, at the alms house, Oct. 4, 1842, a. 23 y.

**MAGEE** (see also McGee). James, Capt., Feb. 4 [2. dup.], 1801, a. 51 y.
——, ch. James, Nov. 26 [28. dup.], 1800, a. 15 m.

**MAGRATH** (see also McGraw), Edward, m., b. Ireland, consumption, Jan. 17, 1849, a. 44 y.

**MAHAN,** Michael, unm., laborer, b. Ireland, lung fever, Jan. 21, 1847, a. 26 y.

**MAHONEY** (see also Mahony), John, Aug. 5, 1834, a. 53 y. C. R. 5.

**MAHONY** (see also Mahoney), Daniel, b. Ireland, fever, Mar. 18, 1848, a. 22 y.

MAHONY, James, b. Ireland, s. John and Catherine, scarlet fever, Jan. 17, 1849, a. 12 y.

**MALAWN** (see also Maloon), Denis, s. Denis and Catherine, lung fever, Apr. 1, 1848, a. 6 m.

**MALKAM,** Winneford, d. Michael and Winneford, decline, Aug. 17, 1849, a. 1 m. 14 d.

**MALLON** (see also Maloon), ——, inf. ch. Kendall and Adeline E., fits, Dec. 6, 1846, a. 18 d.

**MALONEY** Michael, m., b. Ireland, fever, Oct. 23, 1847, a. 40 y.

**MALOON** (see also Malawn, Mallon), Michael, laborer, b. Ireland, sun struck, July 13, 1849, a. 26 y.
Nathaniel, s. Benj[amin] and Mary A., lung fever, Dec. 31, 1849, a. 8 m.

**MANAHAN** (see also Monnahan), Bridget, m., b. Ireland, child bed, May 20, 1848, a. 30 y.

**MANCHESTER,** Hephzabah Dana, w. William, Sept. 17, 1811.
William, Sept. 24, 1813.

**MANDELL,** Samuel W., b. Braintree, s. John and Caroline, at Brookline, bur at Roxbury, croup, Mar. 3, 1849, a. 3 y. 8 m.

**MANLY,** Patrick, b. Ireland, dysentery, June 7, 1848, a. 37 y.

**MANN,** Mary A., b. Ireland, cramp, at the alms house, June 15, 1847, a. 37 y.

**MANNING,** Agnes Gifford, d. Charles and Susan, dysentery, Aug. 16, 1848, a. 10 m. 22 d.
Patrick, at the alms house, Jan. 27, 1839, a. 29 y.

**MANSFIELD,** Nelson French, s. Capt. Joseph, Nov. 21, 1833, a. 6 m.
Thomas N. F., s. Joseph and Caroline, Mar. 24, 1836, a. 18 m.
Willie, s. Sylvester and Elizabeth, cholera infantum, Aug. 4, 1848, a. 1 m. 14 d.
——, s. Stephen, Nov. 7 [9. dup.], 1800, a. 6 y.

**MARDEN,** Mary Ann, d. David and Mary Ann, disease of the spine, Feb. 21, 1847, a. 2 y. 3 m.

**MAREAN** (see also Mareene), Susannah C., Nov. 26, 1826, a. 17 y.

**MAREENE** (see also Marean), ——, inf. ch. Dorman, an Irishman of Muddy River, bur. 20 : 3 m : 1681. C. R. 1.

**MARKHAM,** Catherine, Mrs., bur. June 16, 1845, a. 39 y. C. R. 5.
Robert, bur. Feb. 12, 1845, a. 39 y. C. R. 5.

**MARN,** —— [Mar. dup], s. James, foreigner, scarlet fever, July 1 [June 14. dup.], 1846, a. 7 y. [a. 6 y. dup.]

**MARSH,** Charles, bur. Jamaica Plain, bilious fever, Sept. 5, 1849, a. 45 y.
Hannah Withington, d. Warren, Oct. 16, 1826, a. 14 y.

**MARSHALL,** John James, s. Benj[amin] and Susannah, Dec. 23, 1798.
John James, s. Benjamin and Susanna, Nov. 9, 1801, a. 2 y.
——, ch. Benja[min], Sept. 10, 1802, a. 8 m.
——, ch. Benja[min], Sept. 20, 1807, a. 9 m.
——, inf. ch. H. and Lucretia, Sept. 4, 1846, a. 14 d.

**MARSTON,** David S., old age, Mar. 28, 1844, a. 83 y.
Elizabeth, a stranger, from Boston, consumption, Jan. 26, 1825, a. 34 y. C. R. 3.
Phebe Jane, d. John C., sore throat, bur. Feb. 14, 1832, a. 6 y. C. R. 2.
Sarah, w. David S., Mar. 11, 1841, a. 92 y.

**MART,** ——, Mrs., ——, 176-. G. R. 1.

**MARTIN,** John [polypus on the heart. C. R. 3.], Sept. 24, 1809, a. 45 y. G. R. 1. [a. 50 y. C. R. 3.]
Mary, d. Dennis and Catherine, decline, Jan. 3, 1849, a. 6 m.
Patrick, b. Ireland, ship fever, at the alms house, Oct. 1, 1847, a. 47 y.
William, s. John, Apr. 21, 1809, a. 7 m. G. R. 1.

**MARTY,** ——, w. W[illia]m, Nov. 12, 1803, a. 27 y.

**MASCRAFT** (see also Mashcraft), Mary [Marscraft. C. R. 1.], wid. Daniel, June 30, 1703.

**MASHCRAFT** (see also Mascraft), ——, inf. ch. Daniel, bur. 11 : 5 m : 1687. C. R. 1.

**MASON,** Elisabeth, d. Robert and Elisabeth, ——, 1686.

Elizabeth A., Aug. —, 1848. C. R. 6.

George, unm., laborer, b. Charlestown, s. Thomas and Mary, consumption, Oct. 30, 1848, a. 19 y.

Han[n]ah, w. ——, bur — : 11 m : or 12 m : 1687-8. C. R. 1.

John [inf. C. R. 1.], s. Robert and Elisabeth, July 26, 1687. ·

Mary, m., b. England, dysentery, Sept. 6, 1847, a. 60 y.

——, w. Robert, bur. Apr. —, 1637.

——, ch., still born, Thomas, jr. and Mary Ann, Feb. 14, 1849.

**MATHER** (see also Mathers), Jeremiah, Mar. 1, 1718.

**MATHERS** (see also Mather), Hannah, wid., b. Plymouth, d. Lemuel and Sarah Marshall, consumption, Feb. 24, 1848, a. 32 y.

**MATTHEWS,** John, Mar. 14, 1823, a. 75 y. C. R. 2.

Lucy, w. Gardner, Apr. 2, 1801, a. 25 y.

——, ch. Gardner, Feb. 19 [22. dup.], 1801, a. 11 w.

——, w. Gardner, Apr. 2, 1801, a. 25 y.

——, ch. James, diarrhoea, Aug. 15, 1846, a. 11 m.

**MATTOCK,** Elizabeth [Mattocks. CT. R.], d. David, July 5, 1655.

**MAUZ,** Christiana, b. Germany, w. Philip, palsy, Aug. 14, 1848, a. 48 y.

**MAXFIELD,** Ann, Jan. 12, 1843, a. 68 y.

Elizebeth, Sept. 1, 1807, a. 75 y.

**MAXWELL,** Hervey N., Feb. 16, 1826, a. 31 y.

**MAY** (see also Mayes, Mays, Mayse), Abigail, wid. Ebenezer, Jan. 26, 1763, in her 70th y. G. R. 1.

Abigail, w. Lemuel, Jan. 23, 1772, in her 23d y. G. R. 1.

Abigail [wid. Benjamin. G. R. 1.], June 15, 1799, a. 74 y. [a. 75 y. G. R. 1.]

Benjamin, Dec. 8, 1774, a. 67 y. G. R. 1.

Benj[ami]n [intemperance. C. R. 3.], Aug. 5, 1833, a. 52 y.

Ebenezer, May 2, 1752, in his 60th y. G. R. 1.

Eleazer, slain by the Indians, Apr. 29, 1689.

Gideon, s. Samuell, Feb. 27, 1671. [1671-2. C. R. 1.]

John, blind, bur. 11 : 7 m : 1671, a. abt. 40 y. C. R. 1.

John, s. Samuel and Abigail, of Boston, Dec. 3, 1672, a. 1 y. G. R. 1.

MAY, John, Dea., Feb. 24, 1729-30 [a. 67 y. 8 m. 4 d. G. R. 1.]

John, s. William and Margarett, Feb. 15, 1798.

Lemuel, Capt. [consumption. C. R. 3.], Nov. 19, 1805, a. 67
 y. G. R. 4. [a. 57 y. C. R. 3.]

Mary, d. Samuel and Katherine, of Boston, Jan. 15, 1749, a.
 6 w. 3 d. G. R. 1.

Mary, w. Benjamin, May 7, 1750, in her 32d y. G. R. 1.

Mary, cancer, May 13 [5. G. R. 1.], 1794, a. 49 y. C. R. 3. [a.
 48 y. G. R. 1.]

Noah Perrin, s. Moses and Mary, Feb. 2, 1766, a. 3 y. G. R. 1.

Olevia, consumption, Oct: 25, 1796, a. 19 y. C. R. 3.

Prudence, w. Dea. John, Sept. 26, 1723.

Samuel, s. Eleaser and Sarah, Dec. 26, 1688.

Samuel, July 12, 1697.

Samuel, jr., s. Samuel and Abigail, of Boston, Dec. 3, 1762,
 a. 7 y. G. R. 1.

Samuel, s. Samuel and Abigail, Sept. 22, 1768, a. 17 m. G. R. 1.

Sarah, w. Eleaser, Jan. 5, 1688-9.

Solomon, s. Ebenezer and Susanna, Feb. 26, 1759. [1760. a.
 1 y. G. R. 1.]

Solomon, nervous fever, —— 23, 1800, a. 38 y. C. R. 3.

Stephen, s. Benja[min] and Mary, Oct. 20, 1745, a. 2 y. 3 d.
 G. R. 1.

Stephen, s. Benja[min] and Mary, June 30, 1750, a. 11 m.
 G. R. 1.

Susannah, decay of nature, Mar. 19, 1811, a. 87 y. C. R. 3.

William, Mar. 3, 1829, a. 69 y.

**MAYBLE,** Elezabeth, d. Entris and Rosanna, bowel complaint,
 Aug. 10, 1848, a. 2 y.

**MAYES** (see also May), ——, "Sister," 18 : 4 m : 1651. C.
 R. 1.

——, ch. John, jr., bur. [bet. 4 m : and 10 m:], 1662. C. R. 1.

**MAYHALL,** James S., s. James and Caroline, disease on brain,
 July 29, 1848, a. 1 y. 3 m.

Miles Edgar [s. Miles and Polly. G. R. 5.], small pox, May 14,
 1846, a. 2 y. [a. 2 y. 2 m. G. R. 5.]

**MAYO,** Abel, Nov. 13, 1785, a. 18 y. C. R. 2.

Anne, wid., Apr. 16, 1816, a. 76 y. C. R. 2.

Anne, June 23, 1816, a. 51 y. C. R. 2.

MAYO, Benjamin, s. John, Oct. 1, 1672.

Catharine, w. Capt. [old age. C. R. 3.], Aug. 4, 1803, a. 81 y. G. R. 1.

Elizabeth, w. [Capt. G. R. 1.] Joseph, Feb. 7, 1734. [1734-5, in her 65th y. G. R. 1.]

Elizabeth, w. Thomas, jr., Jan. 27, 1748. [in her 34th y. G. R. 3.]

Elizabeth, d. Thomas and Mary, Jan. 1, 1753.

Hannah, d. John, Sept. —, 1658.

Hannah, wid John [w. John G. R. 1.], Oct. 5, 1699. [a. 63 y. G. R. 1.]

John [Maio. C. R. 1.], sr., Apr. 28, 1688. [a. 58 y. G. R. 1.]

John, Dea., Feb. 25, 1732-3, a. 74 y. G. R. 1.

John, shot by a cannon ball, Mar. 6, 1776, a. 34 y. C. R. 2.

Joseph, s. Thomas and Elizabeth, July 9, 1717.

Joseph, Capt., Mar. 5, 1747, a. 82 y. G. R. 1.

Joseph, s. Joseph and Esther, Oct. 22, 1748.

Joseph, Esq., Feb. 14, 1776, a. 55 y. C. R. 2.

Lemuel, s. Thomas, Nov. 10, 1791, a. 22 y. C. R. 2.

Mary, d. Thomas and Elizabeth, Sept. 9, 1718.

Mary, wid., Dec. 17, 1782, a. 41 y. C. R. 2.

Polly, w. J., Feb. 4, 1828, a. 51 y. C. R. 2.

Rebeca, d. John, Esq. [vomiting. C. R. 1.], Apr. 1, 1685.

Rebecka, d. John, jr., July 18, 1686.

Rebeckah, d Thomas and Elizabeth, Nov. 29, 1739. [in her 29th y. G. R. 3.]

Rebeckah, d. Thomas, jr. and Elisabeth, Dec. 26, 1744.

Rebeckah, d. Thomas, jr. and Elizabeth, June 17, 1747.

Samuel, Sept. 15, 1775, a. 18 y. C. R. 2.

Sarah, d. John and Sarah, June 30, 1688.

Sarah, d. Thomas, jr. and Elizabeth, Apr. 27, 1749. [in her 11th y. G. R. 3.]

Sarah Day, w. Aaron D., Mar. —, 1842, a. 47 y.

Thomas, s. John, Oct. 17, 1672.

Thomas, May 26, 1750, a. 72 y.

Thomas, Capt., Nov. 30, 1792, a. 79 y. C. R. 2.

Thomas, jr., Mar. 15, 1804, a. 40 y.

Thomas, Capt., Feb. 25, 1805. [a. 64 y. C. R. 2.]

Thomas, Sept. 15, 1822, a. 55 y.

——, inf. ch. John, bur. 5 : 12 m : 1686-7. C. R. 1.

——, s. John [and Sarah. dup.], Feb. 23, 1686. [a. abt. 4 or 5 y. dup.]

MAYO, ——, w. Maj., Aug. 26, 1775, a. 50 y. C. R. 2.
——, ch. John and Mary, Oct. 30, 1798, a. 6 m. C. R. 2.
——, ch. John and Mary, Feb. 13, 1804, a. 5 m. C. R. 2.

**MAYS** (see also May), John [May. C. R. 1.], sr., Apr. 28, 1670. [a. abt. 80 y. C. R. 1.]
Samuel, July 17, 1677.
Sarah [May. C. R. 1.], w. John, sr., May 4, 1670.

**MAYSE** (see also May), John, inf. s. John, bur. 29 : 8m : 1685. C. R. 1.

**MEAD** (see also Mede), Rebeca [Meade. C. R. 1.], wid. William [old. C. R. 1.], Nov. 6, 1683.
William [Meade. aged. C. R. 1.], Oct. 29, 1683.

**MEAG,** Osward, s. Peter and Ellen, teething, Jan. 10, 1849, a. 1 y. 2 m.

**MEAKINS** (see also Mekins), Katherin [Meakings. C. R. 1.], mother of Thomas [an aged woman. C. R. 1.], bur. Feb. 3, 1650. [1650-51. C. R. 1.]
Sarah, w. Thomas [child birth. C. R. 1.], bur. Jan. 25, 1650. [1650-51. C. R. 1.]

**MEARS,** Amos A., Dec 19, 1832, a. 48 y.
Ann, Mrs., Mar. 3, 1805.
James, June 6, 1804, a. 73 y.
James, Mar. 10, 1808, a. 49 y.
John, May 17, 1769, a. 37 y. G. R. 1.
John, Mar. 2, 1797, a. 35 y.
Mary, d. James and Mehitabel, Sept. 18, 1729.

**MECUEN** (see also McCuen), Edward Frances, s. John and Lois, Aug. 14, 1813.
John, Aug. 21, 1831, a. 43 y.
Lois, wid. John, d. Jacob Whittemore, dec., Jan. 17, 1839, a. 46 y.
Sarah L., d. John and Lois, heart complaint, Apr. 7, 1847, a. 24 y.

**MEDE** (see also Mead), Richard, Feb. 21, 1689-90.

**MEE,** Hugh, s. Hugh and Ann, bowel complaint, Nov. 8, 1848, a. 1 y. 2 m.
Peter, June 23, 1833.

**MEHAR,** Edmund, a pauper, Nov. 30, 1834, a. 65 y.

**MEKINS** (see also Meakins), John, s. Thomas, 10 : 3 m : 1649. C. R. 1.

**MELLER,** William, widr., florist, b. England, disease of the brain, Apr. 15, 1849, a. 64 y.

**MELLESH** (see also Mellish), ——, wid., Jan. 27, 1804, a. 49 y.

**MELLISH** (see also Mellesh, Mellus), Samuel [officer in U. S. Army. N. R. 4.], Sept 7 [9. G. R. 1.], 1797, a. 42 y.

**MELLON,** Mary, m., child bed, Dec. 9, 1848, a. 28 y.

**MELLUS** (see also Mellish), Mary, m., b. Olna, Me., d. John and Mary Averill, lung fever, Mar. 24, 1847, a. 48 y.

**MENDON,** Robert, widr., trader, b. Kittery, N. H., cancer, Dec. 29, 1849, a. 73 y.

**MERCY,** John, dwelt at Ebenezer Bernard's, last of July, 1716.

**MERIAM,** Eliza, d. John, Oct. 25, 1829, a. 25 y.
John, Oct. 28, 1833, a. 64 y.
Louisa, d. Maj. Abijah, Oct. 11, 1823, a. 1 y. 8 m.
Lucy, w. Nathaniel, bur. May 5, 1795, a. 56 y. N. R. 4.
Samuel, s. Maj. Abijah and Caty, July 18, 1824, a. 1 m.

**MERRIFIELD,** Benjamin [Merrsfield. N. R. 4.], July 26, 1796, a. 35 y. C. R. 2. [a. 34 y. N. R. 4.]

**MERRILL,** Walter R., s. Ezekil [s. Ezekiel and Hannah. C. R. 5.], Feb. 13, 1840, a. 6 y. 10 m. [a. 7 y. C. R. 5.]

**MESSER,** Francis, d. W[illia]m D., and Sarah Ann, croup, Jan. 27, 1848, a. 2 y. 6 m.

**METZLER,** Rebecca, m., fever, Dec. 12, 1846, a. 23 y.
——, ch. still born, George and Mary, July 1, 1849.

**MILES,** Katherine, d. Capt. [John and Sarah. G. R. 1.], "the beginning of" Jan. 1702-3. [a. abt. 3 y. G. R. 1.]
Mary, d. Capt. [John and Sarah. G. R. 1.], Dec. 20, 1702. [a. 8 y. 8 m. G. R. 1.]
Samuel, Mar. 11, 1813, a. 50 y.

**MILLER,** Catherine, d. George and Catherine, bowel complaint, Aug. 1, 1849, a. 11 m. 16 d.

Charles, Apr. 9, 1823, a. 34 y.

Charles, s. Frederick and Margaret, Mar. 12, 1849, a. 5 d.

Ellen A., d. John F. and Harriet, scarlet fever, Apr. 18, 1848, a. 2 y. 5 m.

James, an Irishman, Sept. 9, 1724.

Leven E., d. George and Caroline, bowel complaint, Aug. 31, 1847, a. 1 m. 21 d.

Menda, b. Germany, ship fever, at the alms house, Aug. 23, 1847, a. 38 y.

Rosa, b. Germany, ship fever, at the alms house, Aug. 7, 1847, a. 37 y.

———, w. Capt., Apr. 30, 1807, a. 55 y.

**MILLETT** (see also Millit), Henry Jewell [s. Morris and Esther. G. R. 4.], convulsion fits, Aug. 24, 1836, a. 2 y. C. R. 3.

**MILLIT** (see also Millett), Morris B., Aug. 4, 1840, a. 32 y.

**MILLS,** John, Jan. 21, 1822, a. 19 y. G. R. 5.

Mary Ann, d. Lemuel and Lucy, Mar. 19, 1836.

**MILNER,** Ann F. H., w. Joseph F., June 12, 1836, a. 27 y.

**MILTON,** Betsey, w. Thomas, Aug. 23, 1838, a. 51 y.

**MINGRIEL,** Catherine, m., b. Germany, consumption, Aug. 27, 1848, a. 38 y.

**MIRICK** (see also Myrick), Benjamin [Mereck. dup.], s. Benjamin and Sarah, Sept. 25, 1805. [a. 20 m. dup.]

Benjamin [Merrick. dup.], s. Benjamin and Sarah, Oct. 13, 1806. [a. 11 m. dup.]

Sarah, w. Capt. Benjamin, Oct. 8, 1825, a. 44 y.

**MIRRY** (see also Murray), Robert D. C., s. Robert D. C. and Sarah A., consumption, Sept. 9, 1847, a. 16 y.

**MITCHELL,** Mary Ann, b. Ireland, w. James, dysentery, Oct. 4, 1848, a. 54 y.

**MOFFETT,** Sarah, d. Affa, measles, July 20, 1849, a. 2 y. 2 m.

**MOLAN,** Michael, s. Patrick and Bridget, disease of the brain, July 15, 1849, a. 6 y.

**MOLINEUX,** Henry Clark, s. Robert W. and Paulina, bur. Oct. 10, 1839, a. 14 m. C. R. 5.

Mary Gilman, d. Robert W. and Paulina, Oct. 10, 1839, a. 3 y. 6 m.

——, ch. W. and Paulina, Sept. 15, 1846, a. 1 y. 6 m.

**MONK,** Charlotte, b. England, d. James and Charlotte, diarrhoea, July 5, 1849, a. 2 m. [a. 2 y. C. R. 5.]

**MONNAHAN** (see also Manahan), Julia, d. James and Ann, brain fever, Jan. 21, 1849, a. 1 y. 8 m.

**MONTGOMERY,** Mary, d. W[illia]m and Mary, bowel complaint, Aug. 18, 1848, a. 1 y. 8 m.

William, Oct. 1, 1805, a. 60 y.

——, ch. ——, Oct. 12, 1796, a. 2 y. 6 m.

**MOODY,** Dearborn, killed by a wagan passing over him, Nov. 24, 1826.

**MOONAN,** John, s. Thomas and Mary, measles, Feb. 22, 1849, a. 1 y.

**MOORE,** D. W., s. A. M., measles, June 12, 1846, a. 4 y. 5 m.

Edwin A., m., baker, d. Seth and Margarett, fits, Apr. 14, 1849, a. 43 y.

George R., s. Augustus M. and Sarah B., typhoid fever, Sept. 19, 1849, a. 13 y. 9 m.

James Peabody, s. Joseph, Sept. 15, 1817, a. 14 m.

John, bur. 27 : 8 m . 1679, a. 99 y. C. R. 1.

Levi A., s. Augustus M. and Sarah B., cholera morbus, Sept. 14, 1849, a. 9 y. 9 m.

Lydia Ann, d. Capt. J. H., Mar. 17, 1838, a. 7 m.

Margaret Ann, d. Seth H. and Margaret, Jan. 22, 1824, a. 16 y.

Mary J., d. Capt. J. H., Mar. 3, 1838.

Seth H., May 10, 1831, a. 55 y.

——, s. ——, Aug. 12, 1834, a. 6 h. C. R. 3.

**MORAN** (see also Moren, Morin), Eliza J., d. Michael and Sarah, bowel complaint, Sept. 5, 1849, a. 1 y. 2 m.

**MOREN** (see also Moran), Margarett, m., b. Ireland, bowel complaint, Oct. 8, 1847, a. 33 y.

**MOREY** (see also Mory), Abigail, d. John and Hannah, Dec. 24, 1741.

MOREY, Reuben, m., laborer, b. Charlton, Ct., s. J., erysipelas, Dec. 15, 1848, a. 61 y.

**MORGAN** (see also Morgaren), Abraham, bur. 2 : 6 m : 1649, a. abt. 1 y. C. R. 1.

Mary, m., b. Ireland, burnt, Jan. 28, 1848, a. 19 y.

Polly White, w. James H., July —, 1839.

——, inf. d. James, 20 : 9 m : 1650. C. R. 1.

**MORGAREN** (see also Morgan), James, m., laborer, b. Ireland, drowned, Aug. 14, 1849, a. 33 y.

**MORIL** (see also Morrill), Isaac, 18 : 10 m : 1662, a. 74 y. G. R. 1.

**MORIN** (see also Moran), Timothy, b. Ireland, fever, Jan. 13, 1848, a. 24 y.

**MORREL** (see also Morrill), Ezekiel, of Reading, bur. May 22, 1663.

Sarah, wid. Isaac, bur. 9 : 11 m : 1672-3, a. 72 y. C. R. 1.

**MORRELL** (see also Morrill), Abraham, 13 : 8 m : 1661, a. abt. 21 y. C. R. 1.

Abraham, s. Isacck, Sept. 28, 1661.

Abraham, of Salisbury, bur. 20 : 4 m : 1662. C. R. 1.

Isaac, s. Isaac, bur. —, 11 m : 1632. CT. R.

Isacck [Morell, "an aged brother." C. R. 1.], Dec. 20, 1661.

**MORRICK**, ——, wid. 25 : 6 m : 1650. C. R. 1.

**MORRILL** (see also Moril, Morrel, Morrell, Morroll), Abner, s. Joseph, June 30, 1840, a. 16 y.

Amos, Aug. 31, 1835, a. 36 y.

George, Sept. —, 1836, a. 24 y.

**MORRIS** (see also Morriss), Emanuel, m., mason, b. Ireland, consumption, Sept. 17, 1847, a. 36 y.

George, bur. Dec. 30, 1844, a. 71 y. C. R. 5.

Hannah, w. Isaac, Nov. 5, 1701.

Isaac, Lt., Oct. 21, 1715.

Mehitabel, w. Samuel, Feb. 8, 1702-3.

——, ch. Emanuel and Abigail, whooping cough, Sept. 6, 1846.

——, ch. Emanuel and Abigail, whooping cough, Sept. 11, 1846, a. 3 m.

**MORRISON,** Alexander, cancer, July 8, 1813, a. 86 y. C. R. 3.
John, s. John and Julia, inflammation of bowels, Aug. 24,
1849, a. 10 m. 15 d.

**MORRISS** (see also Morris), Elisabeth, d. Edward, jr., Feb.
19, 1683.
Grace, wid. Edward, sr., June 6, 1705.

**MORROLL** (see also Morrill), Elizabeth, d. Isaack, bur. May
—, 1638.
Isaack, s. Isaack, bur. Jan. 30, 1633.
Isaack, s. Isaack, bur. Jan. 31, 1639.

**MORSE,** Adam, at the alms house, May 11, 1837, a. 52 y. [a.
51 y. G. R. 5.]
Adeline d. Luther, 2d, Jan. 5, 1823, a. 2 y.
Amos, Nov. 24, 1823, a. 51 y.
Elizabeth, Sept. 8, 1834, a. 19 y.
Ezra, Oct. 17, 1826, a. 61 y.
Ezra, unm., gentleman, s. Ezra and Rebecca, consumption,
Mar. 31, 1849, a. 27 y.
Ezra Dwight, s. Luther and Elizabeth, Sept. 25, 1817.
George, s. Luther, 2d, Dec. 16, 1831.
Harford, Oct. 28, 1830, a. 43 y.
Lewis, Aug. 2, 1830, a. 52 y.
Luther, m., yeoman, b. Sharon, at Sharon, bur. at Roxbury, old
age, Dec. 4, 1848, a. 79 y.
Martha, Sept. 26, 1809.
Mary, w. Lewis, May 25, 1815, a. 31 y.
Mary Holmes, d. Luther and Mary, Apr. 22, 1799.
Sally, May 13, 1812.
——, ch. Lewes, Aug. 20, 1805, a. 11 m.
——, w. Lewis, Apr. 3, 1806, a. 27 y.
——, ch. still born, George, Dec. 29, 1846.

**MORTON,** Harriet, m., lung fever, Sept. 1, 1847, a. 20 y. 11
m. 15 d.
Joseph E., s. Joseph and Mary S. [fever and measles. C. R. 3.],
May 2, 1810. [a. 3 y. C. R. 3.]

**MORY** (see also Morey), Elizabeth Leavit, d. Thomas, Nov.
23, 1712.
John, Sept. 16, 1771, a. 86 y. N. R. 2.
Nathanael, s. Thomas, Jan. 9, 1717.

Mory, Nathaniel, Jan. 7, 1717-18, in his 24th y. G. R. 1.

Thomas, s. Thomas, May 19, 1678.

Thomas, Dec. 25, 1717. [in his 71st y. G. R. 1.]

Timothy, b. Ireland, ship fever, at the alms house, Jan. 10, 1848, a. 25 y.

**MOSIER,** Mary, Sept. 17, 1818, a. 44 y.

**MOULTON,** Ellen, b. Ohio, d. Albenus and Julia, bowel complaint, Aug. 9, 1848, a. 8 y. 6 m.

George, s. George and Phebe J., disease on the brain, Oct. 11, 1847, a. 2 y.

James, internal tumor, Oct. 27, 1832, a. 15 y. c. R. 3.

Leander, s. Jonathan and Olive, bowel complaint, Aug. 26, 1848, a. 2 y. 5 m.

**MOUNTAIN,** James, s. Patrick and Ellen, bowel complaint, Aug. 31, 1848, a. 4 m.

**MOUNTFORT,** Lucretia, Mrs., Oct. 26, 1823, a. 37 y.

**MULDRY,** William, at the almshouse, Oct. 17, 1839, a. 38 y.

**MULLIGAN,** John, s. Thomas and Jane, croup, Apr. 22, 1848, a. 2 y. 7 m.

**MULRAIN,** Michael, m., laborer, b. Ireland, convulsions, Oct. 27, 1849, a. 34 y.

**MUNCREAF** (see also Muncrief), Joseph, Dec. 23, 1805, a. 76 y.

**MUNCREEFF** (see also Muncrief), Sarah, w. Joseph, June 13, 1764, a. 32 y. G. R. 1.

**MUNCRIEF** (see also Muncreaf, Muncreeff), Amy Baker [Muncreaf, d. Joseph and Anna. G. R. 5.], May 19, 1831, a. 2 y. 5 m.

Joseph [Moncrief, jr. dup.], s. Joseph and Abigail, Oct. 10, 1797. [a. 4 y. dup.]

Joseph, Oct. 24, 1823, a. 56 y.

**MUNROE,** Daniel, July 23, 1827. G. R. 1.

Nehemiah, Dea., Aug. 18, 1828, a. 83 y.

Rebecca, Mrs., ——, 1832, a. 30 y.

——, d. John and Sarah, teething, Aug. 26, 1846, a. 1 y. 6 m.

**MURDOCK,** Charity, w. Ebenezer, May 8, 1802, a. 31 y. c.
r. 2.

Charity, Sept. 23, 1804, a. 58 y. c. r. 2.

Ebenezer, Sept. 6, 1807, a. 37 y. c. r. 2.

Ebenezer, s. wid. Hannah, Mar. 23, 1808, a. 4 y. c. r. 2.

Eph[rai]m, Dea., Aug. 23, 1803, a. 66 y.

Hannah, d. Robart and Hannah, Jan. 23, 1692-3.

Mary H., w. Geo[rge], June 14, 1837, a. 37 y.

Sarah, Oct. 3, 1779, a. 76 y. c. r. 2.

——, s. Dea., Feb. 9, 1776, a. abt. 3 y. c. r. 2.

——, s. Dea., Aug. 16, 1778, a. 19 m. c. r. 2.

——, s. Dea., Feb. 9, 1783, a. 2 y. c. r. 2.

——, d. Dea., Aug. —, 1783, a. 4 y. c. r. 2.

——, inf. ch. Ebenezer and Charity, May 4, 1802. c. r. 2.

——, ch. Ebenezer and Hannah, Sept. 14, 1806, a. 9 w. c. r.
2.

**MURPHY,** Catherine, d. Owen and Joanna, decline, Apr. 7,
1849, a. 11 m.

David, unm., laborer, b. Ireland, dysentery, Oct. 3, 1848, a.
26 y.

Francis, s. Martin and Hannah, bowel complaint, Aug. 30,
1848, a. 8 m.

Mary, m., b. Ireland, fever, Sept. 23, 1847, a. 28 y.

Mary A., b. Maine, St. Anthony's dance, at the alms house, Jan.
25, 1849, a. 39 y.

Patrick, m., laborer, b. Ireland, consumption, Mar. 17, 1849,
a. 32 y.

——, ch. Margaret, at the alms house, Oct. 28, 1842.

**MURRAY** (see also Mirry, Murrey, Murry), Catherine, b. Ireland, May 8, 1848, a. 28 y.

Mary, d. John and Julia, fits, July 13, 1849, a. 22 y.

Michael, s. Alick and Catherine, teething, Sept. 6, 1849, a.
10 m.

Peter, b. Ireland, accidental, June 7, 1848, a. 25 y.

Timothy, b. Ireland, ship fever, at the alms house, June 12,
1848, a. 21 y. [a. 28 y. dup.]

——, ch. still born, John and Mary, May 13, 1848.

**MURREY** (see also Murray), Caroline Elizabeth Abbott, d.
William, Sept. —, 1837, a. 13 m.

Michael, ship fever, at the alms house, July 18, 1847, a. 1 y.

**MURRY** (see also Murray), James, s. James and Ann, by a fall, July 26, 1848, a. 5 m.

**MUSENORE,** John, s. John and Johanna, fits, Aug. 7, 1848, a. 8 m.

**MUTOCHLER,** Michael, m., cabinet maker, b. Germany, dysentery, Sept. 6, 1849, a. 32 y.

**MYRICK** (see also Mirick), Benjamin, Capt., Sept. 30, 1838, a. 62 y.

**NAFF** (see also Neafe), Adeline, d. Lewis and Catherine, fits, July 21, 1848, a. 3 m.

**NARVAN,** John, m., laborer, b. Ireland, bowel complaint, Nov. 17, 1847, a. 55 y.

**NASH,** Caroline M., d. David R., July 16, 1839, a. 5 y.
Ellen A., d. Cha[rle]s W. and Amoretta, scarlet fever, June 24, 1849, a. 4 y.
Louisa M., d. Cha[rle]s W. and Amoretta, scarlet fever, June 28, 1849, a. 6 y.

**NASON,** Elizabeth A., Mrs., July 9, 1831, a. 42 y.
Emely C., b. Cambridge, w. James, inflammation of bowels, Aug. 6, 1848, a. 41 y.
Harriet, d. Jabez and Elizabeth, Feb. 19, 1826, a. 6 m.
Jabez, Apr. 24, 1834.
James Henry, s. James, July —, 1833, a. 22 m.
Nancy Josephine, d. James, Feb. 14, 1840, a. 3 y. 5 m.
——, ch. Andrew, bowel complaint, Aug. 23, 1846, a. 1 y 6 m.

**NAUGHLIN,** Hugh, s. Hugh and Bridget, dysentery, Aug. 28, 1848, a. 3 m.

**NAUGHTON** (see also Norton), George, m., laborer, b. Ireland, Sept. 16, 1849, a. 35 y.
Mary, b. Ireland, w. Patrick, consumption, July 7, 1849, a. 26 y.

**NEAFE** (see also Naff), Theo. Kain, inf. ch. Henry and Maria, Sept. —, 1834. C. R. 5.

**NELSON,** Catherine, b. Germany, w. Casper, dysentery, Aug. 27, 1848, a. 47 y.

NESSUCKLE, ———, ch. George, July 3, 1816, a. 21 m.
C. R. 2.

NEWCOMB, Mary, m., b. Cornwallis, Nova Scotia, d. John
and [James, sic], child bed, Jan. 26, 1847, a. 26 y.

NEWEL (see also Newell), Abigail, d. Abraham, jr., Apr. 3,
1682.
Abigail, w. Abraham, jr., May 12, 1686.
Abigail, d. Isaac, jr. and Sarah, Jan. —, 1697.
Abraham, sr., June 13, 1672, a. 91 y.
Abraham [Newell. c. r. 1.], s. Isaac [small pox. c. r. 1.], Dec.
25, 1678. [a. 11 y. c. r. 1.]
Abraham, Oct. 9, 1726.
Abram, sr., Aug. 17, 1692.
Ebenezer, s. Ebenezer, May 25, 1701.
Elisabeth, d. Abraham, jr., Mar. 20, 1683.
Elizabeth, d. Ebenezer and Mary, Sept. 1, 1717.
Experience, d. Ebenezer and Mary, Dec. 8, 1706.
Isaac, sr., Dec. 8, 1707.
Jakob, small pox, 30 : 10m : 1678. c. r. 1.
John, s. Abraham, bur. 3 : 6m : 1673. c. r. 1.
John, Mar. 18, 1694.
John, Feb. 25, 1785, a. 75 y. c. r. 2.
Mary, d. Jakob, small pox, 5 : 12m : 1678-9. c. r. 1.
Mehetabel, w. Robert, Nov. 4, 1739, a. abt. 70 y. g. r. 2.
Robert, Feb. 17, 1741, in his 68th y. g. r. 2.
Thomas, s. Abra[ham], suddenly, 26 : 5m : 1675. c. r. 1.
———, ch. Abram, bur. 10 : 3m : 1686. c. r. 1.

NEWELL (see also Newel, Newells), Abag[ai]l, wid., Nov.
16, 1804, a. 86 y.
Daniel, Nov. 5, 1829, a. 55 y.
Ebenezer, Ens., Oct. 16, 1746. [in his 73d y. g. r. 1.]
Frances, Jan. 13, 1682-3.
Harriet P., d. Willard, Jan. 19, 1837, a. 3 y.
Jonathan A[mory Newall. c. r. 3.], Esq. [typhus fever. c. r.
3.], Sept. 14, 1832, a. 61 y.
Joseph, s. Abram, bur. Dec. 10, 1651.
Josiah, s. Isaac, Nov. 26, 1678.
Luther, Dec. 27, 1832, a. 44 y.
Nathaniel, grand s. Ebenezer, Dec. 8, 1746, in his 4th y. g. r. 1.
Samuel, Apr. 24, 1779, a. 36 y. c. r. 2.
Thomas, s. Abraham, Aug. 1, 1674.

NEWELL, William, bur. Mar. 23, 1796, a. 17 y. N. R. 4.
———, inf. ch. Jacob, bur. May 25, 1657. CT. R.
———, "Mother," bur. 16 : 11m : 1682-3, a. abt. 100 y. C. R. 1.
———, w. John, July 21, 1780, a. 63 y. C. R. 2.
———, ch. Joshua, July 6, 1781, a. 9 w. C. R. 2.
———, ch. Joshua, May 20, 1782, a. 5 h. C. R. 2.
———, ch. Dan[ie]l, Dec. 27, 1802, a. 2 m.
———, ch. Dan[ie]l, Sept. 26, 1807, a. 18 m.

**NEWELLS** (see also Newell), ———, inf. ch. Ja[c]ob, bur.
May 25, 1660.

**NEWMAN,** Andrew, Nov. 2, 1802, a. 59 y.
Andrew, Capt., Mar. 11, 1812, a. 33 y. [a. 34 y. G. R. 1.]
Edward, Dec. 21, 1811, a. 11 m. G. R. 1.
Elizabeth, Mar. 11, 1817.
Elizabeth S., Mrs., July 26, 1827, a. 82 y.
William, s. William J. and Sarah, Feb. 22, 1814. [a. 2 y. 11 m.
G. R. 1.]
William, J., Apr. —, 1838, a. 52 y.
———, ch. still born, Andrew W. and Caroline, Feb. 16, 1847.

**NEWTON,** Antipas, m., soap boiler, b. Westborough, s.
Barnabas and Eunice, dysentery, Aug. 26, 1847, a. 66 y.
David, Nov. 29, 1812, a. 58 y. C. R. 2.
Hannah, Jan. 8, 1827, a. 32 y. C. R. 2.
James C., s. Antipas and Elizabeth, Nov. 20, 1839, a. 30 y.
Leonard, widr., yeoman, lung complaint, Jan. 7, 1849, a. 51 y.
Warren F., s. Alvin and M., croup, Dec. 18, 1849, a. 1 y. 2 m.
———, s. Stephen and Sarah F., croup, Mar. 19, 1847, a. 2 m.

**NICHOLS** (see also Nickols), William, s. William and Mary,
lung fever, Oct. 10, 1847, a. 2 m.

**NICKERSON,** Mary Smith, d. David and Emily, Nov. —,
1825, a. 15 m.

**NICKOLS** (see also Nichols), Julia Florina, d. William and
Mary, bur. Mar. 21, 1837, a. 5 w. C. R. 5.

**NILES,** Daniel, Sergt., of Easton, Nov. 2, 1775, a. 41 y. G. R. 4.

**NINCHOLSON,** William, Apr. 12, 1812, a. 29 y.

**NIXON,** Sarah F.. b. Salem, N. H., w. George, consumption,
Jan. 8, 1848, a. 41 y.

**NOBLE,** Arthur, rheumatism, Nov. —, 1807, a. 71 y. c. r. 3.

**NOLAN** (see also Nolen), James, s. Thomas and Catherine, dysentery, Aug. 9, 1848, a. 9 m. 8 d.

**NOLAND** (see also Nolen), James, Dr., "came sick from Anapolis Royal," July 8, 1713.

**NOLEN** (see also Nolan, Noland), Elizabeth, wid. Thomas, sr., Feb. 2, 1802, a. 62 y.
Thomas, Dec. 26, 1801, a. 37 y. [1802. dup.]

**NORCROSS,** Jane E[liza. c. r. 3.], d. Otis, Esq., of Boston, dec. [consumption. c. r. 3.], Apr. 22, 1840, a. 17 y.

**NORCUTT,** Experience, at her mother Johnson's, Mar. 23, 1710.

**NORRIS,** Abraham, b. England, cholera, at the alms house, Aug. 19, 1849, a. 35 y.
Hugh, Nov. 22, 1789. c. r. 2.
Michael, m., laborer, b. Ireland, suicide [at the alms house. dup.], Aug. 26, 1848, a. 40 y.
————, ch. still born, Abraham B. and Agnes, Jan. 3, 1849.

**NORTON** (see also Naughton), Ann, b. Ireland, ship fever, at the alms house, May 29, 1847, a. 22 y.
Bridgett, unm., b. Ireland, consumption, Sept. 29, 1848, a. 25 y.
Hugh, m., laborer, b. Ireland, lung complaint, Mar. 19, 1848, a. 45 y.
John, b. Ireland, lung complaint, at the alms house, Jan. 30, 1849, a. 14 y.
Lawrence [unm., laborer. dup], b. Ireland, ship fever, at the alms house, June 20 [19. dup.], 1847, a. 32 y. [a. 27 y. dup.]
Mary, d. Patrick and Bridget, small pox, Sept. 13, 1849, a. 1 y. 2 m.
Thomas, b. Ireland, ship fever, at the alms house, July 15, 1847, a. 22 y.
Thomas, b. Baltimore, ship fever, at the alms house, Mar. 31, 1849, a. 58 y.

**NOYES,** Esther, w. John E., May —, 1826, a. 33 y.
Isaac, s. George and Margarett, small pox, at the alms house, May 14, 1849, a. 7 y.
James, suddenly, Feb. —, 1827. c. r. 4.

Noyes. Martha, Dec. —, 1830. c. r. 4.

Michael, May —, 1842. c. r. 4.

Moses, Apr. 1, 1831, a. 14 y.

Simeon, May —, 1842.

———, inf. ch. Benj[ami]n, Sept. —, 1840.

**NUDD,** Hannah, m., b. Stratham, N. H., July 24, 1847, a. 18 y.

**NUSZ,** Anthony, m., laborer, b. Germany, brain fever, Dec. 10, 1848, a. 41 y.

**NUTE,** ———, ch. still born, Josiah and Abby, dysentery, Aug. 20, 1847.

**NUTSPITTLE,** ———, inf. d. ———, Feb. 19, 1809. c. r. 2.

**NUTTALL,** ———, ch. W[illia]m, cholera morbus, Sept. 30, 1833, a. 2 y. g. r. 2.

**NYE,** Henry Toby, s. Oliver C., Dec. 25, 1840, a. 6 y.

Lydia, Mrs., July —, 1829, a. 53 y.

**NYHAN,** Michael, unm., laborer, b. Ireland, bowel complaint, Aug. 9, 1849, a. 21 y.

**O'BEIRNE** (see also O'Brine), Catherine, d. Francis and Ellen O., water on the brain, Nov. 16, 1849, a. 1 y. 1 m.

**O'BRINE** (see also O'Beirne), Cornelius, s. John and Mary, brain fever, Jan. 21, 1849, a. 2 m. 3 d.

Edward, s. John and Catherine, bowel complaint, Oct. 25, 1848, a. 1 y. 1 m.

John, dropsy in the head, at the alms house, Oct. 31, 1847, a. 10 m.

Malachi, unm., b. Ireland, of poisoning, in New Bedford, bur. at Roxbury, Nov. 11, 1848, a. 30 y.

Martin, m., b. Ireland, fits, July 27, 1849, a. 28 y.

**OCKINGTON,** Polly [Mary Orkington, Mrs. n. r. 4.], Apr. 17, 1799 [bur. at Jamaica Plain. n. r. 4.], a. 25 y. [a. 24 y. n. r. 4.]

**O'CONNOR** (see also Conner, Connor), Edith, bur. Oct. 23, 1844, a. 2 y. 9 m. c. r. 5.

**O'DONAL** (see also O'Donnell), John, b. Ireland, bowel complaint, at the alms house, Sept. 14, 1847, a. 81 y.

**O'DONNELL** (see also O'Donal), Margarett, wid., b. Ireland, consumption, Sept. 27, 1848, a. 53 y.

Patrick, m., laborer, b. Ireland, consumption, Jan. 21, 1849, a. 33 y.

**O'FLARETY,** Matthew, s. Michael and Catherine, erysipelas, Oct. 9, 1848, a. 6 y.

**OGIN,** Lucy, Sept. 15, 1798, a. 48 y.

**OLIVER** (see also Olivers), Daniel, Rev., Sept. 14, 1840, a. 89 y.

Henry J., m., merchant, s. Edward and Ann, consumption, Sept. 5, 1847, a. 59 y.

———, ch. Stephen, May 8, 1807, a. 3 y.

**OLIVERS** (see also Oliver), Stephen [Oliver. dup.], Oct. 2, 1800, a. 18 m.

**ONION,** Mary, w. Robart [childbirth. c. r. 1.], bur. Apr. 4, 1643.

Samuel, s. Asa and Susan, fits, Nov. 15, 1846, a. 1 y. 3 m.

———, ch. still born, Robart, bur. Mar. 22, 1642.

———, inf. ch. Robert, bur. —: 2m: 1643. ct. r.

**ORCUTT,** Betsey, Mrs. [paralytic. c. r. 3.], Feb. 7, 1835, a. 73 y.

———, Miss, July 29, 1837, a. 70 y. c. r. 2.

———, w. Henry, fit, May 8, 1846. c. r. 3.

**ORKFORD,** James, laborer, b. Ireland, s. Bridget, typhus fever, Feb. 16, 1848, a. 19 y.

**ORNE,** Elizabeth, Mrs., Nov. 11, 1836, a. 81 y. [a. 84 y. c. r. 5.]

**O'ROUKE** (see also Rook), Margarett, b. Ireland, w. Thomas, consumption, Mar. 24, 1849, a. 35 y.

**ORR,** Mary, wid., old age, Mar. 21, 1844, a. 85 y.

Rebecca, d. James and Elizabeth, Aug. 7, 1765, a. 5 m. g. r. 1.

**ORROK,** James L. P., hung himself on the chamber door, Feb. 17, 1843, a. 42 y.

Joseph Tacher, s. J. L. P., Jan. 9, 1840, a. 9 m.

**OSBORN,** Martha, w. John, June —, 1825, a. 30 y.

**OSGOOD,** Abigail, w. Henry, dysentery, Sept. 17, 1848, a. 34 y.

Amelia, b. Eaton, L. C., d. Benj[amin] and Lucinda, consumption, Nov. 13, 1847, a. 22 y.

Mary, instructress, d. Peter and Mary, heart complaint, Oct. 16, 1849, a. 46 y.

Sally, July 13, 1826, a. 40 y.

**PACKER,** Dolly, wid., old age, Feb. 25, 1844, a. 78 y.

Walter C., s. George, Feb. 1, 1843, a. 2 y.

————, ch. Charles A., diarrhoea, July 10, 1846, a. 14 m.

**PAGE,** Francis Dana, scarlet fever, June 15, 1849, a. 5 y. 4 m.

John, inf. s. John, a stranger, bur. 7 : 9m : 1685. C. R. 1.

Mary, wid., b. N. Y., old age, Feb. 19, 1848, a. 84 y.

Samuel Dana, scarlatina, Dec. 16, 1842, a. 3 y. 9 m. C. R. 3.

————, inf. ch. Nathaniel, bur. 31 : 5m : 1687. C. R. 1.

————, ch. Kilby. Dec. —, 1842.

**PAIN** (see also Paine), Mary, wid. Samuel, Dec. 26, 1753, in her 70th y. G. R. 1.

**PAINE** (see also Pain, Payne), Joseph C., Dec. —, 1839, a. 24 y.

Mary, Oct. 2, 1800, a. 26 y. C. R. 2.

————, Mr., Jan. —, 1840, a. abt. 60 y.

**PALMER,** Ann, unm., b. Bridgewater, dropsy, May 4, 1847, a. 67 y.

Joseph, Hon., Dec. 25, 1788, in his 70th y. N. R. 3.

Joseph, Capt., Aug. —, 1824, a. 62 y.

**PALSEY,** ————, ch. still born, John and Rebecca, Aug. 21, 1849.

**PALSGRAVE,** Anne, Mrs., bur. 17 : 1m : 1668-9, a. 75 y. C. R. 1.

**PARK** (see also Parke, Parkes, Parks), John, bur. Apr. 5, 1688. C. R. 1.

John, b. Ireland, consumption, July 21, 1848, a. 21 y.

William, s. Willia[m], 14 : 5m : 1656. C. R. 1.

William, Dea., May 11, 1685. [1683, a. 79 y. G. R. 1.]

**PARKE** (see also Park), Martha [Park. G. R. 1.], wid. Dea. W[illia]m, Aug. 25 [10. G. R. 1.], 1708, in her 94th y.

**PARKER,** Abby M[ary. c. r. 3.], d. John, Esq., dec. [consumption. c. r. 3.], Oct. 23, 1838, a. 50 y. [a. 49 y. c. r. 3.]

Abigail, w. Jonathan, Mar. 23, 1773, in her 40th y. G. R. 1.

Abigail [M. consumption. c. r. 3.], Apr. 22, 1840, a. 16 y. [a. 17 y. c. r. 3.]

Abram, Sept. 17, 1693.

Alfred, s. Caleb and Susan P., dysentery, Aug. 18, 1848, a. 16 y.

Anna C., w. Benj[ami]n M., d. Dea. Abner and Betsey Childs [nervous brain fever. c. r. 3.], Nov. 7, 1826, a. 24 y. [a. 25 y. c. r. 3.]

Benjamin F., Dr., consumption, Feb. 27, 1844, a. 33 y.

Caleb, widr., farmer, paralytic, Nov. 26, 1846, a. 75 y.

Deborah, Mrs., July 22, 1838, a. 85 y.

Fanny, Mrs., of Amsterdam, Holland, Feb. 3, 1826, a. 20 y.

Fanny, w. Caleb, Sept. —, 1827, a. 53 y.

Fanny W[arner. G. R. 5.], wid., b. Hardwick, dysentery, Sept. 24, 1847, a. 69 y.

Frances [Warner. G. R. 5.], wid., dysentery Sept. 4, 1847, a. 46 y.

George B., s. John and Rebecca, dysentery, Aug. 27, 1847, a. 3 y. 5 m.

Hannah [consumption, Oct. 11. c. r. 3.], 1830, a. 43 y.

Hannah, w. Charles, Mar. 19, 1836, a. 46 y. c. r. 2.

Jacob, s. Jacob and Thankfull, Apr. 26, 1691.

Jeremiah, Jan. 8, 1778, in her 60th y. G. R. 1.

Jeremiah, Lt., Apr. 29, 1780, in his 36th y. G. R. 1.

Jeremiah [by a fall under a trip hammer, at Dedham. c. r. 3.], May 9, 1797, a. 17 y.

John, collier [of Muddy River. c. r. 1.], Jan. 30, 1684-5.

John, Esq.. [consumption of lungs. c. r. 3.], Apr. 21, 1828, a. 68 y.

John A., s. Joseph, Apr. 22, 1819, a. 40 y. G. R. 1.

John A[ndrews. G. R. 5.], clerk, b. Charlestown, s. Nehemiah and Frances W., dysentery, Sept. 23, 1847, a. 21 y.

John W., s. John and Rebecca, dysentery, Aug. 21, 1847, a. 1 y. 10 m.

Joseph, May 30, 1782, a. 30 y. G. R. 1.

Lydia, typhus fever, Jan. 31, 1811, a. 54 y. c. r. 3.

Lydia, w. Abraham G., consumption, June 1, 1846, a. 56 y.

PARKER, Martha, d. Jeremiah and Martha, Jan. 29, 1780, in his 23d y. G. R. 1.

Martha wid. [Jeremiah. G. R. 1.; pluerisy fever. C. R. 3.], Dec. 18, 1805, a. 81 y.

Mary, w. Jeremiah, Mar. 11, 1749, in her 27th y. G. R. 1.

Mary, d. Jere[mia]h and Martha, May 15, 1779, a. 23 y. G. R. 1.

Mary E., d. Solomon B. and Sarah B., dysentery, Aug. 5, 1847, a. 1 y. 6 m. 6 d.

Peter, Nov. 15, 1765, in his 46th y. G. R. 1.

Samuel, Capt., June 9, 1831, a. 54 y.

Sam[ue]l W., Oct. 16, 1838, a. 47 y.

Sarah, Jan. 23, 1710-11.

Susan Miria, d. Dea., Nov. 1, 1831, a. 5 y.

Thankfull, d. [inf. ch. C. R. 1.], Jacob and Thankfull, Feb. 19, 1687-8.

Thomas, jr., of Amsterdam, Mar. —, 1830.

Timothy, Apr. 8, 1785, a. 31 y. G. R. 1.

William, widr., s. Nath[anie]l and Hannah, old age, Mar. 28, 1849, a. 86 y.

————, inf. twin chn. [Dea. C. R. 1.] William, bur. June 1, 1653.

————, ch. still born, ————, bur. 27 : 9m : 1686. C. R. 1.

————, ch. Charles, influenza and croup, Dec. 24, 1834, a. 2 y. 4 or 5 m. C. R. 2.

**PARKES** (see also Park), Deborah [Park. C. R. 1.], d. William, bur. Aug. 14, 1649.

Hanna [Parke. d. Dea. C. R. 1.], d. W[illia]m, June 24, 1655.

John [Parke. inf. C. R. 1.], s. William, bur. June 17, 1646.

Sarah, d. William, bur. Sept. 8, 1644.

**PARKINSON,** Edward Davis, s. John and Ann, croup, Nov. 30, 1827, a. 2 y. 3 m. C. R. 3.

John Austin, s. John, Esq., Nov. [bur. Nov. 12. C. R. 5.], 1839, a. 15 y.

**PARKS** (see also Park), John [Parke. C. R. 1.], s. Dea., bur. May 3, 1663.

**PARMENTER** (see also Parmeter), John, formerly Deacon at Sudbury, bur. 1 : 3m : 1671, a. 83 y. C. R. 1.

**PARMETER** (see also Parmenter), Annis [Parmiter, "old mother." C. R. 1.], wid. John, Mar. 15, 1683.

**PARSONS,** ———, ch. W. G., Aug. —, 1837, a. 7 w.

**PARTERIDGE** (see also Partridge), William, s. Thaddeus and Jane, Nov. 12, 1772, a. 3 y. G. R. 1.

**PARTRICK** (see also Patrick), ———, ch. Phin[ea]s, Nov. 24, 1803, a. 10 d.

**PARTRIDGE** (see also Parteridge), Abigail, d. Thad[deu]s and Fane, Dec. 26, 1780, a. 1 y. 5 m. G. R. 1.
Jane w. Thaddeus, Feb. 13, 1782, in her 43d y. G. R. 1.
Sarah, Mrs., Sept. —, 1817, a. 80 y.
Thaddeus, Aug. 20, 1801, a. 67 y.

**PASON** (see also Payson), Anna [Anne. CT. R.], w. Edward, bur. Sept. 10, 1641.
Ann [Anne Paison. C. R. 1.], d. Edward, bur. Feb. 15, 1650.
Benjamin, s. Benjamin and Mary, July 23, 1716.
Daniell, s. Benjamin and Mary, Oct. 24, 1719.
Elisha, s. Jacob and Martha, Aug. 21, 1718.
Elizabeth, d. Giles, bur. Mar. 8, 1639.
Elizabeth, d. Benjamin and Mary, Aug. 7, 1715.
Jacob [Payson. G. R. 1.], small pox, Dec. 7, 1721. [in his 27th y. G. R. 1.]
Joanna, d. Edward, bur. 27 : 1m : 1668. C. R. 1.
John, s. John, jr. and Elizabeth, June 29, 1707.
John [Payson. G. R. 1.], Dea., Nov. 15, 1719. [in his 77th y. G. R. 1.]
Jonathan, small pox, bur. 7 : 11m : 1666-7. C. R. 1.
Josiah, s. Jacob and Martha, Nov. 3, 1717.
Martha [W. Jacob. G. R. 1.], Aug. 20, 1718. [a. 24 y. G. R. 1.]
Mary, w. Edward, Mar. 24, 1697.
Samuel, Apr. 12, 1697.
Susan [Susana. C. R. 1. ; Pawson. CT. R.], d. Edward, Sept. 29, 1654.

**PATCHEN** (see also Patchin), Egleden, d. in-law, Joseph, bur. 20 : 8m : 1646, a. abt. 10 y. C. R. 1.

**PATCHIN** (see also Patchen), ———, ch. Joseph, bur. —: 3m : 1649. C. R. 1.

**PATRICK** (see also Partrick), James, m., ship carpenter, b. Gloucester, old age, Sept. 9, 1849, a. 81 y.
John, s. Phinehas and Betsey, Sept. 12, 1800.

PATRICK, Phineas, at the alms house, Sept. 19, 1842, a. 70 y.

Sarah, wid., Oct. 5, 1823, a. 88 y.

**PATTEN,** Caroline, d. Nathaniel and Nancy, Sept. 11, 1801.

George Deneale, s. William and Sally, Jan. 19, 1810.

Mary Sumner, d. William and Sally, Aug. 23, 1844, a. 41 y. 3 m. [a. 40 y. C. R. 5.]

Nancy Williams, d. William and Sally, June 13, 1816.

Nathaniel, [Capt. N. R. 4.], July 5, 1790, a. 39 y. G. R. 1. [a. 57 y. N. R. 4.]

Thomas, s. William and Sally, Sept. 26, 1805. [Sept. 25, a. 4 m. dup.]

**PATTISON,** James, living at Maj. Whiting's, Sept. 9, 1777, a. 60 y. C. R. 2.

**PAUL,** Hanna [d. —— Woodee. C. R. 1.], Nov. 10, 1658.

**PAYNE** (see also Paine), Mary, of the alms house, Apr. 25, 1828, a. 81 y.

Samuel, a pauper, May 8, 1830, a. 86 y.

**PAYSON** (see also Pason), Abigail, w. Henry, Nov. 27, 1786, a. 53 y. G. R. 1.

Abigail, Mrs., ———, 1829, a. 80 y.

Benjamin, Capt., May 31, 1769, a. 81 y. G. R. 1.

Ebenezer, June 9, 1781, a. 70 y. C. R. 2.

Elisabeth, w. Dea. Giles, Jan. 8, 1677.

Giles, Dea., Jan. 28, 1688-9, a. 78 y.

Hannah, wid. Dea. John, Nov. 25, 1724. G. R. 1.

Henry, bur. Mar. 27, 1795, a. 62 y. N. R. 4.

Isaac, June 27, 1743, in his 24th y. G. R. 1.

John, s. Benjamin and Mary, Dec. 9, 1720.

John, Dea., Jan. 6, 1747, in his 72d y. G. R. 1.

John, Jan. 23, 1748, in his 29th y. G. R. 1.

John, Jan. 14, 1819, a. 6 y. G. R. 4.

John Gill, s. John and Maria, croup, Jan. 17, 1819, a. 4 y. C. R. 3.

Joseph, s. Samuel, May 25, 1831, a. 11 m.

Lydia, w. Samuel, Dec. 26, 1842, a. 46 y.

Mary, w. Capt. Benjamin, July 30, 1767, a. 80 y. G. R. 1.

Mary, July 28, 1804, a. 14 y.

Rachel, w. John, May 23, 1770.

Sarah, w. Ebenezer, June 23, 1761, in her 45th y. G. R. 1.

PAYSON, Stephen, s. Stephen, mortification of the bowels, Nov. 27, 1803, a. 27 y. C. R. 3.
——, ch. Asa, Jan. 23, 1774, a. 3 m. C. R. 2.
——, w. Asa, Feb. 4, 1774, a. 40 y. C. R. 2.
——, ch. Edward, July —, 1830.

PEABODY, Oliver [Rev. C. R. 1.], (ordained Nov. 7, 1750), May 29, 1752, a. 32 y. G. R. 1.

PEACOCK, William [Peacocke. CT. R.], s. William, Dec. 29, 1655.

PEAK (see also Peake), John, s. Jonathan, bur. July 15, 1665.
Joseph, s. Jonathan, bur. 14 : 6m : 1672. C. R. 1.

PEAKE (see also Peak, Peek), Christopher [Peak. C. R. 1.], sr., May 22, 1666.
Christopher, s. Jonathan, bur. Oct. 12, 1666.
Hama [Hanna. C. R. 1.], d. Christopher, Oct. [5. C. R. 1.], 1660.
Jonathan, sr., June 2, 1700.
Sarah, June 12, 1715.
——, inf. ch. Christopher, bur. Mar. 30, 1647.
——, inf. ch. Christopher, 13 : 2m : 1647. C. R. 1.
——, inf. ch. Christopher, bur. Apr. 6, 1648.
——, inf. ch. ——, bur. 10 : 3m : 1649. C. R. 1.

PEAR, John, Mar. 23, 1820, a. 60 y.

PEARCE (see also Pierce), Eliza, d. James and Sarah, Jan. 3, 1846, a. 6 y. 9 m. G. R. 5.

PEARSE (see also Pierce), Rebecca, d. Martin and Kezia, Oct. 18, 1792, a. 2 y. 4 m. G. R. 1.

PEARSON (see also Pearsons), Abigail, d. Thomas, jr. and Nancy, Sept. 25, 1817.
Louisa, d. W[illia]m and Ellen, whooping cough, Aug. 2, 1847, a. 4 m. 2 d.
Thomas, m., victualler, dropsy, Sept. 9, 1846, a. 77 y.

PEARSONS (see also Pearson), ——, ch. still born, W[illia]m and Ellen, July 17, 1848.

PECK, [Elizabeth. G. R. 1.], Mrs., "at her kinswomans Mrs. Corbetts," Mar. 23, 1710. [1709-10, a. 63 y. G. R. 1.]
Samuel, m., victualler, cholera morbus, Sept. 3, 1849, a. 72 y.

PECK, Theoda, wid. Stephen, formerly w. Dea. Wiliams, Aug. 26, 1718, a. 81 y. G. R. 1.

William, Jan. 14, 1840, a. 28 y.

PEEK (see also Peake), Dorcas, Oct. 14, 1694.

PEEPER (see also Pepper), Benjamin [Pepper. C. R. 1.], s. Robert, bur. Jan. 16, 1669. [1669-70. C. R. 1.]

PEIRCE, (see also Pierce), Anna K., Apr. 18, 1841, a. 86 y.

John, m., laborer, b. Ireland, consumption, Dec. 22, 1848, a. 32 y.

PEIRPONT (see also Pierpont), Charles [Pierpont. dup.], at the alms house, Sept. 11, 1838, a. 73 y. [a. 74 y. dup.]

John [Peirpoynt, sr. C. R. 1.], Dec. 7, 1682, a. 64 y. [a. 65 y. G. R. 1.]

William, Apr. 23, 1769. N. R. 5.

PELLHAM, William, ulcers, at the almshouse, Oct. 3, 1847, a. 50 y.

PELTON, Harriet G., b. Dedham, w. Joel W., consumption, May 3, 1849, a. 25 y. 7 m. 18 d.

PENDELBERRY, Thomas [Pendlebury] [b. Boston, Eng. G. R. 5.], m. machinist, consumption, Sept. 9, 1846, a. 43 y.

PENDERGRASS, Margarett, d. W[illia]m and Alice, croup, Apr. 1, 1849, a. 1 y. 4 m.

PENNY, Benj[ami]n, Feb. 17, 1841, a. 22 m.

PEPPER (see also Peeper), Benjamin, s. Jacob and Elizabeth, Feb. 17, 1713.

Elisabeth ["old Sister." C. R. 1.], w. Robert, Jan. 5, 1683. [1683-4. C. R. 1.]

Elizabeth, d. Robert, 8 : 1 m : 1643-4. C. R. 1.

John, s. Rob[er]t, Mar. 18, 1669. [1669-70. C. R. 1.]

Joseph, s. Robert [under the command of Capt. Sam[ue]ll Wadsworth. dup.], slain by the Indians [at Sudbury. dup.], Apr. 21, 1676.

Mary, d. Jacob and Elizabeth, Apr. 21, 1708.

Mary, d. Jacob and Mary, Apr. 6, 1715.

Robert [old. C. R. 1.], July 7, 1684.

Robert, s. Jacob and Elisabeth, Jan. 4, 1685-6.

Robert, s. Robert and Elisabeth, May 24, 1687.

——, inf. ch. Jakob, bur. 24 : 3 m : 1687. C. R. 1.

**PERCY**, Mary, at the almshouse, July 27, 1842, a. 28 y.

**PEREPOINT** (see also Pierpont), Thankfull, d. John, — : 10 m : 1649. C. R. 1.

——, "young" ch. ——, 28 : 5 m : 1651. C. R. 1.

**PERIN** (see also Perrin), Mary, d. Noah and Patience, Sept. 1, 1714.

Patience, d. Noah and Patience, Sept. 7, 1744, in her 19th y. G. R. 1.

**PERKINS**, Elizabeth R., b. Pittsfield, N. H., consumption, Apr. 8, 1848, a. 30 y.

James, inflammation on the lungs, Aug. 1, 1822, a. 61 y. C. R. 3.

James, s. James, Esq. [brain fever. C. R. 3.], Aug. 24, 1824, a. 10 y.

James, Sept. 4, 1830, a. 21 y.

John B. L., s. Benjamin, July 21, 1839, a. 6 m.

Sam[ue]l, Oct. —, 1828, a. 22 y.

William, s. William, bur. Dec. 23, 1639.

William T., Nov. 5, 1827, a. 20 y.

**PERREN** (see also Perrin), Patience [Perin. G. R. 1.], w. Noah, Nov. 28, 1730. [in her 45th y. G. R. 1.]

**PERRIN** (see also Perin, Perren), Harriet, wid. Augustus, inflammation of lungs, July 9, 1846, a. 56 y.

John, s. Noah, July 22, 1731.

Margaret, w. Noah, June 29, 1743. [in her 46th y. G. R. 1.]

Martha, d. Noah and Mary, Apr. 2, 1760, in her 22d y. G. R. 1.

Mary, w. Noah, Mar. 18, 1773, in her 63d y. G. R. 1.

Mary Zeigler, w. George, June —, 1835, a. 34 y.

Noah, s. Noah and Mary, July 18, 1749.

Noah, Oct. 15, 1754, in his 75th y. G. R. 1.

Noah, Apr. 4, 1788, in his 80th y. G. R. 1.

Thankfull [Thankful Perin. G. R. 1.], d. Noah [and Patience. G. R. 1.], Oct. 27, 1730. [in her 4th y. G. R. 1.]

**PERRY**, Adelaide A., d. Levi and Susan, dysentery, Aug. 3, 1849, a. 8 y. 3 m.

Adelia, at the alms house, Nov. 24, 1842, a. 88 y.

Christianna, m., b. Oxford, consumption, Sept. 19, 1847, a 54 y.

Cordelia, m., b. Paris, Me., d. Gideon and Charlotte, diarrhoea, Sept. 6, 1849, a. 22 y.

PERRY, Emely, w. Benj[amin] F., consumption, Jan. 7, 1849, a 25 y.

James Appleton, unm., merchant, b. Brunswick, Me., typhus fever, Nov. 2, 1846, a. 24 y.

John, householder [consumption. C. R. 1.], bur. Sept. 21, 1642.

John, Oct. 8, 1779, a. 65 y. C. R. 2.

Nathanael, s Samuel and Sarah, Feb. 2, 1686.

Nathanael, s. Thomas and Sarah, Feb. 5, 1716.

Nath[ani]el, Jan. 25, 1806, a. 62 y.

Samuel, Apr. 16, 1706.

Sarah, d. Samuel [?], Feb. 14, 1683.

Sarah, w. Thomas, Mar. 10, 1715-16.

Sarah, wid., June 9, 1775, a. 84 y. C. R. 2.

Walter F., s. Benj[amin] and Emily, disease of lungs, July 25, 1847, a. 5 m. 6 d.

William H., s. Joseph H., Mar. 22, 1842, a. 9 m.

——, w. Samuel, Sept. 20, 1775, a. 65 y. C. R. 2.

——, wid., Mar. 27, 1792, a. 72 y. C. R. 2.

——, Mr., Mar. —, 1837.

PETERS, ——, ch. still born, John and Sarah, Mar. 2, 1848.

PETTES, Joseph Bass, m., physician, b. Brooklyn, Ct., s. Joseph and Sarah, disease of heart, Oct. 14, 1848, a. 68 y.

PEVEAR (see also Peveare), ——, ch. Bradbury, Sept. 29, 1840.

——, ch. Charles, Aug. 17, 1846, a. 7 m.

PEVEARE (see also Pevear), ——, ch. Bradbury, May 7, 1830, a. 3 m.

PHELPS, Amos A., m., clergyman, b. Farmington, s. Clarissa, consumption, July 29, 1847, a. 43 y.

PHILBRICK (see also Philbrook), Ruth [Philbrook. C. R. 4.], unm., b. Thomaston, Me., cancer, July 11, 1847, a. 31 y.

PHILBROOK (see also Philbrick), Elizabeth N., d. Levi and Mary Ann, diarrhoea, Oct. 24, 1849, a. 1y. 1 m. 12 d.

PHILIPS (see also Phillips), John, [inf. C. R. 1.] s. Caleb, Apr. 6, 1684.

Malinda [Phillips. dup.], b. Nova Scotia, ship fever, at the alms house, July 14, 1848, a. 31 y. [a. 30 y. dup.]

**PHILLEBROWN,** Sarah, Mar. 7, 1808, a. 77 y.

**PHILLEPS** (see also Phillips), John, s. twin, Caleb and Hannah, July 10, 1707.
Joshua, s. twin, Caleb and Hannah, Aug. 28, 1707.
Mary, d. Caleb and Elizabeth, June 9, 1716. [a. 28 y. G. R. 1.]

**PHILLIPS** (see also Philips, Philleps), Abigail, w. Hon. William, Nov. 14, 1777, in her 32d y. N. R. 2.
Caleb., Lt., in the Army, Mar. 28, 1776, a. 36 y. C. R. 2.
Hiram K., Aug. 22, 1840, a. 19 y.
Thomas, Dec. 18 [15. dup.], 1801, a. 49 y. [1802. dup.]

**PHILLPAIL,** ——, inf. ch. Sam[ue]l and Elizabeth, Oct. 2, 1847, a. 1 d.

**PHIPPEN,** Joshua, Aug. —, 1833.

**PHIPPS,** Daniel S., Jan. 25, 1839, a. 6 m.
Lucy Amelia, d. William, Oct. —, 1830, a. 10 m.
Rosanna, b. Ireland, consumption, at the alms house, Apr. 15, 1849, a. 33 y.

**PIERCE** (see also Pearce, Pearse, Peirce), Cynthia [Peirce. dup.], w. George W., Jan. 26, 1843. [a. 26 y. dup.]
Ellen P., d. William and Ellen, Oct. 2, 1836, a. 16 m.
James, s. [James and Hannah. different ink.], July 9, 1722.
James, May 21, 1826, a. 71 y.
John Calvin, s. Otis and Mary, scarlet fever, Oct. 10, 1847, a. 4 y. 3 m.
Levi, cancerated stomach, Dec. 25, 1843, a. 56 y. C. R. 3.
Mary, d. Edward and Eliza Ann, Sept. 6, 1836, a. 17 m.
Mary, m., b. Ireland, intemperance, at the alms house, June 12, 1847, a. 39 y.
Sila, Oct. 13, 1837, a. 30 y. G. R. 4.
William, consumption, at the alms house, Aug. 10, 1847, a. 1 y.
William H., s. Otis and Mary, scarlet fever, Sept. 12, 1847, a. 6 y. 5 m. 13 d.
——, inf. ch. Bradford K. and Hannah W., June 10, 1848, a. 7 d.

**PIERPOINT** (see also Pierpont), Ezra, s. Robert, bur. 21 : 7 m : 1669. C. R. 1.
Jonathan, s. Robert, bur. 23 : 8 m : 1663. C. R. 1.
Thankful, 11. : 5 m : 1664, a. 9 m. G. R. 1.

**PIERPOINTE** (see also Pierpont), Thankefull, d. John, Dec. 16, 1649.

**PIERPOINTS** (see also Pierpont), ——, inf. ch. John, bur. July 28, 1651.

——, [Pierpont. CT. R.], inf. ch. John, Aug. 9, **1657.**

**PIERPONT** (see also Peirpoint, Peirpont, Perepoint, Pierpoint, Pierpointe, Pierpoints, Pirepont), Ann, w. Ebenez[e]r, July 12, 1745.

Ann, Feb. 6, 1836, a. 82 y.

Ebenezer, Oct. 24, 1767, a. 42 y. G. R. 1.

Elizabe[t]h, d. Robert and Hannah, Aug. 22, 1750, in her 2d y. G. R. 1.

Ezra, s. Robert, Oct. 10, 1669.

Hannah, d. Robert and Hannah, Sept. 28, 1742. [in her 3d y. G. R. 1.]

Hannah, w. Ebenez[e]r, Oct. 10, 1747.

Hannah, w. Robert, of Boston, May 23, 1751, in her 32d y. G. R. 1.

Hannah [Madam. N. R. 4.], Feb. 26, 1799, a. 72 y. [a. 73 y. N. R. 4.]

Jam[e]s, s. Robert, Nov. 30, 1657.

James, 2d, s. Robert, Oct. 14, 1676.

James, small pox, Dec. 4, 1721.

John, s. Ebenezer and Ann [Feb. 15, 1789. different ink.]

Jonathan, s. Robert, Oct. 24, 1663.

Margaret, d. Robert, Mar. 24, 1659.

Margaret, 2d, d. Robert, Mar. 28, 1661.

Mary, d. Ebenezer and Mary, Feb. —, 1696, a. 5 m. G. R. 1.

Mary, d. Ebenezer and Ann, July 22, 1724.

Rebecca, Mrs., Sept. 2, 1828, a. 65 y.

Robert [Peirpoynt. C. R. 1.], s. [inf. ch. C. R. 1.] Robert [falling from lap of a girl. C. R. 1.], Feb. 2, 1678 [1678-9. C. R. 1.]

Robert, s. Robert and Susannah, Nov. 2, 1763, a. 6 y. G. R. 1.

Robert, Esq., Nov. 25, 1786, a. 73 y. N. R. 3.

Sarah, d. Robert, Nov. 29, 1671.

Sarah, d. Robert and Hannah, Sept. 5, 1742. [in her 1st y. G. R. 1.]

Sarah, d. Robert and Hannah, Mar. 9, 1749, in her 4th y. G. R. 1.

Susannah, w. Robert, Aug. 28, 1760, a. 29 y. G. R. 1.

——, ch. Robert, Sept. 15, 1802, a. 1 y.

**PIGG,** Thomas [Pig. C. R. 1.], householder [dropsy and a fall which injured his kidneys. C. R. 1.], bur. Dec. 30, 1643.

**PIKE,** Edwin, s. Thomas and Harriet, dysentery, Aug. 8, 1848, a. 1 y. 10 m.

Ellen F. [Hellen Frances. G. R. 5.], b. Providence, R. I., d. W[illia]m G. and Miranda [at West Danvers. G. R. 5.], croup, Apr. 18, 1847, a. 3 y. 3 m.

John, s. Jarves and Abigail, June 30, 1713.

Thomas, m., rope maker, b. Charlestown, inflammation of stomach, Apr. 10, 1848, a. 45 y.

**PIREPONT** (see also Pierpont), Ebenezer [Pierpont. G. R. 1.], Dec. 17, 1696. [a. 35 y. G. R. 1.

John, Dec. 30, 1690.

Robert, May 16, 1694.

**PITTS,** Henry, July 17, 1803, a. 28 y.

**PLAFF,** Walbarga, m., b. Germany, bowel complaint, Apr. 20, 1848, a. 42 y.

**POLLARD,** Edith, Feb. 6, 1845, a. 89 y.

Frances R., d. A. W., bilious diarrhoea, Aug. 24, 1849, a. 5 y.

Jeffrey A., Oct. 22, 1837, a. 40 y.

**POLLEY** (see also Polly), Hannah [Polly. C. R. 1.], w. John, June 8, 1684.

Jane, wid. John, Oct. 24, 1701.

John, Apr. 2, 1689, a. 71 y.

**POLLY** (see also Polley), John, small pox, Oct. 11, 1721.

Mary, w. John, smallpox, 30 : 6 m : 1666. C. R. 1.

Susanna, w. John, bur. 30 : 2 m : 1664. C. R. 1.

——, inf. ch. John, bur. 11 : 11 m : 1665-6. C. R. 1.

**POMROY,** Elizabeth C., m., b. Haverhill, d. William and Huldah Batchelder, paralysis, Mar. 28, 1848, a. 38 y.

——, worms, Nov. 14, 1809, a. 15 m. C. R. 3.

**POND,** Elizabeth, d. Moses and Elizabeth, Dec. 28, 1812.

Thomas, May —, 1827, a. 70 y.

William, s. Moses and Elizabeth, Dec. 13, 1815.

William H., a pauper, Nov. 16, 1831, a. 5 y.

**POOL** (see also Poole), George E., s. Ebenezer and Clarissa, croup, Oct. 24, 1846, a. 2 y.

Martha S., small pox, Dec. 14, 1827, a. 21 y.

**POOLE** (see also Pool), Martha Shed, d. Samuel, May —, 1833, a. 3 y. 9 m.

**POOR,** ——, ch. still born, Charles A. and Percis, Oct. 4, 1846.

**PORTER,** Eliphalet, Rev. D. D. [ordained Oct. 2, 1782. G. R. 1.], Dec. 7, 1833, a. 75 y. [a. 75 1-2 y. C. R. 1.]

John, A. M., s. Rev. Huntington, of Rye, N. H., Mar. 28, 1825, a. 33 y.

Patty, w. Rev. Eliphalet, Dec. 2, 1814, a. 38 y. 10 m.

**PORTIS,** ——, "Father," of Boston, at his daughter's —— Weld, bur. — : 5 m : 1681. C. R. 1.

**POTTER,** Judith, wid., Oct. 22, 1683.

Robart ["brother." C. R. 1.], householder, bur. June 17, 1653.

**POTTLE,** Simon, Sept. 12, 1805, a. 45 y.

**POWERS,** Mary Ann, Dec. 28, 1836, a. 15 m.

Richard [laborer. dup.], m., b. Ireland, heart complaint [consumption. dup.], Jan. 28, 1849, a. 38 y. [a. 35 y. dup.]

Sarah, June 9, 1836, a. 44 y.

William, s. John and Adeline, fits, Sept. 16, 1847, a. 28 d.

**PRATT,** Ann, Nov. 25, 1835, a. 23 y.

Ann Newell, d. twin, William and Mary, May 29, 1811.

Isabella, d. Jerahmeel C. and Isabella, Apr. 12, 1834, a. 17 d. G. R. 5.

Issabella, w. Jerahmiel C., Mar. 31, 1834, a. 23 y.

John, widr., book binder, s. Simeon and Phebe, consumption, Feb. 15, 1848, a. 66 y.

Maria L., d. John C., congestion of the brain, Dec. 19, 1849, a. 1 m. 17 d.

Martin C., s. Henry, May 7, 1837, a. 17 d.

Mary, Mrs., Oct. 10 [7. dup.], 1797, a. 21 y.

Mary P., d. William, dec., Nov. 29, 1827, a. 26 y.

Phebe, w. Simeon, July 9, 1794, a. 46 y. N. R. 4.

Ruth, a pauper, Aug. 5, 1834, a. 70 y.

Sarah, Mrs., Apr. 16, 1830, a. 85 y.

Sarah Whiting, d. William and Sarah, Sept. 19, 1804.

PRATT, Sarah Whiting, d. William and Mary, Apr. 8, 1823, a. 17 y.
Simeon, Mar. 6, 1805.
Willard, a pauper, Mar. 10, 1829, a. 26 y.
William, Feb. 5, 1826, a. 50 y.
William, m., s. William and Mary, insanity, July 16, 1849, a. 56 y.
William Wirt, s. Jerahmeel and Julia Ann, croup, Dec. 17, 1846, a. 2 y. 6 m.
——, ch. W[illia]m, Nov. 12, 1804, a. 12 m.
——, Mrs., at the alms house, Aug. —, 1834, a. 70 y.
——, d. Jerahmeel and Julia Ann, lung fever, Apr. 17, 1847, a. 6 m.

PREBLE, Adeline, wid., b. Germany, dropsy, Dec. 3, 1848, a. 69 y.

PRENTICE (see also Prentiss), Rob[er]t, bur. 3 : 12 m : 1665-6. C. R. 1.

PRENTISS (see also Prentice), Abigail, d. [Dr. dup.] Nath[anie]l S. and Abigail, Apr. 25, 1802. [a. 4 y. dup.]
Abigail, w. Nath[anie]l S., Mar. 6, 1807, a. 41 y.
Abigail, Mrs., Aug. 29, 1825, a. 80 y. 10 m. 6 d.
Abigail, w. Dr. Nath[anie]l S., Mar. 6, 1827, a. 62 y.
James A. M., s. Dr. Nath[anie]l S., Aug. 26, 1828, a. 33 y.
Nath[anie]l S., Jr., s. Dr. Nath[anie]l S., July 2, 1819, a. 26 y.
Sarah, w. Hugh K., July 14, 1838, a. 35 y.

PRESCOT (see also Prescott), Harriet Maria, d. Jonathan, infantile disease, June 9, 1828, a. 6 m. C. R. 3.
Jerome, s. Jerome, Dec. 8, 1839, a. 6 m.

PRESCOTT (see also Prescot), James, s. Isaac, Aug. —, 1828.
Jerome W., s. Jerome, Apr. 10, 1837, a. 8 m. 14 d.

PRESTON, Hannah, w. Edward, Aug. 26, 1747, in her 24th y. G. R. 1.

PRICHARD, ——, inf. ch. ——, bur. 10 : 3 m : 1649. C. R. 1.

PRINCE, Daniel McCarty, Mar. 24, 1806, a. 26 y.
John, hernia, June 26, 1816, a. 82 y. 6 m. C. R. 3.
John, apoplexy, Aug. 13, 1843, a. 73 y. C. R. 3.
Martha, w. John, Esq. [apoplexy. C. R. 3.], Jan. 22, 1832, a. 58 y. [a. 68 y. C. R. 3.]

PRINCE, Mary D[erby. c. r. 3.], d. John, Esq. [apoplexy, May 16. c. r. 3.], 1836. [a. 34 y. c. r. 3.]
Nathan, m., lumber merchant, b. Salem, apoplexy, Nov. 15, 1847, a. 56 y.

**PROCTER,** Sarah, Mar. 14, 1806, a. 47 y.

**PROUT** (see also Prouty), Elizabeth B., Oct. 6, 1837, a. 21 y.

**PROUTY** (see also Prout), [Jacob D. c. r. 3.], inf. ch. Dwight [and Mary R. of Boston, grandson —— Gould, lung fever, Mar. 22. c. r. 3.], 1835 [a. 9 m. c. r. 3.]

**PURCHASE,** Hannah, a pauper, Apr. 9, 1831, a. 48 y.

**PUTMAN** (see also Putnam), Eliza, d. Rev. George and Elizabeth Anne, Sept. 6, 1834. [a. 2 y. 3 m. dup.]

**PUTNAM** (see also Putman), Allen, at the alms house, Nov. 29, 1841, a. 40 y.
Hannah D., w. Allen, consumption, Nov. 30, 1843, a. 28 y.
Matilda Golding, cholera infantum, Oct. 3, 1819, a. 1 y. c. r. 3.

**QUIDLEY,** Mary, m., b. Ireland, consumption, Nov. 13, 1847, a. 28 y.

**QUINCY,** Ann, w. Edmund, jr., merchant, d. Ellis Husk, Esq., of Portsmouth, postmaster, dec., small pox, June 8, 1764, in her 41st y. n. r. 2.

**QUINN,** Jane, wid., b. Ireland, accidental, Apr. 27, 1848, a. 60 y.

**RACHFORD,** Mary, d. James and Catherine, croup, Apr. 23, 1848, a. 1 y.

**RAFTER,** Sarah, b. Marblehead, consumption, at the alms house, Oct. 31, 1847, a. 78 y.

**RAMSDELL** (see also Rumsdill), Mesheck [Meshech. dup.], Oct. 27, 1800.

**RAMSEY,** Eunice, June 5, 1707.
Eunice, d. John [and Anna. g. r. 1.], July 7, 1734. [a. 16 y. 9 m. g. r. 1.]

**RAND,** Anna, July —, 1833, a. 17 m.

Emily A., drowned, May 13, 1840, a. 34 y.

Ezra D., s. Nahum and Dolly C., dropsy on brain, Nov. 8, 1847, a. 2 y. 3 m.

Francis Arnold, s. Edward S., of Boston, July —, 1840, a. 18 m.

Joseph J., s. Obed and Anna Y., July 4, 1844.

Julia Elisabeth, d. William and Helen, bur. June 28, 1839, a. 2 1-2 y. c. r. 5.

Mary Jarvis, d. William and Helen, bur. June 8, 1839, a. 6 m. c. r. 5.

**RANDALL,** Abraham [old age, Apr. 6. c. r. 3.], 1834, a. 78 y.

James B., a pauper, Mar. 14, 1831, a. 4 y.

John, m., carpenter, s. Abram and Sarah, consumption, Sept. 11, 1846, a. 66 y.

Jonas, Jan. 16, 1833, a. 54 y.

Joseph, s. Abraham, of Brookline, Oct. 9, 1793, a. 14 m. c. r. 3.

Reuben, Feb. 7, 1817, a. 35 y.

Sarah Ann, w. Stephen [child bed fever. c. r. 3.], Dec. 1, 1814, a. 25 y.

Stephen, m., s. Abraham and Zebia, cancer, Apr. 16, 1847, a. 58 y. 8 m.

Zibiah, w. Abraham [old age. c. r. 3.], Mar. 18, 1833, a. 78 y. g. r. 4. [a. 76 y. c. r. 3.]

**RAWLIN,** Polley, Nov. 10, 1804.

**RAYNOLDS** (see also Reynolds), Mary, b. Ireland, cholera morbus, at the alms house, Sept. 26, 1849, a. 23 y.

**REA,** Isabel W., d. W. A., Sept. —, 1838, a. 3 m.

**READ** (see also Reed), Charles, Dec. 16, 1827, a. 41 y.

Hannah, d. John, Feb. 18, 1815, a. 31 y.

John, Esq., Jan. 13, 1813, a. 85 y.

Joseph, Nov. 24, 1814, a. 21 y.

Peter, of Woodstock, Dec. 29, 1751, a. 27 y. 2 d. g. r. 1.

Rebecca, w. George, May 9, 1834, a. 34 y.

Sally, d. John, jr. and Mary, Sept. 25, 1801.

——, ch. Jon[athan], Oct. 15, 1803, a. 18 m.

**RECKARD** (see also Reckards), Rosanna, d. Sam[ue]l T. and Rosanna, inflammation of bowels, Mar. 22, 1849, a. 8 m.

**RECKARDS** (see also Reckard), Josiah, typhus fever, Oct. 17, 1820, a. 37 y. C. R. 3.

**REED** (see also Read), Adelaide E., b. Bedford, d. W[illia]m N. and Lucy Ann M., lung fever, Mar. 30, 1847, a. 1 y. 8 m.

Betsy, only d. John, Nov. 16, 1784, a. 15 y. N. R. 2.

Harriet, w. John, July —, 1835.

Henrietta B., d. Levi, Jan. 13, 1842.

Henrietta M., d. Levi and Louisa C., scarlet fever, June 21, 1849, a. 2 y. 10 m.

Louisa, consumption, Nov. 19, 1840, a. 22 y. C. R. 3.

**REILY** (see also Riley), David, oppression at the stomach by eating green fruit, Oct. 10, 1794, a. 15 y. C. R. 3.

**REMINGTON,** John, bur. 8 : 4 m : 1667. C. R. 1.

**REORIDEN,** Catherine, d. Jeremiah and Julia, brain fever, Sept. 13, 1848, a. 2 y.

**REYNOLDS** (see also Raynolds), W[illia]m J., jr., s. W[illia]m J. and Martha P., June 14, 1847, a. 12 d.

**RHOADES** (see also Rhodes), Nabby, w. Aaron, Feb. 6, 1812.

**RHODES** (see also Rhoades), Abigail, canker in bowels, Mar. 23, 1812, a. 33 y. C. R. 3.

**RICE,** Alanson, h. Caroline, Nov. 29, 1840. P. R. 5.

Amos, June 2, 1804, a. 22 y. C. R. 2.

Caroline, w. Alanson, Oct. 4, 1840. P. R. 5.

Charles W[illia]m, s. Isaac N. and Mary, Dec. 6, 1844, a. 5 2-3 y.

Harriet Newell, d. Timothy B., May 8, 1824, a. 10 m.

Luther, lock jaw, issue of Sept. 9, 1795, a. 21 y. N. R. 4.

Timothy B., Sept. 2, 1829, a. 34 y.

**RICH,** George L., s. Nepthali and Betsey, Jan. 29, 1849, a. 1 m. 16 d.

**RICHARD** (see also Richards), John [Richards. dup.], Dec. 26, 1801, a. 24 y. [1802. dup.]

**RICHARDS** (see also Richard), Abagail, Mrs., consumption, bur. Dec. 25, 1831, a. 83 y. C. R. 2.

Bulah, w. Lemuel, Aug. 31, 1818 , a. 33 y. C. R. 2.

RICHARDS, Caroline Frances Child, d. John and Hannah, Jan. 25, 1827, a. 18 m. C. R. 2.

Caroline F. C., Jan. 4, 1842. C. R. 7.

Cynthia, w. Lemuel, Sept. 22, 1812, a. 26 y. G. R. 3.

David, Mar. 11, 1782, a. 37 y. C. R. 2.

Davy, "old," bur. 1 : 7 m : 1680. C. R. 1.

Deborah, wid., June 27, 1826, a. 48 y. C. R. 2.

Ebenezer, Mar. 10, 1776, a. 55 y. C. R. 2.

Edward, m., farmer, lung complaint, Apr. 4, 1847, a. 74 y.

Edwin, s. Walter W., dec., Feb. 1, 1837.

Eliza, w. Lawrence, of Charlestown, d. Edward Turner, June 8, 1823, a. 27 y.

Hannah, wid., May 9, 1782, a. 82 y. C. R. 2.

Hannah, d. wid. Tabitha, June 29, 1794, a. 28 y. C. R. 2.

Hannah, w. Jesse, of Dedham, Aug. 24, 1832, a. 70 y.

Henry Lincoln, b. Hillsborough, Ill., s. Geo[rge] H. and Irene H., dysentery, Sept. 9, 1849, a. 6 y. 4 m. 17 d.

Jeremiah, Capt., Aug. 4, 1763, in his 83d y. N. R. 5.

Jeremiah, jr., Feb. 25, 1774, in his 43d year. C. R. 2.

Jeremiah, Jan. 14, 1776, a. 70 y. C. R. 2.

Jeremiah, May 3, 1799, a. 29 y. C. R. 2.

Joel, Dec. 31, 1800, a. 27 y. C. R. 2.

John, s. L., Mar. 8, 1828, a. 3 y. C. R. 2.

John Warren, s. Lemuel, whooping cough, May 25, 1833, a. 20 m. C. R. 2.

Jonathan, Dea. [from Dedham, old age. C. R. 3.], July 21, 1837, a. 77 y.

Joseph, Nov. —, 1790, a. 74 y. C. R. 2.

Joseph, Apr. 14, 1815, a. 72 y. C. R. 2.

Joseph, a pauper, Mar. 21, 1833, a. 51 y.

Joshua, Dec. 31, 1820, a. 57 y.

Levi, Feb. 18, 1805, a. 34 y. [a. 31 y. C. R. 2.]

Lucie, d. Nath[anie]l and Mary, Oct. 15, 1746.

Lucy, d. David and Melatiah, Jan. 10, 1788, a. 14 y. C. R. 2.

Lucy Elizabeth, d. Geo[rge] H. and Irene H., dysentery, Sept. 7, 1849, a. 1 y. 4 m. 23 d.

Mark, June 1, 1826, a. 42 y.

Mary, w. Nath[anie]l, Nov. 20, 1746.

Mary, wid., Apr. 17, 1814, a. 84 y. C. R. 2.

Nath[anie]l, s. Nath[anie]l and Mary, Oct. 3, 1746.

Nathaniel, Mar. 25, 1786, a. 74 y. C. R. 2.

RICHARDS, Noah Davis, s. Jeremiah and Abigail, Mar. 15, 1798. [a. 13 y. C. R. 2.]

Persis, Mrs., May 31, 1833, a. 74 y.

Samuel, June 26, 1776, a. 25 y. C. R. 2.

Sarah, June 6, 1791. C. R. 2.

Sarah, wid. Giles, Apr. —, 1836, a. 67 y.

Solomon, Oct. 9, 1834, a. 83 y.

Susan, d. Joseph and Susannah, May 30, 1816, a. 5 y. C. R. 2.

Tabitha, wid., July 19, 1798. C. R. 2.

Thomas, s. Jeremiah, jr. and Hannah, July 22, 1742.

Walter W., Nov. 4, 1836, a. 32 y. [a. 33 y. G. R. 5.]

Walter E., s. Walter W., Feb. 1, 1837, a. 14 w. G. R. 5.

——, ch. Joseph, jr., Dec. 18, 1779, a. 2 d. C. R. 2.

——, youngest s. Mark, kicked by a horse, Sept. 16, 1794, a. 4 y. N. R. 4.

——, ch. Lemuel, Sept. 13, 1808, a. 12 h. C. R. 2.

——, ch. Joshua and Deborah, Mar. 15, 1809, a. 7 d. C. R. 2.

——, ch. Lemuel and Cinthia, Apr. 3, 1812, a. 12 m. C. R. 2.

——, ch. Danforth, Aug. 17, 1833, a. 4 m. C. R. 2.

——, ch. Lemuel, Feb. 22, 1834, a. 10 d. C. R. 2.

**RICHARDSON**, Abigail, wid. John, Esq., at Boston, Sept. 22, 1770, a. 81 y. G. R. 1.

Abigail, wid. Joseph, Nov. 7, 1816, a. 62 y. G. R. 1.

Albert, s. Josiah and Martha, Jan. 26, 1829. [a. 14 y. dup.]

Frances T. A., Mar. —, 1823, a. 18 y.

George, dysentery, Oct. 31, 1822, a. 3 y. C. R. 3.

Jesse P., suicide, May 29, 1840, a. 46 y.

John, Esq., Jan. 17, 1752, in his 67th y. G. R. 1.

John [s. Joseph and Abigail. G. R. 1.], Feb. 14, 1824, a. 45 y. [a. 46 y. G. R. 1.]

Joseph, Mar. 12, 1790, a. 41 y. G. R. 1.

Maria M., d. Henry H. and Celia, disease on the brain, Oct. 20, 1848, a. 1 y.

Maria A., b. Jamaica Plain, d. John and M. M., dropsy on brain, Nov. 23, 1849, a. 1 y. 10 d.

Martha, w. Josiah, Oct. 25, 1842, a. 57 y.

Mary, d. John, Esq. and Abigail, Aug. 24, 1745, in her 22d y. G. R. 1.

Nathaniel, Apr. 18, 1812, a. 32 y.

Peter, Jan. —, 1819.

Susanna, wid., Jan. 24, 1802, a. 79 y.

RICHARDSON, ——, ch. Luther, Dec. 5, 1806, a. 1 m.
——, s. Geo[rge], Sept. 24, 1836, a. 5 m. C. R. 3.

RICKS, Thomas, Mar. 25, 1802.

RIDDELL (see also Riddle), John [Riddle, July 24. G. R. 4.],
     1836, a. 28 y. [a. 29 y. G. R. 4.]

RIDDLE (see also Riddell), Andrew [consumption. C. R. 3.],
     Dec. 14, 1830, a. 58 y. G. R. 4.
Jane, w. Andrew [cancer. C. R. 3.], Sept. 18, 1830, a. 56 y.
     G. R. 4.

RIDER, Caroline, w. Adolphus, inflammation, May 29, 1846,
     a 35 y.
Sarah, w. Thomas, Aug. 15, 1714. [a. abt. 40 y. G. R. 1.]

RIGGS, Edward, bur. 5 : 1 m : 1671-2. C. R. 1.
Elizabeth, d. Edward, bur. May ——, 1634.
Elizabeth, w. Edward, bur. Oct. ——, 1635.
Elizabeth, w. Edward, bur. 2 : 7 m : 1669. C. R. 1.
John, s. Edward, bur. Oct. ——, 1634.
Lidea, d. Edward, bur. Aug. ——, 1633.

RIGNE (see also Rigney), Anthony, s. Anthony and Catherine,
     croup, Feb. 29, 1848, a. 7 m.

RIGNEY (see also Rigne), William, s. W[illia]m and Hannah,
     decline, Jan. 2, 1849, a. 21 d.

RILEY (see also Reily), Adison Ware, s. James and Avis, Nov.
     13, 1831, a. 2 y. 7 m. G. R. 5.
James, Nov. 6, 1829, a. 39 y.
James, s. James, dec., Nov. ——, 1831, a. 5 y.
James Whipple, s. James and Avis, Nov. 26, 1831, a. 7 y. G.
     R. 5.
Hannah, unm., b. Ireland, consumption, Dec. 12, 1848, a. 28 y.
Richard, s. Thomas and Bridget, croup, Apr. 8, 1849, a. 11 m.

RIPLEY, Christiana, m., b. Germany, consumption, June 2,
     1848, a. 38 y.

RIUE, ——, June 2, 1804, a. 22 y.

ROACH, Daniel, s. D. and Winneford, teething, Sept. 6, 1849,
     a. 9 m.
Edward, b. Ireland, ship fever, at the alms house, Aug. 5, 1847,
     a. 25 y.

ROACH, James, s. James and Ellen, bowel complaint, Aug. 7, 1848, a. 2 m. 15 d.

John, s. Thomas and Mary, bowel complaint, May 14, 1848, a. 2 y.

Michael, b. Ireland, ship fever, at the alms house, June 19, 1847, a. 22 y.

**ROAKS,** Margarett, d. Thomas and Margarett, decline, Aug. 17, 1849. a. 6 m.

**ROBBINS** (see also Robins), Aaron, at the alms house, Oct. 10, 1828, a. 28 y.

Andrew G., s. A., consumption, July 4, 1846, a. 14 y.

Elisha, Oct. 23, 1805, a. 26 y.

John, Oct. 11, 1797, a. 23 y. N. R. 4.

Matilda Caroline, d. Aaron and Susana, Sept. 8, 1811, a. 6 w. G. R. 1.

Rebecca, Sept. 7, 1805, a. 18 y. C. R. 2.

Susanna W., d. Aaron and Susana, Aug. 29, 1807, a. 3 m. G. R. 1.

**ROBERTS,** John, dropsy, 27 : 9 m : 1651. C. R. 1.

John, under the command of Capt. Sam[ue]ll Wadsworth, slain by the Indians at Sudbury, Apr. 21, 1676.

————, "Old Mother," a Welch woman, bur. 7 : 11m : 1645-6, in her 103d y. C. R. 1.

**ROBERTSON,** Hannah, wid., b. Scotland, old age, Mar. 19, 1847, a. 85 y.

Thomas, of Aberdeen, Scotland, June 27, 1824, a. 75 y.

**ROBINS** (see also Robbins), W[illia]m, Mar. 20, 1805.

————, ch. Elisha, Aug. 28, 1807, a. 3 m.

**ROBINSON,** Ellenor [Elenor, a pauper. dup.], w. William, May 15, 1834. [May 14, a. 33 y. dup.]

John P., s. J. P., Oct. 2, 1837, a. 6 m.

Leah, Nov. 15, 1804.

Sarah, wid. Thomas, Nov. 15, 1710.

————, ch. Elenor, June 2, 1834, a. 27 d.

**RODGERS** (see also Rogers), Harriet B., May 20, 1834, a. 5 y.

William, fever, Nov. 20, 1809, a. 25 y. C. R. 3.

**ROGERS** (see also Rodgers), Emogine C., d. Russell and Ann S., bowel complaint, July 29, 1849, a. 3 m. 7 d.

James, Dec. 31, 1751, a. 19 y. 10 m. G. R. 1.

John, s. Jeremiah and Elizabeth, Apr. 13, 1708.

John, s. Jeremiah and Elizabeth, Sept. 15, 1712.

Jona[than] P., m., counsellor at law, b. Augusta, Me., consumption, Nov. 26, 1846, a. 46 y.

Mary B., Mrs., Sept. 5, 1839, a. 67 y.

Mary C., d. Ammon and Mary, consumption, Feb. 11, 1847, a. 19 y.

Samuel, unm., gentleman, paralysis, May 31, 1849, a. 40 y.

———, ch. still born, Jeremiah and Elizabeth, Sept. 21, 1705.

**ROOK** (see also Rorke, Rourke, O'Rouke), Elizabeth C., w. William H., consumption, Jan. 3, 1847, a. 33 y.

Mary, b. Ireland, w. Patrick, at Dorchester, bur. at Roxbury consumption, Sept. 7, 1848, a. 30 y.

**ROONEY,** James, s. William and Esther, consumption, Sept. 11, 1849, a. 1 y. 9 m.

John, b. Ireland, s. Patrick and Mary, accidental, Apr. 25, 1848, a. 9 y.

Thomas, s. Bernard and Bridget, croup, Feb. 15, 1849, a. 1 m. 15 d.

**ROOTE,** ———, "Old Moth[e]r," wid. Tho[mas] Ruggles, bur. 14:12m: 1674-5, in her 89th y. C. R. 1.

**RORKE** (see also Rook), Edward, m., laborer, b. Ireland, jaundice, Mar. 21, 1849, a. 34 y.

**ROSE,** Esther, w. Henry, of Hartford, Conn., dropsy, Oct. 3, 1836, a. 31 y. C. R. 3.

**ROSEMEYER** (see also Rosemyer), Hannah, b. Sharon, w. Henry C., typhus fever, Oct. 6, 1846, a. 28 y.

Monroe B., ch. H. C., Sept. 13, 1841, a. 6 w.

Sarah B., w. Henry C., Sept. 6, 1841, a. 24 y.

**ROSEMYER** (see also Rosemeyer), ———, ch. H. and C., typhus fever, Aug. 29, 1846, a. 3 y.

**ROSS,** Charles L., s. John and Elizabeth, lung fever, June 14, 1849, a. 3 y.

**ROURK** (see also Rook), James, s. Patrick and Mary, convulsions, Aug. 8, 1848, a. 3 m.

Maria, d. John and Ann, decline, Aug. 30, 1849, a. 2 m.

Margarett, d. Michael and Bridget, measles, Oct. 24, 1849, a. 1 y. 6 m.

**ROUSE,** Oliver, Jan. 16, 1824, a. 40 y.

**ROWE,** Catharine, w. Thomas, dropsy, June 29, 1822, a. 36 y. c. R. 3.

Harriet, erysipelas, May 3, 1842, a. 5 w. c. R. 3.

———, ch. still born, Elihu and Sophia, Aug. 18, 1847.

**RUGGLE** (see also Ruggles), Hanna [Hannah Ruggles. CT. R.], d. Samuell, Mar. 16, 1655. [1655-6. CT. R.]

John [Ruggles, Sergt. c. R. 1.], jr., s. Tho[mas], Sept. 15, 1658.

Sarah [Ruggles. c. R. 1.], d. Samuell, bur. Nov. 11, 1664.

———, inf. ch. John, bur. 22 : 12m : 1687-8. c. R. 1.

**RUGGLES** (see also Ruggle, Rugle), Anna, wid. Capt. Samuel, Sept. 5, 1711. [in her 68th y. G. R. 1.]

Edward, Dea., Sept. 16, 1765, in his 74th y. G. R. 1.

Elizabeth, w. John, July 21, 1740. [a. abt. 81 y. G. R. 1.]

Hannah, w. Samuell, Oct. 24, 1669.

Hannah, d. Samuell, Nov. 6, 1669.

Hannah, w. Sergt. John, Dec. 17, 1700.

Hannah w. [Dea. G. R. 1.] Edward, Mar. 11, 1731-2. [a. 35 y. G. R. 1.]

Henry, s. Capt. Samuel [and Ann. G. R. 1.], Dec. 9, 1702. [a. 21 y. G. R. 1.]

Henry, s. Nath[anie]l, Esq., Oct. 27, 1806.

Joanna, wid. Joseph, Esq., at Fort Constitution, N. H., June 16, 1829, a. 81 y.

John, sr., bur. 6 : 8m : 1663. c. R. 1.

John, Dec. 16, 1694.

John, Sergt., Feb. 28, 1711-12. [a. abt. 55 y. G. R. 1.]

John, Mar. 4, 1718.

John Fairfield, s. Nath[anie]l and Sally, small pox, Sept. 25, 1792.

Jonathan, s. John, cut his throat, Nov. 26, 1715.

Joseph, s. Samuel, bur. 6 : 12m : 1664-5. c. R. 1.

Joseph, Capt., Sept. 9, 1742, in his 47th y. G. R. 1.

Joseph, June 9, 1765, a. 40 y. G. R. 1.

RUGGLES, Joseph, s. Nath[anie]l and Sally, Aug. 16, 1795.

Joseph, s. Nath[anie]l and Sally, May 21, 1798.

Joseph, s. Nath[anie]l and Martha, Sept. 12, 1800.

Joseph, s. Joseph and Joanna, Jan. 3, 1819.

Martha, d. Nathaniel and Martha, Sept. 22, 1770, a. 2 y. 16 d.

Martha, Mrs., Jan. 26, 1829, a. 83 y.

Martha Fairfield, d. Nath[anie]l and Sally, Feb. 7, 1796.

Mary, w. John, sr. [fever and ague. c. r. 1.], Dec. 5, 1673.
     [1674. c. r. 1.]

Nathaniel, Esq., Jan. 14, 1780. [in his 50th y. N. R. 2.]

Nathaniel, June 15, 1806, a. 32 y.

Nath[anie]l W., at Wilmington, N. C., Sept. 5, 1807, a. 21 y.
     4 m. 16 d.

Nathaniel, Hon., a Representative in Congress for the Norfolk
     District, Dec. 19, 1819, a. 58 y.

Nathaniell, s. Lt. Samuel, May —, 1676.

Ruth, w. John, sr., Apr. 11, 1710.

Sally, d. Nathaniel and Sally, Apr. 25 [24. dup.], 1802. [a
     14 y. dup.]

Sally, d. Nath[anie]l, Aug. 30, 1805.

Samuel, Capt., Aug. 15, 1692. [a. 63 y. G. R. 1.]

Samuel, Capt., Feb. 25, 1715-16. [a. 57 y. G. R. 1.]

Sarah, d. Samuell, Nov. 17, 1669.

Sarah, w. John, sr., May 2, 1687.

Stephen, s. John and Sarah, June 28, 1714.

Thomas, householder [consumption. c. r. 1.], bur. Nov. 16,
     1644.

Thomas, Rev., June 1, 1728.

———, s. still born, John and Barbara, —: 11m: 1636. c. r. 1.

———, inf. ch. Samuel, bur. 3 : 8m : 1668. c. r. 1.

———, ch. Joseph, jr., Oct. 25, 1802, a. 13 m.

———, ch. Nath[anie]l, Aug. 28, 1805, a. 1 m.

———, ch. Nath[anie]l, Oct. 26, 1807, a. 4 m.

RUGLE (see also Ruggles), Joseph, s. Samuell, bur. Feb. 5,
     1664.

Mary [Ruggle. dup.], d. Samuell [Samuel. dup.], bur. Mar. 31,
     1658. [1657. dup.]

RUMRELL (see also Rumrill), Charles, s. Thomas, at New
     Bedford, Jan. 8, 1840.

RUMRILL (see also Rumrell), Aaron, Apr. 1 [Mar. 31. dup.],
     1800, a. 65 y.

RUMRILL, Aaron, July 9, 1811, a. 42 y. G. R. 1.

Abigail[Abagail. dup.], w. Tho[ma]s, d. Jos[eph] and Abigail Richardson, Oct. 16 [24. dup.], 1801. [a. 27 y. dup.]

[Abigail R. G. R. 1.], ch. A., Sept. 14, 1803, a. 20 m.

Elizabeth, a pauper, Dec. 25, 1834, a. 68 y.

Henary A., Sept. 24, 1800, a. 2 m. G. R. 1.

Mary Ann, d. Aaron and Ann, July 17, 1801.

Samuel M., s. Samuel and Jane, bowel complaint, Sept. 8, 1848, a. 1 y. 6 m.

Thomas, s. Tho[ma]s and Abigail, Nov. 25, 1808.

Thomas, jr., painter, s. Thomas and Sally, typhoid fever, Sept. 25, 1849, a. 41 y. 3 m.

Thomas, m., pensioner of the revolution, b. Dorchester, s. Aaron and Elizabeth, old age, Nov. 10, 1849, a. 87 y.

W[illia]m D., s. W[illia]m and Nancy [(Young. P. R. 6.)], croup, June 9, 1846, a. 2 y.

———, ch. A., Sept. 23, 1805, a. 21 m.

———, wid. James, Dec. —, 1834.

**RUMSDILL** (see also Ramsdell), Sarah, Jan. 1, 1804, a. 56 y.

**RUPALL,** ———, Mr., Aug. 30, 1830.

**RUSSELL,** Abby S., w. True, Feb. 4, 1847, a. 36 y. G. R. 5.

Abigail, m., b. Gray, Me., d. Stephen Thayer, typhus fever, Feb. 4, 1847, a. 36 y.

Catherine, paralytic, Sept. 5, 1847, a. 75 y.

Chapin William, s. True and Abby S., Oct. 21, 1846, a. 19 m. G. R. 5.

Edward True, s. True and Abigail [Abby S. G. R. 5.], dysentery, Sept. 29, 1846, a. 3 y. 8 m. [a. 4 y. G. R. 5.]

Thomas, Oct. 4, 1805, a. 20 y.

William Chapin, s. True and Abigail, canker, Oct. 11, 1846, a. 1 y. 7 m.

**RYAN** (see also Ryon), Ellen, b. Ireland, ship fever, June 20, 1848, a. 19 y.

Margar[e]tt, unm., b. Ireland. consumption, Apr. 16, 1849, a. 17 y.

**RYON** (see also Ryan), ———, ch. ———, Sept. 8, 1805.

**SALTER,** Elizabeth, d. Thomas and Mary, Dec. 28, 1698, a. 2 y. 9 m. G. R. 1.

Thomas, s. Thomas and Mary, July 11, 1699, a. 13 d. G. R. 1.

SALTER, William, Apr. 17, 1780, a. 55 y. C. R. 2.
———, Mrs., Aug. 29, 1786. C. R. 2.

SAMPSON, Mehitable, w. Stephen, Mar. 6, 1803. [a. 33 y. dup.]
Nancy, w. Joshua, May 12, 1828.
———, ch. still born, Joseph and Rachel, Apr. 28, 1848.

SANBORN (see also Sanburn, Sandborn), Asa, Dec. —, 1839. C. R. 4.
———, ch. still born, Solomon and Elizabeth, Dec. 14, 1848.

SANBURN (see also Sanborn), Sarah, b. N. H., tumor, at the alms house, Feb. 27, 1849, a. 54 y.

SANDBORN (see also Sanborn), Rebecca, w. Abraham, stoppage in stomach, Feb. 23, 1832, a. 33 y. C. R. 2.

SANDERSON, Daniel, Jan. 25, 1829, a. 83 y.
Sarah, b. Canton, wid. Dan[ie]l, old age, Jan. 14, 1849, a. 98 y. [a. 97 y. 5 m. G. R. 1.]

SANFORD, ———, inf. ch. ———, Aug. 9, 1846.

SANGER, Abner, m., laborer, b. Watertown, pleurisy fever, May 7, 1847, a. 72 y.
———, [Sangor. inf. C. R. 1.], s. Nathanael, Feb. 7, 1684-5.

SARGENT, Elizabeth L., d. Epes, consumption, May 14, 1847, a. 17 y. 3 m.
Mary Turner, d. Lucius M., Esq., Aug. 2, 1841, a. 23 y.
———, ch. Epes, consumption, June 22, 1846, a. 18 y.

SAUAGE (see also Savage), Mary, Oct. 5, 1806, a. 69 y.

SAVAGE (see also Sauage), Isaac, Apr. 23, 1782, a. 87 y. G. R. 1.
Richard J., June 3, 1824, a. 24 y.

SCALLON, Mary, bur. May 27, 1841, a. 57 y. C. R. 5.

SCARBOROW (see also Scarbrough), John [Scarbarrow. CT. R.; Scarbro. inf. C. R. 1.], s. John [convulsions. C. R. 1.], bur. Aug. 12, 1642.
John [Scarbrough. C. R. 1.], slain with a gun, June 9, 1646.

SCARBROUGH (see also Scarborow, Scarbrow), Bethiah, wid. Dea. Samuel, Sept. 10, 1728, a. 73 y. G. R. 1.

SCARBROUGH, Jeremia[h] [Scarbro. inf. c. r. 1.], s. Samuel
  and Bethia, Sept. 7, 1686.
Joseph, Feb. 5, 1737-8. [a. 55 y. G. R. 1.]
Mary, d. Samuel and Bethia, Aug. 12, 1693.
Samuel, Dea., Mar. 18, 1714. [a. 69 y. 2 m. G. R. 1.]
Samuell, small pox, Nov. 2, 1721. [in his 41st y. G. R. 1.]
Theoda, wid. Samuel, Sept. 19, 1724.

**SCARBROW** (see also Scarbrough), ———, "sister," consumption, bur. 30 : 4m : 1679. C. R. 1.

**SCHAFER** (see also Schaffer), Margarett, d. Frederic and
  Mariah, fits, Mar. 28, 1849, a. 7 m. 15 d.

**SCHAFFER** (see also Schafer), Elizabeth, d. John and
  Chirstiana, scarlet fever, July 17, 1849, a. 5 y.
John, s. John and Christiana, scarlet fever, July 27, 1849, a. 3
  y. 10 m.

**SCHEEL,** Catherine, d. Jacob and Catherine, measles, Mar. 6,
  1849, a. 1 y.

**SCHNAPH,** Antonia, m., b. Germany, typhus fever, Oct. 15,
  1848, a. 38 y.

**SCHNEIDER** (see also Shnider, Shneider, Shnider, Snider).
  John, m., carpenter, b. Germany, accidental, Oct. 15,
  1846, a. 56 y.

**SCOT** (see also Scott), Mary, bilious fever, Sept. —, 1809, a.
  20 y. C. R. 3.

**SCOTT** (see also Scot), Ann R., wid. Ebenezer, Jan. 16,
  1840, a. 57 y. 6 m.
Eben, s. George and Harriet, cholera infantum, July 24, 1848,
  a. 21 d.
Hannah, d. John, Aug. 7, 1674.
Hannah, 2d, d. John, Aug. 26, 1678.
John, s. John, Nov. 11, 1675.
John [Scot. inf. c. r. 1.], s. John, Nov. 16, 1683.
John, Oct. 6, 1779. G. R. 2.
John, drowned, May 17, 1806, a. abt. 40 y.
Judith, Madam, Feb. 4, 1819, a. 82 y. C. R. 2.
Lawrence, s. Patrick and Ellen, croup, Jan. 2, 1849, a. 4 y.
  6 m.

SCOTT, Margarett [Scot. inf. ch. C. R. 1.], d. John, Jan. 14, 1680. [1680-1. C. R. 1.]

Mary [Scot. inf. ch. C. R. 1.], d. John, July 30, 1679.

Mary B., Dec. —, 1836. C. R. 4.

Peter Chardon, Feb. 22, 1798, a. 28 y. C. R. 2.

Robert C., s. John and Alice, scarlet fever, Apr. 23, 1848, a. 5 y.

Sarah, d. John, Jan. 26, 1676, a. 6 h.

Sarah, d. John, Nov. 10, 1684.

Sarah, w. Joseph, Jan. 1, 1705-6.

Susannah, wid. Peter C., Esq., Apr. 16, 1834, a. 67 y.

Thomas W., May 1, 1824, a. 30 y.

———, d. still born, Char[le]s C. and Sarah R., Mar. 18, 1847.

SEABURY, Lucretia, b. Granby, d. John, consumption, Mar. 12, 1848, a. 27 y.

Maria P., b. Granby, d. Dr., consumption, Nov. 12, 1848, a. 26 y.

SEARL (see also Searle), Hannah, w. Philip [Phillip. dup.], small pox, Jan. 3, 1721-2. [a. 63 y. G. R. 1.]

SEARLE (see also Searl, Searles), Anne, w. Thomas, bur. Dec. 18, 1841. C. R. 5.

Ebenezer, s. Philip and Hannah, Jan. 26, 1719-20. [in his 26th y. G. R. 1.]

Elizabeth, w. Philip, sr., Feb. 5, 1708.

Hannah, w. Phillip, sr., Dec. 16, 1691.

Hannah, d. Philip and Hannah, Aug. 7, 1693.

Mary, w. John, Sept. 20, 1712.

Philip, sr., May 3, 1710.

Philip [Phillip Sarle. G. R. 1.], Dec. 17, 1722. [a. 62 y. G. R. 1.]

Rebecca, d. John and Mary, June 2, 1709.

———, ch. twin, John, Mar. 7, 1684-5.

———, inf. ch. John, bur. 10 : 1m : 1684-5. C. R. 1.

SEARLES (see also Searle), Philip, issue of Mar. 8, 1773, a. 88 y. N. R. 2.

SEARS, David C., s. Paul, jr., and Eunice T., lung fever, Mar. 24, 1848, a. 5 m. 7 d.

Sarah G., w. Peter, Sept. 14, 1837, a. 36 y.

———, d. still born, Paul and Eunice, Nov. 14, 1846.

———, ch. still born, Paul, jr. and Eunice, Nov. 30, 1848.

**SEAVER** (see also Seaverns, Seavers, Sever), Abijah, May 5, 1823, a. 23 y.

Benjamin, June 29, 1815, a. 48 y. 9 m.

Caleb, s. Thomas and Elizabeth, small pox, July 4, 1730.

Deborah, Mrs., Nov. 18, 1789, a. 74 y. c. r. 2.

Ebenesar, Hon., yeoman, old age, Mar. 1, 1844, in his 81st y.

Ebenezer, s. Shubael and Abigail, Feb. 14, 1736-7, in his 17th y. G. R. 1.

Ebenezer, May 8, 1773, a. 86 y. G. R. 1.

Ebenezer, Lt., Mar. 26, 1785, a. 64 y. G. R. 1.

Ebenezer, scrofula, Feb. 3, 1839, a. 21 y. c. R. 3.

Ebenezer, consumption, July 31, 1845, a. 54 y. c. R. 3.

Elijah, at the work house, Feb. 1, 1810, a. 82 y.

Elisha, Apr. 7, 1813, a. 45 y.

Elizabeth, w. Hon. Ebenezer, Feb. 22, 1838.

Elizabeth G., Dec. 4, 1813, a. 17 y. G. R. 1.

Ellen, d. John and Abigail, July 9, 1835, a. 9 m.

Emma Frances, d. William D. and Catherine, canker, Sept. 1, 1848, a. 21 d.

George, s. George and Elizabeth W., Aug. 10, 1825, a. 15 m.

George, consumption, July 27, 1843, a. 26 y. c. R. 3.

George Henry, s. John C. and Mary, Oct. 9, 1827, a. 8 m.

George Henry, s. Joshua and Elizebeth, Dec. 29, 1837.

Hannah, d. Robert, bur. 3 : 4 m : 1648. c. r. 1.

Harriet, d. John and Betsey, Feb. 13, 1809.

Harriet, d. John and Betsey, Nov. 1, 1813.

Jonath[a]n, Dec. 18, 1753, in his 54th y. G. R. 1.

Joseph, Capt. Aug. 17, 1811.

Joseph, dropsy of brain, Mar. 10, 1821, a. 15 m. c. R. 3.

Joshua, Mar. 27, 1730, in his 88th y. G. R. 1.

Joshua, Sept. 4, 1773, a. 45 y. G. R. 1.

Joshua [Seever, affection of liver. c. R. 3.], Aug. 11, 1833, a. 54 y.

Lucy, d. Hon. Ebenezer, Oct. 16, 1822, a. 17 y.

Margaret, w. Ebenezer, Nov. 30, 1765, a. 72 y. G. R. 1.

Martha P., d. W[illia]m and Martha, fits, Mar. 13, 1847, a. 21 d.

Mary, inf. d. Joshua, bur. 24 : 3m : 1683. c. R. 1.

Mary, w. Ebenezer, May 8, 1766, a. 35 y. G. R. 1.

Nancy, wid. Joshua, Esq. [broken leg. c. R. 5.], Oct. 23, 1837, a. 57 y.

Nathaniel, s. Caleb, bur. Mar. 8, 1687-8. c. R. 1.

SEAVER, Nathaniel, July 4, 1806, a. 33 y.

Nathaniel, s. Hon. Eben[eze]r, July 16, 1832, a. 25 y.

Robert, aged, bur. 6 : 4m : 1683. C. R. 1.

Robert, s. Robert and Abby, tumor on the brain, June 23, 1847, a. 7 y. 6 m. 10 d.

Rufus Kelton, s. Joshua and Nancy, canker fever [bet. Aug. 20 and Nov. 21], 1805, a. 11 m. C. R. 3.

S., Mrs., Mar. 3, 1804, a. 66 y.

Sally, issue of Nov. 3, 1792, a. 13 y. N. R. 4.

Sarah, d. Nathaniel, bur. 18 : 2m : 1674. C. R. 1.

Seth Sumner, teething, Feb. 21, 1817, a. 7 m. C. R. 3.

Susanna, d. Ebenezer and Margaret, Sept. 22, 1769, a. 39 y. G. R. 1.

Susannah, d. Ebenezer and Elizabeth, Sept. 3, 1801.

Tabitha, wid. Ebenezer, Mar. 1, 1804, a. 67 y. G. R. 1.

Willard Henry, s. Joshua and Elizabeth, Dec. 6, 1844, a. 6 m.

William, Apr. 12, 1818, a. 84 y. 6 m. [a. 85 y. G. R. 1.]

————, w. Robert, bur. 18 : 10m : 1669-70. C. R. 1.

————, inf. ch. Caleb, bur. 29 : 5m : 1685. C. R. 1.

————, [Seavers. dup.], ch. Nath[anie]l, Sept. 10, 1801.

————, ch. W[illia]m, jr., Jan. 23, 1803, a. 12 d.

————, ch. Nath[anie]l, Sept. 15, 1803, a. 10 m.

————, Mrs., Sept. 20, 1804, a. 85 y.

————, ch. W[illia]m, jr., Nov. 15, 1805, a. 3 m.

————, w. W[illia]m, Feb. 10, 1807, a. 37 y.

————, wid., Feb. 23, 1808, a. 32 y.

————, ch. R., lung fever, Jan. 9, 1846, a. 6 m. C. R. 3.

**SEAVERNS** (see also Seaver), Abijah, July 29, 1838, a. 74 y.

Catharine, Mar. 30, 1831, a. 24 y.

Elisha, fall from scaffold, Nov. 18, 1821, a. 45 y. C. R. 3.

Joel, Feb. 12, 1827, a. 61 y.

Josiah, m., farmer, s. Josiah and Naomi, liver complaint, Jan. 20, 1847, a. 76 y. [73 y. C. R. 3.]

Luther [epilepsy. C. R. 3.], Aug. 23, 1825, a. 52 y.

Luther S., s. Luther and Hannah, Oct. 14, 1836.

Mary, Mrs. [consumption. C. R. 3.], Jan. 16, 1821, a. 36 y.

Olive D., Mrs., Aug. —, 1830.

Peres, s. Abijah, drowned in Jamaica pond [bet. Aug. 20 and Nov. 21], 1805, a. 11 y. C. R. 3.

Samuel, Apr. 29, 1810, a. 28 y. G. R. 1.

Samuel, throat distemper, Mar. 24, 1813, a. 3 y. C. R. 3.

SEAVERNS, Susannah, b. Brookline, wid. Abijah, old age, Oct. 26, 1849, a. 81 y. 5 m.

Thomas W., s. Josiah and Rebecca, Jan. 29, 1802, a. 4 m. G. R. 4.

Thomas White, s. Josiah and Rebecah, July 4, 1802.

————, d. Abijah, nervous fever and canker rash, Oct. 27, 1801. C. R. 3.

————, inf. ch. Josiah and Rebecca, convulsion fits, Dec. 21, 1807, a. 1 w. C. R. 3.

SEAVERS (see also Seaver), [Francis Seaver. G. R. 1.], ch. Benja[min] [and Deborah. G. R. 1.], June 20, 1803, a. 17 m.

————, ch. John, Feb. 12, 1806, a. 4 m.

————, ch. Richard, July 29, 1807, a. 5 m.

SEDRICK, Marius, mariner, consumption, July 28, 1846, a. 40 y.

SEGARS, Francis, at the alms house, Sept. 9, 1842, a. 42 y.

SEGASKA, Elizabeth, at the alms house, Nov. 19, 1837, a. 5 m.

SESSIONS, Chester, m., gentleman, b. Brimfield, s. Joseph A. and Sarah F., Nov. 23, 1848, a. 68 y.

Sarah, w. Chester, June 18, 1834.

SEVER (see also Seaver), Caleb, sr., Mar. 6, 1713.

Elizabeth [Seaver. C. R. 1.], w. Robart, June 6, 1657.

Elizabeth, d. Thomas and Elizabeth, Feb. 6, 1739-40.

Hanna, d. Robart, June 3, 1647.

Hanna [Seaver. C. R. 1.], d. Robart, bur. Mar. 3, 1653. [1653-4. C. R. 1.]

Hannah, w. Shubael, Feb. 13, 1721-2, a. 75 y. G. R. 1.

Hannah, w. Caleb, Aug. 26, 1721, a. 42 y. G. R. 1.

Mary, d. Joshua and Mary, May 22, 1683.

Mary, wid. Peter, Sept. 9, 1768, a. 51 y. G. R. 1.

Nathanael, under command of Capt. Sam[ue]ll Wadsworth, slain by the Indians at Sudbury, Apr. 21, 1676.

Robert, May 13, 1683, a. abt. 74 y.

Sarah, w. Caleb, sr., Jan. 31, 1708.

Sarah, d. Caleb and Hannah, Oct. 6, 1714.

Sarah, d. Joshua and Mary, Sept. 13, 1736, in her 47th y. G. R. 1.

SEVER, Shubael, Jan. 18, 1729-30, a. 92 y. G. R. 1.

SEWAL, Hull, s. Samuel and Rebecca, Dec. 11, 1703.
Rebecca, d. Samuel and Rebecca, Aug. 3, 1710.

SHAFER, ——, ch. still born, John and Anna, Dec. 9, 1849.

SHANNON, Mary E., d. Thomas and Martha, canker rash,
    June 16, 1849, a. 3 m.

SHAPLEIGH, Benj[amin] F., canker, Sept. 27, 1837, a. 10 m.
    C. R. 3.

SHARKEY (see also Tharkey), Daniel, Oct. —, 1837.

SHARPE, John, under the command of Capt. Sam[ue]ll Wads-
    worth, slain by the Indians at Sudbury, Apr. 21, 1676.
Robart, householder, bur. July —, 1653.

SHATTUCK, William B., Oct. —, 1836; a. 26 y.

SHAW, Ann Heath, d. Joseph P. and Sarah H., Sept. 13, 1833.
    [Aug. 12, a. 3 m. dup.]
Nancy, July 29, 1804, a. 19 y.
Nancy Brown, w. Isaac, Oct. 7, 1810, a. 35 y. 5 m. 6 d.
Nathan, June 3, 1797, a. 44 y.

SHEA, Ann, m., b. Ireland, heart complaint, Dec. 8, 1847, a.
    34 y.
Cary, a pauper, Aug. 20, 1831, a. 33 y.
Morris, s. Morris and Ellen, consumption, Nov. 30, 1848, a.
    21 d.
——, ch. still born, Thomas and Ann, Aug. 18, 1847.

SHEAD (see also Shed), Elisabeth [Elizabeth Shed. G. R. 1.],
    w. James, Apr. 18, 1743. [in her 72d y. G. R. 1.]

SHED (see also Shead, Shedd), Betsey, Jan. 9, 1795.
Frances, May 18, 1794.
Grace, Mrs., Aug. —, 1834, a. 79 y.
Henry Augustus, s. Oliver, Sept. —, 1820, a. 1 y.
James, Dec. 29, 1749, in his 69th y. G. R. 1.
James, Oct. 7, 1796, a. 49 y.
Mary, w. James, Jan. 21, 1716.
Mary, Dec. 10, 1799, a. 81 y.
Oliver, Jan. 26, 1799, a. 48 y.
——, s. wid., Sept. 23, 1802, a. 7 y.

**SHEDD** (see also Shed), James, b. Brookline, dropsy, at the alms house, Mar. 24, 1849, a. 28 y.

**SHEDDON,** Sarah, w. William, Sept. 30, 1823, a. 35 y.
William, Jan. 17, 1824.
William, Mar. —, 1832.

**SHEHAR,** Catherine, d. Timothy and Julia, measles, Feb. 4, 1849, a. 3 y. 6 m.

**SHEPARD** (see also Sheperd), Joseph S., unm., morocco dresser, s. Eliphalet, scarlet fever, June 15, 1846, a. 17 y.
Rhoda, wid., b. Canton, d. John and Hepzibeth Taunt, old age, Sept. 6, 1849, a. 90 y.

**SHEPERD** (see also Shepard), Julia, d. John M. and Susan, lung fever, Apr. 9, 1847, a. 1 y. 1 m.

**SHEPHERD,** William, convulsion fits, Aug. 30, 1801, a. 42 y. c. r. 3. [a. 38 y. g. r. 4.]

**SHERIDAN,** Judith, wid., b. Ireland, old age, Sept. 17, 1849, a. 75 y.

**SHINNICK,** John, June 18, 1804.

**SHIRLEY,** Francis, b. Ireland, fever, at the alms house, Aug. 31, 1849, a. 10 y.
John, butcher, issue of Aug. 30, 1773. N. R. 2.
William, Esq., formerly Gov. and Commander in chief, Mar. 24, 1771, in his 77th y. N. R. 2.

**SHNEIDER** (see also Schneider), Emily, w. Jacob, Apr. 14, 1845, a. 21 y. 7 m. G. R. 5.

**SHNIDER,** (see also Schneider), Caroline, d. Peter and Caroline, scarlet fever, Sept. 6, 1849, a. 8 y.
John W., s. Jacob W. and Henrietta, fits, Jan. 5, 1849, a. 1 y. 6 m.
Peter, jr., b. Germany, s. Peter and Caroline, scarlet fever, Sept. 9, 1849, a. 12 y.

**SHOEMAKER,** Charles, s. Randell, bowel complaint, Aug. 12, 1848, a. 1 y. 10 m.
Eliza, d. Rudolph and Eliza, lung fever, Mar. 3, 1847, a. 2 y.
Elizabeth, b. Germany, w. Hirman, dysentery, Sept. 9, 1848, a. 40 y.

**SHORTELL,** Michael, m., laborer, b. Ireland, fever, Nov. 2, 1847, a. 38 y.

**SIAS,** Elvira, d. Sam[ue]l P. and Eunice, typhus fever, Feb. 18, 1849, a. 2 y. 4 m.

**SIBLEY,** ——, ch. W., Aug. 8, 1804, a. 12 y.

**SILSBY,** Emeline, d. Enoch and Alice, consumption, Oct. 18, 1848.

**SIMMONS** (see also Skimmons), Benjamin, Oct. —, 1831. c. R. 4.

Joseph L., s. Joseph L. and Mary, inflammation of bowels, Sept. 13, 1848, a. 4 y. 5 m.

Maria Eastburn, d. George A. and Belinda P., Sept. 10, 1839.

——, ch. George, Sept. 27, 1798, a. 2 y.

——, s. George, Jan. 6, 1806, a. 15 y.

**SIMPSON,** Joshua P., s. Horatio G. and Charlotte, dysentery, Sept. 28, 1848, a. 10 m.

Martha L., Apr. 29, 1838, a. 14 y.

**SIMS,** Charlotte, Mrs., a pauper, Dec. —, 1829, a. 46 y.

Thomas, at the almshouse, May 5, 1828, a. 2 m.

William T., at the almshouse, May 10, 1838, a. 33 y.

**SINCLAIR,** Susan E., d. John T. and Minerva, dysentery, Dec. 15, 1849, a. 1 y. 3 m.

——, s. W[illia]m and Lucy J., July 31, 1847, a. 14 d.

**SKILLEN,** ——, ch. Pollidore, Sept. 15, 1798, a. 14 y.

**SKIMMONS** (see also Simmons), Eben[eze]r, Nov. 6, 1807, a. 15 y.

**SKINNER,** John [apoplexy, Sept. 25. c. r. 2.], 1833, a. 65 y.

Joseph, June 9, 1840, a. 26 y.

Mary Sampson, d. Jacob and Mary, Oct. 3, 1803. [a. 1 m. dup.]

**SLEPER,** ——, Mrs., old age, May 13, 1801, a. 84 y. c. r. 3.

**SLOAN** (see also Sloane, Sloun), John, Sept. 24, 1810, a. 56 y.

John, s. Thomas D. and Sally, May 22, 1812.

Polly B., painter, w. William P., consumption, May 19, 1846, a. 45 y.

Samuel W., May 17, 1826, a. 35 y. g. r. 5.

——, ch. David and Elizabeth, July 17, 1801.

**SLOANE** (see also Sloan), Elizabeth, May —, 1824. C. R. 4.

**SLOUN** (see also Sloan), Elizabeth, Mrs., Mar. 9, 1836, a. 73 y.

**SMITH,** Abiel, at the almshouse, Apr. 2, 1828, a. 43 y.

Abigail [Peele, Mrs., old age. C. R. 3.], Jan. [6. C. R. 3.], 1825, a. 80 y.

Abigail, a pauper, Oct. 27, 1834, a. 17 y.

Abigail, wid. Eben[eze]r, May —, 1837, a. 77 y.

Amos, Mar. 17, 1826, a. 77 y.

Andrew, s. Francis, Mar. 15, 1639.

Anthony, Apr. 1, 1800, a. 46 y.

Benjamin, Oct. 1, 1775, a. 82 y. C. R. 2.

Ebenezer, intemperance, Oct. 4, 1795, a. 47 y. C. R. 3.

Elisha F., s. Francis and Lydia M., July 7, 1841, a. 4 y. 17 d. G. R. 5.

Emma, d. Robert and Hannah, fits, Sept. 20, 1849, a. 1 y. 1 m.

Francis, s. Reuben, Oct. 15, 1830, a. 18 m.

George, worm fever, Sept 17, 1830, a. 1 y. 11 m. C. R. 3.

Hannah, w. John, Sept. 25, 1713. [1714, a. 55 y. G. R. 1.]

Hannah B., b. Scarborough, Me., d. George T. and Hannah, typhus fever, Sept. 24, 1847, a. 18 y.

Isaac, a stranger, at Maj. Whiting's, Sept. 10, 1811. C. R. 2.

James, s. John and Mary, Feb. 25, 1721-2, in his 21st y. G. R. 1.

James, s. James and Jane, bowel complaint, Sept. 16, 1848, a. 11 m.

James, s. James and Catherine, Jan. 20, 1849, a. 2 y.

James E., s. James W., May 8, 1836, a. 9 m.

James L., June 25, 1838, a. 58 y.

John, innholder, Aug. 17, 1714. [a. abt. 52 y. G. R. 1.]

John, Jan. 9, 1728-9, in his 76th y. G. R. 1.

John, at the almshouse [bet. Aug. and Nov.] 1, 1837, a. 65 y.

John, scarlet fever, at the alms house, Dec. 30, 1848, a. 11 m.

John M., s. Matthew and Margarett, teething, Oct. 4, 1848, a. 8 m.

John W. S., Aug. 2, 1841, a. 23 y.

Joseph, Jan. 26, 1804, a. 60 y.

Joseph, s. Henry and Elizabeth, disease of the lungs, Jan. 18, 1848, a. 5 m.

Levenia, b. England, d. David and Maria, whooping cough, May 13, 1849, a. 21 y.

SMITH, Lidea, wid., Mar. 4, 1748, a. 83 y. C. R. 2.

Lucy L., w. James L., Jan. 11, 1836, a. 44 y.

Margaret, Mrs., Sept. 25, 1812, a. 47 y. G. R. 4.

Margaret, complication of disorders, Feb. 29, 1813, a. 54 y.
C. R. 3.

Mary, w. Ralph, Oct. 8, 1777.

Mary, eldest d. Reuben, Jan. 1, 1831, a. 18 y.

Mary, w. Reuben, Feb. 17, 1833, a. 43 y.

Mary, m., b. Ireland, dysentery, Oct. 23, 1847, a. 38 y.

Mehitable, Mrs., Apr. 3, 1835, a. 78 y.

Michel, Oct. 19, 1775, a. 19 y. C. R. 2.

Nathaniel Ruggles, s. Ralph and Sarah, Sept. 2, 1782.

Polly, d. Ralph and Mary, Aug. —, [after 1772.]

Rachel R., w. Reuben, July 21, 1835, a. 47 y.

Ralph, bur. 7 : 6m : 1672, a. 95 y. C. R. 1.

Ralph, s. Ralph and Mary, at Dedham, Sept. 20, 1776.

Ralph, Aug. 17, 1812, a. 65 y.

Richard C., a native of England, veterinarian, Jan. —, 1830,
a. 64 y.

Sarah, w. Ralph, Dec. 23, 1799.

Sarah, w. William, Mar. —, 1840, a. 39 y.

Solomon, Mar. 10, 1837, a. 72 y.

Susannah, wid., lung fever, Dec. 8, 1846, a. 90 y. 7 m.

William N., Oct. 8, 1827.

——, w. Francis, bur. 13 : 3m : 1667, a. abt. 84 y. C. R. 1.

——, ch. Henry, throat distemper, Apr. 10, 1777, a. 8 y. C. R. 2.

——, ch. Henry, throat distemper, Apr. 10, 1777, a. 4 y. C.
R. 2.

——, s. Henry, Aug. 17, 1778, a. 2 y. C. R. 2.

——, Dec. 24, 1805.

——, w. Parker, Oct. 10, 1806, a. 22 y.

——, Mrs., consumption, Aug. 27, 1844, a. 50 y.

——, ch. Andrew H., fits, Aug. 11, 1846, a. 5 m.

——, inf. ch. John T. and Eliza, Jan. 31, 1849, a. 3 d.

SNELL, Elizabeth, wid., d. Nehemiah and Elizabeth ——,
cholera morbus, Sept. 6, 1849, a. 42 y.

Seth, Feb. 28, 1837, a. 28 y.

SNIDER (see also Schneider), Elizabeth, d. Peter and Elizabeth, decline, July 13, 1849, a. 8 m.

——, ch. still born, Jacob, Aug. 9, 1846.

**SNOW,** Nathaniel, Capt., May 3, 1822, a. 40 y.

**SOLEY,** Nathaniel, Jan. —, 1840, a. 42 y.
Russell, Lt., bur. Nov. 3, 1845, c. r. 5.

**SOREN,** Charles, s. John J. and Fanny, lung fever, Mar. 26, 1847, a. 4 y.
John J., s. John J., May 8, 1838, a. 4 m.

**SOUTHACK,** Maria Augusta, d. George, Apr. —, 1839.
Sarah Louisa, d. George, May 9, 1839, a. 2 1-2 y.

**SOUTHER,** Caroline V., d. William and M., dysentery, Oct. 4, 1848, a. 10 m.

**SOUTHWORTH,** Hannah, Nov. —, 1831. c. r. 4.

**SOWDEN** (see also Sowdon), ——, ch. P., Jan. —, 1831, a. 3 m. c. r. 3.

**SOWDON** (see also Sowden), Susan, Dec. 14, 1828, a. 21 y.

**SPALDING,** William Tileston, s. Jeremiah, Sept. 11, 1839, a. 13 1-4 m.

**SPARHAWK** (see also Sparhawks), Frances, w. Nathaniel, merchant, Mar. 30, 1791, in her 24th y. n. r. 4.
Maria, Dec. 1, 1805, a. 22 y.
Mary, w. Nathaniel, bur. Aug. 4, 1787. n. r. 3.
Nath[anie]l, Nov. 16, 1802, a. 21 y.

**SPARHAWKS** (see also Sparhawk), ——, ch. Cotten, Oct. 11, 1797, a. 3 d.

**SPEAR,** Caroline Weston, d. W[illia]m H. and Catharine H., Aug. —, 1837, a. 15 m.

**SPEED,** Joseph, Feb. —, 1819.

**SPELMAN,** Edward, s. John and Mary, croup, Sept. 9, 1849, a. 3 y. 3 m.
John, s. Daniel and Bridget, diarrhoea, Aug. 23, 1849, a. 1 y. 3 m.

**SPOONER,** Caroline, w. Capt. William H., Sept. 7, 1824, a. 21 y.
Harriet, consumption, May 5, 1844, a. 39 y. c. r. 3.

**SPRAGUE,** Hannah W., w. Isaac, Apr. 19, 1843, a. 39 y.
Nath[anie]l, Oct. 25, 1804, a. 18 y.

**SPRING** (see also Springs), Peter, Mar. 15, 1808, a. 55 y.

**SPRINGER,** Lyman [Asa Lyman, ulcerated bowels. c. R. 3.],
Nov. 25, 1839, a. 34 y. [a. 32 y. 11 m. G. R. 4.]

**SPRINGS** (see also Spring), ——, w. W[illia]m, Sept. 21,
1806, a. 22 y.

**SPROWLS,** Margaret, d. James and Catherine, decline, Dec.
31, 1848, a. 3 m.

**SRADER,** Andrew, b. Germany, consumption, at the alms
house, Oct. 31, 1847, a. 40 y.

**STACK,** Samuel, Sept. 28, 1829, a. 64 y.

**STAFFORD,** ——, Aug. 12, 1798, a. 21 y.
——, ch. M., Jan. 12, 1799, a. 3 y.

**STANIELS,** Harriet, w. Edw[ard], Jan. 27, 1835, a. 30 y.

**STANIFORD,** Elvira H., Mar. 31, 1832, a. 15 y.
Lucy, Mrs., July 24, 1829, a. 50 y.

**STANWOOD,** Charles W., s. H. B. and Ellen, cholera infantum, Aug. 26, 1849, a. 4 m. 10 d.

**STARR,** Daniel [intemperance. c. R. 3.], Aug. 1, 1813, a. 61 y.
Martha, w. Daniel, bur. Apr. 25, 1791. N. R. 4.
Susannah, mortification, May 24, 1813, a. 60 y. c. R. 3.

**STEARNS,** Caroline E., d. Henry M., dec., Oct. —, 1839, a.
2 y.
Sarah, w. Joshua B., Dec. 2, 1840, a. 33 y.
William Pierce, s. William, Oct. —, 1836, a. 10 w.

**STEBBENS** (see also Stebbins), Anna [Stebbin. c. R. 1.;
Stebbins. G. R. 1.], w. John, Apr. 3, 1680. [a. 50 y. G. R. 1.]

**STEBBINS** (see also Stebbens), Elisabeth Hawkins, d. Mrs.,
Sept. 24, 1683.
John [Stebbin. c. R. 1.], Dec. 4, 1681, a. 70 y.

**STEDMAN,** Caleb, June 26, 1746, in his 28th y. G. R. 1.
Caleb, Sept. 24, 1748, in his 77th y. G. R. 1.
Hannah, w. Caleb, Aug. 24, 1743, in her 69th y. G. R. 1.

**STEELE,** Charles S., s. Eleazer F. and Elizabeth M., dysentery, Sept. 24, 1849, a. 1 y. 5 m.

Charlotte Richards, b. New York, d. Jonathan D. and Charlotte. consumption, Oct. 23, 1848, a. 18 y.

——, ch. still born, W[illia]m and Mary, Nov. 11, 1849.

**STEPHENS** (see also Stevens), Stephen, May 21, 1814.

**STETSON,** Jesse, widr., wheelwright, b. Quincy, old age, Aug. 16, 1847, a. 67 y.

Sarah, Mrs., May 3, 1820, a. 39 y.

Sarah, d. Jesse, Feb. 1, 1826, a. 22 y.

**STEVENS** (see also Stephens), Abigail, d. Lt. Joseph and Joanna, [after Mar. 31, 1712.] G. R. 1.

Dorothy, w. Samuel, Oct. 26, 1710. [in her 27th y. G. R. 1.]

Elizabeth, Nov. 7, 1798, a. 72 y.

Joanna, w. Joseph, May 10, 1715.

John, Apr. —, 1750, in his 27th y. G. R. 1.

John, jr., May 6, 1839, a. 25 y.

Joseph, Sept. 16, 1755, in his 35th y. G. R. 1.

Joseph, Lt., Nov. 6, 1756, in his 84th y. G. R. 1.

Lucy, w. Joseph, June —, 1750. G. R. 1.

Mary, w. Capt. Samuel, Nov. 8, 1764, a. 78 y. G. R. 1.

Mary, d. Lt. Joseph and Joanna [after Nov. 22, 1707.]. G. R. 1.

Nathan, s. Timothy and Sarah, Aug. 9, 1689.

Samuel, Capt., Feb. 23, 1768, a. 85 y. G. R. 1.

Sarah, w. Capt. Timothy, Apr. 5, 1695. [a. abt. 48 y. G. R. 1.]

Silence, d. Henry, bur. 1 : 12m: 1668-9. C. R. 1.

Thomas, s. [Lt. G. R. 1.] Joseph and Joanna, Jan. 13, 1703-4.

Timothy, Capt., Jan. 31, 1707. [1707-8, a. abt. 68 y. G. R. 1.]

Timothy, s. [Lt. G. R. 1.] Joseph and Joanna, June 3, 1712.

——, small pox, 13 : 10m: 1678. C. R. 1.

——, ch. John, Dec. 4, 1830, a. 2 y.

**STEVENSON,** ——, bur. Dec. 28, 1849, a. 6 w. C. R. 5.

**STEWART,** Adam, Oct. 15, 1842, a. 66 y.

**St. HENRY,** Mary, Mrs., Oct. 18, 1834, a. 23 y.

**STIMPSON,** Abigail, dysentery, Sept. 21, 1817, a. 56 y. C. R. 3.

Charles, drowned, Aug. 15, 1800, a. 25 y. C. R. 3. [a. 27 y. G. R. 4.]

**St. JOHN,** Margaret Ann, at the alms house, Jan. 28, 1837, a. 4 m.

**STOCKMAN,** Maria, d. Silas and Maria, bowel complaint, Sept. 29, 1847, a. 10 m.

Marietta, d. John and Mary C., bowel complaint, Sept. 12, 1848, a. 1 y. 8 m.

**STODDARD** (see also Stodder), Agnes S., b. New York, d. Robert and Emeline, fever, May 11, 1849, a. 5 y. 8 m.

William E., s. William and Sarah E., inflammation of bowels, Jan. 30, 1849, a. 2 m.

——, Capt., at sea, Oct. —, 1807.

**STODDER** (see also Stoddard), Almira Rebecca, d. William and Almira, Feb. 17, 1826, a. 5 y. 6 m.

**STON** (see also Stone), John [Stone, "an old Kentish man." c. R. 1.], a householder, bur. Oct. 26, 1643.

**STONE** (see also Ston), Alonzo Potter, s. Jonas E., July 25, 1840, a. 4 y. 8 m.

Charles W., s. Warren W. and Eliza A., Oct. 26, 1845, a. 2 y. 3 d. G. R. 5.

Elizabeth Waldo, d. Rev. Cyrus [and Atossa (b. Calcutta, Oct. 26, 1827, left motherless at Bombay, Aug. 7, 1833. Arrived in this country with her younger sister Atossa F., Apr. —, 1834). G. R. 5.], May. 26, a. 11 y. 7 m.

Samuel Fenwick, s. E. W. and Catharine [scarlatina, Nov. 18. c. R. 3.], 1835, a. 27 m.

Sophia C[larke. c. R. 3.], d. Ebenezer W. [convulsion fits. c. R. 3.], Feb. 24, 1838, a. 2 y. 5 m.

**STONHARD,** John, middle aged, bur. 13: 6m: 1649. c. R. 1.

**STOREY** (see also Story), Charles James, s. Charles W. and Elizabeth Moorfield, (bur. in Newbury), Aug. 2, 1844, a. 14 m. 22 d.

**STORY** (see also Storey), Susanna, w. William, June 4, 1707.

**STOW,** Elizabeth, w. John, bur. Aug. 24, 1638.

**STOWELL,** Samuel, Oct. 26, 1825, a. 49 y.

**STRATFORD,** Eleanor, at the alms house, July 20, 1837, a. 36 y.

**STRATTEN** (see also Stratton), Jona[than], Sept. 26, 1805, a. 33 y.

**STRATTON** (see also Stratten, Stretton), Martha H., w. W[illia]m F., Feb. 24, 1837, a. 33 y.

**STRETTON** (see also Stratton), Elizabeth, d. Joseph and Sally, Apr. 4, 1809.

**STRONG,** Deborah, unm., b. Nova Scotia [b. Germany. dup.], typhus fever, Oct. 29, 1846 [Oct. 30, 1847. dup.], a. 19 y. 8 m.

**STUART,** Elizabeth, Mrs., mother of Gilbert, the celebrated painter, Jan. 28, 1819, a. 91 y.

**STUBERT,** Mary Ann, d. Sosis and Mary Ann, dysentery, July 28, 1848, a. 2 y.

**STURTEFANT** (see also Sturtevant), George Clinton, "on the Havana," July 17, 1801, a. 18 y. 7 m.

**STURTEVANT** (see also Sturtefant, Sturtiphant, Stutefant), Rebecca, Mrs., June 7, 1827, a. 69 y. G. R. 4.

**STURTIPHANT** (see also Sturtevant), Isaac [Sturtevant, Capt. G. R. 4.; Sturtivant, consumption. C. R. 3.], July 10, 1806, a. 66 y. [a. 60 y. C. R. 3.]

**STUTEFANT** (see also Sturtevant), Sarah [d. Isaac and Rebecca], May 6, 1790, a. 5 y.

**STYMER,** John, Aug. 4, 1803.
William, Jan. 15, 1825.

**SULLIVAN,** Dennis, m., b. Ireland, hemorrhage, Jan. 25, 1849, a. 63 y.
Martha, m., b. Ireland, sunstruck, June 23, 1849, a. 35 y.
Richard, b. Ireland, consumption, at the alms house, Sept. 14, 1848, a. 60 y.

**SUMNER,** Abigail, m., d. Edward, dec., Feb. 18, 1838, a. 24 y.
Abigail, d. Dea. Samuel, dec., Aug. 18, 1838, a. 54 y.
Amey, d. Samuel and Abigail, Sept. 13, 1753, in 12th m. of her age. G. R. 1.
Arthur, Nov. 1, 1842, a. 76 y. 4 m. C. R. 4.
Austin P., s. Austin and Julia, bowel complaint, Aug. 17, 1848, a. 1 y. 1 m.

SUMNER, Ebenezer, Lt., s. Edw[ar]d, Nov. 13, 1745.
Edward, Oct. 28, 1829, a. 83 y.
Elisabeth, w. Edward, Sept. 26, 1758, a. 79 y.
Elizabeth, d. Edward and Elizabeth, June 19, 1704.
Increase, Nov. 27, 1774, a. 62 y. N. R. 2.
Increase [Gov. dup.], s. Increase and Sarah, June 7, 1799, a. 53 y.
Job, Sept. 23, 1844, a. 20 y.
Maria, w. W[ilia]m H., formerly w. of D. Greenough, consumption, Nov. 14, 1843, a. 51 y. C. R. 3.
Martha, Apr. 30, 1807, a. 22 y.
Nancy, Sept. —, 1826.
Nicholas Burnham, s. Samuel and Abigail, Aug. 7, 1749, a. 3 w. 4 d. G. R. 1.
Polly, d. Clement, canker fever, July 21, 1793, a. 3 y. C. R. 3.
Rufus, s. Clement, canker fever, July 12, 1793, a. 6 y. C. R. 3.
Ruth, d. Clement, consumption, Jan. 29, 1804, a. 18 y. C. R. 3.
Samuel, Dea., Oct. 11, 1813, a. 81 y.
Sarah, wid. Increase, issue of June 25, 1796, a. 77 y. N. R. 4.
Susanna, w. John, Feb. 2, 1732-3. [in her 24th y. G. R. 1.]
Susanna, d. Increase and Sarah, Apr. 29, 1742.
Susanna, 2d, d. Increase and Sarah, June 3, 1742.
Susanna, 3d, d. Increase and Sarah, June 22, 1745.
——, Mrs., w. E. S., Nov. 13, 1804, a. 40 y.
——, w. Clement [dysentery. C. R. 3.], Sept. 20, 1805, a. 55 y.

SURPLUS, ——, ch. Patrick, croup, Sept. 18, 1847, a. 3 y. 3 m.

SUTTON, Rachel, w. Richard, Nov. 10, 1572.
Sarah, w. Rich[ar]d, bur. 12:9m: 1672. C. R. 1.

SWAB, ——, inf. s. still born, Jacob and Catherine, Dec. 30, 1847.

SWAIN, Angelina, d. Joseph, Oct. 23, 1831.
Joseph, s. Joseph and Elizabeth S. W., Oct. 12, 1821.

SWALLOW, Ezra [consumption. C. R. 2.], Oct. 21, 1832, a. 38 y.
——, ch. Abel and Dorcas, July 24, 1815, a. 2 w. C. R. 2.

SWAN, Dorothy, bur. 6:8m: 1675, a. 2 1-2 y. C. R. 1.
Elizabeth, w. Thomas [consumption. Mar. 11. C. R. 3.], 1829, a. 49 y.

SWAN, Peter, bur. 28 : 7m : 1675. C. R. 1.

Peter, s. Thomas, Dec. 10, 1684.

Sarah, cancer in the breast, Nov. 13, 1824, a. 73 y. C. R. 3.

Thomas, s. Thomas, bur. 2 : 11m : 1668-9. C. R. 1.

Thomas, Dr., bur. 8 : 12m : 1687-8. C. R. 1.

Thomas, Dr., at the Castle, Oct. 19, 1710. [a. 42 y. G. R. 1.]

SWANY (see also Sweeney), Michael, b. Ireland, fever, Feb. 25, 1848, a. 17 y.

SWAYSEY, Emanuel, a pauper, Apr. 27, 1834, a. 68 y.

SWEAT (see also Swett), Abigail W., Mrs., Nov. 11, 1828, a. 48 y.

Mark P., Dea., Mar. 9, 1837, a. 60 y.

SWEENEY (see also Swany), John, m., b. Ireland, drinking water, Aug. 11, 1848, a. 36 y.

John, s. Jeremiah and Mary, bowel complaint, Sept. 3, 1848, a. 1 y. 2 m.

John [m., laborer. dup.], b. Ireland, ship fever, at the alms house, Mar. 21, 1849, a. 40 y. [a. 34 y. dup.]

SWEET (see also Swett), Mary, d. Thomas and Nancy, scarlet fever, July 12, 1849, a. 3 y. 6 m.

SWETT (see also Sweat, Sweet), Mary A., d. Thacher and Eliza M., scarlet fever, Aug. 7, 1849, a. 2 y. 10 m. 20 d.

Polly, unm., old age, Aug. 7, 1846, a. 75 y.

William B., Esq., Apr. 4, 1838, a. 48 y.

SWIFT, Polly, Mrs., May 5, 1828, a. 42 y. G. R. 5.

SWINBURN, John, Apr. —, 1830, a. 57 y.

SYLVESTER, Charles C., May —, 1835, a. 24 y.

SYMMS, ——, ch. L., Sept. 27, 1806, a. 11 m.

TABER, Abigail H., May 1, 1834, a. 22 y.

TABLE, Mary, d. Thomas and Abigail, May 27, 1725, in her 2d y. G. R. 1.

TAFT, Dandridge, Aug. 10, 1832, a. 45 y.

Mary Ann, d. Read, Sept. 28, 1840, a. 27 y.

——, ch. Reid and Mary, Oct. 16, 1721 [1821?], a. 16 m. C. R. 2.

——, Mrs., old age, Jan. 16, 1846, a. 80 y. C. R. 3.

**TALBOT,** Sarah, w. Daniel, Jan. 28, 1782, a. 37 y. G. R. 1.
Sarah, Dec. 2, 1793, a. 16 y. C. R. 2.
Sarah, Apr. 21, 1805, a. 62 y. C. R. 2.
Susanna S[oaper, cancer in the breast. C. R. 3.], Aug. 16, 1825,
    a. 47 y.

**TAPPAN,** George Hepburn, s. Tho[ma]s P., July —, 1832, a.
    2 y. 3 m.
Martha P., wid. Tho[ma]s, Oct. 29, 1835, a. 36 y.
Sarah, b. Newburyport, chronic diarrhoea, Oct. 4, 1846, a. 67 y.

**TARBOX,** ——, inf. s. ——, Feb. —, 1842.

**TATMAN** (see also Totman), Elizabeth, inf. d. Jabesh, small
    pox, 30 : 9m : 1678. C. R. 1.
Johannah, w. John, Sept. 29, 1668.
John, Oct. 28, 1670.

**TAUSLEY,** Thomas, servant to Joshua Hues, bur. 23 : 10 m :
    1641. CT. R.

**TAYLER** (see also Taylor), Abigail, w. Peter, Aug. —, 1752,
    a. 66 y. G. R. 1.
Peter, May —, 1753, a. 63 y. G. R. 1.

**TAYLOR** (see also Tayler), Fillmore Z., foundling, infantile,
    at the alms house, Dec. 27, 1849, a. 4 m.
Hale Cass, foundling, cholera infantum, at the alms house, July
    25, 1849, a. 5 m.
John, teething, Oct. 20, 1840, a. 14 m. C. R. 3.
William, Esq., Apr. —, 1838, a. 74 y.

**TEBBETS** (see also Tibbetts), Matilda [w. Enoch. G. R. 3.],
    b. Carlisle, inflammation on the brain, May 3, 1848, a.
    34 y.

**TERNEY,** Michael, s. John and Margaret, lung complaint,
    Dec. 18, 1848, a. 2 y.

**TERRY,** Mary Louisa, d. Henry G. and Mary H., Aug. 14,
    1845, a. 5 m. C. R. 5.

**THACHER,** Elizabeth, d. Oxenbridge and Elizabeth, Oct. —,
    1721. [Oct. 1, in her 5th y. G. R. 1.]

**THANG,** John A., m., coppersmith, b. Germany, dysentery, Oct.
    1, 1848, a. 34 y.

**THARKEY** (see also Sharkey), Felix, drowned, Feb. —, 1843.

**THAYER,** Adam, Nov. 9, 1798, a. 50 y.

George, m., master mariner, b. Taunton, fit, June 26, 1847, a. 50 y.

Jane, at the almshouse, Sept. 7, 1843, a. 77 y.

Sarah, w. Rev. Ebenez[e]r, Feb. 8, 1733.

William, Aug. 5, 1797, a. 21 y. [1798. dup.]

**THOMAS,** Clement ["old Mother." c. r. 1.], wid. Hugh, Sept. 24, 1683.

Frances A., d. Capt. John, dec., [nervous affection. c. r. 3.], June 5, 1837, a. 21 y.

Hugh ["old." c. r. 1.], May 6, 1683, a. abt. 76 y.

Lucy, Mrs., Apr. 10, 1835, a. 77 y.

Malissa S., b. Chelsea, s. Saunders and Julia, fits, Oct. 7, 1848, a. 10 m.

Mary, servant to Hugh Prichard, 10:4m:1643. ct. r.

Rebecca A., Mrs. [paralytic stroke. c. r. 3.], Oct. 25, 1828, a. 70 y.

Thomas K., m., gentleman, old age, Feb. 20, 1849, a. 78 y.

William, m., laborer, b. Ireland, consumption, Mar. 16, 1847.

——, inf. d. Winslow and Ruth S., Feb. 7, 1847, a. 8 d.

**THOMPSON** (see also Tompson), Julia A., d. Augustus C. and Sarah E., Apr. 22, 1848, a. 1 d.

Sarah Hooker, d. Augustus C. and Elizabeth, dropsy on the brain, Feb. 10, 1847, a. 11 m. 17 d.

William J., machinist, consumption, Feb. 9, 1844, a. 29 y.

——, ch. still born, David V. and Joannah, Apr. 20, 1848.

**THURSTON,** Eli [nervous fever. c. r. 3.], Oct. 28, 1817, a. 39 y.

Lucy, d. Joseph and Lucy, Jan. 15, 1808. [a. 11 m. dup]

**THWING,** Elsey F., w. Supply C., Sept. 5, 1844, a. 39 y. 9 m. 25 d. p. r. 1.

James, Esq., Nov. 8, 1835, a. 72 y.

Sarah [Homer. p. r. 1.], Mrs., Aug. 20, 1833, a. 64 y.

**TIBBETTS** (see also Tebbets), ——, 2 chn. still born, Sept. 22, 1846.

**TICKNOR,** Delia Letitia, b. Lebanon, N. H., consumption, May 15, 1849, a. 24 y. 10 m.

**TIDD,** Rhoda, Mrs., Aug. 22, 1693, a. 86 y.

**TIFFANY,** Dexter, Oct. 18, 1822, a. 40 y.

**TILDEN,** L. C. [Ziba C. c. r. 3.], w. Bryant P., Esq., [liver complaint. c. r. 3.], Mar. 26, 1842, a. 58 y.

**TILER,** ——, inf. ch. twin, Job, 28 : 1m : 1646. c. r. 1.

**TILESTON,** Elizabeth, wid. Nath[anie]l, Jan. —, 1838, a. 68 y.
Nath[anie]l [gravel. c. r. 2.], Oct. 6, 1835, a. 72 y.
Rebecca, w. John, June 22, 1840, a. 42 y.

**TILLSON,** ——, s. still born, Isaiah and Deborah, Jan. 31, 1848.

**TILT,** William H., s. John and Mary, consumption, Sept. 29, 1849, a. 3 y.

**TIMONS,** ——, ch. ——, Mar. 23, 1797, a. 2 m.

**TITCOMB,** Antoinette J., d. Joseph P. and Lucy D., scarlet fever, Mar. 19, 1849, a. 2 y. 10 m.
Eliza Ann, d. George and Charlotte, Sept. 20, 1836, a. 1 y.
Joseph P., m., b. Newburyport, consumption, Nov. 27, 1847, a. 30 y.
Joseph P., Nov. —, 1846. c. r. 4.

**TITMAN** (see also Totman), ——, inf. ch. Jabesh, bur. 6 m : 1679. c. r. 1.

**TITTERMAN,** Charity, Feb. 18, 1835, a. 77 y.
Margaret, wid., June 12, 1801, a. 81 y. c. r. 2.

**TOBY,** Jacob, July 30, 1829, a. 22 y.
John, Aug. 21, 1829, a. 18 y.

**TOLLE,** Nancy, Nov. —, 1828, a. 45 y.

**TOLMAN,** Elisha, s. Elisha and Henrietta, May 13, 1826, a. 10 m.
Henry, cancers, Aug. 29, 1843, a. 63 y. c. r. 3.
Henrietta, d. Elisha, jr. and Henrietta H., Feb. 10, 1836 [a. 13 m. dup.]

**TOMPSON** (see also Thompson), Benjamin [schoolmaster and physician. g. r. 1.], Apr. 9, 1714. [a. 72 y. g. r. 1.]

TOMPSON, Elanor Elinor. [G. R. 1.], d. Philip and Mary, Jan. 13, 1720-21. [a. 2 m. 6 d. G. R. 1.]

Joseph, s. Philip and Mary, Oct. 27, 1739, in his 13th y. G. R. 1.

Mary, d. Benjamin, Mar. 28, 1700.

Mary, d. Benjamin and Elizabeth, Sept. 10, 1716. [a. 1 y. 6 m. 13 d. G. R. 1.]

Mary, w. Philip, Jan. 25, 1739, a. 49 y. G. R. 1.

Susanah, d. Philip and Mary, Apr. 7, 1721. [a. 2 y. 5 m. 18 d. G. R. 1.]

——, Dr., July —, 1742. G. R. 1.

**TOOTHAKER,** see Tuthaker.

**TORRY** (see also Tory), Philip [Tory. C. R. 1.], May —, 1686.

Samuel R[dams Torrey. C. R. 5.], s. Joseph G., Dec. [12. C. R. 5.], 1839, a. 3 y. 3 m.

**TORY** (see also Torry), Joseph, a young ch., cough, bur. 6 : 7 m : 1649. C. R. 1.

**TOTMAN** (see also Tatman, Titman), Deborah, w. Jabez, May 31 [June 31. dup.], 1689.

Elizabet, Dec. 11,1677. G. R. 1.

Jabez, Apr. 16, 1705.

Joana, Aug. 2, 1722.

Mahitabel, d. Jabesh, bur. 15 : 7 m : 1682. C. R. 1.

Mary, inf. d. Jabesh, bur. 7 : 6 m : 1681. C. R. 1.

Sarah, d. Jabez, June 16, 1685.

Sarah, d. John and Mary, July 27, 1721.

**TOURTELOTT,** George, b. Connecticut, delirium tremens, at the alms house, July 14, 1847, a. 54 y.

**TOWER,** John, servant of Thomas Cheny, drowned, July 2, 1690.

**TOWNE,** Andrew S., unm., laborer, s. Jonathan and Rebecca P., consumption, Mar. 9, 1849, a. 25 y.

**TOWNSEND,** Isaac P., m., merchant, b. Chester, N. H., s. Ebenezer and Ann, paralytic, Nov. 3, 1846, a. 62 y.

**TOY,** Grace, Mrs., Apr. 11, 1712, in her 91st y.

**TRACY,** Ellen, b. Ireland, sun struck, at the alms house, July 13, 1849, a. 35 y.

TRACY, James, unm., laborer, b. Ireland, at N. H., bur. at Roxbury, Aug. 21, 1848, a. 22 y.

TRAIN, Fanny Gore, d. Sam[ue]l F. and Fanny, scarlet fever, June 16, 1849, a. 3 y. 1 m.

TRASK, George W., s. Sam[ue]l, Aug. 19, 1837, a. 9 y.
Lyman T., m., laborer, s. Samuel and Betsey, cholera morbus, Aug. 28, 1849, a. 47 y.
Samuel, widr., b. Braintree, a soldier of the Revolution, old age, Feb. 7, 1849, a. 90 y.
William, Dec. 19, 1834.
William E., s. Sam[ue]l, jr., Jan. 24, 1837, a. 2 y.
——, w. Sam[ue]l, Dec. 14, 1832.

TRAVACE, Joshua, consumption, at the alms house, Feb. 3, 1849, a. 70 y.

TREBENT, Christian, s. Henry and Louisa, bowel complaint, Aug. 11, 1848, a. 1 y. 1 m.

TROBRIDGE, Experience, d. wid. Thankfull, June 9, 1707.

TROTT, Charles Henry, s. Charles E., Jan. 25, 1836, a. 7 m.

TRULL, Abigail, d. Jonathan, dysentery, Sept. 11, 1803, a. 8 y. C. R. 3.
Hannah R., consumption, May 9, 1827, a. 58 y. C. R. 3.
Jonathan, consumption, June 6, 1819, a. 53 y. C. R. 3.
Jonathan, unm., shoemaker, apoplexy, June 16, 1847, a. 42 y.
Lucretia, d. Jonathan, dysentery, Sept. 26, 1803, a. 10 m. C. R. 3.
——, s. Jonathan, dysentery, Sept. 16, 1803, a. 4 y. C. R. 3.

TRUMBULL, Elizabeth, Mrs., July 12, 1832, a. 66 y.

TUCKER, Ann, d. Benjamin and Elizabeth, Apr. 24, 1707. [in her 7th y. G. R. 1.]
Benjamin, Lt., Feb. 27, 1713-14. [a. abt. 69 y. G. R. 1.]
Benjamin, Oct. 8, 1728, in his 58th y. G. R. 1.
Beza, Esq., May 16, 1820, a. 48 y.
Daniel, s. Seth and Hannah, Nov. 29, 1738.
Edward, Nov. 8, 1754.
Elijah [gradual decay, Dec. 1. C. R. 3.], 1831, a. 67 y.
Elizabeth, wid. Benjamin, Sept. 11, 1740.

Tucker, Hannah, d. Ebenez[e]r and Margaret, by a fall of a tree, June 16, 1731. [a. about 7 y. n. r. 1.]

Hannah, at the almshouse, Aug. —, 1828, a. 90 y.

Joseph, at the almshouse, June 12, 1837, a. 59 y. [a. 58 y. c. r. 5.]

Lemuel, Nov. 15, 1789, a. 43 y. c. r. 2.

Lorenzo, s. Seth, Sept. 20, 1839.

Loxley, s. Noah M. and Mary Ann, dysentery, Oct. 1, 1848, a. 1 y. 9 m.

Mary, d. Beza, June 26, 1823, a. 16 y.

Nehimiah, s. Ebenezer and Margaret, June 18, 1725.

Tho[ma]s W. [enlargement of the heart, at Milford, N. H., July 2. c. r. 3.], 1836, a. 30 y.

William, s. Jonathan and Hannah, Aug. 28, 1718, a. 7 y. 10 m. 14 d. g. r. 1.

——, d. twin, Ebenezer and Margarett, Jan. 7, 1713.

——, s. twin, Ebenezer and Margarett, Jan. 14, 1713.

——, ch. ——, Aug. 24, 1817. c. r. 2.

——, ch. ——, Aug. 28, 1846.

**TUCKY** (see also Tukey), John E., s. John B. and Harriet, diarrhoea, June 24, 1848, a. 3 m.

**TUKEY** (see also Tucky), ——, ch. John and Harriet M., Mar. 28, 1849, a. 1 d.

**TULLY** (see also Turley), James, s. James and Mary, bowel complaint, July 26, 1849, a. 6 m. 20 d.

**TUPPER,** Henery, s. Ezra and Penelope, Oct. 15, 1813, a. 1 y. 5 m. g. r. 1.

**TURKINGTON,** Elizabeth, b. England, at the alms house, Dec. 19, 1849, a. 66 y.

**TURLEY** (see also Tully), William, m., b. Ireland, lung fever, Dec. 8, 1849, a. 53 y.

**TURNER** (see also Turnor), Elizabeth, Mrs., Jan. —, 1832, a. 58 y.

Edward, jr. [s. Edward and Lucy. g. r. 1.], Nov. 23, 1803, a. 18 y.

Edward, Dec. 25, 1838, a. 83 y.

Thomas, bur. Nov. 22, 1849, a. 10 w. c. r. 5.

——, childbirth, bur. 7 : 8 m : 1647. c. r. 1.

TURNER, ——, Mrs., a stranger, at Maj. Ebenezer Whiting's, Oct. 5, 1788. C. R. 2.
——, wid. Edward, Jan. —, 1843, a. over 80 y.

TURNOR (see also Turner), Elizabeth, w. John, Oct. 2, 1647.

TUTHAKER, Mary, a pauper, Apr. 13, 1832, a. 60 y.

TUTTLE, Charles W., clerk, b. New York, s. Daniel and Lydia, typhoid fever, Dec. 3, 1847, a. 17 y.
Dorephus, July —, 1830, a. 25 y.
Theodore, drowned, Sept. —, 1837.
——, inf. ch. Theodore, Dec. 24, 1830.

TYLER, see Tiler.

UMBERHAND, Francis, s. John and Catherine, Apr. 16, 1849, a. 3 m.

VALENTINE, William, b. Ireland, dysentery, Sept. 11, 1847, a. 35 y.

VAUX, Thomas, shot himself, at alms house, May 20, 1847, a. 74 y.

VICKLEY, Barny, laborer, b. Germany, palsy, Mar. 16, 1849, a. 63 y.

VILA, Daniel, July 7, 1846, a. 84 y.

VINAL, Ellen Matilda, June —, 1830, a. 11 m.

VOGLE, ——, ch., still born, Sept. 13, 1846.

VOSE, Kezia, wid., Aug. 27, 1816, a. 75 y. C. R. 2.
Oliver, Capt., Sept. 2, 1810, a. 76 y. C. R. 2.
Theodea, w. James W., May 26, 1809, in her 23d y. G. R. 1.

WACH, Matthew, s. John and Mary, measles, Mar. 18, 1849, a. 9 m.

WADE, John, s. W[illia]m and Mary, measles, Mar. 8, 1849, a. 3 y.

WAINWRIGHT, Elizabeth M[ayhew, inf. C. R. 5.], d. Peter, Jan. 7, 1838, a. 6 m. [1833. C. R. 5.]
——, ch. Peter, jr., Sept. —, 1831.

**WAISNER,** John H., s. John G. and Eliza J., bowel complaint, July 23, 1849, a. 3 m.

**WAIT,** David, issue of Aug. 3, 1791, a. 55 y. N. R. 4.
Mary, wid. Samuel, Esq., Oct. 12, 1835, a. 88 y. 6 m.
Rebecca, Dec. 2, 1807, a. 70 y.
Samuel, Mar. 3, 1826, a. 65 y.
Sophia, d. Benj[ami]n, deceased, Sept. —, 1817, a. 8 y.

**WALCUTT,** Alice W., Mrs., May —, 1839, a. 32 y.

**WALDO,** William, bur. May 28, 1844, a. 51 y. C. R. 5.

**WALES,** Abigail, d. William and Mary [fever. C. R. 3.], Jan. 20, 1810. [a. 4 y. 6 m. C. R. 3.]
Benjamin, an Englishman who lived with Elisha Whitney, May 13, 1721. [1821 ?], a. 46 y. C. R. 2.
E., wid., Feb. 14, 1808, a. 45 y.
Elizabeth, from Boston, consumption [bet. Mar. — and June 29], 1808, a. 47 y. C. R. 3.

**WALKER,** Abel, m., b. England, lung fever, June 23, 1848, a. 47 y.
Dorcas, bur. Apr. 17, 1640.
Estelle Viola, d. Samuel and Mary Louisa, measles, Mar. 4, 1844, a. 7 y. 4 m.
Mercy, Oct. 28, 1833, a. 20 y.
William Wallace, s. Samuel, Sept. 22, 1834, a. 17 m.

**WALL,** Thomas, laborer, b. Halifax, N. S., s. Nicholas and Ellen, consumption, Oct. 8, 1849, a. 19 y.
Thomas Houghton, s. Thomas and Jane, June 16, 1839, a. 4 y. 9 m. G. R. 5.

**WALLACE,** Mary Ann, at Chelsea, Jan. —, 1841. C. R. 4.
Susan L., Mrs. [consumption. C. R. 2.], Feb. 16, 1838, a. 38 y. [a. abt. 30 y. C. R. 2.]

**WALLAY** (see also Walley), Frederic J., m., carpenter, b. England, consumption, Jan. 26, 1848, a. 65 y.

**WALLEY** (see also Wallay), Elizabeth [wid. Rev. J. N. R. 4.], Oct. 11, 1798, a. 71 y.
Samuel, s. Sam[ue]l H., jr., Sept. 13, 1837, a. 1 y.
Sarah, w. John, d. Rev. Nehemiah Walter, May 23, 1740, a. 45 y. G. R. 1.

WALLEY, W[illia]m E. Prescott, s. Elizabeth, teething, Sept. 8, 1849, a. 1 y.

**WALLINGFORD,** Louisa, w. Samuel S., May 8, 1837, a. 28 y. G. R. 5.

**WALTER** (see also Walters), Nath[anie]l, Rev., Mar. 11, 1776, in his 65th year, and 42d year of his ministry. C. R. 2.
Nehemiah, s. Nehemiah, Apr. 17, 1702.
Nehemiah, s. Nehemiah and Sarah, Mar. 21, 1707.
Nehemiah [Rev., s. Rev. Nathaniel and Rebecca. G. R. 3.], (ordained Oct. 17, 1688), Sept. 17, 1750, a. 87 y. G. R. 1.
Rebecca, Jan. 11, 1780, a. 58 y. C. R. 2.
Rebecca, Madam [wid. Rev. Mr. N. R. 3.], Apr. 30, 1790, a. 78 y. C. R. 2.
Susanna, w. Samuel, July 5, 1736, a. 28 y. G. R. 1.
Thomas, Rev., (ordained Oct. 29, 1718), Jan. 10, 1724-5, a. 28 y. 1 m. 3 d.

**WALTERS** (see also Walter), Amey, wid. Will[ia]m, May 29, 1754, in her 53d y. G. R. 1.

**WARD,** Ann, w. James, Oct. 7, 1811, a. 31 y. G. R. 1.
Ann M., d. Patrick and Alice, consumption, Jan. 7, 1849, a. 12 y. 4 m.
Bridget, d. John and Mary, bowel complaint, Aug. 12, 1848, a. 2 m.
Ebenezer P. [consumption. C. R. 3.], Sept. 23, 1834, a. 26 y.
Elisabeth, wid. John, Mar. 3, 1843, a. 87 y.
Eliza, w. James O., Feb. 12, 1838, a. 29 y.
Elizabeth, d. Col. Joseph, deceased, Apr. 10, 1813, a. 28 y. G. R. 1.
Charles H., s. Samuel and Martha, lung fever, Mar. 18, 1847, a. 1 y. 3 m.
Hannah G., Mrs., May 6, 1830, a. 19 y.
Hannah G. P., d. Henry S., Sept. 1, 1838, a. 3 y. 6 m.
John, Apr. 29, 1828, a. 80 y.
John Jackson, s. Samuel and Joana, Apr. 6, 1811.
John Ross, s. Henry S., Sept. —, 1838, a. 5 y. 2 m.
Lyman, m., soap manufacturer, b. Athol, consumption, Mar. 5, 1847, a. 36 y.
Lucy, w. James, Sept. 1, 1827, a. 52 y.
Mary E., Sept. —, 1848. C. R. 4.
Mira, d. Col. Joseph, dec., May 26, 1812, a. 23 y. G. R. 1.

WARD, Nabby M., d. Henry S., Aug. 25, 1838, a. 9 m.

Samuel [contraction of bowels. c. r. 3.], Jan. 3, 1830, a. 59
y. [a. 57 y. c. r. 3.]

——, w. John, Dec. 25, 1806, a. 53 y.

——, Mr., Nov. 7, 1839.

**WARDSWORTH** (see also Woodworth), ——, ch., teething,
Sept. 2, 1846, a. 1 y. 6 m.

**WARE** (see also Wares), George, May 12, 1820, a. 28 y.

Joseph, July 22, 1830, a. 50 y.

Mary S., d. Joseph, June 30, 1820, a. 8 y.

**WARES** (see also Ware), ——, ch. Mrs., Dec. 29, 1807, a.
11 m.

**WARNER,** Ellen R., d. John, Aug. —, 1833, a. 20 m.

**WARREN,** Calvin, Capt., May 3, 1819, a. 34 y.

Deborah, Oct. 6, 1743, [in her 41st y. g. r. 1.]

Deborah, Mrs., Aug. 23, 1749. [a. 82 y. g. r. 1.]

Ebenezer, Dec. 9, 1756, a. 57 y. g. r. 1.

Joseph, July 13, 1729, a. 66 y.

Joseph [fell from a ladder, broke his neck. n. r. 2.], Oct. 23,
1755, a. 60 y. g. r. 1.

Marey, wid., Jan. 7, 1803, a. 90 y.

Mary, Mrs., at the alms house, Aug. 29, 1829, a. 97 y.

Samuel, s. Joseph and Deborah, Sept. 1, 1694.

Samuel, Nov. 1, 1805, a. 62 y.

**WASON** (see also Watson), Joanna, Mrs., June 12, 1842. c.
r. 7.

**WATERMAN,** Ann [Hannah. ct. r.], w. Thomas, June 5,
1641.

Henry Cornelius, s. Melzar, Feb. 3, 1833, a. 2 m.

Mercy, w. Melzar, Oct. 2, 1830, a. 32 y.

Thomas, Jan. 22, 1675.

**WATERS,** Anna Wilhemina, w. Williams, jr., May 27, 1813, a.
22 y.

William, m., laborer, lung fever, June 20, 1846, a. 75 y.

**WATKER,** Sarah Jane, w. Samuel, Nov. —, 1826, a. 34 y.

**WATKINS,** W[illia]m, servant of William Philleps, Dec. 7,
1713.

**WATSON** (see also Wason), Henry, s. Lawrence and Maria, convulsions, June 15, 1849, a. 2 m.

John, Dec. 2, 1671, a. 77 y. G. R. 1.

John, sr., bur. 5 : 11 m : 1671-2. C. R. 1.

John [jr. G. R. 1.], Aug. 13, 1693. [a. 59 y. G. R. 1.]

Josuah [Joshua. C. R. 1.], s. John [suddenly. C. R. 1.], bur. Apr. 30, 1649. [a. 11 y. C. R. 1.]

Leander, s. James and Abigail, Feb. 18, 1814. [a. 16 m. C. R. 2.]

Lucy, d. Matthew and Margarett, fits, Sept. 28, 1848, a. 7 m.

Margaret, Oct. 6, 1829, a. 22 y.

Martha, Aug. 26, 1840, a. 77 y.

Nathan, s. Nathan and Hannah, Sept. 12, 1801.

William, s. Nathan and Hannah, Sept. 20, 1799.

——, s. Nathan, June 19, 1802, a. 7 m.

——, ch. N., Sept. 23, 1804, a. 10 m.

**WEATHERBEE** (see also Weatherby), ——, d. ——, Jan. 16, 1818, a. 10 y. C. R. 2.

**WEATHERBY** (see also Weatherbee), Benja[min], Oct. 22, 1805, a. 21 y.

**WEATHERS** (see also Wethers), Helena F., d. John and Martha, dropsy in the head, Mar. 3, 1847, a. 9 m.

**WEBB**, Theodore L., Dr. [of Detroit, Mich., bur. Sept. 18. C. R. 5.], 1838, a. 30 y.

William, m., engineer, b. Dedham, consumption, July 15, 1848, a. 34 y.

**WEBBER** (see also Webbers), James F., b. Maine, s. James and M., cholera infantum, Oct. 3, 1846, a. 7 m. 2 d.

John, 3d, s. John, jr. and Elizabeth, accidental drowning, Oct. 28, 1848, a. 7 y. 10 m.

Josiah D., s. John, Oct. 11, 1823, a. 10 m.

——, ch. John A., June 14, 1807, a. 1 m.

**WEBBERS** (see also Webber), ——, ch. John A., Aug. 27, 1805.

**WEBSTER**, Mrs., Apr. 3, 1813, a. abt. 67 y.

**WEIFFENBACK**, Christiana E., d. George and Mary Ann, bowel complaint, July 20, 1847, a. 2 m.

**WEING,** Lydia A., d. Charles and Emily, cholera infantum, Aug. 13, 1849, a. 9 y. 13 m.

**WELCH,** Ann, d. John and Mary, Apr. 25, 1849.

Deborah, b. Ireland, inflammation of bowels, at the alms house, May 8, 1849, a. 20 y.

Edward, Feb. 5, 1847, a. 2 m.

Edward, m., grocer, b. Ireland, accidental, Mar. 8, 1849, a. 55 y.

Martin, laborer, b. Ireland, dysentery, July 20, 1848, a. 23 y.

**WELD** (see also Welde), Aaron D[avis, Esq., consumption, June 28. c. r. 3.], 1835, a. 56 y.

Ann, d. Daniel and Elizabeth, Feb. 5, 1738, a. 7 d. g. r. 3.

Benjamin, s. Daniel, Jan. 11, 1657.

Benjamin, s. Benjamin and Elisabeth, Oct. 3, 1802. [a. 1 y. g. r. 1.]

Betsey, w. Aaron D[avis. c. r. 2.], Apr. 10 [12. dup.], 1807, a. 23 y.

Catharine, Mrs., Oct. 4, 1815, a. 80 y. c. r. 2.

Clemence, wid. Edmund, Dec. 8, 1766, a. 67 y. g. r. 1.

Daniel [Welde. c. r. 1.], s. Thomas, bur. June 25, 1663.

Daniel, Lt., Jan. 20, 1761, in his 64th y. g. r. 3.

Daniell, July 22, 1666, a. 81 y. [a. 80 y. c. r. 1.]

David, Dea., Jan. 5, 1821, a. 86 y.

Dorothy, wid. Thomas, July 31, 1694. [in her 66th y. g. r. 1.]

Dorothy, d. John and Hannah, July 9, 1695.

Ebenezer, s. Samuel and Susanna, Sept. 19, 1693.

Ebenezer, s. Ebenezer and Mary, Feb. 8, 1731-2.

Ebenezer, Sept. 24, 1767, a. 65 y. g. r. 3.

Ebenezer [old age. c. r. 3.], Mar. 28, 1822, a. 76 y. [a. 75 y. c. r. 3.]

Edmund, June 13, 1748, in his 54th y. g. r. 1.

Edward, s. Joseph and Sarah, Feb. 25, 1700-1701.

Edward [fell off his cart and run over. n. r. 2.], Oct. 13, 1761, in his 29th y. g. r. 3.

Eleazer, Col., asthma, May 19, 1800, a. 63 y. c. r. 3.

Elijah [consumption. c. r. 3.], Sept. 24, 1805, a. 51 y. [a. 42 y. c. r. 3.]

Elijah, bilious fever, May 27, 1811, a. 28 y. c. r. 3.

Elisabeth, w. Joseph [small pox. c. r. 1.], Feb. 15, 1678. [1678-9. c. r. 1.]

Elisabeth, w. Edmond, small pox, Dec. 20, 1721.

WELD, Elizabeth, w. Joseph, bur. Oct. —, 1638.

Elizabeth, w. Joseph, Sept. 21, 1719.

Elizabeth, wid., Jan. 6, 1784, in her 83d y. C. R. 2.

Elizabeth, Mrs., June 20, 1833, a. 72 y.

Elizabeth, w. Benjamin, Esq., Aug. 28, 1838, a. 69 y.

Esther, d. John, bur. 10 : 11 m : 1664-5. C. R. 1.

Esther, w. Thomas [liver complaint. C. R. 3.], July 1, 1811. [a. 56 y. C. R. 3.]

Esther, w. Dea. Nath[aniel], black jaundice, July 9, 1811, a. 58 y. C. R. 3.

Francis, s. Jacob, May 10, 1801, a. 11 y. C. R. 3.

Hanah, w. John, Dec. 10, 1721.

Hannah [inf. C. R. 1.] d. John [jr. C. R. 1.], glazier, Oct. 6, 1683.

Hannah, d. Joseph and Elizabeth, Nov. 5, 1713.

Hannah, d. John and Mehitabell, July 18, 1721.

Hannah, putrid fever and throat distemper, Oct. 24, 1824, a. 17 y. C. R. 3.

Jabez Hatch, s. Eleazer and Mary, July 7, 1762.

Jacob, s. Joseph and Elizabeth, Feb. 8, 1716.

Jacob, a selectman and assessor [paralytic stroke. C. R. 3.], Dec. 30, 1819, a. 67 y.

Jane, d. Benjamin and Elizabeth, July 1, 1809.

John, s. John and Hannah, Apr. 28, 1680.

John, inf. s. John, jr., bur. 4 : 10 m : 1683. C. R. 1.

John, s. John, glazier, Nov. 27, 1683.

John, jr., bur. 1 : 6 m : 1686. C. R. 1.

John, s. Thomas, July 25, 1686. [a. 29 y. G. R. 1.]

John, Sept. 20, 1691.

John, glazier, Feb. 21, 1737-8.

John, July 18, 1807, a. 77 y.

John Rugles, s. Joseph, [after 1765.] G. R. 1.

Joseph [inf. C. R. 1.], s. Joseph, bur. Dec. 7, 1645.

Joseph, householder [cancer. C. R. 1.], bur. Oct. 7, 1646.

Joseph [inf. C. R. 1.] s. John, bur. Oct. 23, 1649.

Joseph, s. Edmund and Elizabeth, Feb. 21, 1693-4.

Joseph, Lt., Feb. 14, 1711-12, in his 62d y. [a. 63 y. G. R. 1.]

Joseph, Sept. 27, 1765, a. 32 y. G. R. 1.

Joseph [intemperance. C. R. 3.], Apr. 2, 1822, a. 30 y. [a. 32 y. C. R. 3.]

Josiah, s. Daniel and Elizabeth, Feb. 27, 1738, a. 29 d. G. R. 3.

WELD, Margaret [Marget. C. R. 1.], d. Joseph and Elisabeth [small pox. C. R. 1.], Feb. 12, 1678.

Margarett, wid. John, Sept. 13, 1692.

Martha, d. Capt. Joseph and Martha, Aug. 23, 1736. [in her 5th y. G. R. 3.]

Martha, Mrs., May 13, 1831, a. 93 y.

Martha, wid. Aaron D., d. Joseph and Susannah Williams, dropsy, Jan. 28, 1847, a. 67 y. 7 m.

Mary, w. Ebenezer, Oct. 10, 1763, in 58th y. G. F. 3.

Mary, d. Eleazer and Mary, Dec. 2, 1766.

Mary, d. Benja[mi]n and Elizabeth, July 3, 1801. [a. 16 m. G. R. 1.]

Mary Ann [Maryanne. C. R. 3.], d. Jacob and Sally, Nov. 29, 1799. [Nov. 3, a. 5 m. C. R. 3.]

Mehitabel, d. Daniel, bur. 12 : 11 m : 1679-80. C. R. 1.

Mehitabel, d. Daniel, Sept. 5, 1657.

Nathaniel, Dea. [rupture of bowels. C. R. 3.], Dec. 4, 1817, a. 78 y.

Rebecca, d. Ebenezer and Mary, Mar. 15, 1727, a. 2 m. 15 d. G. R. 3.

[Rebecca. C. R. 3.], Mrs., old age, June 18, 1844, a. 98 y. [a. 97 y. C. R. 3.]

Sally, d. David and Sarah, Dec. 28, 1791, a. 19 m. C. R. 2.

Samuell, s. Thomas, bur. Aug. 26, 1653.

Samuel, s. [inf. ch. C. R. 1.] Samuel and Susanna, Aug. 9, 1686.

Samuel, s. Samuel and Susanna, Apr. 20, 1689.

Samuel, s. John and Hannah, Nov. 11, 1697.

Samuel, s. Edmund and Elizabeth, Mar. 29, 1698.

Samuel, s. Thomas, minister of Dunstable, and Mary, Jan. 18, 1715-16. [in his 15th y. G. R. 1.]

Samuel, Sept. 2, 1737. [a. 82 y. G. R. 1.]

Samuel, consumption, Feb. 23, 1813, a. 27 y. C. R. 3.

Samuel, June 8, 1826, a. 71 y.

Samuel W., Aug. 16, 1829, a. 40 y.

Sarah, d. Joseph and Sarah, Dec. 30, 1685.

Sarah, d. John and Hannah, Jan. 16, 1708.

Sarah, wid. Ebenezer, Dec. 22, 1767, a. 60 y. G. R. 1.

Sarah D., d. Aaron [Davis. C. R. 2.] and Betsey, Apr. 12, 1815. [a. 8 y. C. R. 2.]

Sarah, w. Dea. David, Sept. 29, 1817, a. 80 y.

Sarah, scrofula, July 21, 1823, a. 64 y. C. R. 3.

WELD, Sarah, wid. [old age. c. r. 3.], Mar. 12, 1824, a. 91 y.

Stephen, s. Daniel and Elizabeth, Aug. 16, 1745, in his 23d y. G. R. 3.

Susannah, w. Samuel, Apr. 20, 1729, a. 67 y. G. R. 1.

Susannah, w. Aaron D., Oct. 24, 1816, a. 40 y. [a. 38 y. c. R. 2.]

Thomas, s. Joseph, Sept. 9, 1649. [a. abt. 17 y. c. R. 1.]

Thomas, sr. [fever. c. R. 1.], Jan. 17, 1682-3, a. 56 y.

Thomas, s. Thomas and Elizabeth, July 21, 1704. [in her 21st y. G. R. 1.]

Thomas, s. Capt. Joseph, drowned in New River, North Carolina, Apr. 10, 1740.

Thomas [lung fever. c. R. 3.], May 12, 1821, a. 70 y.

Thomas McCarthy, pulmonary consumption, Aug. 24, 1818, a. 33 y. c. R. 3.

——, ch. still born, Daniel, — : 4 m : 1653. c. R. 1.

——, inf. ch. Dan[iel], bur. 10 : 1 m : 1681-2. c. R. 1.

——, w. Daniel, 15 : 1 m : 1681-2. c. R. 1.

——, ch. Ebenezer and Mary, ——, 1732, a. 2 y. 2 m. 1 d. G. R. 3.

——, s. Dea., May 26, 1782, a. 16 y. c. R. 2.

——, s. ——, thrown from a cart of Mr. Star's, died instantly, [bet. June and Oct.], 1798. c. R. 3.

——, ch. Stedman, Feb. 1, 1804, a. 3 y.

——, wid., Jan. 30, 1805.

——, w. Aaron D., Apr. 12, 1807.

——, ch. G. M. and Harriet, Apr. 13, 1836, a. 5 w. c. R. 3.

——, inf. ch. Geo[rge] and Mary E., Nov. 26, 1849, a. 1 d.

**WELDE** (see also Weld), Abigail, d. John, bur. 24 : 12 m : 1667-8. c. R. 1.

Margaret, d. John, bur. 27 : 4 m : 1674, in her 17th y. c. R. 1.

**WELLES** (see also Wells), Alfred, bur. Jan. 5, 1847. c. R. 5.

**WELLINGTON**, ——, Mrs., Apr. 15, 1830.

**WELLS** (see also Welles), Lowell Bumsted, bur. Aug. 18, 1848, a. 1y. 6 m. c. R. 5.

**WELTON**, Bethel Thomas, b. England, s. T. and Mary, scarlet fever, Nov. 14, 1846, a. 7 y. 7 m.

Henry Alfred, b. England, s. T. and Mary, scarlet fever, Nov. 11, 1846, a. 5 y. 8 m.

WELTON, Sary Ann, b. England, d. Thomas and Mary, scarlet fever, Nov. 21, 1846, a. 4 m.

Thomas, b. England, s. Thomas and Mary, scarlet fever, Nov. 17, 1846, a. 2 y. 7 m.

WENTWORTH, Edward, bur. July 10, 1794. N. R. 4.

Mary M., b. Yarmouth, w. Philip M., consumption, May 19, 1849, a. 29 y.

Sally, d. Philip, Mar. 9, 1838, a. 43 y.

WEST, Elisabeth, d. Benjamin and Joannah [C. dup.], July 29, 1724. [1723. dup.]

Elizabeth, Mar. 23, 1799, a. 78 y.

Joseph, s. Benjamin and Joanna, Jan. 3, 1736-7.

Mary Ann, bur. Dec. 22, 1846, a. 6 w. C. R. 5.

WESTERN, Sarah, w. George, smallpox, Oct. 25, 1792, a. 82 y. G. R. 1.

WETHERS (see also Weathers), Margarett J., b. Troy, N. Y., d. James and Margarett, consumption, May 26, 1847, a. 20 y.

WHALEN (see also Whalin), Mary, b. Ireland, at the alms house, Mar. 31, 1849, a. 31 y.

Mary, b. Ireland, w. Michael, child bed fever, May 1, 1849, a. 38 y.

Michael, b. Ireland, ship fever, at the alms house, June 25, 1847, a. 1 y.

Michael, s. John and Mary, infantile, at the alms house, Apr. 3, 1849, a. 7 d.

Michael, m., b. Ireland, gravel, May 1, 1849, a. 70 y.

Michael, s. Michael and Mary, May 2, 1849, a. 3 d.

WHALIN (see also Whalen), Martin, b. Ireland, consumption, Mar. 9, 1849, a. 70 y.

WHALL, Nicholas, m., laborer, b. Ireland, consumption, Oct. 11, 1847, a. 60 y.

WHEELER, Addison N., ch. ——, of Grafton, grand ch. Mrs. Norcross, Sept. 7, 1845, a. 7 m. C. R. 3.

Ansel T., s. Thaddeus, Sept. 13, 1840, a. 4 y.

Charles H., s. Thaddeus, Aug. 26, 1836.

Deborah, old age, Oct. 18, 1795, a. 78 y. C. R. 3.

Deborah, Apr. 22, 1839, a. 83 y.

WHEELER, Henry, s. Elisha and Betsey, Oct. 27, 1813, a. 1 y. 11 m. G. R. 1.

**WHEELWRIGHT,** John, merchant, issue of Nov. 21, 1792. N. R. 4.

**WHIPPLE,** John, jr., s. John, Esq., of Providence, July —, 1832, a. 21 y.

**WHISTON,** Eliza G., w. Francis C., Oct. —, 1836, a. 37 y.

**WHITAMORE** (see also Whittemore), —— [Whittamore. C. R. 1. ; Whittamore. CT. R.], w. Lawrence [apoplexy and palsy. C. R. 1.], Feb. 18, 1642. [a. abt. 60 y. C. R. 1.]

**WHITCOMB,** Henry, s. Joseph and Eliza, bowel complaint, June 11, 1847, a. 5 m. 11 d.
Le[o]pold H., s. H., bowel complaint, Oct. 13, 1848, a. 2 m.

**WHITE** (see also Whyte), Aaron, Dec. 18, 1809. [a. 69 y. G. R. 1.]
David, black jaundice, Apr. 30, 1816, a. 71 y. C. R. 3. [a. 70 y. G. R. 4.]
Elizabeth, wid. Lt. John, Jan. 7, 1699-1700, in her 48th y. G. R. 1.
Elizabeth, May —, 1824. C. R. 4.
Elizabeth, wid. Aaron, Feb. [6. G. R. 1.], 1827, a. 80 y.
Elizabeth, Mrs., Sept. 6, 1834, a. 83 y.
Elizabeth G., d. Isaac D. and Elizabeth H., dropsy on the brain, June 5, 1848, a. 1 y. 3 m.
Frances A., d. W[illia]m H. and Frances, teething, Oct. 7, 1847, a. 1 y. 5 m. 15 d.
Isaak, s. John, jr., bur. 12: 1m: 1683-4. C. R. 1.
James, Aug. 9, 1815, a. 70 y. G. R. 1.
John, Lt., Mar. 28, 1695, a. 53 y. G. R. 1.
John, May 13, 1798, a. 13 y.
Julia F., m., b. New Hampden, N. H., fever, Mar. 7, 1849, a. 26 y.
Louisa L., w. W[illia]m, apoplexy, June 5, 1849, a. 40 y.
Margarett [Mrs. G. R. 4.], old age, July 19, 1844, a. 92 y. [1841. G. R. 4.]
Mary, d. John, bur. 26: 3m: 1669, a. abt. 17 y. C. R. 1.
Mary [d. Aaron and Elizabeth. G. R. 1.], Aug. 27, 1805, a. 18 y.
Samuel, Sept. 8, 1793, a. 52 y. G. R. 4.
Sarah, cholera morbus, Aug. 30, 1815, a. 68 y. C. R. 3.

WHITE, Thomas, s. A[aron and Elizabeth, suddenly. G. R. 1.], May 31, 1802, a. 27 y.

William, suicide, Aug. —, 1833.

——, inf. ch. Joseph, bur. 29 : 8m : 1683. C. R. 1.

——, w. John, Sept. 27, 1778, a. 27 y. C. R. 2.

——, ch. Luther and Rebecca, Oct. 21, 1805. C. R. 2.

——, inf. ch. Richard, Sept. —, 1838.

——, ch. Franklin, Aug. —, 1839, a. 2 m.

——, inf. ch. W[illia]m H. and Frances, fits, May 21, 1847, a. 7 d.

**WHITEMORE** (see also Whittemore), Ann, a pauper, Sept. 10, 1835, a. 90 y.

Samuel, s. Michael, Nov. 27, 1826, a. 37 y. C. R. 2.

**WHITING** (see also Whitings, Whitney), Benajah, June 24, 1777, a. 39 y. C. R. 2.

Caroline Ann, consumption, Jan. 14, 1849, a. 5 m. 2 d.

Caroline Prentiss, d. Moses, Apr. 5, 1835, a. 15 y.

Ebenezer, Sept. 13, 1779, a. 79 y. C. R. 2.

Eben[eze]r, Maj., Sept. 24, 1817, a. 86 y.

Ebenezer [consumption, Mar. 3. C. R. 2.], 1832, a. 44 y.

Eliphalet, s. Jonathan and Rachel, Nov. 30, 1693.

Elsy Davis, d. William and Nancy F., June 9, 1824.

Elsy Thwing, d. William and Nancy F., Oct. 31, 1825.

Hannah, w. Nathaniel, Apr. 4, 1788, a. 70 y. C. R. 2.

Henry Oxnard, s. William and Nancy F., Aug. 23, 1831.

Isaiah, May 2, 1785, a. 53 y. C. R. 2.

Lenard, s. Benajah, Apr. 18, 1784, a. 16 y. C. R. 2.

Leonard, Capt., Jan. 29, 1830, a. 43 y.

Mary, Nov. 8, 1814, a. 21 y.

Mary, wid., May 7, 1843. C. R. 7.

Mehitable, wid., Sept. 4, 1796. C. R. 2.

Moses, Capt., Jan. 2, 1796, a. 53 y. C. R. 2.

Moses, Mar 19, 1842, a. 62 y.

Nathaniel, jr., June 21, 1760, in his 22d y. G. R. 2.

Nathaniel, Jan. 19, 1790, a. 87 y. C. R. 2.

Nathan[ie]ll, s. Nathan[ie]ll and Hannah, July 30, 1744.

Polly Williams, d. Joel and Abigail Sumner, Oct. 31, 1812.

Prudence, Nov. 4, 1800, a. 20 y. C. R. 2.

Rachel, wid., Dec. 15, 1721 [1821?], a. 88 y. C. R. 2.

Rebeckah, d. Nathan[ie]ll and Hannah, May 6, 1743.

Rhoda, w. Ebenezer, Nov. 10, 1746. [in her 42d y. G. R. 2.]

WHITING, Robert Davis, s. John and Mary, Sept. 14, 1798. C.
R. 2.

Sally, d. wid., Oct. 2, 1791, a. 20 y. C. R. 2.

Seth, Feb. 11, 1831, a. 73 y.

Seth T., unm., farmer, s. Seth T., consumption, May 25, 1847,
a. 51 y.

——, w. Benajah, Feb. 20, 1776. C. R. 2.

——, w. Isaiah, July 8, 1777, a. 43 y. C. R. 2.

——, w. Ebenezer, Dec. 23, 1778, a. 68 y. C. R. 2.

——, ch. Leonard and Sukey, Dec. 26, 1810, a. 2 w. C. R. 2.

——, 3d, d. William and Nancy F., Aug. 3, 1826.

WHITINGS (see also Whiting), ——, ch. Benajah, Apr. 13,
1776, a. 9 m. C. R. 2.

WHITMAN, Simeon, May 2, 1830, a. 77 y.

WHITMARSH, Thomas, a pauper, —, 1829, a. 48 y.

WHITMORE (see also Whittemore), Sarah Elizabeth, Sept.
—, 1831, a. 8 y.

WHITNEY (see also Whiting), Caroline Eliza, d. John H.,
Sept. —, 1838, a. 4 y.

Daniel Hammond, s. Maj. Asa, Oct. 6, 1817, a. 8 y.

Elisha, s. Elisha, jr. and Sally, Mar. 17, 1810.

Elisha, May 18, 1815, a. 67 y.

Elisha, Capt., Feb. 22, 1823, a. 43 y. C. R. 2.

Elizabeth Eustis, d. Rev. George [whooping cough. C. R. 2.],
Apr. 26, 1834, a. 3 y. 7 m.

Elizebeth, d. [Lt. G. R. 1.] Elisha and Aba[gail], Mar. —,
1793. [Apr. 20, a. 6 w. G. R. 1.]

Experience, d. Lt. Elisha and Abigail, Sept. 17, 1777, a. 8 m.
G. R. 3.

George [Whiting. C. R. 2.], s. Seth T. [and Lucy. C. R. 2.], Oct.
9, 1815. [a. 12 y. C. R. 2.]

George, Rev. [bilious fever. C. R. 3.], Apr. 2, 1842, a. 38 y.

Hannah, July 14, 1789, a. 18 y. C. R. 2.

Isaac, small pox, Jan. 4, 1777, a. 40 y. C. R. 2.

Jacob, Jan. 14, 1803, a. 66 y. C. R. 2.

John, Mar. 4, 1726-7, a. 83 y.

Josiah, Oct. 3, 1839, a. 62 y.

Moses, hip complaint, Aug. 30, 1825, a. 20 y. C. R. 3.

Samuel, Aug. 15, 1805, a. 22 y.

Sarah, July 4, 1689.

WHITNEY, Timothy, s. Timothy and Margaret, July 8, 1721.
——, d. Isaac, Dec. 26, 1776, a. 15 y. C. R. 2.
——, ch. ——, canker rash, Feb. —, 1810, a. 3 y. C. R. 3.

**WHITTEMORE** (see also Whitamore, Whitemore, Whitmore, Whittomore), Agnes, d. Sam[ue]l, infantile humor, June 24, 1822, a. 1 m. C. R. 3.
Asa, Aug. 4, 1825.
Augusta, w. Thomas, consumption, June 12, 1846.
Elizabeth, d. William and Betsy, Sept. 4, 1817, a. 5 y.
Elizabeth, Mrs., Sept. 8, 1829, a. 76 y.
John, nervous fever, issue of Sept. 28, 1793, a. 24 y. N. R. 4.
Mary, wid., Nov. 18, 1804, a. 78 y.
Nath[anie]l, July 5, 1829, a. 38 y.
Rebecca, w. Michael, old age, Apr. 12, 1835, a. 80 y. C. R. 2.
Samuel, Aug. 7, 1816.
William, Aug. 14, 1832, a. 45 y.
William, Mar. 28, 1837, a. 50 y.
——, ch. Michael, Dec. 12, 1789, a. 22 m. C. R. 2.
——, ch. Michael, Aug. 24, 1795, a. 7 m. C. R. 2.
——, ch. Jacob, Sept. 30, 1803. [a. 1 y. C. R. 2.]
——, Mrs., Oct. 20, 1805, a. 26 y.
——, Mr., a stranger, at Mrs. Ayers', May 24, 1808. C. R. 2.
——, ch. Polly, Nov. 4, 1808, a. 6 m. C. R. 2.
——, ch. Amos, Jan. 25, 1830, a. 20 d.
——, d. Sam[ue]l, June 15, 1837, a. 1 1-2 y. C. R. 2.
——, ch. Capt. John, ——, 1837. C. R. 2.

**WHITTOMORE** (see also Whittemore), Lawrence [Whittamore. C. R. 1.; Wittamore. CT. R.], householder, bur. Nov. 24, 1644. [a. 80 y. C. R. 1.]

**WHITWELL,** Lucy, w. Nath[anie]l P., July 28, 1808, a. 31 y.
Mary, Madam, old age, Dec. 15, 1799, a. 77 y. C. R. 3.
Nathaniel, Feb. 9, 1814. [a. 41 y. G. R. 1.]
Sarah, Madam, bur. at Jamaica Plain, Dec. 19, 1799, a. 77 y. N. R. 4.

**WHOLETOWER,** Bennet, unm., b. Germany, lock jaw, Dec. 17, 1847, a. 30 y.

**WHYTE** (see also White), Oliver, Aug. 6, 1844. C. R. 6.

**WIGGIN** (see also Wiggins), James A., s. James and Mary, scarlet fever, May 9, 1847, a. 1 y. 1 m. 5 d.

WIGGIN, John, from Sanbornton, N. H., in D. S. Greenough's family, typhus fever, Oct. 16, 1826, a. 24 y. C. R. 3.

**WIGGINS** (see also Wiggin), Elizabeth J., d. James and Mary, scarlet fever, May 5, 1847, a. 5 y. 8 m.

**WILBAR,** Sarah E., d. Francis and Charlotte, lung fever, Nov. 13, 1849, a. 2 y. 4 m.

**WILDER,** Marion, b. Hingham, d. Thomas and Bethia, cholera morbus, Sept. 23, 1849, a. 52 y.
Steward, m., laborer, b. Ireland, consumption, Aug. 25, 1847, a. 40 y.

**WILKINS,** John H., Apr. 24, 1842.
Joseph H., Apr. 24, 1842, a. 24 y. G. R. 5.

**WILKINSON,** George, s. Arthur and Martha Ann, whooping cough, Sept. 6, 1849, a. 11 m. 8 d.

**WILLARD,** Aaron, May 20, 1844, a. 87 y. G. R. 1.
Ada L., b. Dorchester, d. Benjamin and Emeline, dysentery, at Haverhill, Sept. 3, 1848, a. 9 y.
Benj[amin] F., m., clock maker, s. Simon and Mary, liver complaint, at Dorchester, Mar. 12, 1847, a. 43 y.
Catharine, w. Aaron, July 30, 1785, a. 22 y. G. R. 1.
Harriot, Dec. —, 1883, a. 48 y.
John M., s. Simeon, July 11, 1824, a. 24 y.
Julia, d. Simon and Mary, Nov. 27, 1799, a. 1 y. 2 m.
Mary, w. Simon, July 13, 1823, a. 60 y.
Mary, wid. [Aaron. G. R. 1.], old age, Oct. 10, 1846, a. 85 y.

**WILLIAMS,** Abagail, d. Samuel and Abagail, Sept. 4, 1750, a. 3 m. 4 d. G. R. 1.
Abigail, wid. Samuel, small pox, Jan. 1, 1793, a. 70 y. G. R. 1.
Ann, w. John, of Dorchester Brook, Apr. 9, 1767, in her 43d y. G. R. 1.
Ann, w. William, Mar. 11, 1771, in her 38th y. G. R. 1.
Ann M., d. Thomas, jr., Esq., issue of Aug. 20, 1796, a. 2 y. 7 m. N. R. 4.
Ann V., d. Capt. Stephen, June 6, 1832, a. 20 y.
Anna, Mar. 15, 1827, a. 88 y.
Anna Maria Savage, d. Tho[ma]s, jr. and Elizabeth, Aug. 5, 1799.
Augustus, s. Augustus and Mary, teething, Sept. 29, 1849, a. 1 y.

WILLIAMS, Benjamin, s. Henry and Mary, Nov. 11, 1752, in his 13th y. G. R. 1.

Benjamin, Aug. 4, 1775, a. 46 y. G. R. 1.

Benj[amin] P., farmer, heart complaint, Sept. 15, 1844, a. 56 y. [a. 57 y. C. R. 3.]

Betsey, w. Stedman, June 5, 1838, a. 62 y.

Bridget, a pauper, Oct. 19, 1834, a. 29 y.

Caleb, s. John and Sarah, Mar. 21, 1725-6.

Caleb, s. Stephen and Sarah, Jan. 18, 1729.

Catherine, Apr. 5, 1776, a. 21 y. G. R. 1.

Charlota, d. William and Anne, Sept. 13, 1769, in her 3d y. G. R. 1.

Cumberland D., at Boston, July —, 1840, a. 60 y.

Daniel, Jan 7, 1771, a. 76 y. G. R. 1.

Daniel Thomas, s. Thomas, jr., Esq., at Calcutta, Oct. 28, 1812, a. 20 y.

Deborah, wid. Samuel [thrown from a chaise against a stone. N. R. 2.], Oct. 23, 1761, in her 73d y. G. R. 1.

Dwight, s. Dr. Thomas, Aug. 10, 1812.

Eben A., b. Chelsea, s. Ebenezer and Elizabeth R., scarlet fever, June 10, 1849, a. 10 y. 10 m. 4 d.

Ebenezer, s. [Lt. G. R. 1.] John and Sarah, Dec. 12, 1736. [in his 16th y. G. R. 1.]

Edward, Dec. 5, 1812.

Elcy, d. Jonathan and Nancy, Nov. 17, 1813.

Eleanor, w. John, Nov. 16, 1824, a. 47 y.

Eliakim, s. John and Abigail, of Deerfield, Jan. 23, 1724-5, a. 14 y. G. R. 1.

Elisabeth, w. Benjamin, Apr. 7, 1763, a. 32 y. G. R. 1.

Elizabeth, d. Sam[ue]ll, 10 : 1 m : 1644. CT. R.

Elizabeth, d. Samuell, Mar. 10, 1653.

Elizabeth, d. Sam[ue]l, bur. 10 : 1m : 1654-5. C. R. 1.

Elizabeth, w. Robart, July 28, 1674. [a. 80 y. C. R. 1.]

Elizabeth, w. Capt. John, Nov. 17, 1746, a. 31 y. G. R. 1.

Elizabeth, old age, Sept. 21, 1834, a. 88 y. C. R. 3.

Elizabeth, wid., late W[illia]m, formerly w. Elijah Weld, old age, Jan. 31, 1849, a. 89 y.

Elizabeth Davis, d. Benjamin Payson and Margaret [consumption. C. R. 3.], Feb. 11, 1817. [a. 5 m. C. R. 3.]

Ellen M., w. John Sumner, Mar. 19, 1843, a 31 y.

Ellenor Maria, d. John, June 1, 1824, a. 17 y.

Emily M., d. Joseph D., Apr. 13, 1840, a. 8 y.

WILLIAMS, Frances, wid. Thomas, Esq., Apr. 10, 1824, a. 56 y.

Frances Lydia, d. Thomas, jr., Esq., Sept. 3, 1813, a. 2 y. 7 m. 11 d.

George E., s. Dudley and Isabella, dysentery, Aug. 22, 1847, a. 1 y. 3 m.

Gideon, Esq., late of Taunton, Jan. —, 1830, a. 84 y.

Hannah, w. Samuel, 4th d. Hon. John Chandler, Esq. of Worcester, May 30, 1761, in her 34th y. N. R. 2.

Hannah, w. Daniel, May 7, 1764, a. 65 y. G. R. 1.

Hannah, wid. Samuel, formerly wid. Ebenezer Pierpont, May 22, 1804, a. 76 y. G. R. 1.

Hannah, wid. John Davis, old age, Mar. 15, 1844, a. 92 y. 3 m.

Henry [inf. ch. C. R. 1.], s. Stephen and Sarah, Aug. 25, 1686.

Henry [jr. G. R. 1.], s. Henry and Mary, Feb. 13, 1749-50. [1748, in his 12th y. G. R. 1.]

Henry, s. Jeremiah and Catharine, Jan. —, 1752, a. 8 m. G. R. 1.

Henry, May 22, 1781, a. 70 y. 3 m. 28 d.

Henry Howell, at Colerain [Sept.?] —, 1832, a. 65 y.

Isaac, s. Isaac, bur. 7: 1m: 1660-61. C. R. 1.

Isaac, Capt., June 27, 1739, in his 78th y. G. R. 1.

Isaac, Dea. [decay of nature. C. R. 3.], Feb. 5, 1815, a. 71 y.

Jacob, Capt., formerly a sea commander, younger brother to Dea. Jonathan, Dec. 14, 1735, a. 56 y. N. R. 1.

Jane, a pauper, Aug. 14, 1835, a. 1 y.

Jeremiah, s. Jeremiah and Katharin, Oct. 15, 1748, a. 10 m. G. R. 1.

Jeremiah, s. Jeremiah and Katherine, Apr. 17, 1759, a. 3 m. G. R. 1.

John, s. John and Sarah, Aug. 29, 1710.

John, Lt., Jan. 22, 1733-4, in his 51st y. G. R. 1.

John, Nov. 5, 1742, in his 58th y. G. R. 1.

John, Capt., Apr. 9, 1777, a. 65 y. G. R. 1.

John, Feb. 8, 1794, a. 74 y. G. R. 1.

John D[avis, s. Capt. John and Elizabeth. G. R. 1.], May 26, 1807, a. 68 y.

John, June 16, 1809, a. 65 y.

John C., Hon., a graduate of Harvard College, at Pittsfield, Jan. —, 1831, a. 77 y.

John Davis, widr., merchant, old age, Aug. 27, 1848, a. 78 y.

Jonathan, Mar. 27, 1743, in his 30th y. G. R. 1.

Jonathan, Feb. 11, 1825, a. 49 y.

WILLIAMS, Joseph Ens., Aug. 17, 1720. [in his 39th y. G. R. 1.]

Joseph, Col. [Esq. N. R. 4.], May 29, 1798, a. 90 y.

Joseph, Capt., Mar. 5, 1822, a. 84 y.

Joseph D., Nov. 29, 1840, a. 38 y.

Joshua, s. Stephen and Sarah, Oct. 28, 1729.

Joshua [s. Capt. John and Elizabeth. G. R. 1.], Dec. 30, 1801, a. 58 y.

Joshua, Dec. 30, 1802.

Joshua H., Aug. 7, 1841, a. 49 y.

Katherine, d. Stephen and Sarah, June 14, 1707.

Lucy, d. Jeremiah and Katherine, Dec. 18, 1758, a. 2 y. G. R. 1.

Lucy, w. Samuel, d. Hon. Hezekiah Huntington, Esq., of Norwich, Oct. 1, 1763. N. R. 5.

Lucy, d. Sam[ue]l S., Apr. 14, 1838, a. 21 y.

Martha, d. Sammuel, Feb. —, 1660. [1660-1. C. R. 1.]

Mary [2d w. G. R. 1.] Lt. Samuell, Feb. 7, 1718. [1718-19, a. 54 y. G. R. 1.]

Mary, w. Capt. Isaac, Oct. 13, 1732, a. 80 y. G. R. 1.

Mary, Mrs., w. Henry. dup.; old age. C. R. 3.], Feb. 18, 1794, a. 77 y. [a. 76 y. 3 m. 24 d. dup.]

Mary, w. Stephen, jr. [consumption. C. R. 3.], Jan. 30, 1799, a. 50 y. 5 m. 25 d.

Mary, wid. John, Sept. 9, 1824, a. 80 y.

Mary Ann, d. Nath[anie]l W., dec., Apr. —, 1818.

Mary Ann, m., d. Moses and Rebecca Davis, dropsy, Mar. 27, 1848, a. 55 y.

Mary Ann S., b. Portsmouth, N. H., w. James, consumption, July 2, 1849.

Mary E., d. Maj. Neh[emia]h D., Oct. 29, 1836, a. 12 y.

Mary W., d. Aaron D., Apr. 13, 1841, a. 24 y.

Mercy, wid. Capt. Joseph, Dec. —, 1824, a. 78 y.

Milroe, Jan. 7, 1836, a. 44 y.

Nabby Langdon, d. Stephen, jr. and Mary, Mar. 17, 1776, a. 2 y. 3 m. 9 d.

Nath[anie]l W., typhus fever, Oct. 2, 1844, a. 14 y. 6 m. [a. 15 y. C. R. 3.]

Nicholas, Aug. 27, 1693.

Patty, d. Stephen, jr. and Mary, May 25, 1783, a. 3 m. 8 d.

Polly, Mrs., Mar. 6, 1837, a. 64 y.

Prissilla Langdon, May 18, 1788, a. 2 m. 6 d.

Rebecca, w. John, "at the brook," Aug. 11, 1788, in her 46th y. G. R. 1.

WILLIAMS, Robert [inf. C. R. 1.], s. Stephen, Oct. 30, 1680.

Robert, Sept. 1, 1693.

Rob[er]t, Sept. 13, 1778. in his 62d y. G. R. 1.

[Robert. C. R. 3.], s. William, Nov. 10, 1800. [a. 12 y. C. R. 3.]

Sally, d. Stephen and Abigail, Dec. 29, 1802.

Sally, w. Maj. Nehemiah D., Sept. —, 1832.

Samuel, Dea., Sept. 28, 1698. [a. 65 y. G. R. 1.]

Samuel, Aug. —, 1735.

Samuel, Aug. 13, 1751.

Samuel, June 1, 1779, in his 21st y. G. R. 1.

Samuel, Dec. 21, 1786, in his 76th y. G. R. 1.

Samu[e]ll, s. John and Sarah, Oct. 28, 1719.

Sam[ue]l S., Sept. 7, 1839, a. 52 y.

Sarah, w. [Lt. G. R. 1.] Samuel, sr., Dec. 29, 1712. [a. 54 y. 3 m. G. R. 1.]

Sarah, d. Samu[e]ll and Deborah, Sept. 12, 1719.

Sarah, w. John, Oct. 13, 1742, a. 57 y. G. R. 1.

Sarah, w. William, June 21, 1754, a. 24 y. G. R. 1.

[Sarah. C. R. 3.], w. W[illia]m [consumption. C. R. 3.], July 23, 1804, a. 42 y. [a. 43 y. C. R. 3.]

Sarah, d. Nehemiah D. and Sarah, Sept. 14, 1822.

Sarah, w. Noah Perrin, consumption, Mar. 22, 1844, a. 71 y.

Sarah Jane, d. John, of Charlestown, June 27, 1823, a. 9 y.

Sarah Jane, June 14, 1834, a. 1 m. C. R. 3.

Smith, s. Benjamin and Anna, Apr. 2, 1775, a. 9 y. G. R. 1.

Stephen, s. Joseph and Abigail, Aug. 21, 1720. [a. 3 y. 11 m. G. R. 1.]

Stephen, Capt., May 13, 1768, a. 90 y. G. R. 1.

Stephen, s. Stephen, jr. and Mary, May 14, 1776, a. 11 m. 13 d.

Stephen, s. Stephen and Abigail, Sept. 16, 1782.

Stephen, 4th [jr. N. R. 4.], Sept. 9, 1797, a. 30 y.

Stephen, jr., Mar. 12, 1807, a. 60 y.

Stephen, jr., s. Stephen and Abigail, Jan. 9, 1815, a. 30 y.

Stephen, May 23, 1844, a. 62 y. 10 m. 27 d. G. R. 1.

Steven [Stephen. G. R. 1.], Capt., Feb. 15, 1719-20. [in his 80th y. G. R. 1.]

Susy, Nov. 18, 1804. C. R. 2.

Theoda, small pox, bur. 8:12m: 1678-9. C. R. 1.

Thomas, s. Stephen, Sept. 1, 1694.

Thomas, s. John and Sarah, Aug. 31, 1718.

Thomas, Esq., Sept. 20, 1823, a. 59 y.

William, Mar. 6, 1791, a. 71 y. G. R. 1. [1790. N. R. 3.]

WILLIAMS, William [dsentery and old age. C. R. 3.], Feb. —, 1838, a. 78 y.

——, inf. ch. Samuel, bur. 17 : 2m : 1680. C. R. 1.

——, ch. still born, Sam[ue]l, sr., bur. 29 : 3m : 1683. C. R. 1.

——, ch. still born, Samuel, Jan. 1, 1686.

——, w. Robert, Dec. 22, 1690.

——, ch. still born, Samuel, Mar. 16, 1696-7.

——, ch. still born, Samuel and Sarah, July 25, 1704.

——, wid. Eleazer, issue of Aug. 2, 1786, a. 84 y. N. R. 3.

——, s. William, Nov. 12, 1800, a. 9 y.

——, ch. Tho[ma]s, jr., Sept. 26, 1801, a. 20 d.

——, ch. Hen[r]y H., Apr. 27, 1802, a. 10 m.

——, ch. Stephen, 3d, Aug. 28, 1802, a. 3 y.

——, ch. Dudley, Oct. 16, 1802, a. 10 m.

——, wid. H., May 23, 1804, a. 76 y.

——, w. Tho[ma]s, jr., Esq., Aug. 26, 1807, a. 36 y.

——, ch. wid., Sept. 12, 1807, a. 1 y. 2 m.

**WILLINGER**, Martin, m., laborer, b. Germany, consumption, July 14, 1847, a. 50 y.

**WILLIS**, Polly, w. Allen, Feb. 18, 1801, a. 22 y. C. R. 2.

Sarah E., d. Thomas and Salina, canker, July 18, 1848, a. 1 y. 7 m.

——, ch. Allen and Polly, Dec. 23, 1800, a. 4 m. C. R. 2.

**WILLSON** (see also Wilson), Bethia, w. Andrew, May 8, 1702, a. 46 y. G. R. 1.

John, s. Barnabas and Margaret, Aug. 13, 1739.

Sally P., Mrs., May 26, 1839, a. 60 y.

Sarah, d. Barnabus and Margaret, June 15, 1738.

**WILSON** (see also Willson), Aaron, July 18, 1814, a. 64 y. C. R. 2.

Benja[min], Mar. 22, 1803, a. 41 y.

Benjamin, of Newton, Oct. 7, 1806, a. 89 y. C. R. 2.

Benjamin, Jan. 26, 1834, a. 29 y.

Elizabeth, dysentery, Oct. 7, 1821, a. 8 y. C. R. 3.

Ephraim, July —, 1806, a. 53 y. C. R. 2.

Frederick Augustus, cholera infantum, Sept. 29, 1819, a. 1 y. C. R. 3.

Hannah, childbirth, bur. 9 : 12m : 1645-6. C. R. 1.

Joseph, s. John and Sarah, Apr. —, 1725. C. R. 2.

WILSON, Mary L., d. Alexander and Mary L., dysentery, Sept. 1, 1848, a. 1 y 11 m.

Samuel, Aug. 17, 1811, a. 29 y. C. R. 2.

Sarah Emily, d. Alexander and Mary L., dysentery, Sept. 1, 1848, a. 1 y. 2 m.

——, inf. ch., ——, bur. 4 : 1m : 1679-80. C. R. 1.

——, ch. Ephraim and Abigail, Aug. 28, 1793. C. R. 2.

WINCH, Elvina, inf. ch. ——, May 28, 1848, a. 1 m.

Matilda, d. Henry and Barbara, July 17, 1848, a. 3 m.

WINCHESTER, Ann [Anna. G. R. 4.], w. Gulliver, fever, Apr. 22, 1797. C. R. 3.[ a. 60 y. G. R. 4.]

Artemas, from Boston, consumption, Nov. 25, 1814, a. 43 y. C. R. 3.

Ebenezer, s. Josiah, Aug. 10, 1684.

Elvira, d. Franklin and Sarah, dysentery, July 11, 1848, a. 1 y. 2 m.

Gulliver, old age, Nov. 13, 1811, a. 79 y. C. R. 3.

Hannah, Mrs., Sept. 8, 1822, a. 31 y.

Henry, consumption, June 23, 1801, a. 42 y. C. R. 3. [a. 40 y. G. R. 4.]

Jonathan, fever, bur. 8 : 1 m : 1678-9. C. R. 1.

Luther Seaverns, s. Will[iam] and Mary, croup, Dec. 5, 1830, a. 4 y. C. R. 3.

Luther S., Oct. 6, 1838, a. 3 y. C. R. 3.

Mary P., w. William [child bed consumption, Sept. 4. C. R. 3.], Aug. 4, 1839, a. 36 y.

Nath[anie]l, Capt., Jan. 25, 1819, a. 27 y.

Sarah, w. John, jr., Jan. 31, 1715-16, a. abt. 36 y. G. R. 1.

Sarah Ann, d. Franklin and Sarah, July —, 1836, a. 1 y.

Thead., consumption, bur. Oct. 9, 1795, a. 28 y. C. R. 3.

William, s. William, of a scald, Dec. 30, 1804, a. 3 y. 6 m. C. R. 3.

——, Mr., Dec. 15, 1798, a. 80 y.

——, ch. William and Mary P., Sept. 1, 1839, a. 3 w. C. R. 3.

WING, ——, Mrs., Aug. 9, 1710.

WINGATE, George Raleigh D., s. Gen. Joshua, of Portland, Me., Apr. 24, 1826, a. 19 y.

WINGLER, Mary E., d. David and Mary, consumption, June 1, 1847, a. 1 y. 2 m.

**WINKLEY,** Cecilia H., d. James A. and Mary Ann, teething, Aug. 28, 1849, a. 9 m. 15 d.

**WINSHIP,** ——, Mrs., b. Proctor, w. Joseph, dropsy, May 4, 1848, a. 34 y. 7 m. 11 d.

**WINSOR,** Hannah, d. Joseph and Betsey, croup, Apr. 8, 1847, a. 2 y. 4 m.
——, d. still born, Henry and Mary Ann, Mar. 29, 1847.

**WINTHROP,** Elizabeth, d. John and Anne, Sept. 12, 1714.

**WISE,** Benjamin, s. Joseph, bur. 4 : 10m : 1660. C. R. 1.
Benjamin, s. Joseph, bur. 1 : 3m : 1664. C. R. 1.
Jane, wid., bur. —: 1637. CT. R.
Jeremiah, small pox, 17 : 9m : 1678. C. R. 1.
Joseph, sr., Sept. 12, 1684.
Mary, Aug. 4, 1693.

**WISTLE,** Mary Ann, b. England, w. William, cholera, Aug. 25, 1849, a. 22 y.

**WISWALL,** Charles Edwin, s. Amasa C., Sept. 22, 1832, a. 8 m.
Frederick A., s. Amasa C., Aug. 12, 1841, a. 5 y. 6 m.
——, ch. Am[a]sa C., July —, 1841, a. abt. 11 m.

**WITHERLEE,** Joshua, at the almshouse, Aug. 7, 1841, a. 64 y.

**WITHERS,** James Apr. 25, 1844, a. 46 y. G. R. 5.
William, June 13, 1844, a. 22 y. G. R. 5.

**WITHINGTON,** A. M., s. A. M., Mar. 29, 1831, a. 18 y.
Abiel, Mar. 3, 1804.
John [Whitington. typhus fever. C. R. 2.], Dec. 15, 1835, a. 33 y.
Sarah, d. Lewis and Sarah, Aug. 7, 1800.
——, Mrs., Sept. 6, 1805, a. 19 y.

**WOLLY,** ——, Mar. 2, 1784, a. 68 y. C. R. 2.

**WOOD** (see also Woods), Almira, June 21, 1807. C. R. 2.
Edwin B., s. Abijah and Hannah, dysentery, Sept. 11, 1847, a. 7 y. 2 m.
Lemuel, Aug. 20, 1812, a. 68 y. C. R. 2.
Mary, Mrs. [dropsy, Oct. 23. C. R. 3.], 1828, a. 79 y. [a. 69 y. C. R. 3.]

Wood, Mary L., d. Micajah and Hannah F., complaint in head, July 9, 1848, a. 4 y. 4 m.

Sarah, w. John, issue of May 7, 1796, a. 79 y. N. R. 4.

Walter M., s. M. and Hannah, dysentery, Nov. 9, 1846, a. 11 m.

——, d. Lemuel, Dec. 29, 1783, a. 12 y. C. R. 2.

**WOODARD** (see also Woodward), Hannah, Sept. 24, 1800, a. 9 y. C. R. 3.

Joseph, lung fever, Mar. 2, 1794, a. 33 y. C. R. 3.

Mary, dropsy in the head, Mar. 13, 1803, a. 4 y. C. R. 3.

Relief, w. John C., Dec. 10, 1827, a. 72 y. C. R. 2.

**WOODBRIDGE**, Ann, Mrs., Feb. 28, 1700-1701.

Lucy Ann, May 31, 1840. C. R. 6.

William C., Rev., at Boston, Nov. 9, 1845, a. 51 y. C. R. 6.

**WOODDIE** (see also Wooddy, Woody), John, smallpox, 23 : 3 m : 1650. C. R. 1.

Thomas, s. Richard, 13 : 7 m : 1650. C. R. 1.

**WOODDY** (see also Wooddie), ——, ch. stillborn, Rich[ard], abt. 2 : 9 m : 1647. C. R. 1.

**WOODMAN,** Jenette S., d. William and Mary Jane S., July 7, 1848, a. 3 d.

**WOODS** (see also Wood), Abigail, d. Richard and Hannah, Sept. 26, 1712.

Abigail, d. Richard and Hannah, Jan. 23, 1715-16.

Benja[min], s. John and Jemima, Feb. 12, 1736-7, a. 1 y. 3 m. G. R. 1.

Charlotte Ann, d. Harvey and Rebekah, Oct. 1, 1811. [a. 4 m. G. R. 1.]

Dolly, cholera morbus, Sept. 12, 1843, a. 94 y. C. R. 3.

Elizabeth, w. John, jr., Mar. 21, 1744, a. 24 y. G. R. 1.

George [indigestion. C. R. 3.], Oct. 15, 1815, a. 73 y. G. R. 4.

Hannah, d. Richard and Hannah, Dec. 21, 1712.

Hervey, Sept. 25, 1820, a. 35 y.

Jemima, wid. John, May 4, 1768, a. 88 y. G. R. 1.

John, May 24, 1747, a. 58 y. G. R. 1.

John, Oct. 12, 1799, a. 84 y.

Jonathan, s. Richard and Hannah, Nov. 22, 1713.

Jonathan, s. John and Jemima, Aug. 4, 1741, in his 20th y. G. R. 1.

Woods, Polly, July 12, 1788, a. 19 y. C. R. 2.

Polly [Mary. G. R. 4.], d. George, Apr. 19, 1795, a. 5 y. C. R. 3. [a. 5 y. 6 m. G. R. 4.]

Rebecca, w. Hervey, May 29, 1818, a. 31 y.

Rufus, stone cutter, b. Groton, consumption, Apr. 4, 1848, a. 45 y.

Silvanus [Sylvanus. G. R. 4.], s. George and Elizabeth [Dolly. G. R. 4.], dropsy of the brain, [Mar. 25. G. R. 4.], 1808, a. 16 y. C. R. 3. [a. 17 y. G. R. 4.]

**WOODWARD** (see also Woodard), David, widr., carpenter, b. Newton, dysentery, Sept. 22, 1847, a. 69 y.

Emma J., b. Newton, typhoid fever, dysentery, Dec. 26, 1848, a. 5 y. 3 m.

Joanna, w. Abraham, Aug. 12, 1718. C. R. 2.

Josiah, Oct. 23, 1817, a. 63 y.

Thomas, sr., Oct. —, 1685.

——, bur. 26 : 10 m : 1678. C. R. 1.

——, d. Peter, of Dedham, killed by her horse, Aug. 11, 1683.

**WOODWORTH** (see also Wardsworth), Ebenezer F., s. Ebenezer and Ann, dysentery, Oct. 3, 1846, a. 3 y. 6 m.

**WOODY** (see also Wooddie), Ann [Woodee. C. R. 1.], w. Rich[ard], sr., Apr. 4, 1656.

Richard [Woodie, Sr. C. R. 1.], "Ould," Dec. 6, 1658.

**WOOLEY,** Henry, drowned in Jamaica Pond, bur. July 15, 1839, a. 19 y. C. R. 5.

**WORLEY,** ——, Oct. 12, 1804, a. 14 y.

**WORMWOOD,** Ivory, Nov. 15, 1837.

**WORSELEY** (see also Worsley), Sally, d. Joseph and Mary, Oct. 15, 1792, a. 8 m. G. R. 1.

**WORSLEY** (see also Worseley), William, at the almshouse, Dec. 14, 1838, a. 88 y.

—— [Worseleys. dup.], ch. Joseph and Molly, Sept. 15, 1801, a. 4 m.

**WRIGHT,** Charlotte, w. Jabash, Jan. 19, 1819, a. 28 y.

——, "Old Mother," old age, 17 : 10 m : 1678, a. nearly 100 y. C. R. 1.

**WRIN,** Ann, d. James and Mary, Mar. 12, 1849, a. 15 d.

**WUFFENBACH,** Christina, d. George and Mary, ——. G. R. 5.
Samuel, s. George and Mary, ——. G. R. 5.
Sophia, d. George and Mary, ——. G. R. 5.

**WYMAN,** Aaron Davis, s. Capt. W[illia]m and Ruth, Feb. 18, 1811.
Aaron Davis, s. Capt. William, jr., Nov. 26, 1817, a. 2 y. 8 m.
Ann, wid. Rufus, M. D., May 22, 1843, a. 59 y.
Ann, wid., d. Joseph and Abigail Payson, dysentery, Sept. 16, 1847, a. 73 y.
Charles Hammond, s. W[illia]m, July 1, 1826, a. 9 y.
Frederick W., s. Asa, jr. and Louisa A., cholera infantum, Aug. 11, 1849, a. 9 m.
Harriott, d. Thomas, jr. and Sarah, Dec. 22 [25. dup.], 1801.
John, at the almshouse, Jan. 2, 1842, a. 73 y.
Joshua, s. Thomas and Sarah, Apr. 1, 1802.
Joshua, s. Isaac and Catharine, Sept. 28, 1831, [a. 13 m. dup.]
P. W., w. Capt. W[illia]m, Aug. 7, 1804, a. 56 y.
Rufus, M. D., Dea., June 23, 1842, a. 64 y.
Simeon, Apr. 25, 1825, a. 60 y.
Thomas, Sept. 7, 1802, a. 70 y.
William, Capt., an officer in the Revolution, Mar. 3, 1820, a. 81 y.
——, ch. Tho[mas], Oct. 18, 1806, a. 1 m.
——, wid., Nov. 10, 1806, a. 70 y.
——, ch. John W., Nov. 11, 1807, a. 5 y.

**YOUNG,** Caroline, d. Lott and Keziah (Pierce), Oct. 4, 1840. P. R. 5.
Catherine, unm., b. Ireland, cramp, July 31, 1848, a. 28 y.
Joseph, Oct. 14, 1825, a. 33 y. C. R. 2.
Josephine J., d. Joseph B. and Mary B. P., measles, May 21, 1849, a. 4 y. 5 m.
Mary, wid., b. Hingham, decline, Jan. 13, 1849, a. 70 y. 10 m. 27 d.
——, ch. James, Oct. 11, 1803, a. 18 m.
——, ch. Ja[me]s, Sept. 17, 1805, a. 17 m.

**YOUNGMAN,** Francis, July 23, 1712.
John, s. Francis and Anna, July 26, 1711.
Leah, d. Francis and Ann, May 28, 1701.

ZEIGLER (see also Zeigley, Ziegler, Zigler), George, Jan. 29, 1819, a. 59 y.

Mary, d. George and Mary, Aug. 10, 1789, a. 7 w. G. R. 1.

Polly, Mrs., Oct. 8, 1805, a. 43 y.

ZEIGLEY (see also Zeigler), Caroline, d. John and Susan, fits, Aug. 5, 1848, a. 9 m. 29 d.

ZIEGLER (see also Zeigler), Jos[eph], s. G. Z., Feb. 3, 1808.

——, ch. G., Oct. 26, 1804, a. 7 m.

ZIGLER (see also Zeigler), George, issue of Oct. 9, 1793, a. 7 y. N. R. 4.

ZUMGRAULE, Joseph, m., b. Germany, varioloid, Dec. 13, 1849, a. 46 y.

## SURNAMES MISSING

——, Barbara, w. ——, childbirth, — : 11 m : 1636. C. R. 1.

——, Elizabeth, an old maid, at John Parker's, [bet. Feb. 5 and Dec. 21], 1807. C. R. 3.

——, Jane, wid., bur. Apr. —, 1637.

——, Mary, servant of Hugh Pritchard's, June 10, 1643.

——, Sam ——, jr., Feb. —, 1746, in his 23d y. G. R. 1.

——, ——, inf ch., ——., sojourner, at Sister Lamb's, small pox, abt. 16 : 10 m : 1649. C. R. 1.

——, ——, servant of Brother Porter, 28 : 2 m : 1651. C. R. 1.

——, ——, a servant of Brother Hely, bur. 2 : 9 m : 1652. C. R. 1.

——, ——, inf. grand ch. John Chandler, bur. 12 : 4 m : 1686. C. R. 1.

——ngton, ——, Nov. 10, 1750, in his 71st y. G. R. 1.

——, ——, a child, at Capt. John Baker's, Mar. 27, 1785, a. 3 y. 3 m. C. R. 2.

——, ——, ch. ——, Mar. 29, 1789, a. 24 h. C. R. 2.

——, a stranger at Mr. Lewis', Oct. 26, 1793. C. R. 2.

——, ——, a stranger at Martin's, Nov. —, 1804.

——, ——, ch. living at Eben[ezer] Murdock's, Mar. 12, 1805, a. 11 y. C. R. 2.

——, a man from Capt. Jos[eph] Curtis, Oct. 6, 1807, a. 26 y.

——, ——, a stranger, killed, bur. from Capt. Dunster, Nov. 30, 1811. C. R. 2.

——, ——, a pauper, Sept. 9, 1834, a. 40 y.

——, ——, ch. foreigner, dropsy on the brain, July 15, 1846, a. 4 y.

——, inf. ch. ——, German, July 28, 1846, a. 35 d.

——, ——, inf. ch. consumption, Aug. 1, 1846 a. 35 d.

——, ——, Irish boy, consumption, Aug. 1, 1846, a. 7 y.

——, ——, ch. German, Aug. 14, 1846.

——, ——, ch. teething, Sept. 11, 1846, a. 1 y. 6 m.

——, ——, a stranger, delirium tremens, Aug. 14, 1847, a. 30 y.

——, ——, ch. still born, Gilbert and Mary, July 7, 1849.

——, ——, ch. "still," Daniel and Elizabeth, July 21, 1849.

——, ——, inf. s. Peter and Eliza, Aug. 10, 1849, a. 7 d.

——, ——, ch. still born, Geo[rge] W. and Louisa C., Sept. 5, 1849.


## INDIANS

**EZBON,** bur. 6 : 6 m : 1646. C. R. 1.

**NAN,** a captive of Mr. Weld, bur. 7 : 6 m : 1646. C. R. 1.

**PETER** [Pete. C. R. 1!], servant to Joseph Dudley, Esq., Aug. 14, 1687.

——, w. Andrew, of Natick, June 6, 1655.

——, a boy of Holbrook's, small pox, 5 : 11 m : 1678-9. C. R. 1.

——, a girl of Mr. Dudly, "neer well of a pox, fell a bleeding and bled to death," 18 : 2 m : 1679. C. R. 1.


## NEGROES

**BLANEYS,** ——, May 10, 1805.

**BLONT,** Jack, African, June 9, 1807.

**BOWELS,** ——, ch. ——, June 5, 1712.

**BRACKETT,** Rose, Mar. 8 [6. dup.], 1801, a. 30 y.

**BRIDGHAM** (see also Brigham), Peter, old age, Dec. 1, 1801, a. 87 y. C. R. 3.

Simon, old age, Dec. 3, 1837, a. 80 y. C. R. 3.

**BRIGHAM** (see also Bridgham), David, cholera morbus, Oct. 22, 1832, a. 33 y. C. R. 3.
Hannah, inflammation of wind pipe and bronchia, June 13, 1834, a. 50 y. C. R. 3.

**COLBURN,** Scipio, consumption, Feb. 22, 1821, a. 22 y. C. R. 3.

**CUMMINGS,** Patience, Jan. 9, 1823, a. 60 y.

**CUTLER,** Othello, dropsy, July 10, 1812, a. 45 y. C. R. 3.

**CYRUS,** servant of wid. Lyons, Dec. 16, 1774, a. 80 y. C. R. 2.

**DEBORAH,** a mulatto, at the poor-house, Feb. 1, 1801.

**DINAH,** in the family of Hon. John Lowell [Lovell. dup.], Esq., Nov. 10, 1801, a. 85 y. [1802, a. 81 y. dup.]

**DINAH,** from the work house, Dec. 15, 1801. [1802. dup.]

**DIX,** Polly, Nov. 10, 1804.

**ELIZABETH,** Dec. 17, 1802, a. 55 y.

**EUNICE,** servant of Joseph Richards, Aug. 6, 1775, a. 32 y. C. R. 2.

**FILLADE,** servant of Hon. John Lowell, Esq., Jan. 18, 1802, a. 56 y.

**FLORA,** an African, Sept. —, 1786, a. abt. 28 y. C. R. 2.

**GARDNER,** Grace, wid., domestic, b. Providence, d. Spears, cholera, Aug. 18, 1849, a. 52 y.

**GILES,** Dinah, at the work house, Dec. 15, 1801, a. 80 y.
Joseph, s. Simeon, typhus fever, June 24, 1835, a. 13 y. C. R. 3.
Phebe, bilious colic, Apr. 17, 1818, a. 71 y. C. R. 3.

**HANNAH,** servant to Edmund Weld, Feb. 21, 1715-16.

**HANNAH,** at the work house, Jan. 8 [7. dup.], 1801.

**HARTWICK,** Betsey, May 5 [3. dup.], 1801, a. 31 y.

**HEMMENWAY,** Nancy, belonging to Mr. Durant, consumption, Oct. 9, 1806, a. 35 y. C. R. 3.

**HOLLAND,** ——, ch. Jupiter, Dec. 6, 1798, a. 3 y.

**JOHNSON,** Betty, at the work house, Apr. 23, 1809.

**LEWIS,** Phillis (before the Revolution a slave in the family of Mr. Morey of Jamaica Plain), at the almshouse, Mar. 22, 1843, a. abt. 100 y.

**LOGAN,** Quasha, at the work house, Feb. 26, 1809.

**MINOR,** Drover, Nov. 26, 1802, a. 61 y.
——, wid. Drover, Jan. 7, 1803.

**MORRIS,** Charlotte, June 26, 1810, a. 18 y.
——, ch. Charlotte, June 22, 1810.

**ROBERTS,** Richard, Feb. 10, 1804, a. 25 y.

**ROGER,** Nov. 19, 1798, a. 60 y.

**SCARBOROUGH,** Phillis, at the work house, Dec. 4, 1809.

**SMITH,** Thomas, at the work house, Oct. 4, 1809, a. abt. 50 y.
——, Mrs., Dec. 3, 1819. c. r. 2.

**STEVENS,** Pompy [Pompey. dup.], Oct. 11, 1797, a. 77 y.

**SUMNER,** Cuff, Mar. 5, 1838, a. 67 y.
Dean S., Sept. 15, 1805, a. 14 y.
——, w. Cuff, Nov. 25, 1804, a. 27 y.

**THOMAS,** Hannah, lung fever, May 14, 1835, a. 22 y. c. r. 3.

**THOMPSON,** ——, ch. Henry, July 30, 1820, a. 3 y. c. r. 2.

**WILLIAMS,** Phillis, Feb. 1, 1799, a. 75 y.
——, a mulatto, at Samuel Lewis', Dec. 28, 1778, a. 26 y. c. r. 2.
——, ——, "a girl," June 28, 1802.
——, woman, from P. Spring, Dec. —, 1805.
——, servant to Mr. Prescott, Jan. 8, 1806, a. 32 y.

83